FOOTBALL

EDITED BY JOHN SCHULIAN

FOOTBALL

GREAT WRITING ABOUT
THE NATIONAL SPORT

A Special Publication of
THE LIBRARY OF AMERICA

Introduction, headnotes, and volume compilation
copyright © 2014 by Literary Classics of the United States, Inc.,
New York, N.Y. All rights reserved.
www.loa.org

Some of the material in this volume is reprinted with the
permission of holders of copyright and publishing rights.
Acknowledgments are on page 447.

Photograph on page 46 by Marvin E. Newman,
courtesy of *Sports Illustrated*/Getty Images.

Distributed to the trade in the United States by Penguin Random
House Inc. and in Canada by Penguin Random House Canada Ltd.

A hardcover edition of this book was published
by The Library of America in 2014.

First paperback edition published in 2015.

Library of Congress Control Number: 2014956331

ISBN 978–1–59853–417–7

1 3 5 7 9 10 8 6 4 2

Printed in the United States of America

Contents

Preface to the Paperback Edition ix

Introduction
   by John Schulian xi

GRANTLAND RICE
   from The Tumult and the Shouting 1

W. C. HEINZ
   The Ghost of the Gridiron 4

MYRON COPE
   from The Game That Was: Johnny Blood 17

SHIRLEY POVICH
   The Redskins' Longest Day 25

RED SMITH
   The Most Important Thing 28
   The Lost Cause 30

FREDERICK EXLEY
   from A Fan's Notes 34

STUART LEUTHNER
   from Iron Men: Pat Summerall 38

GARY SMITH
   Moment of Truth 47

FRANK DEFORD
   The Best There Ever Was 65

JOHN SCHULIAN
   Concrete Charlie 71

DAVID MARANISS
   from When Pride Still Mattered 85

JIMMY CANNON
   Greatness 91

JIMMY BRESLIN
...The One Last Good One That Wasn't to Be 94

GEORGE PLIMPTON
from Paper Lion 102

DAN JENKINS
An Upside-Down Game. 112

JERRY IZENBERG
A Whistle-Stop School with Big-Time Talent. 119

JERRY KRAMER AND DICK SCHAAP
from Instant Replay 135

JENNIFER ALLEN
from Fifth Quarter 144

AL SILVERMAN
Gale Sayers: The Hard Road Back. 155

JIM MURRAY
Don't Look Now . . . but the Funny Little League is No. 1 . . . 167

LARRY MERCHANT
from . . . And Every Day You Take Another Bite. 170

ARTHUR KRETCHMER
Butkus. 179

PAUL HEMPHILL
Yesterday's Hero. 203

GARY CARTWRIGHT
Tom Landry: Melting the Plastic Man 213

TOM ARCHDEACON
Smith Hates for It to End Like This. 224

RICHARD PRICE
Bear Bryant's Miracles 229

RICK REILLY
A Matter of Life and Sudden Death 246

LEIGH MONTVILLE
   A Miracle in Miami 259

H. G. BISSINGER
   from Friday Night Lights 263

MARK KRAM
   No Pain, No Game 272

CHARLES P. PIERCE
   Legends of the Fall 285

IRA BERKOW
   The Minority Quarterback 294

PETER RICHMOND
   Flesh and Blood 314

JOHN ED BRADLEY
   The Best Years of His Life 328

WRIGHT THOMPSON
   Pulled Pork & Pigskin: A Love Letter to Southern Football . . 341

RICK TELANDER
   Atkins a Study in Pride and Pain 351

PAT FORDE
   Broncos Earn Respect With Improbable Victory 355

MICHAEL LEWIS
   The Kick Is Up and It's . . . a Career Killer 360

JEANNE MARIE LASKAS
   G-L-O-R-Y! 377

NATE JACKSON
   from Slow Getting Up 395

PAUL SOLOTAROFF
   The Ferocious Life and Tragic Death of a Super Bowl Star . . . 401

BRYAN CURTIS
   Friday Night Tykes 413

ROY BLOUNT JR.
   Immaculate Memory 435

SOURCES AND ACKNOWLEDGMENTS 447

INDEX 451

Sunday's Other Heroes

IF IT WAS AN AUTUMN SUNDAY BACK THEN, we knew there would be a touch football game. Without benefit of cell phones, texts, or computers, we just showed up in early afternoon and took it from there. Sometimes we played three on three, sometimes four on four. Anything beyond that felt out of scale for the park that was our home field, a humble patch of grass with a swing and a sandbox for the mothers and small children who lay claim to it during the week. But for those two or three hours when the rest of the town was getting religion or staring numbly at the Chicago Bears' Fred Flintstone offense on TV, the park belonged to us, come rain, snow, or frozen tundra.

Our game materialized when most of us were playing on a high school team whose state championship dreams would be dashed by a penalty that remains stuck in the craw more than fifty years later. Nothing much changed when we drifted to college a few blocks up the street, still living at home, sublimely ignorant of the world opening up to the kids who had gone off to Yale and Berkeley and Columbia, schools that would have seemed as distant as the dark side of the moon if we had bothered to think about them. But we had more pressing concerns—the fly pattern, the hook-and-ladder, and especially the out-of-bounds lines that floated unseen between two towering trees to the east and bumped up against a couple of hostile shrubs and a sad excuse for a softball diamond to the west. O, the arguments that raged every Sunday. O, the infinitives that got split.

And yet it was all so innocent, even when McCarthy, the athletic prodigy who was the heart and soul of the action, began sampling life's temptations. Martinez, who once won a high school game with a forty-seven-yard field goal, always rolled up in the Studebaker he called his Maserati. Butch, a dentist's son who was too slight for varsity football, scored style points with turtleneck sweaters, stocking caps, and socks pulled high. Me, I soaked it all in as I killed time until baseball season. There were the neighborhood kids who were summoned when our ranks were thin, and McCarthy's younger brothers, future all-state linebackers who could hold their own even when they were in junior high. But those Sundays began and ended with us, the guys who were there from Day One.

When the hardback edition of *Football* came out, I inscribed a copy for the dentist's son, who, by the way, no longer calls himself Butch. It seemed only natural I should mention the games we used to play, but he caught me off guard when he said my few scrawled words were what he would treasure most about the book. Only then did I begin to truly appreciate the staying power of those games and the Sundays remembered by no one but us. Once again we are young and McCarthy is still alive. His youngest brother is, too. I don't know what the score is or who is in bounds or out of bounds, but I do know the paperback edition now has something the hardback doesn't. It has a dedication, and this is it.

—John Schulian

Introduction

by John Schulian

Tackling Football

I THINK OF THE OLD FOOTBALL PRESS BOXES FIRST, the ones where you'd look up from scribbling something in your notebook and find a guy in the crowd staring at you through the window, probably wondering if it was your story that made him choke on his cornflakes the other morning. When the scoreboard clock hit 0:00, he'd be gone, win or lose, and you'd join the media procession down to the locker room bent on making sense of what you'd seen and praying you didn't get coldcocked by some joker wielding a TV camera. The head coach would tell you he wouldn't know anything until he saw the game films, and then you'd get the truth from the players, who provide football with its great thumping heartbeat. You'd stay for as long as you could before the threat of your deadline forced you back to the press box to start stringing sentences together. Everybody else's day was done but work was just beginning for you and the cleanup crew.

The writers of my generation toiled on portable typewriters that were built for punishment and on primitive computers that could scar you for life where technology was concerned. One frozen afternoon in Minnesota, the Vikings turned off the heat after they won on a Hail Mary, and the three of us left in the press box, all out-of-towners, had to write with fingers we couldn't feel. Better to have been in Baltimore the day a small plane crash-landed in Memorial Stadium's upper deck barely ten minutes after a game ended. At least you could get a story out of the plane.

The story was always the thing. It was what we lived for: re-creating the drama every game is built on, pillaging our notebooks for the perfect quote, forever searching for something in the people we wrote about that maybe even they weren't aware of. Our working quarters could be cramped and our deadlines tighter than the wrong pair of shoes, but the men and women who ran this gauntlet every week still felt the jolt of inspiration. If you cared about what you were doing, if you felt a connection to the game and wanted your contribution to its deadline literature to truly matter, you had to write like your pants were on fire even when you were risking frostbite.

It's my hope that the spirit of those press boxes infuses this book. Some of the pieces gathered here were written in them, the early stuff mostly, the stories that bear such legendary bylines as Red Smith and Jimmy Cannon. You don't have to search the Internet for long before you find photos of the old-timers in overcoats and fedoras as they hunched over their typewriters, cigarette smoke curling around their heads, banging out page after page and shouting for Western Union to come get it and send it. It seemed a romantic life. It *was* a romantic life. Those of us who got the chance to live it carry the memories no matter how far we have traveled from the press box. Yes, we cursed our forgotten field glasses, jeopardized our health with bad box lunches, and kept an eye on the clock, always the clock, but in return we covered games that people would talk about for decades to come. And with those games we got the characters and the craziness and the occasional sadness that we would turn into what so many wonderful writers shrugged off as "typing." It was, at its best, much more than that.

* * *

Forgive me if I sound as puffed up as the former University of Oklahoma president who wanted a school his football team could be proud of, but the stories you are about to read go beyond scores and championships and the zeal for money, money, money that increasingly drives every aspect of the sport. What we have here is full-blooded prose that is smart, funny, poignant, impassioned, and insightful. Some stories are steeped in the relative innocence of the past. Others address the hard and uncomfortable truths that are forcing lovers of the game to reevaluate the thrill they get from a tackle that separates someone from his senses. And always there are the yarns that will live as long as tailgaters have brats on the grill.

Time unwinds in these pages, taking us all the way back to Grantland Rice, the granddaddy of modern sportswriting, as he reminisces about how he mythologized Notre Dame's Four Horsemen in 1924. Hard on his heels is the master craftsman W. C. Heinz recalling the magic of a hero from his youth, Red Grange, football's first great broken-field runner. And then there is Myron Cope, an impish wordsmith and broadcaster turned oral historian, tracking down Johnny Blood, the footloose halfback who personified what it meant to be a tramp athlete when the game dwelled on the margins of respectability. Each writer comes out of a different era—Rice the Roaring Twenties, Heinz postwar America, Cope the rebellious '60s and '70s—and yet they are bound by the history that provides the road map for this book.

It's the history of football, of course, but it's also the history of football writing. Rice's florid dispatches aside, the press started out treating the game like a ne'er-do-well brother-in-law. To come to some understanding of its past, your safest bet in most cases is to rely on writers of more recent vintage. So it is that two of the very best grace these pages with stories that look back at football in the middle of the last century. Gary Smith delivers a meditation on an unforgettable photo of the Texas Christian University team taken moments before its 1957 Cotton Bowl collision with Jim Brown, perhaps the greatest running back ever. Frank Deford, Smith's venerable stablemate at *Sports Illustrated*, taps into his hometown roots to define what Johnny Unitas meant to him and to the city of Baltimore.

Such pieces propel us to a basic truth about football coverage: what the roaring crowds and TV cameras see may not amount to half of what you can get from writers with an eye for detail, an ear for the vernacular, and a gift for asking the right questions. There are small moments, too, and small moments define football for us in ways the scoreboard never will. They demystify the coaches who scheme and rage along the sideline, and the players whose Darth Vader helmets render them faceless, and the support troops who dwell on the periphery of the heroism and the violence and the cacophony.

Coaches offer a particular challenge, for they find an odd kind of comfort in secrecy, paranoia, and workdays that last twenty hours, with four off for sleeping in their offices. The game that consumes them only seems as elemental as eleven brawny young men trying to knock the snot out of eleven other brawny young men. Beneath the surface, football is complicated in a way that coaches embrace intellectually and use as a cudgel to ward off writers they consider either too dim to understand or too smart to fall for their obfuscation and prevarication. It's a tribute to Gary Cartwright, a freewheeling Texan, that he could get past Tom Landry's "Ice Age smile" and provide readers with essential truths about the Dallas Cowboys' legendary coach, not the least of which is this one: "Tom did not see a contradiction between the terms *pride* and *humility*, any more than politicians and military men see a rift in slogans like 'Bombs for Peace.'"

Writers worth remembering always dig deepest for the truth. The evidence is here before you whether it's John Ed Bradley, an ex-LSU football captain, coming to terms with the game he can never put behind him, or Jennifer Allen spending her New Year's Eve watching her father, George Allen, a formidable and controversial NFL coach, endure the agony of being fired. Michael Lewis, as comfortable in the world of football as he is in high finance, captures the precarious life of a professional placekicker, and Jeanne Marie Laskas gives us a story that only a woman with her big heart could have written properly, a story that paints the Cincinnati Bengals' cheerleaders as human beings, not kewpie dolls. And then there are the unforgettable games that get the telling they deserve: Dan Jenkins tweaking Notre Dame for playing for a tie in a battle to be number one, Leigh Montville recalling the prayer that Doug Flutie answered for Boston College, Tom Archdeacon finding uncommon grace in the wake of a dropped pass in the Super Bowl, Rick Reilly re-creating an overtime duel that looked as though it would never end and a life that threatened to end too soon.

The one piece that may seem an odd fit is plucked from Frederick Exley's *A Fan's Notes*. Though it won a National Book Award and depicts football as a lost soul's rock to cling to, it was published as "a fictional memoir," and fiction is for someone else's anthology. We deal in facts here. But Exley's biographer, Jonathan Yardley, tells us that the author dealt in facts, too, when he revisited his boozy, hilarious, heartbreaking life to write the first draft of his masterpiece as pure memoir. The result was too bold for his publisher, who backed away for fear of lawsuits. Exley, left with no other choice, reworked the book as a novel, but the truth of it remained. That's a fact.

* * *

As unfathomable as it seems in an era when football blots out the sun for every other sport, there was a time when the nation's newspapers treated it as little more than an afterthought. The excitement over, say, Red Grange playing in New York for the first time or Jim Thorpe and the Carlisle Indians upsetting Army would last for a day or so, and then it was back to baseball, boxing, and horseracing, the sports that ruled the headlines. All were woven into the fabric of everyday life, and all were platforms for the storytelling that seemed as foreign to football as an ode on a Grecian urn.

The salvation of football writing began after World War II when the press box ceased to be Mount Olympus and its denizens took it upon themselves to troop down to the locker room and find out what they didn't know, which was usually just about everything. Baseball writers blazed the trail and their brethren in football followed as a matter of survival. They didn't want to open the competition's sports section and find a mediocre insight they didn't have, much less a memorable quote. Sports editors, even those who booked bets or took payoffs from wrestling promoters, wouldn't put up with that. So the reporting got better, and so, by the mid-'50s and early '60s, did the writing. There were more and more stories with style, attitude, and touches that suggested writers had not only read Hemingway but also were copping his moves.

Wonder of wonders, the revolution wasn't confined to New York. In fact there's a school of thought that the city's entire football writing corps couldn't match what was going on at the ragged, largely unread *Fort Worth Press*. Its sports editor, Blackie Sherrod, who could be gruff and funny in the same sentence, had populated his staff with hugely talented young cutups, introduced them to the sly humor and high style of *Newsweek*'s John Lardner, and turned them loose. As Jones Ramsey, the University of Texas publicist and self-proclaimed "world's tallest fat man," liked to say, the only sports in the state were football and spring football. Dan Jenkins, Edwin (Bud) Shrake, and Gary Cartwright didn't need to be told what to write about.

It was no accident that Jenkins and Shrake went on to become stars at *Sports Illustrated* and that Cartwright's byline would appear in the magazine when he wasn't writing best-selling crime books and achieving exalted status at *Texas Monthly*. Jenkins in particular influenced a generation of writers with his cool, knowing, sacred-cow-tipping football coverage. In his case timing was everything. He landed at the magazine in 1962, as it was becoming the epicenter of a sportswriting revolution that emphasized literary flair, distinctive voices, and long pieces that could probe the psyche or find the fun in the games. In a roundabout way, however, it was a distinctly unstylish story written four years before Jenkins's arrival that showed *SI*'s brain trust the truth and the light. The story was about the Baltimore Colts' sudden-death overtime victory over the New York Giants in what the magazine's headline proclaimed "the best game ever played." Never mind that those words didn't appear in the story itself. If it was passion that football fans wanted, *SI* would give them passion.

While sportswriting was getting its house in order artistically, it also had to meet the challenge of print journalism's great nemesis: TV. *Twentieth Century*, CBS's amiable predecessor to the confrontational *60 Minutes*, delivered "The Violent World of Sam Huff," a jargon-rich, feel-the-blocks-and-tackles 1959 feature about a crew-cut, camera-ready Giants linebacker. The network could not have cared less that in a time of prime beef at that position—Ray Nitschke in Green Bay, Chuck Bednarik in Philadelphia, Joe Schmidt in Detroit, Bill George in Chicago—Huff was perfectly ordinary. The proof could be found in a goal-line stand against Cleveland and its battering ram, Jim Brown. The Giants stopped him on two straight plunges, with Huff shouting, "You stink, Brown! You stink!" But Brown's third try was a charm as he barged into the end zone standing up. Then it was his turn to ask a question: "Hey, Sam, how do I smell from here?"

CBS provided the answer: Huff played in New York, so he smelled just fine. But there was something far bigger than provincialism at work in the 1960s, and it stirred football's cosmos in ways it hadn't been stirred before. Working out of Philadelphia's New Jersey suburbs, the father-son team of Ed and Steve Sabol founded NFL Films, which captured games and great plays and players with such imagination and so many cameras that Hollywood couldn't match it, only borrow from it. The upstart American Football League may have been even more photogenic than the NFL, but it didn't have any Sabols of its own to immortalize its scoreboard-melting alternative to the NFL. The 57–53 game ruled in towns like Houston and Kansas City, frontier outposts that gained a certain contrary glamour when two-thousand-year-old George Blanda was defying age with his throwing arm and Otis Taylor was going long on thoroughbred legs. But even then New York horned in on the AFL's action when Broadway Joe Namath took off his full-length mink coat to guarantee the Jets would beat Baltimore in Super Bowl III, and got away with it.

Namath personified what football had become by the early '70s: show business. Those who resisted the transformation had their noses rubbed in it by ABC's *Monday Night Football*, where Howard Cosell parked his ego at center stage and Dandy Don Meredith, still a blithe spirit after nine seasons as the Dallas Cowboys' quarterback, sang Willie Nelson songs. Frank Gifford, once a golden boy at USC and with the New York Giants, would slip in whenever he could to describe a play or give the score, but on many a Monday night the score was hardly the thing.

With TV big and getting bigger, writers responded by jousting for position with camera crews in crowded locker rooms and laughing at talking heads who couldn't function without hairspray. Those, however, were border skirmishes in a war that called for more serious journalistic muscle. Football was making giant strides toward sports-world domination and press coverage had to get better and broader. Suddenly, it wasn't just *SI* and *Sport* magazine providing football stories to remember. There was *Life*, *Look*, and *The Saturday Evening Post* as well as such hairy-chested newsstand favorites as *True*, *Argosy*, and *Saga*. You had *Esquire* weighing in more than it ever had, too, and, beginning in the mid-'80s, *GQ* doing what no one ever thought it would. The name of the game was football even in *Playboy*, where a preseason forecast was as much a part of the magazine as the staple in the Playmate of the Month's navel and Arthur Kretchmer's portrayal of Dick Butkus as man and beast was a classic by any standard.

From the world of nonfiction books came George Plimpton's *Paper Lion*, Myron Cope's *The Game That Was*, and *Instant Replay*, Dick Schaap's unforgettable collaboration with Jerry Kramer, an All-Pro guard for Vince Lombardi's Packers. Here was football as TV had yet to show it, rich not just in immediacy but in history, lore, and personalities. The public response was a demand for more and even better books that led to David Maraniss's state-of-the-art Lombardi biography, *When Pride Still Mattered*, and H. G. Bissinger's *Friday Night Lights*, a brave, empathetic study of high school football in small-town Texas that became an admirable movie and an even better TV series.

But if you wanted to feel the pulse of football during the last forty years of the twentieth century, you had to read newspapers. They were there every day until technology and their reluctance to acknowledge it began eating them alive. They gave readers the scores and the scoop on sprained ankles, and they opened their pages for reporters and columnists to put a face on coaches and players. There were opinions, too, of course—no season was complete without a quarterback controversy or rumblings that the head coach might be fired—but opinions had been around since Walter Camp drew up his first play. What made newspapers different in this golden age was the space they devoted to magazine-length features that strived for *Sports Illustrated*'s excellence and showcased such stars in the making as Gary Smith of the *Philadelphia Daily News* and John Ed Bradley of the *Washington Post*. And yet such excellence could get lost in the excess exemplified by the mob of writers, reporters, photographers, and editors who descended on the Super Bowl every year. Never mind that it was the worst week in the season for doing first-rate work, everyone herded onto buses at dawn, fed rubbery scrambled eggs at each team's hotel, and numbed into near comas by the same answers they'd heard the day before, and the day before that. But still they came from the *Los Angeles Times*, *Boston Globe*, *Washington Post*, and *Dallas Morning News*, ten, twelve, fourteen at a time, reveling in their success as if it would never end.

And then it did. Papers began going out of business, budgets were slashed, staff reductions became part of the equation (*reduction* being a euphemism for *firing*), and finally the people in charge were happy just to have one writer at the Super Bowl. For those of us who had written about football in the good times, it wasn't so much the end of overkill that hurt; it was the absence of the time and space for storytelling and the decline of what we considered our high standards. Surely, we told one another, there would never be another generation of writers like us.

But there is, and they're out there now. For all I know, they're better than we ever were. Not many write for newspapers, and if they do, they're likely plotting a move to a magazine or website where they can dig into fearless, imaginative stories like the one Bryan Curtis wrote for *Texas Monthly* about youth football in the age of concussions. In the Internet's wide open spaces, ESPN.com, Grantland, SBNation, and Deadspin are emphasizing the kind of work that will fill a volume like this twenty years from now. You'll see what I mean when you read Wright Thompson's rambunctious ode to Southern football. It's simply too much fun to leave for someone else to anthologize.

* * *

I can still hear Bear Bryant, the ayatollah of Alabama, invoking his wife's name as he offered the assembled media a folksy invitation the day before the Sugar Bowl: "If you ever down in Tuscaloosa in the summer, come on by the house and Mary Harmon and I'll turn the hose on you."

And I'll never forget Walter Payton, restless as a hummingbird, convincing an in-and-out Bears quarterback named Vince Evans they could use their idle moments in practice to set up ten yards apart and fire a ball at each other as hard as they could. First one to drop it was a chump or a punk or whatever they called the unmanly back then. Evans had a bazooka for an arm, but Payton threw just as hard, laughing, radiating pure joy. I wasn't surprised—he could do anything. I saw him run for 275 yards one afternoon, and throw two touchdown passes on another. But it was his smile during that blistering game of catch that made me understand how every day was Christmas as long as he had a football in his hands.

Memories like those are made every season, great memories inspired by kids who come from out of nowhere in college ball or steely-eyed old pros like Peyton Manning and Tom Brady. Problem is, there are also storm clouds hanging over both the NFL and the NCAA, and they are bigger and more ominous than any before them. To be honest, I don't like either institution, and when I was writing a newspaper sports column in Chicago and Philadelphia, I'm not sure either institution liked me. In fact I know the NFL didn't. "You're not a friend of the league," one of its bright-eyed, rosy-cheeked young factotums once told me. I had enough friends.

But the imperious lad from the NFL assumed everyone wanted to be in the league's good graces. The NCAA was similarly deluded. Now look at the mess they're in. No sooner did the colleges figure out a playoff system than players started talking about being paid for helping to make fortunes for their schools. Powerhouse conferences, meanwhile, are going public with doubts that the NCAA is necessary at all. With the NFL, things are infinitely more complicated, so much so that even its iron grip can't prevent its wheels from wobbling. Gambling is up—Super Bowl betting in Las Vegas is approaching a hundred million dollars—but the league, taking its cue from Captain Renault in *Casablanca*, acts as if gambling doesn't exist. It can't be as willfully blind about the shrinking attendance that afflicts some of its less glamorous franchises. The blame for that lies most obviously with ticket prices beyond the ordinary fan's budget, but you must also factor in the increasingly appealing parallel universe football has spawned. The Madden video games, John Madden's unlikely legacy, have replaced *Monday Night Football* in the lives of teenaged boys and young adults. It's even said that more than a few NFL players prefer fantasy football to watching *MNF*, and I think I know at least part of the reason why: when the game is imaginary, no one gets a concussion or ends up a cripple, and no one lands in jail, either.

The NFL's dark side, on the other hand, is as real as the murder trial that almost ensnared Baltimore's Ray Lewis and the murder conviction that brought down Carolina's Rae Carruth, as memorably depicted in these pages by Peter Richmond. Look around and you'll find a multitude of other examples of players run amok—the drug beefs and the wives and girlfriends who get brutalized, the guns that go off in nightclubs and the twisted metal and bloody highways that signify death by speeding auto.

The extent of the pathology by itself would ordinarily be enough to bedevil the NFL, but the NFL happens to be facing the mother of all its problems. The violence on which the game is built—the violence the league has blissfully marketed and turned into billions upon billions of dollars—has been turned against it with a vengeance. It got lucky when the 4,500 former players who had sued it agreed to a 765 million-dollar settlement roundly described as modest. But the NFL must still contend with the epidemic of degenerative brain disease it has unsuccessfully and shamefully sought to pretend doesn't exist. Too many players have had their lives ruined. Too many others have taken their lives, none more dramatically than Dave Duerson, the Super Bowl star Paul Solotaroff writes about here so unflinchingly. There's no pill or injection to make Duerson's kind of pain go away— but there are pills and injections available for almost everything else in a league with a flimsy drug policy. When you read the excerpt from former Denver Bronco Nate Jackson's memoir *Slow Getting Up*, you'll see that human growth hormone is more than another storm cloud. It's a storm, and it's already here.

What will become of the NFL after the deluge, I can't tell you. I'm equally short on clairvoyance when it comes to college football in the seemingly inevitable post-NCAA era. All I know for sure is that the game is on the verge of major change, and that this seems the right time to salute what is beautiful and soul stirring about it while taking an honest look at its highly visible failings. I hope the stories gathered here serve both purposes and remind you of the resilience that is football's backbone. In good times and bad, there is a quintessentially American toughness about the game that triggers the imagination. When you were a kid picturing yourself as Unitas dropping back to pass, you did it with a hero's limp. When you played touch football on a field booby-trapped with a bush that could impale you at any second, you named the bush after the toughest linebacker you could think of.

Even now, I can close my eyes and think back to the magic that ensnared me when I was five or six years old. The Rams played in Los Angeles then—it was the early 1950s and they were relative newcomers—and somehow, though I was the only child of parents who changed addresses frequently and cared not a whit about football, I became aware of the players' nicknames. There was Tank Younger and Night Train Lane, Deacon Dan Towler and Vitamin T. Smith, and then there was the best of all: Crazylegs Hirsch. *Crazylegs!* Not even *Dick Tracy* could have improved on that. What visions it conjured up, what majestic fantasies. Kids have welcomed football into their lives with far less inspiration, but the spell I was under after hearing that nickname turned out to be a harbinger of the life ahead of me. As proof, I offer this book.

Grantland Rice

Of the millions upon millions of words lavished on football, the most famous, quoted, and parodied may be those written by Grantland Rice (1880–
1954) as he feverishly transformed Notre Dame's backfield into mythological
heroes: "Outlined against a blue-gray October sky, the Four Horsemen rode
again. In dramatic lore they are known as Famine, Pestilence, Destruction
and Death. These are only aliases. Their real names are Stuhldreher, Miller,
Crowley and Layden. They formed the crest of the South Bend cyclone before
which another fighting Army football team was swept over the precipice at
the Polo Grounds yesterday afternoon as 55,000 spectators peered down on
the bewildering panorama spread on the green plain below." Rice was just getting warmed up. His column for the October 18, 1924 edition of the *New York
Herald Tribune* is, by contemporary standards, a hallucinogenic stew of gaudy
prose and carpet-sample metaphors. But it was a product of a different time—
no TV, not everyone had a radio—and Rice piled on the adjectives as he tried
to paint the most vivid word picture possible. A courtly former Vanderbilt
football player, he was the star of the *Herald Trib*'s sports page throughout the
Roaring Twenties and the Depression, and one of the nation's most beloved
syndicated columnists. In the following excerpt from his 1954 memoir *The
Tumult and the Shouting*, he trots out Ring Lardner, Knute Rockne, and George
Gipp before explaining his inspiration for those four overwrought but unforgettable horsemen.

from

The Tumult and the Shouting

COACH JESSE HARPER of Notre Dame took the real forward pass
east in 1913. He brought it to West Point where Army and Notre
Dame met that year for the first time. Harper gave the ball to quarterback Gus Dorais, who threw it to his broken-nosed roommate, Knute
Rockne. Rockne caught it and Army was slaughtered 35–13. I didn't
meet Rockne on that trip. I met him some years later when I returned
to the Point after he became head coach at Notre Dame.

Ring Lardner, a keen Notre Dame and midwestern rooter, went
with me on that trip to the Point in the fall of 1920. We ran into John
J. McEwan, the big Army assistant coach. John J. was loaded with
confidence. One of Army's all-time centers, John coached the Cadet

line. Army's strong squad was headed by the flying Walter French, who earned his spurs—and an appointment to West Point—at Rutgers.

"I understand," said Lardner, "that Rockne is coming in again with that kid named Gipp."

"Who the hell is Gipp?" snorted McEwan.

"You'll find out at ten minutes to two tomorrow," replied Lardner.

McEwan did. With Army and the irrepressible French leading 17–14 at half time, Gipp put on a second half one-man rodeo as the Irish pulled out the game 27–17.

"How'd you like Gipp as a football player?" I asked McEwan after the game.

"Gipp is no football player," retorted McEwan. "He's a runaway son of a bitch!" One of the more volatile English instructors in West Point's long history, McEwan's descriptives remain as pungent as they are concise.

Self-reliant as a wild mustang, George Gipp came out of the iron-ore country near Calumet, Michigan, on Lake Superior's Keweenaw peninsula. He came up the hard way, but at making his point on a football field, Gipp could open with sevens and keep rolling 'em. He had more than his share of speed, power, daring and deception. At times he even baffled Rock. The following, told to me by a former Notre Dame star and assistant coach, occurred during the intermission of the historic 1920 Army game.

"Being behind by three points, Rock was really laying into the boys," he said. "He had about finished and Gipp, standing nearby, asked me for a drag of my cigarette. Rock looked up and spotted Gipp leaning against the door, his helmet on the back of his head, puffing the cigarette.

"Rock exploded, 'As for you, Gipp,' he crackled, 'I suppose you haven't any interest in this game...?'

" 'Listen, Rock,' replied Gipp, 'I've got five hundred dollars bet on this game; I don't aim to blow any five hundred!' "

Rock was younger then. Later, not even Gipp would have got away with it.

One of Rock's greatest gangs was his 1924 team that featured a veteran array of backs functioning behind a powerful, combative line.

In the fall of 1923, Army met Notre Dame at Ebbets Field because the World Series between the Yankees and the Giants was taking place at the Polo Grounds. I preferred the football game. That afternoon I took along "Brink" Thorne, Yale's great 1895 captain. We had only sideline passes so Brink and I watched from the rim of the playing field. In one wild end run, the Irish backfield of Harry Stuhldreher, Jim Crowley, Don Miller and Elmer Layden, swept off the field over the sideline. At least two of them jumped over me, down on my knees.

"It's worse than a cavalry charge," I said to Brink. "They're like a wild horse stampede."

That thought occurred to me a year later at the Polo Grounds when that same backfield beat Army 13–7 en route to an undefeated year, and the "Four Horsemen" emerged on my copy paper. I'm afraid it was those four football players who averaged only 157 pounds and the glory they won that made the phrase stick.

They were an amazing four men. Fullback Elmer Layden, better than a 10-second sprinter, weighed 164 and was the heaviest of the lot. Quarterback Stuhldreher, at 154 pounds, was the lightest; and the halfbacks Miller and Crowley were in between. Layden could run, block, kick and handle a forward pass. Fast and shifty, the Four Horsemen had a brand of rhythm that was beautiful to watch. They were a hardy lot and were seldom hurt. They could all block and tackle and carry the ball—the memory of them made me scoff a little during the days of platoon football, with offensive and defensive specialists cluttering up the premises each Saturday afternoon.

All were keen and smart. Rockne liked players on his squad like these four—all individualists who did their own thinking.

W. C. Heinz

When W. C. Heinz (1915–2008) returned from covering World War II in Europe, it was an honor for a copy boy just to open the crate in which his typewriter had been shipped back to the *New York Sun*. The paper's editors tried to reward Heinz by posting him in the Washington bureau, but he had other ideas, and they involved sports. He wanted to write about more than wins and losses; he wanted to dig deep into the games that transfixed the nation, and the men who played and coached them, and the forces that drove those men, sometimes to the limits of courage and nobility. In doing so he refined a style that employed the techniques of fiction—scenes, dialogue, character—and would two decades later be hailed as the New Journalism. But Bill Heinz never claimed to be doing anything more than writing as well as he could, whether it was for his *Sun* sports column, magazines like *Life*, *True*, and *Sport*, or his memorable collaboration with Vince Lombardi, *Run to Daylight!* (1963), which detailed a week in the life of the legendary coach as he remade the Green Bay Packers in his image. When you read Heinz's profile of Red Grange, pro football's first great broken-field runner—written for *True*'s November 1958 issue—his artistry won't be conspicuous, but it is there between the lines.

The Ghost of the Gridiron

WHEN I WAS TEN YEARS OLD I paid ten cents to see Red Grange run with a football. That was the year when, one afternoon a week, after school was out for the day, they used to show us movies in the auditorium, and we would all troop up there clutching our dimes, nickels or pennies in our fists.

The movies were, I suppose, carefully selected for their educational value. They must have shown us, as the weeks went by, films of the Everglades, of Yosemite, of the Gettysburg battlefield, of Washington, D.C., but I remember only the one about Grange.

I remember, in fact, only one shot. Grange, the football cradled in one arm, started down the field toward us. As we sat there in the dim, flickering light of the movie projector, he grew larger and larger. I can still see the rows and rows of us, with our thin little necks and bony heads, all looking up at the screen and Grange, enormous now, rushing right at us, and I shall never forget it. That was thirty-three years ago.

"I haven't any idea what film that might have been," Grange was saying now. "My last year at Illinois was all confusion. I had no privacy. Newsreel men were staying at the fraternity house for two or three days at a time."

He paused. The thought of it seemed to bring pain to his face, even at this late date.

"I wasn't able to study or anything," he said. "I thought and I still do, that they built me up out of all proportion."

Red Grange was the most sensational, the most publicized, and, possibly, the most gifted football player and greatest broken field runner of all time. In high school, at Wheaton, Illinois, he averaged five touchdowns a game. In twenty games for the University of Illinois, he scored thirty-one touchdowns and ran for 3,637 yards, or, as it was translated at the time, 2 miles and 117 yards. His name and his pseudonyms—The Galloping Ghost and The Wheaton Iceman—became household words, and what he was may have been summarized best by Paul Sann in his book *The Lawless Decade*.

"Red Grange, No. 77, made Jack Dempsey move over," Sann wrote. "He put college football ahead of boxing as the Golden Age picked up momentum. He also made the ball yards obsolete; they couldn't handle the crowds. He made people buy more radios: how could you wait until Sunday morning to find out what deeds Red Grange had performed on Saturday? He was 'The Galloping Ghost' and he made the sports historians torture their portables without mercy."

Grange is now 55 years old, his reddish brown hair marked with gray, but he was one with Babe Ruth, Jack Dempsey, Bobby Jones and Bill Tilden.

"I could carry a football well," Grange was saying now, "but I've met hundreds of people who could do their thing better than I. I mean engineers, and writers, scientists, doctors—whatever.

"I can't take much credit for what I did, running with a football, because I don't know what I did. Nobody ever taught me, and I can't teach anybody. You can teach a man how to block or tackle or kick or pass. The ability to run with a ball is something you have or you haven't. If you can't explain it, how can you take credit for it?"

This was last year, and we were sitting in a restaurant in Syracuse, New York. Grange was in town to do a telecast with Lindsey Nelson of the Syracuse-Penn State game. He lives now in Miami, Florida, coming out of there on weekends during the football season to handle telecasts of college games on Saturdays and the Chicago Bears' games on Sundays. He approaches this job as he has approached every job, with honesty and dedication, and, as could be expected, he is good at it. As befits a man who put the pro game on the map and made the whole nation football conscious, he has been making fans out of people who never followed the game before. Never, perhaps, has any one man done more for the game. And it, of course, has been good to him.

"Football did everything for me," he was saying now, "but what people don't understand is that it hasn't been my whole life. When I was a freshman at Illinois, I wasn't even going to go out for football. My fraternity brothers made me do it."

He was three times All-American. Once the Illinois students carried him two miles on their backs. A football jersey, with the number 77 that he made famous and that was retired after him, is enshrined at Champaign. His fellow students wanted him to run for Congress. A Senator from Illinois led him into the White House to shake hands with Calvin Coolidge. Here, in its entirety, is what was said.

"Howdy," Coolidge said. "Where do you live?"

"In Wheaton, Illinois," Grange said.

"Well, young man," Coolidge said, "I wish you luck."

Grange had his luck, but it was coming to him because he did more to popularize professional football than any other player before or since. In his first three years out of school he grossed almost $1,000,000 from football, motion pictures, vaudeville appearances and endorsements, and he could afford to turn down a Florida real estate firm that wanted to pay him $120,000 a year. Seven years ago the Associated Press, in selecting an All-Time All-American team in conjunction with the National Football Hall of Fame, polled one hundred leading sportswriters and Grange received more votes than any other player.

"They talk about the runs I made," he was saying, "but I can't tell you one thing I did on any run. That's the truth. During the depression, though, I took a licking. Finally I got into the insurance business. I almost starved to death for three years, but I never once tried to use my football reputation. I never once opened a University of Illinois year book and knowingly called on an alumnus. I think I was as good an insurance man as there was in Chicago. On the football field I had ten other men blocking for me, but I'm more proud of what I did in the insurance business, because I did it alone."

Recently I went down to Miami and visited Grange in the white colonial duplex house where he lives with his wife. They met eighteen years ago on a plane, flying between Chicago and Omaha, on which she was a stewardess, and they were married the following year.

"Without sounding like an amateur psychologist," I said, "I believe you derive more satisfaction from what you did in the insurance business, not only because you did it alone, but also because you know how you did it, and, if you had to, you could do it again. You could never find any security in what you did when you ran with a football because it was inspirational and creative, rather than calculated."

"Yes," Grange said, "you could call it that. The sportswriters used to try to explain it, and they used to ask me. I couldn't tell them anything."

I have read what many of those sportswriters wrote, and they had as much trouble trying to corner Grange on paper as his opponents had trying to tackle him on the field....

Grange had blinding speed, amazing lateral mobility, and exceptional change of pace and a powerful straight-arm. He moved with high knee action, but seemed to glide, rather than run, and he was a master at using his blockers. What made him great, however, was his instinctive ability to size up a field and plot a run the way a great general can map not only a battle but a whole campaign.

"The sportswriters wrote that I had peripheral vision," Grange was saying. "I didn't even know what the word meant. I had to look it up. They asked me about my change of pace, and I didn't even know that I ran at different speeds. I had a cross-over step, but I couldn't spin. Some ball carriers can spin but if I ever tried that, I would have broken a leg."

Harold Edward Grange was born on June 13, 1903, in Forksville, Pennsylvania, the third of four children. His mother died when he was five, and his sister Norma died in her teens. The other sister, Mildred, lives in Binghamton, New York. His brother, Garland, two and a half years younger than Red, was a 165-pound freshman end at Illinois and was later with the Chicago Bears and is now a credit manager for a Florida department store chain. Their father died at the age of 86.

"My father," Grange said, "was the foreman of three lumber camps near Forksville, and if you had known him, you'd know why I could never get a swelled head. He stood six-one and weighed 210 pounds, and he was quick as a cat. He had three hundred men under him and he had to be able to lick any one of them. One day he had a fight that lasted four hours."

Grange's father, after the death of his wife, moved to Wheaton, Illinois, where he had relatives. Then he sent the two girls back to Pennsylvania to live with their maternal grandparents. With his sons, he moved into a five-room apartment over a store where they took turns cooking and keeping house.

"Can you recall," I said, "the first time you ever ran with a football?"

"I think it started," Grange said, "with a game we used to play without a football. Ten or twelve of us would line up in the street, along one curb. One guy would be in the middle of the road and the rest of us would run across the street to the curb on the other side. Then the kid in the middle of the street tackled one of the runners, the one who was tackled had to stay in the middle of the street with the tackler. Finally, all of us, except one last runner, would be in the middle of the street. We only had about thirty yards to maneuver in and dodge the tackler. I got to be pretty good at that. Then somebody got a football and we played games with it on vacant lots."

In high school Grange won sixteen letters in football, basketball, track and baseball. In track he competed in the 100 and 220 yard dashes, low and high hurdles, broad jump and high jump and often won all six events. In his sophomore year on the football team, he scored 15 touchdowns, in his junior year 36—eight in one game—and in his senior year 23. Once he was kicked in the head and was incoherent for 48 hours.

"I went to Illinois," he was saying, "because some of my friends from Wheaton went there and all the kids in the state wanted to play football for Bob Zuppke and because there weren't any athletic scholarships in those days and that was the cheapest place for me to go to. In May of my senior year in high school I was there for the Interscholastic track meet, and I just got through broad jumping when Zup came over. He said, 'Is your name Grainche?' That's the way he always pronounced my name. I said, 'Yes.' He said, 'Where are you going to college?' I said, 'I don't know.' He put his arm around my shoulders and he said, 'I hope here. You may have a chance to make the team here.' That was the greatest moment I'd known."

That September, Grange arrived at Champaign with a battered second-hand trunk, one suit, a couple of pairs of trousers and a sweater. He had been working for four summers on an ice wagon in Wheaton and saving some money, and his one luxury now that he was entering college was to pledge Zeta Phi fraternity.

"One day," he was saying, "they lined us pledges up in the living room of the fraternity house. I had wanted to go out for basketball and track—I thought there would be too much competition in football— but they started to point to each one of us and tell us what to go out for: 'You go out for cheerleader. You go out for football manager. You go out for the band.' When they came to me, they said, 'You go out for football.'

"That afternoon I went over to the gym. I looked out the window at the football practice field and they had about three hundred freshman candidates out there. I went back to the house and I said to one of the seniors, 'I can't go out for football. I'll never make that team.'

"So he lined me up near the wall, with my head down, and he hit me with this paddle. I could show you the dent in that wall where my head took a piece of plaster out—this big."

With the thumb and forefinger of his right hand, he made a circle the size of a half dollar.

"Do you remember the name of that senior?" I said.

"Johnny Hawks," Grange said. "He was from Goshen, Indiana, and I see him now and then. I say to him. 'Damn you. If it wasn't for you, I'd never have gone out for football.' He gets a great boot out of that."

"So what happened when you went out the next day?"

"We had all these athletes from Chicago I'd been reading about. What chance did I have, from a little farm town and a high school with three hundred students? I think they cut about forty that first night, but I happened to win the wind sprints and that got them at least to know my name."

It was a great freshman team. On it with Grange was Earl Britton, who blocked for Grange and did the kicking throughout their college careers, and Moon Baker and Frank Wickhorst, who transferred to Northwestern and Annapolis, respectively, where they both made All-American. After one week of practice, the freshman team played the varsity and were barely nosed out, 21–19, as Grange scored two touchdowns, one on a 60 yard punt return. From then on, the freshmen trimmed the varsity regularly and Zuppke began to give most of his time to the freshmen.

"That number 77," I said to Grange, "became the most famous number in football. Do you remember when you first got it?"

"It was just handed to me in my sophomore year," he said. "I guess anybody who has a number and does well with it gets a little superstitious about it, and I guess that began against Nebraska in my first varsity game."

That game started Grange to national fame. This was 1923, and the previous year Nebraska had beaten Notre Dame and they were to beat "The Four Horsemen" later this same season. In the first quarter Grange sprinted 35 yards for a touchdown. In the second quarter he ran 60 yards for another. In the third period he scored again on a 12 yard burst, and Illinois won, 24–7. The next day, over Walter Eckersall's story in the Chicago *Tribune*, the headline said: GRANGE SPRINTS TO FAME.

From the Nebraska game, Illinois went on to an undefeated season. Against Butler, Grange scored twice. Against Iowa, he scored the only touchdown as Illinois won, 9–6. In the first quarter against Northwestern, he intercepted a pass and ran 90 yards to score the first of his three touchdowns. He made the only touchdown in the game with the University of Chicago and the only one in the Ohio State game, this time on a 34 yard run.

"All Grange can do is run," Fielding Yost, the coach at Michigan, was quoted as saying.

"All Galli-Curci can do is sing," Zuppke said.

Grange had his greatest day in his first game against Michigan during his junior year. On that day Michigan came to the dedication of the new $1,700,000 Illinois Memorial Stadium. The Wolverines had been undefeated in twenty games and for months the nation's football fans had been waiting for this meeting. There were 67,000 spectators in the stands, then the largest crowd ever to see a football game in the Midwest.

Michigan kicked off. Grange was standing on his goal line, with Wally McIlwain, whom Zuppke was to call "the greatest open field blocker of all time," on his right, Harry Hall, the Illinois quarterback, on his left, and Earl Britton in front of him. Michigan attempted to aim the kickoff to McIlwain, but as the ball descended, Grange moved over under it.

"I've got it," he said to McIlwain.

He caught it on the 5-yard line. McIlwain turned and took out the first Michigan man to get near him. Britton cut down the next one, and Grange started under way. He ran to his left, reversed his field to avoid one would-be tackler, and, then, cutting back again to the left, ran diagonally across the field through the oncoming Michigan players. At the Michigan 40-yard line he was in the open and on the 20-yard line, Tod Rockwell, the Michigan safety man, made a futile dive for him. Grange scored standing up. Michigan never recovered.

In less than twelve minutes, Grange scored three more touchdowns on runs of 67, 56 and 44 yards. Zuppke took him out to rest him. In the third period, he re-entered the game, and circled right end for 15 yards and another touchdown. In the final quarter, he threw a pass for another score. Illinois won, 39–14. Against a powerful, seasoned and favored team, Grange had handled the ball twenty-one times, gained 402 yards running, scored five touchdowns and collaborated, as a passer, in a sixth.

"This was," Coach Amos Alonzo Stagg, the famous Chicago mentor, later wrote, "the most spectacular singlehanded performance ever made in a major game."

"Did Zuppke tell you that you should have scored another touchdown?" I asked Grange.

"That's right," Grange said. "After the fourth touchdown we called a time-out, and when Matt Bullock, our trainer, came with the water, I said to him, 'I'm dog tired. You'd better tell Zup to get me out of here.' When I got to the bench Zup said to me, 'You should have had five touchdowns. You didn't cut right on one play.' Nobody could get a swelled head around him."

"And you don't recall," I said, "one feint or cut that you made during any one of those runs?"

"I don't remember one thing I ever did on any run I made. I just remember one vision from that Michigan game. On that opening kickoff runback, as I got downfield I saw that the only man still in front of me was the safety man, Tod Rockwell. I remember thinking then, 'I'd better get by this guy, because after coming all this way, I'll sure look like a bum if he tackles me.' I can't tell you, though, how I did get by him."

When Grange started his senior year, Illinois had lost seven regulars by graduation and Harry Hall, its quarterback, who had a broken collarbone. Zuppke shifted Grange to quarterback. Illinois lost to Nebraska, Iowa and Michigan and barely beat Butler before they came to Franklin Field in Philadelphia on October 31, 1925, to play Pennsylvania.

The previous year Penn had been considered the champion of the East. They had now beaten Brown, Yale and Chicago, among others. Although Grange's exploits in the Midwest had been widely reported in Eastern papers, most of the 65,000 spectators and the Eastern sportswriters—Grantland Rice, Damon Runyon and Ford Frick among them—came to be convinced.

It had rained and snowed for 24 hours, with only straw covering the field. At the kickoff, the players stood in mud. On the third play of the game, the first time he carried the ball, Grange went 55 yards for his first touchdown. On the next kickoff he ran 55 yards again, to the Penn 25-yard line, and Illinois worked it over the goal line from there. In the second period, Grange twisted 12 yards for another score and in the third period he ran 20 yards to a touchdown. Illinois won, 24–2, with Grange carrying the ball 363 yards, and scoring three touchdowns and setting up another one, in thirty-six rushes.

Two days later when the train carrying the Illinois team arrived in Champaign, there were 20,000 students, faculty members and townspeople waiting at the station. Grange tried to sneak out of the last car but he was recognized and carried two miles to his fraternity house.

"Do you remember your feelings during those two miles?" I asked him.

"I remember that I was embarrassed," he said. "You wish people would understand that it takes eleven men to make a football team. Unless they've played it, I guess they'll never understand it, but I've never been impressed by individual performances in football, my own or anyone else's."

"Do you remember the last touchdown you scored in college?"

"To tell you the truth, I don't," he said. "It must have been against Ohio State. I can't tell you the score. I can't tell you the score of more than three or four games I ever played in."

I looked it up. Grange's last college appearance, against Ohio State, attracted 85,500 spectators at Columbus. He was held to 153 yards on the ground but threw one touchdown pass as Illinois won, 14–9. The following afternoon, in the Morrison Hotel in Chicago, he signed with Charles C. (Cash and Carry) Pyle to play professional football with the Chicago Bears, starting immediately, and he quit college. Twenty-five years later, however, he was elected to the University of Illinois Board of Trustees for a six-year term.

"I had a half year to finish when I quit," he said. "I had this chance to make a lot of money and I couldn't figure where having a sheepskin would pull any more people into football games."

"How were your marks in college?"

"I was an average student. I got B's and C's. I flunked one course, economics, and I made that up in the summer at Wheaton College. I'd leave the ice wagon at 11 o'clock in the morning and come back to it at 1 o'clock. There was so much written about my job on the ice wagon, and so many pictures of me lugging ice, that people thought it was a publicity stunt. It wasn't. I did it for eight summers, starting at 5 o'clock every morning, for two reasons. The pay was good—$37.50 a week—and I needed money. I didn't even have any decent clothes until my junior year. Also, it kept me in shape. After carrying those blocks of ice up and down stairs six days a week, my legs were always in shape when the football season started. Too many football players have to play their legs into shape in the first four or five games."

Grange played professional football from 1925 through the 1934 season, first with the Bears, then with the New York Yankees in a rival pro league that Pyle and he started, and then back with the Bears again. He was immobilized during the 1928 season with arm and knee injuries, and after that he was never able to cut sharply while carrying the ball. He did, however, score 162 touchdowns as a professional and kicked 86 conversion points, for a total of 1,058 points.

What the statistics do not show, however, is what Grange, more than any other player, did to focus public attention and approval on the professional game. In 1925, when he signed with the Bears, professional football attracted little notice on the sports pages and few paying customers. There was so little interest that the National Professional Football League did not even hold a championship playoff at the end of the season.

In ten days after he left college Grange played five games as a pro and changed all that. After only three practice sessions with the Bears, he made his pro debut against the Chicago Cardinals on Thanksgiving Day, November 26. The game ended 0–0 but 36,000 people crowded into Wrigley Field to see Grange. Three days later, on a Sunday, 28,000 defied a snowstorm to watch him perform at the same field. On the next Wednesday, freezing weather in St. Louis held the attendance down to 8,000 but on Saturday 40,000 Philadelphians watched him in the rain at Shibe Park. The next day the Bears played in the Polo Grounds against the New York Giants.

It had been raining for almost a week, and, although advance sales were almost unknown in pro football in those days, the Giants sold almost 60,000 before Sunday dawned. It turned out to be a beautiful day. Cautious fans who had not bought seats in advance stormed the ticket booths. Thousands of people were turned away but 73,651 crammed into the park. Grange did not score but the Bears won, 19–7.

That was the beginning of professional football's rise to its present popularity. At the end of those first ten days, Grange picked up a check for $50,000. He got another $50,000 when the season ended a month later.

"Can you remember," I asked him now, "the last time you ever carried a football?"

"It was in a game against the Giants in Gilmore Stadium in Hollywood in January of 1935. It was the last period, and we had a safe lead and I was sitting on the bench. George Halas said to me, 'Would you like to go in, Red?' I said, 'No, thanks.' Everybody knew this was my last year. He said, 'Go ahead. Why don't you run it just once more?'

"So I went in, and we lined up and they called a play for me. As soon as I got the ball and started to go I knew that they had it framed with the Giants to let me run. The line just opened up for me and I went through and started down the field. The farther I ran, the heavier my legs got and the farther those goal posts seemed to move away. I was thinking, 'When I make that end zone, I'm going to take off these shoes and shoulder pads for the last time.' With that something hit me from behind and down I went on about the 10-yard line. It was Cecil Irvin, a 230-pound tackle. He was so slow that, I guess, they never bothered to let him in on the plan. But when he caught me from behind, I knew I was finished."

Grange, who is 5 feet 11 and ¾ inches, weighed 180 in college and 185 in his last game with the Bears. Now he weighs 200. On December 15, 1951, he suffered a heart attack. This motivated him to give up his insurance business and to move to Florida, where he and his wife own, in addition to their own home in Miami, land in Orlando and Melbourne and property at Indian Lake.

"Red," I said, "I'll bet there are some men still around whose greatest claim to fame is that they played football with you or against you. I imagine there are guys whose proudest boast is that they once tackled you. Have you ever run into a guy who thought he knew everything about football and didn't know he was talking with Red Grange?"

"Yes," he said. "Once about fifteen years ago, on my way home from work, I dropped into a tavern in Chicago for a beer. Two guys next to me and the bartender were arguing about Bronko Nagurski and Carl Brumbaugh. On the Bears, of course, I played in the backfield with both of them. One guy doesn't like Nagurski and he's talking against him. I happen to think Nagurski was the greatest football player I ever saw, and a wonderful guy. This fellow who is knocking him says to me, 'Do you know anything about football? Did you ever see Nagurski play?' I said, 'Yes, and I think he was great.' The guy gets mad and says, 'What was so great about him? What do you know about it?' I could see it was time to leave, but the guy kept at me. He said, 'Now wait a minute. What makes you think you know something about it? Who are you, anyway?' I reached into my wallet and took out my business card and handed it to him and started for the door. When I got to the door, I looked back at him. You should have seen his face."

Mrs. Grange, who had been listening to our talk, left the room and came back with a small, gold-plated medal that Grange had won in the broad jump at the Interscholastic track meet on the day when he first met Zuppke.

"A friend of mine just sent that to me," Grange said. "He wrote: 'You gave me this away back in 1921. I thought you might want it.' Just the other day I got a letter from a man in the Midwest who told me that his son just found a gold football inscribed, 'University of Illinois, 1924' with the initials H. G. on it. I was the only H. G. on that squad so it must have been mine. I guess I gave it to somebody and he lost it. I wrote the man back and said: 'If your son would like it, I'd be happy to have him keep it.'"

Mrs. Grange said, "We have a friend who can't understand why Red doesn't keep his souvenirs. He has his trophies in another friend's storage locker in Chicago. The clipping books are nailed up in a box in the garage here and Red hasn't looked at them in years."

"I don't like to look back," Grange said. "You have to look ahead."

I remembered that night when we ate in the restaurant in Syracuse. As we stood in line to get our hats and coats, Grange nudged me and showed me his hat check. In the middle of the yellow cardboard disk was the number 77.

"Has this ever happened to you before?" I said.

"Never," he said, "as far as I know."

We walked out into the cold night air. A few flakes of snow were falling.

"That jersey with the 77 on it that's preserved at Illinois," I said, "is that your last game jersey?"

"I don't know," Grange said. "It was probably a new jersey."

"Do you have any piece of equipment that you wore on the football field?"

"No," he said. "I don't have anything."

The traffic light changed, and we started across the street. "I don't even have an I-sweater," he said.

We walked about three paces.

"You know," Grange said, "I'd kind of like to have an I-sweater now."

Myron Cope

Myron Cope (1929–2008) was the radio voice of the Pittsburgh Steelers for thirty-five seasons, and what a voice it was—an adenoidal screech punctuated by a language that was partly local patois, partly Yiddish, and partly his own creation. He invented the "Terrible Towel" during the 1975 playoffs to give a stadium full of fans something to wave while he translated the excitement into such Cope-isms as "Yoi!" and "Okel-dokel!" Too often overlooked was the work Cope did as a sportswriter before he gave broadcasting his full attention. He learned his way around a sentence at the *Pittsburgh Post-Gazette* and zeroed in on eccentrics in every sport for such magazines as *True*, *Sport*, *The Saturday Evening Post*, and *Sports Illustrated*. His reward was an *SI*-financed trip around the country to interview the men who were present for the creation of pro football, a hardy, rough-hewn band that played, as Cope put it, "when there were no offers to endorse shaving cream." The result was *The Game That Was* (1970), an oral history every bit as rich as Lawrence Ritter's epic work on baseball's early days, *The Glory of Their Times* (1966). In the following excerpt, Cope encounters one John Victor McNally (1903–1985), better known as the vagabond halfback Johnny Blood. Starting in 1925, Blood played for fourteen seasons, in Green Bay and Pittsburgh as well as Milwaukee, Duluth, and Pottsville, Pa., and at every stop, he made a point of proving what he proudly called his "high resistance to culture."

from

The Game That Was: Johnny Blood

I COULDN'T SAY, particularly, that I was the black sheep in my family, though some people were inclined to view some of my episodes with less than applause. Well, by way of explanation, there *is* a difference between pro football now and pro football then. I'm referring to, say, the early 1930s, during the Depression. In 1931 I was All-Pro right halfback. I had scored thirteen touchdowns, which at that time was a league record, and I was in the All-Pro backfield along with Red Grange, Ernie Nevers, and Dutch Clark. I had played for Green Bay three years and we had won three championships. But when it came time to go back to Green Bay for the '32 season, I had no money to get across the state from my home in New Richmond. I had only a dollar or two in my pocket.

So I decided to ride free on the train. They called it the Soo Line, but its real name was the Minneapolis, St. Paul & Sault Sainte Marie Railroad, and in order to get to Green Bay you would have to change trains at Amherst Junction to the Green Bay & Western. I got on the Soo Line and rode the blinds down to a place called Stevens Point, where there was a stop. I got off and inquired about connections at Amherst Junction and was told that the Green Bay & Western would get into Amherst Junction a couple of minutes before the Soo Line but if you wired ahead they would hold the train. They did this for passengers. So I wired ahead and then got back on the blinds again and rode to Amherst Junction. There I got off the Soo and ran down a cut and grabbed on to the blinds of the Green Bay & Western. After the trainmen waited around for a few minutes for the passenger who had wired ahead, they gave up and started the train.

Well, about ten miles from Green Bay, the door of a freight car opened and one of the crew looked out and saw me and said, "John, what are you doing out there?" Everybody on the Green Bay & Western knew the Packer football players. The guy said, "Come on in and wash up." So I got me a bowl of water, and while I was washing up, he looked at me and said, "Say, where did you get on?" I said, "Amherst Junction." And he started laughing. He said, "Oh, so you're the guy who wired ahead! Well, you're the first hobo I ever heard of holding a train for." And this, in essence, shows you the difference between pro football in 1932 and pro football today.

By the way, when I told Ollie Kuechle, a Milwaukee sportswriter, how I got to camp, he said, "We're going to call you the Hobo Halfback." I didn't say anything. That was his business if he wanted to call me the Hobo Halfback. But Curly Lambeau, our coach, didn't like it. He thought we were on the big time and going to win another championship. He didn't like the term. So Ollie said, "Well, okay. We'll call him the Vagabond Halfback." For years after, I was known as the Vagabond Halfback, and maybe all this is a partial answer to your question as to whether my relatives regarded me as the black sheep.

I'm a schizophrenic personality. I was born under the sign of Sagittarius, which is half stud and half philosopher. The stud, of course, is the body of a horse, and I was always full of *run*. Running all the time when I was a kid. In the sign of Sagittarius the body of the horse joins with the chest of a man, who is aiming a bow and arrow. This is a man who's looking for a target and is going to hit it, which I take represents the philosopher in him. So with that combination of philosopher and stud, I always felt I was going two ways. My life illustrates it. Let me put it this way. I had an aunt, a big, husky doll, and one day she asked me, "John, what are you really interested in?"

"Well," I said, "I guess I'm really interested in the theory of morals and the theory of money."

She started to laugh. I said, "What are you laughing at, Aunt?" And she said, "Well, isn't that funny! You'll never have any of either!"

I come from a group of Irish people. The names of my eight great-grandparents were McNally, Barrett, Reilly, McCormick, Murphy, McGraw, McGannon, and McGough. Our outfit came over and settled in Wisconsin because it was just opening up around 1850, and from that group, some of them succeeded quite well and some did not. They all stayed out of jail and all got decent funerals, and some of them did quite well, that's correct. My father was a McNally and my mother was a Murphy. Father became the general manager of a successful flour mill, and my mother's two brothers became publishers of the Minneapolis *Tribune*. But I claim my poor relatives as well as my rich ones.

I got out of high school at fourteen and a half, really. It wasn't that I was precocious but that I was *pushed* along by my mother, who had been a schoolteacher. I had no signs of athletic ability, because I was too small. Even later, when I matured, I matured late. My parents had tried to make me master the violin and be a debater and recite poems. They wanted to make a cultured individual out of me, but I had a high resistance. In the seventh or eighth grade I once put on a very poor public performance with the violin, playing "Turkey in the Straw," which was a very humiliating experience for me. I haven't gotten over it yet.

Well, as I say, I was a runner. I used to run away from home. I'd catch freights. The fact is, I can remember my father giving me several memorable drummings with a shillelagh, which I recall with no malice at all. I was still in knee pants when I graduated from high school and a little young to go to college, so I studied bookkeeping and typewriting, and the following year, 1919, my parents sent me to River Falls State Normal, about twenty miles away. They went to California and left me with a checkbook, which turned out to be a mistake. Because of that, I eventually decided to join the Navy to avoid a confrontation with my parents.

The Navy, however, turned me down because my eyesight wasn't up to standards, although I subsequently made a living in football with my eyesight, and in World War II, when they weren't quite so choosy, the Army took me and I served as a cryptographer in China. Anyhow, I left River Falls State Normal and went to work in a packing plant at New Richmond and then went up to Dakota to put in the crops. I slept in a wagon. I can remember that on the longest day of the year, June 21, 1919, after I got up and finished getting the bugs off me, I fed the horses before the sun came up and then spent the entire day, till sundown, alone on a section of half-broken land, which I was cultivating—"disking," they called it. So I figured out that this was too tough a way to make a living. That was my terminal experience on the farm.

From there I went to St. John's University in Minnesota, which was where Eugene McCarthy later went to school. At the time, there were about six hundred students in the university, but that's what they called it—a university. It was a Benedictine institution, but I was an antitheological misfit. However, I played my first football game there, in the intramural league. I played for a team called the Cat's Pajamas. That was an expression current at the time—it meant something like "a superior guy." Anyway, I was an immediate success with the Cat's Pajamas. By that time I was sixteen and a half. I was tall but frightfully skinny, but the summer up in Dakota had toughened me up. We won the intramural league, and later I started competing for the college team.

After three years there, I had a little confidence in myself and felt ready for a bigger sphere. I went down to Notre Dame and went out for the freshman squad. The Four Horsemen were playing for Notre Dame that season, and as it turned out, the only contribution I made to Notre Dame football was that I wrote Harry Stuhldreher's poetry assignments. You see, they wanted to make a tackle out of me. I was six feet tall, but I weighed only 160 pounds and felt that my function was to avoid contact rather than to make it. So I did not stay long on the football squad, and the following St. Patrick's Day I took a little trip and had an unexplained absence from school. When the officials began investigating my absence, they discovered that in addition to my dormitory room, I kept another room in town. They took exception to the nature of my existence and suspended me. So I got a motorcycle and took a big trip. About thirty years later, when I decided to resume my education, I went back to Notre Dame to inquire about my credits, if any. They showed me my record. Inscribed upon it was no mention of any accomplishments but only the words, "Gone, never to return."

After the motorcycle trip, I went to work on a Minneapolis newspaper as a stereotyper, but it didn't take me long to see that a stereotyper's work was not for me. Meanwhile, I heard that there was a way of making a little money in the fall playing football. There were four teams in a semi-pro league in Minneapolis, and one of these teams was called the East 26th Street Liberties. They had a small practice field alongside the railroad track with one light, which was in the center of the field. That was the lighting by which they practiced. Well, I and another stereotyper decided to try out. As we went out to the field, riding my motorcycle, we went by a theater where the marquee advertised a picture titled *Blood and Sand*. Being that both of us still felt we might have some college eligibility left, and knowing that semi-pro football would ruin our amateur standing, I realized we had to have fake names if we played semi-pro ball. So when the East 26th Street Liberties asked us what our names were, it popped into my head right there. I said, "My name is Blood and this guy's name is Sand."

We won the league championship that fall, and then were paid for the entire season. We got ten dollars for our effort. We spent it that night.

The following year, 1925, I got an offer to play for a team in Ironwood, Michigan, for seventy-five dollars a game. I played three games there, then jumped the team for an offer from the Milwaukee Badgers of the National Football League. I remember we played in Steubenville, Ohio—that was really quite a fun city—and it was there that I became convinced that I might have a future in pro ball. Steubenville had a guy named Sol Butler, who had been a broad jumper in the Olympics. I caught a pass and ran away from Sol Butler, and that was the first time I really thought I was a ball player. Nobody believed in the future of pro ball at that point, but I believed I was a pro ballplayer.

You see, I had been drifting along in the sense that I was looking for my life-style, as they say nowadays. I wanted a life in which I could do something I enjoyed and still have leisure to do other things that I enjoyed. Football was an escape, certainly, but an escape into something that I enjoyed. In the off-season I would ship out to the Orient as an ordinary seaman and enjoy the beauty of the Pacific islands. Or I would winter on Catalina Island off the coast of Los Angeles. Understand, I was not afraid of work. I had sufficient energy that work did not bother me at all. I was a hard worker. To me, freedom did not mean being able to do only the nondifficult but, rather, to do what I chose to do. One winter in Catalina, I worked three shifts. I worked in the brickyard all day, making bricks. I worked the next eight hours in a gambling hall as a bouncer. And the next eight hours, I "honeymooned" with a redhead.

The football season was a great time of year. During the seasons I played for Green Bay, the ball players stayed at the Astor Hotel. They'd sit around the hotel and gossip, or they'd go to libraries—well, maybe one out of a hundred pro ballplayers would go to a library. We played golf, we went hunting, we drank—the ordinary activities of young men when they're at leisure. We had no difficulty passing the day. The fall weather in Green Bay was beautiful, and just to do *nothing* was marvelous. Just watching the autumn turn golden was a pleasure.

The ordinary ball player made seventy-five to a hundred dollars a week, but it was tax-free and it was a dollar worth twice as much as the dollar is worth today. There weren't too many people getting that kind of money at our age. And right across the street from the hotel was the YWCA, where you could get a good dinner for seventy-five cents. That's where we usually ate. The boys from the South watched their money, because things were tough down South and they were trained that way. But as for myself, I can say that in spite of my interest in monetary theory, I always remembered that "they who harvested the golden grain, and they who flung it to the winds like rain, alike to the same aureate earth are borne." It takes a guy who's really loose with money to think about it freely.

Curly Lambeau used to say that I trained harder than anybody on the club. That is, I spent more energy on the training field than the average guy, and I believe that to be true or I would not repeat it. But in 1933 Lambeau fired me. We were in New York that year to play the Giants, and we were having a medium season, with about three or four games to go. It was a Friday night, about eight o'clock, and I got a call at the hotel from some millionaire's wife—the wife of some millionaire from the Fox River Valley around Green Bay. She wanted me to meet her at the Stork Club.

I said, "Oh, no. I couldn't do that. The game's only day after tomorrow." So I got ready to go to bed, and here two goddamned nurses rapped on the door. So my roommate and I ordered up a few drinks. Well, we got pretty loaded. Next morning, I went out to practice in not the best of condition. Alcohol, you see, hangs on to me. I don't sober up real fast. It's a family characteristic—I have plenty of recuperative power, but alcohol doesn't fall out of me. It hangs on to me.

So I went out to practice and got ready to punt, and the first ball I kicked, I fell flat on my ass. Lambeau sent me back to the hotel. He came up afterward and said, "I've got to let you go." I didn't argue with him. I never argued. Well, the team played New York without me and lost the game, but the fact was that I was fired. I went over to Paterson, New Jersey, and played a couple games with a Paterson semi-pro team, and finally the Packers were playing Chicago in their last game of the season, and Lambeau got in touch with me to come back. He got to thinking about next year, I suppose, and that I'd be a free agent if I was still fired. About June the next year, 1934, he sold me to Pittsburgh.

Art Rooney, the Pittsburgh owner, had taken a fancy to me. He liked Irishmen. But after I got to Pittsburgh he no doubt was a little disappointed in me. He pressed me to go to confession, to make a better Roman Catholic of me. Let's just say that I came under the heading, but spell it with an *i*, an *n*, and an apostrophe. I *was* a roamin' Catholic.

Anyway, after a season in Pittsburgh I decided the next summer that I wanted to get back with Green Bay. I knew that the Packers were training up in northern Wisconsin and that they had scheduled an exhibition game with the Chippewa Falls Marines and two more with the La Crosse Loggers. So I got on with both of those semi-pro teams and played three games against Green Bay and did all right. I talked to Art Rooney and told him I had a chance to go back with the Packers, and he said okay, go ahead. But it was from that point on that I started having real trouble with Lambeau.

He began to push me around. This was because I had gotten quite a reputation around Green Bay. Lambeau was football in that town. He became jealous of me. He would sit me on the bench. The game would be practically lost and the fans would be hollering, "Put him in! Put Blood in!" So then, when we were just about dead, he'd say to me, "Get in!" I'd have to come up with a big play, and that's how I got the reputation of being a clutch player. Lambeau wouldn't play me unless he had to play me!

After two years of that, I went back to Pittsburgh as a player and head coach, and later, in the early 1950s, I was head coach at St. John's for three years. We won about 75 percent of our games. I'm neither awfully proud of my coaching record nor am I ashamed of it. But I would not say that my temperament was designed for coaching. A coach can't be concerned with the poor ballplayer. If the player can't make it, he's got to be out right away. It's a very tough aspect of coaching, and in this aspect I was weak. Also, some guys get fat on coaching—they get healthy and strong—but other guys get ulcers. At St. John's, I got ulcers. All those guys in black suits who had been there all their lives, they'd say, "We know all about this coaching. We have the best boys. We know our boys are the best boys. *Why* are they the best boys? They're at St. John's, *that's* why they're the best boys." So I got ulcers, which is not necessarily inconsistent with my temperament. A lot of clowns have ulcers.

I gave up coaching in 1953 and since then have spent the years meditating. I inherited enough money to take it a little easier. I wrote a book called *Spend Yourself Rich,* which deals with my theory that riches consist of consuming products. Actually, I wrote the book a long time ago, in 1940, and then got it out to rework it twenty years later. The first time, I had written it in a madhouse. Yes, in a madhouse. See, I had some friends who once said, "John, you've been on a big song and dance. Maybe you'd better slow down." At Winnebago there was a hospital run by the State of Wisconsin, so I went there and stayed ninety days and dashed off this tome. Twenty years later I went back to the manuscript to see if there was anything wrong with it, and I decided there wasn't anything wrong with it. The book is now out of print. Well, actually, it was never published. But hell, it didn't do me any harm to get it off my chest. I'd been carrying a typewriter in the back of my car for years, not knowing why.

Shirley Povich

No kinder or more decent man ever graced a press box than Shirley Povich (1905–1998)—and yes, he was definitely male, even though he was once included in *Who's Who of American Women*. Shirley was a common boys' name in his native Maine (and close enough to "Sorella," a Yiddish transliteration of his grandmother Sarah's name). Povich, meanwhile, was an uncommon talent. He was all of twenty when he became the *Washington Post's* sports editor in 1926, but after seven years he stepped down to focus on his daily "This Morning" column. Even after he announced his retirement in 1974, he couldn't stop writing, filing some five hundred columns after his career had officially ended. He filed the last one the day before he died, at ninety-two.

In tasteful, unobtrusive prose, Povich chronicled the giants in every sport, from Babe Ruth to Bobby Jones to Muhammad Ali. In his football coverage he didn't shy away from criticizing the Washington Redskins' outlandish impresario of an owner, George Preston Marshall, and campaigned relentlessly against Marshall's refusal to integrate the team. The essential Povich shines through in the piece that follows, a consoling column written after the Redskins lost the 1940 NFL championship game to the Chicago Bears 73–0, the worst defeat in any title game in any sport. Had it taken place today, there would be a multimedia outpouring of vituperation and cheap jokes. But Povich went in a different direction entirely, offering compassion and a subtle reminder that all that separates even the best of us from ignominy is a simple twist of fate.

The Redskins' Longest Day

Washington, D.C., December 9, 1940

IF YOU'RE WANTING TO KNOW what happened to the Redskins yesterday, maybe this will explain it: The Bears happened to 'em.

The Redskins' 73–0 defeat by a team that they had licked a month ago doesn't add up. But there it was. It reminds us of our first breathless visit to the Grand Canyon. All we could say is: "There she is, and ain't she a beaut." When they hung up that final score at Griffith Stadium yesterday, all we could utter was: "There it is and wasn't it awful."

We're going to win one title right here—the championship for understatement—by saying that the Redskins didn't play good football yesterday. But somehow, we can't get mad at the Redskins. It was an agonizing experience for those poor fellows who probably are more angry at themselves than you or us could ever be toward them.

We saw Redskins in tears after the ball game. Some of these elder players weren't sorry for themselves. They were ashamed of the way they let their Washington fans down. They were the fellows who lived through those lean days at Boston where they were playing under sufferance and who couldn't quite get over the friendliness and the warmth of Washington fans who tried to make big heroes of them.

We can't put in with the folks who say that the Redskins loafed and took it on the lam. They played a lot of bad football, and they were a picture of complete demoralization, but they were trying to play football, if blindly. The Bears, incidentally, are no gentle playmates.

That 73–0 score, of course, is no true comparison of the two teams. The Bears on their great day caught the Redskins on a horrible one. The Redskins, forced to gamble after they were two touchdowns behind in the first five minutes, profaned their game, and the avalanche of Bear touchdowns that followed came easy. The Bears were pouring it on a team that didn't need one or two touchdowns. The Redskins needed four by the end of the first half.

We're paying no attention to the latest telephone query from some gagster who remembers those eight passes the Bears intercepted and wants to know how far behind the line a Redskin back must stand this year before he can throw a pass to a Bear. This is no time for cracks, men, those poor fellows were suffering.

We'll never think that the Redskins could have won that ball game in the light of what happened, because the Bears—well, no team living, or deceased for that matter, could have beaten 'em yesterday. But the Redskins might have made a battle of it if the receiver had held onto that pass on the Bears' 4-yard line. When the Redskins muffed that touchdown, the Bears were relieved of pressure and went townward.

Those Bears were wonderful, weren't they? That "T" formation is really dread stuff and Coach George Halas comes pretty close to being the No. 1 offensive genius in the land. The Bears' ball carriers were under way at full speed before they had their hands on the ball and at the rate they were galloping when they hit something, it didn't make a difference whether there was a hole in the Redskins' line or not.

Halas' man-in-motion play was shaking his ball carriers loose through the middle, at the tackles and around the ends. The Redskins scarcely knew where the Bears would strike; and if they did know it didn't make much difference. The Bears' power plays were ghastly concentrations of blockers in front of ball carriers. The Redskins were first confused and then so weakened physically by the pounding they were taking that they were helpless.

Halas turned back the clock to beat the Redskins. The Bears were getting their wondrous effects with the old "T" formation that was popular early in the century when the boys were playing the game in turtle-necks. Halas embellished it with some variations, but its form was basically the same with the quarterback taking the ball from center and handing it gently to a big back who was already in motion. The Redskins could never get set for that kind of an attack.

All of which brings up that game of a month ago when the Bears with the same sort of system couldn't score a touchdown against the Redskins. The Redskins knew how to meet the Bears' running game that day, obviously. How come, then, they were such foils for the same attack yesterday? Pardon us, please, if we sidestep that one, beyond noting that the Redskins yesterday simply played bad football.

The first 55 seconds of play were a shock to folks who knew the Redskins. We mean when Bill Osmanski scored that 68-yard touchdown on the Bears' second play from scrimmage. On Osmanski's heels were Ed Justice and Jimmy Johnston, who finished noses apart in a race earlier in the season to decide the fastest Redskin. When neither Justice nor Johnston could catch Osmanski, the Redskins were obviously in for a sorry afternoon.

Red Smith

Elegance is a rare word in any discussion of sportswriters and yet it is the first word that comes to mind when remembering Walter Wellesley "Red" Smith (1905–1982). One thinks back to his self-effacing graciousness, his Brooks Brothers sport coats, and, most of all, his crystalline prose. Reading Smith was like discovering that E. B. White knew what an onsides kick is. After apprenticing in Milwaukee, St. Louis, and a decade in Philadelphia, Smith arrived at the *New York Herald Tribune* in 1945 and was quickly embraced for the keen eye and gentle wit he brought to his daily column. His virtues are on full display in the pieces that follow, about two football rivalries—Harvard-Yale and Army-Navy—when America still cared about them. It's easy to imagine the joy he must have felt when he described grins "as broad as Kate Smith" and President Truman as a "prominent fancier of hopeless causes." Smith outlived the *Herald* and moved on to write for the *New York Times*, where his "Sports of the Times" columns won him a Pulitzer Prize in 1976 that most felt was long overdue. To those who shook his hand afterward, his response was vintage Red Smith: "Well, God bless. Don't let anything happen to you."

The Most Important Thing

New Haven, Conn., November 22, 1947

"GENTLEMEN," THE sainted Tad Jones is alleged to have said in the cathedral hush before a Yale-Harvard game, "you are about to play football for Yale. Never again in your lives will you do anything so important—"

America has been through two world wars, a world-wide depression, and had a couple of flings at inflation since then and yet, corny as it seems, the young Yales appeared actually to feel that T. Jones was right when today's affair with the Harvards ended.

As the last whistle blew, a great passel of Yales swarmed onto the field to hug the combatants to their bosoms and even from the press box you could see grins as broad as Kate Smith upon the soiled faces of the belligerents. There was a brief, ecstatic huddle, and then Levi Jackson, the tall, dark, and handsome fullback of the Yales, broke away from his companions and raced across the field to pump any and all Harvard hands within reach. Meanwhile, a small boy snatched the cap of G. Frank Bergin, the umpire, and fled with the official in pursuit.

The cap-snatch was brought off on Harvard's 20-yard line. The small miscreant fled to Yale's goal line on a long, clean, 80-yard dash, circled to his right and raced back ten yards, then angled off into the crowd with the stolen haberdashery still in his possession. Mr. Bergin, puffing, gave up.

This was far and away the most spectacular play of the long, gray day. But such post-game shenanigans were no more than frosting on an extraordinarily fancy cake. The show itself was the thing, and it was the greatest thing since the invention of the wheel.

Here were two teams that had made a career of failure and had enjoyed staggering success at it. One had lost four games, the other three. Neither had beaten anyone of importance. And so, between them, they drew a crowd of 70,896, biggest gathering this holy of holies has attracted in seventeen years.

It was a hairy crowd, wrapped thickly in the skins of dead animals and festooned with derby hats, pennants and feathers of crimson and blue. It wore the pelts of mink and beaver and raccoons. Indeed, counting the coon coats in any section of the Bowl, you could be excused for assuming Coolidge was still President. Here and there a moth took wing as some fur-bearing customer flapped his arms in an effort to keep warm. It was concluded that although the science of offensive football was advanced by every play, the entertainment set the fur industry back thirty years. There were enough crew haircuts in evidence to supply the Fuller Brush Company for the next generation.

All the appurtenances of elegance were present. The bands paraded and postured between halves according to the strictest dictates of tradition. The Harvard tootlers wore crimson jackets and ice cream pants. From the waist up they looked like a road company chorus out of *Rose Marie*. From there down, they suggested Good Humor men on holiday.

The Yales came oompah-ing onto the scene after their guests were done. Yale costumes its bandsmen to impersonate bellhops in a good but unpretentious hotel. The somber ranks of blue shifted and twitched and maneuvered, deploying into fascinating but undecipherable formations. The only one which could be spelled out from the press loft seemed to be a salute to the Reliable Jersey House. It appeared to read: "Yale minus 7."

Critics agreed the Yale band was two steps faster than Harvard's. This was approximately the difference between the two teams. Harvard passed, but Yale ran. Rather, Yale marched, driving relentlessly in short, savage bursts, chewing out yardage with a persistence which Harvard couldn't resist. Thus Yale scored first, and was tied scarcely more than a minute later when Harold Moffie raced down from his flanker position on the right side, got behind Ferd Nadherny and made a casual catch of Jim Kenary's pass into the end zone.

Yale clawed down for another touchdown and Harvard responded with one of its own, fashioned chiefly on two plays. One was a forward pass to Chip Gannon, who faked two tacklers out of their underwear on a slick run. The other was a bolt through the middle by Paul Lazzaro on a fake pass-and-buck play which is called the bear trap because the Chicago Bears no longer use it.

So the score was tied again, but it stood to reason it wouldn't stay that way. You couldn't expect Harvard to keep on coming up with one-play touchdowns to match a team that could grind out gains as Yale was doing. Harvard finally gave Yale an unearned chance by roughing the New Haven kicker and drawing a penalty for same. This resulted in the winning touchdown. A little later, a low snapback from center loused up a Harvard punt, giving the ball to Yale for the score that made the game safe.

It was noted that the incredibly erudite Harvard coach, Dr. R. Harlow, made unique use of the free substitution rule. He would haul a guy out of the game, give him special instructions and run him back in again, all in one pause between plays. He did this with a couple of his key men just before the first half ended. The results were significant. On the next play, Yale intercepted a Harvard pass.

The Lost Cause

Philadelphia, Pa., November 27, 1948

A SLIGHT, FOUR-EYED MAN stood teetering on tiptoe down near the 40-yard line in Municipal Stadium, his pearl-gray hat bobbing like a floating cork as he craned and twisted and strained to see over the wall of blue Navy overcoats and white Navy caps whose owners towered in front of America's Commander in Chief.

Harry Truman, of Independence, Missouri, a former haberdasher and prominent fancier of hopeless causes, was struggling to focus his lenses on the hopeless Navy football team, a team that had lost thirteen successive games and now, with fifty-eight seconds of its season remaining, stood tied with undefeated Army, champion of the East, third-ranking power of the nation, and twenty-one-point favorite in the trustworthy Minneapolis line.

Fifty Secret Service men fidgeted, watching protocol go down the drain. For safety's sake, it has been their custom to get the President clear of the crowd two minutes before an Army-Navy game ends. Hot or cold, out he goes with two minutes to play.

But Harry Truman wouldn't budge. Like the 102,580 others present at the forty-ninth meeting of service academies, he simply had to see Navy fire the last shot in its locker.

Pete Williams took a pitch-out and lost three yards. Bill Hawkins went twisting and wrestling through the line, gaining five. The clock showed thirty-three seconds left. Slats Baysinger, the quarterback, tried to sneak around end. He lost six. Navy huddled once more, rushed up to the line for one more play, but the referee stepped in, waving his arms.

The red hand of the clock stood at zero, and the best, most exhilarating and least plausible Army-Navy game in at least twenty years was over. The score, 21 to 21, was the same as that of 1926, the year historians always mention first when they try to name the finest of all Army-Navy games.

And even if you'd seen it, it was fearfully hard to believe. While the referee tossed a coin to decide on permanent possession of the ball, Baysinger walked around the periphery of huddled players, shook hands with Army's Tom Bullock and then with Arnold Galiffa. Army's guys walked off hurriedly, but Navy's froze to attention while the midshipmen's band played "Navy Blue and Gold."

Then all the players save two departed, as civilians and non-combatant midshipmen and cadets swarmed over the field. Dave Bannerman, Navy's substitute fullback, and Ted Carson, left end, just stayed there where the deed had been done. When small boys came asking for autographs, they signed abstractedly and kept rubbering around through the crowd. Maybe they were looking for a couple of peach cakes to share an evening's liberty. But it seemed more likely they were waiting in the hope that someone would give them one more crack at Army.

The great, sunswept crowd that paid six dollars a head hadn't expected anything like this. The customers had come for the show, the spectacle, the pageant of youth that always is about as thrilling as anything in American sports. They had thought to get their money's worth out of just being there; out of seeing the magnificent parade these kids always bring off superbly before the game; out of the shiver that scampers along the spine when the colors are brought to midfield and the band plays the national anthem and the packed stands are a frozen block of color, with the bright blue-gray of the Army on one side and the shimmering white of Navy caps on the other.

They figured to get a chuckle out of the kids' musty nonsense. And of course they did. There was a Navy dreadnought that rolled around the cinder track and shot off cannon and went down in flames. There was a huge papier mâché goat and a huge papier mâché mule. There were signs in the Navy stands: "Gallup Picks Army" (to which the Army stands replied with a cheer: "Gallup, Gallup, Gallup!") and a sly reference to the difference between Army and Navy schedules: "When do you play Vassar?" ("Vassar, Vassar, Vassar!") and then after the Navy scored first: "Send in Alan Ladd"; (no response to this).

But nobody expected a ball game, except the few people who bore in mind an old, old truth which the game restated dramatically. That is, that there never can be between undergraduate football teams of the same league a gap in ability too great to be bridged by spirit alone. Navy proved that beyond remotest doubt, and the guy who did most to prove it was a fellow playing on spirit and very little else. Bill Hawkins, ill a long while this season with a blood disorder that doctors call acute infectious mononucleosis, was entirely out of action for three weeks in midseason. Without preparation, he came back to play against Michigan on November 6. Then he played three minutes against Columbia and was hurt November 13. Since then he hadn't a minute of physical contact until today.

But today he was a bull, and a mad bull into the bargain. He ran the ball fourteen times and made fifty important yards. He scored two touchdowns. He backed up the line, his blocking was like a crime of passion, and he played almost all afternoon.

It wasn't exactly a football game, it was an exhibition of pure, unbridled fury on both sides for both sides persistently moved the ball against incredibly savage resistance. It was, altogether, as good a thing as could possibly happen to football.

Thirty-two Navy players got into the game, which means—if there is such a thing as justice—that the Navy added thirty-two full admirals today. For the guys down there on the field today were officer material, as ever was. It goes without saying that there are more than thirty-two full admirals in Philadelphia tonight.

Frederick Exley

It seemed like a perfect match when *Inside Sports* magazine sent Frederick Exley (1929–1992) to cover Super Bowl XIII with the defiant, self-flagellating style that made his "fictional memoir" *A Fan's Notes* (1968) so compelling. Exley showed up in Miami in January 1979 only to hear NFL minions say there wasn't a press credential for him. *And what was that name again? Never heard of the guy.* It was a classic Exley moment. He had turned to writing for the validation he couldn't find on the athletic fields where his father had starred, and by now had a second published book to his credit, *Pages From a Cold Island* (1975), but still he was being told he might as well not exist. In the past, lesser affronts had plunged him into bouts of "foodless, nearly heroic drinking," but this time he hung onto his Bloody Mary and the NFL eventually came up with a credential. It's doubtful that many people connected to the league realized that Exley understood the essence of fandom as fully, even profoundly as anyone ever has. In the following excerpt from *A Fan's Notes*, Exley finds his way to New York's Polo Grounds in the fall of 1954 to watch Frank Gifford and the Giants in the company of strangers who become more than just his fellow fans. They are the closest thing he has to friends.

from

A Fan's Notes

IN THE YEAR I SPENT IN NEW YORK, I became a fan. I became hooked. I didn't intend it that way, or, for that matter, didn't comprehend it when it did happen. But happen it did; it was in those days that Sundays began to take on for me a frantic and nervous exhilaration. I would purchase all the Sunday newspapers, drop those sections I didn't read into the gutter along the way, then take my Sunday breakfast at a diner on Third Avenue. It was not a clean place, but the food was cheap and edible and abundant, mountains of scrambled eggs and thick-cut bacon and home-fried potatoes and great mugs of fresh coffee (the place is gone now, given way to a pastel lemon and orange Hot Shoppe). After breakfast I used to go back to my iron cot at the Y, reread the articles about the Giants over and over again, and plan my strategy. Steve Owen was gone, and the new coach, Jim Lee Howell, wasn't "showing" me very much. About noon I would rise and head for the Polo Grounds.

The crowds at the Polo Grounds were nothing whatever like the crowds one sees in Yankee Stadium today. The sportswriters hadn't as yet convinced the public that something very special was taking place on autumn Sunday afternoons, something that in its execution was at times beautiful, at times almost awesome, at times almost art. The writers were beginning to clamor, but the tone of most sportswriting is a clamor, making it difficult for the fan to isolate the real from the fantastic. Still, these writers are a tough breed to tune out, the public would eventually listen, and in a few seasons the Giants would have moved to the Yankee Stadium, would have changed their jerseys from a crimson to a formal navy blue, would have added to their helmets a snooty *N.Y.* emblem, and would be playing, week in and week out, to sell-out crowds of Chesterfield-coated corporation executives and their elegant-legged, mink-draped wives. The Polo Grounds was never sold out.

Arriving at the field shortly before one, I would buy a bleacher seat for a buck, then for another dollar bribe my way into a seat between the forty-yard lines. With the wind at my back I had to stand at the back of the stadium during the first part of the game until the usher, having decided what seats were going to go unoccupied throughout the afternoon (usually near the end of the first period), steered me to an empty. Waiting, I always stood with a group of men from Brooklyn who also paid the bribe. An Italian bread-truck driver, an Irish patrolman, a fat garage mechanic, two or three burly longshoremen, and some others whose occupations I forget—we were a motley, a memorable picture. Dressed as often as not in skimpy jackets, without gloves, we were never dressed warmly enough. Our noses ran. To keep warm we smoked one cigarette after another, drank much beer, and jogged up and down on the concrete. The Brooklyn guys talked all during the game, as much as Brooklyn guys ever talk, which is to say hardly at all. Brooklyn guys issue statements. There is a unity of tone that forbids disagreement. "Take duh fucking bum outa deah!" or "Dat guy is a *pro*"—that designation being the highest accolade they allowed a player for making some superb play. Hollow-chested, their frigid hands stuffed deep into their pockets, their eyes and noses running, they looked about as fit to judge the relative merits of athletes as Ronald Firbank. Still, because of the cocksure, irrefutable tones in which they issued their judgments, I was certain they knew everything about football, and I enjoyed being with them immensely.

And they liked me. I was so alien to their hard, sophisticated, and wordless enthusiasms that they—oh, grand irony!—considered *me* a freak! Especially because I was so partial to Gifford. Whenever, smiling, I joined their conclave, sneaking sort of shyly among them, one of them would always say, "Hey, boys, here's duh Gippeh. How we gonna make out today, Gippeh?" or "Don't stand next to me, Gippeh—my fucking back's still achin' from last week!" Everyone would laugh like a goddam hyena. Me too. As the season progressed, we found we enjoyed each other so much that we decided, quite tacitly, to stand the entire game. Had we moved into the empty seats, we would have had to split up, one here, two or three there, wherever the seats were available. So we braved the wind at our backs, our noses ran, we had large laughs—that laughter haunts me still—and sometimes, at those moments when the play on the field seemed astonishingly perfect, we just fell quiet. That was the most memorable picture of all. We were Wops and Polacks and Irishmen out of Flatbush, along with one mad dreamer out of the cold, cow country up yonder, and though we may not have had the background, or the education, to weep at Prince Hamlet's death, we had all tried enough times to pass and kick a ball, we had on our separate rock-strewn sandlots taken enough lumps and bruises, to know that we were viewing something truly fine, something that only comes with years of toil, something very like art.

They were right about my churlish, extravagant partiality to Gifford; though I suspect they never understood it, it amused them, and they liked me for that. Already that fall I had drawn parallels between Gifford's life and mine, our having been at USC together, our having come East almost simultaneously, and the unquestionable fact that we both desired fame, perhaps he even more than I, for he had already eaten, in a limited way, of that Bitch at school. Throughout that autumn, throughout those long, lovely afternoons, there was only one number for me, 16, and I cheered frantically for it, pounding my Brooklyn buddies on the back, and screaming, "Atta boy, Frank! Atta way, you bastard!" I caught passes with him, and threw blocks with him, and groaningly sucked in my breath as he was being viciously tackled. Watching him rise after such a tackle, I piddled back to the huddle with him, my head cranked back at the recent executor of the tackle, my voice warning, "Next time, you bastard—"

It was very simple really. Where I could not, with syntax, give shape to my fantasies, Gifford could, with his superb timing, his great hands, his uncanny faking, give shape to his. It was something more than this: I cheered for him with such inordinate enthusiasm, my yearning became so involved with his desire to escape life's bleak anonymity, that after a time he became my alter ego, that part of me which had its being in the competitive world of men; I came, as incredible as it seems to me now, to believe that I was, in some magical way, an actual instrument of his success. Each time I heard the roar of the crowd, it roared in my ears as much for me as him; that roar was not only a promise of my fame, it was its unequivocal assurance.

He was hurt a good deal in 1954; but there were days when he was fine, and all that season I tried to get my Brooklyn friends to bestow on him the name of pro. In the very last game I saw at the Polo Grounds—for I was suddenly to be transferred by the railroad to Chicago—they did so. I don't remember the play, but it was one of those incredible catches that have characterized his career; that awesome, forbidding silence had descended immediately on our group. We looked at each other pop-eyed, shaking our heads in wonder. Then we stared at the Italian truck driver, the swarthy little man who was the arbiter of our fuzzy enthusiasms. He was a very theatrical little guy. He didn't say anything for a long time. Then he looked up at me and smiled apologetically, as though he were giving in. "He's a pro," he proclaimed. "*He is a pro.*" Then all the rest of them shook their heads knowingly and repeated, "*He is a pro!*" Lunatic tears brimmed my eyes and I smiled a lunatic smile from ear to ear; we all roared at my sentimentality and roughed each other affectionately with our hands, dancing round and round in the cold winds of the Polo Grounds.

Stuart Leuthner

John Madden was the noisy one, a voluble, strategy-savvy former coach who spoke a *bif!-bam-boom* language straight out of a comic book. Pat Summerall (1930–2013) was, as someone once put it, "the calm alongside Madden's storm"—understated, dignified without being stuffy, a true Southern gentleman. Together, they were the premier football broadcasting team in television for twenty-one years, on CBS and then the FOX network. When Summerall said goodbye to the business in 2002, he did it by calling a last-second field goal in the restrained style that was his trademark: "It's right down the pipe. Adam Vinatieri. No time on the clock. And the Patriots have won Super Bowl XXXVI. Unbelievable." What many viewers never knew was that the man born George Edward Summerall had been a superb placekicker for the Chicago Cardinals (1952–57) and New York Giants (1958–61) before he took a seat behind the microphone. Old Giants fans still remember his game-winning field goal against the Browns in a snowstorm in 1958. But the story of his playing days was best told by Summerall himself in the oral history *Iron Men* (1988) compiled by Stuart Leuthner (b. 1939). In the following excerpt, he recalls an NFL so primitive it's hard to imagine its ever existing.

from

Iron Men: Pat Summerall

I GREW UP IN LAKE CITY, FLORIDA, a little country town seventy miles west of Jacksonville. My parents were divorced and I grew up with my father. I was born with a club foot. My right foot was completely backward; the heel was around front and the toes pointed in the opposite direction. A doctor in Lake City, Dr. Harry Bates, broke my leg and turned the foot around. My entire leg was in a cast for what seemed forever to a kid. In time I began to walk correctly, but Dr. Bates told me, "You'll never be able to run and play with the rest of the children." The most ironic thing about the whole experience is that my right foot was my kicking foot.

My father worked in a bank until it went under during the Depression. He spent a few years in an ice plant, went back to the bank when it reopened, and worked his way up from custodian to cashier. He had an eighth-grade education and thought I was wasting my time playing high school athletics. I think he saw me play one basketball game and

38

one football game the whole time I was in high school. He felt I should be working instead of playing.

My first interest in athletics was probably like a lot of other kids, throwing a ball against the house and seeing if I could catch it. I was always a fan and read every word in the sports section. As far as organized sports, I guess I started playing football in the seventh grade. Lake City was a small school, there were ninety boys in my senior class, and if you wore long pants you were almost obligated to play every sport they had. Especially if you were bigger than just about anybody else, or at least taller, like I was. I played football, basketball, baseball, ran track, and was the Florida tennis champion when I was sixteen. A man named Jim Melton was our football and basketball coach during my junior and senior years and I think he was one of the most influential people in my life. I was a rather passive, reticent individual and Jim helped me go from a guy who was afraid to shoot the basketball to a leader on the team.

I was all-state or all-conference, whatever those deals were, in football and basketball my last two years in high school. When I graduated I can't remember how many opportunities I had for scholarships. My dad wanted me to go to West Point, but when I went up there for a visit it looked a little too much like a prison. The first thing they said to me was, "Yes, we'd like to have you, but we don't think you can pass the entrance exam." They wanted to send me to some military institute in Kentucky to prepare for the exam and I didn't like the sound of that at all.

The gentleman who had been my high school football coach in my sophomore year, Hobart Hooser, had left Lake City and was the line coach at the University of Arkansas. He was good friends with my family and when Hobart came back to Lake City to recruit me, they felt I would be in good hands if I was wherever he was. I ended up at Arkansas with the stipulation in my scholarship that I would play both basketball and football. I did that for a couple of years, but it was too time-consuming and it wasn't long before I realized any future I had in sports was not going to be in basketball.

We had a lot of football talent at Arkansas, but I don't think the coaching was the best. Eleven guys from my senior team ended up playing in the pros. Fred Williams played with the Bears. Dave "Hog" Hanner was with the Packers for a long time and we had the Carpenter brothers, Louis and Preston. I forgot who else was drafted. Our best year we were 7–3, but I don't think we ever got the maximum out of the talent that was available.

In my sophomore year one of the coaches announced that they were unhappy with the player who was kicking off. He asked anybody who wanted to try for the job to come out thirty minutes before practice. I showed up, happened to do pretty well, and that was how I got started place-kicking. While I was at Arkansas field goals weren't an important part of the game. If I recall correctly, when I was a senior I led the nation with four field goals. The guy I beat out was Vic Janowicz, who was at Ohio State. You didn't really work at kicking; it was just sort of an afterthought. You had a tough time getting somebody to hold the ball for you in practice, much less trying to get somebody to run it down each time you kicked. There weren't that many good holders around because I think a lot of players thought it was a demeaning job. It was also dangerous. The holder was squatting on all fours and had a real good chance of getting belted before he could get up. It wasn't until I got into the pros that people started to realize the importance of the kicking game. I suppose that was because of the significance of Lou Groza and the way Paul Brown used him. Everybody started to pay attention to field goals when the Browns started to win games with them.

I graduated from Arkansas in 1951 and signed a baseball contract with the Cardinals. They sent me to a Class C team in Oklahoma. During that summer, I realized that my future wasn't going to be in baseball either. I found out I couldn't hit a curveball, and worse than that, the opposing pitchers found out too. That same year the Detroit Lions drafted me to play pro football and then traded me to the Chicago Cardinals. When the guy from the Cardinals came down to Fayetteville, Arkansas, to sign me, I was playing a pinball machine in a place called Hog's Heaven. He probably thought, "This rube is going to be a soft touch." He gave me the line—I guess it was pretty standard at the time—that for equity and happiness on the team they had arrived at an average salary. The figure they came up with was $5,500. Later on I found out that was an out-and-out lie because Charley Trippi, the Cardinals' star quarterback, was obviously making a lot more than $5,500.

I called my father and told him that the Cardinals wanted to pay me $5,500 to play professional football. He said, "I thought you were going to have to go to work for a living." I told him, "Dad, they also want to give me $250 if I'll sign." He said, "Son, if somebody is willing to pay you that kind of money to play anything, take it." That was the extent of my negotiations. No agents, no lawyers, no anything. I used the $250 bonus to pay a beer bill I had at the University of Arkansas, but I didn't tell the Cardinals that.

I can still remember my introduction to pro football. It was a Monday, the team's day off, and I walked into the locker room at Comiskey Park. There sat Plato Andros in the whirlpool. He had been an All-American guard at Oklahoma and was a very thick heavy-chested guy. Plato filled up the entire whirlpool and had a cigar in his mouth, was reading the daily racing form, and sitting on the edge of the whirlpool was a pint of whiskey. Almost everybody who went into pro football was a pretty good beer drinker in college, but when practice started you didn't drink beer, you didn't do anything. You abided by the training rules and there was no question whatsoever because it was something you had been brought up with since you first started playing in high school. If you were an athlete, you didn't smoke, drink, or stay out late, and the guys who did were considered disgraces. We had two guys at Arkansas—both went into the pros—and when the coaches found out they drank some beer during the season they were suspended. Right off the team. It was quite a shock for me when I walked into that locker room and saw Plato doing everything you weren't supposed to do. Welcome to pro football.

The Cardinals' head coach at that time was Joe Stydahar. He was the only man I have ever known who could smoke a cigar, chew tobacco, and drink whiskey at the same time. He had been a great player with the Bears and had a very violent temper. Joe was also a tremendous physical specimen. He was one of those guys who look bigger than they are. He must have weighed about 265 and his head was as big as a toilet. We didn't have much of a team and Stydahar would go berserk when we lost. At the top, we had some pretty good talent—Ollie Matson, Johnny Olszewski, Charley Trippi—but once you got past those names, we didn't have much. To be very honest about it, we were pretty bad.

In 1953 we were 0–10–1 (we had managed to tie the Steelers) and were going to play our last game, which was traditionally against the Bears. We drew them at Wrigley Field and the week before the game

Stydahar said, "I've always thought you guys were a bunch of gutless losers and I'm going to tell you something. If you don't beat the Bears on Sunday, none of you get paid." There was an open revolution and we had a team meeting. A couple of the guys said we should talk to the Bidwells, the owners at the time, but nobody had the guts to go to them. We beat the Bears, 24–17.

The next year was almost as bad, I think we won two games, and that was Stydahar's swan song. He used to pay us on Tuesday. He would come down to the locker room and have each of our checks in a little brown envelope. There would always be some kind of editorial comment about your performance on the envelope. "You're not worth shit," something like that. This one particular Tuesday he was about half an hour late and when he came in the locker room it was obvious he had a late night. Blurry eyes, stuff dripping out of his mouth. He had everybody's paychecks wrapped up with a rubber band and threw them across the locker room. He growled, "Fight for them, you bastards," turned around, and walked out.

After Stydahar left the Cardinals, one of his assistants, Ray Richards, took over and he was just the opposite. Ray was a real gentleman and we had a couple of good years. The coaching was better and we got some better players, but I wasn't enjoying pro football. The Cardinal organization was always trying to save pennies and by the time the season ended we were sometimes down to twenty-five players. At one point we almost didn't have enough footballs to practice with. It just wasn't much fun, losing every weekend, and if I hadn't been traded to the Giants I was going to retire.

During the off-season I had been going back to Lake City and teaching school. My undergraduate degree was in physical education and I also have a master's degree in Russian history. When I was an undergraduate, I had a history professor, Dorsey Jones, who taught history like it was a novel. His classes were so interesting I even enjoyed the tests. He was teaching Russian history at the graduate level and I went back to Arkansas while I was playing. That's how I ended up with that degree. The fellow who was the principal of the school I was teaching at had been a long-time friend of mine and I got involved in some farming ventures with him. We were basically doing truck farming, raising watermelons and tomatoes. I wasn't getting rich, but it was a comfortable living.

"Pop" Ivy was named head coach of the Cardinals in 1958. I called him up and asked him where I was going to fit into his plans. As I said, I wasn't having a very good time in Chicago and was thinking seriously of not playing anymore and getting involved full-time in the farming business. I had gotten married and had one child. My wife, Kathy, didn't like living up north because of the cold weather, so I wanted to hear what Ivy had to say. He told me, "Pat, you're one of our key guys and I want you to come back because we're going to do this and that." It was all very encouraging, so I decided I would play another year. A short time later I went down to the post office in Lake City to pick something up and bought the afternoon paper. There was a story in the sports section that said I had been traded to the Giants. Some "key guy"!

I called Jim Lee Howell, the Giants' head coach, and asked him what he wanted me to do in New York. He said, "We need somebody who can do more than kick." Ben Agajanian was the Giants' kicker and he had a garbage disposal business in Los Angeles. He was busy with that during the week and wanted to fly in on the weekends to play. Katcavage and Robustelli were the Giants' defensive ends and if one of them went down Jim Lee thought I could fill in for them. They also had only one tight end, Bob Schnelker, and he thought I could also cover that spot. When you only had thirty-three players, a team didn't have the luxury of somebody who just kicked field goals.

Going to the Giants was like going from the outhouse to the penthouse. There was a whole new attitude on the team that I hadn't run into before. Those guys expected to win and they almost considered it a personal insult if they didn't. I had never played in that kind of atmosphere before and it helped me become a better kicker, especially under pressure. I just didn't want a loss to be my fault.

That first training camp I felt like a rookie because the veterans were all suspicious of me. Charlie Conerly was the quarterback and it was a big deal to have him hold for the kicker. At first he wouldn't hold for me because I was trying to take Agajanian's job. For a while I had the backup holder, but I guess that Charlie decided I knew what I was doing. He finally started holding for me and that really helped. At Chicago I never had the same holder two years in a row.

Tom Landry was the defensive coordinator and kicking coach at New York and he really made a difference. Tom is a great coach and he worked with Ray Wietecha, the center, Charlie, and myself. Ray was a terrific center and I never remember having to kick a ball when I was with the Giants where I could see the laces. That helped my accuracy. In 1958 I was 12 for 23. The year before with the Cardinals I was 6 for 17. In 1959 I was number one in the league with 20 for 29.

What was probably my most embarrassing moment in broadcasting involved Tom Landry. We are forever changing the way we produce and show football games and one year they had me down on the field introducing each member of the teams like they do in college football. The Cardinals were playing the Cowboys and I got through the Cardinals fine, including Wally Lemm, who was the coach at that time. Then I started on the Cowboys and when I got to Tom Landry I couldn't remember his name. I had known him for thirty years, played against him, had him as a coach, and there we were, on national television, plus a full house at the Cotton Bowl. I stumbled around and finally said, "...and the coach of the Dallas Cowboys." Tom realized I was having a problem and handled it very gracefully.

My first year with the Giants was probably the high point of my career. We needed to win all of our last five games to get into a play-off with Cleveland to see who would play the Colts. Every field goal seemed to be crucial and I think four of those games were decided in the last two minutes. We played Cleveland in Yankee Stadium and there was almost a blizzard. I had been having trouble with my knee and hadn't even worked out. Don Chandler, the Giants' punter, had been practicing field goals all week. Before the game I told Jim Lee that I could play. The score was tied 10–10 with about four minutes to play, and I missed a field goal from the forty. When I went back to the bench, I was thinking that I had blown it and the rest of the guys, especially the defense, said, "Don't worry about it. We're going to get the ball back." They did get the ball back and we had third down on the fifty-yard line. Howell told me to attempt a field goal and I couldn't believe it. That would be the longest kick I had made for the Giants. The field was bad and most of the guys on the bench couldn't believe it either. They wanted Charlie to throw the ball.

I knew as soon as I kicked it that it was going to be far enough and they credited me with a fifty-yard field goal. You couldn't see the yard markers because of the snow and some people say it was longer. But like a lot of things, as time goes by, the snow gets deeper and the kick gets longer. Everybody was yelling and running around and I felt somebody tugging on my arm. It turned out to be Vince Lombardi, who was coaching the Giants' offense. He looked at me and said in that voice of his, "Summerall, nobody can kick a football that damned far."

Gary Smith

It wasn't just the quality of his prose that made people pay attention to Gary Smith (b. 1953) when he was making his bones as a newspaper sportswriter nearly forty years ago. It was the intensity he brought to his reporting even when he was working in a steamy, crowded locker room after a game. Once he had zeroed in on his subject, everything else ceased to matter. Other, older writers would come and go, but Smith was going to get the details and grace notes that would lift his story far above deadline mediocrity. To no one's surprise, he rode the express train from the *Philadelphia Daily News* to the *New York Daily News* to *Inside Sports*, which gave him a national stage for his early magazine work. But it was at *Sports Illustrated* that his style and voice evolved and he took his place alongside Frank Deford and William Nack as a virtuoso of the long features known as bonus pieces. Smith's work became increasingly idiosyncratic as he sought out such unexpected subjects as deep-sea divers and Native American basketball players, spent enormous amounts of time with each of them, and eschewed quotes in stories that burrowed deep into psyches. For *SI*'s July 26, 1999 issue, Smith took as his starting point Marvin E. Newman's photograph of Texas Christian University's football team in the moments before the 1957 Cotton Bowl. The story won him the third of his four National Magazine Awards, but more important than that, it takes readers places the photo never could.

Moment of Truth

YOU HEARD ME RIGHT: Come in. No, you won't disturb a soul in this locker room. They're all lost in that place most folks go maybe once or twice in a lifetime, when their mamas or daddies die or their children are born, a place they don't go nearly as often as they should. Trust me, these boys will never know you're here. All right, maybe that fellow in white will notice, the one looking your way, but Willard McClung would be the last to make a peep.

See, that's one reason we picked this, out of all the crackerjack sports pictures we might've chosen, as our favorite of the century. Not claiming it's better than that famous one of Muhammad Ali standing and snarling over Sonny Liston laid out like a cockroach the morning after the bug man comes. Or that picture of Willie Mays catching the ball over his shoulder in the '54 World Series, or any number of others. But you can walk around inside this picture in a way you can't in those others, peer right inside the tunnel these boys have entered. Their boxer shorts are hanging right there, on the hooks behind their heads, but their faces are showing something even more personal than that. Almost reminds you of a painting by Norman Rockwell.

Can you smell it? No, not the jockstrap sweat, or the cigar reek wafting off the coach, Orthol Martin—better known as Abe, or Honest Abe—in the brown hat. It's the smell of men about to go to war. What I'm inviting you into is 12:50 P.M. at the Cotton Bowl on January 1, 1957, just a few minutes after the boys have returned from pregame warmups, just a quarter of an hour before a legend is born. A roomful of young men from Texas Christian University are about to try and stop the best football player in history, a fellow from Syracuse by the name of Jim Brown, in his last college game—but only his second in front of the entire nation, thanks to the NBC cameras waiting outside.

No denying it, a lot of folks might whip right past this in a collection of sports pictures, rushing to get to those slam-bang plays at home plate or those high-flying Michael Jordan circus shots. But it's funny. The older you get, the more you realize that *this* is what sports are most about: the moments *before*, the times when a person takes a flashlight to his soul and inspects himself for will and courage and spirit, the stuff that separates men such as Jordan and Ali from the rest more than anything in their forearms or their fingers or their feet. *Who am I?* And, *Is that going to be enough?* That's what you're peeking at through the door, and believe me, those are two big and scary questions, the two best reasons for all of god's children to play sports, so they can start chewing on them early. Because once the whistle blows and a game begins, everything's just a blur, a crazy ricochet of ball and bodies that springs—inevitably, you might say—from whatever it is that these boys are discovering right here, right now.

But you're still hesitating, a little intimidated by all those cleats and helmets and knees. Come on, there are things I want to show you. See? Told you nobody would bat an eye. You're *in*.

Maybe it was like this for you, too, back when you played. All the posturing and bluffing and the silly airs that human beings put on get demolished in a moment like this. A team is never more a *team* than it is now, yet look at the looks on the Horned Frogs! Ever see so many guys look so alone?

Look at Buddy Dike, number 38, just behind old Abe. He's the Frogs' starting fullback and inside linebacker, and he's just gotten a good look at Jim Brown's 46-inch chest and 32-inch waist in warmups. Doctors advised Buddy never to play football again after he ruptured a kidney tackling another phenom of the era, Penn State's Lenny Moore, two years earlier. The kidney healed and hemorrhaged four more times, doubling Buddy over with pain, making blood gush out his urethra, bringing him within a whisker of bleeding to death, yet here he is, with a look on his face that might not be seen again until the day he loses his 18-year-old son in a car wreck.

There are 32 more young men suited up in this room, besides the 17 you're looking at. Almost every one's a kid from a small town or ranch or farm in west or south Texas, where all his life he's watched everyone drop everything, climb into automobiles and form caravans for only two occasions: funerals and football games. Nine of the 11 TCU starters—remember, they have to play both ways—are seniors, most of them staring into the biggest and last football game of their lives. Eleven wars are about to burst out on every play, because that's what football is, and what those wars hinge on, more than most folks realize, is the question lurking in the shadows of this room: Who has the most tolerance for pain?

That's a loaded question about manhood, and a matter of geography too. Jim Brown be damned, the Southwest Conference team that loses to an Eastern school in the Cotton Bowl in the 1950s might as well run right past the locker room door at the end of the game, exit the stadium and just keep going, till it's lost in the prairie.

Let's take a good look at old Abe. Country boy from Jacksboro, Texas, who played end at TCU in the late 1920s and kept to the grass on campus, claiming the sidewalk was too hard for his feet. Some folks take him for a hick, but be careful, every shut eye isn't asleep. Notice, Abe's not working the boys into one of those tent-preacher lathers. Not his style. The season after this one, just before the Horned Frogs take the field at Ohio State with 80,000-plus fans licking their fangs, all Abe will tell his boys is "Laddies, you're playin' the best team in *the* United States of America"—then walk away. Another game, what he'll say is, "These are big guys. Hope you don't get hurt." He's a master of the subtle psychological ploy, a man who lacks both the strategic genius and the double-knotted sphincter of your other big football honchos, but who maneuvers a college of 4,700 students, most of them female, into three Cotton Bowls in four seasons between '55 and '58 and humbles elephants such as Southern Cal and Penn State and Texas along the way. "You just believe in human beings, that they're all pretty good folks, and you just try to keep 'em that way"—that's how Abe sums up his coaching philosophy in the Cotton Bowl program they're hawking outside that locker room right now.

In practice he'll drop to his hands and knees and crawl into the huddle, gaze up at his gang like a gopher and declare, "Boys, run a 34." Late in a game, when the Froggies are driving for a score they need desperately, old Abe will come down off the chair he always sits on—fanny on the seat back, feet on the seat—take another chomp of the unlit cigar he alternately sucks and rolls between his palms until it disintegrates, and walk down the sideline murmuring to his troops, "Hold your left nut, laddies—we need this one."

Oh, sure, Abe can get riled. But the vilest oath he ever musters— with his fist clenched and his thumb in an odd place, on top of his index finger instead of around his knuckles—is "Shistol pot!" which is a spoonerism for *pistol shot*, in case you need a translation. Usually Abe just walks a player away from the group with an arm around the boy's shoulders and quietly says, "Now, you know better 'n that." You know what troubles the fellows most at a moment like this, 15 minutes before kickoff? The thought that they might let Abe down.

All right, let's be honest, not everyone's dying to please the boss, not in any locker room in the world. See number 67, Norman Ashley, sitting third from the left against the back wall? He's in Abe's dog-house for late hits in practice and for tackling quarterback Chuck Curtis so hard one day that Curtis peed blood. Ashley will never play a lick, and he knows it. He'll end up spending four decades in Alaska flying a Piper Super Cub just big enough for him, his rifle, his rod and his hunting dog, searching for places where there are no whistles and no prey that a man can't bring down. And over on the other side, second from your right, that's center Jim Ozee, who started all season till today. Damn near half a century later, when he's a grandpa toss-ing raisins to the mockingbird that visits him in his backyard in Fort Worth each day, he'll still remember, "That's despair on my face. I'm offended by Abe at this moment. I couldn't figure why I wasn't start-ing. I didn't hear anything he said...."

"...wanna thank you fellas. Seniors in this room... no need to tell you how I feel 'bout you. You were my first recruitin' class, came in green just like me, and accomplished some great things. Now you're 'bout to split up, go your separate ways, and this'll be the game you remember the rest of your days. Life's about to change, laddies. You're never gonna capture this moment again...."

Two in this room will end up in early coffins when their hearts quit: Dick Finney, on your far right, and John Mitchell, second from your left, the lad inspecting the fingernails he's just chewed. Two other players will lose sons in car accidents, which is worse than a heart attack. Another, Jack Webb, seated in the deep corner just to the left of the youngster holding his chin in his hand, will relish the tension of moments like this so much that he'll become a fighter pilot, only to lose his life when his jet crashes in the Philippines. Two will get rich, then go bankrupt. Allen Garrard, number 84, the guy seated on the floor near the corner, will get multiple sclerosis and draw on moments like this 40 years from now, when his car blows a tire in a rainstorm in the dead of night and he has to hobble painfully on his cane far beyond the 200 feet he's usually able to walk. Of course, Abe himself, when he's in his 70s, will be found draped across his bed by his wife one morning when his ticker quits.

See that fellow on the floor behind Abe, number 53, Joe Williams? Can you tell? A year ago he lost his mom, who attended every game he ever played, in a car accident, and he's worried sick about his dad, sleepwalking awake ever since she died, who's somewhere in the stands high above this room. Here's what Joe will say 42 years from now, when his hair's as white as snow and arthritis has racked his joints with pain and stolen his right hand: "I should've expressed my gratitude to Abe. I'm still living by the principles he taught us. I'm not gonna give in. I'm still coming out of bed swinging even though I might not hit a thing. He guided us through those years. He looked out for us the way our parents presumed he would.

"You know something? Nothing ever again will match the intensity, the passion of moments like this. What it takes to overcome yourself—because if you listen to your body, you'll always be a coward. Don't get me wrong, I love my wife and kids, but I'd give anything to go back. More than who you're looking at now, that guy in the picture, *that's* me. *That's* who I really am."

"...Hasn't been an easy road for us this season, laddies. Stubbed our toe real bad, and a lot of folks started calling us a second-rate team. But we didn't roll up in a ball, and by going through what we did and coming together, we're more a team now 'n we've ever been...."

This is how the boys will recollect Abe's speech four decades later. His sermon doesn't dwell on details, but here are the facts: You're listening to a coach who was hung in effigy and made it to the Cotton Bowl in the same season. Right now, as Possum Elenburg, the fellow gnawing his knuckles on your far left, puts it, "Abe's done a rare thing—got all his coons up the same tree." He's got them all ruminating on a season that began with the Horned Frogs as heavy favorites in the Southwest Conference, returning a slew of starters from the nation's sixth-ranked team the year before, busting out to a 3–0 start with a 32–0 blitzing of Kansas, a 41–6 crushing of Arkansas and a 23–6 spanking of Alabama. Next came TCU's blood enemy, Texas A&M, with Bear Bryant at the wheel, the team that had handed the Frogs their only regular-season defeat the year before.

So now it was payback time, a gorgeous Saturday in College Station, the Aggies' stadium jammed and the 3–0 Frogs cross-eyed crazy in their locker room. And what happened? Sometime during the first quarter, all the friction between the two squads was more than the sky could hold, and the ugliest wall of black clouds you ever saw came rolling in from the north. The wind began to howl so hard that flagpoles bent into upside-down L's, and the ref had to put a foot on the ball between plays to keep it from sailing to Mexico. The rain came in sheets so thick that the subs on the sideline couldn't see the starters on the field, and then the rain turned to hail so helmet-drumming heavy that the linemen couldn't hear the signals from the quarterback screeching at their butts. Postpone the game? This is Texas, y'all! This is football!

The Frogs knifed through winds that gusted up to 90 mph, penetrated the A&M two-yard line on three drives behind their All-America running back, Jim Swink—and couldn't get it in! On one series Swink crossed the goal line twice—the Frogs had the film to prove it—but either the refs couldn't see or it was too slippery to get a good grip on your left nut in a monsoon. TCU finally scored in the third quarter but missed the extra point, and the Aggies stole the game with a fourth-quarter touchdown, 7–6.

Ever drive a car into the exit of a drive-in theater when you were 16, not knowing about those metal teeth? That's the sound that leaked out of the Froggies after that. Miami rocked them 14–0 the next week, Baylor scared the daylights out of them before succumbing 7–6, and then Texas Tech, a team that didn't belong in the same county with the Frogs, pasted them 21–7. Another ferocious storm fell on the team bus on the way home from Lubbock, and the Frogs crawled through it, wondering if their senior-laden squad had lost focus, become more concerned with the honeys they were fixing to marry and the careers they were fixing to start than with the mission at hand.

Back on campus, there dangled poor Abe from a rope lashed to a tree not far from the athletic dorm, brown hat and sport coat over a pillow head and sheet body. It was a startling sight at a university that many players had chosen because it had the homey feel of a big high school, a cow-town college where guys wore cowboy hats and boots, or jeans rolled up at the cuffs and penny loafers. Just like that, the dispirited Frogs had a cause. Their starting quarterback, Chuck Curtis—that's him, number 46, sitting two to the left of Abe—along with end O'Day Williams and backup end Neil Hoskins, the youngster two to the left of Curtis, with his chin in his hand, went out to do a little rectifyin'. Curtis slashed down the effigy with a pocket knife, then led his mates, rumor by rumor, to the perpetrator, who turned tail after a little shouting and shoving. Two days later the Frogs called a players-only meeting at the dining hall, where the subs vented their frustration over lack of playing time, and Cotton Eye Joe Williams, the captain, promised to take their beef to Abe. The players all agreed that an attack on Abe was like an attack on their daddies, and they closed ranks.

To Cotton Eye's suggestion that the second fiddlers fiddle more, Abe said, Great idea. To the notion that the boys were steamed about the hanging effigy, Abe said, Couldn't've been me, I'm a lot better lookin' than that. To the proposition that the Froggies might still make it to the Cotton Bowl—A&M had been hit with NCAA sanctions for recruiting violations and wouldn't be eligible—Abe said, Let's go make hay. That's what the Frogs did, slapping Texas in the face 46–0, elbowing a ripsnorting Rice squad by three and thumping SMU 21–6 to finish 7–3, second to A&M, and scoop up the Aggies' fumbled Cotton Bowl bid. Then came a month to heal and prepare, a half-hour

Greyhound bus ride to Dallas a few days before the big one, the formal dance and then the downtown parade on the fire engine, eyeing that big load on the other fire truck, the one that scored a record-breaking 43 points against Colgate: Jim Brown.

Finally all the buildup is over. The Southwest Conference princesses in convertibles and the high-stepping high school bands are drumming up one last buzz among the 68,000 waiting outside the locker room. But here inside there's only quiet, broken by a soft sob just outside the frame, from the Frogs' All-America lineman Norman Hamilton— who'll swear decades later that no matter what his teammates recollect, he didn't cry before games.

Quiet, broken by the calm drawl of Honest Abe. Whose calm is a lie, so keep your eye on him, because any minute he might just sneak off to the john and throw up. That's what Virgil Miller—he's number 18, the little guy in the dark corner with his head down—will find Abe doing before a game a few years later, when Virgil returns to visit the coach. "Ever get nervous like that?" Abe will ask Virgil. It's safe, since Virgil has graduated and gone.

It's almost like going to church, being here, isn't it? Nope, it's more religious than church, because half of the people here aren't faking it. Maybe folks who never played can't understand how you can be 15 minutes from tearing somebody's head off, 15 seconds from vomiting and a half inch from God, all at the same time. But Chuck Curtis knows. Forty-two years from now, when this picture is placed under his eyes, he'll say, "Look at us. Compared to players today? We weren't great athletes. But we were a team from top to bottom, all giving entire respect to our leader and wanting the same thing wholeheartedly. A sincere group of young men. It'd take a miracle to get the feeling we had in that moment again. With that attitude, there's not a sin that's not erased." When he looks up, there will be tears in his eyes.

Henry B. (Doc) Hardt, he'd understand. He's the old-timer wearing his brown Sunday best and that purple-and-white ribbon on his left arm, so lost in his meditation that he doesn't know that his pants leg is climbing up his calf and that three decades have vanished since he last suited up for a football game—he'd snatch a helmet and storm through that door if Abe would just say the word. That's reverence, the look of a man with four Methodist minister brothers and a missionary sister. Doc's the head of the TCU chemistry department and the Frogs' NCAA faculty representative, the man who makes sure the flunkers aren't playing and the boosters aren't paying, and he's so good at it that he'll become president of the NCAA a few years after this game. Huge hands, grip like a vise and a kind word for everyone, even when he hobbles on a cane to Frogs games a quarter century later. Nice to know he'll make it to 90.

But you need to meet the rest of the boys. Just behind Doc's left shoulder is Mr. Clean: Willard McClung, the quiet assistant to renowned trainer Elmer Brown. Brown's busy right now shooting up guard Vernon Uecker's ankle with novocaine, but Willard would be glad to go fetch a glass of Elmer's concoction for those whose steak and eggs are about to come up, a cocktail the boys call "the green s---." Trouble is, Elmer's green s--- usually comes up along with everything else.

Willard's the only man here who never played, the only one not crawled inside himself—no coincidence there. His ankles were too weak for him to play ball, but he was determined to jimmy his way into moments like this, so he climbed aboard a train his senior year of high school, a fuzzy-cheeked kid from Minden, La., and rode all day to reach the National Trainers' Convention, in Kansas City. Trainers were so thrilled to see a kid show up that Elmer Brown finagled him a scholarship at TCU.

That's Frankie Hyde just behind Doc Hardt's right shoulder, the blond studying the hairs on his left calf. He's the Frogs' scout-team quarterback and an all-around good guy. Doesn't know that he'll hurt his shoulder a few months from now in spring training, that he'll never suit up for a football game again. Doesn't know that Abe's steering his rudder, that he'll end up coaching football just like six of the 17 players in the picture. That he'll end up guiding wave after wave of teenage boys through this moment, some who'll start chattering like monkeys, some who'll go quieter than the dead, some who'll slam their shoulder pads into lockers and poles, some who'll pray like a priest on his third cup of coffee, some who'll get too sick to play. Take it from Frankie: "People who don't experience this don't know themselves like they should."

Or take it from Hunter Enis, the handsome raven-haired boy leaning forward in the dark corner, the one who'll make a bundle in oil: "Sure, there's times in business when you'll work together with a

group of men to meet a goal. But that's not about anything as important as this. It's just about money."

Or Possum Elenburg, the sub on the far left, sitting there thinking,
Heck, yes, it'd be nice to get in and quarterback a few plays on national
TV, but heck, no, I don't want to have to play defense and risk getting
burned deep like I did against Texas Tech. Forty-two years later, here's
Possum: "This is reality stripped to its nakedness. There's no place to
hide. Time is standing still. It's funny, but all your life people tell you
that football's just a game, that so many things more important will
happen to you in life that'll make sports seem insignificant." Listen
to Possum. He's a man who came within a quarter inch of losing his
life in '60 when an oil rig crashed into his skull and paralyzed his
right side for a year, a man who lost a fortune overnight when oil
prices crashed on his head two decades later. "But it's not true, what
people tell ya," he says. "I'm fixing to be tested in this moment, and
I'm gonna be tested again and again in my life, and I'm gonna get
nervous and wonder about myself every single time. Your priorities
as a kid are just as important to you as your priorities as a 60-year-old
man, because all your aspirations and goals are on the line. At any age,
each thing that's important to you... is important to you, and each
fight needs to be fought with every effort."

We're looking at a roomful of bladders fixing to bust, but it's just a
hoax—any doctor could explain the phenomenon. It's just anxiety
sending a surge of adrenaline to the nerve endings in the bladder,
causing it to tighten and creating the feeling that you gotta go. These
boys are like a pack of hunting dogs spraying all over the place just
before the hunt, only dogs are lucky enough not to have all those laces
and hip pads and jockstraps to fumble with.

"...don't need to remind you, laddies, what happened to us in the Cotton Bowl last year, and what that felt like. Not many folks in life get a
second chance, but we've got it right here, today... the chance to redeem
ourselves...."

Redemption. That's all that thumps through the hearts and heads
of two players who happen to be sitting elbow to elbow: Chuck Curtis
and, on his right, Harold (Toad) Pollard, number 16, with the dirty-
blond crew cut and the eye black. See, Toad's missed extra point was
the margin of defeat in TCU's 14–13 Cotton Bowl loss to Mississippi

last year. And Toad's missed extra point in the monsoon at A&M cost the Frogs that 7–6 heartache. Before you get the idea that Toad's a lost cause, you need to know that he led the nation's kickers in scoring last season and that his nickname is Abe's bungled version of Toad's true moniker, the Golden Toe. But ever since that wide-right boot in the Cotton Bowl, Toad has walked around imagining that the entire campus is thinking or saying, "There goes the guy who missed the extra point." Every morning last summer, before his 3-to-11 shift as a roughneck in the oil fields, he toted a tee to a high school field and kicked 40 through the pipes, alone, to prepare for his redemption. "It's a lot more hurt," he'll admit years later, "than a person would realize." Especially since Toad always seems to be clowning, doing that dead-on Donald Duck imitation. But right now he's more nervous than he's ever been, trying to swallow back the notion that he could bungle another critical extra point and be stuck with seeing himself in the mirror every time his hair needs combing the rest of his life.

It's a double-wide hot seat over there, cooking Chuck Curtis's fanny too. Because it was in this very room, at this very moment at the Cotton Bowl last year, that Abe concluded his pregame talk by reminding Chuck-a-luck, as he was fond of calling his quarterback, that he was absolutely *not* to run back the kickoff, that he was to pitch it back to Swink. But Chuck-a-luck, who believed fiercely in his ability to perform or charm his way out of any fix, walked out of this room and fielded that kickoff on the run, down near his shins, and decided that all that forward momentum shouldn't be wasted on a backward lateral, and actually traveled a few yards before—*crunch!*—he took a lick that cracked three ribs and partially dislocated his shoulder, and the Frogs' star quarterback was gone on the game's first play.

Of course, Dick Finney, the backup quarterback—that's him on your farthest right, the one who used to call audibles with fruits instead of numbers ("Apples! Oranges! *Bananas!*")—came trotting into the huddle with that bird-eating grin of his and declared, "Have no fear, Finney's here." But fear truly was in order, because although Diamond Dick ran like a jackrabbit, he also passed like one, and Ole Miss stacked everybody but the trombone players on the line to create a terrible constipation that day.

Imagine what that did to Chuck Curtis, a strapping 6'4", 200-pound All-Conference signal-caller, a Pentecostal preacher's son who could sell a bikini to an Eskimo. In a few years he'll be buying cattle like crazy, owning a bank, winning three state championships as a high school coach and selling automobiles to boot, joking with a former Frogs teammate who protests that he can't afford to pay for a car, "Hey, ol' buddy, I didn't ask you to *pay* for a car—I just wanna *sell* you a car." In the '70s, when he comes up on charges of making false statements on bank-loan applications, there will be preachers preaching in his favor on the courthouse steps, alongside his Jacksboro High football team, cheerleaders and band, all crooning the school's alma mater, and he'll get off with a $500 fine. But no amount of preaching or singing or selling can hide the fact that Chuck-a-luck's ego, more than Toad's blown extra point, cost his teammates the '56 Cotton Bowl, and that he'll have to wear that around like a stained pair of chaps for the rest of his life... unless, in about 10 minutes, he can maneuver the Frogs past Jim Brown.

Now turn around. It's long past time you met Marvin Newman, the well-groomed fellow with the side of his snout pressed against that camera. Nearly forgot about him, he's been so quiet, but none of this would've been possible without him. Funny guy, Marvin: your classic pushy New Yorker when there's something he really wants, but when what he really wants is to disappear into the woodwork—presto, Marvin's a mouse. You can barely hear the click of that Leica he's pointing toward Abe.

He can't use a flash—that would be like taking a hammer to a moment like this. So he has to spread his legs, brace his knees, lock his elbows against his sides and hold his breath to keep that camera stone still. He has to become the tripod, because the quarter second that the shutter needs to be open to drink in enough light is enough to turn Chuck-a-luck and Toad and Buddy and Joe into a purple smear if Marvin's paws move even a hair. Doesn't hurt that he's only 29, because the hands won't let you do that at 59. Doesn't hurt that he rarely drinks, either, because more than a few magazine shooters would still have the shakes at 10 minutes to one in the afternoon on New Year's Day.

He's a Bronx kid, a baker's only son who knew at 19 that he wasn't going to keep burying his arms to the elbows in a wooden vat of rye dough, wasn't going to do what his father and grandfather and great-grandfather had done, even if his old man nearly blew a fuse when that first $90 camera was delivered to the door.

Who knows, maybe that's why he lies in hotel beds for hours, boiling with plans A, B, C and Z on the night before an assignment, brainstorming about how to come home with an image nobody else would have thought of. Maybe that's why he has to come up with something at this Cotton Bowl as heart-touching as the picture he nailed at last year's, that classic shot of Ole Miss's Billy Kinnard coming off the field after beating TCU by one point and planting a kiss on Ole Miss cheerleader Kay Kinnard, who just happened to be his new bride. So, recollecting from last New Year's Day how mouthwatering the light was in that locker room, Marvin made it his first item of business when he saw Abe in Dallas to start schmoozing, start persuading Abe how discreet he'd be, how lickety-split he'd get in and get out, and how much his boss was counting on him... so could he *please* slip into the Frogs' locker room just before kickoff? Heck, Abe didn't need schmoozing. *Sure, Marvin! Why not drop by at halftime too?*

Sure, he'll take snaps more famous than this. He'll bag that black-and-white shot of the World Series-winning homer soaring off Bill Mazeroski's bat as the scoreboard shows all the pertinent facts—3:36 p.m, ninth inning, score tied—of Game 7 between the Pittsburgh Pirates and the New York Yankees in 1960. He'll catch eyes all over the country with his picture of the newly widowed Jackie Kennedy clutching John-John's hand as they watch JFK's coffin go by. But 40-plus years after this New Year's Day in Dallas, he'll remember this picture almost as if he took it yesterday.

"They completely forgot about me," he'll say, sitting over the photo in his Manhattan apartment at age 71. "When photography works well, you can go inside the psyche of the people in the picture. You can see beyond the moment. I always loved this picture. I knew it was special. There hadn't been many photographs taken inside locker rooms, so I knew I was privileged. I couldn't have been standing more than 10 feet from Abe Martin...."

"...but we're not gonna shut down Jim Brown, boys. Not with one tackler. We're gonna have to swarm him. We'll slow him down. We'll go right at him when we've got the ball. He's not a great defensive player. We'll tire him out. We won't stop him. We'll outscore him. This game can put us right back

where we belong, with the best teams in the country. Look inside yourselves and ask, Do I really want it? If you do, laddies, the goose hangs high. Now let's have the prayer."

Some of you might not quite grasp what's sitting and waiting for the Frogs in the room down the hall. Jim Brown stands 6'2" and weighs 225 pounds, which is at least 35 pounds more than the average halfback of his day, not to mention 22 pounds heavier than the average player on the biggest line in the country, Notre Dame's. He runs 100 yards in 10 seconds flat, high-jumps 6'3", hurls the discus 155 feet and once won six events for Syracuse in a track meet, which gave him the notion that it might be fun to enter the national decathlon championship, which he did on 10 days' practice and placed fifth. He scored 33 in a Syracuse basketball game and will be drafted by the NBA's Syracuse Nationals, not bad for a fellow who at the time was considered to have been the greatest lacrosse player in U.S. history. He's just finishing up a senior season in which he averaged 6.2 yards per carry, and he will average a record 5.2 yards per carry for the Cleveland Browns over the next nine years, leading the NFL in rushing in eight of those, before he'll hang it up, as MVP, at age 30. Forgive me if you knew all that, but some legends get so large, the particulars get lost.

Now, some of the Frogs are deeply worried about Brown. Others have been fooled by the three game films they've seen, because Brown looks slower on celluloid than he does when you're reaching for his heels. Still others think he's very good, but he can't possibly be better than John David Crow of Texas A&M.

Brown's sitting very still and silent right now. He's the sort of man who contains a lot more than he lets out, till he steps on the field, and maybe some of what he's holding in has to do with a question that's struck you already, looking around the TCU locker room: Where are all the black folks? There's not one playing football in the Southwest Conference, and there won't be one on scholarship till nine years down the road, after Chuck Curtis becomes an SMU assistant coach and recruits Jerry Levias. In fact, it was only two years before this that the first blacks played in TCU's stadium, when Penn State brought Lenny Moore and Rosey Grier to town and they had to sleep at a motel way out on Jacksboro Highway, because the team couldn't find a downtown Fort Worth hotel that would have them.

That wasn't going to happen to Brown. He decided before the Orangemen arrived in Dallas that he'd refuse to be separated from his teammates, but it hadn't come to that. Syracuse was staying in a hotel on the edge of Dallas that accepted the whole squad.

Sure, Brown's thoughts are fixed on football right now, 15 minutes before kickoff, but it would be a lie to say that another question isn't nibbling on his mind: What's going to happen when he's circled by nearly 70,000 white Texans, some of them wearing cleats? Abe hasn't said a thing to his boys about color. Before the game against Moore and Grier in '54, all he said was, "They're darn good football players, so it wouldn't make much sense to say something to get 'em mad."

Brown will never be the sort to live on the fumes of his past, or reminisce much at all. But even at 63, when he's running across America directing Amer-I-Can—an organization he founded to tackle gang problems and help prisoners get ready for life outside the walls—some of what coursed through him in that Cotton Bowl locker room will still be with him.

"I was concerned how their players would carry themselves, if there'd be any epithets," he'll say. "But I wasn't going to make that any kind of extra motive, or try to prove something. Racism is sickness, and I'm not gonna prove something to sickness. I was a performer with my own standards, and living up to them was all I worried about. For me, the time just before a game was always tense, like going to war without death. I always felt humbled. It's a very spiritual moment. I'd try to go into a pure state. No negative thoughts, even toward the other team. No rah-rah, because rah-rah's for show. Your butt's on the line, and you either stand up and deal with it, or... or you can't. You become a very difficult opponent for anyone or anything when you know that you can."

Let me tell you what happened that day, right after Marvin's last click. Chuck Curtis went wild. He called a run-pitch sprint-out series that no one expected from a drop-back quarterback without much foot speed, and he threw two touchdown passes to stake the Frogs to a 14–0 lead.

Then it was Brown's turn. The tip that TCU coaches had passed on to the Frogs after studying film—that just before the snap Brown leaned in the direction he was about to go—was accurate, but it wasn't worth a Chinese nickel. As Brown carried a couple of more Frogs for rides, Abe spun toward his boys on the sideline and nearly swallowed his cigar, then howled, "Shistol pot! Can't anybody tackle him?"

Against Brown, everything the Frogs had learned about hitting a man in the thighs and wrapping him up went down the sewer—there was just too much power there. First tackler to reach him had to hit him high, delay him for a second, take some of the forward momentum out of those thighs, then wait for reinforcements to hit him low.

Brown bashed in from the two for Syracuse's first touchdown, kicked the extra point, then hurled a 20-yard pass that set up his own four-yard touchdown run and booted another point after to tie the ball game 14–14 just before intermission. Lonnie Leatherman, a backup end for the Frogs, would shake his head from here to the year 2000, yelping, "He ran through the whole stinkin' team! That man was bad to the bone! He was unbelievable! These are great football players, and they couldn't tackle him. Norman Hamilton was an All-America and couldn't tackle him."

A savage moment came early in the second half. Syracuse was on the TCU 40 and rolling—Brown had just made another first down on a fourth-down plunge—when Buddy Dike, with his battered kidney, threw caution to the wind. He hit Brown head-on, producing a sound Hamilton would never forget. "Like thunder," he'd recall. "Never heard a sound that loud from two men colliding. I thought, How can they ever get up?"

Dike's face mask snapped in two, the pigskin burst from Brown's grasp and TCU recovered it. Brown would not miss a play. The inspired Froggies again targeted Brown when he was on defense, flooding his side of the field with three receivers. Years later Leatherman would make no bones about it. "Brown was horrible on defense," he'd say. Joe Williams would be a trifle kinder: "Maybe their coaches didn't want to offend him by teaching him defense."

Curtis closed a drive by sweeping around the left end for a score, and Jim Swink found paydirt for the Frogs a few minutes later. Toad Pollard stepped on the field for the extra point. He was 3 for 3, and his side was up 27–14, but with nearly 12 minutes left and Brown yet to be corralled, the kicker's gut quivered with evil memories. To Jim Ozee, finally getting a few minutes at center, it seemed like eternity between his snap and the thud of Toad's toe against the ball. "What took you so long?" Ozee demanded seconds after the kick sailed true.

"I wanted to be sure," Toad said, breathing heavily—as if he knew that Brown would rip off a 46-yard return on the kickoff, then slam in from the one and bust open Toad's lip a few moments later. As if he knew that Syracuse would roar right down the field on its next possession, finally figuring a way to reach the end zone without Brown, on a touchdown pass with 1:16 left. As if he knew that Chico Mendoza, the lone Mexican-American on the Frogs' roster, would storm in from right end just after Syracuse's third touchdown and block Brown's point-after try, making the team that lost by one extra point in the Cotton Bowl in 1956 the winner by one extra point in 1957, by a score of 28–27. "All those white boys out there," Leatherman would point out, "and the Mexican and the black were the key players."

Brown would finish with 132 yards on 26 carries, three kickoff returns for 96 more yards, three extra points, the whole country's admiration... and no slurs. "They were nice human beings," he'd say of the Frogs. But Chuck-a-luck, who finished 12 of 15 through the air, would see Brown speak at the University of Texas-Arlington years later and leave sniffing that "he sounded like one of those Black Panthers."

Toad would remember "floating" at the postgame banquet, thinking he was saved from a lifetime of negative thoughts, but in his 60s that extra point he missed in the '56 Cotton Bowl would still occupy his mind more than the four he made in '57, and every kick he watched on TV would make his foot twitch up, as if the kick were his.

TCU? The Frogs wouldn't win another bowl game for 41 years. The rules changed on Abe: Free substitution and the end of the two-way player meant that a college needed at least 22 studs, and that a small school with a scrawny budget and even less national TV exposure had almost no prayer, no matter how sincere its players were 15 minutes before kickoff. When Abe quit nine years later, people said the game had passed him by.

Come 1999, that bare locker room would no longer be a locker room, that Southwest Conference would no longer exist, and that New Year's Day game would be known as the Southwestern Bell Cotton Bowl Classic, with a website.

One last thing. There's a saying Texans used to share about men in locker rooms awaiting battle, and pardon my French, but it goes like this: Brave men piss, cowards s---.

Which were you? Which was I? Guess I just can't walk out of this picture without asking questions like that. But I'll shut up now, in case you want to go back and catch Chuck-a-luck going watery-eyed as he leads the team prayer. Hurry, though. It's going hard on nine minutes to one.

Frank Deford

In the days when words mattered more than anything else, the defining feature in *Sports Illustrated* was a weekly back-of-the-book treasure called the "bonus piece"—long and smart and beautifully written whether it was fact or fiction, insightful or controversial, funny or poignant or just a damn good read. For more than two decades Frank Deford (b. 1938) was the master of the bonus piece, writing with a heart surgeon's precision and a social worker's compassion, profiling complicated characters like Bob Knight and Jimmy Connors, and taking an occasional busman's holiday with the Roller Derby and a circus act called Irvy the Whale. Deford left *SI* in 1989 to help launch *The National Sports Daily*, and after that noble experiment failed, his byline could be found in *Newsweek* and *Vanity Fair* and his presence could be felt on NPR and HBO's *Real Sports*. But when he resumed writing for *SI* not long before the turn of the century, there was a genuine sense that he was home again. And when, in 2002, he wrote the following essay about meeting Johnny Unitas years after the quarterback had been his boyhood hero, Deford filled it with the love Baltimore once felt for the Colts and his own love for the city where he grew up.

The Best There Ever Was

SOMETIMES, EVEN if it was only yesterday, or even if it just feels like it was only yesterday....

Sometimes, no matter how detailed the historical accounts, no matter how many the eyewitnesses, no matter how complete the statistics, no matter how vivid the film....

Sometimes, I'm sorry, but....

Sometimes, you just had to be there.

That was the way it was with Johnny Unitas in the prime of his life, when he played for the Baltimore Colts and changed a team and a city and a league. Johnny U was an American original, a piece of work like none other, excepting maybe Paul Bunyan and Horatio Alger.

Part of it was that he came out of nowhere, like Athena springing forth full-grown from the brow of Zeus, or like Shoeless Joe Hardy from Hannibal, Mo., magically joining the Senators, compliments of the devil. But that was myth, and that was fiction. Johnny U was real, before our eyes.

65

Nowadays, of course, flesh peddlers and scouting services identify the best athletes when they are still in junior high. Prospects are not allowed to sneak up on us. But back then, 1956, was a quaint time when we still could be pleasantly surprised. Unitas just surfaced there on the roster, showing up one day after a tryout. The new number 19 was identified as "YOU-ni-tass" when he first appeared in an exhibition, and only later did we learn that he had played, somewhere between obscurity and anonymity, at Louisville and then, for six bucks a game, on the dusty Pittsburgh sandlots. His was a story out of legend, if not, indeed, out of religious tradition: the unlikely savior come out of nowhere.

The quarterback for the Colts then was George Shaw, the very first pick in the NFL draft the year before, the man ordained to lead a team that was coalescing into a contender. Didn't we wish, in Baltimore! Didn't we dream! The Colts had Alan (the Horse) Ameche and Lenny (Spats) Moore and L. G. (Long Gone) Dupre to carry the ball and Raymond Berry and Jim Mutscheller to catch it and Artie Donovan and Big Daddy Lipscomb and Gino Marchetti to manhandle the other fellows when they had the pigskin. Then one day, as it is written, Shaw got hurt in a game, and YOU-ni-tass came in, hunched of shoulder, trotting kind of funny. He looked *crooked*, is how I always thought of him. Jagged. Sort of a gridiron Abraham Lincoln.

And on the first play the rookie threw a pass that went for a long touchdown. Only it was an interception; the touchdown went the other way.

For those of us in Baltimore, this seemed like the cruelest fate (however likely). Finally Baltimore was going to amount to something, and then, wouldn't you know it, Shaw gets taken from us. It seemed so terribly unfair, if perhaps exactly what we could expect for our workingman's town, where the swells passed through, without stopping, on their way to Washington or New York.

But then, there couldn't have been a mother's son anywhere who knew exactly what Unitas had in store for us. Marchetti, apparently, was the first one to understand. It was a couple of weeks later, and he was lying on the training table when the equipment manager, Fred Schubach, wondered out loud when Shaw might come back. Marchetti raised up a bit and said, "It doesn't matter. Unitas is the quarterback now."

Evidently all the other Colts nodded; they'd just been waiting for someone to dare express what they were beginning to sense. Marchetti had fought in the Battle of the Bulge when he was a teenager and thus, apparently, had developed a keen appreciation for things larger than life.

Of course, no matter who John Constantine Unitas had played football for, it would've been Katie-bar-the-door. But perhaps never has greatness found such a fitting address. It wasn't only that Baltimore had such an inferiority complex, an awareness that all that the stuck-up outlanders knew of our fair city was that we had crabs and white marble steps in profusion and a dandy red-light district, the Block. Since H. L. Mencken (he who had declared, "I hate all sports as rabidly as a person who likes sports hates common sense") had died, the most famous Baltimorean was a stripper, Blaze Starr. The city hadn't had a winner since the Old Orioles of a century past. For that matter, until very recently Baltimore hadn't even *had* a major league team in the 1900s. Before the Colts arrived in 1947, the best athlete in town was a woman duckpin bowler named Toots Barger. Football? The biggest games in Baltimore had been when Johns Hopkins took on Susquehanna or Franklin & Marshall at homecoming.

But no mother ever took her children to her breast as old Bawlmer, Merlin (as we pronounced it), embraced the Colts. It wasn't just that they played on Sundays and thus finally made us "big league" in the eyes of the rest of a republic that was rapidly becoming coaxial-cabled together. No, the Colts were just folks, all around town, at crab feasts and bull roasts and what-have-you. Why, I knew I could go a few blocks to Moses' Sunoco station on York Road and see a bunch of Colts there, hanging out, kicking tires. Had I had a good enough fake I.D., I could've even gotten into Sweeney's, up Greenmount Avenue, and drunk beer with them. The Colts were real people, so we loved them even more as they went on their merry way to becoming champions of the world.

With each passing game, though, Unitas elevated above the others until, on December 28, 1958, he entered the pantheon of gods. 'Twas then, of course, in Yankee Stadium itself, that he led us from behind to an overtime victory over the despised New Yorkers in the Greatest Game Ever Played. Yet even as we deified him, we still had it on the best authority that he remained one of the boys. Just because he was quarterback, he wasn't some glamour-puss.

Certainly he didn't look the part of a hero. This is how his team-mate Alex Hawkins described Unitas when Hawkins first saw him in the locker room: "Here was a total mystery. [Unitas] was from Pennsylvania, but he looked so much like a Mississippi farmhand that I looked around for a mule. He had stooped shoulders, a chicken breast, thin bowed legs and long, dangling arms with crooked, mangled fingers."

Unitas didn't even have a quarterback's name. All by himself he redrew the profile of the quarterback. Always, before, it had been men of Old Stock who qualified to lead the pros. Baugh and Albert and Van Brocklin and Layne and Graham. (All right, Luckman was a Jew, but he was schooled in the WASP-y Ivy League.) Unitas was some hardscrabble Lithuanian, so what he did made a difference, because even if we'd never met a Lithuanian before, we knew that he was as smart a sonuvabitch as he was tough. Dammit, he was *our* Lithuanian.

They didn't have coaches with headphones and Polaroids and fax machines then, sitting on high, telling quarterbacks what plays to call. In those halcyon days, quarterbacks were field generals, not field lieutenants. And there was Unitas after he called a play (and probably checked off and called another play when he saw what the ruffians across the line were up to), shuffling back into the pocket, unfazed by the violent turbulence all around him, standing there in his hightops, waiting, looking, poised. I never saw war, so that is still my vision of manhood: Unitas standing courageously in the pocket, his left arm flung out in a diagonal to the upper deck, his right cocked for the business of passing, down amidst the mortals. Lock and load.

There, to Berry at the sideline. Or Moore. Or Jimmy Orr real long. Lenny Lyles. John Mackey. Hawkins. Ameche out of the backfield. My boyhood memory tells me Johnny U never threw an incompletion, let alone an interception, after that single debut mistake. Spoilsports who keep the numbers dispute that recollection, but they also assure me that he threw touchdown passes in 47 straight games. That figure has been threatened less seriously than even DiMaggio's sacred 56. Yes, I know there've been wonderful quarterbacks since Unitas hung up his hightops. I admit I'm prejudiced. But the best quarterback ever? The best player? Let me put it this way: If there were one game scheduled, Earth versus the Klingons, with the fate of the universe on the line, any person with his wits about him would have Johnny U calling the signals in the huddle, up under the center, back in the pocket.

I've always wondered how people in olden times connected back to their childhoods. After all, we have hooks with the past. When most of us from the 20th century reminisce about growing up, we right away remember the songs and the athletes of any particular moment. Right?

A few years ago I saw Danny and the Juniors performing at a club, and all anybody wanted them to sing was *At the Hop*, which was their No. 1 smash back in 1958, the year Unitas led the Colts to that first, fabled championship. About a year after I saw Danny, I read that he had committed suicide. I always assumed it was because no matter how many years had passed, nobody would let him escape from singing *At the Hop*, exactly as he did in 1958.

Unlike songs, athletes, inconveniently, get on. They grow old. Johnny U couldn't keep on throwing passes. He aged. He even let his crew cut grow out. Luckily for me, after I grew up (as it were) and became a sportswriter, I never covered him. Oh, I went to his restaurant, and I saw him on TV, and I surely never forgot him. Whenever Walter Iooss, the photographer, and I would get together, we would talk about Johnny U the way most men talk about caressing beautiful women. But I never had anything to do with Unitas professionally. That was good. I could keep my boy's memories unsullied.

Then, about five years ago, I finally met him for real, at a party. When we were introduced he said, "It's nice to meet you, Mr. Deford." That threw me into a tailspin. *No, no, no. Don't you understand? I'm not Mr. Deford. You're Mr. Unitas. You're Johnny U. You're my boyhood idol. I can't ever be Mr. Deford with you, because you have to always be number 19, so I can always be a kid.* But I didn't explain that to him. I was afraid he would think I was too sappy. I just said, "It's nice to meet you, too, Mr. Unitas," and shook his crippled hand.

A couple of years later I went down to Baltimore and gave a speech for a charity. What they gave me as a thank-you present was a football, autographed by Himself. When you're not a child anymore and you write about athletes, you tend to take 'em as run-of-the-mill human beings. Anyway, I do. I have only one other athlete's autograph, from Bill Russell, who, along with Unitas, is the other great star of the '50s who changed his sport all by himself.

After I got that autographed Unitas football, every now and then I'd pick it up and fondle it. I still do, too, even though Johnny Unitas is dead now, and I can't be a boy anymore. Ultimately, you see, what he conveyed to his teammates and to Baltimore and to a wider world was the utter faith that he could do it. He could make it work. Somehow, he could win. He *would* win. It almost didn't matter when he actually couldn't. The point was that with Johnny U, it always seemed possible. You so very seldom get that, even with the best of them. Johnny U's talents were his own. The belief he gave us was his gift.

John Schulian

When he left the *Philadelphia Daily News* to try Hollywood on for size in 1986, John Schulian (b. 1945) assumed he was finished with sportswriting. But sportswriting had a funny way of sneaking back into his life even when he was churning out scripts for such memorable TV series as *L.A. Law, Miami Vice,* and *Wiseguy.* He wrote regularly for *GQ* and *Sports Illustrated,* just as he had since he came to prominence as a sports columnist for the *Chicago Sun-Times* and *Chicago Daily News* in the 1970s. In 1993, before he struck gold as one of the creators of *Xena: Warrior Princess,* *SI* asked if he was interested in profiling Chuck Bednarik, the NFL's last full-time two-way player and a symbol of the hearty breed that endured the Depression and World War II. Schulian didn't have to be asked twice. But his enthusiasm didn't convince Bednarik that a mere writer could find his way to his subject's home in those pre-GPS days. Better they should meet at a large shopping center and proceed from there. The first person Schulian saw when he pulled into the parking lot was a senior citizen with a face like a clenched fist wearing a Philadelphia Eagles jersey and standing in front of a white van, arms the size of Smithfield hams folded across his chest. Bednarik, of course. And he turned out to be a writer's dream: a man without an unexpressed thought.

Concrete Charlie

H E WENT DOWN HARD, left in a heap by a crackback block as naked as it was vicious. Pro football was like that in 1960, a gang fight in shoulder pads, its violence devoid of the high-tech veneer it has today. The crackback was legal, and all the Philadelphia Eagles could do about it that Sunday in Cleveland was carry a linebacker named Bob Pellegrini off on his shield.

Buck Shaw, a gentleman coach in this ruffian's pastime, watched for as long as he could, then he started searching the Eagle sideline for someone to throw into the breach. His first choice was already banged up, and after that the standard 38-man NFL roster felt as tight as a hangman's noose. Looking back, you realize that Shaw had only one choice all along.

"Chuck," he said, "get in there."

And Charles Philip Bednarik, who already had a full-time job as Philadelphia's offensive center and a part-time job selling concrete after practice, headed onto the field without a word. Just the way his father had marched off to the open-hearth furnaces at Bethlehem Steel on so many heartless mornings. Just the way Bednarik himself had climbed behind the machine gun in a B-24 for 30 missions as a teenager fighting in World War II. It was a family tradition: Duty called, you answered.

Chuck Bednarik was 35 years old, still imposing at 6'3" and 235 pounds, but also the father of one daughter too many to be what he really had in mind—retired. Jackie's birth the previous February gave him five children, all girls, and more bills than he thought he could handle without football. So here he was in his 12th NFL season, telling himself he was taking it easy on his creaky legs by playing center after all those years as an All-Pro linebacker. The only time he intended to move back to defense was in practice, when he wanted to work up a little extra sweat.

And now, five games into the season, this: Jim Brown over there in the Cleveland huddle, waiting to trample some fresh meat, and Bednarik trying to decipher the defensive terminology the Eagles had installed in the two years since he was their middle linebacker. Chuck Weber had his old job now, and Bednarik found himself asking what the left outside linebacker was supposed to do on passing plays. "Take the second man out of the backfield," Weber said. That was as fancy as it would get. Everything else would be about putting the wood to Jim Brown.

Bednarik nodded and turned to face a destiny that went far beyond emergency duty at linebacker. He was taking his first step toward a place in NFL history as the kind of player they don't make anymore.

The kids start at about 7 A.M. and don't stop until fatigue slips them a Mickey after dark. For 20 months it has been this way, three grandchildren roaring around like gnats with turbochargers, and Bednarik feeling every one of his years. And hating the feeling. And letting the kids know about it.

Get to be 68 and you deserve to turn the volume on your life as low as you want it. That's what Bednarik thinks, not without justification. But life has been even more unfair to the kids than it has been to him. The girl is eight, the boys are six and five, and they live with Bednarik and his wife in Coopersburg, Pa., because of a marriage gone bad. The kids' mother, Donna, is there too, trying to put her life back together, flinching every time her father's anger erupts. "I can't help it," Bednarik says plaintively. "It's the way I am."

The explanation means nothing to the kids warily eyeing this big man with the flattened nose and the gnarled fingers and the faded tattoos on his right arm. He is one more question in a world that seemingly exists to deny them answers. Only with the passage of time will they realize they were yelled at by Concrete Charlie, the toughest Philadelphia Eagle there ever was.

But for the moment, football makes no more sense to the kids than does anything else about their grandfather. "I'm not *one* of the last 60-minute players," they hear him say. "I am the last." Then he barks at them to stop making so much noise and to clean up the mess they made in the family room, where trophies, photographs and game balls form a mosaic of the best days of his life. The kids scamper out of sight, years from comprehending the significance of what Bednarik is saying.

He really was the last of a breed. For 58½ minutes in the NFL's 1960 championship game, he held his ground in the middle of Philly's Franklin Field, a force of nature determined to postpone the christening of the Green Bay Packers' dynasty. "I didn't run down on kickoffs, that's all," Bednarik says. The rest of that frosty December 26, on both offense and defense, he played with the passion that crested when he wrestled Packers fullback Jim Taylor to the ground one last time and held him there until the final gun punctuated the Eagles' 17–13 victory.

Philadelphia hasn't ruled pro football since then, and pro football hasn't produced a player with the combination of talent, hunger and opportunity to duplicate what Bednarik did. It is a far different game now, of course, its complexities seeming to increase exponentially every year, but the athletes playing it are so much bigger and faster than Bednarik and his contemporaries that surely someone with the ability to go both ways must dwell among them. It is just as easy to imagine Walter Payton having shifted from running back to safety, or Lawrence Taylor moving from linebacker to tight end. But that day is long past, for the NFL of the '90s is a monument to specialization.

There are running backs who block but don't run, others who run but only from inside the five-yard line and still others who exist for no other reason than to catch passes. Some linebackers can't play the run, and some can't play the pass, and there are monsters on the defensive line who dream of decapitating quarterbacks but resemble the Maiden Surprised when they come face mask to face mask with a pulling guard.

"No way in hell any of them can go both ways," Bednarik insists.

"They don't want to. They're afraid they'll get hurt. And the money's too big, that's another thing. They'd just say, 'Forget it, I'm already making enough.'"

The sentiment is what you might expect from someone who signed with the Eagles for $10,000 when he left the University of Pennsylvania for the 1949 season and who was pulling down only 17 grand when he made sure they were champions 11 years later. Seventeen grand, and Reggie White fled Philadelphia for Green Bay over the winter for what, $4 million a year? "If he gets that much," Bednarik says, "I should be in the same class." But at least White has already proved that someday he will be taking his place alongside Concrete Charlie in the Hall of Fame. At least he isn't a runny-nosed quarterback like Drew Bledsoe, signing a long-term deal for $14.5 million before he has ever taken a snap for the New England Patriots. "When I read about that," Bednarik says, "I wanted to regurgitate."

He nurtures the resentment he is sure every star of his era shares, feeding it with the dollar figures he sees in the sports pages every day, priming it with the memory that his fattest contract with the Eagles paid him $25,000, in 1962, his farewell season.

"People laugh when they hear what I made," he says. "I tell them, 'Hey, don't laugh at me. I could do everything but eat a football.'" Even when he was in his 50s, brought back by then coach Dick Vermeil to show the struggling Eagles what a champion looked like, Bednarik was something to behold. He walked into training camp, bent over the first ball he saw and whistled a strike back through his legs to a punter unused to such service from the team's long snappers. "And you know the amazing thing?" Vermeil says. "Chuck didn't look."

He was born for the game, a physical giant among his generation's linebackers, and so versatile that he occasionally got the call to punt and kick off. "This guy was a football athlete," says Nick Skorich, an Eagle assistant and head coach for six years. "He was a very strong blocker at center and quick as a cat off the ball." He had to be, because week in, week out he was tangling with Sam Huff or Joe Schmidt, Bill

George or Les Richter, the best middle linebackers of the day. Bednarik more than held his own against them, or so we are told, which is the problem with judging the performance of any center. Who the hell knows what's happening in that pile of humanity?

It is different with linebackers. Linebackers are out there in the open for all to see, and that was where Bednarik was always at his best. He could intercept a pass with a single meat hook and tackle with the cold-blooded efficiency of a sniper. "Dick Butkus was the one who manhandled people," says Tom Brookshier, the loquacious former Eagle cornerback. "Chuck just snapped them down like rag dolls."

It was a style that left Frank Gifford for dead, and New York seething, in 1960, and it made people everywhere forget that Concrete Charlie, for all his love of collisions, played the game in a way that went beyond the purely physical. "He was probably the most instinctive football player I've ever seen," says Maxie Baughan, a rookie linebacker with the Eagles in Bednarik's whole-schmear season. Bednarik could see a guard inching one foot backward in preparation for a sweep or a tight end setting up just a little farther from the tackle than normal for a pass play. Most important, he could think along with the best coaches in the business.

And the coaches didn't appreciate that, which may explain the rude goodbye that the Dallas Cowboys' Tom Landry tried to give Bednarik in '62. First the Cowboys ran a trap, pulling a guard and running a back through the hole. "Chuck was standing right there," Brookshier says. "Almost killed the guy." Next the Cowboys ran a sweep behind that same pulling guard, only to have Bednarik catch the ballcarrier from behind. "Almost beheaded the guy," Brookshier says. Finally the Cowboys pulled the guard, faked the sweep and threw a screen pass. Bednarik turned it into a two-yard loss. "He had such a sense for the game," Brookshier says. "You could do all that shifting and put all those men in motion, and Chuck still went right where the ball was."

Three decades later Bednarik is in his family room watching a tape from NFL Films that validates what all the fuss was about. The grandchildren have been shooed off to another part of the house, and he has found the strange peace that comes from seeing himself saying on the TV screen, "All you can think of is 'Kill, kill, kill.'" He laughs about what a ham he was back then, but the footage that follows his admission proves that it was no joke. Bednarik sinks deep in his easy chair. "This movie," he says, "turns me on even now."

Suddenly the spell is broken by a chorus of voices and a stampede through the kitchen. The grandchildren again, thundering out to the backyard. "Hey, how many times I have to tell you?" Bednarik shouts. "Close the door!"

The pass was behind Gifford. It was a bad delivery under the best of circumstances, life-threatening where he was now, crossing over the middle. But Gifford was too much the pro not to reach back and grab the ball. He tucked it under his arm and turned back in the right direction, all in the same motion—and then Bednarik hit him like a lifetime supply of bad news.

Thirty-three years later there are still people reeling from the Tackle, none of them named Gifford or Bednarik. In New York somebody always seems to be coming up to old number 16 of the Giants and telling him they were there the day he got starched in the Polo Grounds (it was Yankee Stadium). Other times they say that everything could have been avoided if Charlie Conerly had thrown the ball where he was supposed to (George Shaw was the guilty Giant quarterback). And then there was Howard Cosell, who sat beside Gifford on *Monday Night Football* for 14 years and seemed to bring up Bednarik whenever he was stuck for something to say. One week Cosell would accuse Bednarik of blindsiding Gifford, the next he would blame Bednarik for knocking Gifford out of football. Both were classic examples of telling it like it wasn't.

But it is too late to undo any of the above, for the Tackle has taken on a life of its own. So Gifford plays along by telling what sounds like an apocryphal story about one of his early dates with the woman who would become his third wife. "Kathie Lee," he told her, "one word you're going to hear a lot of around me is Bednarik." And Kathie Lee supposedly said, "What's that, a pasta?"

For all the laughing Gifford does when he spins that yarn, there was nothing funny about November 20, 1960, the day Bednarik handed him his lunch. The Eagles, who complemented Concrete Charlie and Hall of Fame quarterback Norm Van Brocklin with a roster full of tough, resourceful John Does, blew into New York intent on knocking the Giants on their media-fed reputation. Philadelphia was leading

17–10 with under two minutes to play, but the Giants kept slashing and pounding, smelling one of those comeback victories that were supposed to be the Eagles' specialty. Then Gifford caught that pass. "I ran through him right up here," Bednarik says, slapping himself on the chest hard enough to break something. "*Right here.*" And this time he pops the passenger in his van on the chest. "It was like when you hit a home run; you say, 'Jeez, I didn't even feel it hit the bat.'"

Huff would later call it "the greatest tackle I've ever seen," but at the time it happened his emotion was utter despair. Gifford fell backward, the ball flew forward. When Weber pounced on it, Bednarik started dancing as if St. Vitus had taken possession of him. And as he danced, he yelled at Gifford, "This game is over!" But Gifford couldn't hear him.

"He didn't hurt me," Gifford insists. "When he hit me, I landed on my ass and then my head snapped back. That was what put me out—the whiplash, not Bednarik."

Whatever the cause, Gifford looked like he was past tense as he lay there motionless. A funereal silence fell over the crowd, and Bednarik rejoiced no more. He has never been given to regret, but in that moment he almost changed his ways. Maybe he actually would have repented if he had been next to the first Mrs. Gifford after her husband had been carried off on a stretcher. She was standing outside the Giants' dressing room when the team physician stuck his head out the door and said, "I'm afraid he's dead." Only after she stopped wobbling did Mrs. Gifford learn that the doctor was talking about a security guard who had suffered a heart attack during the game. Even so, Gifford didn't get off lightly. He had a concussion that kept him out for the rest of the season and all of 1961. But in '62 he returned as a flanker and played with honor for three more seasons. He would also have the good grace to invite Bednarik to play golf with him, and he would never, ever whine about the Tackle. "It was perfectly legal," Gifford says. "If I'd had the chance, I would have done the same thing to Chuck."

But all that came later. In the week after the Tackle, with a Giant-Eagle rematch looming, Gifford got back at Bednarik the only way he could, by refusing to take his calls or to acknowledge the flowers and fruit he sent to the hospital. Naturally there was talk that Gifford's teammates would try to break Concrete Charlie into little pieces, especially since Conerly kept calling him a cheap-shot artist in the papers. But talk was all it turned out to be. The Eagles, on the other hand, didn't run their mouths until after they had whipped the Giants a second time. Bednarik hasn't stopped talking since then.

"This is a true story," he says. "They're having a charity roast for Gifford in Parsippany, N. J., a couple of years ago, and I'm one of the roasters. I ask the manager of this place if he'll do me a favor. Then, when it's my turn to talk, the lights go down and it's dark for five or six seconds. Nobody knows what the hell's going on until I tell them, 'Now you know how Frank Gifford felt when I hit him.'"

He grew up poor, and poor boys fight the wars for this country. He never thought anything of it back then. All he knew was that every other guy from the south side of Bethlehem, Pa., was in a uniform, and he figured he should be in a uniform too. So he enlisted without finishing his senior year at Liberty High School. It was a special program they had; your mother picked up your diploma while you went off to kill or be killed. Bednarik didn't take anything with him but the memories of the place he called *Betlam* until the speech teachers at Penn classed up his pronunciation. Betlam was where his father emigrated from Czechoslovakia and worked all those years in the steel mill without making foreman because he couldn't read or write English. It was where his mother gave birth to him and his three brothers and two sisters, then shepherded them through the Depression with potato soup and second-hand clothes. It was where he made 90 cents a round caddying at Saucon Valley Country Club and $2 a day toiling on a farm at the foot of South Mountain, and gave every penny to his mother. It was where he fought in the streets and scaled the wall at the old Lehigh University stadium to play until the guards chased him off. "It was," he says, "the greatest place in the world to be a kid."

The worst place was in the sky over Europe, just him and a bunch of other kids in an Army Air Corps bomber with the Nazis down below trying to incinerate them. "The antiaircraft fire would be all around us," Bednarik says. "It was so thick you could walk on it. And you could hear it penetrating. *Ping! Ping! Ping!* Here you are, this wild, dumb kid, you didn't think you were afraid of anything, and now, every time you take off, you're convinced this is it, you're gonna be ashes."

Thirty times he went through that behind his .50-caliber machine gun. He still has the pieces of paper on which he neatly wrote each target, each date. It started with Berlin on August 27, 1944, and ended with Zwiesel on April 20, 1945. He looks at those names now and remembers the base in England that he flew out of, the wake-ups at four o'clock in the morning, the big breakfasts he ate in case one of them turned out to be his last meal, the rain and fog that made just getting off the ground a dance with death. "We'd have to scratch missions because our planes kept banging together," he says. "These guys were knocking each other off."

Bednarik almost bought it himself when his plane, crippled by flak, skidded off the runway on landing and crashed. To escape he kicked out a window and jumped 20 feet to the ground. Then he did what he did after every mission, good or bad. He lit a cigarette and headed for the briefing room, where there was always a bottle on the table. "I was 18, 19 years old," he says, "and I was drinking that damn whiskey straight."

The passing of time does nothing to help him forget, because the war comes back to him whenever he looks at the tattoo on his right forearm. It isn't like the CPB monogram that adorns his right biceps, a souvenir from a night on some Army town. The tattoo on his forearm shows a flower blossoming to reveal the word MOTHER. He got it in case his plane was shot down and his arm was all that remained of him to identify.

There were only two things the Eagles didn't get from Bednarik in 1960: the color TV and the $1,000 that had been their gifts to him when he said he was retiring at the end of the previous season. The Eagles didn't ask for them back, and Bednarik didn't offer to return them. If he ever felt sheepish about it, that ended when he started going both ways.

For no player could do more for his team than Bednarik did as pro football began evolving into a game of specialists. He risked old bones that could just as easily have been out of harm's way, and even though he never missed a game that season—and only three in his entire career—every step hurt like the dickens.

Bednarik doesn't talk about it, which is surprising because, as Dick Vermeil says, "it usually takes about 20 seconds to find out what's on

Chuck's mind." But this is different. This is about the code he lived by as a player, one that treated the mere thought of calling in sick as a betrayal of his manhood. "There's a difference between pain and injury," Baughan says, "and Chuck showed everybody on our team what it was."

His brave front collapsed in front of only one person, the former Emma Margetich, who married Bednarik in 1948 and went on to reward him with five daughters. It was Emma who pulled him out of bed when he couldn't make it on his own, who kneaded his aching muscles, who held his hand until he could settle into the hot bath she had drawn for him.

"Why are you doing this?" she kept asking. "They're not paying you for it." And every time, his voice little more than a whisper, he would reply, "Because we have to win." Nobody in Philadelphia felt that need more than Bednarik did, maybe because in the increasingly distant past he had been the town's biggest winner. It started when he took his high school coach's advice and became the least likely Ivy Leaguer that Penn has ever seen, a hard case who had every opponent he put a dent in screaming for the Quakers to live up to their nickname and de-emphasize football.

Next came the 1949 NFL champion Eagles, with halfback Steve Van Buren and end Pete Pihos lighting the way with their Hall of Fame greatness, and the rookie Bednarik ready to go elsewhere after warming the bench for all of his first two regular-season games. On the train home from a victory in Detroit, he took a deep breath and went to see the head coach, who refused to fly and had one of those names you don't find anymore, Earle (Greasy) Neale. "I told him, 'Coach Neale, I want to be traded, I want to go somewhere I can play,'" Bednarik says. "And after that I started every week—he had me flip-flopping between center and linebacker—and I never sat down for the next 14 years."

He got a tie clasp and a $1,100 winner's share for being part of that championship season, and then it seemed that he would never be treated so royally again. Some years before their return to glory, the Eagles were plug-ugly, others they managed to maintain their dignity, but the team's best always fell short of Bednarik's. From 1950 to '56 and in '60 he was an All-Pro linebacker. In the '54 Pro Bowl he punted in place of the injured Charley Trippi and spent the rest of the game winning the MVP award by recovering three fumbles and running an interception back for a touchdown. But Bednarik did not return to the winner's circle until Van Brocklin hit town.

As far as everybody else in the league was concerned, when the Los Angeles Rams traded the Dutchman to Philadelphia months before the opening of the '58 season, it just meant one more Eagle with a tainted reputation. Tommy McDonald was being accused of making up his pass patterns as he went along, Brookshier was deemed too slow to play cornerback, and end Pete Retzlaff bore the taint of having been cut twice by Detroit. And now they had Van Brocklin, a long-in-the-tooth quarterback with the disposition of an unfed doberman.

In Philly, however, he was able to do what he hadn't done in L.A. He won. And winning rendered his personality deficiencies secondary. So McDonald had to take it when Van Brocklin told him that a separated shoulder wasn't reason enough to leave a game, and Brookshier, fearing he had been paralyzed after making a tackle, had to grit his teeth when the Dutchman ordered his carcass dragged off the field. "Actually Van Brocklin was a lot like me," Bednarik says. "We both had that heavy temperament."

But once you got past Dutch's mouth, he didn't weigh much. The Eagles knew that Van Brocklin wasn't one to stand and fight, having seen him hightail it away from a postgame beef with Pellegrini in Los Angeles. Concrete Charlie, on the other hand, was as two-fisted as they came. He decked a teammate who was clowning around during calisthenics just as readily as he tried to punch the face off a Pittsburgh Steeler guard named Chuck Noll. Somehow, though, Bednarik was even tougher on himself. In '61, for example, he tore his right biceps so terribly that it wound up in a lump by his elbow. "He hardly missed a down," says Skorich, who had ascended to head coach by then, "and I know for a fact he's never let a doctor touch his arm." That was the kind of man it took to go both ways in an era when the species was all but extinct.

The San Francisco 49ers were reluctant to ask Leo Nomellini to play offensive tackle, preferring that he pour all his energy into defense, and the Giants no longer let Gifford wear himself out at defensive back. In the early days of the American Football League the Kansas City Chiefs had linebacker E. J. Holub double-dipping at center until his ravaged knees put him on offense permanently. But none of them ever carried the load that Bednarik did. When Buck Shaw kept asking him to go both ways, there was a championship riding on it. "Give it up, old man," Paul Brown said when Bednarik got knocked out of bounds and landed at his feet in that championship season. Bednarik responded by calling the patriarch of the Browns a 10-letter obscenity. Damned if he would give anything up.

All five times the Eagles needed him to be an iron man that season, they won. Even when they tried to take it easy on him by playing him on only one side of the ball, he still wound up doing double duty the way he did the day he nailed Gifford. A rookie took his place at center just long enough to be overmatched by the Giants' blitzes. In came Bednarik, and on the first play he knocked the red-dogging Huff on his dime. "That's all for you, Sam," Bednarik said. "The big guys are in now."

And that was how the season went, right up to the day after Christmas and what Bednarik calls "the greatest game I ever played." It was the Eagles and Green Bay for the NFL championship at Franklin Field, where Bednarik had played his college ball, and there would be no coming out, save for the kickoffs. It didn't look like there would be any losing either, after Bednarik nearly yanked Packer sweep artist Paul Hornung's arm out of its socket. But there was no quit in Vince Lombardi's Pack. By the game's final moments, they had the Eagles clinging to a 17–13 lead, and Bart Starr was throwing a screen pass to that raging bull Taylor at the Philadelphia 23. Baughan had the first shot at him, but Taylor cut back and broke Baughan's tackle. Then he ran through safety Don Burroughs. And then it was just Taylor and Bednarik at the 10. In another season, with another set of circumstances, Taylor might have been stopped by no man. But this was the coronation of Concrete Charlie. Taylor didn't have a chance as Bednarik dragged him to the ground and the other Eagles piled on. He kicked and cussed and struggled to break free, but Bednarik kept him pinned where he was while precious seconds ticked off the clock, a maneuver that NFL rulemakers would later outlaw. Only when the final gun sounded did Bednarik roll off him and say, "O.K., you can get up now."

It was a play they will always remember in Philadelphia, on a day they will always remember in Philadelphia. When Bednarik floated off the field, he hardly paid attention to the news that Van Brocklin had been named the game's most valuable player. For nine-of-20 passing that produced one touchdown—an ordinary performance, but also his last one as a player—the Dutchman drove off in the sports car that the award earned him. Sometime later Bednarik caught a ride to Atlantic City with Retzlaff and halfway there blurted out that he felt like Paul Revere's horse.

"What do you mean by that?" the startled Retzlaff asked.

"The horse did all the work," Bednarik said, "but Paul Revere got all the credit."

In the mornings he will pick up his accordion and play the sweet, sad "etnik" music he loves so much. As his football-warped fingers thump up and down the keyboard, he often wishes he and Emma and the girls had a family band, the kind Emma's father had that summer night he met her at the Croatian Hall in Bethlehem. Not what you might expect, but then Bednarik is a man of contradictions. Like his not moving any farther than his easy chair to watch the Eagles anymore. Like his going to 8 A.M. Mass every Sunday and saying the Rosary daily with the industrial-strength beads that Cardinal Krol of Philadelphia gave him. "I'm a very religious person, I believe in prayer," Bednarik says, "but I've got this violent temper." Sixty-eight years old and there is still no telling when he will chase some joker who cut him off in traffic or gave him the finger for winning the race to a parking place. If anybody ever thought he would mellow, Bednarik put that idea to rest a few years back when he tangled with a bulldozer operator almost 40 years his junior. As evening fell the guy was still leveling some nearby farmland for housing sites, so Bednarik broke away from his cocktail hour to put in a profane request for a little peace and quiet. One verb led to another, and the next thing Bednarik knew, he thought the guy was going to push a tree over on him. He reacted in classic Concrete Charlie fashion and got a fine that sounded like it came from the World Wrestling Federation instead of the local justice of the peace: $250 for choking.

That wouldn't change him, though. It slowed him down, made him hope that when he dies, people will find it in their hearts to say he was a good egg despite all his hard edges. But it couldn't stop him from becoming as gnarly as ever the instant a stranger asked whether he, Chuck Bednarik, the last of the 60-minute men, could have played in today's NFL. "I wasn't rude or anything," he says, "but inside I was thinking: I'd like to punch this guy in the mouth."

Of course. He is Concrete Charlie. "You know, people still call me that," he says, "and I love it." So he does everything he can to live up to the nickname, helping to oversee boxing in Pennsylvania for the state athletic commission, getting enough exercise to stay six pounds under his final playing weight of 242, golfing in every celebrity tournament that will invite Emma along with him, refusing to give ground to the artificial knee he got last December. "It's supposed to take older people a year to get through the rehab," he says. "I was done in four months." Of course. He is the toughest Philadelphia Eagle there ever was.

But every time he looks in the mirror, he wonders how much longer that will last. Not so many years ago he would flex his muscles and roar, "I'm never gonna die!" Now he studies the age in his eyes and whispers, "Whoa, go back, go back." But he can't do it. He thinks instead of the six teammates from the 1960 Eagles who have died. And when he sees a picture of himself with six other Hall of Fame inductees from 1967, he realizes he is the only one still living. It is at such a moment that he digs out the letter he got from Greasy Neale, his first coach with the Eagles, shortly after he made it to the Hall. "Here, read this out loud," Bednarik says, thrusting the letter at a visitor. "I want to hear it."

There is no point in asking how many times he has done this before. He is already looking at the far wall in the family room, waiting to hear words so heartfelt that the unsteady hand with which they were written just makes them seem that much more sincere. Neale thought he hadn't given Bednarik the kind of introduction he deserved at the Hall, and the letter was the old coach's apology. In it he talked about Bednarik's ability, his range, his desire—all the things Neale would have praised if his role as the day's first speaker hadn't prevented him from knowing how long everybody else was going to carry on.

"If I had it to do over again," he wrote in closing, "I would give you as great a send-off as the others received. You deserve anything I could have said about you, Chuck. You were the greatest."

Then the room is filled with a silence that is louder than Bednarik's grandchildren have ever been. It will stay that way until Concrete Charlie can blink back the tears welling in his eyes.

David Maraniss

It would have been easy to assume that everything had been written about Vince Lombardi, who coached the Green Bay Packers to five NFL championships in nine years and became a legend in the process. Then David Maraniss (b. 1949) heard about the words tattooed on the knuckles of the iron hands with which Lombardi's father had ruled the family: "W-O-R-K" and "P-L-A-Y." No one had ever reported that, which made Maraniss wonder what else had slipped through the cracks. By the time he finished digging, he had written *When Pride Still Mattered* (1999), an engrossingly human, richly detailed biography of Lombardi that reveals how the Old Man, as he said in his introduction, "was more complex and interesting than the myths that surround him." It was one more triumph for Maraniss, who won a Pulitzer Prize for his *Washington Post* coverage of the 1992 presidential campaign and has written highly praised biographies of presidents Clinton and Obama as well as *They Marched Into Sunlight* (2003), a study of two days in the life of a fractured America during the Vietnam War. Maraniss, an associate editor at the *Post*, was so thorough that he even showed that Lombardi wasn't the first to utter his most famous quote: "Winning isn't everything; it's the only thing." Those words can be found in an otherwise forgettable John Wayne movie called *Trouble Along the Way* (1953). And here's the kicker: It isn't the football coach Wayne portrays who utters them; it's the coach's precocious twelve-year-old daughter.

from

When Pride Still Mattered

H E STRUGGLED IN OBSCURITY for twenty years and then fame arrived, and it came to him in a rush. He had been in Green Bay for only two seasons. His Packers had won 15 games and lost 10. He had captured a conference crown but not a league championship. His achievements as a professional football coach were solid but not singular, not in the same class as those of George Halas, the Papa Bear who had been running things in Chicago since the league's creation forty years earlier, or Paul Brown, who had won an average of ten games a year over fourteen seasons with his Cleveland Browns, or even Weeb Ewbank, who had led the Baltimore Colts to consecutive championships at the end of the fifties. Yet by the first few months of 1961, Vince Lombardi was a transcendent figure in football, worshiped as the Pope in Green Bay, coveted by other teams, held up by national sportswriters as the model of leadership. He was so hot that John F. Kennedy, the new president, who had first met him on the steps of St. Willebrord during the 1960 Wisconsin primary, talked about him admiringly and wrote notes to him and invited him to the inauguration in Washington (missed it; league meetings to attend), and Robert F. Kennedy, the attorney general, made plans to see the Packers the next time they came east.

What was it about Lombardi that set him apart? It could not have been style over substance in any conventional sense. He was innately shy, sometimes painfully so, according to Marie. He had to screw up his courage every day to be a public figure; the witty chatter and glad-handing did not come naturally to him. He was literal, not subtle. If you invited him to a six-thirty cocktail party, peer out the window at 6:25 and you would see him pulling up in his Pontiac, ignoring Marie's plea that they drive around the block a few times to avoid being the first guests ringing the doorbell. Straight ahead with Vince. He did not fake or seduce or charm his way into celebrity. Nothing flashy about his looks: squat and sturdy build, gap-toothed smile, broad and fleshy nose, thick-lens glasses, short wavy dark hair, salted with whitish gray, always fresh from the barber's chair. In dress he was indistinguishable from the State Farm agent on Monroe Street or the cheese broker over at the Bellin Building or the floor manager at H. C. Prange's Department Store: invariably neat, with his big class ring and wristwatch and tie clasp and button-down short-sleeved white shirt.

The furthest thing from Kennedy cool. He wore hats and galoshes and rain slickers made of translucent plastic, and played golf and gin rummy and cried and screamed and smoked and sweated and watched *Tom and Jerry* cartoons and laughed so hard that tears squirted out of his eyes like windshield wiper spray. He fell asleep in the recliner chair in his den and snored away until supper.

No way around it, Lombardi was a square. And yet look again and something else emerges. Here he is, on the Wednesday evening of April 5, 1961, making his way through the banquet hall of Tappen's Restaurant at the corner of Ocean and Voorhies in Sheepshead Bay, guest of honor at a testimonial dinner-dance sponsored by his home-town board of trade. Chris Schenkel, the network sportscaster, has just introduced him. Sellout crowd, the place buzzing. Frank Gifford is there, and the Maras, and Father Tim, and Harry and Matty and all the Izzos. Uncle Pete and Uncle Frank, in black tie and tails, lead him up to the front, this way, this way, past the Kiwanis Club table and the Knights of Columbus table, band playing the Fordham Ram fight song, Lombardi walking with his left fist clenched in triumph, a white carnation shining in the lapel of his dark gray suit, the suggestion of a smile creasing his face—his confirmation day smile, four decades later.

These are his people, yes, and he is their favorite son, former altar boy at St. Mark's, grandson of Tony the Barber. His homecoming harks back to a Sheepshead Bay that is fading from view, like Brooklyn, stores closing, families moving out to Jersey and Staten Island, Dodgers gone to the California sun. Like any aging small town now, a departure place, not a destination. As the program for the evening states: "Since we cannot root for a home team, we root for home talent. We are grateful, Vince, your deeds have done us proud." But if there is, unavoidably, a touch of sentimentalism to the occasion, there is more to Lombardi as he strides through the room. Square and awkward he might be, yet he overpowers people with his will as he walks by. Character is the will in action, his Fordham tutors used to say, and here it is, embodied, magnetism of the will, asserting that life is not merely fleeting luck or chance, that discipline and persistence can prevail, even if it takes twenty years, and as he presses forward the crowd seems certain that he knows the way, the right way, that even if he has not won everything, he will, that he is beyond Sheepshead Bay and Green Bay, and the applause wells up in the hall, deafening now, and it lifts them out of their seats as he goes by and they want to follow him.

It was a snap to draw the organizational chart of the Green Bay Packers then: Vince Lombardi in a box at the top, alone, everyone else below him at about the same level. If he was the Pope, there was no College of Cardinals. Assistant coaches, ticket office clerks, players, members of the executive committee—they were all equally afraid of him. As one assistant later explained, "It became a reciprocal thing: Don't tell on me and I won't tell on you. Sooner or later you knew you were going to screw up in a way he wouldn't like if he found out. That bonded everyone together." When Dominic Olejniczak confided that he would rather have his legs amputated than lose Lombardi, the sentiment was one-sided. "No other club had given a coach as much authority as we gave Vince," the Packers' president said. Lombardi seized the opportunity and wanted as little to do with the executive committee as possible. "He'd let a few on the plane with us, but they were more like the players," according to Bob Skoronski. "If we lost they wanted to sit in the back with us."

During the off-season, grateful that Lombardi had not fled to New York, Ole and his executive committee rewarded him with a new five-year contract, tearing up his original pact, which still had three years to run. His salary was not revealed at the time, but records indicate the raise pushed it above $50,000. The new contract only strengthened his iron rule. Even his closest pals on the committee, Tony "the Gray Ghost" Canadeo and Dick Bourguignon, understood the imbalance in the relationship. "If you don't agree with me, I'll take away your vote," Lombardi once said to them. It was a joke, but he meant it; he expected a rubber stamp from the board of directors. At league meetings he and attorney Fred Trowbridge did most of the talking for the club, with one notable exception; at sessions limited to owners, Olejniczak stayed in the room and Vince was asked to leave. It always "bothered the hell out of him" to face this reminder that he was not complete master of his universe.

Lombardi was not the sort of boss who slipped into the office unnoticed. People sensed him coming before he arrived, like a meteorological phenomenon, a weather front rolling into Green Bay from Saskatchewan. His mood, high pressure or low, was going to define their day. If he smiled as he hung his camel's hair coat on the rack near the Crooks Street entrance, and began with a pleasant "Good morning, Ruth," to Ruth McKloskey, the staff responded in kind, with great relief. If he tramped in with a scowl, they tried to steer clear of him until the storm passed. The storm in most cases featured a sudden tirade, often directed at Tom Miller, the mild-mannered publicist. If Lombardi strolled over to the duplicating machine and told one of his corny jokes and laughed loudly, they all laughed with him. Although he seemed to have a one-track mind, the track was long and wide—anything to do with his football operation. Lorraine Keck had been working at H. C. Prange's that year when she was told that "the Packers needed a girl" to help with secretarial duties. She walked over to the team's downtown office—and there was Lombardi, waiting to ask her how fast she typed and whether she could take shorthand.

Keck quickly learned Lombardi's philosophy of perfecting the little things, a trait that he had acquired from Colonel Blaik at West Point. When he spoke into the dictaphone, he meticulously included all punctuation. After letters were typed they went back to him so that he could double-check the spelling. He demanded precision—letters answered quickly, documents neatly filed, no unfinished tasks lingering at the end of the day. The office hours were nine to five, but anyone arriving at nine was considered fifteen minutes late—the same Lombardi Standard Time that his players had encountered. One morning, before leaving for an off-season vacation with Marie, he called the staff into his office. "While I'm gone, I don't want any slovenly work around here. Do what you're supposed to do!" he said. A few days later he called from the Caribbean to check on them.

One young receptionist was "scared to death" of Lombardi. Whenever she got near him, her hands shook uncontrollably. She could not speak when she saw him coming. At night she dreamed about him, all nightmares. Finally, after a few weeks of torment, she went to Ruth McKloskey and said she had to quit. For the most part, though, Lombardi knew when to pull back. After lecturing McKloskey one morning on the proper way to list assets and liabilities—a subject she knew more about than he did—he approached her at the mail counter later and poked her on the arm. "Still mad at me?" he asked, breaking into a grin. She laughed and said no. There were other saving graces that counterbalanced his autocratic bearing. He was a "softie at heart," according to Keck, and would not hesitate to send people home to attend to sick relatives. Though it was impossible not to hear him swearing in the film room, he was courteous around the women. McKloskey approached his desk once when he was screaming into his phone at a league official—"What the hell is going on, goddamn it!"—until he saw his secretary, covered the receiver, turned to her and said, "Excuse me, Ruth." Keck discovered that the more outspoken she was around Lombardi, the more he seemed to enjoy it, as long as she did her work. "I was dumb enough and green enough that if I thought something was not right, I would tell him. He got so little of that pushing back. Everyone was 'Yes, sir. Yes, sir.' He liked a little 'No, sir.'"

That was true only when it served his purposes. Lombardi was decidedly less open to argument when it came time to negotiate new contracts with his players, and he would thwart their efforts by any means necessary. The players' union was not yet a bargaining force, there were no agents to haggle with and players had little freedom or security. Along with these advantages, Lombardi brought to the negotiations the skills of a psychologist. He knew just when to stroke and when to intimidate. When Bob Skoronski began making a case for a raise, Lombardi pulled a piece of paper from his drawer and said, "You had a pretty good year, but, heh, heh, against the Rams we had a third and one and we ran a 36 and you didn't get the job done, did you, Bob?" As Skoronski tried to counter by citing a crucial block he had made against San Francisco, Lombardi rose from his chair, walked around the desk and affectionately rubbed his tackle's crew-cut scalp. The tactic silenced Skoronski and settled the debate—a preemptive strike that compelled Skoronski the following year to open by saying, "Coach, I want you to sit in that chair and not come over and touch me during these negotiations."

Gary Knafelc was so certain that he would be tongue-tied that he came in with a typed sheet of accomplishments. As Knafelc later recounted: "I walked in and he acted like he was on the phone and left me just standing there. I was just perspiring. He looked at me and said, 'Sit down!' I sat down. I said, 'Coach, I have this...' He stopped me and said, 'Just a minute.' He had to make another call. I knew I was dead already. He hung up and said, 'Yes?' And I said, 'Please read this.' It listed my passes caught to passes thrown, blocking awards, grasping anything I could. He didn't look at it a second and a half and then threw it back to me and with that big finger he had he pointed clear across the table at me and said, 'Gary, all you played was offense. You were not on the kickoff team. You were not on the punt return team. All you played was offense!' He said he would give me two thousand instead of four. And I got up and left the room. I was so happy just to be invited back to training camp. But that's the kind of guy he was. He would build you up, but never to the point too high where you thought you could tell him what to do. He was still the master and you were the slaves."

Jimmy Cannon

For two decades after World War II, Jimmy Cannon (1910–1973) was the quintessential New York sports columnist, a cranky press box presence for the *Post* and the *Journal-American* who had a chip-on-his-shoulder persona and wrote mesmerizing, even poetic prose when he was at the top of his game. He took his lead from the legendary Damon Runyon and then spun his style in his own singular fashion. He called boxing "the red light district of sports" and had the inside track on Joe DiMaggio from day one. Not bad for a guy who was a high school dropout and the son of a low-level Tammany Hall politician. But as much as he loved the glamorous nights at Toots Shor's and 21 with Ernest Hemingway and Marlene Dietrich, Cannon never cheated his readers or forgot where he came from. You can see it in what he wrote for the *Journal-American*'s October 14, 1963 edition after watching the Cleveland Browns' great Jim Brown trample the New York Giants. No wonder one of his acolytes at the *Post*, Maury Allen, once recalled his time in the Army by saying, "I used to sit in a cold pup tent in Korea and read thirty Cannon columns a month. A friend of mine used to send me a package of Cannon. Nothing else. Cannon."

Greatness

WATCHING JIMMY BROWN play football yesterday took me back to my boyhood in the old neighborhood. It had nothing to do with Cleveland beating the Giants, 35–24, and yet this is what it was all about. The memory of greatness lasts forever.

It hasn't happened often since. When it does I hear that glorious voice singing in a language I couldn't understand. But I realized how special it was without knowing why. Joe the Barber had a three-chair shop on Spring Street off Varick, and yesterday I could smell the witch hazel again and hear the plume of steam rise tittering from the boiler where the hot towels were stacked.

My old man shaved himself with a straight razor until the day he died. But he went to Joe's every Saturday for a low trim. I'd go along and listen to the talk about horses and fights and the doorway crap games. On this day Joe said come in the backroom. We talked through the ropes of beads which were the curtain. Joe put a record on one of those hand-cranked phonographs that had a tulip horn.

"Wait'll you hear this guy sing," Joe said. "He's the champion of the world."

I figured it would be John McCormack. We were Irish. Who else could it be? I wasn't an opera man, then or now. But I knew Joe the Barber was right. This wasn't just singing. It was something more. I found out then why Joe shut up the store and stood on line all day for gallery seats when Caruso played the Met. It was like watching Jack Dempsey fight.

The Browns haven't been beaten yet and in their first five games the bookkeepers got Jimmy Brown carrying an average of 157 yards a game. Yesterday he used his legs to travel 123 and grabbed four passes for 86 more. But the numbers can't define it. Ask the Giants and they'll tell you that Brown is killing you even when he is just standing around and someone else is running with the ball. He doesn't block either.

"He puts pressure on you with or without the ball," said Allie Sherman who coaches the Giants.

Other guys ran on the Giants this season. The Steelers busted them open. No one's supposed to do that to their defensive unit. Age may be turning them the other way. But it was how Brown put it to them that shook them. It was like being in a dark room with a guy after you with a ball and bat. They had no chance.

In modern football you don't key on a man and ignore the other guys. They tell themselves that. But it's different with Jimmy Brown. If Brown isn't moving the ball, he's pretending he might. As a decoy he pulls some of the other people off the runner. You better wait. The hesitation hurts and, in that way, Brown's mixed up in every play the Browns call.

That improved Ernie Green, and he had a hell of a Sunday. He's an accomplished back but he was going with the best of it. They were setting their ambushes for Brown. They couldn't come with a rush at Frank Ryan either. They gave him more time to pass and Ryan threw 16 times and hit his people with 12 of them. There's no way you can cheat with Jimmy Brown.

The new coach, Blanton Collier, has a lot to do with it. The old one, Paul Brown, made Jimmy Brown's exciting skills subservient to his domineering will. But Collier turned Jimmy loose. Now he uses his impulses to find his way if the defense anticipates his intentions.

"They beat Jimmy like a dog and whipped him like a pup," a guy shouted in the Cleveland dressing room. "But he showed them."

They worked him over, and there was blood crusted on his muddy white uniform. But he praised Sam Huff for the hard tackles. Once in the first quarter Brown pushed five of them ahead of him for 4 yards when he reached a hole that was sealed by their slamming bodies. The third time he scored wasn't as spectacular as the second touchdown when he ran 72 yards with that bent-knee shrugging gait after catching a screen pass.

But they were at him and he shouldn't have gone the 32 yards. He angled along, stepping lightly, as if he were afraid his big positive feet would bruise the grass. Patiently, Brown waited for the blockers, like a guy under an awning hoping a shower will pass. He stalled until he got his shot, and then went across field, turning it on with a sudden clap of speed.

"You got to honor him," Sherman said, speaking for everyone who ever played football against Jimmy Brown.

It's been forty years since I heard Enrico Caruso sing in Joe the Barber's place. Since then I've seen many of the best in numerous fields. None in any line ever did what they were paid to do better than the singer and the football player. Each, in his own thrilling way, is the greatest of his kind. They never come two at a time.

Jimmy Breslin

For four decades, Jimmy Breslin (b. 1930) served as a cantankerous, chain-smoking role model for aspiring newspaper columnists who saw him battling Chicago's equally crusty Mike Royko for the title of best ever. There was magic in Breslin's street-smart prose and heart and soul in the way he championed the downtrodden. He could write about the man who dug JFK's grave one day and an arsonist known as Marvin the Torch the next. Breslin made his bones as a sportswriter for newspaper chains he called "the Sing-Sing, Leavenworth, and Folsom" of the business and became the *New York Herald Tribune*'s star city columnist. He eventually wrote a column for each of the city's major dailies except the *Times* and somehow also found the time and energy to be a novelist (*The Gang That Couldn't Shoot Straight*, 1969), a memoirist (*I Want To Thank My Brain for Remembering Me*, 1996), and the author of hilarious baseball nonfiction (*Can't Anybody Here Play This Game?*, 1963). His guiding principle was something he had learned covering sports: Work the loser's locker room. Of course, when he set out to chronicle New York Giants quarterback Y. A. Tittle's last game, Breslin had no idea the loser's locker room would be his final destination. But there he was, and there was Tittle, a picture of grace and dignity even in defeat. Breslin seized the moment—and the day—and turned it into a memorable piece of deadline writing for the December 13, 1964 edition of the *Herald Tribune*.

...The One Last Good One That Wasn't to Be

New York, N.Y., December 13, 1964

THEY BOTH WOKE UP before the hotel operator rang for them. Y. A. Tittle didn't move. He looked up at the ceiling. This was the last time he would wake up to play a game of football because he has made up his mind to retire. "Costello dogs," he said to himself. He could see the No. 50. A brown 50 on a white jersey. Vince Costello, the Cleveland Browns' linebacker, red-dogs the passer a lot and it was the first thing Y. A. Tittle thought about when he woke up in an eighth-floor room of the Hotel Roosevelt yesterday morning.

It is like that after 27 years. You don't wake up and say "I'm playing today," you wake up and say, "Costello dogs."

Aaron Thomas, the end, was in the bed closest to the door. He got up and walked past Tittle and went to the window.

"Rain," Thomas said.

"Heavy?" Tittle asked.

"Enough," Thomas said. Thomas opened the window. Tittle could hear the taxicabs down on Madison Avenue, their low pressure tires whining on the wet street. He reached over to the night table and picked up a thick blue-covered looseleaf notebook. The complete set of Giants' plays are on diagram sheets in the book and Tittle turned to a sheet that said "double dive 39" on the top. It is a straight ahead play and Tittle began to study it. You use straight ahead plays on a muddy field and Y. A. Tittle began to go over every one that the Giants use. The amateur whines and curses the weather that's going to bother his passing. Y. A. Tittle looked up football plays that should be used in the mud.

He studies his plays through brown horn-rimmed glasses that were perched on a big nose that caves in halfway down the left side. Patches of shaved gray hair runs down the sides of his bald head. In the back of the neck, the grey runs into deep criss-cross lines. He says he is 38; the deep wrinkles in the back of the neck tell you that the 38 is just a number that he puts down when they ask him how old he is.

He had spent Friday night the same as he has spent every night before a game since they put television sets into hotel rooms.

Right after dinner, Tittle came back to the hotel room, took off his clothes and sat down to watch television. He was dressed as he always is for television on the night before a game. In his shorts with the glasses on, a filter-tip cigarette in his hand and his socks on. The socks always are on.

"Lot of years," somebody said to him.

He shook his head. "Twenty-seven," he said. "That's just about my whole life."

"What do you do after tomorrow, give it up?"

"I don't know," he said. "I haven't said anything about it. But this game tomorrow is important to me for a lot of reasons. A lot of reasons. I want to have a good day tomorrow so much...."

He wanted to have a good day because it was going to be his last. Y. A. had made up his mind before yesterday's game that he was through. The last thing they like to do is stand and tell strangers who work for newspapers that they are finished with the business. But they tell each other, and Y. A. Tittle had told them in the dressing room that yesterday was going to be his last game. That would do it, he told them, and on Friday night Tittle sat in his hotel room and he watched television and he kept thinking about the last shot he would ever get. No comebacks. No Cleveland next year. It was Cleveland now, and the career now, so go out right.

Now, it was 9:15 in the morning and Tittle put down the playbook and got up and got dressed for breakfast. He put on a white shirt and solid black tie and dark slacks. He reached into the closet and took out an olive green checked sports jacket.

"Still raining?" he said to Thomas.

Thomas looked out the window. "Raining pretty good," he said.

He took the elevator down to the lobby and walked into the Roosevelt Grill. It is a supper club, but yesterday morning the Giants used it for breakfast. Red-coated waiters served steak and scrambled eggs and the players ate quietly. When they were through, Allie Sherman, the coach, stepped up onto the bandstand. He smoked a cigar and he was in shirt sleeves. A green blackboard had been set up, with red stagelights playing on it.

"Now, once we get to pinch blocking, let each other know when they go back into a zone," Sherman began. He chalked in plays on the board.

In the background, Andy Robustelli's voice could be heard. He was in the back of the room, with the defensive team.

"Remember," his voice said, "we got to kick his rear end in. Remember, kick his rear end in for him."

When Sherman finished, the players filed out. Then Tittle moved over to Sherman's table, put the playbook on it and sat down. Gary Wood, the young one, sat on a chair behind him.

"Well, what do you think?" Tittle asked.

"The Green Bay special should be the best," Sherman said.

"Uh-huh."

Sherman put the cigar in his mouth and waited for another question.

"How do we block on the slant 34?"

"Two-on-one," Sherman said.

Tittle picked up a knife and ran it across the tablecloth. "Now, the biggest frequency of dogging..."

"Costello," Sherman said.

"I know," Tittle said.

"This isn't a game you win with the big play," Sherman said. "We have to go straight ahead at them. The longer we have it the less he does." He was talking about Jimmy Brown; when they are as big as this one they say "he" and never his name.

"Certain types of screens wouldn't be advisable today," Tittle said.

"What ones do you mean?" Sherman asked.

"Well, I don't think to the Frisco side is advisable."

"The Frisco side is all right here."

"I guess I keep thinking of Chicago," Tittle said. He meant last year in the championship game. He tried to throw a sideline screen pass to Phil King and Ed O'Bradovich, a Chicago lineman, intercepted it and ran for a touchdown.

Sherman smiled. "No, it's different here," he said.

Tittle nodded. "I guess I keep matching a play with a game," he said. "I got a game I can remember for every play that we got. That's the trouble when you've been around a little while. You remember too many games."

It was just like a business conference. There was no talk of "we've got to win" or no worry about getting hurt or how hard he belts when you let him get going for two or three steps. Just two guys sitting at a table and calmly going over technical things.

Football, when you do it for money, is like this. It is a trade, a job for money, and in all of New York few people ever have done their jobs better than Y. A. Tittle. They brought him into this town to pass a football and he did it well enough to bring the Giants to three championship games. But this year, with age taking a step away from him, and leaving him standing there a target for a lineman, he has done little.

John Baker of Pittsburgh got to him in the second game and tore two of his ribs loose, and after that the Giants were through and Y. A. Tittle had to gasp for breath every time he tried to pass. Yesterday, he was ready. The pain was gone, and there was a shot of cortisone in him to keep it out. The Browns were coming in for a game which meant the league title for them. Tittle was coming in after something, too.

He had done too much around here to walk out of town a loser. He plays football in the big place, New York, the only town in the world worth talking about, and yesterday he wanted to go out of the town on top.

"You only know what it's like to play around here if you've played someplace else first," he was saying at the table. "This is the city for an athlete. I don't think I can remember a game I think is as important as this one to me."

The bus left for the ball park at 11:15. Tittle sat in the back, on the right, a thumbnail between his teeth, looking out the window. He ran a hand over the glass so he could see out. He looked down at the sidewalk. Rain splashed into a puddle alongside the doorman.

Tittle began to move his lips.

The opener, he was saying to himself. Open with a double dive 39. Wheelwright right at them. Straight ahead. And watch Costello. Watch what he does on the play. You want to know what he's doing.

In the stadium, in the light green-carpeted dressing room, he put on a gray sweatshirt and sat on a stool and looked down at his legs. Tittle's legs are smooth-shaven, so tape can be put all over them and then ripped off once a day. His toes stick together, with corns on the sides, the toenails black from 260-pound linemen stepping on them all year.

"I saw you in the first game you ever played here," somebody said to him. "It was on a Thursday night, against the Yankees." Tittle smiled. The guy was talking about the old football Yankees.

"What about the kids?" he was asked. "Do they think it's funny that this might be your last game?"

"I don't know," he said. "They're used to this business. Kids can adjust when they're used to things. My daughter now, she takes American history here. Then next week we get back to Palo Alto, she'll be having world history. Everything changes and she just keeps up with it."

Then he got up and started to get dressed, and the thumbnail came up to his teeth again and he began to think about another play.

At 12:45, a buzzer rang in the room. It meant the players had to get up and get ready to go on the field and everybody came around and tapped Y. A. on the shoulder and wished him luck and he sat there quietly and said thank you, and pulled on a cigarette he had cupped in his hand so photographers wouldn't catch him smoking. It was, it seemed, just another working day for him.

Then you shook hands with him and your hand closed on wetness. His whole palm was wet.

"What's this?" he was asked.

"This?" He smiled. "This is the business."

And a few minutes later, clapping his hands together, Tittle came trotting out of the dressing room, down the runway to the baseball dugout and then up the stairs and onto the field and there was a huge roar from the crowd when he came running through the goalposts and over to the bench. He waited while the Giants took the kick-off and when that was over Y. A. came running on the field for the last big shot of his career. He wanted to go out of this city the way the good ones always do. The field was all right, and the rain was almost gone. He had a shot at it. A good shot at going out of this town on top. He bent his head into the huddle and called the first play of the game—a double dive 39.

Tittle took the snap, spun, handed the ball to Ernie Wheelwright and then kept going back, faking a pass. He kept looking over his shoulder at the Browns as he did. What he saw was no good. Their line jumped the Giants on this first play and Wheelwright ran into three or four white jerseys and right away, yesterday afternoon, you could see Y. A. Tittle was going to have trouble.

For the Browns kept getting that first step on the Giants' line and they stacked up runs and their halfbacks were all over the Giants' receivers. And on offense, they simply shoved everybody out and let him smash. He smashed and spun off them, Jimmy Brown did, and they were defenseless against him, and the Browns had the ball too much of the time.

In the second quarter, with the Browns ahead, 3–0, Tittle went back and saw nobody open and then he said the hell with it. He took off on his own to the right and got to the Browns' 18. Ross Fichtner got to him near the sideline and tried to break him in half. Y. A. went down face first into the mud, but he pulled himself up right away. The referee was yelling about a personal foul and the ball was going to be put on the Cleveland 9. Now Tittle didn't hurt at all from the tackle.

On the second play, somebody was after him from the side, and Tittle ran straight up. Then he stopped and threw to Dick James, who was a yard behind the goal line. That put the Giants ahead, 7–3, and Tittle had spring in his legs when he came back to the bench.

The Browns came back and scored. Ryan, their quarterback, was having a big day. Then Tittle was on the field again and he hit Joe Morrison on the Browns' 49 and now noise came down out of the three-decked green stands. Tittle clapped his hands and bent down in the huddle. He wanted Gifford this time, he told them. They broke out of the huddle and Tittle loped up to the line, looking over the Browns as he came. Steam was coming off his face and out of his mouth into the dark, wet air. He stood behind the center, Mickey Walker, and looked around. The old pro was working his trade now.

Mickey Walker's gray pants were straining as he bent over the ball. The others were there, too. Bookie Bolin, Darrell Dess. At the snap, they would be coming back to make a pocket for Y. A. Tittle. Gifford was out on the right. Tittle put his hands down. The Cleveland halfbacks, Walter Beach, over on the left, and Bernie Parrish, on the right, were deep. They go even deeper when you show pass. Good. Tittle had called Gifford on a square-cut to the sidelines in front of Parrish.

Y. A. got the ball on the two-count and went straight back. Walker, Dess and Bolin came back with him and the white jerseys rushed at the three and grunted and slammed and tried to get through. Tittle turned around and held the ball up. Here was Gifford faking deep, throwing his head to the left, then cutting in one motion and running for the sideline, and Y. A. Tittle threw it at him and everything he wanted out of yesterday afternoon was in that pass.

Gifford was at the Browns' 34 and he had his hands out and the ball was coming right to him when Parrish came running right by him and grabbed the ball and took off down the sidelines with the Browns' bench screaming "Ball!" to let their players on the field know there was an interception and to start blocking.

Tittle already was on his way over to the sidelines. You learn how to do this back in high school, in Marshall, Tex. You always get over there and cover the sidelines when you throw a pass out there. Y.A. Tittle put his head down and ran straight for the sidelines, at the Giants' 30, and Parrish was trying to get past that spot and into the open. Tittle came up and he threw his body at Parrish's legs, and Parrish went up in the air and came down on his shoulder. The two of them skidded in the deep mud and then Parrish jumped up and clapped his hands and the Browns' offensive team was coming on the field and it was over.

Sometimes, it goes like that. Everything can be all right and you can know just what has to be done and how to do it, and you've done it a lot of times before and it has worked, and then when you do it this time the whole thing falls apart. It is like that in any business office in the city. Even the best in the place falls apart on something. Y. A. Tittle, who worked at his trade in New York as well as any ever worked, had just blown it all on a play called a square-cut. He has been pulling these off for 27 years.

At the end, Tittle was on one knee in front of the Giants' bench, a blue hood thrown over his shoulders, his hands scraped and mud caked. The lights were reflecting off the puddles in the mud around him. Out on the field, Gary Wood was running the team and the Browns, scoring nearly every time they got the ball, ran up a 52–20 victory.

"How is it?" he was asked.

He shook his head.

"I'm sorry," somebody said to him.

"I'm sorry I couldn't give you something better," he said. "You people here have been awful nice to me."

He walked out of the stadium an hour later, in a black raincoat and black tyrolean hat with a red feather in it. He carried a brown leather attaché case and he looked like a businessman coming home from work, which is what he is going to be from now on. This was the last shot of a career that went 27 years and he blew it on a play called a square-cut. Y. A. Tittle said he was sorry he couldn't have given the people a little more. Professionals think that way.

George Plimpton

Participatory journalist sounds too stiff and fusty to describe what George Plimpton (1927–2003) had such a grand time being. He was best described as "a collector of experiences," and the simple grace of that explanation makes it easy to understand how the public at large could embrace this lanky, floppy-haired son of privilege, plummy accent and all. He cofounded *The Paris Review* and served as its unpaid editor, which seemed like something a Harvard graduate should do. But he also portrayed a bad hombre who got shot dead by John Wayne in *Rio Lobo* (1970), which was definitely out of the norm, as were his role as New York City's fireworks commissioner and his second-place award for playing the piano on amateur night at the Apollo Theater in Harlem. It was Plimpton's misadventures in sports, however, that sealed his connection to everyday guys. Following the lead of Paul Gallico, the New York sports columnist who blazed the trail in the 1920s, Plimpton sparred with boxer Archie Moore (and got his nose bloodied), pitched to a team of baseball all-stars (and failed to go the distance), and took his lumps in hockey, tennis, golf, even bridge. He wrote about them all with charm and wit, but he achieved a personal best when he turned his experiences as the Detroit Lions' "last-string quarterback" into the 1966 best seller *Paper Lion.*

from

Paper Lion

JACK BENNY used to say that when he stood on the stage in white tie and tails for his violin concerts and raised his bow to begin his routine—scraping through "Love in Bloom"—that he *felt* like a great violinist. He reasoned that, if he wasn't a great violinist, what was he doing dressed in tails, and about to play before a large audience?

At Pontiac I *felt* myself a football quarterback, not an interloper. My game plan was organized, and I knew what I was supposed to do. My nerves seemed steady, much steadier than they had been as I waited on the bench. I trotted along easily. I was keenly aware of what was going on around me.

I could hear Bud Erickson's voice over the loudspeaker system, a dim murmur, telling the crowd what was going on. He was telling them that number zero, coming out across the sidelines was not actually a rookie, but an amateur, a writer, who had been training with the team for three weeks and had learned five plays, which he was now going to run against the first-string Detroit defense. It was like a nightmare come true, he told them, as if one of *them*, rocking a beer around in a paper cup, with a pretty girl leaning past him to ask the hot-dog vendor in the aisle for mustard, were suddenly carried down underneath the stands by a sinister clutch of ushers. He would protest, but he would be encased in the accoutrements, the silver helmet, with the two protruding bars of the cage, jammed down over his ears, and sent out to take over the team—that was the substance of Erickson's words, drifting across the field, swayed and shredded by the steady breeze coming up across the open end of Wisner Stadium from the vanished sunset. The crowd was interested, and I was conscious, just vaguely, of a steady roar of encouragement.

The team was waiting for me, grouped in the huddle watching me come. I went in among them. Their heads came down for the signal. I called out, "Twenty-six!" forcefully, to inspire them, and a voice from one of the helmets said, "Down, down, the whole stadium can hear you."

"Twenty-six," I hissed at them. "Twenty-six near oh pinch; on three. *Break!*" Their hands cracked as one, and I wheeled and started for the line behind them.

My confidence was extreme. I ambled slowly behind Whitlow, poised down over the ball, and I had sufficient presence to pause, resting a hand at the base of his spine, as if on a windowsill—a nonchalant gesture I had admired in certain quarterbacks—and I looked out over the length of his back to fix in my mind what I saw.

Everything fine about being a quarterback—the embodiment of his power—was encompassed in those dozen seconds or so: giving the instructions to ten attentive men, breaking out of the huddle, walking for the line, and then pausing behind the center, dawdling amidst men poised and waiting under the trigger of his voice, cataleptic, until the deliverance of himself and them to the future. The pleasure of sport was so often the chance to indulge the cessation of time itself—the pitcher dawdling on the mound, the skier poised at the top of a mountain trail, the basketball player with the rough skin of the ball against his palm preparing for a foul shot, the tennis player at set point over his opponent—all of them savoring a moment before committing themselves to action.

I had the sense of a portcullis down. On the other side of the imaginary bars the linemen were poised, the lights glistening off their helmets, and close in behind them were the linebackers, with Joe Schmidt just opposite me, the big number 56 shining on his white jersey, jumpjacking back and forth with quick choppy steps, his hands poised in front of him, and he was calling out defensive code words in a stream. I could sense the rage in his voice, and the tension in those rows of bodies waiting, as if coils had been wound overtight, which my voice, calling a signal, like a lever would trip to spring them all loose. "Blue! Blue! Blue" I heard Schmidt shout.

Within my helmet, the schoolmaster's voice murmured at me: "Son, nothing to it, nothing at all..."

I bent over the center. Quickly, I went over what was supposed to happen—I would receive the snap and take two steps straight back, and hand the ball to the number two back coming laterally across from right to left, who would then cut into the number six hole. That was what was designated by 26—the two back into the six hole. The mysterious code words "near oh pinch" referred to blocking assignments in the line, and I was never sure exactly what was meant by them. The important thing was to hang on to the ball, turn, and get the ball into the grasp of the back coming across laterally.

I cleared my throat. "Set!" I called out—my voice loud and astonishing to hear, as if it belonged to someone shouting into the earholes of my helmet. "Sixteen, sixty-five, forty-four, *hut* one, *hut* two, *hut* three," and at three the ball slapped back into my palm, and Whitlow's rump bucked up hard as he went for the defensemen opposite.

The lines cracked together with a yawp and smack of pads and gear. I had the sense of quick, heavy movement, and as I turned for the backfield, not a second having passed, I was hit hard from the side, and as I gasped the ball was jarred loose. It sailed away, and bounced once, and I stumbled after it, hauling it under me five yards back, hearing the rush of feet, and the heavy jarring and wheezing of the blockers fending off the defense, a great roar up from the crowd, and above it, a relief to hear, the shrilling of the referee's whistle. My first thought was that at the snap of the ball the right side of the line had collapsed just at the second of the handoff, and one of the tacklers, Brown or Floyd Peters, had cracked through to make me fumble. Someone, I assumed, had messed up on the assignments designated by the mysterious code words "near oh pinch." In fact, as I discovered later, my *own man* bowled me over—John Gordy, whose assignment as offensive guard was to pull from his position and join the interference on the far side of the center. He was required to pull back and travel at a great clip parallel to the line of scrimmage to get out in front of the runner, his route theoretically passing between me and the center. But the extra second it took me to control the ball, and the creaking execution of my turn, put me in his path, a rare sight for Gordy to see, his own quarterback blocking the way, like coming around a corner in a high-speed car to find a moose ambling across the center line, and he caromed off me, jarring the ball loose.

It was not new for me to be hit down by my own people. At Cranbrook I was knocked down all the time by players on the offense—the play patterns run with such speed along routes so carefully defined that if everything wasn't done right and at the proper speed, the play would break down in its making. I was often reminded of film clips in which the process of a porcelain pitcher, say, being dropped by a butler and smashed, is shown in reverse, so that the pieces pick up off the floor and soar up to the butler's hand, each piece on a predestined route, sudden perfection out of chaos. Often, it did not take more than an inch or so off line to throw a play out of kilter. On one occasion at the training camp, practicing handoff plays to the fullback, I had my chin hanging out just a bit too far, something wrong with my posture, and Pietrosante's shoulder pad caught it like a punch as he went by, and I spun slowly to the ground, grabbing at my jaw. Brettschneider had said that afternoon: "The defense is going to rack you up one of these days, if your own team'd let you *stand* long enough for us defense guys to get *at* you. It's aggravating to bust through and find that you've already been laid flat by your own offense guys."

My confidence had not gone. I stood up. The referee took the ball from me. He had to tug to get it away, a faint look of surprise on his face. My inner voice was assuring me that the fault in the tumble had not been mine. "They let you down," it was saying. "The blocking failed." But the main reason for my confidence was the next play on my list—the 93 pass, a play which I had worked successfully in the Cranbrook scrimmages. I walked into the huddle and I said with considerable enthusiasm, "All right! All *right*! Here we *go*!"

"Keep the voice down," said a voice. "You'll be tipping them the play."

I leaned in on them and said: "Green right" ("Green" designated a pass play, "right" put the flanker to the right side), "three right" (which put the three back to the right), "ninety-three" (indicating the two primary receivers; nine, the right end, and three, the three back) "on *three... Break!*"—the clap of the hands again in unison, the team streamed past me up to the line, and I walked briskly up behind Whitlow.

Again, I knew exactly how the play was going to develop—back those seven yards into the defensive pocket for the three to four seconds it was supposed to hold, and Pietrosante, the three back, would go down in his pattern, ten yards straight, then cut over the middle, and I would hit him.

"Set!...sixteen!...eighty-eight...fifty-five...*hut* one...*hut* two... *hut* three..."

The ball slapped into my palm at "three." I turned and started back. I could feel my balance going, and two yards behind the line of scrimmage I *fell down*—absolutely flat, as if my feet had been pinned under a trip wire stretched across the field, not a hand laid on me. I heard a great roar go up from the crowd. Suffused as I had been with confidence, I could scarcely believe what had happened. Mud cleats catching in the grass? Slipped in the dew? I felt my jaw go ajar in my helmet. "Wha'? Wha'?"—the mortification beginning to come fast. I rose hurriedly to my knees at the referee's whistle, and I could see my teammates' big silver helmets with the blue Lion decals turn toward me, some of the players rising from blocks they'd thrown to protect me, their faces masked, automaton, prognathous with the helmet bars protruding toward me, characterless, yet the dismay was in the set of their bodies as they loped back for the huddle. The schoolmaster's voice flailed at me inside my helmet. "Ox!" it cried. "Clumsy oaf."

I joined the huddle. "Sorry, sorry," I said.

"Call the play, man," came a voice from one of the helmets.

"I don't know what happened," I said.

"Call it, man."

The third play on my list was the 42, another running play, one of the simplest in football, in which the quarterback receives the snap, makes a full spin, and shoves the ball into the four back's stomach—the fullback's. He has come straight forward from his position as if off starting blocks, his knees high, and he disappears with the ball into the number two hole just to the left of the center—a straight power play, and one which seen from the stands seems to offer no difficulty.

I got into an awful jam with it. Once again, the jackrabbit-speed of the professional backfield was too much for me. The fullback—Danny Lewis—was past me and into the line before I could complete my spin and set the ball in his belly. And so I did what was required: I tucked the ball into my own belly and followed Lewis into the line, hoping that he might have budged open a small hole.

I tried, grimacing, my eyes squinted almost shut, and waiting for the impact, which came before I'd taken two steps—I was grabbed up by Roger Brown.

He tackled me high, and straightened me with his power, so that I churned against his three-hundred-pound girth like a comic bicyclist. He began to shake me. I remained upright to my surprise, flailed back and forth, and I realized that he was struggling for the ball. His arms were around it, trying to tug it free. The bars of our helmets were nearly locked, and I could look through and see him inside—the first helmeted face I recognized that evening—the small, brown eyes surprisingly peaceful, but he was grunting hard, the sweat shining, and I had time to think, "It's Brown, it's *Brown!*" before I lost the ball to him, and flung to one knee on the ground I watched him lumber ten yards into the end zone behind us for a touchdown.

The referee wouldn't allow it. He said he'd blown the ball dead while we were struggling for it. Brown was furious. "You taking that away from *me*," he said, his voice high and squeaky. "Man, I took that ball in there good."

The referee turned and put the ball on the ten-yard line. I had lost twenty yards in three attempts, and I had yet, in fact, to run off a complete play.

The veterans walked back very slowly to the next huddle.

I stood off to one side, listening to Brown rail at the referee. "I never scored like that befo'. You takin' that away from me?" His voice was peeved. He looked off toward the stands, into the heavy tumult of sound, spreading the big palms of his hands in grief.

I watched him, detached, not even moved by his insistence that I suffer the humiliation of having the ball stolen for a touchdown.

If the referee had allowed him his score, I would not have protested. The shock of having the three plays go as badly as they had left me dispirited and numb, the purpose of the exercise forgotten. Even the schoolmaster's voice seemed to have gone—a bleak despair having set in so that as I stood shifting uneasily, watching Brown jawing at the referee, I was perfectly willing to trot in to the bench at that point and be done with it.

Then, by chance, I happened to see Brettschneider standing at his corner linebacker position, watching me, and beyond the bars of his cage I could see a grin working. That set my energies ticking over once again—the notion that some small measure of recompense would be mine if I could complete a pass in the Badger's territory and embarrass him. I had such a play in my series—a slant pass to the strong-side end, Jim Gibbons.

I walked back to the huddle. It was slow in forming. I said, "The Badger's asleep. He's fat and he's asleep."

No one said anything. Everyone stared down. In the silence I became suddenly aware of the feet. There are twenty-two of them in the huddle, after all, most of them very large, in a small area, and while the quarterback ruminates and the others await his instruction, there's nothing else to catch the attention. The sight pricked at my mind, the oval of twenty-two football shoes, and it may have been responsible for my error in announcing the play. I forgot to give the signal on which the ball was to be snapped back by the center. I said: "Green right nine slant *break*!" One or two of the players clapped their hands, and as the huddle broke, some of them automatically heading for the line of scrimmage, someone hissed: "Well, the signal, what's the *signal*, for Chrissake."

I had forgotten to say "on two."

I should have kept my head and formed the huddle again. Instead, I called out "Two!" in a loud stage whisper, directing my call first to one side, then the other *"two! two!"* as we walked up to the line. For those that might have been beyond earshot, who might have missed the signal, I held out two fingers spread like a V, which I showed around furtively, trying to hide it from the defense, and hoping that my people would see.

The pass was incomplete. I took two steps back (the play was a quick pass, thrown without a protective pocket) and I saw Gibbons break from his position, then stop, buttonhooking, his hand, which I used as a target, came up, but I threw the ball over him. A yell came up from the crowd seeing the ball in the air (it was the first play of the evening which hadn't been "blown"—to use the player's expression for a missed play), but then a groan went up when the ball was overshot and bounced across the sidelines.

"Last play," George Wilson was calling. He had walked over with a clipboard in his hand and was standing by the referee. "The ball's on the ten. Let's see you take it all the way," he called out cheerfully.

One of the players asked: "Which end zone is he talking about?"

The last play of the series was a pitchout—called a flip on some teams—a long lateral to the number four back running parallel to the line and cutting for the eight hole at left end. The lateral, though long, was easy for me to do. What I had to remember was to keep on running out after the flight of the ball. The hole behind me as I lateraled was left unguarded by an offensive lineman pulling out from his position and the defensive tackle could bull through and take me from behind in his rush, not knowing I'd got rid of the ball, if I didn't clear out of the area.

I was able to get the lateral off and avoid the tackler behind me, but unfortunately the defense was keyed for the play. They knew my repertoire, which was only five plays or so, and they doubted I'd call the same play twice. One of my linemen told me later that the defensive man opposite him in the line, Floyd Peters, had said, "Well, here comes the forty-eight pitchout," and it *had* come, and they were able to throw the number four back, Pietrosante, who had received the lateral, back on the one-yard line—just a yard away from the mortification of having moved a team backward from the thirty-yard line into one's own end zone for a safety.

As soon as I saw Pietrosante go down, I left for the bench on the sidelines at midfield, a long run from where I'd brought my team, and I felt utterly weary, shuffling along through the grass.

Applause began to sound from the stands, and I looked up, startled, and saw people standing, and the hands going. It made no sense at the time. It was not derisive; it seemed solid and respectful. "Wha'? Wha'?" I thought, and I wondered if the applause wasn't meant for someone else—if the mayor had come into the stadium behind me and was waving from an open-topped car. But as I came up to the bench I could see the people in the stands looking at me, and the hands going.

I thought about the applause afterward. Some of it was, perhaps, in appreciation of the lunacy of my participation, and for the fortitude it took to do it; but most of it, even if subconscious, I decided was in *relief* that I had done as badly as I had: it verified the assumption that the average fan would have about an amateur blundering into the brutal world of professional football. He would get slaughtered. If by some chance I had uncorked a touchdown pass, there would have been wild acknowledgment—because I heard the groans go up at each successive disaster—but afterward the spectators would have felt uncomfortable. Their concept of things would have been upset. The outsider did not belong, and there was comfort in that being proved.

Some of the applause, as it turned out, came from people who had enjoyed the comic aspects of my stint. More than a few thought that they were being entertained by a professional comic in the tradition of baseball's Al Schacht, or the Charlie Chaplins, the clowns, of the bullfights. Bud Erickson told me that a friend of his had come up to him later: "Bud, that's one of funniest goddamn... I mean that guy's *got* it," this man said, barely able to control himself.

I did not take my helmet off when I reached the bench. It was tiring to do and there was security in having it on. I was conscious of the big zero on my back facing the crowd when I sat down. Some players came by and tapped me on the top of the helmet. Brettschneider leaned down and said, "Well, you stuck it... that's the big thing."

The scrimmage began. I watched it for a while, but my mind returned to my own performance. The pawky inner voice was at hand again. "You didn't stick it," it said testily. "You funked it."

At half time Wilson took the players down to the band shell at one end of the stadium. I stayed on the bench. He had his clipboards with him, and I could see him pointing and explaining, a big semicircle of players around him, sitting on the band chairs. Fireworks soared up into the sky from the other end of the field, the shells puffing out clusters of light that lit the upturned faces on the crowd in silver, then red, and then the reports would go off, reverberating sharply, and in the stands across the field I could see the children's hands flap up over their ears. Through the noise I heard someone yelling my name. I turned and saw a girl leaning over the rail of the grandstand behind

me. I recognized her from the Gay Haven in Dearborn. She was wearing a mohair Italian sweater, the color of spun pink sugar, and tight
pants, and she was holding a thick folding wallet in one hand along
with a pair of dark glasses, and in the other a Lion banner, which she
waved, her face alive with excitement, very pretty in a perishable,
childlike way, and she was calling, "Beautiful; it was beautiful."

The fireworks lit her, and she looked up, her face chalk white in the
swift aluminum glare.

I looked at her out of my helmet. Then I lifted a hand, just
tentatively.

Dan Jenkins

Dan Jenkins (b. 1929) has been mining sports for laughs since his days at the *Fort Worth Press*, when he said the sound of his alarm clock at three A.M. made his hair hurt. The *Press* in the mid-1950s was a ragged operation, but its sports staff was a thing of beauty, with a Texas legend named Blackie Sherrod riding herd on Jenkins and his fellow stars in the making, Edwin (Bud) Shrake and Gary Cartwright. The next stop for all four was the *Dallas Times Herald*. After that, the countdown was on the day in 1962 when Jenkins told Sherrod, "The Yankees just called." He was talking about *Sports Illustrated*, which turned him loose on golf and college football and gave him an expense account that made him the toast of every saloon he walked into. For twenty years, his readers could count on lines like the one that described God and a particularly religious golfer strolling "hand in hand through the valleys and pines of Augusta." As for Jenkins's ability to make old alums foam at the mouth, one need only read the following story, about Notre Dame's infamous 10–10 tie with Michigan State in 1966. Jenkins shifted gears six years later when he wrote *Semi-Tough*, a raunchy, hilarious best seller about pro football that gave him a new career in fiction. But even with ten novels to his credit (plus one cowritten with Shrake) and *SI* far behind him, he may be best known as one of sportswriting's greatest humorists, alongside Jim Murray, Ring Lardner, and Ring's son John. Indeed, it was John Lardner whose column in *Newsweek* lit the way for him. "All he did," Jenkins said, "was give me a career."

An Upside-Down Game

OLD NOTRE DAME WILL TIE OVER ALL. Sing it out, guys. That is not exactly what the march says, of course, but that is how the big game ends every time you replay it. And that is how millions of cranky college football fans will remember it. For 59 minutes in absolutely overwrought East Lansing last week the brutes of Michigan State and Notre Dame pounded each other into enough mistakes to fill Bubba Smith's uniform—enough to settle a dozen games between lesser teams—but the 10–10 tie that destiny seemed to be demanding had a strange, noble quality to it. And then it did not have that anymore. For the people who saw it under the cold, dreary clouds or on national television, suddenly all it had was this enormous emptiness for which the Irish will be forever blamed.

112

Forget everything that came before, all of that ferocious thudding in the line that was mostly responsible for five fumbles, four interceptions, 25 other incompletions, a total of 20 rushing plays that either lost yardage or gained none, and forget the few good plays—the big passes. Put the No. 1 team, Notre Dame, on its own 30-yard line with time for at least four passing plays to break the tie. A No. 1 team will try *something*, won't it, to stay that way?

Notre Dame did not. It just let the air out of the ball. For reasons that it will rationalize as being more valid than they perhaps were under the immense circumstances, the Irish rode out the clock. Even as the Michigan State defenders taunted them and called the time-outs that the Irish should have been calling, Notre Dame ran into the line, the place where the big game was hopelessly played all afternoon. No one really expected a verdict in that last desperate moment. But they wanted someone to try. When the Irish ran into the line, the Spartans considered it a minor surrender.

"We couldn't believe it," said George Webster, State's savage rover back. "When they came up for their first play we kept hollering back and forth, 'Watch the pass, watch the pass.' But they ran. We knew the next one was a pass for sure. But they ran again. We were really stunned. Then it dawned on us. They were settling for the tie."

You could see the Spartans staring at the Irish down there. They had their hands on their hips, thoroughly disdainful by now. On the Michigan State sideline, the Spartans were jeering across the field and waving their arms as if to say, "Get off the field if you've given up." And at the line of scrimmage the Michigan State defenders were talking to the Notre Dame players.

"I was saying, 'You're going for the tie, aren't you? You're going for the tie,'" said Webster. "And you know what? They wouldn't even look us in the eyes. They just turned their backs and went back to their huddle." Bubba had hollered, "Come on, you sissies," while other Spartans were yelling at Parseghian.

Notre Dame Coach Ara Parseghian made the decision to end the so-called "game of the century" that way. The players only followed instructions, some of them perhaps reluctantly. "We'd fought hard to come back and tie it up," Ara argued. "After all that, I didn't want to risk giving it to them cheap. They get reckless and it could have cost them the game. I wasn't going to do a jackass thing like that at this point."

Thus ended a game that had been slowly built up for five long weeks into the biggest collegiate spectacle in 20 years. The last game to create such pre-kickoff frenzy was between Notre Dame and Army in 1946 at Yankee Stadium. That battle of the century was as full of as many fluky things as this one. It ended in an unsatisfactory 0–0 tie, with both teams claiming No. 1, and left thousands bewildered by the fact that such folklore characters as Johnny Lujack, Glenn Davis and Doc Blanchard had not performed the one remarkable deed that would have decided it.

So when the 1966 season is over, who will deserve to be No. 1? Duffy Daugherty thought Michigan State should be 1 and Notre Dame only 1A. He then said he would even accept a "co-championship," thinking of the Spartans' lesser voting power in the polls. "Last year," he said, "we won on the field and lost at the polls." The reference was to Alabama capturing the AP award after the bowl games and slipping into a tie with the Spartans in the Football Writers' postbowl voting. Ara Parseghian, obviously, believed the Irish could outpoll Michigan State and everyone else, or he would not have been so willing to settle for a tie. Alabama's best chances lie ahead. So do Nebraska's. Both teams could wind up undefeated and, should one beat the other in a bowl game, the winner would have an 11-0 record to glisten against the 9-0-1 of Notre Dame and Michigan State, neither of whose schedules was *that much* fiercer than Alabama's or Nebraska's. Finally, there is mounting dissatisfaction with Notre Dame's policy of shunning bowls while at the same time gunning for a national championship, and with the irritating Big Ten rule that forbids a team from going to the Rose Bowl two years in a row. So long as Notre Dame and the Big Ten teams keep these policies, they perhaps deserve to be out-polled by an Alabama—as punishment.

Last week's game was decided a dozen punishing times, it seemed, the two national powers heaping heroics onto boners, and vice versa— as Michigan State surged to a 10–0 lead and Notre Dame struggled back to the indecisive tie that was earned but unapplauded.

The game was marked by all of the brutality that you somehow knew it would be when such gladiators were to be present as Michigan State's 6-foot-7, 285-pound Bubba Smith, "the intercontinental ballistic Bubba," a creature whose defensive-end play had long ago encouraged Spartan coeds to wear buttons that said KILL, BUBBA, KILL.

Bubba killed, all right. He killed Notre Dame quarterback Terry Hanratty early in the first quarter. When Hanratty, a sensational sophomore for eight games, slid off right tackle on a keeper, Bubba Smith whomped him in the left shoulder and separated it. He caught him just right, as they were falling. It looked as if Hanratty had been smacked by a giant swinging green door.

"That didn't help us any," Bubba said later. "It just let them put in that O'Brien who's slippery and faster and gave us more trouble. The other guy just sits there and waits, and that's what we wanted."

That is what Ara Parseghian wanted, too. Hanratty may sit and wait, but he also throws deep better than O'Brien, though Coley O'Brien threw well enough to get the tie. Ara not only would have liked to have had Hanratty but halfback Nick Eddy and center George Goeddeke as well. Like Hanratty, Goeddeke was valuable, one of Notre Dame's more accomplished blockers. He went out with a first-quarter ankle injury, also courtesy of Bubba. But Eddy, the best Irish ball-carrier, never even got into the game. The Grand Trunk got Eddy.

The Grand Trunk is not another name for Bubba Smith. It is the railroad train that Notre Dame rode from South Bend to East Lansing on Friday. When the train arrived, Eddy fell off the steps right onto an already injured shoulder, and sophomore Bob Gladieux was quietly told that he would start the biggest game of the 1966 season at left half.

As Notre Dame lives with the tie in the weeks and months ahead, it will never forget these injuries and the alibis they strongly suggest. But the Irish do not exactly substitute with girls from Sweet Briar, and Coley O'Brien and Bob Gladieux—the *new* Baby Bombers, somebody said—did marvelously well. "Considering everything, I thought they played super," said Parseghian. O'Brien, who must receive two insulin shots a day for diabetes, hit Gladieux with a 34-yard pass on a deep pattern straight to the goalpost. The ball barely cleared a defender's fingertips but brought Notre Dame's touchdown in the second quarter. The score narrowed the Irish deficit to 10–7 at half time.

The combination of Eddy's injury and the pressure of the game made Notre Dame an extraordinarily grim-looking group upon arrival in East Lansing. Usually loose and smiling, the Irish checked into the

Jack Tar Hotel beneath a marquee that said WELCOME TO THE BIG ONE, with frozen, dedicated expressions that for some indescribable reason did not spell confidence. End Jim Seymour, the startling pass catcher and outgoing personality of earlier Saturdays, was rigid, deeply concentrating. In the game itself Seymour was double covered so well all day that he was scarcely noticeable. He had one decent chance at a pass but dropped it.

The Irish should have been happy to leave South Bend, even on the Grand Trunk, after the week of attention they got. On Monday there were dozens of reporters and photographers on hand, the number swelling each day. It was the same for the Spartans, of course. Both Parseghian and Daugherty had to hold daily press conferences and play the game over and over ahead of time. They certainly thought the game was an honor and a privilege. Parseghian said it looked like a product of Hollywood since Notre Dame was 8-0 and No. 1 and Michigan State was 9-0 and No. 2. Daugherty said it was a shame that such games come along only every few years in college football; that there could be one every year if the NCAA would only hold a football playoff. They said they were simply going to remind their players that Saturday was going to be one of the greatest days in their lives.

The two teams were so talented and physically imposing, and had beaten their opponents so easily, that it was impossible to foretell how the game would go. It was anticipated that neither could run much but that both could strike in the air if their quarterbacks had a spare second to get the ball away. No one wanted a freak play to decide it; everyone wanted a clear winner. The last thing anyone thought about, especially the coaches, was a tie. No, that was the next to last thing. The last thing was all of the mistakes that occurred.

It seemed the two teams would never settle down and begin to look like Nos. 1 and 2 instead of Nos. 42 and 43. Of the four passes Terry Hanratty threw before he met Bubba Smith, three were atrociously off target, one a simple screen that went into the turf. The runners went nowhere, primarily because of Webster, linebacker Charlie Thornhill, guard Jeff Richardson and Bubba. And Notre Dame failed to get off a fourth-down punt because of a poor snapback. Michigan State countered with a fumble, a delay penalty, a clip and a penalty for interfering on a punt catch. It looked like the big intramural game at Columbia.

One interesting thing had happened, though. On an aborted sprint-out pass by Spartan quarterback Jimmy Raye, a flighty junior with a mustache, State had seen something. Split end Gene Washington, one of the surest and fastest receivers in the country, had beaten the Notre Dame deep defenders by 10 yards. Washington, the Big Ten hurdles champion, can outrun most people.

"I can look in a man's eyes and know whether I can beat him," Washington said afterward. "I knew I could beat those guys all day."

Near the end of the first quarter, on first down at his own 27, Raye called the play again. He raced to the right, stopped and fired a bomb. Washington got it for a 42-yard gain. Nine battering ground plays later, with merciless double-team blocking on Notre Dame's fine tackle, Kevin Hardy, State scored. Regis Cavender, who was in for Bob Apisa, crashed over, and it was 7–0.

On its next possession in the second quarter, the Spartans scored again. Raye got away for 30 yards outside right end. And he hit Washington again for 17 yards to reach Notre Dame's 26. A couple more passes failed, however, and the Spartans had to be content with barefoot place-kicker Dick Kenney's 47-yard field goal.

Michigan State, though it continually appeared as if it might, never got beyond Notre Dame's 47-yard line the rest of the day. John Ray, Notre Dame assistant, felt he knew why. "We weren't getting out of our tracks in the first half," he said. "Maybe we were tight. We told our kids to just start hitting people."

Notre Dame's defense, led by Hardy and linebackers Jim Lynch and John Horney, finished the day with a record of having jammed the talented Spartan runners for either minus-yardage or for no gain on no less than 16 rushing plays. Clinton Jones, of all people, was held to 13 yards on 10 carries, and this is the equivalent of stopping Cassius Clay at mid-punch. Jones and Jim Lynch came together in what may have been the loudest collision of the game. Lynch intercepted a Raye pass and stormed upfield, only to be met by Jones. The halfback hit him at the knees as Lynch tried to hammer into him simultaneously. In the next instant Lynch was turned a perfect flip. He landed on his headgear, fumbled and Jones recovered. The dizzy play, one of many, enabled Michigan State to keep possession and subsequently to get its field goal.

Then, late in the third quarter, Coley O'Brien cranked up a Notre Dame drive that looked like it would surely send the Irish ahead 14–10. With Jim Seymour decoying, he passed to Rocky Bleier for nine yards and to fullback Larry Conjar, whose blocking was evident all day, for 18 yards right over the center. He passed out in the deep flat to halfback Dave Haley. Short runs by Haley, Bleier and Conjar moved the ball to the Michigan State 10. With third and three—one of those calls that makes Ara chew his gum like a rabbit—O'Brien tried to pass but did well to scramble to the line of scrimmage. Joe Azzaro then came on to kick the 28-yard field goal that tied the game.

By now, with slow subtlety, the look of things had changed. Michigan State, certainly the better team in the first half, did not seem so sure anymore. Notre Dame had come back. A break or something freaky would decide it now and the wrong team would win. Whoever it was would be wrong. You knew that.

Instantly, the play that *should* have settled the game did in fact happen. Notre Dame safety Tom Schoen picked off a wild Jimmy Raye pass—unlike the Irish, the Spartans gambled—and skittered back with it 31 yards to the Spartan 18. Anyone who thought the Irish would pull something besides three straight Larry Conjar plunges and a winning field goal from about the 10- or 15-yard line was in a closed ward somewhere.

Conjar did run on first down. He dug out two yards. But now what's this? Here's Haley going wide to the left on second down, and here's Phil Hoag, completely unmolested, knifing through with Bubba Smith to crack him for an eight-yard loss! The ball isn't on the 16 anymore; it is back on the 24. Now O'Brien fails with a frantic pass and it is fourth down. Joe Azzaro's field-goal try has to be from 42 yards out. It is a couple of feet off to the right, and the swoon of relief in Spartan Stadium makes the structure lean a little.

"That Haley play," said Parseghian, a total wreck in the locker room after the game. "That was just leakage. We leaked a guy through—blew an assignment." He stared down at the floor. "Damn," he said.

And back outside the Notre Dame door, a pretty Michigan State coed going through the tunnel looked blankly at her boy friend. "Damn," she said. "Damn, damn, damn."

Jerry Izenberg

Jerry Izenberg (b. 1930) learned his first serious lessons in sportswriting from Stanley Woodward, arguably the greatest sports editor ever, and then he went out and practiced them. (Rule No. 1, according to Woodward: "Stop godding up the athletes.") Izenberg broke in as a reporter at the *Newark Star-Ledger*, followed the authority-challenging Woodward to the *New York Herald Tribune*, and returned to Newark in 1962 to write a column for the next half century. Izenberg was tireless, pugnacious, trusted by the people who counted in sports, and the possessor of a finely tuned social conscience that some editors weren't ready for in a time of freedom marches and antiwar demonstrations. Case in point: his 1967 story on Grambling, a small black college in Louisiana that was then sending some large talent to the NFL. Izenberg wrote the story for *The Saturday Evening Post* only to see a top editor there shoot it down. But he bounced back by taking the story to *True* magazine, where it found a home and went on to be selected for publisher E. P. Dutton's annual *Best Sports Stories* anthology and to inspire the groundbreaking ABC documentary *Grambling: 100 Yards to Glory*.

A Whistle-Stop School with Big-Time Talent

IT IS NOT AN EASY PLACE TO FIND. Once a day, a train will wheeze to a coughing stop next to the deserted wooden depot if you get the flagman to go out on the tracks and stop it. But the train won't take you anywhere except deeper into the heart of sharecropper country.

If you are lucky and plan well, you can go by airplane. Coming from New York, your plane will stop at Birmingham, Alabama, and Jackson, Mississippi, and when it touches down at Shreveport, Louisiana, you will still be an hour and a half away.

But the men who scout the colleges for America's 25 major-league pro football teams know the way. This fall, as they have done every year since a man named Eddie Kotal first played pathfinder back in 1947, they will climb into their rented cars at the Shreveport airport and drive 61 miles east into the red clay country and pull off the highway at Grambling, Louisiana (population: 3,600). Grambling is one of the few all-Negro incorporated towns in the United States. Years ago it was a sawmill town but the mill is long since gone. Today the town has no major industry, no office buildings and no motels. But it fronts the campus of Grambling College and some of the Grambling students have had a harder time getting there than the scouts. The length of their journey and the new road they hope it will open for them cannot be measured in terms of highway markers.

Mostly the students come from the hard, bedrock country of northern Louisiana or from the teeming cosmopolis which is Greater New Orleans, some 300-odd miles to the south. Some have made the long trek from the dark ghettos of Houston, Dallas and Birmingham and some from the mule-and-a-cabin sharecropper plots which ring the Mississippi Delta. When you ask members of the football team about themselves, you learn almost casually that most of their parents will live their entire lives without ever having earned more than $3,000 in a single year.

The thing which brings them to Grambling is a get-away dream and its vehicle is the promise of the affluent world of professional football. Among the Negro kids who play segregated high-school football in the Deep South, the word has been out for 20 years now: the logical starting point is Grambling College, where a slender, determined 47-year-old coach named Eddie Robinson recruits his team like a psychologist, runs his practice sessions like a paratroop jump-master and guards his players' rights like Clarence Darrow.

Together, Grambling College and Eddie Robinson broke through the amber light professional football used to hold up for all Negroes and the red one it displayed to kids from all-Negro colleges. Today Grambling honor graduates can be seen operating summa cum laude on television screens all over America any fall Sunday. People like Willie Davis of the Packers and Ernie Ladd of Houston; Junious Buchanan of Kansas City and Roosevelt Taylor of the Bears; Mike Howell of the Browns and Willie Williams of the Oakland Raiders.

The list is long and you have to move fast to update it because from last year's team, one of the poorest Robinson has ever had in won-lost records (6-2-1), eight more players signed professional contracts.

Since he sent his first kid off to challenge pro football's then antiquated racial policy, Robinson has seen more than 60 sign with professional teams in both the United States and Canada. Last year, for example, the National League alone had 11, more than it had from

UCLA or Texas or Alabama. This year 32 Grambling players reported to pro football training camps in the NFL, AFL and Canada.

Today every professional roster is dotted with players from all-Negro colleges like Florida A&M, Jackson State, Prairie View, Morgan State, Maryland State, Tennessee State and Southern U., to name just a few. The scouts know them all now and the underground railway they provide for kids with little hope of otherwise obtaining equal job opportunities grows each year.

But in the beginning, there was only Grambling and Robinson, then a neophyte coach, plus a man by the name of Dr. Ralph Waldo Emerson Jones, who was and still is the school president. There was also a yellowed old newspaper clipping which somehow found its way to the front office of the Los Angeles Rams.

That was in 1947 and the impact which an insurgent league called the All-America Conference would have on the employment of Negro football players had not yet made itself felt on the old guard National League. Kenny Washington, who should have had the shot when he was younger, was dragging his aching legs through the tail end of his career as the Rams' showpiece (and only) Negro performer.

And then somebody sent Kenny Washington the clipping from a Negro newspaper which told about a young fullback named Paul Younger who had scored 25 touchdowns in a single season for a school called Grambling. Washington took the clipping to Eddie Kotal, the Rams' chief scout.

"I had never heard of Grambling much less of Paul Younger," Kotal, now retired, recalled recently, "but I could multiply and 25 times six is still 150 points and I don't care if a guy scores them against The Little Sisters of the Poor. I got me a plane ticket and a road map and I went down to see that boy play."

Paul "Tank" Younger was out of Ruston, Louisiana, which is the nearest sizeable town to Grambling. By a strange coincidence, his family had moved to Los Angeles several years earlier. Younger stayed behind and was raised by Doctor Jones right on the Grambling campus. Like all Grambling football players, he was large and hungry and the first time Eddie Robinson ever saw him in a football uniform he marked him down as a tackle. It was a natural mistake because Younger looked as though he should be up front where he could knock people down.

But it could have been a costly mistake because the only player who could possibly attract enough attention to make pro football change its racial ways would surely have to be a boy who ran with the ball. And if Eddie Robinson hadn't tried to teach Paul Younger a lesson one afternoon, all of this might have begun somewhere else. Eddie Robinson got the message in the middle of a punt-return drill.

This is a basic football exercise in which a kicker lofts a high spiral at a group of backs who are waiting for it in a column of twos. The receiver is immediately rushed by a pair of large linemen. On this afternoon, Tank Younger dutifully thundered downfield and made his tackle but instead of rejoining the other serfs, he hid behind the remaining backs. When the next kick arched downfield, Younger elbowed the other receivers aside, slipped in front, caught the ball and returned it unmolested.

"You simply cannot allow that kind of foolishness at practice and expect to get things done," Robinson says, "so I called the linemen together and I told them we were going to straighten this out right now. If Younger wanted to play games, we'd let him. I told them to run down under that next kick and bust him up but good."

Thunk went the ball, down went the tackles, and then Paul Younger was running and laughing at the same time and both linemen were rolling on the ground with acute knee problems.

"Dammit," Robinson said, feeling a great deal of heat beginning to spread under the collar of his sweat shirt, "do it again." *Thunk, bang, ouch.* Exit two more linemen.

"I went home that night," Robinson recalls, "and I said to myself 'Man, you got to be the world's biggest dope. You are going to kill every lineman you got just to prove a point and Old Tank Younger has already proved one for you. That boy has got to be a back.'"

Which is how that yellowed newspaper clipping had its genesis. Switched to the backfield, Tank Younger scored 60 touchdowns in three seasons and Eddie Kotal (who went down to see him play four times) knew the school song by heart before Younger graduated.

In June of 1948, Kotal, Younger, Doctor Jones and Robinson began to rewrite athletic and social history on a lonely road between Grambling and Ruston. They rode around in Doctor Jones' old car and they talked salary terms and when they finally returned to the campus several hours later, they had begun to bury an incredibly shortsighted professional football myth. For the first time the pros were going to offer a kid from an all-Negro college a chance to play football for a living.

Kotal remembers leaving Grambling with Eddie Robinson's parting remark still fresh in his mind. "Just give him the ball in practice," Robinson had said. "You make sure they get to see him run and then stop worrying because nobody is going to cut that boy off your squad."

They gave Tank Younger the ball and he became an All-Pro. Then they took it away from him and played him on defense and he was an All-Pro there as well. By that time other scouts from other teams were on their way South to put their organizations into the 20th century. Nobody had to wait for the new day dawning after that. Grambling had set the thing in motion.

And when CBS and NBC poured thousands of dollars and millions of decibels into advertising what they called "Super Sunday—the Super Bowl Showdown," Dr. Ralph Waldo Emerson Jones, a small gray-haired man of 62 with rimless glasses, flew out to Los Angeles last January to see it.

In the first half, he saw Junious Buchanan (Grambling '64), a magnificent 6-7, 285-pound tackle, play brilliant football as Kansas City stunned people all over the country by dinging within striking distance of heavily favored Green Bay. In the second half, he saw Willie Davis (Grambling '58) come thundering in from his defensive end position to raise great bruises on Len Dawson, the KC quarterback. And at intermission, he saw the world's fastest-stepping college musical aggregation, the Grambling Tiger Marching Band, steal the half-time show away from a cast of hundreds without straining a single grace note.

"It was," Doctor Jones said afterwards, "a very nice afternoon for all of us."

It had taken a long time for Grambling to get there. In 1936, Doctor Jones became the college's second president. He took over a school with 120 students, six frame buildings and a mountain of debts.

Under Doctor Jones the school has grown to a dazzling collection of colonial brick buildings on a 380-acre campus with 4,000 full-time students (roughly one-third male) and a 70,000-volume library. It is fully state supported, offers several different degrees and supplies more than half the teachers for Louisiana's still heavily segregated school systems.

But in the beginning, Doctor Jones not only taught and adminis-
tered, he also coached football, basketball and baseball. In 1941, with
great reluctance, he gave up coaching football and basketball. He kept
baseball, however, and Tommie Agee, the American League's rookie
of the year in 1966 with the Chicago White Sox, is a Ralph Waldo
Emerson Jones player. So 1941 becomes a very large year in Grambling
history. It was the year in which Doctor Jones hired a young man
named Eddie Robinson.

As a kid, Eddie Robinson had played segregated high-school football in Baton Rouge, Louisiana, and spent a brief period haunting the
local gym because "I figured all I needed was a little training and I
could be a regular Joe Louis and go out and conquer the world." His
widowed mother insisted that he go to college and since Leland, a
now defunct Baptist school, was handy in nearby Baker, Louisiana,
geography suddenly brought him into contact with the man who gave
him a direction.

Leland did not have a very good football team. For three years,
Eddie Robinson was its 170-pound tailback and nobody was much
impressed. But when classes recessed at the conclusion of Robinson's
junior year, a man named Rubin Turner hit town. Eddie Robinson had
just been elected football captain and he had taken a job on the ice
wagon for three dollars a week that summer to raise the money for
his fall school clothes.

"Turner hit that town like a hurricane," Eddie Robinson says. "He
was a preacher. But he wasn't just any preacher. Man, he was *the*
preacher. When he got to preachin' there just wasn't anyone could
touch him. He could outpreach you and outdance you and outtalk you
and outjoke you and, if he had to, he could outfight you.

"One day I came home from work and my mother said that Mr.
Turner was the new football coach at Leland and that he wanted me
to take a trip with him that summer looking for football players.

"I told her that I needed my job and that I wasn't going to go off
on some crazy trip but she just looked me in the eye and she told me
that yes I was because Reverend Turner knew what was right for me
and he was such a nice man and she had already packed my bag. And
right there I learned a little something about recruiting which I never
forgot. If you want a boy badly enough and if you think he is right for

your school, then just you never mind about that boy. You go out and sell his momma and if you convince that fine lady, well, you aren't going to lose many prospects."

So Eddie Robinson piled his stuff into Reverend Turner's old Chevy and they set off on an 800-mile trip through cities and over dirt roads and past one-store towns like New Iberia, Delhi and Tallulah. In Eddie Robinson's words, "that old boy just kept selling Leland College to all those parents and little by little he was putting together a football team."

In between stops he preached to Eddie Robinson about the role of the pencil and the notebook in football, something which Negro college football, for the most part, had sadly neglected.

Then one day, on a muddy road near a small town named Jennings, Rubin Turner stopped the car, turned to Eddie Robinson and said:

"Son, up 'til now we've been living with the alumni and gettin' a little help from those good people. But we don't have any more money now and we don't have any alumni in this town and I am going to have to hold a little prayer meeting tonight. You," he said, "are going to lead the prayers."

At first, Robinson flatly refused but then at first (still sulking about the new school clothes this trip would cost him) he had also refused to address potential football candidates. "But after three days," Robinson remembers, "he had me makin' those damned stump speeches all by myself and I got so good I began to believe them." So Rubin Turner held his prayer meeting and he spoke about the good Christian upbringing at Leland College and the next thing he knew, Eddie Robinson was right up there in front leading the prayers.

Rubin Turner got his football team and with Eddie Robinson throwing the passes from his tailback position, Leland won its conference championship. The rest of 1940 was the best of possible years for Eddie Robinson and the glow carried on through the spring of '41. He married Doris Lamott, his childhood sweetheart. Then he graduated and all of a sudden he realized what year it was and where he was and that nobody in Louisiana was rushing out to hire Negro college graduates. He went to work in a Baton Rouge feed mill, loading 150-pound sacks. Reverend Turner's lessons on the value of the pencil in football didn't mean much to him then. The Robinsons did not have the price of too many pencils.

But Doris Lamott's aunt was a student at Grambling and when she learned that Doctor Jones was thinking of giving up his duties as football coach, she marched into his office and told him about her nephew.

"I knew the boy," Doctor Jones says. "He had shown great self-control when a boy named Riley Smith dropped a touchdown pass he had thrown against us the year before." ("The reason I didn't holler at Riley Smith," Eddie Robinson will tell you, "is because I was mad enough to kill him if I got started.")

Doctor Jones went down to Webb's Barbershop on 13th Street in Baton Rouge where Eddie Robinson used to spend his free hours. He asked a lot of questions about him and then he called Robinson and hired him.

Except for the Robinsons, who immediately began to eat better, the rest of the state took little note of the change. Robinson was eager and young and bursting to put Rubin Turner's theories to the test. The results were, to say the least, discouraging. Grambling did not win a single game that season and in the faculty dining room one noon, Eddie Robinson heard one of his co-teachers ask Doctor Jones:

"President Jones, when are you going to fire that man? No man can coach football with a pencil."

"I'm not going to fire him," Doctor Jones said. "He will be so good one of these days that he will probably be here longer than either of us."

The following year, Robinson won every game. (Ironically, this has been his only undefeated season despite the fact that his teams have won 162 games, lost only 63 and tied 11.) Then the war came along and Grambling dropped intercollegiate football. But Robinson had that pencil in the back of his mind and when the school put in a high-school unit, he had the boys playing intramural ball. (Many of them would ultimately move to the college varsity later.) He also had the girls playing touch football. And he spent long nights through those years, diagramming and refining and diagramming all over again.

His first postwar team was 5-5. Then Tank Younger became a back and Robinson was 9-1 the following year. Meanwhile Doctor Jones, scraping in every direction to get the funds Grambling required, still managed to find the money to send Robinson off to the major national coaching clinics.

"It was embarrassing," Eddie recalls. "We'd have to introduce our-selves and I'd say I was from Grambling and they'd all laugh and call it Gambling or Grumbling or something like that and I'd say to myself 'go ahead and laugh, damn you. Give me a couple of years and we'll see who's laughing.' "

At the University of Iowa in 1947, Eddie Robinson, who was finish-ing up some credits for his masters in the off-season, walked into a national coaching clinic where Frank Carideo, the old Notre Damer, was speaking about the Michigan single wing. After 10 minutes, Rob-inson raised his hand and said: "No, you don't do it that way."

"Who are you?" Eddie Anderson, who was then the Iowa football coach, asked.

"I'm, well, I coach Grambling College."

"Oh," Doctor Anderson said. "Really? Well, perhaps you would like to tell us how the formation is run."

Slowly at first and then with a great firmness as his embarrassment died, Eddie Robinson explained it step-by-step. Afterward Anderson approached him and asked him where Grambling was and what type of football they played. He asked for some films. With great trepi-dation, Eddie Robinson asked Doris to mail him some game films immediately.

"I had to show them to the coaches in that class," Robinson remem-bers, "and they were supposed to criticize them. I was a Negro coach and I felt they were waiting to tear me apart. I knew the quality of our films was poor alongside of what they were used to seeing. And then, as I was threading the projector, I said to myself 'maybe I'm in too deep. Maybe I talk too much. Maybe they are going to laugh.' And then I flipped the switch and there was good old Paul Younger run-ning back a kick and the interference was chopping the other people down and Doctor Anderson yelled:

"Stop the film. Stop it right there. Gentlemen, you have just seen a classic demonstration of how a man is supposed to run with a football."

That was when Robinson realized that he must be doing a pretty good job. But not good enough. Rubin Turner's theories had paid off with Tank Younger and, while Grambling won and kept on winning, the pros were not signing up Grambling players. Something was lack-ing and the coach decided he had better find out what it was.

"College coaches won't like this," he says candidly, "but the pros do it all the best. That's what they're paid to do." So Robinson started trying to get some pros to help him out.

The first pro to join Grambling's corps of volunteer consultants was Dub Jones. He had been one of the best pass receivers in football history. Since Jones lived in nearby Ruston, Eddie Robinson had followed his career with great interest. Jones has a lumber business and one day in 1953, Robinson drove over to Ruston, and asked him if he would help with spring practice at Grambling.

Jones is white and a native Louisianan. He realized that Robinson's request was quite unusual. But he didn't hesitate. He was delighted to help coach the Negro team.

The big Browns end came over to practice and mostly he planned to work with the receivers. The results were immediate. More important, every time he showed a boy something, he would look up and there would be Eddie Robinson at his elbow saying, "When you get a minute, Dub, let's talk." By the time Jones left to rejoin the Browns, Robinson had absorbed most of the Cleveland system.

"Eddie Robinson," Dub Jones said in a New York hotel last year, "works harder than the average coach. First, he has to do more coaching. Most of the kids he gets do not have the grounding in fundamentals because Negro youngsters playing high-school ball in the South do not get the quality coaching the white kids do. But he gets them big. He gambles on their size. He works with them and he makes them go. Football is an emotional game. The boy with the most desire makes it. The Negro boy has that desire and he has the hunger. Given the chance, he'll make good.

"And Eddie... well, Eddie Robinson could coach anywhere... at any school... and with any kind of kid."

Dub Jones was the first but not the only pro to have his brain pumped by Eddie Robinson. Many of the others have been Grambling graduates. Their coach reminds them that they have a debt to pay and they are glad to pay it. Many pro players from Grambling finish up their degrees after their pro careers have already started, so they are on campus studying during spring practice.

Robinson gets them out on the field. There you can hear Junious Buchanan explaining, "On the rush, you know, you just don't blow the man over. You learn to read the play. What you do is sort of immobilize him on the first blow and then you have time to hold up a second and see what's happening."

You can hear Willie Davis on the trap play: "If you don't feel pressure coming at you, it's a trap. So then you turn and trap the trapper and drive him back onto that hole and bust that play."

Of course, it's not all coaching. No matter how many pros Robinson had helping him, he still wouldn't turn out winning teams if he didn't have winning material. And to get winning material, you have to recruit. Eddie Robinson is a top recruiter. The lessons he learned from Rubin Turner stayed with him.

A good example is Ernie Ladd, a Grambling All-Pro now with the Houston Oilers. He was a young giant as a high-school senior in Orange, Texas. His uncle, Garland Boyette, was at Grambling. He and Ladd would play on Robinson's 1960 team, the showpiece of all Grambling football teams, a fantastic collection of talent which won nine of 10 games and which produced 11 professional football players. But when Boyette told Robinson about Ladd, every school in Grambling's Southwestern Athletic Conference was already after him.

Robinson sent Dr. C. D. Henry of the phys ed department down to bring Ladd in for a visit. Ladd was a growing boy and breakfast cost Doctor Henry $9.85. He called Robinson collect.

"Listen, I have never seen an eater like this kid in my life. I have 37 cents left and a tank full of gas. What do I do if he wants lunch?"

"Why, you just bring him on in," Eddie said, "even if you have to bring him in hungry." Then he skipped over to the school dining hall and had a little talk with the staff.

When Ernie Ladd arrived, Robinson took him in for lunch. As Ladd moved through the school cafeteria, his tray grew higher and higher. It was an Everest of mashed potatoes, an Eiffel Tower of meat. At the bread station, the girl behind the counter counted out five slices of bread. Then she looked at Robinson who was shaking his head behind Ladd. She hesitated, then put half-a-loaf into Ladd's free hand.

"Coach," Ernie Ladd smiled, "you sure feed good here." He spent four years knocking down other football players for Robinson.

One of Robinson's great victories in recruiting came in the spirited battle for a fullback from southern Louisiana. He had to outtalk and outmaneuver a Big Ten school and Southern U.

"I didn't worry too much about that old boy from the Big Ten," Robinson explains, "because he was living up at the hotel and driving that big car. The man from Southern was more difficult. I had to outwait him and get invited to supper.

"Well, finally it got to be suppertime and the boy's mother said she have didn't much and I'd have to take potluck but I said, 'Listen, that's country cooking if I ever smelled it and I am just really a country boy and you lead me to it.' Then she brought in the graham-cracker pie and I just had to tell her it was better than anything my wife makes but I hoped she'd keep that our little secret.

" 'Southern is a fine school,' I told her after dessert, 'and I'm sure that your boy will do all right even if he is in a big city while at Grambling he'd probably be bored because all there is to do is to study all week and go to church on Sunday.' "

Eddie Robinson got his fullback.

So it's recruiting and coaching and tough, hungry kids whose parents are very, very poor. For the most part, they are kids without big reputations. They come to Robinson with large hands and feet and "then we fill in the rest right there in our dining hall. I have never coached a rich boy. But if he's big and mean and poor, I want him." That's the essence of Robinson's coaching system and of Grambling's football success.

But there is only one way to find out what Grambling football is all about and why it has produced so many top pros. You have to go down there and see it and once you have seen it played, it is something you do not forget.

On this particular weekend, Grambling will play Bishop College in New Orleans' Sugar Cup Classic. On Thursday, Robinson sends his team through the final contact drill and the hitting is positively brutal. Robinson has three part-time assistants. ("An improvement," he explains. "My first year, the whole coaching staff was me and old Jess Applegate, the night watchman.") He is everywhere, racing furiously from one end of the practice field to the other, wearing sweat clothes and an old army field jacket. Several scouts have dropped by to watch practice and Doctor Jones, sitting in his car at the edge of the field, says:

"Some coaches get irritated by the scouts. That's ridiculous. This is a chance for these boys. Our job is to place them in life according to their skills and this is part of it. Pro sports are just another avenue of making a living. There are few enough of such avenues for some."

That night there will be a skull session in the big classroom underneath the stadium and in between practice and the evening's work, the visitor goes down to the town of Grambling to learn something about its association with the school.

Its Main Street is a two-block north-south drag, containing Mike's Cafe, Hawthorne's Novelty and Record Shop and Dan's Dairy Bar. In the evening, the men gather at Gallo's Barbershop to discuss the football team or the fall rains and what they will mean to the men who cut pulpwood in Hodge or Jonesboro.

Over at Calvin Wilkerson's College Shop, a clothing store with the accent on campus fashions, the proprietor explains why Grambling football has a special place for a lot of people.

"We take great pride in the college. When the boys go out and make a name for themselves we feel we're a part of it because it couldn't happen to us on our own. Some of our people are day laborers who cut pulpwood and when the rains come in the fall, their take-home pay could be as little as $15 a week. It costs $1.50 to see Grambling play and that can buy an awful lot when you only start with $15. But they go anyway. This town is empty when Grambling plays—home or away."

That night the Grambling football team sprawls around the large classroom and listens to a scouting report. Midway through it, Robinson interrupts the scout. "Now you all have young minds so I know you are all going to remember this without writing it down. But I am old and tired so I am going to take this notebook and I am going to write down, 'red formation run... brown formation... pass.'" Around him 50 pencils have suddenly come to life.

"But, Elie," Robinson says to a player, "Elie, when they run all over you on Saturday because you didn't listen here and you are stretched out on the ground and the captain looks down at you and patiently asks what do they like to do from the red formation, then when you move your bloody lips, what will you answer?"

"Run," Elie says meekly.

"Well, dog, you hit it right on the nose. Maybe we can play this game after all."

The game is played at City Park Stadium in New Orleans and it has rained the entire night before. It will be a tough, dirty afternoon. Still, the game attracts a happy, partisan crowd. It begins to file in early... co-eds with traditional chrysanthemums flit from seat to seat to socialize while the 110-piece Grambling band marches down the sidelines in gold and black uniforms.

Bishop arrives first. It is not a small team and it moves briskly through its exercises. The visitor wonders if he may not have been deluded somewhat about the enormous size Grambling is supposed to have year after year.

Suddenly, the Grambling band breaks into "Hold that Tiger." It is not a Dixieland beat. It is a let's-all-go-out-to-the-Crusades stomp. The girls in the grandstand jump to their feet and wave black and gold pompons. The Grambling football team lines up quietly in the runway. Then it moves forward through the far goal posts. From tackle to tackle it averages 241 pounds. It spills onto the field and a popeyed visitor on the bench swears that the earth moves.

"It's muddy out here," Robinson says solicitously, "let me get you a pair of football shoes."

"Size nine," the visitor mumbles.

"I don't know," the coach says, "the last time I looked all we had left were a couple of pairs of 17 triple E and some 16's. Maybe I could dig up a 14 somewhere."

During the first half, Eddie Robinson does more person to person coaching in two periods than most head coaches at major colleges do in a decade. When a player fumbles, he takes him aside and shows him how to carry the ball. When a man blows a pass pattern, Robinson draws it for him in the mud. While he teaches, Grambling plays in spurts and runs up a 14–0 lead on sheer size. The players clatter down the runway to the locker room with heads down.

It is here that Eddie Robinson is at his absolute best. He speaks quietly with Fred Hobdy, the basketball coach, who mans the press-box telephone for him. Then he steps forward and looks around him. He wears a single-breasted gray suit and a soft-brim hat, which he pushes toward the back of his head.

"Now we do not have to score 100 points today," he begins. "We are not by nature greedy. But we must score enough to win and we haven't done this yet. Now, please... please... if you help me then maybe... just maybe... I can help you. But somebody is not doing his job. Somebody hasn't paid attention to the scouting reports. What are we doing wrong?"

It doesn't take long to find out. Suddenly everyone is rushing forward to confess for the Good of the Party. Tackles blame themselves for missed blocks. Linebackers repent for being lured away from screen passes. Quarterbacks are especially hard on themselves.

"What do we do," Robinson says, closing the confessional booth, "when their middle linebacker goes for the motion?"

"Run," the quarterbacks chorus.

"Good," Robinson says, "and what do we run?"

"We run the inside counter."

Then they go back out and the middle linebacker from Bishop College goes for the motion and they run the inside counter for 63 yards and six points and "Hold that Tiger." At the finish, they win, 43–13.

Late the following night a visitor packs his bags in the visitors' wing of Grambling's modern student union building while Eddie Robinson sits on the bed.

You do not get the clichés from him you will get at other more prominent schools. It is obvious that there is more to this for him than the job (which pays about $14,000) or the neat house he lives in hard by the campus. He will tell you that he and Doctor Jones have sat in on something like 100 salary discussions with the pros because "if it were a white boy from a big school, he'd have his lawyer. We owe it to these kids to get them the best deal we can."

"Well, sometimes," the visitor said, "you must wonder a little about yourself. I mean you started something down here and it spread to a lot of other schools just like this one but there must have been a time somewhere when you thought of what it might be like to coach in a major, integrated college."

"If you're human," Eddie Robinson said after a long pause, "you do wonder. There isn't a Negro coach in this country today who doesn't wonder. You get to asking yourself how you would react on a Saturday if there were 80,000 people up in those seats instead of 20,000. You have to daydream a little. You look at Woody [Hayes] and Bear [Bryant] and you have to ask yourself 'what do you think?' And deep down you like to think, yes, you could have done it."

But sing no sad songs for Eddie Robinson who is doing what he wants to do and doing it exceptionally well. The scouts will be back this year to see Richie Lee, his 6-5, 275-pound tackle; and Bob Atkins, his 6-6, 215-pound safety and, most of all, a junior named James Harris, who at 6-2, 208 pounds, will be the first Negro quarterback to make it big in the pros, according to Robinson.

The thing has come full cycle now. At the Super Bowl, Doctor Jones and Collie J. Nicholson, the school's publicist, were saying they were extremely anxious to get some white athletes into Grambling.

"We have to get them," Collie Nicholson said emphatically.

"Have to?" a man asked.

"If we don't get them, we could lose some of our federal funds."

Now that, baby, that's a cycle.

Jerry Kramer and Dick Schaap

It was just in passing that an editor asked Dick Schaap (1934–2001) if he knew a professional football player who could keep a diary of the 1967 season. Schaap did, of course. He knew everybody from Muhammad Ali to Lenny Bruce to Robert F. Kennedy. So it figured that he also knew Jerry Kramer (b. 1936), an All-Pro for the Green Bay Packers and, with his fellow guard Fuzzy Thurston, the muscle in the seemingly unstoppable Packer Sweep. Just as important, Kramer was cerebral, insightful, and a splendid observer. Though he loved coach Vince Lombardi and his teammates in the us-versus-the-world way of athletes everywhere, he was able to step back and see the whole picture. That he was involved in the biggest play of the Packers' "Ice Bowl" victory over Dallas—described in the following excerpt—was a bonus. Or maybe it was proof that Schaap possessed a divining rod for great stories like those Kramer gave him to weave into the best seller *Instant Replay* (1968). It was the most successful of the thirty-three books Schaap edited or authored and made him the king of as-told-to nonfiction. Not that he needed any more jobs. He was, at one time or another, sports editor of *Newsweek*, city editor and columnist of the *New York Herald Tribune*, correspondent for nightly newscasts on NBC and ABC, editor of *Sport* magazine, and ringmaster of ESPN's *The Sports Reporters*. He attributed his prolific moonlighting as an author to one thing: the demands of alimony.

from

Instant Replay

December 31

W HEN I WOKE UP THIS MORNING, after a good night's sleep, I knew it was cold. "It must be 10 below zero," I told Barbara. I thought I was kidding.

During breakfast, I found out the temperature was 16 degrees below zero, the coldest December 31st in Green Bay history, and I started to shiver. Still, I figured it would warm up a little by noon. It warmed all the way up to 13 below by game time.

Chandler and I bundled up driving over to the stadium and we didn't realize quite how bitter the cold was. As we ran into the dressing room we saw a helicopter hovering over the stadium, blowing snow off the seats.

When I got inside and began dressing, Gilly came over to me and said, "You gonna wear gloves?"

I hadn't thought of it. I'd never worn gloves before in a football game. I was about to say no, and then I thought, "Who the hell am I kidding? I don't use my hands out there."

"Hell, yeah," I told Gilly.

Maybe, if it were 5 above zero or 10 above, I would have passed up the gloves and tried to psych the Cowboys into thinking that the cold wasn't bothering me. But at 13 below I wasn't going to be psyching anyone. Everybody in the whole United States was going to know I was cold.

Gilly, Forrest, Ski, and I—the interior linemen—got gloves from Dad Braisher, the equipment manager. We're the only ones who don't have to use our hands in a game. We decided we'd wear the gloves outside to loosen up and see if we needed them for the game.

"With this cold," Ron Kostelnik mentioned to me, "it's gonna hamper us on defense. We won't be able to grab, to use our hands too well. You won't have to be afraid of popping people, Jerry. They won't be able to throw you with their hands." The thought warmed me up slightly.

We got dressed in our long stockings and our silk pants, and when we stepped out on the field—I was wearing my thermal underwear, but only knee-length and elbow-length, so that it wouldn't restrict my mobility—icy blasts just shot right up our skirts. It took Gilly and Forrest and Ski and me about three seconds to decide we'd keep on the gloves. "Hell, let's get another pair," I told Gilly.

I looked over at the Dallas Cowboys and I almost felt sorry for them. As bad as the cold was for us, it had to be worse for them. We were freezing, and they were dying. They were all hunched over, rubbing their hands, moving their legs up and down, trying to persuade themselves that they weren't insane to be playing football in this ridiculous weather.

We kicked off, and our defense held, and when I came out on the field for the first time we had the ball around our own 20-yard line. Bart started right off with the 41-special, the new play we'd put in for the Cowboys. Gilly pulled out to his right, faking Lee Roy Jordan, the middle linebacker, into thinking the play was going that way, and Bob Hyland blocked on Gilly's man and I blocked on Jethro Pugh, and Chuck Mercein, at fullback, leading Donny Anderson into the line, blocked Lee Roy Jordan trying to recover. The play worked just the way we hoped it would. Donny picked up yards before he got hit. He fumbled, which wasn't part of our plan, but Mercein recovered for us. With Bart calling 41-special a couple of times, and with the aid of a few penalties, we marched all the way down the field for a touchdown. Bart passed to Dowler in the end zone, and, midway through the first period, we were leading 7–0.

The cold was incredible, cutting right through us, turning each slight collision into a major disaster, but, for me, the footing on the field wasn't too bad. The ground was hard, but by putting most of my weight on my toes, I could dig in and get a foothold. I handled Jethro pretty well, popping him more than I would under normal conditions, keeping his cold hands away from me, moving him on running plays and checking him on passing plays. We didn't say a word to each other; even if we'd had anything to say, it was too cold to talk.

The only conversation I had all day was with Lee Roy Jordan. When we tried a screen pass, Bob Lilly or one of their linemen read the play and grabbed the back, the intended receiver, by the jersey. Bart had no one to throw to. "Look, he's holding, he's holding," I screamed at the referee. But the referee didn't see the infraction, and Jordan smiled and said to me, "He wasn't holding, Jerry. Your guy just slipped and fell down, and we were just helping him up."

We had more conversation on our own bench, mostly over who'd get the good seats by the warmer. Hornung usually had one of them; the commissioner had said he could sit on our bench. At one point, the warmer ran out of fuel and started to smoke, and we all jumped off the bench. Another time, Donny Anderson was sitting on the bench freezing, and he saw the CBS sidelines microphone, sponge-covered to kill the wind sound, dangling in front of him. He reached up and put his hands around the microphone, thinking it was some new kind of heater.

Early in the second quarter, when we had the ball on a third-and-one situation just past midfield, Bart crossed up the Dallas defense, faded back and threw a long touchdown pass, again to Dowler. We were ahead 14–0, and I felt warmer. I was only worried about our tendency to let up when we get a few touchdowns ahead.

Less than a minute later, Herb Adderley intercepted one of Don Meredith's passes and returned the ball almost to the Cowboys' 30-yard line. If we can get this one now, I thought, we can forget it, the game's over, the whole thing's over. I had a beautiful feeling about the ball game—until we didn't score. Bart lost some yardage eating the ball when he couldn't find an open receiver, and we had to punt. I felt frustrated, terribly let down. I'd been so certain that we were going to get at least something, at least a field goal.

Then, late in the second period, deep in our own territory, again Bart faded to pass and again he couldn't get rid of the ball, and Willie Townes, their big defensive end, hit Bart and knocked the ball loose, and George Andrie, their other defensive end, swooped in and picked up the ball and charged to the end zone for a touchdown.

Forrest Gregg tackled Andrie just as he crossed the goal line, and I was only a step or two behind Forrest, and I suddenly felt the greatest desire to put both my cleats right on Andrie's spinal cord and break it. We had been victimized by these stupid plays—scooped-up fumbles, deflected passes, blocked kicks, high-school tricks—so many times during the season that I felt murderous. I'd never in my career deliberately stepped on a guy, but I was so tempted to destroy Andrie, to take everything out on him, that I almost did it. A bunch of thoughts raced through my mind—I'd met Andrie off the field a few times and I kind of liked him—and, at the last moment, I let up and stepped over him.

We couldn't do a thing when we got the ball—Jethro caught Bart for a loss one time, but I thought I'd checked him long enough; I thought Bart held the ball too long—and they took over again and added a field goal, and so, at the half, instead of leading 17–0 or 21–0 or something like that, we were barely in front, 14–10.

Ray Wietecha chewed us out pretty good between the halves. "One guy's giving the quarterback all the trouble," he told us. "One guy. C'mon. Don't let up out there. There's a lot of money riding. Get tough, dammit, get tough." Ray didn't mention any names, but we all knew that Ski was having a lot of trouble with Andrie, that Andrie was doing most of the damage.

We just couldn't get unwound in the third quarter. I still felt I had Jethro under control, but he caught Bart two more times, not back deep, but out of the pocket, after Bart had had enough time to throw if he could have found anyone open. The ends were having trouble cutting. On the first play of the last quarter, they used the halfback-option—an old favorite play of ours—and Dan Reeves passed 50 yards for a touchdown. We were losing, 17–14, and the wind was whipping us, too.

Five minutes later, my roommate was wide with an attempted field goal, and when the ball sailed by to the left I had a little sinking feeling, a little fear that the clock might run out on us. I thought maybe the time had come for us to lose. Dallas controlled the ball for about ten plays, staying on the ground as much as they could, eating up the clock, and all the time my frustration built up, my eagerness to get back on the field, to have another chance to score.

With five minutes to go, we got the ball on our own 32-yard line, and, right away, Bart threw a little pass out to Anderson and Andy picked up five, six yards. The linebackers were laying back; they were having trouble with their footing, trouble cutting. Chuck Mercein ran for the first down, and then Bart hit Dowler for another first down, and we were inside Dallas territory. I began to feel we were going to make it, we were going to go for a touchdown. At the worst, I figured we'd go down swinging.

On first down, Willie Townes got through and caught Andy for a big loss, and we had second and about twenty. But Bart capitalized on the Dallas linebackers' difficulties getting traction. Twice, with the ends still having problems with their footing, he threw safety-valve passes to Anderson and twice Andy went for about ten yards, and we had a first down on the Dallas 30, and I could feel the excitement building in the huddle. But we had only a minute and a half to play. Bart passed out to Mercein on the left and Chuck carried the ball down to the Dallas eleven. I walked back to the huddle, wondering what Bart was going to call, and he called a give-65, and I thought, "What a perfect call. We haven't used it all day. What a smart call."

It's a potentially dangerous play, a give-65. We block as though we're going through the "five" hole, outside me. Gilly pulls and comes over my way, and everything depends on the tackle in front of him, Bob Lilly, taking the fake and moving to his left. The play can't work against a slow, dumb tackle; it can only work against a quick, intelligent tackle like Lilly. We figured Lilly would key on Gilly and follow his move, but we didn't know for sure. Everybody blocks my way on this play, Anderson coming for the hole as though he's carrying the ball, and nobody blocks the actual target area, Lilly's area. If Lilly doesn't take the fake, if he ignores Gilly pulling, he kills the actual ballcarrier, Mercein.

But Lilly followed Gillingham, and the hole opened up, and Chuck drove down to the 3-yard line. With less than a minute to play, Anderson plunged for a first down on the one, and, with only two time-outs left, we huddled quickly. "Run over there," Gilly said, in the huddle. "Run that 55-special. They can't stop that."

Bart called the 55, and I thought to myself, "Well, this is it, toad. They're putting it directly on your back, yours and Forrest's." I didn't make a very good block, and the five hole didn't open up, and Andy got stopped at the line of scrimmage. We called a time-out with twenty seconds to play. Then Bart called the same play again, and this time Andy slipped coming toward the hole—I don't know whether he could have gotten through—and slid to about the one-foot line, and we called time out with sixteen seconds to play, our last time-out, and everybody in the place was screaming.

We could have gone for the field goal right then, for a tie, hoping that we'd win in overtime. We decided to go for the victory. In the huddle, Bart said, "Thirty-one wedge and I'll carry the ball." He was going to try a quarterback sneak. He wasn't going to take a chance on a handoff, or on anybody slipping. He was going to go for the hole just inside me, just off my left shoulder. Kenny Bowman, who had finally worked his way back to the lineup, and I were supposed to move big Jethro out of the way. It might be the last play of the game, our last chance.

The ground was giving me trouble, the footing was bad down near the goal line, but I dug my cleats in, got a firm hold with my right foot, and we got down in position, and Bart called the "hut" signal. Jethro was on my inside shoulder, my left shoulder. I came off the ball as fast as I ever have in my life. I came off the ball as fast as anyone could. In fact, I wouldn't swear that I didn't beat the center's snap by a fraction of a second. I wouldn't swear that I wasn't actually offside on the play.

I slammed into Jethro hard. All he had time to do was raise his left arm. He didn't even get it up all the way and I charged into him. His body was a little high, the way we'd noticed in the movies, and, with Bowman's help, I moved him outside. Willie Townes, next to Jethro, was down low, very low. He was supposed to come in low and close to the middle. He was low, but he didn't close. He might have filled the hole, but he didn't, and Bart churned into the opening and stretched and fell and landed over the goal line. It was the most beautiful sight in the world, seeing Bart lying next to me and seeing the referee in front of me, his arms over his head, signaling the touchdown. There were thirteen seconds to play.

The fans poured on the field, engulfing us, engulfing the Cowboys, pummeling all of us. Chuck Howley, the Dallas linebacker, got knocked down three or four times accidentally, and he was furious. I had to fight my way through the crowd to the sidelines; Bart came off the field looking like he was crying, and he probably was. The Cowboys still had time to get off two plays, two incomplete passes, and the game was over. I tried to get to the dressing room quickly, but I got caught around the 30-yard line, trapped in a mass of people beating me on the back, grabbing at my chin strap, grabbing at my gloves, trying to get anything for a souvenir. I had a sudden moment of panic, wondering whether I was ever going to get out of that mess alive.

Finally I reached the dressing room and I was immediately aware that the whole place was wired for sound. Cameramen and cameras were all around, and Coach Lombardi cussed the cameramen and ordered them, flatly, to get the hell out. When we were alone, just the team and the coaches, Vince told us how proud he was of us. "I can't talk anymore," he said. "I can't say anymore." He held the tears back and we all kneeled and said the Lord's Prayer, and then we exploded, with shouts of joy and excitement, the marks of battle, the cuts, the bruises, and the blood, all forgotten.

The TV people returned, and I was one of the first men led in front of the cameras. "There's a great deal of love for one another on this club," I said. "Perhaps we're living in Camelot." I was referring to the idea of one for all and all for one, the ideal of King Arthur's Round Table, and I meant it. And then I talked about Lombardi.

I'd been waiting for a chance to talk about Vince. A story had appeared in *Esquire* magazine a few weeks earlier making him look like a complete villain, like nothing but a cruel, vicious man. The story had hurt Vince; I had heard that his mother had cried when she read the story. I thought the story gave a distorted picture of the man; it showed only one of his many sides. "Many things have been said about Coach," I said on TV, "and he is not always understood by those who quote him. The players understand. This is one beautiful man."

I loved Vince. Sure, I had hated him at times during training camp and I had hated him at times during the season, but I knew how much he had done for us, and I knew how much he cared about us. He is a beautiful man, and the proof is that no one who ever played for him speaks of him afterward with anything but respect and admiration and affection. His whippings, his cussings, and his driving all fade; his good qualities endure.

Over and over and over, perhaps twenty times, the television cameras reran Bart's touchdown and my block on Jethro Pugh. Again and again, millions of people across the country saw the hole open up and saw Bart squeeze through. Millions of people who couldn't name a single offensive lineman if their lives depended on it heard my name repeated and repeated and repeated. All I could think was, "Thank God for instant replay."

Kenny Bowman came up to me smiling and said, "Don't take all the credit, Kramer. Don't take all the credit. I helped you with that block."

"Shut up, Bow," I said. "You've got ten more years to play. You've got plenty of time for glory. I ain't telling anybody anything. If they think I made that block alone, I'm gonna let them think it."

I was only kidding Bowman, of course. But I've got to admit that I didn't tell many people about Bowman's part in the block. I stayed around the locker room as long as I ever have, talking to all the reporters, answering all their questions, accepting all their kind words. I felt like a halfback. I stayed till the last dog was dead.

I drove home from the stadium in an icebox. The heating unit in my Lincoln was frozen, and so was I. For an hour or two I relaxed with a few friends and with my family, letting the circulation come back all over my body. I watched part of the American Football League title game, watched the Oakland Raiders kill the Houston Oilers, and then I went in my room and changed into my fancy, black-striped walking suit, putting it on over a white turtleneck sweater. I put on my black cowboy hat and stuck a fat cigar in my mouth, and I felt like a riverboat gambler. And then we all took off for Appleton, about thirty miles away, for the Left Guard Steak House, owned by Fuzzy and Max, for a big, beautiful celebration.

It was 20 degrees below zero outside, and the heating broke down in the restaurant, but the cold didn't bother me at all. I drank toasts with Hornung and toasts with Jordan and toasts with Max, and, somehow,

I managed to notice that Donny Anderson had, for company, a girl who had once been a Playmate-of-the-Month. Donny had certainly earned a big night out; he'd played almost the entire game, while Travis shivered on the bench.

I had a great time. At least everyone told me I had a great time. Fuzzy and I got carried away by the whiskey man, and we ended up the evening greeting the New Year with toasts—toasts, naturally, to the two greatest guards in the history of the whole world.

Jennifer Allen

Jennifer Allen takes care to note that she was born in 1961, the same year the Chicago Bears drafted Mike Ditka, their Hall of Fame tight end and the head coach of their Super Bowl XX championship team. Not every woman embraces such trivia, but Allen is a special case. Her father, George Allen, was then the Bears' defensive coach, a rising star who would eventually become head coach of the Washington Redskins once and the Los Angeles Rams twice. Jennifer Allen was as close to him as she could be, but there was still the distance imposed by "the mere fact that I was a girl in a big man's world." With a sense of purpose that rivaled her father's, Allen set out on a career as a writer that has seen her publish a short-story collection, *Better Get Your Angel On* (1989), and deliver estimable journalism for *Rolling Stone*, the *New York Times*, *The New Republic*, and *George* magazine. She has also written for the HBO comedy *Arli$$*, been a feature reporter for the NFL Network, and taught yoga. When her father died, on New Year's Eve 1990, her world was tilted in a new direction. It led her to what she calls "the most difficult writing project I have ever undertaken": *Fifth Quarter* (2000), a deeply personal book about her connection to her father and her family's tumultuous life in the NFL. The following excerpt shines a light on the love and pain that are the book's hallmarks.

from

Fifth Quarter

Dinner, New Year's Eve, 1968

D AD SAT AT THE DINNER TABLE, sipping his milk. We all watched him sip his milk, his first and only drink of choice. Then he set his glass down on the table where my three older brothers and I sat, while Mom scowled as she stirred a pot of boiling spaghetti on the kitchen stove.

"Listen," Dad said, "a guy who goes out after a loss and parties is a two-time loser." Dad was referring to his ex-boss, Los Angeles Rams owner Dan Reeves. "First, he's a loser for losing, and second, he's a loser for thinking he doesn't look like a loser by partying it up."

Dan Reeves had once said, "I'd rather *lose* with a coach I can drink with and have fun with than *win* with George Allen." Reeves had been drinking all Christmas night at a Hollywood bar when he called my father at home from the bar telephone, the following day, at 8 A.M. "Merry Christmas, George," Reeves had said. "You're fired!"

That was a week ago. Now, on New Year's Eve, Dad sat in his pajamas, talking to us kids at the dinner table. Mom stood in her bathrobe, clanging pot and pans on the stove. This was a rare dinner with Dad since he had taken the job as head coach of the Los Angeles Rams three years before. For my father, getting the Rams to the National Football League Championship meant drinking a tall glass of milk at the office for dinner, then spending the night on his office couch so that he wouldn't waste valuable work time driving home, eating with his family, and sleeping with his wife. The long hours paid off: the 1968 Rams defense had set a new fourteen-game record for fewest yards allowed on offense. But the team finished second in the Coastal Division, falling two games short of reaching the championship play-offs. A week later, Dan Reeves fired Dad. Since then, we had been keeping the TV volume turned down low so as not to disturb Dad's weeklong monologue, which had begun the day after Christmas.

"Heck," Dad said, "Dan Reeves is dying of cancer. Maybe that's his problem. He's drinking to forget he's alive!"

We all knew what came next. When talking about drinking and dying, our father always cited his own father, Earl, who died an unemployed alcoholic. To our father, the only thing worse than losing was dying without a job. "I want to die working," Dad told us all. "That's the only way to die!"

"Dying," Mom said, setting down Dad's plate of spaghetti. "Who's talking about dying? I thought we were going to have a nice dinner together for once in our lives."

"I'm trying to teach these kids a lesson."

"They've learned enough as it is."

"You know," our father said as our mother finished serving dinner, "you kids have a lot to learn about life."

We kids nodded. We twisted our forks into our spaghetti as Dad told us again about his other kids, the players he'd recently coached at the Rams: Deacon, Lamar, Roman, and Jack. Deacon Jones, Lamar Lundy, Roman Gabriel, and Jack Pardee had organized a team strike against Dan Reeves the day after Reeves had fired Dad. Thirty-eight of the Rams' forty players signed a petition saying they would quit if my father was not rehired as head coach. "We won't play if George don't coach" was the slogan they chanted for the television cameras. Dad was so moved by this display of support that he could barely manage more than a few words for the reporters before stepping down off the platform to lean against the shoulders of his men. Dark sunglasses covered his eyes as one by one the players took the microphone to speak for their former coach, whom some called their best friend.

"Now, *those* are men to aspire to," our dad told us. "You kids need something to aspire to." He said television was turning us all into wallpaper. He said we needed to have daily goals besides watching television all day long. "Show me a person without goals and I'll show you someone who's *dead*!"

"Please, George," Mom said, "it's New Year's Eve. Can we please eat a dinner in peace?"

But my father now directed his gaze at the little black-and-white television perched on a stool over my shoulder. A local Los Angeles announcer was summarizing the past year's events: the assassinations of Senator Robert F. Kennedy and Dr. Martin Luther King Jr. and the recent firing of Los Angeles Rams Head Coach George Allen.

"You know," my father said, not taking his eyes off the television, "I'm disappointed in each of you kids." He said there was a lot to be done around the new house and no one was doing anything about it. A few weeks earlier, we had moved into our large new house. It was our third home in three years as we followed Dad, moving from team to team in the NFL. Sealed boxes still filled every room of the house. Pointing to a box in the kitchen, Dad said, "You see a box like that, you unpack it!" Pointing to a scrap of brown paper on the floor, he said, "You see a piece of paper, you pick it up!" Peeling away a strip of packing tape stuck to the edge of the kitchen table, Dad said, "You see a piece of tape, you toss it out!"

We leapt from our dinner chairs to unpack boxes, pick up paper, toss out tape.

Mom stopped us all. "Not now," she said. "Sit down, it's time to eat. Let's eat."

"You know," Dad said, "it would be nice if someone said a little grace for a change."

"I said it last time," my oldest brother, George, said.

"I said it last time," my middle brother, Gregory, said.

"*Bull*, you did," my youngest brother, Bruce, said. "I always say it!"

"*Grace!*" Mom shouted. "There. I said it."

Dad shook his head. "Boy, oh, boy," he said, "here I am fighting to get back my job, and my own family cannot even bow their heads to say a few prayers."

Everyone looked to me. I was almost eight years old. When no one else wanted to say grace, I said it. I bowed my head and closed my eyes and thanked the Lord for our food and shelter and asked the Lord to help Dad get his job back with the Rams.

"Amen," we all said together, and Dad thanked me for my special grace, and George called me Ugly and I called George a Moron and George called me a Dog and I told George to Shut Up and my father said, "You know I don't like that word," and Gregory said, "What word?" and Bruce screamed, "*Shut up!*" and Dad just shook his head, ran his hand through his thick black hair, and said, "Boy, oh, boy, you kids."

"*Now* can we eat?" my mother said.

"Who's stopping you?" my father said. His gaze returned to the television. The announcer was now giving a play-by-play of Senator Robert Kennedy's assassination in the kitchen of the Los Angeles Ambassador Hotel.

"Now *there's* a leader," Dad said. "There's a man this country will never forget."

My father was talking about Rosey Grier, a former Rams defensive lineman who had tackled and helped capture Kennedy's assassin, Sirhan Sirhan, moments after the shooting.

The telephone rang.

"Uh-oh!" said Dad, sitting up. "Uh-oh!" meant "Oh, *no!*" Every time the telephone rang since Dan Reeves called the day after Christmas to say, "Merry Christmas, George, you're fired," my father would say, "Uh-oh!" and refuse to answer the telephone. We knew the call would invariably be for Dad, but still we all sprang to answer it, saying, "Hello? Allen residence? Hello?" and then we would force the receiver into our father's hand. It would usually be just another sports reporter calling to ask Dad about his "uncertain future." Our number was unlisted, yet every sportswriter in the country seemed to have it in his Rolodex.

Earlier that day, our mother, who is French, had intercepted one such call.

"You Americans are so brutal!" she laid into the guy, "so different from the French. At least when a man is standing at the guillotine, we give him a cigarette before cutting off his goddamn head!"

Mom hated reporters. She said reporters were vultures preying on Dad. Dad liked reporters. He often talked to them as if they were long-lost friends, confiding in them recently how much he loved coaching the Rams. That's all Dad wanted, he would tell reporters. Dad would tell them, "I just want to coach, you see?" But this time, tonight, when the telephone rang, Mom answered it. *"Enough!"* she screamed into the receiver and slammed it down, then took it off the hook.

"You think those goddamn reporters care if we're trying to eat our goddamn holiday dinner in peace?" she asked. I looked around the table. Gregory was pouring himself another glass of milk, Bruce was slurping up the last of a long spaghetti strand, and George was licking his plate clean.

Dad hadn't touched his food.

"Starving yourself isn't going to get your job back, so *eat,*" she said. Then she said to all of us, "Your father thinks chewing is a distraction. Your father's afraid chewing might take his mind off football."

Dad nodded his head and sipped his milk. He'd lost fifteen pounds during the last season: skipping meals, getting vitamin shots, drinking milk for dinner. He had two bleeding stomach ulcers: one that acted up during the season and one that bled off-season. He believed milk calmed ulcers. His love of milk was so well known that he became the spokesman for a local dairy that sponsored his weekly pregame radio show. Instead of regular payment, Dad made a deal with the dairy to deliver hundreds of gallons of the stuff to our door daily.

"You know, football was the only thing that didn't bug me," our father said. I knew of a few things that did bug him, beginning with his childhood during the Depression in Detroit, where he and his parents and sister lived in a two-room shack with a single-seat outhouse. His father, Earl, a failed musician, suffered a severe injury on the Ford assembly line that left him with a metal plate in his head and shakes so violent that even alcohol could not sedate his pain. After that, Earl could not keep a job. At ten years old, my father went to work to support the family by planting potatoes for pennies a day. What really bugged my father was allowing his brilliant younger sister, Virginia, to convince him that she should take over the care of their aging parents so that he could pursue his dream of coaching professional football. Only in later years did he realize the depth of her sacrifice when he discovered she had hidden the menial nature of her clerical work in order to allow her brother his rise to fame. These were some of the things that bugged my father.

"Apparently," my mother said.

"That's right," said my father. He said we kids needed to find out what we wanted to do with our lives and then follow that dream. Dad said without a dream, well, maybe we kids weren't really Americans.

"So you better drink your milk, Jen," Dad said to me, "if you want to grow up to be big and strong like Mike Ditka." At such a young age, I had visions of growing up to be big and strong like Mike Ditka. "Iron Mike" Ditka was a solid, six-foot-three, 225-pound tight end who played in five consecutive Pro Bowls, the first tight end selected to professional football's highest honor: the Hall of Fame. My father had drafted Ditka to the Chicago Bears the week I was born in 1961. Our simultaneous entrance into my father's life linked us forever.

When I drank my milk, I envisioned my frilly ballet tutu transforming into sleek football pants, my tight leotard into a loose jersey, my satin slippers into stiff cleated shoes. My long brown hair streamed out of the back of my helmet as I ran onto my field of dreams, and I thought I could hear the announcer scream, "The former Miss America, now the first pro-football girl in the NFL! Jennifer! Jennifer! Jennifer!"

"*Jennifer! Sports!*" everyone around the table was shouting at me.

It was my job to time the turning of the channels on the TV to the sports reports of local television stations. Starting with KTTV Channel 11 at 5:32, I then spun the dial as quickly as I could to catch the 5:35 report on Channel 9; 5:37 on Channel 4; 5:39 on Channel 7; and 5:44 on Channel 2. As one announcer wrapped up hockey, my brothers would shout channels—9! 4! 7! 2!—and I'd get nervous and lose precious seconds of sports news turning to the wrong station. Then I would be called an Idiot, a Moron, and an Ugly Dog, and my father would shake his head, disappointed, once again, in one of his children.

In the days following my father's firing, sports reporters asked the questions we dared not ask: Where was George Allen headed next? Buffalo? Pittsburgh? Washington? How did George Allen, one of the most successful coaches in the league, get fired by Dan Reeves, one of the most respected owners in the league? And most important, would Dan Reeves reinstate George Allen as head coach of the Rams? Just as the morning sports pages might brighten our breakfast, the nightly sportscast could cloud our dinner with new insights we could not expect from our father. Without the media, we kids might never have known which NFL city we would end up in next. An entire day passed after Dad's last firing before I learned about it on the news. Dad had not been able to tell us; Mom was too busy crying. That night after Christmas, I watched my father tell a TV sports reporter, "I haven't told my children yet." So on this New Year's Eve, we all listened attentively to the sports reports.

The first reporter said, "It looks as though George Allen is going to take a year off from football to write the great American novel."

Though this was certainly news to us, it did not sound implausible. We did not even look to our father for any kind of response before I switched channels on the TV. Dad had already written three books. With a master's degree in physical education, my father was known as the resident intellectual of the National Football League. His five-hundred-page master's thesis, "The Technique and Methods Used in Game Scouting by Outstanding Football Coaches," received an A at the University of Michigan. My father often showed me his thesis, letting me feel the weight of the neatly typed and numbered pages. The text spoke a language I would never fully understand—the 34 tab statue right, the 44 tite blast fielder, the 78 ax up and out—but I understood the work that went into making the book. He had typed the entire thesis himself on an old Royal typewriter that he had just given me for Christmas. "To Jeniffer, love, Daddy," read the note taped to the space bar. He always misspelled my name. Sometimes Jeniffer, sometimes Jenifer. Mom said that with over forty men on his Rams roster and over three hundred plays in his playbook, I was lucky my father even remembered my name. I remember wondering that night if my father would want his old Royal typewriter back to write his great American novel.

The next sportscaster said that two years remained on George Allen's contract with the Rams. It would be easy for Dan Reeves to reinstate Allen with the same financial terms. But, the sportscaster wondered, how could Allen know that he would not be fired again?

Though the firing of George Allen shocked many, no one was surprised, he said. The sportscaster reminded us that Dan Reeves had once said, "George Allen is the last coach I will hire." But hadn't Reeves said that about every coach he ever hired—eight in the last twenty-three years—and then given every one the ax?

"What makes George Allen think he is different from any other coach in the National Football League?" the sportscaster asked his viewers. "Coaches are hired to be fired."

"Rot in hell," Mom said to the TV.

Dad rubbed his forehead with the heel of his hand.

Bruce said, "Turn that moron *off*!"

I turned off the little TV.

Now Mom demanded to know the truth. Mom said to Dad, "Do you mind telling me what you plan to do?"

Dad sipped his milk. He gazed at the blank screen of the television.

"Hey, George Allen!" Mom screamed. "Hey, I'm talking to you! Hey, I'm not some goddamn reporter! I'm your goddamn wife!"

Dad finished his milk then. He set his milk glass on the table. He got up from his chair and said, "For cripes sakes, sweetie, all I want to do is coach, you see?"

"Thank you for your insight," Mom said as she got up from the table.

Dad put the telephone receiver back on the hook and said he was going to watch some game films in the basement. One by one, the boys followed Dad down. George followed first. At seventeen years of age, George had a tall, solid build that towered over our six-foot Dad. Gregory followed next. Gregory was only fifteen years old, but his round, hunched shoulders reminded me that Gregory was already burdened by the same posture as Dad. Bruce followed last; with his quick, agile, thirteen-year-old body, he effortlessly raced his father and brothers down the stairs. I stayed upstairs, helping Mom clean the pots and pans. Mom muttered to herself, chain-smoking, flicking ashes into the soapy water that filled the kitchen sink. When we were done, Dad called us down to the basement, where he had set up a PROPERTY OF THE LOS ANGELES RAMS 16-millimeter projector to watch a tall stack of Rams highlight films. Dad wanted us to understand why he was never home for dinners or birthdays or even Christmas. He wanted to teach us the beauty of the sport of football. He wanted us to know the plays as well as he knew them, so well that even with his eyes closed he could decipher what play was run by merely listening to the rhythm of colliding helmets and crashing pads. Remote control in hand, Dad slowed entire games so that we could see, in slow motion, forward, and reverse, the perfection of a particular running back, how his torso remained steady while his hips turned this way and that, faking a defender, twisting out of a tackle, all to gain an extra inch on the grass. Once Dad reran a play so many times that he burned a hole in the film and it caught on fire.

After watching Dad's favorite plays of the 1968 season, he asked us all, "Who wants to watch *The Impossible Dream*?"

We had watched *The Impossible Dream* possibly a thousand times, but we were always willing to see it again. *The Impossible Dream* captured what seemed to be a perfect time in all our lives—our father's second season as head coach in Los Angeles. He had transformed the last-place Rams into a first-place team that led the NFL in defense, earning him his first NFC Coach of the Year award. *The Impossible Dream* was a record of that season set to the music of Dad's favorite Broadway show, *Man of La Mancha*, a musical about Don Quixote.

Even at my young age, I knew the lyrics were corny: "to reach the unreachable star, to right the unrightable wrong." But every time I heard that music while watching those men—Deacon Jones head-slapping his way through a thick mass of linemen, Lamar Lundy making a game-saving tackle, Roman Gabriel gracefully dropping back to pass, Jack Pardee making a diving-interception end-zone catch—my heart would race and my throat would tighten and my legs would curl up under my nightgown and I felt as if we were one family dreaming together in the dark.

The film ended with the next-to-last game of the season: the Rams versus Vince Lombardi's world-champion Green Bay Packers at the Los Angeles Coliseum. Lose, and my father's team would be knocked out of the play-offs; win, and they would be one game closer to entering the play-offs. With fifty-four seconds remaining in the game, the Rams were behind by three points, and the Packers were prepared to punt. My father placed all eleven players on the line to block the punt with not one player back to receive. It was a wild play my father had the Rams practice for days before the game. He determined the only

Packer weak spot to be the team's left-footed punter, and he believed that the game might come down to this very moment—a Rams gamble to block a Packers punt.

The Rams miraculously blocked the punt, and even more miraculously, they recovered the ball and scored a touchdown to win the game.

Seconds later, the film showed my father on the sidelines, crying, shaking his head, as if to say "No, no." My father cried when he lost. He also cried when he won. As he cried, his players toppled him over, lifted him up, and carried him on their shoulders off the field. In another week, he would lead the team to their first play-offs in twelve years.

Watching the film replay these events, I would remember how that night, after the victory, my father was so wound up he needed a sleeping pill to get to sleep. I would also remember how my father awoke the next morning so exhausted that he could not even remember if he had won or lost the game. Still in bed, I could hear him ask my mother, "Did we win or did we lose?"

Now, on New Year's Eve, after *The Impossible Dream*, we all clearly remembered these events. When Gregory turned on the lights, I could see that each one of us had been crying.

When Dan Reeves fired our father, he fired our whole family.

Dad rubbed his eyes.

Mom lit a cigarette.

Gregory rewound the film and carefully placed it in its gray metal canister until the next night's screening.

We all kissed Dad, said "Happy New Year" and "Sweet dreams," and headed upstairs. As I got in my bed, I hoped that maybe what one reporter predicted would come true: that Dan Reeves would change his mind and reinstate my father as head coach of the Rams. More than wanting Dad at home, I wanted to see Dad happy. He just seemed so unhappy to be home with us.

Lying in bed, I listened to my parents talk. Our bedrooms shared a wall. Mom was blaming herself for Dad's firing. She said she knew all along that taking the Rams job had been a mistake. Mom said the moment she saw the Rams colors—gold and blue—she knew we were doomed but didn't dare say anything to Dad then.

"How can you trust a team with such flaky colors?" she asked Dad now. Then she told him, "Look, something good will come out of this—you'll see."

My father kept saying what he had been saying since the morning Dan Reeves had called.

"For cripes sakes, sweetie, don't you understand?" Dad said. "All I want to do is coach. You see?"

Al Silverman

The door to a career opened when Al Silverman (b. 1926) sold his first story to *Sport*, a short item for the front of the book. It was 1947, he'd been out of the Marine Corps for a year, and the magazine, only a year old itself, was helping to revolutionize sportswriting by portraying athletes as human beings and the games they play as a reflection of society. *Sports Illustrated* didn't arrive until 1954, and by then Silverman's byline was appearing in *Sport* regularly next to those of such heavyweights as W. C. Heinz, John Lardner, and Roger Kahn. Silverman eventually segued to editing and ended up running the magazine from 1960 to 1972. He went on become CEO of the Book-of-the-Month Club and editor and publisher of Viking Press. But as prestigious as those jobs were, they meant nowhere near as much to football aficionados as *I Am Third*, his 1970 book with Gale Sayers, the Chicago Bears' poetically fluid running back. It became the genesis of the legendary TV movie *Brian's Song*, the story of the friendship between Sayers, an African American, and his cancer-stricken white teammate and roommate, Brian Piccolo. That same friendship is the backbone of the following story, which Silverman wrote for *Sport's* November 1969 issue. This time, however, it is Sayers who is battling vulnerability as he attempts to come back from his first major knee injury.

Gale Sayers:
The Hard Road Back

GALE SAYERS LAY ON HIS BED in a motel room in Washington, D.C., a day before the Chicago Bears' first exhibition game of the 1969 season. He was wearing white jockey undershorts and glistened like a bronze god. A friend, Henny Young, had come in the room and noted immediately that Sayers' skin was a deeper brown than usual. "You got a tan!" Young exclaimed. "Where'd you get that tan? You been sittin' in the sun?" Sayers laughed, a flashing, self-assured laugh, showing his white teeth and sharing his secret with no one.

The bronze body was hard and lean and the five-inch scar that ran along the inside of his right leg, thigh-bone to knee-bone, knee-bone to leg-bone, that jagged badge of fellowship among professional football players, was not noticeable. But it was there and it filled the room with its presence; unspoken questions, urgent questions, were in the air.

The knee had been cut into last November 10 and cartilage removed and ligaments sewn up and now the finest runner in professional

155

football the last four years—until November 10, 1968—was about to play in his first game since the injury.

Finally, a question was asked, not to Sayers but, warming up, to Sayers' roommate, Brian Piccolo, who lay on his own bed, the whiteness of his skin a startling contrast to Gale's bronze look.

"There's one big difference in Gale now," Piccolo said. "He runs all right until the knee starts to wobble." He laughed and Gale laughed and the visitors in the room laughed and, suddenly, the air was lighter.

Piccolo played fullback at Wake Forest. He was born in Massachusetts but raised, he said, in Fort Lauderdale, Florida.

"By way of He-Hung-High, Mississippi," said Sayers.

Pick grinned. "Don't get me started, Massa Sayers," he said. But he was started. The two had become roommates two years ago in Birmingham, Alabama, before an exhibition game, when the Bears decided hastily to room men according to position.

"Of all the places to spring it on us," said Piccolo. "I came up to the room and saw Gale and said, 'What are you doing here?' But it's been okay. We talk about everything, whatever goes on."

"Mostly race relationships," said Sayers.

"We're okay," said Piccolo, ignoring Sayers, "as long as he doesn't use the bathroom."

Someone asked Sayers, "Who would you want as a roommate if you had a choice?" He replied, "If you're asking me, what white Italian fullback from Wake Forest, I'd say Pick."

Some people find it difficult to understand the black humor, the needling that goes on between Sayers and Piccolo. The two keep it up even on the field. When Ross Montgomery, a rookie running back from Texas Christian, first heard it, he was astonished. Sayers and Piccolo use it therapeutically, as a way of easing into each man's world, a world that has been vastly separate for so long. The needling helps take the strangeness from each man's world, and it lessens tensions.

Sayers said, "Pick, show him the letter you just got." The letter had come from Chicago, from a man who had actually signed his name. It began: "I read where you stay together with Sayers. I am a white man! Most of the people I know don't want anything to do with them. I just don't understand you. Most Italians I have met say that they stink—and they really do."

Piccolo interrupted. "Well, of course that's true. You can't get away from that."

Sayers roared, shaking his head. "I don't like your racist attitude," he said.

The rest of the letter described how the Bears smelled, how they had no quarterback, no receivers, no offensive line. And, it ended: "Sayers will fold up like an accordion when he gets hit."

That was one question Sayers hoped to settle right away in the game with the Redskins. But he was disappointed to learn, earlier in the week, that he would not start, that he would be used only to run back kickoffs and punts.

Jim Dooley, a tall man with curly hair, who wears horn-rimmed glasses and looks more like a scoutmaster than the head coach of the Bears, explained why Sayers would not be starting. "He's fine," Dooley said. "I know he wanted to start this game. I told him, 'Gale, look, we got an inexperienced line. Two of our regulars are out. They make a mistake—boom.' When he scrimmaged last week someone made a mistake and Butkus hit him. He understood afterwards."

Perhaps he understood, but he was not happy. "They're babying me," he said, "I know they are."

All along, Sayers had refused to baby himself. He would not use crutches when his leg was in a cast. Right after the cast was removed, he began to lift weights on the leg. He started jogging in early February. He was examined on February 27 and Dr. Theodore Fox, who had performed the operation, told Sayers, "If there were a game this Sunday, you'd be able to play."

Dr. Fox believes in Sayers. He once defined the special quality that made Sayers the finest runner in football. "Factor X," he called it. "This stands for drive and motivation," he said. "Factor X elevates a player one plateau. It makes a star out of an average player and a superstar out of a star." Dr. Fox said that his operation on Sayers' knee would contribute 60 percent to Sayers' recovery and "Gale's strong desire to return—Factor X—will add the other 40 percent."

There could be no doubt about that desire. "I worked hard to get up there," Sayers had said mid-point in his recuperation period, "and I'm going to work twice as hard to stay up there." At that time, an article in a Chicago newspaper suggested that running backs with knee injuries rarely come back to top form and that Sayers might have to spend the rest of his career as a flanker or at some other position. The article infuriated Gale. "I saved it," he said, "because when I do come back as a runner, I'm gonna show it to him." And then, as if to underscore his determination, he drew out the words—"I . . . Will . . . Be . . . Back."

When rookie camp opened in Rensselaer, Indiana, in mid-July, Sayers was there. His first day in camp, he insisted on taking part in the scrimmage. On one play he started running to his right. Willie Holman, the Bears' huge and mean defensive left end, came across and blindsided Sayers, crashing him to the ground. Others piled on. Sayers got up by himself. He continued to play. Finally, the scrimmage was over. He had carried the ball a half-dozen times, gaining six yards through the middle once, five another time. But no one said a word to him. Sayers felt he was being ignored by the coach, the trainer, the Bears' doctor. But that was the game plan. Trainer Ed Rozy says, "The instructions on him were don't even mention it. Make him forget it."

In desperation Sayers went up to Ed McCaskey, who is the Bears' treasurer, a son-in-law of George Halas and a confidant of Sayers.

"How'd I look?" Sayers asked.

"You're all right," McCaskey said, and turned away.

When the veterans came into camp, Gale was used sparingly. The younger backs, Mike Hull, Ralph Kurek and Montgomery, did most of the hitting. Dooley was going easy with Sayers, but also with veterans Piccolo and Ronnie Bull, who had a record of preseason injuries. But the lack of contact drills worried Gale because of his timing. "With Piccolo or Bull in there," he said, "the timing is different. The guards can be a little slower. But with me in there they've got to go full speed. I'm much quicker, so they have to set up their blocks fast. When I'm in there, I'm running up their backs."

But he did scrimmage a bit. In the Saturday scrimmage before the Redskins' game, he went up the middle. Someone grabbed him by the legs and Dick Butkus rammed him in the chest. Ed Stone, who covers the Bears for *Chicago Today*, was there and says that Sayers seemed to show his old moves. "I talked to Johnny Morris, who's on TV now," Stone says, "and he said that on a sweep it looked like Gale might have the slightest hitch. But," Stone said, "I can't see anything. It looks like it's all there."

On the morning of August 2, at breakfast, Sayers and Piccolo talked about Vince Lombardi and Washington and playing the first exhibition game of the season. Both men were dressed casually, in T-shirts and shorts. A waitress came over to Sayers. "Can I ask you your name?"

she said to him. Pick mumbled loud enough for all to hear, "They all look alike."

Piccolo said he thought he would like to play a little bit for Lombardi before his career was over.

"I can arrange that," Sayers said.

"Would you? I'm tired of playing in your shadow. I want to be a legend in my own time."

The game was less than twelve hours away and they talked about what it meant to them. "You can't treat it as any game," said Sayers. "Do that and you have a short season. Every game is important, and you always like to start off with a win after all that training."

"But it's not like life or death," said Piccolo. "Lombardi and Washington is not the same as Lombardi and Green Bay. Certainly, you want to beat Vince, but it's not the same as beating him with a team that's in your division."

"I know Lombardi's going to be up," Sayers said. "The Redskins are going to be up." His thoughts suddenly became disconnected. "I hate to lose," he said. Then, as if the real meaning of the game had just come to him, he said, "I just want to show people I'm ready."

That was it—to show people that he was ready. It was a secret he had carried around for eight months, and even he did not know the answer. He had jogged, played handball, basketball and touch football. He had run full speed, he had made his patented Sayers cuts, he had been hit in camp and, through it all, the knee had held up. Now there was one more test, contact in battle against another team. He was twenty-six years old with four glorious and rewarding years behind him and now he must know about the future.

While Sayers attended a mid-morning team meeting, I talked with the Bears' trainer, Ed Rozy. He is a grizzled Walter Brennan type who has been with the Bears for twenty-two years. "I'd say Gale's 99 percent now," Rozy said. "The big thing to overcome is the mental attitude, the subconscious feeling—is it or isn't it? See, he's got to believe it. It's got to be proven to him. Better than that, he's got to prove it to himself. That's why he had to go right out that first day in camp and scrimmage and try to get it over with."

Rozy talked with admiration about Sayers' dedication. At Rensselaer, Sayers would come down to the basement at 8 A.M. each day. He would take a whirlpool bath for ten minutes to loosen up the knee, then go into the weight room and lift sixty pounds on the knee, lift those sixty pounds fifty times. Morning and night he would be down there lifting. "That's the mark of a champion," Rozy said. "The guy never quit on himself."

Rozy talked abstractedly about the injury. "It was a beautiful shot," he said of the film clip and still photo of the injury. "It shows Gale planting his foot with pressure applied to the outside of the leg. A beautiful shot," Rozy repeated, as if he were admiring a Picasso painting.

Sayers himself saw little beauty in the shot. One night last March he brought home the Bears' 1968 highlight film to show some friends, including his teammates George Seals and Frank Cornish. When the film came to the injury—the first time Sayers had seen it—Seals hollered, in jest, "Get up! Get up!" And a chill, almost like an electric shock, went through Sayers' body. After the guests had gone, he told his wife, Linda, "I'm never gonna look at that film again as long as I live." A couple of days later when he had to show the film to a group, he left the room just before the injury sequence. Eventually, he got over it, said to himself, the hell with it, and stayed and watched.

It was, no doubt, the most traumatic moment of his life. The Bears were at home and, in the second quarter, held a comfortable 24–6 lead over the 49ers in the ninth game of the season. Sayers had gained 32 yards in ten carries. That gave him 856 yards rushing for the season so far, well ahead of all the NFL runners: he seemed on his way to the best year of his career, perhaps a record-breaking year.

In the huddle, quarterback Virgil Carter called for a toss to Sayers. Gale broke left, hoping to go outside the defense behind the blocking of tackle Randy Jackson. The 49ers' right linebacker, Harold Hays, began to string along the line, keeping his hands on Jackson in order to control him and prevent Sayers from breaking to the outside. Right cornerback Kermit Alexander, who also had the responsibility of turning the play inside, was trying to strip his blocker. Hays was controlling Jackson and defensive tackle Kevin Hardy was barreling down the line toward Sayers. So Gale knew he couldn't go wide and he tried to slip inside the blocker, as he often does.

At the instant he planted his foot, Alexander hit him with a low, rolling block. The cleats of Sayers' right shoe were anchored in the turf, preventing give and the knee took the full shock of the blow.

Sayers knew immediately that the knee was gone. He thinks he turned to Alexander, who was standing over him, and said, "It's gone."

He remembers motioning to the bench to come and get him and putting his arms around a couple of the Bear players. Then he passed out.

He came to as he reached the sidelines. Dr. Fox was there. "It's gone, Doc," Sayers said.

Dr. Fox checked the knee. "It's okay," he said, and started to walk away.

"Come back here!" Sayers screamed. "Tell it to me straight."

Dr. Fox looked at Sayers for a moment, then said, "Yes, you have torn ligaments in your knee."

At that moment, Sayers felt an overwhelming sense of loss, also of self-pity. He asked himself, why me, why did it have to be me? And he began to cry.

He was operated on late that afternoon. The quicker the surgeon can get in there, the better job he can do. "You wait twenty-four hours after one of those things," Dr. Fox said, "and the injury is like a bag of mush. It really would be like trying to stitch together two bags of cornmeal mush."

In medical slang, Sayers' injury is called "The Terrible Triad of O'Donoghue." This describes the tears of the three ligaments in the knee and is named after Dr. Don H. O'Donoghue of the University of Oklahoma, the dean of football physicians. It is a common operation now. The estimate is that there are fifty thousand football victims each year, fifty thousand who require knee surgery.

The operation took three hours and when Sayers came out of it he remembers the doctor saying, everything's okay, and Sayers not believing him. "You wouldn't lie to me? You wouldn't lie to me?" he kept repeating. Linda Sayers was there and she says that Gale actually got up and started screaming to Dr. Fox: *"You wouldn't lie to me?"*

He is much more emotional than has been generally understood. He is much deeper, too. In his first couple of years with the Bears he was very shy, a little frightened, unsure of himself off the field and wary, very wary, of strangers. He began to change about two years ago. Symbolically, he stopped cutting his hair short for football. He wears a natural now and someone wrote him a letter blaming his knee injury on his "long" hair. He became a stockbroker for Paine, Webber, Jackson and Curtis in the Chicago office. He worked on his public speaking. He began to respond to people, and to the world around him. Recently, Ed McCaskey has helped make a reader of Sayers. McCaskey gave Sayers *The Autobiography of Malcolm X* and Sayers devoured it in three days. In quick succession he read a novel, *Siege*, Eldridge Cleaver's *Soul on Ice* and the classic Ralph Ellison novel *Invisible Man*. All are on Negro themes and all seemed meaningful to Sayers. "Something," he says, "keeps you going into books and you don't want to put them down." He seemed to relate most to Malcolm X. "He was a drug addict for so many years and got out of it," Sayers said. "I believe he could do anything he wanted."

He admires people like that, people who can overcome. He is that way himself. In his rookie year, he would vomit before every game. Finally, he decided he had to stop, that he was using up too much nervous energy. "I would go out of the dressing room," he said, "tired, beat." So he started talking to other players, thinking of other things and he disciplined himself to stop vomiting.

Now the discipline, the fight, concerns the knee. He rested in his Washington motel room an hour before the team dinner, which would be followed by the ankle taping and then the bus ride to Robert F. Kennedy Stadium and a football game. The television set was on. The Baltimore Orioles were playing the Oakland Athletics and Sayers watched idly. And as he watched, the question was slipped to him:

"Do you think about the knee?"

"I think about it," he said. "I never stop thinking about it. When I'm in my room listening to records, I think about it. Every day a thought about it goes through my mind. I know it's fine, but I think about it."

He has considered seriously about going to a hypnotist. "I remember Don Newcombe went to one about his fear of flying. If I knew of a hypnotist in Chicago, I would probably go to one." But then he said he was not sure that he was the type to be hypnotized.

His mind was a jumble of emotion. He thought of an old teammate, Andy Livingston, who had hurt a knee against the Packers a couple of years ago, and was never the same again. But he also thought of the old Bear halfback, Willie Galimore, who had survived two knee operations and come back fine (only to die in an automobile crash); and of Tommy Mason, who has had six knee operations and still plays. Gale blamed the failures on human weaknesses. "They didn't work at it," he said. "I worked at it." He groped for words. Finally, words came. "I consider this my game. A damn injury like that is not going to keep me out of it."

Looking at Sayers in the Bear dressing room deep beneath RFK Stadium, the strong statement he had made a few hours earlier seemed remote and irrelevant. He sat slumped in front of his locker. It was five minutes to seven and he would have to go out on the field for pregame drill in fifteen minutes. He was wearing his cleats, his white game pants with the orange piping down the side, and a white T-shirt. He sat on a folding chair in front of his locker. He was bent over. His head was bowed, his eyes were closed. He was leaning on his elbows, holding his head in his hands, his two thumbs resting between his eyes. He sat there quiet as stone, as if in a trance. He was unapproachable.

George Seals, the 265-pound offensive guard, the man Sayers had ridden behind for so many of his long-gainers, was dressing in a corner. A close friend of Sayers, he was asked whether he felt any extra pressure to protect Sayers because of the knee. Seals shook his head. "To me," he said, "that would be conceding something. Football is a very emotional game. When you step out onto that field, you cannot concede a thing. Gale certainly wouldn't want it that way."

Seals, who had his own knee operation last March and was still far from being 100 percent, was with Sayers when the cast was removed from Sayers' leg. He was astonished to see that there was very little atrophy in the leg. "He's not human," Seals said. "After he got that cast off, he'd go out in the afternoon, morning, every night, doing things constantly. Many athletes come back from knee injuries lacking quite a bit. I feel if Sayers comes back, he'll be the one that comes back all the way."

And still Sayers sat there, bent over, trancelike, almost in the fetal position. Bennie McRae, the Bears' veteran defensive back came over, leaned down and whispered to Sayers: "Are you ready, man?" Sayers nodded. "You all right? You're gonna be all right," McRae said soothingly. "You're ready, I know you're ready." He put an arm on Sayers' shoulder. "Hang loose." Sayers nodded again. McRae drifted away and Sayers remained cast in stone.

I was thinking various things. I was thinking about the knee... how it happened, could it happen again, how would it hold up... hoping I could make it through the game. That's the mental torture of football and I think this is going to afflict me as long as I play this game.

Finally, it was 7:10 and the players started out. Backfield coach Ed Cody came close to Sayers and said, "About a minute, Gale."

Sayers shook himself, rose, slipped on his white jersey with the big navy-blue numerals, 40, picked up his helmet and clattered out of the room.

As you come through the runway leading up to the field, a distorted sound hits you, an eerie sound, like a piece of heavy machinery sucking out air. It is only when you get through the runway and hit the dugout that you finally recognize the sound—it is the roar of the crowd.

It was a stifling night. The temperature was in the eighties, there was no breeze stirring and the humidity menaced the soul. The weather forecast was for scattered thundershowers, but the clouds in that Washington twilight looked benevolent.

Sayers was throwing left-handed with Ronnie Bull, he and Bull trotting up and down the field exchanging passes. Then the Washington Redskin players poured out of their dugout and milled around the entrance. Sam Huff was leading them. He stood there, waiting for them all to come out before leading the charge across the field. "Everyone up?" he asked. Vince Lombardi, wearing a shortsleeved shirt, black tie, black pants and the look of a bus driver, grew impatient with Huff. "Okay," Lombardi barked, "let's go, let's take 'em." There was joy and exhilaration in his voice as he ran out on the field with his men. Clearly, he was glad to be back in the game.

Sayers, taking part in a passing drill, caught a short pass and ran by Lombardi. The Redskin coach stopped him. They shook hands. "I'm very glad to see that you've overcome your injury," Lombardi said. Sayers mumbled his thanks.

Sayers remembered meeting Lombardi in Commissioner Pete Rozelle's office in New York last spring, the spring of his recuperation, the spring of his anxieties. Lombardi said to Sayers, "How do you feel, son? I hope to see you out there this fall." And Sayers said, "You'll see me August 2." And so he had.

Now it was 7:30 and two Bear players started the kicking drill. The punts came out of the sky like fireworks, except that the boom was heard first, then the ball was seen soaring in the air. Sayers caught the first punt and ran it back fifteen yards, crouched, darting, making the moves that had thrilled people for the last four years. He caught another punt, then a third, and a fourth. Then he was in another pass drill. He went down and out, toward the Redskin side of the field, taking a long pass over his shoulder. Two skinny Redskin kids, Number 5 and Number 3, the field-goal kickers, were together when he went by. They looked at Sayers, then turned to say something to each other, gossiping like a couple of old maids at a soda fountain.

Finally, the drill was over and the Bears returned to the dressing room to put on their shoulder pads and wait for the start.

It had been raining for five minutes when the teams lined up for the kickoff, a hard, slanting rain with thunder and lightning and a rising wind. The field, especially the skin part, the Washington Senators' infield, was already filling up with puddles.

The Bears were the receiving team. Gale Sayers was deep, at his five-yard line, with Ross Montgomery stationed just in front of him. Just as the kicker moved forward, Sayers hollered to Montgomery to deploy right. Sayers, who captains the kick and punt return team, always tells the other deep back where to go. The idea is for Sayers to cover three-quarters of the field, to make sure that he gets the football.

He got the football. He took it easily on his six-yard line and started straight up the middle. One man broke through the wedge and came on to challenge Sayers. "I feel I can always beat any man one-on-one," Sayers has said, "and two-on-one I can beat 75 percent of the time." Sayers gave the one man his inside move, a head and shoulder fake, and the man was out of it and Sayers was flashing to the right, toward the sidelines.

"The thing that makes Gale different," Brian Piccolo had said earlier, "is the way he's able to put a move on somebody and not lose a step. He gives a guy a little fake and he's full speed. I give a guy a move like that and it takes me fifteen yards to get in stride."

Sayers was in full stride now, streaking down the sidelines. Two Washington defensive backs angled in on him around the Redskin forty. One lunged at him and Sayers just pushed him away with his left arm. The other threw himself at Sayers, jostling him momentarily. But Sayers kept his feet, regained control and sped triumphantly into the end zone. There was a purity, a shining purity to that run, that contrasted in a strange and rather beautiful way with the indecent weather and the spongy field. The first time he had carried the ball in combat since his knee injury, which was the worst kind of a knee injury you can have, he had broken one. It was as if all the questions had been answered, all the doubts resolved about the condition of

Gale Sayers. It was an illusion, of course; it was much too early to form a judgment on Sayers' recovery. But the illusion was heightened by the clap of thunder that accompanied Sayers' last step into the end zone.

One illusion was, however, quickly dispelled. It was not a touchdown after all. The referee ruled that Sayers had stepped out of bounds on the Redskin twenty-five. Sayers said later that he could not see the sideline markers because they had been obscured by the rain. But it was still a sixty-nine-yard run and surely it held some meaning for Gale Sayers, for the Chicago Bears—and maybe for those fifty thousand players who fall victim to a knee injury every year.

And that was all there was to the game, really. Later, the Bear coaches had to throw out the films of the game because nothing could be seen. After the Sayers' run the rain intensified and the entire first half was played in a blinding cloudburst that ruined the field and left the players dispirited. The Redskins won 13 to 7. Sayers came out on the field twelve times, but carried the ball only once more. Dick Butkus took a short kickoff and lateraled to Sayers who piled seventeen yards up the middle before he was pulled down in the glop.

The next morning Sayers was eating breakfast at 7:15. He had hardly slept that night. He says it usually takes him a day and a half to unwind after a game. He ordered ham and eggs but ate sparingly.

He listened while a friend read accounts of the game from the Washington morning newspapers. Sayers, it seemed, had almost gotten equal play with the Redskins. One story began this way: "It took the sellout crowd of 45,988 at RFK Stadium last night only a matter of seconds to see for themselves that Gale Sayers is as good as ever...."

He grinned when he heard that. He thought it was true and now he felt more assured because he had passed the first test. After months of hard work, months filled with doubt and pain and the mental torture that only a knee victim can understand, he had passed his first test. He knew it was only a beginning, but it was a good beginning.

Jim Murray

There was a time when it seemed that every aspiring sportswriter in America wanted to be Jim Murray (1919–1998). He turned his *Los Angeles Times* column into a nationally syndicated comedy club with lines that are quoted and laughed at to this day: "Buster Douglas looked like something that should be floating over a Thanksgiving Day parade." He could even be funny when the subject was serious, as it was at the 1966 Indianapolis 500: "Gentlemen, start your coffins!" Murray warmed up for the sports beat by working as a rewrite man for Hearst's *Los Angeles Herald Examiner* and a Hollywood reporter for *Time* magazine, a gig that once involved taking Marilyn Monroe to dinner and getting an introduction to Joe DiMaggio as a bonus. After seven years writing for *Sports Illustrated*, Murray in 1961 headed to the *Times* and the glory that put him in the same spotlight with Red Smith and Jimmy Cannon. He stayed on the job right up until his death, like Smith and Grantland Rice before him, and all these years later he remains L.A.'s favorite sports columnist. It's easy to understand why when you read what he had to say about the Jets' historic, American Football League–validating victory over the Colts in Super Bowl III. Only Jim Murray could have watched that game and imagined missionaries swallowing cannibals.

Don't Look Now... but the Funny Little League is No. 1

Miami, Fla., January 13, 1969

FIRST OF ALL, are you sitting down? Be sure who you tell this to or they'll think you've been drinking.

On Sunday afternoon, the canary ate the cat. The mailman bit the police dog. The minnow chased the shark out of its waters. The missionaries swallowed the cannibals. The rowboat rammed the battleship. The mouse roared, and the lion jumped up on a chair and began to scream for help. The first thing that's going to surprise you about the Super Bowl game is the closeness of the score. But, hang onto your hat. If you think THAT'S a shocker, wait till I get to the punchline.

The—come closer and let me whisper this—the NEW YORK JETS are the Super Champions of football! Cross my heart! That funny little team from that funny little league they left on pro football's doorstep a few years back. You know the one—the team whose checks bounced and so did their quarterbacks.

And you know that smart-alecky quarterback they got for $400,000 and the NFL sat down and like to have busted laughing? Well, turns out he was a bargain. You know, they called him "Broadway Joe" and he went around wearing women's fur coats and he closed up more bars than Carrie Nation? A sleep-to-noon guy who had been a model youth. He didn't smoke till he started kindergarten and he never drank in high school till the sun went down. And when someone said the Jets had a "Boozer" in the backfield, someone thought it was a description instead of a name.

They said (Normal Van Brocklin did) that Broadway Joe would be playing in his first professional game in the Super Bowl. Well, he likes it better than that game they play over in that other league. He got beat three times over in that league.

They said the Jets were the third-best team in their own league. If so, it's a good thing they didn't send the best. Everybody would have switched over to Heidi.

I would say, on the basis of what we saw Super Sunday, the NFL is a couple of years away. I mean they have INDIVIDUAL performers, but the AFL appears to be better in teams.

Namath said that the Colts' Earl Morrall would be third string on the Jets, but he may have overestimated him. Of the nine passes Morrall completed before his coach invited him to spend the rest of the game resting up for next year, only six went to his own team. He has a good arm, but they might want to check his color perception.

It could be said to be a contest only if you consider a public hanging a contest. As usual, if you want the executioner, you have to give points. But the funny thing in this game was, the books put their expert eyes on this match and said you could have the Jets and 17½ points and there was no limit to what you could bet. If you wanted Baltimore, you had to come up with 18 points. And they wouldn't take a check. Bookmakers are perched on ledges all over America today. For them, the score of the game at the payoff window was Jets 33½, Colts, 7.

I would say the Colts were terrible, but that would be an overstatement. They weren't that good. It's hard to believe this team went through 30 NFL games and only lost two in the past two years.

The Colts started the game as if the other guys hadn't showed up yet. The first three plays gained 36 yards. It looked as if the only thing that might happen to them is that they might get bored to death, or have trouble staying awake. Then, they gradually lost their poise, their tempers, and, finally, the game. Namath picked them apart as though they were a safe he had memorized the combination to. The right side of the Baltimore line was as wide open as a Yukon saloon on a Saturday night. Jet halfbacks were fighting to get to run through it or by it.

The Jets' locker room was awash with the heady bubble of gloat. The Jets wear their names on their backs like most of the teams in the AFL. The other league grudgingly wears numbers. They figure anybody who doesn't know who they are must be as out of touch as Judge Crater.

"Where was their defense? Didn't it show up?" an ex-nobody in the Jets' dressing room named Earl Christy demanded. Larry Grantham, who has been in the league on this team since the days when it wasn't even safe to take cash (without biting on it), was trumpeting, "Let them have the College All-Star game."

"$15,000 apiece!" glowed Gerry Philbin.

Five years ago, you could have bought the franchise for that—maybe the league.

It was like the turkey having the farmer for dinner, the rabbit shooting the hunter, the dove pulling the feathers out of the eagle.

The worm had not only turned, it was chasing the early bird right down the street and up a tree. And Broadway Joe can be singing the old Jimmy Durante tune, "You Know Darn Well I Can Do Without Broadway, But Can Broadway Do Without Me?"

Even at 400 grand, he may be the biggest bargain in Manhattan since they gave those Indians all those beads and started to put in subways. As for the NFL, it will have to start building to catch up.

Larry Merchant

If you go into a certain kind of bar in New York, one where the sports page is read as devoutly as the best (though not necessarily best-selling) new novel, you're liable to find someone who can still recite the lineup the pre-Rupert Murdoch *Post* trotted out in the 1960s and 1970s: Paul Zimmerman, Vic Ziegel, Milton Gross, Leonard Lewin, Neil Offen. There might even be someone who remembers the chill that set in when the engagingly irascible Leonard Shecter left for books and magazines in 1965, and how quickly the temperature went back up once people started reading the columnist who replaced him, Larry Merchant (b. 1931). Smart, funny, irreverent, socially conscious, and a former football star at Brooklyn's Lafayette High, Merchant quickly became the heart of the *Post*'s sports section. That didn't surprise anyone who knew about the revolution he had led as the *Philadelphia Daily News'* sports editor. Now, of course, he is best known for the trenchant commentary he provided on HBO's boxing telecasts for thirty-five years. At midcareer, Merchant wrote two books about football, ... *And Every Day You Take Another Bite* (1971) and *The National Football Lottery* (1973). The former is the source of this look at Joe Namath, a new breed of hero best understood by a new breed of sportswriter.

from

... And Every Day You Take Another Bite

ACROSS THE FIELD he came in that ambling poolroom slouch. For much of America Joe Namath is the only man on the field when he is on a field, but this time he was alone literally, ambling toward a television interview through a valley of boos and hoots. It was half time at an exhibition game between the Jets and the Giants in the Yale Bowl, New Haven, Connecticut, and here came Joe Namath in violet bell bottoms—boo—white sockless loafers—hoot—a flowered shirt—boohoot—helmeted with a beautiful coiffeur—hootboo. He was, as always, one of the truly fantastic species of fauna ever to appear on a playing field. And, as always, he inspired catatonic fits among the multitudes the likes of which we haven't seen since *Marat/Sade*.

Joe Namath, threat to the moral order of the universe, is one of the most important athletes this country has ever spawned.

What foul deed had he done to arouse the natives this time? His annual summer caper. For the fourth straight summer Joe Namath had blasphemed, launching dialogues of righteous debate on his fitness to throw a football in polite society. Having made a movie with Ann-Margret over the winter, a movie with much kissy-kissy and other bad stuff, he arrived weeks late for training. Since walking up stairs was torture for Namath's wrecked knees, they certainly could do with as little training as he could get away with. And exhibitions were a bloody bore anyway; he'd be twice the fool to risk his fool neck and knees in glorified scrimmages.

But he was Joe Namath and so his absence had become an international incident. A teammate, linebacker Al Atkinson, made a delayed appearance too, after threatening retirement, partially, he said, because he'd like to see his quarterback grow up. Laid bare for the fans was another rare view into the body politic of a football team, sliced open by a quarterback who defied every holy-holy about the game.

There is an undercurrent of tribalism on every team, based on race, position, salary, geography, life style, and so on. It rarely is harmful, it seldom comes to the surface, and winning usually keeps it submerged. But the pros and cons of Namath, who had led the Jets to a championship and a division title in the previous two seasons, polarized his teammates. Predictably, with a couple of exceptions, they were split along offensive and defensive lines (although most players liked him personally). One notable exception was Matt Snell, the fullback, who made no secret of his contempt for what he saw as a double standard in the organization's indulgence of Namath. Yet nobody blocked harder or more efficiently for Namath than Snell: that was his job.

Actually there was little the organization could do about Namath except hand him the ball and say, "Play nice," as the Lions did with Bobby Layne, who raised hell in his day, and as many teams have done with many superstars. But the flap over Namath and Atkinson was totally incomprehensible to fans who had been brainwashed to believe that ball teams, especially football teams, are love machines. Unless they play in Green Bay and can't avoid bumping into each other in the street, some players might not talk to each other for years simply because they play on separate units, practice on separate ends of the field, attend separate meetings, live in separate worlds. Maybe that's what the pre-game prayer is all about, a way to introduce the players to each other.

Said Dave Herman, offensive guard, about the anguished cries of dissension rising once more from the ashes of yesterday's newspapers: "When Joe came back I felt like throwing a bouquet of roses to him. He'll be there when we need him."

Joe Namath played four games of football before he suffered a wrist injury and was sidelined for the duration of last season, a season that then needed the heroics of George Blanda, a forty-three-year-old quarterback, and Tom Dempsey, a no-toed place kicker who kicked a 63-yard field goal, to rescue it from a severe depression in drama. Still, America's most admired writer, its most controversial public servant and its most Olympian political columnist dramatized the importance of being Joe Namath.

Norman Mailer on the National Aeronautics and Space Administration's antiseptic promotional approach to moonshots: "Unless they get someone like Joe Namath as an astronaut, they're in terrible trouble," because the public will lose interest.

J. Edgar Hoover: "You won't find long hair or sideburns à la Joe Namath here. There are no hippies in the FBI. The public has an image of what an agent should look like."

James Reston: "Joe Namath is not only in tune with the rebellious attitude of the young, but he doubles it. He defies both the people who hate playboys and the people who hate bullyboys. He is something special: a long-haired hard-hat, the anti-hero of the sports world."

You have to go back to Babe Ruth to find an athlete who had the impact on his game that Namath has. Ruth brought baseball back after the Black Sox Scandal by swinging a bat with theatrical gusto. Namath changed the face of professional football with one orgasmic victory, in the 1969 Super Bowl. Ruth's spats with management were every bit as controversial as Namath's. But Ruth kept his Ruthian boozing and wenching private, and his historic "bellyache" has been identified by some historians as a social disease. The importance of Joe Namath is that there is very little about him that is private.

Bursting on the scene in the age of television, in a hot game, football, and at a time of social upheaval, especially among the young, Namath's impact as old-fashioned *bon vivant* and new-fashioned iconoclast is staggering.

He liberated the athlete from the centuries-old chastity belt of false morality. The athlete doesn't have to list his sexual conquests on the statistical charts, as Namath does, but neither is he compelled any more to present himself as a defender of the faith and neatest of tricks—virile eunuch. He can even cry real tears as Namath did in public when he said he was quitting football because he had been ordered by Pete Rozelle to get rid of his bar.

The immediate visible result was that athletes like Johnny Bench and Derek Sanderson began showing up on television as pleasantly hip flip young men, the new breed of jock, personable entertainers rather than neuter bullet heads. (Although Jack Concannon of the Bears complained, "They want us to play like Joe Namath, but we can't look like him.") Fran Tarkenton observed that it was possible for an athlete to take a drink in public now without being accused of getting roaring drunk. Son of a Georgia preacher, Tarkenton said Namath had broken through his stereotyped ideas about people. Looks and life styles, Tarkenton decided, could be deceiving. He understood better than most that it took more than pure talent to play football the way Joe Namath does.

That message might be trickling out to America subliminally. Meanwhile the fallout from Namath's white-shoes-long-hair-anti-Establishment image was upsetting many parents because it created serious problems in selling athletes as plastic heroes. This was a good thing but the parents didn't think so. Wrote Pete Axthelm in *Newsweek*, in a piece on a heralded rookie quarterback: "Terry Bradshaw looms not only as a potential superstar, but also as a knight-errant of sport, destined to somehow guide the youth of America away from Namath's swinging broads and bars and into a promised land of the clean-cut and the fair." But it's never going to happen again, because the youth simply will defect to the next sonic-boom rock group or whatever, as they may have been about to do when Namath proved to be one of their own.

Finally Namath influenced the uneasy truce between uptight high school and college coaches and their players. The coaches thought the kids were going to hell in a communal bus because they were showing dangerous signs of being part of their generation. With Namath proving their point, players have gotten some concessions in being treated more like real students, i.e., people. They still have a long way to go before coaches concede that their authority isn't challenged by a mustache but total alienation has been averted. (A sociologist at UCLA took a survey that showed there were fewer candidates for football in Los Angeles high schools because the kid who plays the guitar and has a social conscience has as much status among his peers as a kid who plays tackle. Drops in turnouts for high school teams have been reported in other cities. It is something for the coaches to think about.)

Elinor Kaine inadvertently took her own sociological survey—on Joe Namath. Possessed of one Joe Namath white shoe, given to her by a Jet equipment man, she offered it as a prize to her readers in a letter-writing contest. She got a nationwide response from girls who thought it would be better than a glass slipper, from boys who thought it would transform them into passing demons. An entire class in a grade school in Des Moines, Iowa, entered the contest; there's a teacher out there with his or her finger on the pulse of America.

The idea of little boys and girls hero-worshipping Joe Namath was enough to make William Buckley's eyebrows quiver with fear for the decline of Western civilization. For behind much of the paranoia about Namath were clearly defined moral imperatives. Not only did he seem to defy conventions of hard work and team play ethics, but he made the titillating confession that he was an All-Pro at sexual fore and post game play. He was quoted in *Playboy* magazine to the effect that he left the Catholic Church because he didn't see anything wrong with sex. He checked his trophy room and counted three hundred pubic scalps. He put his name to a boorish bump-and-run autobiography that might have been titled "The Sensuous Quarterback." Inexplicably he failed to reveal whether his quick release was a condition of all his bodily functions, or just of his arm. Joe Namath's Beaver Falls Imperative hasn't won any popularity contests with women's liberationists—"You've heard the old saying about there being a boy for every girl in the world?" said comedian Flip Wilson of Namath. 'Well, here's the boy they meant."—but his candor stripped away the last of the jock taboos. Bud Wilkinson once expressed the moral imperative of athletes this way: "Drinking a beer won't hurt a player physically. But it is a chink in his moral armor." But that implies guilt, and there is no guilt if it doesn't violate a personal code of ethics.

There are jocks who could have carnal knowledge of baby sea otters and sleep the sleep of the pure.

Larry Grantham, a teammate of Namath's, said he hardly knew there was an opposite sex until he went to college, so wrapped up in football was he in his small town Mississippi high school. Coaches, as guardians of sex-is-evil morality, used to warn that sex ("Sleep with your hands over the blankets") could steal your energy in the night. What they really were concerned about was that sex, or love, especially love, would divert athletes from the monastic dedication they think is required to score touchdowns. Few if any jocks pay attention to such nonsense in college and none in the pros, for they discovered long before psychologists did that sex is not harmful physiologically and that sex and games are mutually compatible parts of the same world of intense experience.

Weeb Ewbank put the matter in professional perspective when an assistant coach told him that the Jets were being seduced by college girls at their training site. "That's one good thing about this place," Ewbank said. "They don't have to go driving to New York at all hours for it."

But nobody throws touchdown passes every Sunday or scores every Sunday night, and that goes for Joe Namath too. A movie actress with a weakness for quarterbacks, and linebackers, pitchers, forwards, goalies and the rest of the menagerie, tells a touching story. On her first date with a famous unmarried quarterback, at an all-star game, he put her up in a suite in a hotel. But she was stricken by a sudden case of virtue and informed him that he would have to return to his hotel and try again on second down. She retired to her bedroom, only to find, hours later, the quarterback asleep on a couch outside her door. "Get out," she cried. "You're just trying to make those guys think you're sleeping with me." He slinked out, defeated. Football is a game of adversity.

The first hint anyone had that Joe Namath was going to stand astride the land like the Colossus of Rhodes came in 1967, just before his third season. Although the Jets hadn't had a winning season with him, he had already guaranteed the success of the team and the AFL. He did this with an electrifying performance in his last college game, in the Orange Bowl. Sonny Werblin, president of the Jets and a prominent executive in show business, said it was the greatest pilot (test) film he ever saw, and he signed Namath to the celebrated $400,000 contract. Presto: the Jets sold thirty thousand season tickets, the AFL secured its beachhead in New York, television ratings climbed and the merger with the NFL was ordained. The Jets, purchased by Werblin and friends for less than a million dollars in 1963, are valued today at about $20 million.

Now, in the summer of 1967, Namath walked out of pre-season camp because, he said, of personal problems. He spent a night on the town in New York, got into a scuffle with a sportswriter, was fined $500 by the Jets—and made headlines all over the country for three days. He had arrived.

After a winning season, Namath caused another furor the next summer when he missed several exhibitions due to a salary dispute. A sportswriter for the *Times* recommended that the Jets trade him because a team couldn't win with a selfish player like that. It was the funniest story of the year until Tex Maule wrote in *Sports Illustrated* just before the Super Bowl four months later: "Most experts, for unfathomable reasons, have conceded the Jets an edge at quarterback."

There has never been a season quite like 1968 or a game quite like the 1969 Super Bowl for a football player, one twenty-five-year-old presence confronting the country with its moral hangups. Namath grew a Fu Manchu mustache, then a stylish rage, and a dozen Jets followed suit. Milt Woodward, commissioner of the AFL, wrote them a letter saying it was bad for football's image to be identified with extremist elements in society. Joe Namath said that Milt Woodward could tell everyone how extremely brutal and savage football is if he seeks the truth. Someone stuffed a packet of religious literature into Namath's locker; Namath stuffed it back in the donor's hand and said, wrong pew. A black player said Namath was responsible for the racial harmony on the team, because of his unaffected color-blindness. Namath said, "I stink," after he threw five interceptions in a game. And the Jets didn't lose for another year.

Before the heavyweight championship fight between Muhammad Ali and Joe Frazier last March, comedian Bill Cosby said, "I'm so excited I wish they'd fight a whole week." Joe Namath had that kind of week at the Super Bowl.

Joe Namath is no hippie but in January 1969 a young person who questioned authority, religion and society's hypocrisy, and who didn't take a haircut every three weeks, was automatically hooked up with Allen Ginsberg, Haight-Ashbury and dirty feet. Namath drove a Lincoln, lived in a penthouse, was a devout hedonist, affected Frank Sinatra's glass-in-hand insouciance, and would rather go one-on-one with Dick Butkus than sit in the mud for three days at Woodstock to listen to rock music. But America saw him as a hippie—there was no doubt in anyone's mind that if he were a girl he wouldn't wear a brassiere—and that was that. He was ranked alongside the Beatles, Bobby Dylan and Muhammad Ali as symbols of a decade's decadence.

Flying to Miami Namath began a week-long assault on all the time-honored traditions of pregame conduct. He remarked that there were four or five quarterbacks in the AFL superior to Earl Morrall, who was the most valuable player in the NFL. Since Namath obviously was one of the four or five, the interpretation given this candid and accurate appraisal of the talent in the room was that Namath was saying he was better than Morrall. A no-no.

Namath was cast in the role of the villain from that moment on, stealing the role from teammate Johnny Sample, who came by it naturally and eagerly and, what's more, was a former Colt. When Namath failed to show up at a photographer's session the first day in Miami, noting that 10 A.M. was an indecent hour for a civilized man to get up, it was taken as further evidence of his lack of team spirit and disrespect for authority. A second no-no.

When he made headlines after a night-club debate with Lou Michaels of the Colts, insisting the Jets would win, it was feared that Namath had a death wish. Third no-no.

This was followed by his famous "guarantee" that the Jets would win, given at a banquet, and that no-no convinced wizened NFL heads that he should be muzzled for his own safety because he was giving the Colts so much ammunition—newspaper clippings—that they would break his legs like uncooked spaghetti. The Colts started as seventeen-point favorites and gained so much support that the spread soared to nineteen and higher by game time.

What happened on that Sunday, January 12, 1969, was best described by George Sauer, who caught ten passes from Namath. It was, said Sauer, like the day Copernicus told earthlings that the sun didn't rotate around them. "It must have been fantastic to find out you weren't the center of the universe," he said.

For three hours 75 million viewers on television saw the end of the world as they knew it. And it blew minds. They had been convinced that the AFL was a planet to the NFL's sun. They had been convinced by the pro football mystique that a quarterback had to be Bart Starr or Johnny Unitas to win championships, leading by example, modesty, discipline, character and attendance at communion breakfasts. The quarterback was the new American ideal of sound mind and body. Joe Namath might be able to throw a football, but his mind was scattered and his body vulnerable. For the fans who bought that theology whole, it was a three-hour horror show. Attacking a defense that had set NFL records, Namath ran the game as resourcefully as Starr and threw lightning bolts like Unitas. The Jets won 16–7.

Arthur Kretchmer

Arthur Kretchmer (b. 1941) was hired on as an associate editor at *Playboy* in 1966 and, six years later, beat out his fellow Young Turks to become the magazine's editorial director. While Kretchmer was working his way up the masthead, his own byline occasionally graced the magazine. He interviewed Jesse Jackson in 1969 and wrote the following profile of Dick Butkus, the bone-crunchingest linebacker the Chicago Bears ever employed, for *Playboy*'s October 1971 issue. Chicago was first and foremost a Bears town and Butkus was the product of one of its working-class neighborhoods. As fate had it, *Playboy*'s editorial offices were in Chicago, too, which meant Kretchmer was a fan before he put on his journalist's hat. One worries about the transition after seeing him refer to his subject in print as "my man." It's enough to make a practicing skeptic think he was too chummy with Butkus, but skeptics can be wrong. No football anthology should be without Kretchmer's classic story.

Butkus

ICK BUTKUS slowly unraveled his mass from the confines of a white Toronado and walked into the Golden Ox Restaurant on Chicago's North Side. He is built large and hard, big enough to make John Wayne look like his loyal sidekick. When he walks, he leads with his shoulders, and the slight forward hunch gives him an aura of barely restrained power. He always seems to be ready.

As he walked through the restaurant, he was recognized by most of the men sitting at lunch. But the expression on their faces was not the one of childlike surprise usually produced by celebrities. It was of frightened awe. It read: "Holy Christ! He really *is* an ape. He could tear me apart and he might *love* it."

Ten rolling steps into the restaurant, with all eyes fixed on him, he was stopped by an ebullient lady with a thick German accent, a member of the staff. "Mr. Boot-kuss!" she scolded him. "What have you done to yourself? You look so thin."

He smiled shyly. Not even the ferocious Dick Butkus can handle a rampant maternal instinct. "Aw," he said. "I'm just down to my playing weight."

Butkus chose a table in a far corner of the restaurant. It was a Friday afternoon, two days before the Chicago Bears were to meet the

Minnesota Vikings in the first of two games the teams would play in 1970. The Vikings had won the NFL championship the year before and seemed likely to repeat. The Bears were presenting their usual combination of erratic offense and brutal defense and appeared to be on the verge of another undistinguished season. Butkus was joined at the table by a business associate and a journalist. He ordered a sandwich and a liter of dark beer. He doesn't like journalists and is cautious to the point of hostility with them. But he fields the questions, because it's part of his business.

"Do you think you can beat the Vikings?"

Butkus answers, "Yeah, the defense can beat them. I don't know if the offense can score any points. But we can take it to those guys."

"Have you ever been scared on a football field?"

"Scared?" he repeats, puzzled. "Of what?"

Then he smiles, knowing the effect he's had on his questioner. "Just injuries," he says. "That's the only thing to be afraid of. I'm always hurt, never been healthy. If I ever felt really great and could play a hundred percent, shit, nobody'd know what was going on, it would be so amazing."

"Does anybody play to intentionally hurt other guys?"

"Some assholes do. The really good ones don't."

"Dave Meggyesy, the ex-Cardinal, says that football is so brutal he was taught to use his hands to force a man's cleats into the turf and then drive his shoulder into the man's knee to rip his leg apart. That ever happen to you?"

"Hell, no! All you'd have to do is roll with the block and step on the guy's face."

That's my man. Richard Marvin Butkus, 28 years old, 245 pounds, six feet, three inches tall, middle linebacker for the Chicago Bears football team, possibly the best man to ever play the position. To a fan, the story on Butkus is very simple. He's the meanest, angriest, toughest, dirtiest son of a bitch in football. An animal, a savage, subhuman. But as good at his game as Ty Cobb was at his, or Don Budge at his, or Joe Louis at his.

As one of the Bear linemen said to me, "When you try to pick the best offensive guard, there are about five guys who are really close; it's hard to pick one. The same thing's true about most positions.

But Butkus *is* the best. He's superman. He's the greatest thing since popcorn."

The Minnesota game is being played on a warm, sunny autumn day at Chicago's Wrigley Field before a capacity crowd. Both teams have come out to warm up, but Butkus is late, because his right knee is being shot up with cortisone. It was injured three weeks before in a game with the New York Giants. Butkus was caught from the blind side while moving sideways and the knee collapsed. Until then, the Giants had been playing away from him. When they realized he was hurt, they tried to play at him and he simply stuffed them. Giant quarterback Fran Tarkenton said afterward, "Butkus has the most concentration of any man in the game. He's fantastic. And after he was hurt, he dragged that leg around the whole field. He was better after the injury than before—better on that one damn leg than with two."

When Butkus finally comes out, his steps are hesitant, like he is trying to walk off a cramp. You notice immediately that he looks even bigger in pads and helmet—bigger than anyone else on the field, bigger than players listed in the program as outweighing him. He has the widest shoulders on earth. His name seems too small for him; the entire alphabet could be printed on the back of his uniform and there'd be room left over.

Both teams withdraw after warm-ups and the stadium announcer reads the line-ups. The biggest hand from the restless fans comes when Butkus' name is announced. In the quiet that follows the applause, a raucous voice from high in the stands shouts, "Get Butkus' ass."

The players return to the field and string out along the side line. Both team benches at Wrigley Field are on the same side of the field, the Bears to the north and the Vikings to the south. Near midfield, opposing players and coaches stand quite close to each other, but there is almost no conversation between them, abusive or otherwise. As the Vikings arrange themselves for the national anthem, linebacker Wally Hilgenberg roars in on tight end John Beasley, a teammate, and delivers a series of resounding two-fisted hammer blows to Beasley's shoulder pads, exhaling loud whoops as his fists land. Beasley then smashes Hilgenberg. Everyone is snarling and hissing as the seconds tick away before the kickoff. Butkus is one of the few who show no signs of nervousness. That is true off the field and on. He does not fidget nor pace. Mostly, he just stands rather loosely and stares.

After the anthem, the tempo on the side line increases. The Bears will be kicking off. Howard Mudd, an offensive guard who was All-Pro when the Bears obtained him in a trade from San Francisco, is screaming, "KICKOFF KICKOFF KICKOFF," trying to get everyone else up as well as discharge some of his own energy. Mudd is a gap-toothed, blue-eyed 29-year-old with a bald spot at his crown who arrives at the field about 8:30 A.M.—fully four and a half hours before the game. He spends a lot of that time throwing up.

As I watch the Vikings' first offensive series from the side line, the sense of space and precision that the fan gets, either up in the stadium or at home on television, is destroyed. The careful delineation of plays done by the TV experts becomes absurd. At ground level, all is mayhem; sophistication and artistry are destroyed by the sheer velocity of the game. Each snap of the ball sets off 21 crazed men dueling with one another for some kind of edge—the 22nd, the quarterback, is the only one trying to maintain calm and seek some sense of order in the asylum.

It's the sudden, isolated noise that gets you. There is little sound just before each play begins—the crowd is usually quiet. At the snap, the tense vacuum is broken by sharp grunts and curses from the linemen as they slam into one another. The sudden smash of a forearm is sickening; and then there is the most chilling sound of all: the hollow thud as a launched, reckless body drives a shoulder pad into a ball carrier's head—a sound more lonely and terrifying than a gunshot.

After receiving the kickoff, the Vikings are forced to punt when a third-down pass from Gary Cuozzo, the Viking quarterback, to Gene Washington falls incomplete. As the Bears come off the field, Butkus is screaming at left linebacker Doug Buffone and cornerback Joe Taylor, because Washington was open for the throw. Luckily, he dropped it. They are having a problem with the signals. There is something comical about Butkus screaming with his helmet on. His face is so large that it seems to be trying to get *around* the helmet, as if the face were stuffed into it against its will.

That third-down play was marked by a lapse in execution by both offense and defense. It was one of those plays where all the neatly drawn lines in the playbook are meaningless. The truth about football is that, rather than being a game of incredible precision, it is a game of breakdowns, of entropy. If all plays happened as conceived, it would be too easy a sport. But the reality is that the timing is usually destroyed by a mental error, by a misstep, by a defenseman getting a bigger piece of a man than he was expected to, by the mere pace of the action being beyond a man's ability to think clearly when he's under pressure. Or by his being belted in the neck and knee simultaneously while he's supposed to be running nine steps down and four steps in.

The Bears don't get anywhere against the Viking defense and Butkus is back out quickly. On the field, his presence is commanding. He doesn't take a stance so much as install himself a few feet from the offensive center, screwing his heels down and hunching forward, hands on knees. His aura is total belligerence. As Cuozzo calls the signals, all of Butkus goes into motion. His mouth is usually calling signals of his own, his hands come off his knees, making preliminary pawing motions, and his legs begin to drive in place. No one in football has a better sense of where the ball will go, and Butkus moves instantly with the snap.

Two Cuozzo passes under pressure set up a Viking touchdown. On the Bears next set of offensive plays, they can't get anything going, and the defense is back out. On the second play from scrimmage, the Vikings set up a perfect sweep, a play that looks great each time you put it on the blackboard but works right one time in ten. This is one of those times. Guards Milt Sunde and Ed White lead Clint Jones around the left side with no one in front of them except Butkus, who is moving over from his position in the middle. All four bodies are accelerating rapidly. The play happens right in front of me and Butkus launches himself around Sunde and smashes both forearms into White, clawing his way over the guard to bring Jones down for no gain. He has beaten three men.

The Vikings are forced to punt after that and the Bears get their first first down. Then, on first and ten, Bear quarterback Jack Concannon lobs a perfect pass to halfback Craig Baynham, who is open in the Viking secondary. Baynham drops it. And that is about as much as the Bear offense will show this day.

With 56 seconds left in the half, the Vikings have the ball again. Cuozzo is trapped in the backfield trying to pass, and as he sets to throw, the ball falls to the ground and the Bears pick it up. The officials rule that Cuozzo was in the act of throwing and therefore the Vikings maintain possession on an incomplete pass. The Bears and all of Wrigley Field think it's a fumble and are expressing themselves accordingly. Butkus is enraged and is ranting at all the officials at once. But the Vikings keep the ball and a few seconds later try a field goal from the Bear 15. Butkus is stunting in the line, looking for a place to get through to block the kick. At the snap, he charges over tackle Ron Yary but is savagely triple-teamed and stopped. The field goal is good. When Yary comes off the field, he is bleeding heavily from the bridge of his nose but doesn't seem to notice it.

As the half ends, a ruddy-looking gray-haired man who had been enthusiastically jeering the officials on the Cuozzo call slumps forward in his seat. Oxygen and a stretcher are dispatched immediately and the early diagnosis is a heart attack. He is rushed from the stadium, but the betting among the side-line spectators—an elite group of photographers, friends of the athletes and hangers-on—is that he won't make it. They are right: the man is taken to a hospital and pronounced dead on arrival. A spectator, watching the game from behind a ground-level barricade, says, "If he had a season ticket, I'd like to buy it."

The second half is more of the same for the Bears' offense. Concannon throws another perfect touchdown pass, but it's dropped; and the Vikings maintain their edge. The surprising thing is that the Bears never give up. With the score 24–0, the Bear offensive line is still hitting and, God knows, so is the defense. The Bears have a reputation as a physical team, and it's justified. They have often given the impression, especially in the days when George Halas was coaching them, of being a bunch of guys who thought the best thing you could do on a Sunday afternoon was go out and kick a little ass. Winning was a possible but not necessary adjunct to playing football.

As Butkus comes off the field at the end of the third quarter, he's limping noticeably, but it hasn't affected his play. Cuozzo has had most of his success throwing short passes to the outside, but he continues to run plays in Butkus' area. The plays begin to take on a hypnotic pattern for me. Every three downs or so, there is this paradigm running play: Tingelhoff, the center, charges at Butkus, who fends him off with his forearms. Then Butkus moves to the hole that Osborne or Brown has committed himself to. Butkus, legs driving, arms outstretched, seems to simply step forward and embrace the largest amount of space he can. And he smothers everything in it—an offensive lineman, possibly one of his own defensive linemen and the ball carrier. Then he simply hangs on and bulls it all to the ground.

Finally, the game ends with a sense of stupefying boredom, because everyone seems to realize at once that there was never any hope. As the fans file out, one leans over a guardrail and screams at Bear head coach Jim Dooley. "Hey, Dooley! Whydoncha give Butkus a break? Trade him!" This is met with approval from his friends.

A few days after the Viking game, Butkus is in another North Side German restaurant. He is quiet, reserved and unhappy, because he feels that the Vikings didn't show the Bears much, didn't beat them physically nor with any great show of proficiency. I can't help thinking that a man of his talent would get tired of this kind of second-rate football.

"Don't you ever get bored? Don't you think of retiring from this grind?"

"No way!"

"But what do you get from it? It's got to be very frustrating. Why do you play?"

"Hell. That's like asking a guy why he fucks."

The following Sunday, the Bears are flat and lose badly to an amazing passing display from the San Diego Chargers. But they have been pointing toward their next big game—a rematch with an old and hated rival, the Detroit Lions. Earlier in the year, on national television, the Bears led the Lions for a half but ended up losing. After that game, Lion head coach Joe Schmidt said that his middle linebacker, Mike Lucci, was the best in football and that Butkus was overrated. The Lions generally said that Butkus was dirty rather than good. It added a little spice to a game that didn't need any.

The question of linebacking is an interesting one to consider. To play that position, a man must be strong enough in the arms and shoulders to fight off offensive linemen who often outweigh him, fast enough to cover receivers coming out of the backfield and rangy enough to move laterally with speed. But the real key to the position is an instantaneous ferocity—the ability to burst rather than run. And the man must function in the face of offenses that have been specifically designed to influence his actions away from the ball. Butkus is regarded as the strongest of middle linebackers, the very best at stopping running plays.

I once asked Howard Mudd if the 49ers, his previous team, had a special game plan for Butkus. "Sure," he said. "The plan was to not run between the tackles: always ensure that you block Dick. Once the game started, the plan changed, though. It became, 'Don't run. Just pass.'"

Mudd also pointed out something that belies Butkus' reputation for viciousness. "He doesn't try to punish the blockers," Mudd said. "He doesn't hit you in the head, like a lot of guys. The first time I played against him, I was—well—almost disappointed. It wasn't like hitting a wall or anything. He didn't mess with me, he went *by* me. All he wants is the ball. When he gets to the ball carrier, he really rings that man's bell."

In the Bear defense, Butkus is responsible for calling the signals and for smelling out the ball. If he has a weakness, it's that he sometimes seems to wallow a bit on his pass drops, allowing a man to catch a pass in front of him and assuming that the force of his tackle will have an effect on the man's confidence. It often does.

The night before the Lions game, Butkus was at his home in a suburb about 40 minutes' drive from Wrigley Field. It's an attractive ranch-style brick house. In front of the garage is a white pickup truck with the initials D. B. unobtrusively hand-lettered on the door. Inside the garage is a motorcycle. These are Butkus' toys. The main floor of the house is charmingly furnished and reflects the taste of his wife, Helen, an attractive auburn-haired woman who is expecting their third child early in 1971. She is a lively but reserved woman who runs the domestic side of their lives and attempts to keep track of Nikki, a four-year-old girl, and Ricky, a three-year-old boy—two golden-haired and rugged children.

The basement of the house belongs mostly to Butkus. Its finished, paneled area contains a covered pool table—he doesn't enjoy the game very much nor play it well—and a bar. Along the walls are as many trophies and glory photos as a man could ever hope for. The only photograph he calls to a visitor's attention is an evocative one from *Sports Illustrated* that shows him in profile, looking grimy and tired, draining the contents of a soft-drink cup.

At the far end of the basement is Butkus' workroom. The area is dominated by a large apparatus of steel posts and appendages that looks like some futuristic torture chamber. It's called a Universal Gym and its various protrusions allow him to exercise every part of his body. There is other exercise equipment about and in a far corner is a sauna. Butkus works out regularly but not to build strength. His objective is to keep his weight down and his muscles loose.

After an early dinner with the family, Butkus secluded himself in the bedroom with his playbooks and 16mm projector for a last look at the Lions' offense in its shadowy screen incarnation. Just after ten o'clock, he went to sleep. He woke early the next morning and went to early Mass, at 6:30, so that he didn't have to dress up. He and the priest were the only ones there. He returned home to eat a big steak and, after breakfast, he spent some more time with the playbooks. About ten o'clock he left the house for the drive to the ball park.

"He's real quiet before a game," Mrs. Butkus says, "but he's usually quiet. When he was dating me, my mother used to ask, 'Can't he talk?' I don't think he gets nervous before a game. I think it's just anticipation. He really wants to get at them."

She is remarkably cheerful about football and likes to talk about her husband's prowess. Her favorite story is one that she learned when she met Fuzzy Thurston, one of the great offensive linemen from Vince Lombardi's years at Green Bay. "Fuzzy told me," she says, "that when Dick played against the Packers the first time, Lombardi growled, 'Let's smear this kid's face.' But Fuzzy says they just couldn't touch him. After the game, Lombardi said, 'He's the best who ever played the position.'"

The day of the Lions game is cool and clear. When Butkus comes out, his expression is blank. The Bears are quieter and more fidgety than before the Vikings game. It's immediately apparent that this game will be played at a higher pitch than the previous ones, nearly off the scale that measures human rage. People who play football and who write about it like to talk about finesse, about a lineman's "moves." But when the game is really on, the finesse gets very basic. The shoulder dip and slip is replaced by the clenched fist to the head, the forearm chop to the knee and the helmet in the face.

From the opening play, the fans show they are in a wild mood. They have begun to call Mike Lucci (pronounced Loo-*chee*) Lucy. And when Lucci is on the field, they taunt him mercilessly. "Hey, Lucy! You're not big enough to carry Butkus' shoes."

The Lions are stopped on their first offensive series, and punt. As the ball sails downfield, Butkus and Ed Flanagan, the Detroit center, trade punches at midfield. They are both completely out of the play.

Soon enough, the Bear defense is back out. Butkus seems to be in a frenzy. He stunts constantly, pointing, shouting, trying to rattle Lion quarterback Bill Munson. On first down at the Lions' 20, he stuns Flanagan, who is trying to block him, with his forearm and knifes through on the left side to bring down Mel Farr for a five-yard loss.

On second down, Munson hands off to Farr going to his left. The left tackle, Roger Shoals, has gotten position on defensive end Ed O'Bradovich, as Farr cuts to the side line. Butkus, coming from the middle, lunges around the upright Shoals-O'Bradovich combination like a snake slithering around a tree and slashes at the runner's knees with his outstretched forearm. Farr crumbles.

On third down, Munson tries to pass to Altie Taylor in front of right linebacker Lee Roy Caffey. Caffey cocks his arm to ram it down Taylor's throat as he catches the ball, but Taylor drops the pass and Caffey relaxes the arm and pats him on the helmet.

The Lions set to punt and Butkus lurches up and down the line, looking for a gap. He finds one and gets a piece of the ball with his hand. The punt is short and the Bears have good position at midfield. On the first play from scrimmage, Concannon drops back and drills a pass to Dick Gordon, who has gotten behind two defenders. Gordon goes in standing up for a touchdown and pandemonium takes over Wrigley Field.

The game settles down a bit after that and the only other score for a while is a Lion field goal. Munson is trying to get a running game going to the outside, but Butkus is having an incredible day. He is getting outside as fast as Farr and Taylor. The runner and Butkus are in some strange *pas de deux*. Both seem to move to the same place at the same time, the runner driving fiercely with his legs, trying to set his blocks and find daylight. Butkus seems, by comparison, oddly graceful, his legs taking long lateral strides, his arms outstretched, fending off would-be blockers. But it's all happening at dervish speed and each impact has a jarring effect on the runner. Lucci, when he's on the field, just doesn't dominate the action and is taking abuse from the fans. He's neither as strong nor as quick. He's good on the pass drops, possibly better than Butkus, but he's not the same kind of destructive tackler.

Midway in the second quarter, Detroit cornerback Dick LeBeau intercepts a Concannon pass intended for Gordon. Gordon had gone inside and Concannon had thrown outside. Entropy again. The half ends with the score 7–3, Bears. On the side line after the half-time break, the Bears are back at high pitch. Concannon is yelling, "Go, defense," and Abe Gibron, the Bears' defensive coach, is offering, "Hit 'em to hurt 'em!" A wide man of medium height, Gibron was an All-Pro tackle for many years in pro football's earlier era. He is a coach in the Lombardi mold, full of venom and fire—abusive to foe and friend. He is sometimes comical to watch as he walks the side line hurling imprecations for the entire football game; but his defenses are solid and brutal.

The intensity of the hitting seems to be increasing. Butkus makes successive resounding tackles, once on Farr and once on Taylor. He does not tackle so much as explode his shoulder into a man, as if he were trying to drive him under the ground. The effect is enhanced by his preference for hitting high, for getting as big a piece as he can. Butkus once told a television sports announcer, "I sometimes have a dream where I hit a man so hard his head pops off and rolls down-field." On a third-down play, Munson passes deep and Butkus, far downfield, breaks up the pass with his hand. The fans are overjoyed and have a few choice things to say about Lucci's parentage.

The Bears get the ball, but Concannon is intercepted again and the defense gets ready to go back in. As Butkus and the others stand tensely on the side line, it's clear to everyone that they are Chicago's only chance to win; the offense is just too sluggish. The "Ds," as they are called, have all the charisma on this team, and as they prepare to guts it out some more, I am overcome by a strange emotion. Stoop-shouldered and sunken-chested, weighing all of 177 pounds rather meagerly spread over a six-foot, three-inch frame, I want to join them. Not merely want but feel compelled to go out there and get my shoulder in—smash my body against the invaders. At this moment, those 11 men—frustrated, mean and near exhaustion—are the only possibility for gallantry and heroism that I know. The urge to be out there wells up in me the way it does in a kid reacting to a field sergeant who asks for the impossible—because to not volunteer involves a potential loss of manhood that is too great to face.

The defenses dominate the game for a while, but a short Bear punt gives the Lions good position and they get a field goal. A bit later, Munson passes for a touchdown and the Lions take the lead, 13–7. The Lions were favored in the betting before the game by as much as 16 points, and after the touchdown, the side-liners are murmuring things like, "I'm still all right, I got thirteen and a half."

With four minutes left in the game and the score 16–10 after each team has added a field goal, coach Dooley pulls Concannon in favor of the younger, less experienced but strong-armed Bobby Douglass, his second-string quarterback. A clumsy hand-off on a fourth and one convinced Dooley that Concannon was tired, although Concannon will indicate afterward that he wasn't. Pulling him at this point in the game, when the Bears obviously have only one chance to score and when a touchdown and point after would win, is an unusual thing to do, and Concannon is upset. He is a dark, scraggly-haired Irishman, very high strung, a ballplayer who stares at the fans when they're abusing him. He never feigns indifference. Now he is standing on the side line, head slightly bowed, pawing the ground with his cleats while someone else runs his team. His hands are firmly thrust into his warm-up jacket and all the time he stands there, intently watching the game, he repeats venomously over and over, "Stuff 'em! Stuff 'em! Fuck you, Lions! Goddamn it! Goddamn it! Fuck you, Lions!"

Douglass doesn't move the team and the Lions take over. Gibron is screaming that there's plenty of time. There is one minute, 36 seconds on the clock. Altie Taylor gets a crucial, time-consuming first down. Butkus tackles him viciously from behind, nearly bisecting him with his helmet; but the Bears are losers again.

The Bear defense had played tough football, and Butkus had played a great game. I said as much to him and he replied, "Hell, we're just losin' games again. It don't matter what else happened." But he didn't deny the ferocity of the Bear defense: "You didn't see a lot of that second effort out there," he said, referring to the Lion backs. "They weren't running as hard as they might."

"Do you think you intimidated them?"

"They knew they were getting hit. And when you know you're getting in there, then you really lay it on them."

"What was the reason for the punches with Flanagan?"

"I wanted to let him know he was going to be in a game."

Butkus seemed to talk all the time on the field. Was he calling signals to his own players or yelling at Detroit?

"Mostly it's signals for our side, but every once in a while, I'll say
something to jag them a little."

"Like what?"

"Oh, you know. Call them a bunch of faggots or somethin'. Or I
told sixty-three after a play when I got around him that he threw a
horseshit block."

Butkus says these things in an emotionless voice—almost shrugging the words out rather than speaking them. His speech is filled
with the nasal sounds of Chicago's Far South Side, and he is very much
a neighborhood kid grown up. His tastes are simple—in food, in entertainment, in people. He doesn't run with a fast crowd. If you ask him
what he does for kicks, he shrugs. "I don't know, just goof around, I
guess." He has wanted to play football all his life, and one of his most
disarming and embarrassing statements when he was graduated from
college was, "I came here to play football. I knew they weren't going
to make a genius out of me."

As a kid, Butkus loved to play baseball. Surprisingly, he couldn't hit
but had all the other skills. He pitched, caught and played the infield.
He had the grace of a "good little man," and that may be one key to
his success. Unlike most big football players, who find it hard to walk
and whistle at the same time, and have to be taught how to get around
the field, Butkus has the moves of a quick, slippery small man who
happens to have grown to 245 pounds.

By the time he got to high school, Butkus was committed to football. His high school coach wouldn't let him scrimmage in practice
for fear that the overenthusiastic Butkus would hurt some of the kids
on his own team.

He distrusts worldliness in most forms, except that he knows that
his stardom can make money and he works at it. He has changed his
hair style from the crewcut he wore in his early years to something a
bit longer, but he's far from shaggy. His clothes are without style. He
wears open-collar shirts, shapeless slacks and button-front cardigan

sweaters that he never buttons. A floppy, unlined tan raincoat is his one concession to Chicago winters.

He is genuinely shy and deferential on all matters except football, and his façade is quiet cynicism. He especially dislikes bravado and gung-hoism when he has reason to believe they're false, as he does with many of the Bear offensive players. Although he has a reputation for grimness, he smiles rather easily. And his laugh is a genuine surprise: it's a small boy's giggle, thoroughly disconcerting in his huge frame.

His shyness comes out in odd ways. When asked if, as defensive captain, he ever chews out another player for a missed assignment, he says, "Nah. Who am I to tell somebody else that he isn't doing the job? After all, maybe I'm not doing my job so good." Butkus is serious.

That sort of resignation makes him an ideal employee—sometimes to his own detriment. Butkus thinks, for example, that his original contract with the Bears was for too little money—and he's been suffering financially ever since. But he refuses to consider holding out for a renegotiation or playing out his contract option in order to get a better deal with a new team. "I made my mistake," he says. "Now I gotta live with it." And, although you probably couldn't find a coach in the world who wouldn't trade his next dozen draft choices for him, Butkus thinks that if he did something so downright daring as leave the Bears, no other team would take him, because he'd have marked himself a renegade.

This is not so much naïveté on Butkus' part as it is a deeply conservative strain in the man. When he saw a quote from Alex Johnson, the troubled California Angels baseball player, suggesting that he wanted to be treated like a human being, not like an athlete, Butkus said, "Hell, if he doesn't want to be treated like an athlete, let him go work the line in a steel mill. Ask those guys if they're treated like human beings."

Yet Butkus is not a company man. If anything, he is brutally cynical about established authorities—especially the management of the Chicago Bears football club—but he abhors being in a position where he finds himself personally exposed, and distrusts anyone who would willingly place himself in that position.

He especially dislikes personal contact with the fans. He complains about being stared at and being interrupted in restaurants. He is also inclined to moan about the ephemeral nature of his career. "It could be over any time," he says. "An injury could do it tomorrow. And even if I stay healthy, hell, it's all gonna be over in ten years." I ask if he has any plans for the future. "Not as a hanger-on, trying to live off my name. When it's over, I'm gonna hang up the fifty-one and get out. I'm not gonna fool around as some comedian or public speaker."

For the present, Butkus determinedly, but with no joy, does as much off-field promotional activity as he can get. He attends awards dinners and other ceremonial functions and will appear at just about any sports-related event that comes along. He's done some television appearances and made one delightful commercial for Rise shaving cream. This year, International Merchandising Corporation (the president of IMC, Mark McCormack, is the man who merchandised Arnold Palmer, among others) contacted Butkus and now manages his finances. His name has begun to appear on an assortment of sports gear and may yet make its way to hair dressings and other such men's items. When I told Butkus that he had taken his place in the pantheon of great middle linebackers, along with Sam Huff and Ray Nitschke, he said, "Hell, I'm going to make more money this year than those guys ever thought about."

Over the following six weeks, the Bears played a lot of mediocre football: they won two, lost four—although two of those were very close.

The next time I saw Butkus was on a cold, damp Thursday—a practice day for the Bears' return match with the Packers. The numbing grayness of the Chicago winter day was matched only by the Bears' mood at practice. They were sluggish and disconnected and seemed to be going through motions to run out the string. The Packer game was the next-to-last one of the season. Butkus was working with the defense under coaches Gibron and Don Shinnick. Shinnick is the Bears' linebacker coach and a veteran of 13 years with the Baltimore Colts. He is an enthusiastic, straightforward man who doesn't hassle his players. He is Butkus' favorite coach, and the impression you get from talking to either of them is that they both think that Don Shinnick and Dick Butkus are the only two men in the world qualified to talk about football.

The defense was working on its pass coverage against some second-string receivers. Doug Buffone was bitching to Shinnick because they weren't practicing against the first string and couldn't get their timing right. They had practiced with the first string before their Baltimore game and Buffone said that it was directly responsible for five interceptions in the game. Shinnick agreed but gave Buffone an "I don't make the rules" look and they both went back to the drill.

Gibron was installing some new formations to defend against Green Bay. One was called Duck and the other Cora. They tried out some plays to see if everyone could pick up Butkus' signal. Butkus called "Duck" if he wanted one formation in the backfield and "Cora" for another and they relayed it to one another. Gibron was unhappy with the rhythm and said, "Listen. Don't say 'Duck.' It could be 'fuck' or 'suck' or anything. Say 'Quack quack' instead, OK?" For the next few minutes, the Bears shouted "Quack quack" as loud as they could. Butkus just stared at Gibron. Then they ran some patterns.

Shortly, the defense left the field so Concannon and the first-string receivers could work out without interference. Butkus stood morosely on the side line with Ed O'Bradovich, the only team member he is really close to.

O. B., as he is called, is a huge curly-haired man endowed with a nonchalant grace and good humor. He looks like he's never shown concern for anything, especially his own safety.

A visitor at the practice says to Butkus, "That quack-quack stuff sounds pretty good."

"It's not quack, quack," says Butkus, glowering. "It's Duck."

Butkus is about two weeks into a mustache. "It's for one of those Mexican cowboy movies," he says.

O'Bradovich says, "You're gonna look like an overgrown Mexican faggot."

"Yeah, who's gonna tell me?" At that minute, a burst of sharp, raucous howling rises up where the offensive linemen are working on their pass blocking. "Look at 'em," Butkus says. "Let's see how much noise they make against Green Bay on Sunday."

As I look around the practice field, there seems to be chaos among the players. If I were a betting man, I'd go very heavy against the Bears. They seem totally dispirited. "It's all horseshit," Butkus says. "Everybody wants it to be over."

Just before the practice breaks up, coach Dooley calls everyone together and says, "All right! Now, we've had these three good practices this week. And we're ready. Let's do a big job out here Sunday." All the players leave after a muffled shout—except for Concannon, who runs some laps, and Mac Percival, the place kicker, who has been waiting for a clear field to practice on. One of the coaches holds for Percival, and as I head for the stands, Percival makes nine field goals in a row from the 36-yard line before missing one.

Sunday is sunny, but three previous days of rain have left the side lines muddy, although the field itself is in good shape. The air is damp and cold; it's a day when the fingers and toes go numb quickly and the rest of the body follows. Bear-Packer games are usually brutal affairs, but this game is meaningless in terms of divisional standings: both teams are out of contention. There is speculation, however, that each head coach—Phil Bengtson of the Packers and Dooley of the Bears—has his job on the line and that the one who loses the game will also lose his job.

When the line-ups for the game are announced, the biggest hand is not for Butkus but for Bart Starr, Green Bay's legendary quarter-back. If Butkus is the symbol of the game's ferocity, then Starr is the symbol of its potential for innocence and glory. He is the third-string quarterback who made good—Lombardi's quarterback—an uncanny incarnation of skill, resourcefulness, dedication and humility. He is the Decent American, a man of restraint and self-discipline who would be tough only in the face of a tough job. But he is so much in awe of the game he plays that he wept unashamedly after scoring the *winning* touchdown in Green Bay's last-second victory over Dallas in minus-13-degree weather for the NFL championship in 1967.

The Packers receive and on the first two plays from scrimmage, But-kus bangs first Donny Anderson, then Dave Hampton to the ground. He has come out ferocious. A third-down play fails and the Packers punt. On the Bears' first play from scrimmage, Concannon throws a screen pass to running back Don Shy, who scampers 64 yards to the Packer 15. Concannon completes a pass to George Farmer and then throws a short touchdown pass to Dick Gordon. Bears lead, 7–0.

Green Bay's ball: Starr hands off to Hampton, who slips before he gets to the line of scrimmage. On second and ten, Butkus stunts a bit, then gets an angle inside as Starr goes back to pass. Butkus gets through untouched and slams Starr for an eight-yard loss. The Packers are stopped again, and punt. As Starr comes off the field, he heads for the man with the headset on to find out from the rooftop spotters just what the hell is going on.

On the Bears' next offensive play, Concannon drops back and arcs a pass to Farmer, who has gotten behind Bob Jeter. Touchdown. Bears lead, 14–0, and there is ecstasy in the air. It is a complete turnaround, and my shock at the Bears today—after watching them on Thursday—is testimony to how difficult sports clichés are to overcome. I am obsessed with whether the team is up or down, as if that were the essence of the game. Actually, for all anyone knows, the Packers might have come to Wrigley Field "up" out of their minds. It doesn't matter. The Bears are just good this day; they are at a peak of physical skill as well as emotional drive. Concannon is very close to his finest potential and, for all it matters, might be depressed emotionally. What counts is that his passes are perhaps an eighth of an inch truer as he loops his arm, and that is enough to touch greatness.

All the Bears are teeing off from their heels. When the game began, Bob Brown, the Packers' best pass rusher, sneered at Jim Cadile, Bear guard, the man across the line from him, "I'm gonna kill you."

Cadile drawled, "I'll be here all day."

The Packers now have the ball, third down, on their own 19. Starr drops back to pass and, with no open receiver, starts to run the ball himself. As he gets to the line of scrimmage, he is tripped up with four Bears closing in on him, one of whom is Butkus. I'm watching the play from the side line right behind Starr. From that vantage point Butkus, looking for a piece of Starr, is all helmet and shoulders brutally launched. The piece of Starr that Butkus gets is his head. Starr lies on the ground as the Packer trainer comes to his aid. The crowd noise is deafening.

Starr is helped from the field and immediately examined by the team physician, who checks his eyes to see if there are signs of concussion. The doctor leaves him and Starr, who looks frail at six feet, one inch, 190 pounds in the land of giants, puts his helmet on and says that he's all right. When the Bears are stopped on a drive and punt, he returns and immediately goes to work completing some short, perfectly timed passes. He moves the Packers to the Bear 15. Then, on second down, he is smashed trying to pass and comes off the field again. He is replaced by a rookie named Frank Patrick, who can't get anything going, and the Packers kick a field goal. Starr is now seated on the bench, head in hands, sniffing smelling salts. He's out for the day.

The game turns into a blood-lust orgy for the Bears. O'Bradovich is playing across from offensive tackle Francis Peay. Vince Lombardi had obtained Peay from the New York Giants, predicting that the tackle was going to be one of the greats, and he is good, indeed. But on this day, O'Bradovich is looming very large in Peay's life. In fact, he is kicking the shit out of him, actually hurling Peay's body out of his way each time Patrick tries to set up to pass. The Packer rookie is in the worst possible position for an inexperienced quarterback. He has to pass and the defense knows it. The linemen don't have to protect against the running game and just keep on coming.

Lee Roy Caffey had been traded to Chicago by the Packers. After each set of violent exhibitions by the Bear defense, he comes off the field right in front of Packer coach Bengtson, screaming, "You mother-fucker. You traded me! And we're gonna kill you!"

One of the most impressive pass plays of the game comes in the second quarter, with the score 14–3 and the Bears driving. Concannon throws a short high pass down the side line that George Farmer has to go high in the air to catch. Farmer seems to hang for a moment, as if the football has been nailed in place and his body were suspended from it. In that vulnerable position, Ray Nitschke, the Packers' middle linebacker, crashes him with a rolling tackle that swings Farmer's body like a pendulum. As Farmer turns horizontal, still in the air, Willie Wood, the safety, crushes him and Farmer bounces on the ground. But he holds onto the football.

A few plays later, Concannon, looking for a receiver at the Packer 25-yard line, finds no one open and runs in for a touchdown. It is a day when he can do no wrong.

The hysteria on the field even works its way up to the usually cool stadium announcer. In the third quarter, when Dick Gordon beats Doug Hart for another touchdown pass from Concannon, the announcer, with his mike behind his back, screams in livid rage at the Packer defender, "You're shit, Hart! You're shit!" Then he puts the instrument to his mouth and announces to the fans in his best oratori-cal voice, "Concannon's pass complete to Gordon. Touchdown Bears."

At the Packer bench, Bart Starr is spending the day with his head bowed, pawing the turf with his cleats. It occurs to me that every quarterback I have watched this year has spent a lot of his time in that position: Concannon, Munson, Unitas when the Bears were leading Baltimore, and now Starr.

Behind Starr, Ray Nitschke has just come off the field after the Bear touchdown. Nitschke is one of the great figures from Green Bay's irrepressible teams of the Sixties, and his face looks like he gave up any claims on the sanctity of his body when he decided to play football. He is gnarled, bald and has lost his front teeth. He constantly flexes his face muscles, opening and clamping his jaw in a set of grotesque expressions. He has put on a long Packer cape and is prowling the side line, exhaling plumes of vapor from his nostrils, the cape flowing gracefully behind him. There is something sublime in the image. Nitschke is the caped crusader; had there ever really been a Batman, he could not have been a pretty-boy millionaire—he'd have been this gnarled avenger.

As the game progresses further in the third quarter, the hysteria increases and it's hard to follow the play sequences or the score, and little details intrude on my mind:

- Little Cecil Turner, the swift black return specialist, running back a kickoff after the Packers score a touchdown, is finding daylight. As he works his way upfield, a black Packer screams to his teammates on the field, "Kill that dude!"
- O'Bradovich, coming off the field after hurling Peay around some more, sits down with his sleeves rolled up in a spot where he can avoid the heat from the side-line blowers—on a day when it's so cold that a man standing next to me is warming his hands over the open flame of his cigarette lighter.
- Willie Holman, Bear defensive tackle, barrels into Patrick as he tries to pass. The ball has no speed and is intercepted. Holman's shot actually rings in the ears for a moment. That night on the TV reruns, you can't even tell that Holman caused the interception, because there is no sound, no sense of the brutality of the play.
- Butkus is dumped on his ass by Gale Gillingham as he tries to blitz Patrick. Gillingham is one of the very good offensive guards around and it's an incredible shot. The only time I've seen Butkus go backward all year.

• Jim Ringo, the nine-year All-Pro center who now coaches the Bear offensive line, winces with pain each time a Bear defensive lineman wipes out one of Green Bay's offensive linemen. It's obvious that Ringo simply hates all defensive players, even his own.

Late in the fourth quarter, with the game safely out of reach, 35–10, Butkus comes out and is replaced by John Neidert. Gibron and the defense are now very much interested in the game again. The Packers get a little drive going and are at the Bear 13. Neidert is getting a lot of information from the Bear bench, especially from Gibron. To show some respect for the rule that prohibits coaching from the side line while the clock is running, Gibron wants to call his signals discreetly. He is trying to whisper "Double-zone ax" across a distance of some 25 yards.

Double zone means that the cornerbacks will play the wide receivers tight, one on one. Ax means that the middle linebacker will take the tight end alone on the short drop. On the next play, Patrick completes a pass to the tight end for the score. As Neidert comes off the field, he is heartbroken and Gibron is screaming, "Neidert, whatsamatta witchoo? If you don't know it, say so. Did you have the ax in?" Neidert, who looks too confused to think, only nods and kneels down, looking as if he is close to tears. It's possible that at the end of this already decided football game, on a meaningless score, his football career might be over. It's the one upsetting thought in an otherwise brilliant day for the Bears.

Two months after the Packer game, after a trip to Los Angeles to play in the Pro Bowl, Butkus goes into the hospital to have his knee operated on. He leaves the hospital afterward but suffers great pain for days and finally returns to see if anything can be done about it. Butkus thinks a muscle was strained when the cast was put on; the doctor doesn't agree and can't understand why he is having so much pain. I went to visit Butkus at Illinois Masonic Hospital, a typically ugly yellow-walled institution. When I get to his room, he is playing gin rummy with a friend and is in a very scowly mood.

He doesn't look like a typical patient. He isn't wearing a hospital gown, just a pair of shorts, and his upper body is almost wider than the bed. The impression is that any moment he may get out of bed, pick it up as if it were an attaché case and walk out. He offers me a beer from a large container filled with ice and cans.

He gets bored with the rummy game very quickly and his guest departs.

"How do you feel?"

"Horseshit."

Butkus describes the pain he's been having in the side of his knee and tells me the doctor just keeps saying that Gale Sayers was up and around the day after his knee was operated on. He isn't happy with the doctor. His wife, who is nine months pregnant, enters. We all discuss the pain for a minute and she makes it clear that she thinks it may be partly psychosomatic.

Butkus talks about a condominium he's bought on Marco Island in Florida and a big Kawasaki bike that he hasn't been able to ride because of the operation. He is very uncomfortable and we get into some more beers.

I ask if he was trying to hurt Starr in the Green Bay game. "Nah," he says. "I just went in there with everybody else. That's what you gotta do. But you should see the mail from Wisconsin. I got a letter that said, 'You shouldn't hit old people.' Another one said, 'I hope you get yours.'"

Butkus continually reaches down to massage his leg, which is wrapped from hip to toe in a bandage. A nurse comes in with a paper cup containing an assortment of brightly colored capsules. He asks which one is the painkiller, but the nurse refuses to tell him. She explains that he has been taking a number of sedatives since his arrival in the hospital and Butkus is disturbed that he's been swallowing a lot of stuff that hasn't done any good. "We didn't want to give you anything too strong," she tells him archly. "We thought you were taking care of yourself with the beer." It is apparent that a lot of people are enjoying the fact that the big, mean Butkus is acting like a six-year-old. He looks at the nurse with puzzlement and annoyance. He doesn't think that any of this is the least bit funny and goes back to rubbing his knee.

"Do you think the operation is going to make you cautious?"

"No. But nobody's going to hit this knee again. No way."

During the next few weeks, the knee continued to trouble him. He had an unusual reaction to the catgut that had been used to rebuild the joint and his body was trying to reject it. He was often in pain and became adept at squeezing pus and sometimes chunks of catgut from the suppurating incision. At the end of March, the doctor opened the knee again and cleaned it out. This time, the doctor and Butkus were satisfied and a second operation, planned to rebuild the other side of the knee, was canceled because the joint seemed sound again.

Early in April, Butkus went to Florida to relax. He returned to Chicago after a brief stay and fell into an off-season pattern. Fool with the Kawasaki, have beers with O'Bradovich, spend Sundays with his family. In late May, he started to tune his body on the Universal Gym.

On a hot, rainy morning last June, I arrived at Butkus' house to find him sitting in the kitchen jouncing Matthew Butkus, who had been born in late February (8 pounds, 13 ounces), on his knee. The father was cooing and the son was grinning, as well he should, considering that he was spending much of his first few months surrounded by the protective comfort of those huge hands.

Butkus was still unsure of the knee. "I think I'll really be able to go on it around December first," he said. That would mean missing three months of the season. I didn't know if he was serious, and it occurred to me that he didn't either. He was to see the doctor that afternoon. I had an appointment to visit his parents, who live nearby, and as I left, his wife said, "If that knee isn't OK, I'm moving South. He'll be impossible to live with."

Butkus' parents are Lithuanian. They have seven children (Dick is the youngest and smallest of five boys) and 22 grandchildren; the family is loyal and gathers frequently.

When I got to the house, Mr. Butkus, 80 years old, a bushy-browed, weathered man of medium height, was working with a spade on the grounds. The rain had stopped and the day had turned sunny and hot. He was calmly digging out weeds in a small thicket bordering an expansive lawn that fronted the house. A white-plaster statue sat in the middle of the lawn. Mr. Butkus is a friendly man of few words who has little to say about his youngest son's success. It's simply not something that he relates to easily. The senior Mrs. Butkus is quite another story. She's a big woman who clearly supplied her sons' breadth of shoulder and chest. She is a bit immobilized now from a recent fall and thoroughly fills the armchair she is seated in. Butkus bought the house for his parents a few years ago. The living room is filled with the furniture and remnants of other places and times, and the harsh early-afternoon light seems to be cooled by its journey around the knickknacks to the corner of the room, where she is sitting. His mother says of Dick: "He didn't make any special trouble. He liked practical jokes a lot but never got into any real trouble. He was full of mischief and energy—like any other boy." There is something hard in her attitude, something that comes from raising a lot of children. Life is not wonderful, nor too simple, but it's not too bad, either. It's to be endured—and sometimes bullied. As she stares out the window, thinking about Dick, she says, "When he was a kid, his brothers would take him to the College All-Star game. He'd sit there and say, 'I'm going to play here. This is where I'm going.'" She pauses, and then continues: "You know, his brother Ronnie played for a while with the old Chicago Cardinals. He had to stop because of a knee injury." Then she turns to me and says, "I hope Dick gets well. It's his life."

Paul Hemphill

Paul Hemphill (1936–2009) knew the pain and joy of being a Southerner as well as any writer in the last fifty years. He was a truck driver's son from Birmingham who might never have discovered his gift for the language if he hadn't failed at minor league baseball's bottom rung. Unflinching in his honesty, poetic no matter what his subject, he wrote about honky-tonks and church bombers, failed heroes and flannel-mouthed politicians. He may have been most honest and poetic, however, when writing about his own life—the drinking, the problems raising kids, the memories of being on the road with a father who couldn't get past the prejudices Hemphill spent his career battling. He earned a reputation as the Jimmy Breslin of the South when he was the *Atlanta Journal*'s city columnist in the 1960s, but newspapers couldn't hold him. While on a Nieman Fellowship at Harvard, he began writing his first book, *The Nashville Sound* (1970), still the definitive work on country music. Ten more nonfiction books, including the stunning memoir *Leaving Birmingham* (1993), followed it. There were also four novels, most significantly *Long Gone* (1979), which echoed with memories of his one week as a Class D second baseman. The experience evoked in Hemphill the empathy on display in the following character study, written for *Sport*'s January 1972 issue. His subject is Bob Suffridge, one of college football's all-time great players, now lost in a boozy haze of memories and regret. Hemphill's story reads like fiction. It is as real as an empty bottle.

Yesterday's Hero

"A week never passes that the Alumni Office fails to receive news highlighting the good works of former football players. So many of them reflect credit on our University."

—*University of Tennessee Football Guide, 1970*

What is fame?
An empty bubble;
Gold? A transient,
Shining trouble.

—James Grainger, 1721–1766

THE EVENING BEGAN with an expedition to the friendly neighborhood liquor store four blocks away, where a purchase of four quarts of sticky-sweet Wild Irish Rose red wine was negotiated with a reedy gray-haired man behind the cash register. When the man saw who was shuffling through the front door his jaw tightened and he glanced nervously around, as if checking to be sure everything was nailed down.

"When you start drinking that stuff, Bob?" he asked.

"Since the last time I woke up and didn't know what month it was," said Robert Lee Suffridge, inspiring a doleful exchange about his drinking exploits. It was concluded that cheap wine at least puts you to sleep before you have a chance to do something crazy. Paying for the $1.39-a-quart bottles he trudged back out the door into the dry late-afternoon July heat and nursed the bleached twelve-year-old Mercury back to his apartment.

It is an old folks' home, actually, a pair of matching six-story towers on the outskirts of Knoxville, Tennessee. At fifty-five he isn't ready for an old folks' home yet, but a brother who works for the state arranged for him to move in. Most of the other residents are well past the age of sixty-five, and to the older ladies like Bertha Colquitt, who lives in the apartment next to his and lets him use her telephone, he is their mischievous son. More than once they have had to call an ambulance for him when he was either drunk or having heart pains, but they don't seem to mind. "Honey, if I was about ten years younger you'd have to watch your step around me," he will say to one of them, setting off embarrassed giggles. God knows where he found four portable charcoal grills, but he keeps them in the dayroom downstairs and throws wiener roasts from time to time. He grows his own tomatoes beside his building, in a fiberglass crate filled with loam and human excrement taken from a buddy's septic tank.

Getting off the elevator at the fourth floor, he thumped across the antiseptic hallway. The cooking odors of cabbage and meatloaf and carrots drifted through doorways. Joking with an old woman walking down the hall with a cane, he shifted the sack of wine bottles to his left arm and opened the door to his efficiency apartment. A copy of *AA Today*, an Alcoholics Anonymous publication, rested atop the bureau. A powder-blue blazer with a patch reading "All-Time All-American" hung in a clear plastic bag from the closet doorknob. The bed, "my grandmother's old bed," had not been made in some time. Littering the living room floor were old sports pages and letters and newspaper clippings.

"Not a bad place," he said, filling a yellow plastic tumbler with wine and plopping down in the green Naugahyde sofa next to the wall. "Especially for forty-two-fifty a month."

"What's your income now?"

"About two hundred a month. Social Security, Navy pension."

"You don't need much, anyway, I guess."

He stood up and stepped to the picture window that looks out over the grassy courtyard separating the two buildings. In the harsh light he looked like the old actor Wallace Beery, with puffy broken face and watery eyes and rubbery lips, his shirttail hanging out over a bulging belly. "I'm an alcoholic," he said in a hoarse whisper. "I've done everything. Liquor, pills, everything. I don't even like the stuff. Never did like it, not even when I was playing ball. Hell, only reason I used to carry cigarettes was because my date might want a smoke." He drained the wine from the tumbler and turned away from the window, and there was no self-pity in his gravelly voice. "I came into the world a poor boy," he said, "and I guess I'm still a poor boy."

The 1970 *Tennessee Football Guide* was generally correct, of course, when it boasted about the steady flood of "news highlighting the good works of former football players." The good life awaits the young man who becomes a college football star. He gets an education, or at least a degree, whether he works at it or not. He becomes known and admired. He discovers the relationship between discipline and success. He makes connections with alumni in high places—men who, in their enthusiasm for football, cross his palm with money and create jobs for him. About all he has to do is mind his manners, do what he is told, and he will be presented with a magical key to an easy life after he is finished playing games. The rule applies to most sports. "If it hadn't been for baseball," a pint-sized minor-league outfielder named Ernie Oravetz once told me, "I'd be just like my old man today: blind and crippled from working in the mines up in Pennsylvania." For thousands of kids, particularly poor kids in the South, where football is a way of life, athletics has been a road out. Look at Jim Thorpe, the Native American. Look at Babe Ruth, the orphan. Look at Willie Mays, the black man. Look at Joe Namath.

But look, also, at the ones who couldn't make it beyond the last hurrah. Look at Carl Furillo and Joe Louis and the others—the ones who died young, the ones who blew their money, the ones who ruined their bodies, the ones who somehow missed the brass ring. Fame is an empty bubble, indeed, easily burst if not handled with care. What happens when the legs go, the arm tires, the eyes fade, the lungs sag? Some cope, some don't. The reasons some don't are so varied and sometimes so subtle they require the attention of sociologists. But the failures are there, and they will always be with us.

Few bubbles have burst quite so dramatically as that of Bob Suffridge. A runaway who had been scratching out his own living in the streets of Knoxville since the age of 15, Suffridge went on to be named one of the eleven best college football players of all time. He weighed only 185 pounds, but he had killer instincts and rabbit quickness and the stamina of a mule. "He was so quick, he could get around you before you got off your haunches," says one former teammate. "Suff was the archetype of the Tennessee single-wing pulling guard," says his friend and *Knoxville Journal* sports columnist Tom Anderson. Playing both ways for coach Bob Neyland, averaging more than fifty minutes a game, Suffridge was in on the beginning of a dynasty that became one of the strongest traditions in American college football: the Tennessee Volunteers, the awesome single-wing offense, "The Big Orange," those lean and fast and hungry shock troops of "the General." During three seasons at UT, 1938–40, Suffridge never played in a losing regular-season game (though the Vols did lose two of three bowl games, the first of many postseason appearances for the school). He was everybody's All-American in 1938 and 1940 and made some teams in 1939. In 1961 he was named to the national football Hall of Fame, and during college football's centennial celebration two years ago joined the company of such men as Red Grange and Jim Thorpe and Bronko Nagurski on the eleven-man All-Time All-American team. "Bob," says George Cafego, a Vol tailback then and a UT assistant coach now, "had every opportunity to be a millionaire."

There may be no millionaires among the Vols of that era, but there are few slackers. The late Bowden Wyatt was head coach of the Vols for eight seasons. Ed Molinski is a doctor in Memphis. Ed Cifers is president of a textile company. Abe Shires is a sales coordinator for McKesson-Robbins. Bob Woodruff is the UT athletic director.

All of which makes Suffridge an even sadder apparition as he drifts in and out of Knoxville society today, an aimless shadow of the hyped-up kid who used to blitz openings for George Cafego and who once blocked three consecutive Sammy Baugh punt attempts in a brief fling with the pros. Over the past twenty-five years he has tried working—college coaching, selling insurance, hawking used cars, promoting Coca-Cola, running for public office, and running a liquor store (in that order)—but something would always happen. He hasn't worked now in about five years. He has had two heart attacks, one of them laying him up for eight months. He has engaged in numerous battles with booze, winning some and losing others. He has gone through and survived a period with pills. Now a bloated 250 pounds, he lives alone at the Cagle Terrace Apartments (he lost his wife and four kids to divorce twelve years ago, although now and then one of the children will come to see him), where he seems to have made a separate peace with the world. He made the local papers recently by protesting when two armed guards showed up to supervise a July 4 party there. ("Bob Suffridge, a former All-American football player at Tennessee, complained that elderly residents were frightened at the sudden appearance of the men with guns.... Suffridge serves on a committee to help set up socials for elderly residents and also lives at Cagle Terrace.") He spends his time hanging around the sports department of the *Knoxville Journal*, going fishing with buddy Tom Anderson, writing spontaneous letters to people like Paul ("Bear") Bryant, talking old times with Cafego and publicist Haywood Harris at UT's shimmering new athletic plant, and sitting for hours in such haunts as Dick Comer's Sports Center (a pool hall) and Polly's Tavern and Tommy Ford's South Knoxville American Legion Club No. 138.

Except for a handful of sympathetic acquaintances, some of whom have battled booze themselves, Knoxville doesn't really seem to care much about him anymore. When a woman in the upper-class suburbs heard a magazine was planning a story on Suffridge, she said only, in a low gasp, *"Oh, my God."* There is a great deal of embarrassment on the part of the university, although officials there recognize an obligation to him and have, over the years, with fingers crossed, invited him to appear at banquets and halftime ceremonies. "It's really pretty pitiful," says another Knoxvillian. The newspapers generally treat him gently—"He is now a Knoxville businessman," the *Journal* said after his Hall of Fame selection in 1961—and mercifully let it go at that.

Even when you talk to those who know him best you get little insight into what went wrong. Says Tom Anderson: "He's smarter than you'd think he is, and I thought for a while he was going to straighten up. But I guess you have to regard him as a great athlete who never grew up. It gets worse when he starts talking about the old days. He can get to crying in a minute. Some of those big guys are like that." George Cafego is clearly puzzled by it all: "I don't believe the guy's allergic to work. I've *seen* him work." Ben Byrd of the *Journal* paints a picture of a man who has always marched to a different drummer: "He used to drive into town, park his car anywhere he felt like it, pull up the hood like he had engine trouble, and be gone all day. That time Coke hired him to do PR, he got fired when they had a big board meeting and he put a tack on the chair of the chairman of the board. He doesn't mean to cause trouble. Maybe he just never understands the situation. I mean, like when he was sergeant-at-arms for the state legislature one time and didn't like the way a debate was going, he demanded the floor."

Perhaps the best friend Suffridge has is a lanky Knoxville attorney named Charlie Burks, a friend from college days who is a recovering alcoholic himself and deserves some credit for the occasions when Suffridge is in control of things. "Oh, Bob's a great practical joker all right," says Burks. "But what do you say about him and his troubles? He's looking for something, but he doesn't know what it is."

There was a time many years ago when Bob Suffridge knew exactly what he was looking for: three square meals a day and a place to sleep at night. He was born in 1916 on a farm in Raccoon Valley, then a notorious hideout for bootleggers, situated some twenty miles from Knoxville. As one of seven children he often had to help his father carry sacks of sugar and stoke the fire for a moonshine still, but that didn't last long. Bob wanted to go to school and play football, against his father's wishes, and one day when he was fifteen there was a big fight between the two and Bob left home. He wandered into Fountain City, a suburb of Knoxville, where he fended for himself.

"I was living on a park bench at first," he recalls. "One day I went into this doctor's office and got a job going in early in the morning to sweep out the building and start the fire, for two dollars and fifty cents a week. I noticed they had some bedsprings next to the heater in the basement—no mattress, just springs—and since I had a key to the place I started sleeping there." The doctor, a Dr. Carl Martin, came in unusually early one morning on an emergency call and found Suffridge asleep in his clothes and saw that he got a mattress and some blankets. Soon another doctor hired him to clean up his office, too, meaning an additional $2.50 a week. "For two years I lived like that. I carried newspapers, worked in a factory, cleaned out those offices and even joined the National Guard so I could pick up another twelve dollars every three months. I didn't go hungry. I was a monitor at school, and took to stealing my lunch out of lockers."

In the meantime, he was asserting himself as the football star with the Central High School Bobcats. "Maybe I was hungrier than the rest of them," he says. He was almost fully developed physically at the age of eighteen, an eager kid with tremendous speed and reflexes, and in 1936 he captained the Bobcats to the Southern high school championship. Central won thirty-three consecutive games, and Suffridge became a plum for the college recruiters.

Tennessee was the school he wanted. "They already had a lot of tradition. Everybody wanted to play for General Neyland." Something of a loner, a poor country boy accustomed to fighting solitary battles, he spent every ounce of his energy on the football field. "I couldn't get along with anybody. I couldn't understand them." Although he and Neyland were always at odds, there was a curious, if unspoken, mutual respect between the nail-hard disciplinarian and his moody, antagonistic little guard.

Once the last cheers of the 1940 season had died, Bob Suffridge appeared to have the world in his hands. He earned a degree in physical education ("I guess I thought maybe I'd be a coach one day"), married a UT coed and signed to play with the Philadelphia Eagles. He was named All-Pro for the 1941 season, but more important than that was what happened in the last regular game of the year. It was played on Sunday, December 7. "That was the day I blocked three of Sammy Baugh's punts," he says, "but nobody paid any attention the next day. At halftime somebody had come into the dressing room and told us Pearl Harbor had been bombed by the Japs. I'd have been the hero of the day except for that." Suffridge immediately joined the Navy.

In retrospect, that announcement of the attack on Pearl Harbor was the pivotal moment in Suffridge's life. As executive officer on a troop attack transport, he suffered only a slight shrapnel wound to his right leg and went through no especially traumatic experiences. What hurt was the timing of it all. He was twenty-five and in peak physical condition when he went in, but a flabby thirty when he came out. He tried to make a comeback with the Eagles during the 1946 season, but he weighed 225 and was soon riding the bench. The bubble had burst, and he was confused. There would be occasional periods of promise, but once the 1950s came it was a steady, painful downhill slide.

Giving up on pro football, he tried college coaching—at North Carolina State under ex-Vol great Beattie Feathers, and at the Citadel under his old high school coach, Quinn Decker. Next he went to work as an insurance agent for a company in Knoxville, and after three good years he decided to open his own agency. The business did all right for a while, thanks to his name and his contacts around town, but he started in on the pills and the booze and soon had to unload it. ("I sold out for a good profit," Suffridge says, but others say the business fell flat.) And then the wandering began. He went to Nashville to sell used cars. He blew the public relations job with Coca-Cola. He was divorced by his wife in March of 1960, a year before his election to the football Hall of Fame. The chronology of his life became a blur after that. He ran for clerk of the Knox County court and nearly defeated a man who was considered one of the strongest politicians around and who later became mayor of Knoxville. He had to be literally propped up, to the horror of UT officials, at numerous occasions when he was being paraded around as the Vols' greatest player. He drifted to Atlanta, where, for a year, he drank more than he sold at a friend's liquor store. He worked briefly for the state highway department. Finally, around 1965, shortly after the private publication of a boozy paperback biography entitled *Football Beyond Coaching*—composed in various taverns by Suffridge and a local sportswriter known as Raymond ("Streetcar") Edmunds—he suffered two heart attacks.

"Yeah, me and Streetcar had a lot of fun with that book," Suffridge was saying. It was almost dark now, and we had driven out to Tommy Ford's American Legion club. This is the place where Suffridge's Hall of Fame plaque had hung majestically behind the bar for several months before outraged UT officials finally got it for display in a glass showcase on campus, and the place where Suffridge has spent many a night locked up without anybody knowing he was there. He was saying farewell to his friends, for in the morning he would leave for a month's vacation at Daytona Beach as the guest, or mascot, of his attorney friend Charlie Burks and a doctor from Jamestown, Tennessee. He had dropped a couple of dollars at the nickel slot machine, and now he was sitting at the bar, playing some sort of game of chance for a bottle of bourbon.

"How'd the book do?" somebody asked.

"Damn best-seller," he said. "Hell, I made about seventeen thousand dollars off that thing. Sold it for two bucks. We'd have done better than that if we hadn't given away so many. I'd load a batch in the trunk of my car and head out for Nashville, Memphis, and Chattanooga. Sell 'em to people I knew at stores and in bars. Then I'd come back home and find Streetcar sitting in Polly's Tavern and I'd ask him how many he'd sold while I was gone and he'd say he'd gotten rid of two hundred. 'Well, where's the money?' I'd ask him, and he'd say he gave 'em away. Street was almost as good a businessman as I was."

"Go on, Bob, take another chance," said a blonde named Faye.

"Another? Honey, that's getting to be expensive liquor."

"Price of liquor never seemed to bother you much."

"Guess you're right about that." A phone rang. "Get that, will you?" he said. "Might be somebody."

And so it goes, an evening with Bob Suffridge. They are all like that, they say: aimless hours of puns and harmless practical jokes and, if the hour is late enough and the pile of beer cans high enough, those infinitely sad moments when his eyes water up as he talks on about the missed opportunities and the wasted years. How can anyone pass judgment, though, without having come through the same pressures he has? *I came into the world a poor boy, and I'm still a poor boy.* What a man has to do is be grateful for the good times and try to live with the bad.

We were finishing steaks at a motel dining room, washing them down with beer, when the waitress could stand it no longer. A well-preserved woman near Suffridge's age, she had been stealing glances at him throughout the meal. She finally worked up her nerve as she was clearing the table, turning to me and saying with an embarrassed grin: "Excuse me, but didn't I hear you call him Bob?"

"That's right."

"Well, I thought so." For the first time she looked directly at Suffridge. "You're Bob Suffridge, aren't you?"

He wiped his mouth and said, "I guess I am."

"I was Penny Owens. I went to Central High with you."

"Penny...?"

"Oh, you wouldn't remember me. You never would even look at me twice when we were in school."

They talked for a few minutes about old times and former classmates. There was an awkward silence. "So," she said, "ah, what are you *doing* now, Bob?"

"Nothing."

She flushed. "Oh."

He suppressed a belch and then looked up at her with a mischievous grin. "You want to help me?"

"Aw, you."

"Awww, you."

Gary Cartwright

When Gary Cartwright (b. 1934) reported for his first day of work at the *Fort Worth Press*, squeaky clean at 6 A.M., a grizzled copy editor looked up from the vodka he was sipping out of a paper cup and said, "You'll never make it, kid." Cartwright has gotten a lot of mileage out of that moment, particularly when he was the reigning free spirit of Texas sportswriters. Of course it helped that he did make something of himself. He was a newspaper sports columnist in Dallas; wrote for all the right magazines (*Harper's, Esquire, Rolling Stone, Sports Illustrated*); churned out the inevitable football novel, *The Hundred Yard War* (1968); crashed the best seller list with true-crime books, *Blood Will Tell* (1979) being the most prominent; and wrote the screenplay for the rodeo movie *J. W. Coop* (1972) with fellow Texan Edwin (Bud) Shrake. Cartwright's longest lasting achievement was the twenty-five years he put in as a senior editor at *Texas Monthly*, a run that ended when he retired in 2010 after writing stories on subjects ranging from stripper Candy Barr to dogfighting to the death of his son Mark. The subject he wrote about most, however, was the Dallas Cowboys, the team he began covering as a newspaperman and that fascinated and perplexed him long afterward. In the following 1973 essay, he wrestles with the good and bad of the Cowboys' stoic coach, Tom Landry, still perplexed but, as always, eminently readable.

Tom Landry: Melting the Plastic Man

WHAT WAS THE OLD WORLD COMING TO?, I asked Tom Landry. Landry was at his desk, his back to an autographed picture of Billy Graham, facing the big, silver Super Bowl VI trophy, impassive as a museum director, fielding questions with technical, theological, thermo-regular certainty, impervious to the demons that my senses told me were present in staggering numbers.

I mean *where is it leading us?* This obsession with being first, being best, being No. 1. Tampered transcripts at Ball High in Galveston, rigged Soap Box Derbies in Akron, highly-subsidized 11-year-old Chinamen making a shambles of the Little League World Series, bribes, kickbacks, burglary, perjury, Watergate. Had the monster of our pioneering escaped in the rose garden? It seemed to me that this preoccupation with being No. 1 was rushing us toward the Temple of False Idols, and from there to the paranoiac's ward.

"I don't mean football or even sports in particular," I said, "I'm talking about this country, across the board. This thing, this passion... this *belief* that in the search for success the means justify the end...."

Yeah, Landry knew what I meant. He had been challenged before, and I had heard him expound his beliefs many times—in interviews, press conferences, damp locker rooms, and Fellowship of Christian Athletes banquets. "Take away winning," he had said, "and you take away everything that is strong about America." But I wanted to hear him say it again.

"You're talking now about the negative side of winning," he began, and I fancied that there was a hitch in the toneless economy of his voice. "Generally, achieving goals... which in many cases means winning... is really the ultimate in this life we live in. Being the best at whatever talent you have, that's what stimulates life. I don't mean cheating or doing things that are bad. That's the negative side. But here's the thing: what are the alternatives? If you don't believe in winning, you don't believe in free enterprise, capitalism, our way of life. If you eliminate our way of life, the American way of life, what is the effect... what are the alternatives?"

I said that I couldn't name them all, but humility was probably one. Peace. Joy. Freedom from the stigma of failure. If this country had the same appetite for peace and brotherly love as it had for war and puritanical vengeance... if free enterprise was more than a code word for greed... we might become the beacon of the world that we imagine ourselves to be.

Tom smiled his ice age smile: I had known him for 14 years and we had had this discussion many times. Tom did not see a contradiction between the terms *pride* and *humility*, any more than some politicians and military men see a rift in slogans like Bombs for Peace.

"Achievement builds character," he told me. "People striving, being knocked down and coming back... this is what builds character in a man. The Bible talks about it at length in Paul, in Romans. Paul says that adversity brings on endurance, endurance brings on character, and character brings on hope."

"Then hope... not joy, peace or love... hope is the ultimate goal?"

"That's right," he said. "Character is the ability of a person to see a positive end of things. This is the hope that a man of character has. It's an old cliché in football that losing seasons build character, but there is a great truth in it. I've seen very little character in players who have never had to face adversity. This is part of the problem we see in this country today... young people who have never really had to struggle in life, when they do eventually face problems where they need to turn to character, it's not there. They turn to the alternatives: drugs, alcohol or something."

Drugs, alcohol or something. Hmmm. I wondered what that *something* could be. Al Ward, the Cowboys' assistant general manager who had known Landry since 1945, recalled that Landry's own life was a progression of goals... to make his team at Mission, Texas High School, to make it at the University of Texas, to make it with the New York Giants. "But each time he reached his goal," Ward said, "the kick wasn't there. Then he found religion. Now he is satisfied with life." Though he had been a Methodist since boyhood, Landry claims he didn't become a Christian until 1958, two years before he became the Cowboys' first and only head coach. "I was invited to join a Bible-study breakfast group at the Melrose Hotel in Dallas, and I realized I had never really accepted Christ into my heart. Now I have turned my will over to Jesus Christ," he explained. There is nothing unusual in getting off on Jesus, or even using Holy Scripture to justify any act or event, but in coming to grips with the alternatives—that is, *eliminating* them—Landry seemed to have refined the narcotic qualities of Paul's definition of character.

Landry was relaxed, more than I had ever seen him, strangely relaxed considering that it was less than three hours before game time, perversely relaxed for a man who detests small talk and was now being bombarded with it: 30 minutes, my allotted time, had elapsed and I hadn't yet mentioned football to the man who is supposed to be the finest brain in the business. Landry's cobalt eyes studied me, waiting for a question, and I tried to remember what had happened in the year since I saw him last. He appeared warmer, less regimented, even vulnerable. Why?

Well, two things were obvious. The Cowboys had not repeated as Super Bowl champions, thus laying waste all that talk about a Cowboy dynasty. And 15 of the 40 players who did win the Super Bowl had been traded or forced into early retirement. Unlike previous champions—the Giants, the Packers, the Colts—the Cowboys weren't waiting for the skids, they were rebuilding while they were still near the top.

But there was something else, something Cowboys president Tex Schramm mentioned earlier. We were talking about the criticism that Landry treats his players like so many cards in a computer file.

Schramm said: "You have to remember, Tom is a very honest, straightforward person. He is not a con artist. He treats his players like adults. Some coaches sell their players a bill of goods... you've seen it, they stop just short of holding hands when they cross the street... and these coaches get away with it because their consciences don't bother them. Tom can't do that.

"I think one thing that happened last year was that Tom tried to adapt... he tried to have a double standard. Even though it was against his nature. This year there is one standard and everyone conforms. Tom has gone back to his original concept of gathering about him the type of players he likes."

It *is* staggering, the roster of non-conformers who had gone down the drain. Duane Thomas, Tody Smith, Billy Parks, Ron Sellers, Dave Manders, and in years gone by talents like Don Meredith, John Wilbur, Lance Rentzel, and Pete Gent, to name very few. Landry lifted his eyes and they vanished. Thomas was a landmark in Landry's experiment with the double standard. Thomas got away with things that in Meredith's times would have called for thumb screws. There were those in the Dallas organization (players, especially) who resented Thomas leading them to two consecutive Super Bowls almost as much as they resented not getting there without him last season. The official theory is, the Cowboys paid last year for the sin of putting up with Thomas in two previous campaigns.

Take the case of Billy Parks, heretofore a good white boy with a sterling reputation as a pass receiver. In the aftermath of Duane Thomas, Parks insisted on wearing white football shoes and speaking out against the war. Once, he refused to play because his black friend Tody Smith was hurt, and another time he took himself out of a game because his presence on the field was keeping a black receiver on the bench.

Now they were gone, the non-conformers as well as the non-achievers, and Landry looked more relaxed than I'd ever seen him. You know the illegal smile, the one John Prine sings about? Landry wore what you might call a *legal* smile.

He told me: "I've come to the conclusion that players want to be treated alike. They may talk about individualism, but I believe they want a single standard. Yes, that belief is behind many of the trades we made. If a player is contributing and performing the way he ought to, he will usually conform. Now if he isn't performing well and not conforming to team standards either, he ought not be around. We can put up with someone who is getting the job done as long as he'll conform. But we just can't get along with a player who doesn't conform or perform. No way."

There is a common misunderstanding among football experts that the best team—the team with the most talent—wins. It is true that you don't win without talent, but in the National Football League there are five or six teams of more or less equal ability. In those delirious hours after Super Bowl VI when the Cowboys were drunk with victory and talk of the new dynasty rained down, Landry permitted himself a Virginia reel around the dressing room, then he struck a note of caution. The question, Landry said, is will the Cowboys perform at the same level next year.

"At the championship level," he said, "there is a very narrow edge between winning and losing. You don't have to take much away from a team to keep them out of the Super Bowl. The hunger that makes a player work hard enough to win is inherent in some, but in others it has to be built in. The edge comes from trying to achieve a goal. Once you've achieved it, it is very difficult to look back at the price you've paid and then make yourself do it again."

At the bottom of the sweet cup of Super Bowl VI, Landry read the future. Though they were essentially the same team that won the Super Bowl, the 1972 Cowboys were found lacking. There is only one Super Bowl; and it's no disgrace not to get there: in recent years, only Vince Lombardi's Green Bay Packers have been able to repeat as champions.

That is what hurt, the fact that Lombardi had done it. There had been no double standard at Green Bay. All-Pro guard Jerry Kramer once remarked, "Coach Lombardi treats us all the same—like dogs." Even before his death a few years ago Lombardi was a football legend, a vain, volatile, uncompromising dictator, a living metaphor for Number 1. Could Tom Landry afford to be something less? Not if he had character.

It wasn't Jesus or Paul that Tom Landry had in mind when he did corrective surgery on the 1973 Cowboy team, it was Vince Lombardi.

Lombardi and Landry were guiding forces behind the great New York Giants' teams of the Fifties, and when pro football climbed out of the coal yards into the affluent livingrooms of America in the early Sixties, they were major influences. Jim Lee Howell was the head coach of the Giants, but it was Lombardi's offense and Landry's defense that gave the Giants character. After Lombardi moved on to the head job at Green Bay and Landry took on the new franchise in Dallas, Howell resigned, explaining that "Ten victories don't make up for two defeats."

"Lombardi was a much warmer person than Landry," says Wellington Mara, the Giants' owner. "He went from warm to red hot. You could hear him laughing or shouting for five blocks. You couldn't hear Landry from the next chair. Lombardi was more of a teacher. It was as though Landry lectured the top 40 per cent of the class and Lombardi taught the lower ten per cent."

Landry was still a player-coach when he designed the modern 4-3 Defense, pro football's equivalent of the doomsday machine. Later, at Dallas, Landry pioneered a method of combating that defense—the multiple offense.

"Landry was a born student of the game," says Em Tunnell, the great defensive back who played with (and later for) Landry. "But he was kind of weird. After a game the rest of us would go out for a beer, Tom would disappear. He was always with his family. You never knew what was going through his mind. He never said nothing, but he always knew what was going on. We didn't have words like *keying* (ie: reacting to prearranged schemes) in those days, so Tom made up his own keys and taught them to the rest of us."

By training, Landry was an industrial engineer: he had a need to know what was going on. "I couldn't be satisfied trusting my instincts the way Tunnell did," Landry explained. "I didn't have the speed or the quickness. I had to train myself and everyone around me to key various opponents and recognize tendencies."

"Most of us just played the game," Frank Gifford recalls. "Landry studied it. He was cool and calculating. Emotion had no place in his makeup."

Another former Giant, Dick Nolan, who went on to become head coach of the San Francisco 49ers, says, "I remember one time Tom was at the blackboard, showing me that if their flanker came out on the strong side on a third-down play, and the fullback flared to the weak side, I was to follow the fullback out a few steps and then race back quickly because they would be bringing the wingback inside me to take a pass. 'But Tom,' I said, 'what if I commit myself that completely and the wingback isn't there?' Tom just looked at me without any change of expression and said, 'He will be.' "

Landry's reputation was constantly exposed to ridicule in the mid-1960s, not only because his Cowboys twice lost championship games to Lombardi's Packers, but because Landry himself came across as such a cerebral paradox, a rigid, humorless figure stalking the sidelines of the Cotton Bowl in his felt snapbrim and burial-policy dark suit. Like the team he coached, Lombardi was purely physical, seething, kicking, pushing, openly humiliating those around him; and getting results. If the Packers were the bludgeons of pro football, the Cowboys were the slide rules. Paul Hornung once observed, "Lombardi would be kicking you in the rump one minute and putting his arm around you the next. "

Landry would react to a great play or a poor play in the same dispassionate manner, as though it were ancient history. When a player was down writhing in agony, the contrast was most apparent: Lombardi would be racing like an Italian fishwife, cursing and imploring the gods to get the lad back on his feet for at least one more play; Landry would be giving instructions to the unfortunate player's substitute.

Landry once explained: "The reason I take on the appearance of being unemotional is I don't believe you can be emotional and concentrate the way you must to be effective. When I see a great play from the sidelines, I can't cheer it. I'm a couple of plays ahead, thinking.

"Lombardi's style of play was very different from ours. The Green Bay system of offense—we call it the basic system—was that you were going to run the power sweep regardless of what the other team put up against you. Run that play over and over until you could execute it in your sleep. It was all execution. So Lombardi had to develop the players to an emotional pitch, keep them doing their best all the time against a defense that knew what was coming. The Packers had to stay very high emotionally to win.

"Our system is different. We run a multiple offense and must take advantage of situations as they present themselves. Everything we do from every formation doesn't work against every defense, so we have to concentrate, we have to think. Our defense is also quite compli-cated. It depends on reading movements and formations and knowing where to go. Therefore the nature of response from the sidelines must be very different. The players don't want to see me rushing around and screaming. They want to believe I know what I'm doing."

Lee Roy Jordan, Dallas' middle linebacker, explains: "Landry isn't a praising coach, he's a corrective coach. If you do something right, that's what you oughta do. He only talks when you do some-thing wrong. If Tom says 'damn it', you know something severe has happened."

There were traces of empathy when the Packers referred to Vince Lombardi as *Il Duce*. Landry has been called Old Computer Face, a description that has all but vanished with the non-conformers and non-achievers. Pete Gent used to say he could tell when Landry was mad, the muscles beneath Landry's ears would pop out and his eyes would sort of glaze. "His normal method of discipline is to treat you like a number," Gent said. "He seems to be concentrating on talking to you mainly to keep you from vanishing."

Gent, author of the bitterly-critical pro football novel *North Dallas Forty* [read: Dallas Cowboys], agrees with another ex-Cowboy, Duane Thomas: "Landry *is* a plastic man. And yet, there is this paradox—in Landry's presence you do not feel the cool platitudes of plastic and computers, you feel something more visceral. You feel fear." Meredith and other ex-Cowboys have said the same thing. It is the fear that no matter how hard you try or how much you care you will be found inadequate.

Landry hadn't read Gent's novel and didn't plan to, but he was aware of the general criticism: bigtime football is dehumanizing, bru-tal and unfairly stacked on the side of management.

In rebuttal Landry said: "It's an amazing thing, this whole area of criticism... the one thing a player respects in a coach is that the coach makes him do what he doesn't want to do in order to win. Lombardi had great respect from his players, not because they liked him person-ally but because he made winners of them. That is what all coaches are attempting to do, make players do things they don't want to do in order to achieve success. The people who usually level this sort of criticism [read: Gent] are the people who didn't achieve."

By Landry's code, you could stick Gent's ration of character on the back of a postage stamp. Gent was not a great player, but he hung around for five years. Landry never understood why Gent, Meredith and others sat at the rear of team meetings, laughing hysterically. Gent explains why in his novel: they were cracking and passing snappers of amyl nitrate. Gent once observed of Landry's playbook, "It's a good book, but everyone gets killed in the end." Gent's own book has already earned him more than $500,000. Non-achiever, indeed.

Meredith, the honky-tonk hero, was a special case. From the beginning he was the Cowboys' future. Coming off a brilliant career as an All-American quarterback at SMU, Meredith approached pro football as though he were Popeye saving Olive Oyl from the cannibals. Meredith's quality was leadership, an ability to strike a spark of hope in the most hopeless situation. That is why he was called Dandy Don, a name Landry never appreciated. Meredith could rally a team from certain defeat, or splinter the sobriety of a practice session by perking off his helmet and threatening Cornell Green with bodily harm. He played it for laughs: the notion of Meredith threatening a headhunter like Cornell Green was beautifully absurd, and everyone appreciated it—everyone except Landry, who reminded the Cowboys in the meeting that night: "Gentlemen, nothing funny ever happens on a football field."

I don't know if Landry ever saw it, but beneath all that tomfoolery and searching Meredith was essentially the person he joked about—a good ol' East Texas boy, eaten up with talent and the Protestant vision of material success, fairly begging to excel and be recognized. Meredith endured against his own better judgment. He played many games when he could have rightly been in the hospital.

Meredith's unhappy decision to slide into premature retirement came after Landry supplied an obstacle Meredith wasn't prepared to endure. Landry pulled Meredith from the 1968 playoff game with Cleveland and replaced him with Craig Morton. Ironically, Landry pulled Meredith for throwing an interception that should have been credited against Landry's disciplined system of play. According to Landry's gospel, the Cleveland defensive back who intercepted Meredith's final pass should have been on the other side of the field. Unfortunately, the Cleveland defensive back was in the wrong place.

It wasn't that Landry was wrong; Cleveland just wasn't right. Meredith couldn't endure the consequences—the humiliation that after all these years of enduring he could be benched for non-achievement.

When Meredith went to Landry, his pride crushed and personal problems weighing around him like a 90,000-ton infection, thinking that at last he had made the right choice, a choice that would please Landry, the choice to quit football—then Landry would stay in character and say: straighten up, don't do it, forget it ever happened and smile tomorrow. Instead, Landry looked at him coolly and said: "Don, I think you are making the right decision."

Landry contends that he was "treating Don Meredith as an adult," respecting Meredith's right and ability to decide for himself. But given their relationship, a relationship Landry controlled, that was no way to treat Don Meredith.

When I was a sportswriter in Dallas Meredith and I had this unspoken arrangement whereby he would tell me what I needed to know and I would change his quotes to make both of us appear literate. Meredith had only one reservation to this arrangement. "Watch out for my image," he would caution me after every interview. Meredith saw himself as a 13th-century troubadour persecuted for his good intentions. He saw Landry as the Black Monk, a creature who could swallow himself without changing form. If Landry understood the depth of Meredith's paranoia, he never let on.

Sitting now across the desk from Landry, looking through the man and seeing my own reflection, I wonder: what image does Landry have of himself? I have been in many coaches' offices and observed that the decor is narcissistic—for example, the walls of Bear Bryant's office are papered with pictures of the Coach and his Team, the Coach and his Family, the Coach and Phil Harris, the Coach and his Buick. But there are only two pictures in Landry's office—a small, gold-framed portrait of his family, and the large autographed picture of Billy Graham looking down from infinity. Is it possible that Landry sees himself as a rock?

I ask Landry if he thinks he has changed in the last four years and he takes a long time to answer. "I've tried to," he says. "I think I've become more aware of people as individuals. I know the criticism—that I look at my players as numbers—and I guess there's something to it. People my age... we grew up with the Depression, the War... a time of ICBMs and pinstripe suits and rampant materialism. But times are changing. I see that and I make an effort to change, too."

Has Landry changed? I ask Clint Murchison, Jr., the Cowboys owner. "His hair has gotten shorter," Murchison says. Anything else? "Not that I know of," Murchison says.

They are subtle, befitting their instigator, but the changes are there. There are fewer rules, veteran players tell me. Veteran players (though not rookies) can wear their hair any way they please, and with a few exceptions like Bob Lilly and Roger Staubach, most of them look like candidates for a drug raid. Landry personally sees to it that the word "optional" is printed on the schedule announcing the time and place of the weekly Sunday devotional. And the double standard, while officially reputed, exists as a practical matter.

"Just before training camp," Al Ward tells me, "Walt Garrison asked Landry for permission to ride in a rodeo. Landry has strictly forbidden Garrison to rodeo, but of course Garrison does it anyway. But this time, when he asked permission, Landry just said, 'I don't want to know about it.'"

In the preseason game against Kansas City Landry did something that no one in the press box could remember seeing him do before— he walked over to an injured player and inquired about his health.

What was it that Paul said again... about adversity and endurance and character and hope? Hope for what? More adversity? I look at Tom Landry again and now I know his self image. Landry sees himself as a circle. So be it.

Tom Archdeacon

Newspaper sports sections are noisy precincts these days, overflowing with so much outrage and vitriol that it's hard to separate honestly felt opinions from those manufactured to fit the occasion. The vast majority of columnists and beat reporters take their cues from talk radio and cable-TV yak fests without a thought to what they've abandoned: the art of storytelling. To understand how great the loss is, you need only turn to Tom Archdeacon (b. 1951) of the *Dayton Daily News*, a craftsman committed to finding the humanity in every subject he tackles. Archdeacon is a big, shambling character with a walrus mustache and a willingness to go wherever the wind blows him. He has been operating that way for nearly four decades, since he was writing about football, boxing, horse racing, and oddball characters for the *Miami News*. The *News* ran a distant second to the *Miami Herald* before folding in 1988, but it offered him stylistic freedom and P.M. deadlines, which meant he could stay with a story all night if he had to. For the January 22, 1979 edition he turned his writer's eye on a great player's worst moment. There are no cheap shots at Jackie Smith for dropping a pass that cost the Dallas Cowboys a touchdown in Super Bowl XIII. There is only the restraint that Smith himself shows as he faces wave after wave of reporters, all while his fourteen-year-old son looks on. You come away from the story filled with admiration for him, and for Archdeacon, too.

Smith Hates for It to End Like This

D ARRELL SMITH sat there and listened quietly. What he heard hurt him, but he didn't speak. He looked down at the floor. He fidgeted and fumbled with a small Instamatic camera he had brought to the game.

Six feet away, his dad, just out of the shower, stood nude.

And the sportswriters, dozens of them, swooped in immediately and stripped him even further.

"Why did you drop it?"

"Will this play stand out in your mind 10 years from now?"

"Is this the biggest disappointment of your career?"

"What's going through your head?"

"Are you embarrassed?"

"Do you think you cost Dallas the game?"
"Tell us about it again, will you?"
"Will you watch the play on the films?"

For 45 minutes, Jackie Smith, the veteran tight end of the Dallas Cowboys, stood in front of his Orange Bowl dressing room stall and took it. It hurt him. It hurt his 14-year-old son.

Pittsburgh had just beaten Dallas, 35–31, in Super Bowl XIII.

The biggest heartbreak of the game for Dallas had come with 2:30 left in the third quarter.

The Cowboys, trailing 21–14, had a third down and three yards to go situation on the Pittsburgh 10-yard line. Using a run offense (double tight ends), Dallas completely fooled Pittsburgh's defense. Smith slipped into the end zone and stood there all alone as Cowboy quarterback Roger Staubach floated a pass a bit low to him. It looked like a sure touchdown. But Smith slipped just as he was about to make the catch, and the ball bounced off his hip pad and fell harmlessly onto the painted grass of the end zone.

An incredulous gasp arose from the Dallas fans. Their Pittsburgh counterparts went berserk. And Jackie Smith sat there in the end zone, stunned.

The field goal unit came in and Smith walked off.

Super Bowl XIII was to be the ultimate reward for Smith.

A month shy of 39, he was the oldest man on the field yesterday. He had toiled so long and so well over the years for the St. Louis Cardinals that Cowboys' president Tex Schramm had guaranteed Smith was "sure-fire Hall of Fame" material.

No tight end in the history of pro football has caught more passes (483) or gained more yards on receptions (7,956) than Jackie Smith. But in his 15 seasons with the Cards, he never made it to the pinnacle of his profession.

So after last season, he retired. A Cardinal doctor had warned him that he would risk paralysis if he kept playing with the nagging neck injury he had had for two seasons. When the St. Louis pre-season camp opened this year, Smith wasn't there. He was with his son in the mountains of New Mexico.

"My Boy Scout troop went on a 100-mile hike in the mountains and my dad went along," Darrell said yesterday. "When he was playing with the Cards, he never got any time with us. While we were up there, I asked him if he wished he was back with the Cards and he said 'No,' but I'm sure he missed it.

"But when we got back, he still took his physical. They said he flunked it."

So Smith busied himself in civilian life. He sells real estate. He has a restaurant and bar in St. Louis called "Jackie's Place." And he planned to move his family into the country, where Darrell said they are going to raise horses on 20 acres.

Two clubs called Smith to see if he'd be interested in playing with them. He didn't even return their calls. If he was going to come back to football this year, it was either going to be with the Cards or a club he felt was a sure contender.

"Then, one night, Dad called me from the restaurant," Darrell said. "He was excited. He said he had just gotten a call from Coach Landry. I thought he was kidding. I laughed, but the next day he was on the plane to Dallas."

The Cowboys needed a replacement for Jay Saldi, who had broken his arm. They felt Smith was the best of the crop of free agents available. After all, a year ago, Smith caught the touchdown pass that enabled the Cardinals to beat the Cowboys. Smith passed the physical and joined the club in early October before the first Washington game.

"I was worried when I first came to the Cowboys," Smith said. "I didn't know if I could get in shape. I didn't know how I'd be accepted. I was thinking I might have overloaded myself."

Smith caught no passes during the regular season, but was often used when the Cowboys went to a two tight end formation. His blocking was still effective, so much so, that after the Philadelphia game, he was presented the game ball. In the playoffs, he made three receptions including a touchdown catch in the Cowboys' 27–20 victory over Atlanta.

After the Cowboys 28–0 NFC championship victory over Los Angeles, Smith said, "I looked around and I wasn't with all those people, Irv Goode, Charley Johnson, Larry Wilson, I'd cranked up with all those years [in St. Louis]. Those guys had worked just as hard as I had and they never had it happen. All those years, we'd come into camp saying this will be the year and all we got was frustrated. I had gotten so I almost hated this game [Super Bowl] because we worked so hard. Now it didn't seem fair that I was the lucky one."

The game was an hour past and still the sportswriters and sportscasters pushed in around Smith. They pushed his son, bumping him, not knowing who he was.

Two writers would leave and four would fight to squeeze into the vacant spots. They stuck their notepads and microphones in Smith's face. They stepped on his towel. They'd ask the same questions over and over.

One sportswriter, pushed from behind, began to slip. He tried to brace his fall with his hand. As he did, he brushed his felt tip pen across Smith's back, leaving a black streak of ink on a shoulder blade.

And Jackie Smith stood and took it.

"I was wide open and I just missed it," he said. "It was a little behind me, but not enough that I should have missed the ball. Hell, the coverage had left. I tried to get down. I was trying to be overcautious. On a play like that, you want to get it in your hands and pull it close to your body. My left foot got stuck and my hip went out from under me."

"Did you take your eye off?" a reporter asked.

"I don't remember the ball the last few inches," Smith said quietly. "I don't remember. I promise you, I don't remember. I just missed it."

He sat down. He didn't focus on his interrogators. The crows' feet around his eyes made his face look tired. He pulled on his brown pants and his fancy tooled cowboy boots.

Across the dressing room, Staubach spoke of the same play.

"I saw him open and I took something off it. I didn't want to drill it through his hands," he said. "The ball was low. It could have been better. Chalk that one up to both of us."

Before yesterday's game, Smith was not quite sure whether he'd play again next season or not.

Last night, he had decided.

"I've decided that I don't want to try it again," he said. "I was looking to get away from it last year. It takes a while, but I thought I had done it and then everything got regenerated again. I hate for it to end like this. It's part of what you do when you play the game. It's from the intensity. You have a lot of good times and a lot of bad times. I hope it won't haunt me, but it probably will." His voice trailed off a bit. "I've still got what I've done, who I've met, but I hate going out like this. All these years, all the wait, and this is what they'll remember."

He was fully dressed now and had withstood the barrage.

"I've had about all I can take now," he said quietly to a friend.

He picked up his belongings and excused himself from the new wave of reporters who were still probing away. He walked over to his son, tapped him on the head and said: "Let's go."

The two got to the locker room door, but before Smith got out, a sportscaster with a little tape recorder shoved a microphone up into his face and blurted, "I hate to bring this up Jackie, you've probably answered it already, but why did you drop that pass?"

Jackie Smith sighed.

Richard Price

The mind boggles at the thought of what Bear Bryant's first impression of Richard Price (b. 1949) must have been. Price arrived at the University of Alabama in 1979 to interview the football coach who earned his nickname wrestling carnival bears and almost killed off his early teams with training camps more brutal than anything the Marine Corps ever devised. And here was this skinny, twitchy, baggy-eyed writer with long hair, an earring, and a Bronx accent, and he said he was from *Playboy*, with all those pictures of naked women that can sap a young linebacker's energy faster than lightning. Though only twenty-nine at the time, Price had written three novels—*The Wanderers* (1974), *Bloodbrothers* (1976), and *Ladies' Man* (1978)—all lusty and vivid and brimming with street smarts as foreign to Tuscaloosa as a bagel with a schmear. He has since written five more novels, including *Clockers* (1992) and *Freedomland* (1998); received an Oscar nomination in 1986 for his screenplay of *The Color of Money*; and won an Edgar Award in 2007 for his writing for the brilliant HBO series *The Wire*. None of them, however, may have presented Price with as big a challenge as understanding Bryant when he started speaking in that tobacco-cured mumble of his.

Bear Bryant's Miracles

BECAUSE I GREW UP in a multiethnic environment in New York City, the South has always conjured up some bad news reactions on word-association tests for me: Klan, lynch, redneck, moonshine, speed-trap towns and death... lots of death.

As the years have passed, I've started hearing some flip sides. There's the "New South," with Atlanta as cosmopolitan as New York. I've heard that, despite the headline horrors, Southerners get along racially better than Northerners. And that foreign blacks prefer the upfrontness of the South to the hypocritical liberal bullshit of the North.

But despite all my revisionist thoughts, the only good images that have held up in my head are Southern novelists and the University of Alabama football team. The novelists because they are good or great and the Crimson Tide because, like Notre Dame, they are the New York Yankees of college football. I don't give a rat's ass about football, college or otherwise, and I'm not crazy about regimentation or bullet-head activities. But I do admire winners.

And as ignorant as I am of the "real" South and football in general, even *I* know that the man behind the winning tradition at Alabama is a magnetic, scary John Wayne type named Paul "Bear" Bryant. I would see him every few years on a televised bowl game, standing on the side lines, craggy-faced, in that houndstooth hat. I figured he was some kind of coaching genius. I also got the notion that he was somebody I was very glad not to have as a teacher in any course I was flunking.

On the plane headed for Birmingham, I am armed with two documents: *Bear*, coach Bryant's autobiography; and the 1978 *Alabama Football Crimson Tide Press Guide*. *Bear* doesn't do much for me—it's a little too cagily humble. The *Press Guide*, on the other hand, has me freaking out six ways to Sunday. These guys are *monsters*. Even the handsome fraternity types have that combat-veteran look about them.

The other things that are dizzying in the press book are the win-loss stats. They're almost pornographic. Since Bryant went to Alabama in 1958, the Tide's record has been 193-38-8. In the past eight years, try 85-11—that's almost 11 wins per season. They were in 20 bowl games in a row, won all but one Southeastern Conference title since 1971 ('76 went to Georgia), won five national championships since 1961 and have a home record of 60-1, with 45 straight victories.

Bryant is the winningest active coach, with 284 victories in 34 years at four schools, and is third in total wins only to Amos Alonzo Stagg and Pop Warner as far as the history of the game goes.

At the Birmingham airport, I start wondering why the hell I am keying in so much on the hairdos I see all around me. The Dolly Parton pompadours, the rock-a-billy duck asses, the military knuckle-heads. Then I look in a mirror. With the possible exception of a photo of Duane Allman, I have the longest hair of anybody I've seen all day. I start getting visions of rusty scissors in a sheriff's office. Ah, that's all Hollywood horseshit, I tell myself. But I do go into a men's room and remove my earring.

Bryant Hall is where all the players have to live for the four or five years they're at Alabama. It was among the first sports dorms in the country and it received a lot of flak for special treatment, pampering, athletic elitism. Since then, sports dorms have popped up all over, but the controversy still goes on.

In any event, as I go there for lunch with Kirk McNair, Alabama's sports information director, I expect to see something between a palace and a beachfront condominium. What I see is more like a cross between a dorm and a housing project. The place looks like shit. Off the lobby is a TV room and the dining room. Players walk by. Some are mammoth, with roast-beef shoulders and ham-hock thighs, and they shuffle sway-backed into the dining room: others aren't much bigger than I am. Alabama opts for quickness over bulk; consequently, it's not that big a team.

I eat with McNair and a Birmingham sportswriter, plus a short, heavy Italian guy who runs a restaurant in town, is a freak for the team and supplies everybody with food. He just likes to hang around with the boys.

From where we sit, I can see the guys taking the empty trays to the disposal area. They all seem to shuffle, drag their feet like they're saving it up for practice—or else they have that sprightly pigeon-toed jock walk, as if they're about to sprint across a room keeping a soccer ball afloat with their toes and knees.

I don't hear anybody mention Bear Bryant. In fact he doesn't have that much personal contact with his players. He's got a huge staff of coaching assistants who get down in the dirt with them.

But he's there. He's in that room. He *is* the team and everybody knows it.

A football is laid out with a white pen by the tray-disposal area, and the players sign the ball after they get rid of their trays. Some kid is going to get the best birthday present in the entire state. Or maybe it's for his old man.

Later that afternoon, I'm taken to the grass practice field. The sports offices are in the coliseum and there's a long underground walkway that connects with the closed-to-the-public Astroturf practice field. The first thing I notice as I come up to ground level, slightly drunk on the waft of freshly cut grass, is a tower. A huge 50-foot-high observation post.

And up there is my first shot of Bear, slouched against the railing, wearing a beat-up varsity jacket, a baseball cap, a megaphone hanging from one wrist. He doesn't move, just leans back like he's lost in thought. Below him, there are maybe 100 guys running plays, mashing into one another in the dirt, attacking dummies. A massive division of labor of violence, speed and strength. Assistant coaches are all over, screaming, barking, shoving, soothing (though not too much), encouraging. A sound track of grunts, growls, roars and commands floats in the spring air. And above it all, Bear doesn't move, he doesn't even seem to be interested. It's as though he's a stranded lifeguard, six months off season, wondering how the hell he got up there and how the hell he's gonna get down.

The most terrifying workout I see that day is called the gauntlet drill. You take three linemen, line them up one behind the other about ten feet apart. Then a relatively small running back is placed about five feet in front of the first lineman, and at the sound of a whistle, he tries to get past the first lineman. If he does, the lineman gets the shit chewed out of him by the defensive coach. If he doesn't, the running back gets dumped on his ass by an enormous amount of meat and gear. Either way, he has to set to, go around the second lineman, then the third. Somehow, with that coach bawling and shoving the lineman who fucked up, I feel more anxiety for the lineman than I do for the halfback.

On the Astroturf field, there are two practice scrimmages with referees. I sit on the side-line bench with a number of pro scouts, a few privileged civilians and a bunch of shaggy-haired 12-year-olds who walk up and down the side line imitating that pigeon-toed jock walk, chewing gum and trying to look like future prospects. Like me, every few minutes they sneak a glance at the tower to check out the big man.

The players are wearing jerseys of one of five colors. Red jersey— first-string offense. White—first-string defense. Blue—second-string defense. Green—second-string offense. And gold. Gold signifies "Don't tackle this man," which means the guy is either a quarterback (quarterbacks never get tackled in practice) or nursing an injury.

I look up at the tower. Bear is gone.

The bench we're sitting on divides the pits and the Astroturf from a long, flat grassy field with just a few goal posts at one distant end. Bear makes it down to earth and, head still down, slowly ambles over to the grassy field. Some of the 12-year-olds notice and nudge one another. He's walking away. Going home. Hands in pockets. The bench divides the two shows: the number-one college team working out to the west and the coach slowly walking alone to the east.

I turn my back on the players and watch Bear walk. He gets out about 50 yards toward the walkway back to the coliseum when a player on crutches, hobbling toward the Astroturf, meets him at midfield. They stop, exchange a few words (the crutches do *not* fall away as I would prefer) and the wounded player swings along toward the crowd.

Bear stands there, staring at his shoes, scratching his nose. Then, without looking up, he puts a whistle in his mouth, shoots a couple of weak toots I think only I can hear, and suddenly the earth is shaking and I'm caught in a buffalo stampede. Every player has immediately dropped everything and is tearing ass over to Bear.

They say no one *ever* walks for a second from the beginning to the end of an Alabama practice. Within 20 seconds of his whistle, Bear is surrounded in a square by four perfect lines. Blue jersey, south; white, north; red, east; green, west. Bear squints into the distance. A player leaps forward out of the tense and taut blue south—they're all in a slight crouch, eyes on the blue leader, who jerks his hands toward his helmet and, in a twinkling, they follow suit; he jerks his hands down to his flexed thighs, halfway up to his chest, a half jerk up, down, a feint, finger tips to the helmet. The entire blue squad is frozen except for its arms. Back and knees bent, eyes and neck straight ahead, they play flawless follow-the-leader for 15 seconds, then stand up straight, arching their backs, and clap and cheer for themselves.

As soon as they applaud, the leader of the green west leaps out and leads his squad through a perfect 15-second drill. The green applaud themselves. Bear stands alone in the center of all this, a deity, a religious rock being rapidly salaamed by an army of jocks. The green cheer is immediately followed by the white north, then applause, then red east. Fifteen flawless seconds each of heart-stopping precision—Bear Bryant the centerpiece, looking nowhere, everywhere, watching or lost in thought.

Then every one of them is running back to where he came from. Back to the dirt, the Astroturf, the tackling sled. Back over my head and shoulders. And once again, Bear is alone on the field, hands in pockets just like 120 seconds before. He has not said a thing, seemingly never looked at anyone. Behind me, the practices are in full swing. I watch coach Bryant amble over to his tower and slowly ascend the 50 feet to his platform, resume his slouch against the railing and check out whatever those flinty eyes deem in need of checking out. Holy shit and kiss my ass. That was known as a quickness drill.

In terms of glory, there are no individual stars at Alabama. It really is a team team. It has had plenty of All-Americans, plenty of pro stars such as Lee Roy Jordan, Joe Namath, Ken Stabler, but by and large, you don't hear that much about individuals besides the coach.

How does he do it? The team is composed predominantly of home boys, who must have grown up worshiping Bear Bryant. I think of those 12-year-olds cock-walking the side lines, one-eying the tower. Every year, the coach gets a batch of players who have been spoonfed Bear stories and glories all their lives. So for an adolescent athlete from Birmingham, Florence, Demopolis, Bessemer to hear "Bear wants you"—it would turn him into a raving kamikaze, or at least a stout and loyal fellow. I don't think Bear has to try very hard anymore to get players with the right "attitude."

My first interview the following morning is with Steadman Shealy. We meet under the chandelier in the football dorm. Shealy isn't much bigger than I am, but he's a lot blonder and tanner. He also has a firmer handshake, better manners and a neater appearance. Shealy's the first-string quarterback.

We go up to his room and I get my first gander at the living arrangements. The dorm rooms are tiny, with two beds, cinder-block walls and the usual campus-bookstore assortment of banal posters. Shealy, at least, is average-human-being-sized. I try to imagine two nose guards sharing a room this narrow.

Shealy sits on his bed, confident, serene, courteous, helpful and cheerful. And he's not putting me on. I ask him why he chose to go to Alabama, assuming he could have played anywhere in the South. I expect him to rave about Bear, but instead he says, "I really thought this is where God wanted me to come."

I sit up a little straighter. At first I don't know if he's talking about the Lord or Bear, but then he says the second reason was the opportunity to play for coach Bryant—that Alabama has "something extra" in its winning tradition. And then he says something I will hear in the next several interviews: "And I want to be a winner."

On the cover of *Bear* is the quote "I ain't nothing but a winner."

Shealy talks of Bear's father image, of how the coach applies football to life (another thing I'll hear again), of what it takes to win. All hokey stuff in the abstract—but not to Shealy or the others. The guys talk about these bland notions as though they were tenets of radical politics.

Shealy's religiosity, as exotic to me as Bora-Bora, seems a natural extension of the team spirit. He is a Christian soldier, a leader and a follower. Not many of the guys say they're religious, but—at least in interviews—there are no wise guys, no cynics. Frankly, all this clear-eyed devotion makes me extremely uncomfortable, but maybe that's *my* problem.

And where does Shealy see himself five years from now? "Coachin' or Christian ministry... it all depends on what doors God opens up." None of what he says about the coach, about winning and life is all that insightful, but his eyes and chin tell the story. He has no room in his face for sarcasm, despair or doubt. He loves the coach, he loves the team, he loves Christ: a clean-cut, all-American, God, Bear and 'Bama man if ever there were one.

Attitude. I know Bryant doesn't tolerate any guff from anybody. He suspended two of his most famous players, Namath and Stabler, for infractions. No matter who you are, if you don't toe the line, the man will personally clean out your locker for you. Bear says in his book that he works best with the kid who doesn't know he's not terribly talented but plays his heart out. He's more attuned to that kind of athlete than to the hot-dog natural. Sort of like making the New York Yankees out of a bunch of Rocky types. The great American combo: underdog, superstar.

My next interview is with Don Jacobs, the second- or possibly third-string quarterback. He picked Alabama because, growing up in north Alabama, that's all you hear: "Alabama this, Alabama that." He says in the southern part of the state, boys are partial to Auburn, but Alabama is the "number-one university in your mind."

"The first time I talked with coach Bryant," says Jacobs, "I was scared to death. I was afraid to say anything at all. But he was real nice. He talked about Pat Trammel [a star on the 1961 championship team], 'cause Trammel was from Scottsboro, my home town. Said he hoped I was good as Trammel."

Bear, I'm thinking, is a frightening man, but from what I gather of the impressions and memories of players, he's not a screamer, puncher, growler. He's a man of few words, not even one for pep talks. Jacobs has never seen him get really angry, never lose his cool, never jump on anybody's case.

I ask Jacobs how I should conduct myself when I meet Bear. "Be real courteous," he says. "Say 'Yes, sir, no, sir.' Just be yourself."

"Should I get a haircut?"

"I dunno. *I* wouldn't go in there like that. When you go see him, you always shave, look real nice, don't wear sloppy clothes. Lots of players tell you there's a lot of things you don't do when you see coach Bryant. It's been passed down through history. You always take your hat off in the house, stuff like that."

Awe and respect. Dedication and honor. And, oh, yes, talent.

In the early afternoon, I see a few players hanging out with some girls in front of Bryant Hall. A big dude comes walking in with his dad, mom, sis and his pretty gal. The father looks like a big baggy version of his son. Maybe the present son will come to this dorm 20 years later with *his* son. Football is a family sport. Everybody is proud of everybody. Bryant pushes that a lot in his talks to his players.

This is from a midweek, midseason talk to his 1964 national champs:

After the game, there are three types of people. One comes in and he ain't played worth killing, and he's lost. And he gets dressed and out of there as quick as he can. He meets his girl and his momma, and they ain't too damn glad to see him. And he goes off somewhere and says how 'the coach shoulda done this or that,' and 'the coach don't like me,' and 'I didn't play enough.' And everybody just nods.

And the second type will sit there awhile, thinking what he could have done to make his team a winner. And he'll shed some tears. He'll finally get dressed, but he doesn't want to see anybody. His momma's out there. She puts on a big act and tells him what a great game he played, and he tells her if he had done this or that, he'd be a winner, and that he will be a winner—next week.

And then there's the third guy. The winner. He'll be in there hugging everybody in the dressing room. It'll take him an hour to dress. And when he goes out, it's a little something extra in it when his daddy squeezes his hand. His momma hugs and kisses him, and that little old ugly girl snuggles up, proud to be next to him. And he *knows* they're proud. And why.

That afternoon, I have an interview with one of the black players, a nose guard named Byron Braggs. I have seen only a small photo of him in the press book and know that on the first day of practice his freshman year, he almost died of heatstroke but came back to be a top lineman.

I'm checking out my biceps in the empty lounge of Bryant Hall when I look up and jump 90 feet—there's Braggs, 6′6″, 260 pounds, wearing a Cat-tractor hat. We go up to his room, which consists of a large roommate, a TV, a stereo and a full-size refrigerator. They must sleep standing up.

Braggs is a little different from the others I've talked with—a little less awestruck, more blasé. He came to Alabama because his "folks picked it for me. It's near home."

What does he think about Bryant? "A lot of guys are scared of him," says Braggs. "They're in awe of his presence. But I just look at him like anybody else. I'm just happy he can remember my name. He mixes up a lot of names and faces, but two minutes later, he'll remember and apologize."

Ten years ago, Alabama was segregated. When I ask Braggs if prejudice lingers, he just shrugs. "It doesn't bother me," he says. "There were times when things looked shaky, but there are no major problems."

And is state-wide football fever a white fever, or does it affect black Alabamans, too? "Up until about eight to ten years ago," says Braggs, "it was mainly white. I didn't even *know* about Alabama. I would watch Notre Dame, USC with O. J. Simpson. I didn't really notice Alabama until they beat USC out there. That was the first time I knew they had a team. And since they had black players, a lot more people became fans of the team. My folks and others follow the team now. In my home town, people have become real fans."

How about those things Bryant teaches—about character and football and life? "It's life and death out there on the field sometimes. It all ties in. Some coaches like Bryant, John McKay, Ara Parseghian tend to have a definite pull on which way you're looking after you graduate.

They're sort of like the last shaping process that someone is going to do to you. From then on, you do it from within."

Braggs's advice on how to relate to the coach? "Talk to him straight. Don't beat around the bush. He's not impressed with slickness or guys trying to fool him."

Taking a breather between interviews, I walk around campus a bit, grooving on the coeds in their summer dresses, the chirping of the birds, the flora of the South. Old brick and columns. There's not one physically ugly person on the campus.

Back on campus that afternoon, I interview defensive end Gary DeNiro. The reason I pick him is that he's from Youngstown, Ohio, which is definitely Ohio State turf.

He went to Alabama, he says, because he "didn't like Woody Hayes's coaching that much" and was "always an Alabama fan.

"I like that the coach plays a lot of guys who are small [DeNiro is six feet, 210 pounds]. Up North, they play bigger people. Coach Bryant plays the people who want to play."

"How about your Ohio State buddies? What was the reaction when they found out you were going to play for Alabama?"

"They thought I made a big mistake. That I'd come down here and they'd still be fighting the Civil War. They were wrong."

DeNiro's first impression of Bryant?

"He's a legend. Like meeting someone you always wanted to meet. Once Alabama wanted me, I didn't have no trouble makin' up my mind. I remember one time I was loafin' when I was red-shirted, which is a hard time, 'cause you practice like everyone else, but come Friday night, when the team goes, you stay home. Anyway, I was 'puttin' in a day,' as coach calls it, and he caught me and yelled, 'DeNiro, who you think you're tryin' to fool?' And from then on, I never loafed. There's really no place for it on the field."

"How about contact with the coach?"

"Maybe two or three times a year. He says his door is always open, but I'll go in just maybe to say goodbye before I go home or something—nothing more. He has coaching meetings every day. He tells the coaches what he thinks, then we'll have meetings with the coaches in the afternoon and they'll tell us what we're doing wrong. And then about three, four times a week, we'll have a meeting with coach Bryant. We'll all go in as a group. He'll tell us what he sees overall. I imagine he gets more contact with the upperclassmen, because they're the leaders and they'll get it across to the team."

"Where do you see yourself five years from now?"

"Hopefully, with a lot of money. Maybe pro ball if I'm not too small—coach Bryant proved the little man can work out. Or maybe I'll coach. Coach Bryant is the legend of all coaches. If he is behind you, no telling how many doors can open for you."

No telling is right. There's a club based in Birmingham consisting of all Bear Bryant alumni now in the business world. They meet with graduating senior team members and help them find both summer and career jobs. Many kids want, if not to play pro, which most of them *do* want, to take a crack at coaching. There's also a big business school down there and a strong education program. But whatever they *do* choose, if they stay in Alabama, playing for Bear and then going into anything in athletics or business is like graduating *summa cum laude*. Even outside Alabama, the alumni network is nationwide. I hear that one of the biggest diamond dealers in New York's 47th Street district is an Alabama grad.

These interviews are frustratingly inconclusive. All this nonsense concerning life, character, winners' attitudes—of course it's going to come across bland and boringly obvious on a tape recorder. But it's really a combat camaraderie, a brotherhood of suffering and surviving, a growing together in a violent, competitive world. And being rewarded by being called best. Call it character, call it chicken soup, but it's really love. Love of the boss man. Love of one another and love of victory. All this hoopla about football applied to life comes down to this: *I was the best in the world once. I know what that tastes like. I want more.* Roll, Tide!

In areas of rural poverty, football is the American passion play, the emotional outlet for all the rage, boredom and bad breaks—just as basketball is in urban areas.

In *The Last Picture Show*, an entire Texas town lived for high school football; and that's a common phenomenon. In our dissociated culture—despite whatever grace, glory and beauty they evoke in the best teams and players—contact sports serve two functions: They allay boredom, divert people from thinking about the dreariness of their lives; and they help people channel their rage.

You can go to a revival in Selma on Friday or you can scream your lungs out in Bryant-Denny Stadium in Tuscaloosa on Saturday. The bottom line at both is transference of a lot of anger into a socially acceptable outlet.

Like in football, there's a lot of beatific beauty in Gospel, but it's a bit beside the point. As coach Karl Marx once said, football is the opiate of the people. And not just here: There are soccer riots in the Third World stadiums. Christs for a day bloodying themselves in Latin-American pageants. Millions marching to Mecca. A lady in Selma once told me, "People leave Bryant Stadium like they're in a religious trance."

It's my day to interview Bear, and, to be honest, I'm scared. I consider giving myself a haircut with nail clippers. My heart is calling Kong to the gates.

McNair takes me up to the offices on the top floor of the coliseum, where I sit in the spacious waiting room. The walls are covered with floor-to-ceiling black-and-white blowups of every major bowl stadium—Rose, Orange, Sugar, Bluebonnet, Gator, Tangerine, you name it.

Everybody walking around is named Coach. It's like sitting in a room with all the tall, stately, aging cowboys of Hollywood. A room full of Gary Cooper–Ben Johnson look-alikes, all nodding to one another. "Mornin', coach." "Hey, coach." "Nice day, coach." If I were to scream out "Coach!" there would be a ten-way collision. And everybody looks like Bear Bryant.

Several times I see someone walk in and hear someone say, "Hey, coach," and I jump up, drop my tape recorder and extend my hand. After the fifth false alarm, I ignore the next look-alike. Too bad. That one is the mold.

I walk into his office, a large wood-paneled room with a color TV, a massive cluttered desk and a view of the practice field. Coach Bryant is cordial—patient but distant. He has been interviewed perhaps six times a week since coming to Alabama.

He looks all of his 66 years—his face is like an aerial shot of a drought area. His eyes are glittering hard. His hands are huge and gnarled. He needs a haircut himself.

As I fumble around with the tape recorder, explaining that I'm not a sportswriter, he opens a pack of unfiltered Chesterfields. He's dressed like a retired millionaire entertainer—casual natty. A pale-blue golf sweater, checked blue slacks and spiffy black loafers. When he laughs, all the creases in his face head toward his temples and he lets out a deep, gravelly "Heh-heh." When he's annoyed, his eyebrows meet over his nose and I feel like jogging back to New York. His movements are slow; he seems almost phlegmatically preoccupied.

All in all, I like the guy, though I couldn't see being in a sensory-awareness class together.

The interview is a bit of a bust. I'm glad I have the tape recorder, because I can't understand a damn thing he says. He sort of mutters from his diaphragm in his artesian-well-deep Arkansas drawl and it's like listening to a language you studied for only a year in high school.

Bear sits sideways in his chair, legs crossed, elbow on the back rest, absently rubbing his forehead and smoking those Chesterfields. I sit a few feet away in a pulled-up chair, a spiral notebook in my lap open to my questions. I tentatively slide my tape recorder toward him from the corner of his desk.

"Coach, you're pretty much an American hero these days. I was wondering who *your* heroes are." (Please don't kill me.)

He pouts, shrugs. "Well, my heroes are John Wayne, Bob Hope, General Patton... J. Edgar Hoover, although he ain't too popular, I guess...." He mentions various sports stars through the ages—from Babe Ruth to contemporary players—then he nods toward the tape recorder and says, "I suppose you'd like me to say Einstein."

"Nah, nah, nah. Einstein, no... no, not at all."

"Of course, with my heroes, as I get older, *they* get older."

"Yeah, ha, ha."

I ask a few boring questions about defining character, defining motivation, defining a winning attitude, none of which he can define but all of which he can sure talk about.

"I cain't define character," he says, "but it's important, especially to those who don't have that much natural ability—on the football field or elsewhere."

Next comes my New York hotsy-totsy question.

"In *Bear*, I read about how you motivate players, psych them up. I also read that you understand people better than any other coach.

Comprehension like that seems to be one of the attributes of a good psychiatrist. What do you feel about the field of psychiatry?"

He gives a chuckle. "Well, I don't know nothing about psychiatrists. I prob'ly need one, but I don't know the secret of motivatin' people—an' if I did, I wouldn't tell anyone."

Then he goes on about motivation. At one point, he says, "I remember one time...." And about five minutes later, he says, "That was the damnedest... heh-heh," in that noble garble of his.

Then his face darkens and he says, "I guess that ain't funny to you."

I almost shit. A joke! He told me a joke! Laugh, you asshole! Fake it!

I haven't heard a word he's said. I give a sick grin, say, "Naw, that's funny, that's funny!" and give my own "Heh-heh." My armpits feel flooded.

For a while, I go sociological and non-sports, thinking maybe I can get him to admire my sensitive and probing mind—or at least throw him some questions that are a little more interesting than the traditional Southern sports groupie/journalist fare.

"Are your players... uh... afraid of you?" ('Cause I'm about to do a swan dive out this window, coach.)

He sits up a little.

"Afraid of me? Shit, heh-heh. I'm the best friend they got. Some haven't been around here much. They might be a little reluctant. I dunno. But if somebody's doin' poorly, I'll come after him. But I dunno what they'd be afraid of me about."

One period in college history that has always fascinated me is the late Sixties—mainly because it was a transcendent radical bubble between the Fifties and the Seventies, but also because that's when I was an undergraduate. I wonder what it was like to be a football player then, when regimentation was so reactionary—when long hair and a taste for dope were *de rigueur*. I know that Bryant's worst years since coming to Alabama were 1969 and 1970. Is there any connection?

"I did a real poor job of recruiting and coaching," he says. "Every youngster in America was goin' through a rebellious period. Nobody wanted anybody to tell 'im anything. I remember a boy sittin' right there an' tellin' me, 'I just wanna be like any other student.' Well, shit. He can't *be* like any other student. The players have to take pride in the fact that football means that much to 'em. That's where the sacrificin' comes in. That they *are* willin' to do without doin' some things. Without havin' some things other students have, to be playin' football, to win a championship."

"What was the campus attitude toward football at that time?"

"I really don't know that much about what goes on over there [*nodding toward the window*]. I always tell 'em they're the best in the world, at pep rallies and all. Whether they said anything about me I don't know. I was just doin' a lousy job then."

"As an Alabaman, how do you feel about the image that your state has in the national eye, which is mainly a negative or fearful one?"

He doesn't like that question. His eyebrows start knitting a sweater.

"I dunno if that's true or not. I traveled all over the country. A large percentage of Alabamans consider the Yankees their baseball team, or the Red Sox. The only difference I see is that it ain't as crowded down here, people aren't in such a hurry. I'm afraid of New York City. It ain't just what I heard, it's what I seen. I dunno if we got as many thieves, crooks and murderers down here percentagewise, but, hell, it's so many of them in New York. I don't care to leave the hotel—alone or with money in my pocket."

"How about the football-dorm system? Is it still under fire for separatism?"

"Naw. About ten years ago, we were the first school to build one. They called it Alabama Hilton, Bryant Hilton. But everyone's built one since then."

"Is there any criticism because the players are segregated from the rest of the campus?"

"Well, a lot of coaches don't do that, but I was brought up on it and we're gonna do it. If anyone rules against it, we won't, but I know that's one of the ways that help us win. You live under the same roof together, fightin' for the same thing. If you don't see one another but occasionally, you have other interests, you don't know what's goin' on. And I can see 'em over there, too. I like to see 'em. If one of them lives in an apartment and's sick for a week, his mother's not even there. I want 'em where I can find 'em, look at 'em."

That's it. Bear doesn't move, just gazes out the window. I don't move. I feel stuck. I don't know how to say goodbye. I ask about

Astroturf. About the coming A Day game. Bear says that he'd rather not even have it, but the alumni have things planned around it.

Outside the office, he signs my copy of *Bear*. I say "Howdy-do" and split.

Later in the week, I get a note from Bear via McNair that he wants to add Oral Roberts, Billy Graham, Arnold Palmer and Jack Nicklaus to his list of heroes—all American fat cats who made it through personal enterprise and charisma.

McNair says he's never heard Bear mention Patton before and makes the analogy that in World War Two, to die for Patton was an honor and that the coach is the only other person he knows of whom people feel that way about.

Days later, I'm still smarting about that missed joke. I feel I understand something then about why this man is successful. There is something about him—about *me* in that moment when I blew being an appreciative audience—that goes past embarrassment. I feel like I let him down. I feel like I could have pleased him by laughing, made him like me for a moment, could have broken through the interviewer-interviewee roles for a few seconds in a way that would have made me feel like a million bucks *because it would have given him pleasure.* There is something in Bear's subdued dignity, his cordial distance that got to me. He is a man of *character.* I could see myself having done Mexican tail spins during that interview to get his admiration or just his acknowledgment. And this was just a magazine assignment. If I were one of his five-year players, I could see myself doing 90 mph through a goal post to get a pat on the back. And, frankly, I can't define motivation, either, but whatever it is that he lays on his boys, I got a tiny ray of it myself. The man could literally crush you by letting you know you were a disappointment to him. Shit, maybe I've just seen too many John Wayne movies.

I did go down to McNair's office, though, with the queasy feeling that I've blown it. Not the interview so much, but I'm left with the feeling that if Bryant had to go over Pork Chop Hill, I wouldn't be his first choice in the assault squadron.

"I didn't understand a damn thing he said!" I half complain to McNair.

"Listen to this!" I play back Bear's joke-anecdote for him and two other guys in the office. Instead of commiserating, they are all on the floor, howling with laughter.

"I never heard that one before!" says a trainer, wiping tears from his eyes.

"That's the funniest thing I ever heard!" says McNair.

"Yeah, well, I think you guys are a little funny, too," I mutter.

McNair translates the joke for me. Bear was recalling an old Kentucky-Tennessee game, a real "bloodletter." During the half, a guy named Doc Rhodes (I can't figure out what his relation to the team was) went into the Kentucky locker room and delivered "the damnedest talk I evah heard." He had one big old boy just slobbering at the bit. The only problem was that big old boy wasn't playing.

In the last quarter of the game, Tennessee was down on the Kentucky 15 and the coach finally sent the big old boy in. He ran halfway onto the field; then he went running back to the side lines and said, "Coach, can Doc Rhodes talk at me again?"

I guess you had to be there.

Rick Reilly

It really was a game unlike any other: San Diego and Miami locking up in the 1982 NFL playoffs, playing past regulation, playing overtime after overtime, playing as if they would never stop. Rick Reilly (b. 1958) and his brother watched every glorious, grueling second of it on TV at home in Denver, tackling each other out of sheer joy between commercial breaks, two Broncos fans enthralled by a game in which they ordinarily would have had no rooting interest. "It was more than any fan could ask for," Reilly says. And a fan is what he was that day, and what he becomes whenever he recalls the game. It doesn't matter that he's now a fixture on ESPN or a star columnist for its website, or that he was a marquee name at *Sports Illustrated* for more than two decades, or that he was a whiz kid on the *Los Angeles Times*'s vastly talented sports staff in the 1980s. Reilly knew he had to write about the Miami-San Diego endurance contest someday. While doing so for *SI*'s October 25, 1999 issue, he met Kellen Winslow, a hero for San Diego and Reilly's inspiration when naming his first son. Winslow asked for a picture, the way he always does when he hears about a kid named Kellen because of him. But Reilly went from flattered to flummoxed when Winslow said he kept the pictures in a shoebox. "How many do you have?" Reilly asked. And Winslow said, "A hundred and twenty-nine."

A Matter of Life and Sudden Death

ONE PLAYER sat slumped on a metal bench under a cold shower, too exhausted to take off his blood-caked uniform. Four were sprawled on the floor, IVs dripping into their arms. One of them tried to answer a reporter's questions, but no words would come out of his parched, chalky mouth. And that was the winning locker room.

On January 2, 1982, a sticky, soaked-shirt South Florida night, the Miami Dolphins and the San Diego Chargers played a magnificent, horrible, gripping, preposterous NFL playoff game. For four hours and five minutes, 90 men took themselves to the limit of human endurance. They cramped. They staggered. They wilted. Then they played on, until it was no longer a game but a test of will. "People remember all kinds of details from that game," says San Diego tight end Kellen Winslow, "but they can't remember who won, because it wasn't about who won or who lost." It was about effort and failure and heroics. Each team's quarterback threw for more than 400 yards. Combined the two teams lost four fumbles and missed three easy field goals. They also scored 79 points and gained 1,036 yards. Miami coach Don Shula called it "a great game, maybe the greatest ever." San Diego coach Don Coryell said, "There has never been a game like this." Years later Miami fans voted it the greatest game in franchise history. And their team *lost*.

For his first 24 years Rolf Benirschke may not have had the perfect life, but it was at least in the class photo.

Handsome. Gorgeous smile. Son of an internationally acclaimed patholo-gist. Honor student. Stud of the UC Davis soccer team. Star kicker on the school's football team. Beloved San Diego Chargers kicker—by 1979, he was on course to set the career NFL record for field goal accuracy. Wheel of Fortune host. Spokesman for the San Diego Zoo, best zoo in the country. It was all blue skies and tables by the window. Looking back, maybe he should have seen trouble coming.

It all started with bananas.

Squalls had just blown through Miami, and the weather report called for nasty heat with humidity to match by game time, so Coryell ordered his players to eat bananas to ward off cramps. Lots and lots of bananas.

Problem was, it was New Year's Day in Miami Beach, and except for those being worn by the Carmen Miranda impersonators, bananas were a little hard to come by. Chargers' business manager Pat Curran had to go from hotel to hotel rounding them up at one dollar apiece. Not everybody got enough. "I think I had a couple beers instead," says quarterback Dan Fouts.

The Dolphins were three-point favorites, what with their Killer B's defense and their home field advantage—the dingy, rickety Orange Bowl, where Fouts remembers fans "blowing their nose on you as you walked out of the tunnel." Fouts was the brilliant, belligerent boss of the turbo-charged Chargers offense that knocked pro football on its ear. But the team had started that '81 season 6-5, and was routinely dismissed as a bunch of underachievers. Even Winslow, who led the league in catches for the second straight year, was hearing catcalls.

"They call me the sissy, the San Diego chicken," he said the week before the game. "I'm the tight end who won't block. They say I need a heart transplant... that our whole team has no heart. But I know what I can do."

All of which set the game up as a barn burner: the unstoppable San Diego O versus the immovable Miami D, the two highest-ranked kickers in the AFC—Miami's Uwe von Schamann and San Diego's Benirschke.

On San Diego's opening drive Benirschke hit a 32-yard field goal, which figured. The guy hadn't missed a road kick on grass all year. Then San Diego wideout Wes Chandler returned a short punt for a touchdown to make it 10–0. Benirschke wedged the ensuing kickoff high into the wind, and when it hit the ground, it bounced backward into Chargers' hands. That set up a one-yard touchdown run by bespectacled halfback Chuck Muncie. Three plays later the Dolphins' wunderkind 23-year-old quarterback, David Woodley, fired a beauty straight into the arms of Chargers free safety Glen Edwards, who ran the interception back far enough to set up another easy score—24–zip. And how's *your* Sunday going?

"I wanted to dig a hole and crawl in it," says Miami tight end Joe Rose.

Across the sideline the Chargers' veteran receiver, Charlie Joiner, had his head in his hands. "What's wrong?" Winslow asked.

"Man, you just don't *do* this to a Don Shula team," Joiner moaned. "He's gonna pull Woodley, put in [backup veteran Don] Strock, start throwing the ball, and we're gonna be here all damn day."

Joiner was wrong. Strock kept them there all night.

The year he nearly died, Benirschke was perfect. He opened the 1979 season with four-for-four field goals in four games, then spent the rest of the season in area hospitals. He had what the doctors originally thought was a demon intestinal virus that they eventually identified as ulcerative colitis. Basically it was eating up his intestines, microscopic bite by bite.

Two surgeries, 78 units of blood and 60 lost pounds later, Benirschke wasn't dead, but he was a reasonable facsimile. "After the second surgery," he recalls, "I knew that if I had another, I wouldn't make it."

Three days later the doctors told him he needed a third operation.

Everything changed the instant Don Strock and his mod-squad haircut and double-hinged arm strode on the field three minutes into the second quarter. "You could just sense the difference," says Chargers linebacker Linden King. "Strock had a real presence out there." Calling his own plays, with nothing to lose, Strock drove the Dolphins to a quick field goal, then a touchdown.

The Chargers' O, meanwhile, was suddenly getting battered. The Killer B's strategy was to turn Winslow into a complicated collection of lumps, so on every pass play the defensive end would take a lick at him, linebacker A. J. Duhe would say a quick hello with his forearm, and then one of the defensive backs would take a shot at him. Early in the second quarter Duhe opened up a cut in Winslow's lip that needed three stitches.

Winslow had been a one-man outpatient clinic coming into the game: bruised left shoulder, strained rotator cuff in his right, sore neck from trying to compensate for both. It was so bad that Sid Brooks, the Chargers' equipment guy, had to help him put on his shoulder pads before the game. Brooks would get good at it—Winslow went through three pairs that night.

Ahead 24–10 with just 36 seconds left in the half, Benirschke attempted a 55-yarder that was plenty long, but right. His first miss since November. With good field position off the miss, Strock came back sizzling. In three plays he took Miami to its 40-yard line with six seconds left in the half—too far out for a field goal. Just for fun, Miami called timeout and tried to dream something up. "What about the hook-and-ladder?" said Shula. Interesting idea. *Dumb* idea, but interesting. The Dolphins hadn't tried that play all year, possibly because it hadn't worked once in practice all year.

So they tried it. Strock hit wideout Duriel Harris on a 15-yard curl on the right wing. Nothing fancy. In fact the pass was underthrown, so Harris had to dive to catch it. Every Chargers defensive back on that side rushed to finish Harris off... except that when they got there, Harris was missing one thing: the ball. He'd lateraled to running back Tony Nathan while falling down. Nathan had come straight out of the backfield, cut right and tucked Harris's lateral under his arm without breaking stride. It was the alltime sucker play. "I never saw him," says San Diego corner Willie Buchanon.

Neither did Harris, but buried under the pile of duped Chargers, he could hear a roar. When he finally sat up, he saw Nathan in the end zone, lonely as an IRS auditor, holding the ball over his head. Touchdown. The lead was suddenly just seven.

The Chargers' sideline froze in shock. "It was a beautiful, beautiful play," remembers Coryell. "Perfectly executed."

Said Fouts, to no one in particular: "Aw, f---! Here we go again." Then he went into the locker room and set new records for swearing, punctuated by a heaved helmet that nearly decapitated Chandler.

Not that anybody could hear Fouts ranting. The schoolyard flea-flicker had so inflamed the Orange Bowl crowd that Shula could not deliver his halftime speech in the Dolphins' locker room because of the din. "I've never heard anything like it," says Strock. "It was like we were still on the field. It was *that* loud. We were in the locker room, what—10, 15 minutes?—and it never stopped!"

It would get only louder.

Benirschke never had that third operation. While looking at a pre-op X-ray, doctors noticed that the abscess in his abdomen had disappeared. They couldn't figure it out. Benirschke's father couldn't figure it out. Benirschke, now a devout Christian, calls it a miracle.

Still, the stud college hero was down to 123 pounds and the approximate shape of a rake, and was going to have to learn to live with two tubes coming out of his abdomen for his ostomy pouch. Kick again? He was hoping just to walk again.

He asked the Chargers' conditioning coach, Phil Tyne, to help him get back some strength. Tyne started him on weights—a dumbbell bar with nothing on it. Benirschke couldn't even lift that.

Still he made his way back. By 1980 he not only was a spokesman for sufferers of ulcerative colitis (von Schamann eventually became both a sufferer and a spokesman) and the 120,000 Americans who have ostomy surgery each year, but was also back playing football.

He showed his "bags" to his teammates one day in the shower. It was a little awkward, explaining it all, until special teams captain Hank Bauer finally said, "Hey, Rolf, do you have shoes to match?"

When the second half started, the Orange Bowl fans were still roaring, and Strock was still firing, throwing another touchdown to Rose on

the Dolphins' first possession. The game was now tied at 24 and starting to look like the ultimate no-heart loss for a no-heart team. Except
to Winslow. "No," he said to himself on the sideline. "*No. We are not
going to be the team that blew a 24–0 lead in the playoffs.*"

A whole bunch of Chargers must've felt the same way because this
is when the game *really* got good. "Never in my life," says Eric Sievers,
the second San Diego tight end, "have I been in a game like that, when
nobody took a single play off."

Back came the Chargers. Winslow took a 25-yard touchdown pass
from Fouts to give them the lead again, 31–24. Returning to the bench,
Winslow started to cramp—first in his thighs, then in his calves. "And
I *ate* my bananas," Winslow says.

Back came the Dolphins. Strock hit reserve tight end Bruce Hardy
for a 50-yard touchdown. Now the noise in the Orange Bowl sounded
like a DC-11. "It made my ears pop," recalls Ric McDonald, the Chargers' overworked trainer that day. "It would be at this incredibly loud
level and then it would go *up* about 10 decibels. Guys were coming up
to me and screaming, 'My ears are popping!' You could stand two feet
from a guy and not hear him."

Maybe that's why a Fouts pass was picked off by Lyle Blackwood,
who lateraled to Gerald Small, who ran it to the San Diego 15 to set
up another easy touchdown run by Nathan and a 38–31 Miami lead
less than a minute into the fourth quarter.

That score seemed to kill the Chargers. They tried to put together a
drive on their next possession but had to punt after seven plays, and
Strock, starting on his own 20-yard line, led a brutal, clock-munching
drive that put the Dolphins on the San Diego 21 with five minutes to
play. A three-pointer by von Schamann, the AFC leader in field goal
percentage, would ice it. "We thought they were dead," Rose told NFL
Films. "It was like, C'mon, throw in the towel! It's hot, we're tired. Let
us win the game."

On first down, Nathan ran right for a short gain. On second down
and seven, Andra Franklin took a safe handoff and plunged up the
middle, where he got tortillaed by Gary (Big Hands) Johnson, and the
ball was ripped out of his grip by San Diego's 280-pound lineman
Louie Kelcher. Safety Pete Shaw fell on it. San Diego lived.

San Diego, the city, however, had no idea. Right around then a
storm there caused a huge power outage. It was as if half a million

people were simultaneously stabbed in the knee. All over town, in the wind and rain, fans huddled in their cars listening to the game on the radio. One caller to a TV station threatened to shoot the president of San Diego Gas and Electric if the game didn't come back on. This was the *playoffs*.

Back came the Chargers. Fouts connected with Joiner for 14 yards, Chandler for 6, Joiner for 5 and then 15 more, Winslow for 7 and Chandler for 19. "It seemed so easy," says Fouts. "There was just no pass rush from Miami. They were gassed."

Winslow was really cramping now—his thigh, his calves and now his lower back. If you ever get your choice of cramps, do not pick the lower back. A cramp there means you can't stand and you can't bend over either. "Kind of like paralysis," Winslow remembers. Each time Winslow was helped to the bench by teammates, the San Diego trainers surrounded him like a NASCAR pit crew: one working on his calves, another stretching his shoulder, a third massaging his back, a fourth trying to pour fluids into his mouth through his face mask. Somehow, Winslow got up each time and got back into the game.

First-and-goal from the nine. Fouts dropped back, scrambled and lobbed one toward the corner of the end zone to Winslow, who jumped for it but couldn't get high enough. Fouts had cursed his overthrow the instant he released it, but then something strange happened. James Brooks, the Chargers' sensational rookie running back, had the ball and the grin and the tying touchdown. On his own initiative Brooks had run the back line of the end zone—behind Winslow—just in case.

"That was one of the alltime brilliant heads-up plays I've ever seen," Fouts says. "In all the hundreds of times we'd run that play, I'd never thrown to anybody back there."

When Benirschke added the pressurized extra point, the game was tied at 38. Fifty-eight seconds left. For the first time in more than two hours, the Orange Bowl crowd was silent.

Just when Benirschke figured he had his problems licked, his insides attacked him again. During the 1981 season, the small section of colon the doctors hadn't removed in the previous two surgeries began sloughing blood. More tests. More hospitals. More surgery. More impressions of a rake. And yet he built himself back up—again. He didn't miss a single game that year. "You

discover within yourself a greater courage," he says, "a greater perseverance
than you ever knew you had."
  It would turn out to be a handy trait.

Fouts is still ticked off that Coryell had Benirschke squib the ensuing kickoff. The Dolphins took over at their 40, 52 seconds on the
clock. Strock's first pass was nearly intercepted by Edwards. His second
pass *was* intercepted, by Buchanon, who fumbled it right back. First-
and-10, 34 seconds left, Strock hit Nathan for 17, then running back
Tommy Vigorito picked up six yards, to the San Diego 26. Miami let
the clock run down; Shula called timeout with four seconds to go,
and von Schamann ran out to kick a 43-yard field goal that would
bring this game to an unforgettable end. It was as good as over—von
Schamann had already won three games this season with last-second
kicks. Winslow, who was slumped on the bench trying to hold down
some liquids, ran back onto the field to try to block the kick. He was on
the "desperation" team. Never in his career had he blocked one, and
now he could hardly stand, much less leap, but he went in anyway.
Why not? It was the last play of the season. "Get me some penetra-
tion, guys," Winslow yelled to Kelcher and Johnson, "so I can have a
chance at the block."
  They did. The snap was a little high, but Strock's hold was good.
Winslow summoned everything that was left in him, heaved his 6'6"
body as high as it would go and blocked von Schamann's kick with
the pinkie finger on his right hand. "To get as high as he did after all
he'd been through?" Fouts says. "Amazing."
  When Winslow hit the ground, he got history's first all-body cramp.
He lay on the field, spasming from his calves to his neck. He was carried off again. He would return again.
  Overtime.

Benirschke is a humble man who has spent half his life raising cash for
critters and blood for people, but he seems to have "trouble" on his speed
dial. He nearly lost his wife, Mary, in childbirth after she'd spent the last
five months of her pregnancy in bed. He nearly lost his newborn daughter,
Kari, that same day—the nurses woke him up in the hospital at 4 A.M. so
he could say goodbye to her. Somehow she survived. She has cerebral palsy,
but she's alive and she's happy.

He and Mary adopted a second daughter, Christina, in 1995 and were beside themselves with joy. Eight days later, the biological mother rang their doorbell and took Christina away.

He flew to Russia to bring home an orphan, only to be told he also had to take the boy's brother, who had a cleft lip, refused to eat, was malnourished and infected with scabies. Benirschke was given no health reports. He couldn't reach his wife. He ran out of time. He brought home two orphans.

"We never ask, 'Why us?'" Benirschke says. "We just try to build our patience and resolve as deep as they'll go."

He'd need more.

The idea of overtime on this thick, broiled night was about as appetizing to the players as a bowl of hot soup. Still, the marathon ran on. "You hear coaches say, 'Leave everything on the field,'" says Miami lineman Ed Newman, now a judge. "Well, that actually happened that day. Both teams. We really did give it all we had. Everything."

Even Benirschke was exhausted. Not physically, *mentally*. All game he'd been stretching, running, kicking—always averting his eyes from his teammates. He was the one apart, the one man on the team with the clean jersey, getting himself ready for the moment he knew was coming: when all the gazelles and gorillas would leave the field and ask him to finish what they could not.

San Diego won the flip, took the kickoff and cut through Miami. In five minutes they were at the Miami eight-yard line, second down. Coryell called for Benirschke to kick a 27-yarder. On the sideline, San Diego's Shaw started pulling the tape off his wrists. Rolf just doesn't miss from there, he thought. No lie. Benirschke hadn't missed from inside the 30 all year, and two of those kicks had given the team last-second wins. Come to think of it, Benirschke had kicked a 28-yarder to beat Miami in the Orange Bowl in overtime last season.

But a field goal unit is not one man, it's 11, and some of the sapped men on San Diego's field goal team were getting water and didn't hear the coach's call. They were late getting onto the field and didn't even make the huddle. "Eddie," Benirschke called to his holder, Ed Luther, "We're not set!"

"We're O.K.," Luther said. "Just kick it."

Benirschke prepared for the snap, but his rhythm was off. The ball was snapped, Luther put it down, and Benirschke hooked his kick just left of the goalpost.

Benirschke was nearly sick with regret. "I knew I'd never get a second chance," he remembers. "I thought, How long will I have to live with this?"

That miss was, strangely, a blow to *both* teams. The players were now on a death march. Men in both huddles leaned on one another for support. "Guys would refuse to come out of the game just so they didn't have to run all the way to the sideline," says Sievers. Whatever side of the huddle receivers happened to be on was the side they lined up on, formations be damned.

Neither offense was able to sustain a drive, and the two clubs staggered through what seemed to be a pointless, hopeless, endless dance. There was a punt, a lost San Diego fumble, two more punts. "I remember Kellen had his eyes closed in the huddle, mouth hanging open," Sievers says. "He looked like a slow-motion picture of a boxer—his mouthpiece falling out, saliva dripping from his lip."

Shula was hot that his players were helping Winslow up after a play only to see him beat them with another great catch. (He had 13 in all, for 166 yards.) "Let him get up by himself!" Shula kept yelling.

At one point in this blast furnace of noise and sweat and exhaustion, Winslow was blocking Miami cornerback Gerald Small. When the play ended, both men tried to get off the field for the punt, but they couldn't move. They just leaned on each other for a few seconds, too tired to get out of each other's way. They shoot horses, don't they? "I'd never come that close to death before," Winslow says.

Finally, nine minutes into overtime, Miami made one last Jell-O–legged breakaway. Strock hit wideout Jimmy Cefalo for a big gain, and von Schamann set up for a 34-yarder to win it. Across the field Benirschke looked like a man about to get fitted for a lifetime of goathood. He knelt on the sideline, "waiting for the inevitable," he says. "It was like watching your own execution. Only in slow motion."

"I wanted to get the kick up right away," said von Schamann later, thinking of Winslow's block earlier. He tried too hard. His shoe scuffed the painted green dirt and the ball went straight into the right arm of defensive end Leroy Jones. It was the only NFL field goal attempt Jones ever blocked.

Three times Strock had prepared to ride off into the sunset at the end of the movie—and three times his horse had broken a leg.

In 1998, 19 years after his last surgery, Benirschke took a standard physical for a life insurance policy. Doctors said his blood showed elevated levels of liver enzymes. This time, Benirschke had hepatitis C, which causes an inflammation of the liver that can lead to cancer and, often, death. Doctors told him that one of those 78 units of blood he received during his surgery in 1979 had probably been infected with the hepatitis virus.

Benirschke dug in. Again. As he'd done with the ulcerative colitis, he decided to make himself an expert on hepatitis C. There were days he wished he hadn't.

Back came the Chargers. "You find something deep down inside you," says Winslow, "and you push on." Almost robotically Fouts drove his team again. He hit Brooks and Chandler and Chandler again, and then Joiner for 39 yards, down to the Miami 10.

Fate, in a forgiving mood, presented Benirschke with a second chance. Guard Doug Wilkerson approached Benirschke on the sideline. "You know that giraffe at your zoo?" he asked.

"Yeah?" said Benirschke, warily.

"Well, if you miss this, I'm gonna go down there and cut its throat."

The giraffe lived. This time San Diego's field goal unit was ready and the rhythm was fine. Benirschke says he didn't even have butterflies. The snap was sweet, and the kick perfect. Wasn't it? "There was just this silence," Benirschke remembers. The linemen for both teams were still lying on the ground. Nobody was celebrating. Benirschke turned to Luther and said, "Didn't it go through?"

"Yes!" Luther said, and Benirschke was mobbed by his teammates.

"Hold on! Hold on!" Benirschke yelled. Not every hero has to watch out for his ostomy pouch.

San Diego 41, Miami 38. Sudden death.

At the bottom of the pile Winslow felt a spoonful of joy and a truckful of pain. As players from both teams struggled to their feet, a Miami player gave Winslow a hand up. Winslow took three or four wobbly steps, then fell, wracked by spasms. Sievers and tackle Billy

Shields helped Winslow up and carried him off, a moment recorded in the famous Al Messerschmidt photograph.

At the line of scrimmage, the massive Kelcher and 270-pound Chargers guard Ed White hadn't moved. The photographers and the reporters and Winslow were long gone, and still they lay there. "Louie, you know we're gonna have to get up and walk," White groaned. "They don't carry fat guys off the field."

Both locker rooms looked like field hospitals. Miami's Newman wept. Wilkerson was so overheated, he sat under a shower fully clothed. Despite the IV in his arm, White had no color and couldn't connect his brain to his mouth. "I really thought Ed was gonna go," says McDonald, the trainer. "I'm not kidding. I thought we might lose him."

Winslow's body temperature was up to 105°, and he'd lost 13 pounds. Pretty much everything on the sissy had stopped working—except his heart.

Kelcher, hair matted with sweat, blood caked on his hands, needed someone to cut the socks off his feet. He could not stand. An hour later, he said, "I feel like I just rode a horse from Texas to California."

Said White, "I feel like the horse."

Reporters mobbed Benirschke, who had scored the first and last points in this epic game. Is this your biggest thrill? they asked him. "Yes," he said with a little smile. "In a football game."

No player on either team would ever take himself that far or that high again. There would be more misery: San Diego went to Cincinnati the next week and lost the coldest playoff game in NFL history—a −59° windchill. There would be payback: Miami beat San Diego in the playoffs the next year. There would be sorrow: Miami linebacker Larry Gordon would die the next year jogging; Muncie would be arrested for cocaine trafficking; Woodley would have a liver transplant. And there would be honor: Shula, Coryell, Fouts, Joiner and Winslow all were inducted into the Hall of Fame. But there would never be another game like the one they played that night.

"People come up to me sometimes and say, 'Too bad you never went to the big one,'" says Fouts. "And I say, Really? Well, do you remember who played in Super Bowl XIV? And they'll say, No. Super Bowl XXII? And they'll go, No. How about our playoff game with Miami in 1982? And they all go, Oh, *yeeeah!*"

Winslow retired six years later at 30 with a bum knee and an aura of glory that just won't fade. "Not a day goes by that somebody doesn't bring up that game," he says. "It's wonderful and it's humbling to be remembered for something people see as so heroic."

A motivational speaker now, Winslow has two enduring memories from that day. One is his permanently sore shoulder. The other is a shoebox filled with pictures of kids named after him. Winslow's count was up to 129, until the author showed him a picture of his son, and made it an even 130.

Reach for a can of beer in Benirschke's fridge these days and what you will mostly find are the needles he uses to inject the drugs he hopes will save his life. "There's a chance I'll die," he says, "but we're not focusing on that." Instead, he's a spokesman on hepatitis C. Five million Americans have it, he'll tell you, but only 250,000 are being treated for it. Some people think there's a reason God gave Benirschke all these diseases. Who would handle them better?

Doctors say the virus is undetectable in his system, but he'll be tested again in six months because 65% of those who get rid of it get it back. He may need a liver transplant.

Whatever happens, Benirschke is ready for it. His wife, Mary, says, "People don't realize what you can go through."

Funny, isn't it, how much of Rolf Benirschke's life has been like that game? Up, down, joy, woe, win, lose and start all over again? Would it be asking too much for him to get one more second chance?

Leigh Montville

Whimsy is a constant in what Leigh Montville (b. 1943) writes, and so is wonderment, as if he can't quite believe what he is seeing but finds it highly entertaining nonetheless. When he was a *Boston Globe* sports columnist in the 1970s and 1980s, he claimed to owe as much to Woody Allen as he did to Woodward and Bernstein. A nine-year stand at *Sports Illustrated* launched Montville into the world of books, and he has gone on to write some of the best-selling and best-regarded sports biographies of the past decade. His choice of subjects speaks volumes about his sensibility: not just legends—*Ted Williams* (2004), *The Big Bam: The Life and Times of Babe Ruth* (2006)—but the outsized characters depicted in his 2008 book *The Mysterious Montague* (a world-class golfer with a past that included armed robbery) and most recently in *Evel: The High-Flying Life of Evel Knievel* (2011). For all that, much of what Montville wrote for the *Globe* can stand with his later work. Consider the following column about Boston College's historic upset of Miami at the Orange Bowl in 1984. It was a road game the day after Thanksgiving and Montville would rather have been home with his family. Then, with the clock ticking down to zero, an undersized quarterback named Doug Flutie unfurled a last-gasp pass, magic happened, and Montville started racing against his deadline. "It's like being a contestant on *Beat the Clock*," he said. As his column proves, BC wasn't the only winner that day.

A Miracle in Miami

The two Boston College linemen discussed the bizarre, amazing thing that had happened on the floor of the Orange Bowl. They dealt with the metaphysics of the event.

"That wasn't Gerard Phelan who caught that ball," big Mark MacDonald said. "God caught that ball."

"No," big Jim Ostrowski said softly. "God threw it..."

BC 47, Miami 45

Nov. 23, 1984

MIAMI—The idea does not go away that Doug Flutie simply willed the ball into the end zone. Thought it there.

He threw the ball—sure, he threw it 48 yards on the scoresheet and maybe 65 yards in the air—but that does not begin to explain exactly what happened. Zero seconds left? National television? Forty-eight yards on the last play of the game. To win the game?

This was the kid's biggest trick of all, the trick of tricks yesterday afternoon in the Orange Bowl. Boston College 47, Miami 45. The idea does not go away that something had to be involved that is larger than the simple act of throwing a football.

"Does it seem that somehow good things happen to you?" the 22-year-old BC quarterback was asked after this dizzy moment.

"Oh, yes, definitely," he replied. "There are things that seem to happen... and I don't know why. I'm not going to complain about it."

The most implausible part of this implausible finish was its plausibility. Does that sound right? Doug Flutie did what you somehow figured Doug Flutie would do. The virtual impossible.

He somehow is the embodiment of all those coaching clichés that sound so well when they're spoken, but usually echo in a hollow room. Never over 'til it's over! Winners never quit! Never say never! He somehow makes all that stuff work.

Coming onto that field in the sideways rain with 80 yards to travel and 28 seconds to do the traveling, he already was thinking about how this marathon game could end. He was thinking about his roommate, Gerard Phelan, catching the ball in the end zone. He was thinking about 48 yards, a touchdown at the end that made half the country rub its eyes.

How was he so positive? Why? Who knew? Maybe he didn't have the specifics of that final play filled in, but he had the idea. He communicated that idea.

"Twenty-eight seconds," offensive lineman Mark MacDonald said. "How long is 28 seconds? I couldn't walk from the kitchen in my house to my bedroom in 28 seconds. I couldn't do it... unless, maybe Doug was with me."

"He just settles everybody down," fullback Steve Strachan said. "We go into the huddle and they've just scored and we're down and he's there, saying we can do it. He was talking like it's a Spring Game or something."

"He's saying we can do it," wide receiver Phelan said. "We believe him, because we've done it."

Wheels somehow turn inside this kid's head that don't turn inside other heads. He had been thinking about this final drive as early as midway through the fourth period on a previous touchdown drive.

"I was trying to hurry up on that drive," Doug Flutie said. "Everybody was saying, well, maybe you should bleed the clock and run as much time off as you can. Uh-uh. I was thinking we were going to have to score again. I wanted to score this time as fast as possible."

When Miami had the ball—heading down the field, indeed for a touchdown and a 45–41 lead—the quarterback was asking BC coach Jack Bicknell to call time-out. To keep Miami from using up time before it scored.

"I understood what he was trying to say," Bicknell said, "but I said, 'You just can't do that.' Suppose they botch a play... have to hurry a kick... suppose."

None of that happened. Twenty-eight seconds were left when Miami scored and the Miami people celebrated and BC came onto the field. Twenty-eight seconds.

"All I wanted to do was get the ball to the 50 and have a chance to throw it into the end zone and win the game," Doug Flutie said. "If you do that, you have a 50-50 chance of getting the reception, right? Your guys can catch it. Or their guys can catch it."

There also would be a good chance that no one would catch the ball—right?—but why consider negatives? There was Flutie, talking to his people before each play. Squatting next to his linemen's ears at the line of scrimmage. Talking. Convincing.

He was where he wanted to be when his last shot arrived with six seconds left. Heck, he was at the 48, two yards closer than expected.

"What were you thinking when he ran that play?" coach Bicknell was asked.

"Tell the truth, I'm thinking about what I'm going to say to the kids after the loss." Bicknell said. "I'm thinking about how I'm going to get 'em up for Holy Cross. I mean, you always say you're never out of it, but really..."

How to describe what happened next? Flutie dancing. Flutie throwing. The ball cutting through the rain. Phelan behind three Miami defensive backs. Phelan catching the ball.

"I landed," Gerard Phelan said, "and I saw that there was writing on the ground underneath me. I knew that I was in the end zone. I jumped up fast to show the referee I had the ball."

"I couldn't exactly see what happened," MacDonald said. "I thought I saw the ball hit the ground. I turned to shake the hand of the guy I'd been playing against. To congratulate him. Then I saw him just slump over. I turned back to see what happened."

"I was numb," Bicknell said. "I ran across the field to shake (Miami coach) Jimmy Johnson's hand. His face... his face was the way I suppose my face would have been if something like that happened to me. I actually felt sorry for him."

Flutie could not see the catch. He worried that he might have thrown the ball too far. The referee's upturned arms were the signal that he had not.

He began to run toward Gerard Phelan and the end zone.

"I was under control," he said. "It's funny, but while it all was taking place I was pretty good. I wasn't very emotional at all. It was after it all happened, as I ran down the field, that I got emotional."

The idea now was to celebrate.

H. G. Bissinger

H. G. "Buzz" Bissinger (b. 1954) first imagined what became the best-selling *Friday Night Lights* (1990) long before he came up with its title, or found the Texas oil town where it is set, or possessed the chops to tackle a subject as complex as it was rich. He was a thirteen-year-old boy then, with no idea he would grow up to be a Pulitzer Prize–winning investigative reporter for the *Philadelphia Inquirer*. All he knew was that he was mesmerized by the world conjured up in a *Sports Illustrated* story about a high school quarterback—the roaring crowds, the homespun fame, the college recruiters. Two decades later the fascination led Bissinger to Odessa, Texas, where the sight of Permian High's stadium moved him to say, "This isn't just a stadium, this is really a shrine." *Friday Night Lights* touched on everything from race relations to the enormous pressure placed on the town's football heroes. ESPN called it the best sports book in twenty-five years, *Sports Illustrated* chose it as one of the best of all time, and even Hollywood couldn't ruin it. Bissinger's second cousin, the filmmaker Peter Berg, adapted it for both a well-reviewed movie and a beloved TV series. The following excerpt depicts Permian's first game of the season, an event felt deeply by players and perhaps even more so by the adults who take leave of their better judgment every fall.

from

Friday Night Lights

E VERY SOUND IN THE DRESSING ROOM in the final minutes seemed amplified a thousand times—the jagged, repeated rips of athletic tape, the clip of cleats on the concrete floor like that of tap shoes, the tumble of aspirin and Tylenol spilling from plastic bottles like the shaking of bones to ward off evil spirits. The faces of the players were young, but the perfection of their equipment, the gleaming shoes and helmets and the immaculate pants and jerseys, the solemn ritual that was attached to almost everything, made them seem like boys going off to fight a war for the benefit of someone else, unwitting sacrifices to a strange and powerful god.

In the far corner of the dressing room Boobie Miles sat on a bench with his eyes closed, his face a mixture of seriousness and sadness, showing no trace of what this pivotal night would hold for him. Jerrod McDougal, pacing back and forth, went to the bathroom to wipe his

263

face with paper towels. Staring into the mirror, he checked to make sure his shirt was tucked in and the sleeves were taped. He straightened his neck roll and then put on his gloves to protect his hands, the last touches of gladiatorial splendor. It looked good. It looked damn good. In the distance he could hear the Midland Lee band playing "Dixie," and it enraged him. He hated that song and the way those cocky bastards from Lee swaggered to it. His face became like that of an impulse killer, slitty-eyed, filled with anger. Mike Winchell lay on the floor, seduced by its coldness and how good it felt. His eyes closed, but the eyelids still fluttered and you could feel the nervousness churning inside him.

In the silence of that locker room it was hard not to admire these boys as well as fear for them, hard not to get caught up in the intoxicating craziness of it, hard not to whisper "My God!" at how important the game had become, not only to them, but to a town whose spirits crested and fell with each win and each loss. You wished for something to break that tension, a joke, a sigh, a burst of laughter, a simple phrase to convince them that if they lost to the Rebels tonight it wasn't the end of the world, that life would go on as it always had.

Gary Gaines, the coach of Permian, called the team to gather around him. He was a strikingly handsome man with a soft smile and rows of pearly white teeth somehow unstained, as if by divine intervention, from the toxic-looking thumbfuls of tobacco snuff that he snuck between front lip and gum when his wife wasn't around to catch him. He had beautiful eyes, not quite gray, not quite blue, filled with softness and reassurance. His message was short and sincere.

"Nobody rest a play, men. Don't coast on any play. You're on that field, you give it everything you got."

Across the field, in the visitor's dressing room, Earl Miller, the coach of the Rebels, gave similar advice in his thick Texas twang that made every syllable seem as long as a sentence.

"First time you step out on that field, you go down there as hard as you can and bust somebody."

Brian Chavez's eyes bulged as he made his way to the coin toss with the other captains. On one side was Ivory Christian, belching and hiccupping and trying to stop himself from retching again. On the other was Mike Winchell, lost in a trance of intensity. The three of them held hands as they walked down a ramp and then turned a corner to catch the first glimpse of a sheet of fans dressed in black that seemed to stretch forever into the desert night. The farther they moved into the stadium field, the more it felt as if they were entering a fantastic world, a world unlike any other.

The metamorphosis began to take hold of Chavez. When the game began and he took the field, his body would be vibrating and his heart would be beating fast and every muscle in his body would become taut. He knew he would try to hit his opponent as hard as he possibly could from his tight end position, to hurt him, to scare him with his 215-pound frame that was the strongest on the team, to make him think twice about getting back up again.

It was the whole reason he played football, for those hits, for those acts of physical violence that made him tingle and feel wonderful, for those quintessential shots that made him smile from ear to ear and earned him claps on the back from his teammates when he drove some defensive lineman to the sidelines and pinned him right on his butt. He knew he was an asshole when he played, but he figured it was better to be, as he saw it, an "asshole playin' football rather than in real life."

He had no other expectations beyond the physical thrill of it. He didn't have to rely on it or draw all his identity from it. "I played because I like it," he once said. "Others played because it was Permian football. It was their ticket to popularity. It was just a game to me, a high school game."

As the number-one student in his class, his aspirations extended far beyond the glimmer of expectation that a Texas school, any Texas school, might be willing to give him a football scholarship. He had set his sights differently, zeroing in on a target that seemed incomprehensible to his family, his friends, just about everyone. He wanted to go to Harvard.

When he tried to imagine it, he thought it would be like stepping into a different world, a world that was steeped in history and breathtaking and so utterly different from the finite world of Odessa, which spread over the endless horizon like the unshaven stubble of a beard. When he visited it his senior year, he sat by the window of his hotel and watched the rowers along the Charles with their seemingly effortless grace, the strokes of their oars so delicate and perfectly timed as they skimmed along the water past the white domes and the red brick buildings and all those beautiful trees. It didn't seem real to him when he gazed out that window, but more like a painting, beautiful, unfathomable, unattainable.

But now he wasn't thinking about Harvard. Every bone in his body was focused on beating Midland Lee, and he felt so absolutely confident that he had already ordered a DISTRICT CHAMPS patch for his letter jacket. As the coin was being thrown into the air by one of the officials he stared across at Quincy White, Lee's bruising fullback. At that moment Brian felt hatred toward the Rebels, absolute hatred, and he wanted to prove he was the best there was on the damn field, the very best.

The team left the dressing room and gathered behind a huge banner that had been painstakingly made by the cheerleaders. It took up almost half the end zone and was fortified by the Pepettes with pieces of rope like some scene of war from the Middle Ages. It became a curtain. The players congregated behind it in the liquid, fading light, yelling, screaming, pounding each other on the shoulder pads and the helmets, furious to be finally set loose onto the field, to revel in the thrilling roar of the crowd.

The fans couldn't see the players yet, but they could hear them bellowing behind that banner and they could see their arms and knees and helmets push against it and make it stretch. The buildup was infectious, making one's heart beat faster and faster. Suddenly, like a fantastic present coming unwrapped, the players burst through the sign, ripping it to shreds, little pieces of it floating into the air. They poured out in a steady stream, and the crowd rose to its feet.

The stillness was ruptured by a thousand different sounds smashing into each other in wonderful chaos—deep-throated yells, violent exhortations, giddy screams, hoarse whoops. The people in the stands lost all sight of who they were and what they were supposed to be like, all dignity and restraint thrown aside because of these high school boys in front of them, *their* boys, *their* heroes, upon whom they rested all their vicarious thrills, all their dreams. No connection in all of sports was more intimate than this one, the one between town and high school.

"MO-JO! MO-JO! MO-JO! MO-JO!"

Chants of the Permian monicker, which was taken from the title of an old Wilson Pickett song and stuck to the team after a bunch of drunken alumni had yelled the word for no apparent reason during a game in the late sixties, passed through the home side. The visitor's side answered back with equal ferocity:

"REB-ELS! REB-ELS! REB-ELS!"

Each wave of a Confederate flag by a Lee fan was answered by the waving of a white handkerchief by a Permian fan. Each rousing stanza of "Dixie" by the Lee band was answered by an equally rousing stanza of "Grandioso" by the Permian band, each cheer from the Rebelettes matched by one from the Pepettes. Nothing in the world made a difference on this October night except this game illuminating the plains like a three-hour Broadway finale.

Permian took the opening kickoff and moved down the field with the methodical precision that had made it a legend throughout the state of Texas. An easy touchdown, a quick and bloodless 7–0 lead. But Lee, a twenty-one-point underdog, came back with a touchdown of its own to tie the game. Early in the second quarter, a field goal gave the Rebels a 10–7 lead.

Permian responded with a seventy-seven-yard drive to make it 14–10. Chris Comer, the new great black hope who had replaced Boobie Miles in the backfield, carried the ball seven of nine plays and went over a thousand yards for the season.

Earlier in the season, Boobie had cheered on Comer's accomplishments with a proud smile. As the season progressed and Comer became a star while Boobie languished, the cheers stopped.

He made no acknowledgment of Comer's score. He sat on the bench, his eyes staring straight ahead, burning with a mixture of misery and anger as it became clear to him that the coaches had no intention of playing him tonight, that they were willing to test his knee out in meaningless runaways but not in games that counted. His helmet was off and he wore a black stocking cap over his head. The arm pads he liked still dangled from his jersey. The towel bearing the legend "TERMINATOR X" from the name of one of the members of the rap group Public Enemy, hung from his waist, spotless and unsullied. The stadium was lit up like a dance floor, its green surface shimmering and shining in the lights, and his uniform appeared like a glittering tuxedo loaded down with every conceivable extra. But it made him look silly, like one of those kids dressed to the nines to conceal the fact that they were unpopular and couldn't dance a lick. He sat on the bench and felt a coldness swirl through him, as if something sacred inside him was dying, as if every dream in his life was fleeing from him and all he could do was sit there and watch it disappear amid all those roars that had once been for him.

With 2:27 left in the half, Winchell threw the finest pass of his life, a sixty-yard bomb to Lloyd Hill, to make the score 21–10. But then, with less than ten seconds left, Lee scored after connecting on a forty-nine-yard Hail Mary pass that unfolded like a Rube Goldberg drawing, the ball fluttering off the hands and helmets and shoulder pads of several Permian defenders before somehow settling into the hands of a receiver who had never caught a varsity pass in his life. Lee's try for a two-point conversion failed.

The score was 21–16 at halftime.

The Permian players came off the field exhausted, in for a fight they had never quite expected. The gray shirts they wore underneath their jerseys were soaked. Winchell, who had taken a massive hit in the first half, felt dizzy and disoriented. They grabbed red cups of Coke and sat in front of their locker stalls trying to get their breath, the strange Lee touchdown at the end of the half a weird and scary omen. There was hardly a sound, hardly a movement. The players seemed more shell-shocked than frantic, and few even noticed when Boobie flung his shoulder pads against the wall.

In a furious rage he threw his equipment into a travel bag and started to walk out the door. He had had it. He was quitting at halftime of the biggest game of the year. He couldn't bear to watch it anymore, to be humiliated in those lights where everyone in the world could stare at him and know that he wasn't a star anymore, just some two-bit substitute who might get a chance to play if someone got hurt.

None of the varsity coaches made a move to stop him; it was clear that Boobie had become an expendable property. If he wanted to quit, let him go and good riddance. But Nate Hearne, a black junior varsity football coach whose primary responsibility was to handle the black players on the team, herded him into the trainer's room to try to calm him down, to somehow salvage what little of his psyche hadn't already been destroyed.

Boobie stood in the corner of the darkened room with his arms folded and his head turned down toward the floor, as if protecting himself from any more pain. "I quit, coach, they got a good season goin'," he said, his tone filled with the quiet hurt of a child who can't process the shame of what has happened except to run from it.

"Come on, man, don't do this."

"Why'd [Gaines] play me the last weekend and the weekend before that?"

"I know how hard it is. Don't quit now. Come on."

"That's why I'm gonna quit. They can do it without me."

"Everything's gonna be all right. Everybody knows how it feels to be on the sidelines when he should be out there."

"Could have hurt [my knee] last week, could have hurt it the week before. He didn't think about it then."

"You'll be all right. Just hang tough for now. The team needs you. You know we need you. Use your head. Don't let one night destroy everything."

"Why not just quit?"

"This is one game. We got six games down the line."

"Six games to sit on the sidelines."

"We're almost there and now you want to do this, don't do this."

"Next week it ain't gonna be a new story because I ain't gonna play. Just leave me alone, and I'll get out of here."

"You can't walk off now, in the middle of a game. You just can't walk off in the middle of a game."

"I'm just gonna leave because I ain't gonna sit on the sidelines for no one. I see what it's all about."

"What's it all about?"

"I'm a guinea pig."

It went on a little longer, Hearne's heartfelt understanding in contrast to the attitude of most of the other members of the Permian football staff who derided Boobie, who had grown weary of his emotional outbursts and privately called him lazy, and stupid, and shiftless, and selfish, and casually described him as just another "dumb nigger" if he couldn't carry a football under his arm.

Reluctantly, Boobie left the trainer's room and walked back out to the dressing room. Without emotion, he put on his hip pads and shoulder pads. Carefully, meticulously, he tucked his TERMINATOR X towel into the belt of his pants and put that ridiculous costume back

on again because that's what it was now, a costume, a Halloween outfit. He went back out on the field, but it no longer had any promise.
When players tried to talk to him, he said nothing. The Rebels scored
early in the fourth quarter on a one-yard run to take a one-point lead,
22–21. The Lee band broke into "Dixie" and the taunting chant, now
stronger than ever, resumed:

"REB-ELS! REB-ELS! REB-ELS!"

With about six minutes left Permian moved to a first and ten at the
Lee 18, but the drive stalled and a thirty-yard field goal was blocked.

Permian got the ball back at its own 26 with 2:55 left in the game,
but instead of confidence in the huddle there was fear. Chavez could
see it in the eyes of the offensive linemen. He tapped them on the
helmet and said, "Com'on, let's get it, this is it." But he could tell they
weren't listening. The game was slipping away.

They were going to lose. They were goddamn going to lose and
everything they had worked for for the past six years of their lives,
everything they cared about, was about to be ruined.

Winchell, after the glorious touchdown pass he had thrown, now
seemed hunted by failure. His face was etched in agony, the passes
coming off his hand in a tentative, jerky motion, thrown desperately
without rhythm. The Lee fans were on their feet. There was the inces-
sant beat of the drums from the band. Both sides were screaming their
hearts out.

"REB-ELS! REB-ELS!"

"MO-JO! MO-JO!"

How could a seventeen-year-old kid concentrate at a moment like
this amid the frenzy of fifteen thousand fans? How could he possibly
keep his poise?

With a third and ten at the Lee 41, flanker Robert Brown broke free
down the left sideline after his defender fell down, but the ball was
thrown way out of bounds.

"Fuck! Winchell!" screamed starting linebacker Chad Payne from
the sidelines as ball fluttered helplessly beyond Brown's grasp.
With a fourth and ten, another pass fell incomplete.

It wasn't even close.

Jerrod McDougal watched as the Lee players fell all over each other
on the field like kittens. He watched as they spit contemptuously on

the field, *his* field, goddammit, his fucking field, defiling it, disgracing it, and never in his life had he felt such humiliation. Some gladiator he was, some heroic gladiator. In the dressing room he started to cry, his right hand draped tenderly around the bowed head of linebacker Greg Sweatt, who was sobbing also. With his other hand he punched a wall. Chavez and Winchell sat in silence, and Ivory Christian felt that creeping numbness. With a three-way tie for first and only one game left in the regular season, now Permian might not get into the state playoffs. But that wasn't potentially devastating to Ivory. There had to be something else in life, if only he could figure out what it was.

Boobie officially quit the team two days later. But no one paid much attention. There were a lot more important things to worry about than that pain-in-the-ass prima donna with a bad knee who couldn't cut worth a crap anymore anyway. There were plenty more on the Southside where he came from.

The loss to Lee sent Odessa into a tailspin, so unthinkable, so catastrophic was it. As in a civil war, goodwill and love disintegrated and members of the town turned on each other.

Gaines himself was distraught, a year's worth of work wasted, the chorus against him only growing stronger that he was a very nice man who wasn't a very good coach when it counted. When he got back to the field house he stayed in the coaches' office long past midnight, still mulling over what had happened and why the eighteen-hour days he had spent preparing for the Rebels had not paid off. The idea of a team with this kind of talent not making the playoffs seemed impossible, but now it might happen. And if it did, he had to wonder if he would be in the same job next year.

When he went home late that night, several FOR SALE signs had been punched into his lawn, a not-so-subtle hint that maybe it would be best for everyone if he just got the hell out of town. He took them and dumped them in the garage along with the other ones he had already collected. He wasn't surprised by them.

After all, he was a high school football coach, and after all, this was Odessa, where Bob Rutherford, an affable realtor in town, might as well have been speaking for thousands when he casually said one day as if talking about the need for a rainstorm to settle the dust, "Life really wouldn't be worth livin' if you didn't have a high school football team to support."

Mark Kram

Violence was the flame that Mark Kram (1933–2002) was drawn to. The spilling of blood and the ruination of lives stirred the empathy, outrage, and fascination that made him the premier boxing writer of his time. An autodidact from a factory-whistle neighborhood in Baltimore, Kram was perhaps *Sports Illustrated*'s most memorable stylist in the 1960s and '70s, when no magazine boasted more writing talent. But he was undone by a change in editors and his involvement in the 1977 scandal surrounding Don King's corrupt United States Boxing Tournament. Kram was forced to wander the wastelands of journalism and Hollywood for more than a decade, his reputation in tatters. His salvation came in the form of two young editors, Rob Fleder at *Playboy* and David Hirshey at *Esquire*, who subscribed to the theory that talent conquers all. In the last decade of his life, Kram responded with brilliant work for both as well as for editors at *GQ* and *Men's Journal*, and he capped his comeback with his defiantly contrarian 2001 book *Ghosts of Manila*, which took Joe Frazier's side in his feud with Muhammad Ali. Kram had paid a rare visit to pro football for *Esquire* a decade earlier when he wrote about the Minnesota Vikings' Joey Browner as a symbol of the damage men do to each other in their hundred-yard wars. What makes the story stand out, in addition to Kram's bristling prose, is that it was written more than a decade before it became common for sportswriters—and medical writers—to reveal the destruction and death the game has left in its wake.

No Pain, No Game

OBSERVE, PLEASE, THE HUMAN SKELETON, 208 bones perfectly wrought and arranged; the feet built on blocks, the shinbones like a Doric column. Imagine an engineer being told to come up with the vertebral column from scratch. After years, he might produce a primitive facsimile, only to hear the utterly mad suggestion: Okay, now lay a nerve cord of a million wires through the column, immune to injury from any movement. Everywhere the eye goes over the skeleton, there is a new composition: the voluting Ionic thigh, Corinthian capitals, Gothic buttresses, baroque portals. While high above, the skull roof arches like the cupola of a Renaissance cathedral, the repository of a brain that has taken all this frozen music to the bottom of the ocean, to the moon, and to a pro football field—the most antithetical place on earth for the aesthetic appreciation of 208 bones.

After nine years in the NFL, Joey Browner of the Vikings is a scholar of the terrain and a rapt listener to the skeleton, the latter being rather noisy right now and animated in his mind. It is Monday morning, and all over the land the bill is being presented to some large, tough men for playing so fearlessly with the equation of mass times velocity; only the backup quarterback bullets out of bed on recovery day. The rest will gimp, hobble, or crawl to the bathroom, where contusions are counted like scattered coins, and broken noses, ballooned with mucus and blood, feel like massive ice floes. Browner unpacks each leg from the bed as if they were rare glassware, then stands up. The feet and calves throb from the turf. The precious knees have no complaint. The thigh is still properly Ionic. The vertebral column whimpers for a moment. Not a bad Monday, he figures, until he tries to raise his right arm.

The bathroom mirror tells him it's still of a piece. It's partially numb, the hand is hard to close, and the upper arm feels as if it's been set upon by the tiny teeth of small fish. Pain is a personal insult—and not good for business; he knows the politics of injury in the NFL. Annoyed, his mind caroms through the fog of plays from the day before, finally stops on a helmet, sunlit and scratched, a blur with a wicked angle that ripped into his upper arm like a piece of space junk in orbit. He rubs *dipjajong*—an Oriental balm—on the point of impact, dresses slowly, then slides into an expensive massage chair as he begins to decompress to a background tape of Chopin nocturnes, quieting and ruminative, perfect for firing off Zen bolts of self-healing concentration to his arm.

By the next morning, after re-creating his Monday damage probe, he appears more worried about his garden of collard greens and flower bed of perennials; given the shape of his arm, most of hypochondriacal America would now be envisioning amputation. That is what Browner would like to do, so eager is he to conceal the injury, so confident is he that he could play with one and a half arms. At six-three, 230 pounds, he is a diligent smasher of cupolas, who has made more than one thousand tackles in his career. He is the first $1 million safety in NFL history; a six-time All-Pro; and a two-time conscriptee to the all-Madden team, an honor given out to those who have no aversion to dirt, blood, and freeway collision.

His only peer is Ronnie Lott, with whom he played at USC. Lott put the safety position on the map, invested it with identity, separated it from the slugging linebackers and the butterfly cornerbacks. It is the new glamour position in the NFL, due in part to CBS's John Madden, a joyful and precise bone counter who always knows where the wreckage will lie. With schedule parity, the outlawing of the spear, the clothesline, and the chop block, with excessive holding, and so many tinkerings to increase scoring, pro football veered toward the static on TV. Madden, it's clear, wanted to bring some good old whomp back to the game, and he found his men in players like Lott and Browner. Now the cameras are sensitive to the work of safeties, the blackjacks of the defensive secondary.

Of all hitters, they have the best of it: time and space for fierce acceleration, usually brutal angles, and wide receivers who come to them like scraps of meat being tossed into a kennel. Lott delineates their predatory zest in his book, *Total Impact*, saying that during a hit, "my eyes close, roll back into my head... snot sprays out of my nostrils, covering my mouth and cheeks." His ears ring, his brain goes blank, and he gasps for air. He goes on to broaden the picture: "If you want to find out if you can handle being hit by Ronnie Lott, here's what you do. Grab a football, throw it in the air, and have your best friend belt you with a baseball bat. No shoulder pads. No helmet. Just you, your best friend, and the biggest Louisville Slugger you can find."

Like medical students, pro players do not often dwell on the reality of the vivisection room, so Lott is an exception, a brilliant emoter with a legitimate portfolio, but still a man who has a lot of pages to fill with body parts and brute-man evocations. Browner has no marquee to live up to—except on the field. He is a star, though not easily accessible in media-tranquil Minnesota, distant from the hype apparatus on both coasts, part of a team that always seems to avoid the glory portioned to it annually in preseason forecasts.

Tuesdays are black days at a losing team's quarters, soft on the body and miserable for the mind. It is the day when coaches slap cassettes of failure into machines, vanish, then emerge with performances graded, carefully selecting their scapegoats. Good humor is bankrupt. On this Tuesday, Viking coach Jerry Burns looks much like Livia in *I, Claudius*, who in so many words scorches her gladiators, saying: "There will be plenty of money for the living and a decent burial for the dead. But if you let me down again, I'll break you, I'll send the lot of you to the mines of New Media." Browner smiles at the notion. "That's it—pro football," he says. "You don't need me."

"No tears like Lott?" he is asked.

"No tears," he says. "I guess I don't have much of a waterworks."

"No snot?"

He laughs: "He must have some nose."

"What's total impact?"

"Like a train speeding up your spinal cord and coming out your ear. When it's bad."

"When it's good?"

"When you're the train. Going through 'em and then coming out and feeling like all their organs are hanging off the engine."

"You need rage for that?"

"Oh, yeah," he says. "The real kind. No chemicals."

"Chemicals? Like amphetamines?"

"Well, I don't know that," he says, shifting in his chair. "Just let's say that you can run into some abnormal folks out there. I keep an eye on the droolers."

"Your rage, then?"

"From pure hitting," he says. "Controlled by years of Zen study. I'm like the sun and storm, which moves through bamboo. Hollow on the inside, hard and bright on the outside. Dumb rage chains you up. But I got a lot of bad sky if I gotta go with a moment."

"Ever make the perfect hit?"

"I've been looking for it for years."

"What would it feel like?"

"It would *feel* like you've launched a wide receiver so far he's splashed and blinkin' like a number on the scoreboard. That's what you're after mostly."

"Sounds terrible."

"It's the game," he says, coolly. "If you can't go to stud anymore, you're gone."

"I get the picture."

"How can you?" he asks, with a tight grin. "You'd have to put on the gear for the real picture."

There is no dramaturgy with Browner, just a monotone voice, a somnolent gaze that seems uninterested in cheerful coexistence. Or, perhaps, he is a model of stately calm. His natural bent is to listen. He does come close to the psychological sketch work of Dr. Arnold Mandell, a psychiatrist with the San Diego Chargers some years back who visited the dark corners of a football player's mind. Now in Florida, Mandell says: "Take quarterbacks: two dominant types who succeed— the arrogant limit-testers and the hyperreligious with the calm of a believer. Wide receivers: quite interested in their own welfare; they strive for elegance, being pretty, the stuff of actors. Defensive backs: very smart, given to loneliness, alienation; they hate structure, destroy without conscience, especially safeties."

Is that right? "I don't know," says Joey. "But it's not good for business if you care for a second whether blood is bubbling out of a guy's mouth." Highlighted by cornices of high bone, his eyes are cold and pale, like those of a leopard, an animal whose biomechanics he has studied and will often watch in wildlife films before a game. An all-purpose predator with a quick pounce, no wasted motion, the leopard can go up a tree for a monkey ("just like going up for a wide receiver") or move out from behind a bush with a brutal rush of energy ("just what you need for those warthog running backs"). The mind tries for the image of him moving like a projectile, so massive and quick, hurling into muscle and bone. It eludes, and there are only aftermaths, unrelated to Browner. Kansas City quarterback Steve DeBerg served up the horrors in a reprise of hits he has taken: his elbow spurting blood so badly that his mother thought the hitter used a screwdriver; a shot to the throat that left him whispering and forced him to wear a voice box on his mask for the next six games; and this memorable encounter with Tampa Bay's Lee Roy Selmon: "Lee Roy squared up on me. The first thing that hit the ground was the back of my head. I was blind in my left eye for more than a half hour—and I didn't even know it. I went to the team doctor and he held up two fingers. I couldn't see the left sides of the fingers—the side Selmon had come from. I sat on the bench for a quarter."

Browner offers to bring you closer to the moment of impact. He puts some tape into the machine and turns off the lights. The figures up on the screen are black and white, flying about like bats in a silent, horrific dream. Suddenly, there is Christian Okoye, of the Chiefs, six-one, 260 pounds, a frightful excrescence from the gene pool, rocketing into the secondary, with Joey meeting him point blank—and then wobbling off of him like a blown tire. "*Booooom!*" he says. "A head full of flies. For me. I learned. You don't hit Okoye. He hits you. You have to put a meltdown on him. First the upper body, then slide to the waist, then down to the legs—and pray for the cavalry." Another snapshot, a wide receiver climbing for the ball, with Browner firing toward him. "*Whaaack!*" he says. "There goes his helmet. There goes the ball. And his heart. Sometimes. You hope." The receiver sprawls on the ground, his legs kicking. Browner looks down at him. Without taunting or joy, more like a man admiring a fresco. "I'm looking at his eyes dilating," he says. "Just looking at the artwork. The trouble is, on the next play I could be the painting." Can he see fear in receivers?

"You don't see much in their eyes," he says. "They're con men, pickpockets."

"Hits don't bother them?"

"Sure, but you tell it in their aura. When you're ready to strike, you're impeding it, and you can tell if it's weak, strong, or out there just to be out there."

"So they do have fear?"

"Maybe for a play or two. You can't count on it. They may be runnin' a game on you. Just keep putting meat on meat until something gives. But a guy like Jerry Rice, he'll keep comin' at you, even if you've left him without a head on the last play."

"The film seems eerie without sound."

"That's how it is out there. You don't hear. You're in another zone."

"So why not pad helmets? That's been suggested by some critics."

"Are you kidding?" he says. "Sound sells in the living rooms. Puts backsides in BarcaLoungers for hours. The sound of violence, man. Without it, the NFL would be a Japanese tea ceremony."

The sound, though, is just the aural rumor of conflict, much like the echo of considerable ram horn after a territorial sorting-out high up in the mountain rocks. NFL Films, the official conveyer of sensory tease, tries mightily to bottle the ingredient, catching the thwack of ricocheting helmets, the seismic crash of plastic pads, and every reaction to pain, from gasp to groan. Network coverage has to settle for what enters the living room as a strangulated muffle. But in the end, the sound becomes commonplace, with the hardcore voyeur, rapidly inured in these times, wondering: *What is it really like down there?* It has the same dulling result as special effects in movies; more is never enough, and he knows there is *more*. Like Browner says: "Whatever a fan thinks he's seeing or hearing has to be multiplied a hundred times—and they should imagine themselves in the middle of all this with an injury that would keep them home from work in real life for a couple of weeks."

What they are not seeing, hearing—and feeling—is the hitting and acceleration of 250-pound packages: kinetic energy, result of the mass times speed equation. "Kinetic energy," says Mandell, "is the force that dents cars on collision." He recalls the first hit he ever saw on the sidelines with the Chargers. "My nervous system," he says, "never really recovered until close to the end of the game. The running back was down on his back. His mouth was twitching. His eyes were closed. Our linebacker was down, too, holding his shoulder and whimpering quietly. I asked him at halftime what the hit felt like. He said: 'It felt warm all over.'" TV production, fortunately, can't produce Mandell's response. But there still remains the infant potential of virtual reality, the last technological stop for the transmission of visceral sensation. What a rich market there: the semireality of a nose tackle, chop-shopped like an old bus; the psychotic rush of a defensive end; the Cuisinarted quarterback, and most thrilling of all, the wide receiver in an entrechat, so high, so phosphorescent, suddenly erased like a single firefly in a dark wood.

Quite a relief, too, for play-by-play and color men, no longer having to match pallid language with picture and sound. Just a knowing line: "Well, we don't have to tell you about that hit, you're all rubbing your spleens out there, aren't you, eh?" But for now, faced with such a deep vein of images, they try hard to support them with frenetic language that, on just one series of plays, can soar with flights of caroming analysis. War by other means? Iambic pentameter of human motion? The mysterioso of playbooks, equal to pro football as quark physics? For years they played with the edges of what's going on below as if it might be joined with a 7-Eleven stickup or the national murder rate. It is Pete Gent's suspicion (the ex-Cowboy and author of *North Dallas Forty*) that the NFL intruded heavily on descriptions of violence, as it has with the more killer-ape philosophies of certain coaches. If so, it is a censorship of nicety, an NFL public relations device to obscure its primary gravity—choreographed violence.

But claw and tooth are fast gaining in the language in the booth, as if the networks are saying, Well, for all these millions, why should we struggle for euphemism during a head sapping? Incapable of delicate evasion, John Madden was the pioneer. Ever since, the veld has grown louder in decibel and candid depiction. Thus, we now have Dan Dierdorf on *Monday Night Football*, part troll, part Enrico Fermi of line play and Mother Teresa during the interlude of injury (caring isn't out—not yet). There's Joe Theismann of ESPN—few better with physicality, especially with the root-canal work done on quarterbacks. Even the benignity of Frank Gifford seems on the verge of collapse. He blurted recently: "People have to understand today it's a violent, vicious game." All that remains to complete the push toward veracity is the addition of Mike Ditka to the corps. He said in a recent interview: "I love to see people hit people. Fair, square, within the rules of the game. If people don't like it, they shouldn't watch."

Big Mike seems to be playing fast and loose with TV ratings—the grenade on the head of the pin. Or is he? He's not all *Homo erectus*, he knows the show biz fastened heavily to the dreadful physics of the game. "Violence is what the NFL sells," Jon Morris of the Bears, a fifteen-year veteran, once said. "They say they don't, but they do." The NFL hates the V-word; socially, it's a hot button more than ever. Like drugs, violence carries with it the threat of reform from explainers who dog the content of movies and TV for sources as to why we are nearly the most violent society on earth. Pete Rozelle was quick to respond when John Underwood wrote a superb series in *Sports Illustrated* on NFL brutality a decade back. He condemned the series, calling it irresponsible, though some wits thought he did so only because Underwood explored the possibility of padding helmets.

Admittedly, it is not easy to control a game that is inherently destructive to the body. Tip the rules to the defense, and you have nothing more than gang war; move them too far toward offense, and you have mostly conflict without resistance. Part of the NFL dilemma is in its struggle between illusion and reality; it wants to stir the blood without you really absorbing that it *is* blood. It also luxuriates in its image of the American war game, strives to be the perfect metaphor for Clausewitz's ponderings about real war tactics (circa 1819, i.e., stint on blood and you lose). The warrior ethic is central to the game, and no coach or player can succeed without astute attention to the precise fashioning of a warrior mentality (loss of self), defined by Ernie Barnes, formerly of the Colts and Chargers, as "the aggressive nature that knows no safety zones."

Whatever normal is, sustaining that degree of pure aggression for sixteen, seventeen Sundays each season (military officers will tell you it's not attainable regularly in real combat) can't be part of it. "It's a war in every sense of the word," wrote Jack Tatum of the Raiders in *They Call Me Assassin*. Tatum, maybe the preeminent hitter of all time, broke the neck of receiver Darryl Stingley, putting him in a wheelchair for life; by most opinions, it was a legal hit. He elaborated: "Those hours before a game are lonely and tough. I think about, even fear, what can happen." If a merciless intimidator like Tatum could have fear about himself and others, it becomes plain that before each game players must find a room down a dark and distant hall not reachable by ordinary minds.

So how do they get there, free from fear for body and performance? "When I went to the Colts," says Barnes, "and saw giant stars like Gino Marchetti and Big Daddy Lipscomb throwing up before a game, I knew this was serious shit, and I had to get where they were living in their heads." Job security, more money, and artificial vendettas flamed by coaches and the press can help to a limited point. So can acute memory selection, the combing of the mind for enraging moments. With the Lions, Alex Karras took the memory of his father dying and leaving the family poor, the anger of his having to choose football over drama school because of money kept him sufficiently lethal. If there is no moment, one has to be imagined. "I had to think of stuff," said Jean Fugett of the Cowboys. The guy opposite him had to become the man who "raped my mother."

But for years, the most effective path to the room was the use of amphetamines. Hardly a book by an ex-player can be opened without finding talk about speed. Fran Tarkenton cites the use of "all sorts" of uppers, especially by defensive linemen seeking "the final plateau of endurance and competitive zeal." Johnny Sample of the Jets said they ate them "like candy." Tom Bass even wrote a poem about "the man" (speed), a crutch he depended on more than his playbook. Dave Meggyesy observed that the "violent and brutal" player on television is merely "a synthetic product." Bernie Parrish of the Browns outlined how he was up to fifteen five-milligram tablets before each game, "in the never-ending search for the magic elixir." The NFL evaded reality, just as it would do with the proliferation of cocaine and steroids in the eighties.

The authority on speed and pro football is Dr. Mandell, an internationally respected psychiatrist when he broke the silence. He joined the Chargers at the behest of owner Gene Klein and found a netherland of drugs, mainly speed. One player told him "the difference between a star and a superstar was a superdose." Mandell tried to wean the players off speed and to circumvent the use of dangerous street product. He began by counseling and prescribing slowly diminishing doses, the way you handle most habits. When the NFL found out, it banned him from the Chargers. Mandell went public with his findings, telling of widespread drug use, of how he had proposed urine tests and was rebuffed. The NFL went after his license, he says, and the upshot was that after a fifteen-day hearing—with Dr. Jonas Salk as one of his character witnesses—he was put on five-year probation; he resigned his post at the University of California–San Diego, where he had helped set up the medical school.

"Large doses of amphetamines," he says now, "induce prepsychotic paranoid rage."

"What's that mean?" he is asked.

"The killer of presidents," he says.

"How would this show up on the field?"

"One long temper tantrum," he says. "Late hits, kicks to the body and head, overkill mauling of the quarterback."

"How about before a game?"

"Aberrant behavior. When I first got up close in a dressing room, it was like being in another world. Lockers being torn apart. Players staring catatonically into mirrors. I was afraid to go to the center of the room for fear of bumping one of them."

"Is speed still in use?"

"I don't know," he says. "I'd be surprised if it wasn't, especially among older players who have seen and heard it all and find it hard to get it up. Speed opened the door for cocaine. After speed, cocaine mellows you down." He pauses, says thoughtfully: "The game exacts a terrible toll on players."

Joey Browner is asked: "At what age would you take your pension?"

"At forty-five," he says.

"The earliest age, right?"

"Yeah."

"Should the NFL fund a longevity study for players?"

"Certainly."

"Are they interested in the well-being of players? Long term or short term?"

"Short term."

"Any physical disabilities?"

"Can't write a long time with my right hand. This finger here [fore-finger] can't go back. It goes numb."

"How hard will the transition be from football?"

"I'll miss the hitting," he says.

"If someone told you that you might be losing ten to twenty years on your life, would you do it again?"

"Wouldn't think twice. It's a powerful thing in me."

"They say an NFL player of seven years takes 130,000 full-speed hits. Sound right?"

"Easy. And I remember every one."

Browner was answering modified questions put to 440 ex-players during a 1988 *Los Angeles Times* survey. Seventy-eight percent of the players said they had disabilities, 60 percent said the NFL was not interested in their well-being, and 78 percent wanted a longevity study. Browner was with the majority on each question. What jolted the most was that pro football players (66 percent of them) seem to be certain they are dying before their time, and that 55 percent would play again, regardless. The early death rate has long been a whisper, without scientific foundation. "We're now trying to get to the bottom of this idea," says Dr. Sherry Baron, who recently began a study for the National Institute for Occupational Safety and Health. "From the replies we get, a lot of players are nervous out there."

The Jobs Rated Almanac seemed to put the NFL player near the coal miner when it ranked 250 occupations for work environment. Judged on stress, outlook, physical demands, security, and income, the NFL player rose out of the bottom 10 only in income. With good reason.

The life is awful if you care to look past the glory and the money; disability underwriters, when they don't back off altogether, approach the pro as they would a career bridge jumper. Randy Burke (former Colt), age thirty-two when he replied to the *Times* survey, catches the life, commenting on concussions: "I can talk clearly, but ever since football my words get stuck together. I don't know what to expect next." And Pete Gent says: "I went to an orthopedic surgeon, and he told me I had the skeleton of a seventy-year-old man."

Pro football players will do anything to keep taking the next step. As it is noted in Ecclesiastes, *There is a season*—one time, baby. To that end, they will balloon up or sharpen bodies to murderous specification (steroids), and few are the ones who will resist the Novocain and the long needles of muscle-freeing, tissue-rotting cortisone. Whatever it takes to keep the life. A recent report from Ball State University reveals the brevity and psychic pain: One out of three players leaves because of injury; 40 percent have financial difficulties, and one of three is divorced within six months; many remember the anxiety of career separation setting in within hours of knowing it was over.

What happens to so many of them? They land on the desk of Miki Yaras, the curator of "the horror shop" for the NFL Players Association. It is her job to battle for disability benefits from the pension fund, overseen by three reps from her side, three from the owners. For some bizarre reason, perhaps out of a deep imprinting of loyalty and team, players come to her thinking the game will be there for them when they leave it; it isn't, and their resentment with coaches, team doctors, and ego-sick owners rises. Her war for benefits is often long and bitter, outlined against a blizzard of psychiatric and medical paperwork for and against. She has seen it all: from the young player, depressed and hypertensive, who tried to hurtle his wheelchair in front of a truck (the team doctor removed the wrong cartilage from his knee) to the forty-year-old who can't bend over to play with his children, from the drinkers of battery acid to the ex-Cowboy found wandering on the desert.

"It's very difficult to qualify," Yaras says. "The owners will simply not recognize the degenerative nature of injuries. The plan is well overfunded. It could afford temporary relief to many more than it does. I even have a quadriplegic. The doctor for the owners wrote that 'his brain is intact, and he can move his arm, someday he'll be able to work.' They think selling pencils out of an iron lung is an occupation."

On Saturday, Joey Browner begins to feel the gathering sound of Sunday, bloody Sunday. He goes to his dojo for his work on *iaido*, an art of Japanese swordsmanship—not like karate, just exact, ceremonial patterns of cutting designed to put the mind out there on the dangerous edge of things. He can't work the long katana now because, after thirty needles in his arm a couple of days before, it was found that he had nerve damage. So, wearing a robe, he merely extends the katana, his gaze fixed on the dancing beams of the blade, making you think of twinkling spinal lights. What does he see? The heads of clever, arrogant running backs? Who knows? He's looking and he sees what he sees. And after a half hour you can almost catch in his eyes the rush of the leopard toward cover behind the bush where he can already view the whole terrible beauty of the game, just a pure expression of gunshot hits, all of it for the crowd that wants to feel its own alphaness, for the crowd that hears no screams other than its own, and isn't it all so natural, he thinks, a connective to prehistoric hunting bands and as instinctually human as the impulse to go down and look at the bright, pounding sea.

Charles P. Pierce

To read Charles P. Pierce (b. 1953) is to be in the company of a wordsmith who delights in making the language sit up on its hind legs and do tricks. Each sentence he writes is its own reward, whether it's floating on the helium of mischief or growing thunderous with outrage at hypocrisy and small-mindedness. It has been thus since Pierce broke in as a generalist at the *Boston Phoenix* in the mid-1970s and then moved to the *Boston Herald* to write sports. His insightful features for the short-lived *National Sports Daily* punched his ticket to *GQ* and *Sports Illustrated*. He is now a writer-at-large for *Esquire* and blogs about politics for the magazine's website while writing the occasional book—most recently *Idiot America* (2009)—and keeping his hand in sports at the website Grantland. You'll never want Pierce far from sports after reading his column for *GQ*'s September 1996 issue, a soulful ode to Archie Manning, father of Peyton and Eli and a heroic quarterback in his time, which was a troubled time indeed. There's a music lesson or two along the way and a short course in Mississippi's racial history, but that's just a smart and entertaining writer setting the table for a look at the elder Manning that will help you understand why his sons turned out so well.

Legends of the Fall

A s I EXPLAINED ONCE to an editor friend, my column is like my house. I decide what gets hung on the walls. I decide what gets served for dinner. I decide what gets played on the stereo. If you don't like my paintings, my food or my music, don't come to my house. So, because this is my column, I am going to write right here about Peerless Price, a wide receiver for the University of Tennessee. I am going to do this because you don't often get to talk to someone named Peerless, unless you're Dick Tracy. It is one of the wonders of sportswriting that you occasionally get to meet people named Peerless, a pleasure denied to all those Beltway flatheads, who, I'm telling you, would act a lot less constipated on all those Sunday-morning television shows if they had a few more people named Peerless in their lives. This is my column, and this is my first Peerless, dammit. We will chat with him for a moment.

"Some people call me Peerless," he explains. "My friends usually just call me Peer." Of course they do.

One autumn afternoon, mark it, Peerless Price is going to make some poor Southeastern Conference cornerback leave his lingerie at about the forty-yard line, and a ridiculously gifted young quarterback named Peyton Manning is going to hang the ball on a deep line, and Tennessee is going to score a long and important touchdown. Peyton to Peerless. It rings.

Drop that note into the great chorus that still sings of a firehaired quarterback from Ole Miss who became the greatest legend Mississippi has produced since that July day at Gettysburg when Barksdale's boys failed to get up Little Round Top.

With the football, Archie Manning was juke-mad, a pocket-busting dervish in a time that celebrated the reckless and the improvised. He lit up the SEC to the point where people were writing songs about him; "The Ballad of Archie Who" was a respectable hit. Later he spent his professional career with horrid teams. He was battered, stomped silly all over the NFL, and he still came out of it smiling. He had three sons, and the middle boy is going to win the Heisman Trophy this season, unless he gets injured or General Grant comes back through Tennessee.

Last year Peyton Manning led his team to an 11-1 season. He threw for 2,954 yards and twenty-two touchdowns. He threw only four interceptions. His team's only loss came at Florida, in a game in which Tennessee led 30–21 at halftime before being hopelessly swamped in a driving rain after intermission. On New Year's Day, Manning and Tennessee caught Ohio State flat after the Buckeyes had punted away a national championship by losing to Michigan in the last game of the regular season. Manning caught Joey Kent with a forty-seven-yard touchdown pass that broke Ohio State and that, truth be told, marked the beginning of the 1996 season, in which Tennessee is nearly as solid a favorite for the national championship as Manning is to win John Heisman's trophy.

Peyton Manning's story is happily infused with his father's legend even as he has only begun to create his own. There is a lightness to the way the stories have begun to blend into each other. It is a burden neither to the father nor to his sons.

"I never had a child named after me," Archie muses when asked about the lore that is growing up around his son. "Best I ever did was some dogs and maybe a mule. But up here in Knoxville, they still print all the new babies' names, and there sure are a lot of little Peytons all of a sudden, boys and girls."

"I remember waiting for my dad after one of those bad games," says Peyton. "They'd have lost, and he'd be sore. He'd come out, and he'd hug my mom, and then he'd sign his autographs. I'd be saying, 'Dad, let's go home.' I used to wonder about those people, Don't they know he just lost a game? But he always told me to keep smile on my face. You know, a quarterback's got to be a patient person.

"What I remember most is that he never brought his sorrows home."

Yes, sorrows. For this is a story about a family, a happy family, but one that can trace its history back through one unspeakably sorrowful evening in the Mississippi Delta. There are heroes in the story, and that there may be a spot in the saga even for a minor character named Peerless proves that Providence still wields a deft hand as literature. Peyton Manning is southern, a New Orleanian, but the home of his legend is not there. Just as the wondrous old blues tells us, its home is in the Delta.

Good Christ, this place is the kingdom of weird. It begins near Belzoni, about twenty miles out along highway 49. You start seeing the prisoners, lining the side of the road in their blue jackets reading MDOC CONVICT, picking up the trash while the soft, loose cotton blows around the roadside. A little farther along, you start to see the signs warning you not to pick up hitchhikers. The next set of signs tells you that it is illegal to stop for longer than five minutes. Then you see the prison, shadowy and vast in the morning mist. The Mississippi State Penitentiary at Parchman.

Parchman Farm.

Its history is shot through with almost mythic terror. It was worse to be there than to be sharecropping, worse to be there than back in slavery, the old ones whispered. Young Riley B. King visited his uncle there once, and Parchman scared him so bad that the first chance he got, he moved to Memphis, picked up a guitar and changed his name to B. B. Most of the American popular culture that has been worth a damn in the twentieth century owes something to this haunted land, and Parchman Farm was the hidden charge behind nearly all of it, good and bad, as though that ever mattered at all.

People bought the music and turned away from the bloody history that produced it.

It was Archie Manning's country. He grew up in Drew, the nearest real town to the Farm, which casts its shadow over Drew as surely as it does over nearly everything else in the Delta. He would come to create his own legend in Mississippi, but he would come to do it from a place thick with long legends of its own.

"There were twenty guys on my football team," he recalls, "and six of them came from Parchman."

His father ran a farm-machinery shop in Drew. Buddy Manning was big and bluff and well loved around the town. Archie grew up as the best athlete in a very small place. Often he would go out to dances in the Delta to hear a band called the Gordian Knot, which was fronted by a singer named Jim Weatherly. Weatherly once started at quarterback at Ole Miss, and he ultimately went on to write not only "Midnight Train to Georgia" but also the vastly superior "Neither One of Us (Wants to Be the First to Say Goodbye)" for Gladys Knight and the Pips. The world was beginning to shake in Mississippi, and some of the boys Archie knew went to Ole Miss with the National Guard in order to escort James Meredith through the front gates.

"I'm not sure I really knew what it was all about back in those days," Archie recalls. "I probably should have."

This sounds more disingenuous than it actually is; after all, it beggars belief that he didn't really know what was going on in Mississippi. More likely, his is the cultivated ambivalence of a decent man on whom white Mississippi fastened at a time when it was groping for a white hero for anesthetic purposes. "Mississippi'd been getting beat up pretty good through the 1960s," he says. "The whole state pretty much clung to the team." One thinks of Parchman Farm and determines that Mississippi pretty much deserved what came to it. In a very real cultural sense, the Mississippi of the 1960s was the test track for the Montana of the 1990s, and Ole Miss still sticks in the craw of many talented black athletes because of all those things that went on while Archie Manning was coming up in Drew.

And one day in 1968, Kentucky brought two black players to Memorial Stadium in Jackson, and one of them, Wilbur Hackett, and Archie damned near knocked each other silly, and Archie patted the Kentucky player on the backside while everyone in the stadium went all hushed and still, even the highway patrolmen, not far removed from the days when their jobs entailed protecting the people who blew up little children in churches. Archie Manning's was the next-to-last Mississippi football class to play all four seasons without a black teammate, and it can be fairly said that Archie Manning became a hero to many people who didn't deserve the likes of him.

He had a glorious career, all torchlight and antebellum rituals. He met and romanced a homecoming queen from Williamsville named Olivia Williams. However, one season, he played such a miserable game at—of all places—Tennessee that he came back to school and briefly broke up with Olivia, severely distressing her father, a country shopkeeper named Cooper Williams. The following season Archie helped Mississippi crush Tennessee in a piece of getback that cemented his legend for good, and he turned out to be smart enough to get Olivia back as well, old Cooper Williams being as thrilled as anyone.

Back home in the Delta, however, right before his junior season, in 1969, Archie came home from a wedding reception and found his father's body. Buddy Manning's health had gone and his business was failing, and so he took a gun to his chest. Archie called the doctor. He cleaned the room. This is the way things were done in the Delta, where they learn to deal with death as though it is nothing more than the dry wind that stirs the cotton.

"My father passed away," is the way Archie says it now.

Where he grew up, sorrow is of the land. He does not bring his sorrows home.

He never pushed his sons into football. He knew the game too well for that. Archie and Olivia married in 1971, a huge church wedding that people still talk about, and they had three boys, whom they raised in big houses in the Garden District of New Orleans. Cooper was the first one, a boisterous and hearty sort, a born operator and a gifted wide receiver. Peyton came next. He was more reserved, impeccably organized and something of a grind. "They never talked about the pros," Archie says. "All they ever wanted was to play college football." Both of the older boys (Eli, the youngest, is in high school now) were allowed to take up the game only when they were old enough for organized leagues in which there would be real coaches. They then went on to the Isidore Newman School, a private institution that is almost

universally assumed to be a Catholic high school but which is actually quite secular and housed in what used to be a Jewish orphanage.
Cooper went first, playing well enough to get a ride to Ole Miss, plunging enthusiastically into the heart of his father's legacy. Back in New
Orleans, Peyton had begun to draw attention as a quarterback. With
a Manning who was a quarterback, the stakes went up dramatically.

"He never pushed us into anything," Peyton says of his father. "If
anything, we all took advantage of him. It was like, 'Hey, Dad. Whyn't
you come work out with us? Show us how to do this and that.'" All
along, Peyton had planned to go to Ole Miss, just as his father and his
brother had. When the letters started to pour into the big house in the
Garden District, especially the handwritten one from Bobby Bowden
at Florida State, everything began to change.

The family determined that they would enjoy the recruiting process. Peyton took Cooper along on the visit to Notre Dame. When a
congenital spinal defect ended Cooper's football career in 1992, the
two brothers had become even closer than they'd always been. "It
wasn't a hard call at all," says Archie, who knew the risks all too well
to let his son continue to play. "I'll never forget the night I had to tell
him. Tell you what, though. Cooper, he's a tough booger." Cooper told
Peyton that he would just have to play football through him. So they
both went to South Bend, where Peyton got the full treatment. "They
had a ball," says Archie. "I'm not sure even I know all the stories." I
am fairly sure he does not.

Every night during the recruitment phase, Peyton would lie across
the foot of his parents' bed, and they would ask him if anything had
clicked. He liked Florida. He liked Ole Miss. He even liked Michigan,
although Archie secretly hoped that Peyton would stay in the South,
where so much of his history was. It got ugly at the end, when Peyton
picked Tennessee, nasty phone calls and all. "Ultimately," says Peyton,
"I didn't want to be a celebrity quarterback the minute I walked on
campus."

At Tennessee Peyton won a fierce competition for the job during
his freshman season. Two veteran quarterbacks went down with injuries, and Peyton was given a chance at the job with another highly
recruited freshman. Peyton ground the other guy out, spending endless hours studying film and winning the job so cleanly that his rival
transferred to Texas A&M. During one of his first games, remembering

what Archie had told him about how a quarterback has to be a leader, Peyton started yammering in the huddle. A veteran offensive lineman told him to shut up and "call the fucking play," which is something that has happened to every young quarterback on every football team in recorded time.

The easy comparison is to say that Archie was an instinctive player while Peyton is more calculating. What is more accurate is to say that Peyton has taken Archie's gifts and blended them with his own. He doesn't openly evince his father's reckless daring, but he is cool and precise, and that is a kind of daring, too. It takes courage to maintain enough distance to create your own legend and still not run away from the one into which you were born.

"I sensed pretty quickly that Peyton wasn't going to go to Ole Miss," Archie says. "I was never afraid of his not going there. What I was afraid of was that, in running away from Ole Miss, he might run away from the entire South."

They say he is a terrible spectator. They say he never learned. Archie Manning spent the first half of his football lifetime on the field, and he's spent the second half of it in the broadcast booth, so his sons say that the essential skills of being a fan simply elude him. He wanders, they say. He'll sit in two, three or four different seats in the course of each game, making new friends all the while. Last New Year's Day, as Peyton and Tennessee took apart listless Ohio State, Archie's wandering took him off through the murk and the gloom all the way to the wrong side of the Citrus Bowl. Olivia and the rest of the family considered sending Smokey the Tennessee hound off to find him.

He's disappeared again this bright spring day. They have brought the Volunteers out to sign autographs and to meet all the fans, great and small. The line for Peyton's autograph begins in front of him on the running track that encircles the football field. It extends halfway down the track, turns sharply to the left and then stretches the entire length of the fifty-yard line until it turns left again to run down the far sideline. From high above the field, Peyton's line looks like a spur from the Trans-Siberian Railroad. This line does not include the fans jamming the front row of the stands to take Peyton's picture. This line does not include the various cheaters who try to do things like toss a camera over Peyton's head to one of the security guards, or to Cooper, who is standing not far from his little brother. Archie is nowhere in sight.

"You seen Dad?" Peyton asks Cooper.

Cooper doesn't answer. He is remarkably lifelike this morning, considering that he'd fallen into evil company the night before. An old slyboots country lawyer—friend of Archie's, Matlock on steroids—had home-turfed Cooper somewhere way up in the hills until the sun began to rise. Cooper is not as quick as he might be, but he's showing definite signs of recovery.

"You seen Dad?" repeats Peyton.

"Yeah," Cooper replies. "He's over there, waiting in line for Will Newman." Will Newman is a sophomore and an offensive tackle, and he is famous primarily to the Newman family of New Market, Tennessee. As the brothers convulse, it becomes plain that it is a good thing that Peyton Manning will become a star professional quarterback, because, one day, Cooper Manning's going to own everything else.

"Peyton, he's pretty serious about things," their father muses. "He doesn't just ease into things. We know his commitments. We know what kind of kid he is. We've seen his grades. But we kind of remind him, you know? 'Hey, Peyton. Make sure you have some fun.'

"I don't think I've ever had to say that to ol' Cooper."

Peyton Manning will contend for the Heisman Trophy, and Tennessee will contend for the national championship in a year in which the slightest early slip can dash both hopes. (Indeed, it can be fairly said that the Vols play a one-game season this year. Unless Tennessee beats Florida on September 21 in Knoxville, the team undoubtedly will be judged a disappointment.) He will try to enjoy himself, to catch a piece of the joy present in those moments when his father turned the corner out of the pocket and a cramped and sour world seemed to crack wide open for Archie Manning in all directions, playing for fun even though Archie was playing for mortal stakes.

For he was from a bloody and haunted place, its history clotted thick with the very worst of many things. It struck him young. He did his damnedest to redeem all of it, with his style and his flair, throwing footballs into the darkness of the place, trying to strike it, finally, at its heart. He drew people to him, and away, if only for a time, from all the hate and the anger. His son is a football star in the South now, and one of his teammates is a black kid from Dayton with a great name like Peerless Price. It is so very different from the way it was when Archie left Drew, out of the long shadows of his own past and the legendary prison. There is a sense that Archie Manning is owed this bright time, this peerless, shining day, these golden children, and that the legend is aging even more deeply and sweetly now, in the great oaken cask of the heart.

Ira Berkow

Ira Berkow (b. 1940) was a sports columnist for Miami University of Ohio's campus newspaper when he sent samples of his work to Red Smith and asked for advice and criticism. Smith wrote back, which speaks volumes about the man widely considered the greatest sports columnist ever. But the exchange tells us even more about Berkow's boldness and ambition. Here, clearly, was a young man with his eye on the prize. Once he was out of school, he fell in with the Young Turks who revolutionized sportswriting in the 1960s and '70s. At the Newspaper Enterprise Association he explored such unexpected subjects as a World Series star browbeaten by his father and a tennis phenom hearing boos for the first time in her career. Berkow went on to work at the *New York Times* as a columnist and reporter from 1981 to 2007. He has written eighteen books, including *Red* (1986), a biography of Red Smith. His crowning moment at the *Times* came when he shared a Pulitzer Prize with the other staffers who worked on the paper's 2000 series "How Race Is Lived in America." His contribution was the story that follows, about a white quarterback feeling the pressure when he plays at a predominantly black university.

The Minority Quarterback

A LATE SUMMER MORNING and the sun was already harsh on the dusty high school football field in Baton Rouge, Louisiana. The shirtless blond nineteen-year-old in shorts stained with sweat kept dropping back to pass, his hands at times so wet it was hard to grip the ball. He was throwing to a friend, working "up the ladder," as it is called, starting with short passes and ending long.

But his mind wasn't totally on his receiver. He could feel the eyes of the man in the dark glasses who sat in a car on the other side of a chain-link fence, a hundred yards away. The boy knew the man was watching. It had been subtly arranged. The National Collegiate Athletic Association does not allow tryouts, but if a college coach happens by a field where kids regularly throw the ball around, well, a coach may argue, where's the harm?

At that time, in July of 1996, Southern University, a football powerhouse among black colleges, desperately needed a quarterback, and the boy, Marcus Jacoby, badly needed a place to play quarterback. After half an hour, the man in dark glasses, Mark Orlando, Southern's offensive coordinator, had seen enough and drove off.

It had gone well. The boy was invited to the coach's apartment, where after a short visit he was offered a full football scholarship. The coach explained that the boy had a shot at the starting job, that the intended starter's poor grades had lost him his place on the team, and that the two backups did not have the coaches' confidence.

"Sounds good," Jacoby, who had been a star at Catholic High, one of Baton Rouge's schoolboy powers, recalled saying. "But I have to think about it—talk with my parents."

"Practice starts in four days," the coach responded. "We're going to need an answer soon."

Marcus Jacoby was unaware that if he accepted the scholarship, he would be the first white to play quarterback for Southern University. And he would be the first white to start at quarterback in the seventy-six-year history of the black Southwestern Athletic Conference. Jacoby had grown up in Baton Rouge, and yet he knew practically nothing about Southern, had never even been to the other side of town to see the campus. Until that July day he had spent his life surrounded by whites.

Southern's head coach, Pete Richardson, worked out of a modest wood-paneled office lined with trophies. In his three years there, he had turned a laughingstock into a national force. Southern won eleven of twelve games his first year, 1993, and two years later it was the number one black college football team in the nation.

It is not easy for a black man to become a head coach. Despite his record, Richardson, fifty-four, has never had an offer from one of the 114 Division I-A colleges; only three of them have black head football coaches.

In college he played at the University of Dayton, hardly a football school, and though he had limited natural talent, he reached the professional level, playing three years for the Buffalo Bills. He coached high school ball for a few years, then took the head coach job at Winston-Salem State in North Carolina. Finally, in 1993, he got his big break at Southern, which with its combined campuses is the largest historically black college in the nation.

"I can't get caught up with the thought that, 'Hey, why shouldn't I be at Notre Dame?'" he said in an interview. "I can't get sidetracked or go around with a chip on my shoulder." He is a stoical man and expected stoicism from his players.

That day in his office, the Jacobys said, they were impressed by his quiet intellect, the way he measured his words, his determination. Indeed, the president of Southern, Dr. Dorothy Spikes, often said that she had hired Richardson over better-known candidates not just because his teams had been winners but because of his reputation for integrity, for running a clean program.

Coach Richardson and the Jacobys discussed everything from Southern's rich athletic tradition to the engineering courses that interested Marcus, but for a long while they didn't mention the thing that worried the parents most. The quarterback is team leader. Would a black team accept a white leader? Would the black campus? The night before, at the Jacobys' home in the upper-middle-class white Tara section of Baton Rouge, talk had become heated. "What if they don't like Marcus?" Marian Jacoby had said, tears in her eyes. "What if there's some kind of... action?" Marcus had not been able to sleep he was so upset.

Now his father, Glen, an environmental engineer, asked the coach, "How are you going to protect my son?"

The room went silent, Glen Jacoby said later. "I realize that you're concerned," Richardson began, "but I just don't think it will be that big a deal. Sure, there will be some adjustments from all sides. But Marcus will have the backing of the administration as well as the coaching staff." Coach Richardson pointed out that there were other minorities on campus. He meant that of the 10,500 students, 5 percent were not black, but Mrs. Jacoby kept thinking about how it would feel to be in a stadium with her husband and 30,000 black fans.

The coach didn't say it to the Jacobys, but no one knew better than he about the strain Marcus would feel being in the minority. As a successful black man, Richardson was used to the stares of surprise. "Walking into a place with a suit and tie on, you're always going to get that second look because you're not supposed to be there." When he coached at Winston-Salem, he drove a state government car. "Whites look at you and ask you what you're doing driving the state's car," he said. "You pull over to get some gas and people will address you the wrong way or policemen will look at you funny."

There was something else Richardson didn't say that morning: He was well aware how hostile Southern's fans could be to any newcomer, regardless of creed or color. Many had not wanted him hired. They felt he had come from too small a college; they had wanted a big name in black college football. They had even used race on him. Shortly after he arrived, a rumor started that Richardson's wife, who is light-skinned, was white, and that his white offensive coordinator was his wife's brother. None of it true, but Richardson didn't let it get to him. He knew the best answer was to win, and since he had done so, he was—as Southern's registrar, Marvin Allen, liked to point out—a campus god.

The coach thought he could make this Jacoby thing work. He wasn't sitting there fretting about whether Marcus could learn to be part of the minority. The first game was only six weeks away. As he would say later, he didn't have "ample time to find another black quarterback." Marcus would have to do what all good players did, what the coach himself had done: suck it up.

To reassure the Jacobys, the coach told them about his staff. Of six assistants he had hired when he started in 1993, two were white, one Asian. He was told Southern fans would never stand for that. But after his 11-1 debut season—the year before they had been 6-5—a popular T-shirt on campus featured a photo of the integrated staff, with the phrase "In Living Color."

The parents wanted to think about it overnight, but Marcus did not. He climbed into his Jeep, he said later, and went riding. He was getting his shot, finally. There was nothing he loved like football. As a boy, when he couldn't find a friend, he tossed footballs into lined-up garbage cans in his yard. His parents held him back in ninth grade so he would have time to grow and a better chance to play high school ball. After starring at Catholic, he went to Louisiana Tech, but there, prospects for playing were dim.

Now he envisioned a game night at Southern with a crowd cheering as he threw yet another touchdown pass. When he stopped at a red light, he lifted his head and at the top of his lungs screamed, "Praise God!"

From the Jacobys' home, Southern was a twenty-minute car trip, literally to the other side of the tracks. On the ride to the first practice, as he drove over the Hump—the small hill that is one of the barriers between Southern and white Baton Rouge—the momentousness of what he had done started sinking in. As he looked around, he began imagining himself playing a game, he recalled. "Would I see a white face?"

Southern's decision to sign a white quarterback made headlines, first locally, then nationally, and the reaction of some whites he knew startled him. When Jacoby called his girlfriend to talk about it, her mother answered. "The niggers over there will kill you," he recalled her saying. "There are bullets flying all over the place. It's a war zone." When his girlfriend got on the phone, she said, "Marcus, I don't want you to call me again." To many on the white side of town, who had never visited this campus bustling with middle-class black students on the bluffs of the Mississippi, it was as if Jacoby had voluntarily moved to the ghetto.

Like many white Americans, he knew there was still prejudice— though, he says, not at home. He had been raised to believe that, after generations of injustice, the country was now a fair place when it came to race—a level playing field, so to speak—and he had made a few black friends while playing high school ball.

The Jacobys were considered a little eccentric for Baton Rouge, having moved here from California when Marcus was three. His paternal grandfather was Jewish. His mother had attended Berkeley in the 1960s and still had some of the flower child in her. She was a fitness buff and had even tried putting her family on a vegetarian diet, stocking the refrigerator with so many oat products that Marcus's buddies asked whether they owned a horse. Marcus and his sister at first attended a private school, but their mother felt too many children there were spoiled by wealth. So she taught them at home for five years, until Marcus was a sophomore.

Friends and teachers at Catholic High remember him as hardworking, smart, and moralistic, with a strong Christian bent. "We'd make fun of his being so innocent," said John Eric Sullivan, one of his best friends. "By that I mean, he didn't do anything that most normal high school kids are doing. He'd be, 'Watch out, watch yourself,' when guys would be drinking. We'd say, like, 'Marc, relax, man.'" He told them he was waiting until he was twenty-one to drink.

The Southern coaches were impressed with his arm and had never seen a quarterback learn Coach Richardson's complex offense so fast. Jacoby stayed after practice to do extra throwing and often studied game films well past midnight. Southern at times uses a no-huddle offense, meaning the quarterback has to call plays rapidly right at the line, and Coach Richardson felt that of the three candidates, only Marcus Jacoby knew the system well enough to do that. Within days of arriving, he was first string.

That sparked anger among many of his new black teammates. For over a year they had been friendly with the two quarterbacks now relegated to backup, and they resented the newcomer, complaining that he had not earned his stripes. "He was *given* his stripes," said Virgil Smothers, a lineman. "There was a lingering bitterness."

Several felt the decision was racial. "It just became the fact that we were going to have this white quarterback," said Sam George, a quarterback prospect who was academically ineligible that year. "It wasn't about ability no more." Teammates picked at Jacoby's weaknesses—he didn't have "fast feet" and rarely scrambled—and joked that he was the typical bland white athlete, which angered Coach Richardson. "A lot of minorities, they want the flash," the coach said. "We felt we needed a system in order to be successful and a quarterback to operate within the confines of that system."

Except for the coaches, he was isolated. In the locker room, Jacoby recalled, "I would walk around the corner and people would just stop talking." Even in the huddles there was dissension. Scott Cloman, a Southern receiver, recalled: "The minute Marcus was like, 'Everybody calm down, just shut up,' they were like: 'Who are you talking to? You're not talking to me.' You know, stuff like that. If it was a black person it wouldn't be a problem. They all felt that 'I'm not going to let a white person talk to me like that.' "

His entire time at Southern, Jacoby kept his feelings about all this inside, "sucking it up," repeatedly telling the inquiring reporters what a great experience it was being exposed to a new culture. "As soon as I signed and walked onto the campus," he told one interviewer, "I felt like part of the family. I definitely feel at home here."

On September 7, 1996, Southern opened at Northwestern State, with Marcus Jacoby at quarterback. Of the 25,000 spectators, half had made the three-hour trip from Southern, not unusual for this football-crazy place. "Fans plan their lives around games," Coach Richardson said. "They fight to get schedules, to see where we're going to play so they can take holidays and go to games."

Southern University families like the Morgans will take more than twenty people to an away game, filling several hotel rooms. Mo Morgan, a supervisor at the local Exxon plant who attended Southern in the 1960s, went so far as to buy a motor home just for Southern football, which made him the object of good-natured ribbing. Friends insisted that "black people don't drive Winnebagos." His wife, Wanda, and about twenty-five of their relatives are Southern graduates, and his youngest son, Jabari, a freshman drummer and cymbals player, was on the field for that same opening game.

For the youngest Morgan, the band was only partly about music. More famous than Southern's football team—having performed at five Super Bowls and three presidential inaugurations—it had real power and importance on campus. The 180-piece Southern band thrived on intimidating lesser rivals on the black college circuit. With its hard-brass sound and its assertive style, the group had a militant edge that old-timers on campus attributed to the influence of the civil rights era, when the band's show was honed.

Robert Gray, who played cymbals with Morgan, said: "When people think about Southern band, they think about a bunch of big, tough-looking, tight-looking dudes with psychotic looks on their faces, ready to go to war. I just think—Southern band—black, all male, just rowdy, loud."

Families like the Morgans were fiercely proud of their school and its role in helping generations of blacks into the middle and professional classes—even if the state had long treated it as second-rate. In the early 1900s, legislators planning to create a new campus for Southern considered several locations around Louisiana. But in city after city, white residents rose in protest, and finally the state settled on a site that no one else then coveted. In the 1950s, blacks like Audrey Nabor-Jackson, Wanda Morgan's aunt, were prohibited from attending the big white public campus across town, Louisiana State University. Southern was their only alternative.

Even as late as the 1970s, Louisiana's public higher education system was capable of inflicting deep racial wounds. Wanda Morgan was required to take several courses at LSU as part of a master's program at Southern. In one class, she was one of four blacks, and for every exam, she said, the four were removed by the professor and put in an empty classroom across the hall, one in each corner, while the white students took the exam in their regular seats. The message was missed by no one: black students would cheat.

By the mid-1990s, change was brewing. The year before Jacoby arrived, Southern and LSU settled a twenty-year-old federal desegregation lawsuit. Both institutions pledged sharp minority increases on their campuses, with 10 percent of enrollment set aside for other races—more whites to Southern, more blacks to LSU. Alumni like the Morgans were worried. Would Southern soon become just another satellite campus of LSU? Was the white quarterback the beginning of the end?

Mo Morgan and Audrey Nabor-Jackson agreed with an editorial in Southern's student paper saying that a white quarterback did not belong. "There are plenty of young black athletes," it said, "who could benefit from Jacoby's scholarship." Mo Morgan said, "I didn't like the fact that he was there." About the only Morgan not upset was Jabari. Mo Morgan worried that his eighteen-year-old son was not race-conscious enough. "I came through the movement, I was confronted with things," said the father. "That's one of the things that concerns me—that he hasn't." But it didn't concern Jabari Morgan— he was consumed with the band. Long before starting college, he had begun assembling on his bedroom wall what he called his shrine, a montage about the Southern band that included a picture of the first white band member, in the early 1990s.

Now, in his freshman year, his long-nurtured fantasy was coming true. Standing there that day with cymbals weighing nine pounds each, ready to march into Northwestern State's stadium, he was at the front of the band. The director, Dr. Isaac Greggs, always positioned his tallest and most imposing players—his "towers of terror"—at the front, and Jabari Morgan, at six foot one, was one of them. Football, he said, was about the last thing on his mind.

"It was like winning the lottery." He wouldn't have cared if Marcus Jacoby were purple, as long as Southern won and people stayed in their seats for the halftime show.

Southern lost its first two games. The team was young—ten of eleven offensive starters were new—but what people remembered was the 11-1 record the year before. For fans, the quarterback, more than any other player, is the team—hero or goat. During the second loss, Jacoby recalled, "I heard the entire stadium booing me."

Jean Harrison, the mother of the quarterback prospect Sam George, remembered, "One lady had a megaphone and she was screaming, 'Get that white honky out of there!' It made you sick."

Chris Williams, an offensive lineman, believed that the other team hit Jacoby harder because he was white: "Teams took cheap shots at him. I really believe that. I mean they hit him sometimes blatantly late after the whistle." Scott Cloman recalled that after one Southern loss, opposing players said, "That's what you all get for bringing white boys on the field."

Jacoby was hit so hard and so often during the first game that he was hospitalized with a concussion. Glen Jacoby, Marcus's father, was sure the blockers were sandbagging their white quarterback, but in interviews at the time, the young man denied it. He still says he believes that it was just the mistakes of an inexperienced line.

After Southern's second loss, an angry fan threatened Jacoby. A coach had to jump between them. For the rest of his career, Jacoby would have a police escort at games. There was a disturbance outside the stadium at another game. Gunshots were fired. Jacoby recalls thinking the shots were aimed at him. They were not.

The Tuesday after the second loss, Jacoby rose at 5 A.M., worked out in the weight room, then walked to the cafeteria for the team breakfast. No one was there. He checked his watch. Shortly after he sat down, Coach Orlando came in, took him by the arm and led him through a nearby door. As Jacoby remembered it, the entire team and coaching staff sat squeezed into a small room. All chairs were taken, so he stood alone against a wall. No one looked at him. Coach Richardson stood. "I think Marcus should know what's going on," he said, adding, "Who wants to say something?"

Virgil Smothers, the senior defensive end, rose. The night before, he had talked about staging a strike. Now he mentioned some minor gripes, then added: "We're losing and we feel changes ought to be made. Some guys aren't getting a fair chance."

Someone else said, "Guys are playing who shouldn't."

Coach Orlando walked to the front. As offensive coordinator, he naturally worked closely with the quarterback. But several players felt he favored Jacoby because they were both white. "Let's get this in the open," Orlando said, adding, "This is mostly about Jacoby, isn't it?" Insisting that the quarterback had been chosen fairly, he said: "You have to accept Marcus, he's one of us. We're 0 and 2, but we have to put this behind us."

Lionel Hayes, who had lost the quarterback job to Jacoby, interrupted Coach Orlando. "You're just saying that," Mr. Hayes said, "because you're Jacoby's Dad." It got a laugh, though his tone was angry. Jacoby said later: "There was a lot of hate in that room. I felt like I was falling into a hole, and I couldn't grab the sides."

Coach Richardson spoke again: "We win as a team, we lose as a team. Jacoby's doing what he's supposed to be doing, and he'll get better. We all will." He said practice would be at three. "If anyone doesn't want to be on the team with Jacoby as the starting quarterback, don't come."

Richardson remembered: "What I saw was a frustration by some players—mostly seniors—who weren't playing. They weren't playing because they didn't deserve to. And so they needed a scapegoat."

Jacoby remembers feeling like the invisible man. "It was almost as though I weren't there, and they were talking about me," he said. "I wasn't sure where to turn. I felt they didn't want me there—not me personally, but any white quarterback—that I was just another problem."

Three or four players didn't show up for practice, and Coach Richardson cut them. Not long afterward, Virgil Smothers and one of the coaches argued, and Smothers was told, "Clear out your locker."

When the players gathered the next day at practice, before the coaches arrived, Jacoby said, he stood to talk. A few tried to shout him down, but John Williams, a star senior cornerback and devout Christian who would go on to play for the Baltimore Ravens, rose and said, "Man, let the man talk."

"I don't care if you like me or hate me," Jacoby recalled saying. "All I ask is that we can go out and play football together. This is not a popularity contest. I'm trying to win. I'm just trying to be your quarterback."

Things improved dramatically. Southern won six of its next seven games, beating the two top-ranked black colleges, and was invited to the Heritage Bowl in Atlanta, the black college championship. "I wasn't getting booed nearly as much," Jacoby said. Some teammates began warming to him. More than anything, they were impressed by his work ethic. During a practice break, players drank from a garden hose. "Sorry, Marcus," one teased, "this is the black water fountain." They called him "Tyrone," and "Rasheed."

"I appreciated it," he recalled. "Things had changed to the extent that some of the players were calling me 'the man.'"

Before games, he and John Williams prayed together. One Sunday the two went to the black church where Williams was a minister. Occasionally strangers would wish Jacoby well. One day the band's legendary director, Dr. Greggs, greeted him warmly and urged him to persevere.

He felt he was developing real friendships with teammates and Southern students. When Scott Cloman needed a place to stay for a month, Jacoby had him to his parents' home and the two grew close. "Marcus was the first white person I ever really got to know," Cloman said. "I always felt a lot of tension around whites. I'd go into a store and I could just feel the tension. Sometimes you just feel like, 'I can't stand white people.' I didn't understand them. I really didn't want to be near them."

"His parents treated me like a son," added Cloman. Some players now joked when they saw him, "Where's your brother?"

"And some," he said, "called me 'white lover.' Didn't bother me. I had come to understand the Jacobys. A lot of times people fear what they can't understand. Because of being around the Jacobys my attitude toward whites in general changed."

At the Heritage Bowl that first year, on national television, Southern took a 24–10 halftime lead against Howard University, then fell behind, 27–24. In the closing minute, Southern drove to Howard's 15-yard line. On third down, with forty-two seconds left, Marcus Jacoby dropped back and, under pressure, threw off the wrong foot, floating a pass into the end zone.

"I heard the crowd gasp," he said. "I couldn't believe this was happening." He'd been intercepted. "Their fans must have cheered, but I remember everything being silent." A camera captured Coach Richardson on his knees, hands over his head.

"I dragged myself off the field and sat on a bench and buried my head in my arms," Jacoby said. "A few people, like John Williams, came by and patted me on the back, to be encouraging. But I heard, 'You screwed up real bad this time, Whitey,' and, 'You're as dumb as they come.' It was the lowest point of my life."

After the game, Coach Orlando received an anonymous call: "If Jacoby ever plays for Southern again, we'll kill him—and you." The coach said he averaged a threat a week that season. Later, as Coach Orlando and Jacoby headed to their cars, the coach pointed to several trees. In the light of the street lamps, Jacoby could see a yellow rope hung from each tree. The ropes were tied in nooses.

On campus, Jacoby struggled with all the daily irritations that go with being in the minority. As a white who grew up among whites, he was used to being inconspicuous. Here, he always felt on display. "I hated that," he said, "because it was like I had become just a novelty act."

He found that things he had done unconsciously all his life were suddenly brought to his attention and analyzed. One was the way he dressed. He liked to wear a T-shirt, shorts, and flip-flops to class; most students at Southern dressed up for class in slacks. Another was that the way he spoke, his slang, was different from the black majority's. "Many times I would say something at Southern and they would repeat it and I wouldn't get my point across," he said. "It would get lost in the mocking of how I said it instead of what I said. I might walk into a room and I'd say, 'Hey, how y'all doin'?'" Instead of answering, someone would do an imitation of a white person talking, enunciating slowly. "They'd say 'Hi, guy, how are you doing?' So I just learned to say, 'Hey.'" He believed the classmates were only needling him, but being constantly reminded was exhausting.

"People's eyes were on him," said Chris Williams, a teammate. "He just didn't blend in. I mean, like me, I just blended in wherever I went."

A white with a different personality might have fared better. There was one other white on the seventy-man squad, Matt Bushart. And though as a punter he was at the periphery of the team and little noticed by fans, Bushart had the personality and experience to cope better as a minority. While Marcus had seemed protected and naive even to the middle-class white students at Catholic High, Matt's years at a local public high school where most of his football teammates were black had taught him how to live comfortably among them. While Marcus was more introspective, a loner, a little too sensitive for some of his coaches' tastes, Matt was noisy, funny, sometimes crude—so outgoing, his girlfriend said, that he could talk to a wall.

When Bushart's teammates made fun of the country music he liked, he gave it right back to them about their rap, and kept listening to his music. "I get kidded about it," he said, "but there's been a song that's been playing and one of the black guys will come by and say, 'Play that again, that's actually not too bad.'"

Jacoby loved music, too; playing guitar was an important outlet for relieving the pressure, but he would not play on campus. As he put it: "At times the rap just blared from the dorms; I longed for something that was my own. I couldn't play it on campus because for most of the time I was apologizing for who I was. I didn't want to cause any more turmoil than there was. I didn't want to make myself look like I was any more separate than I was."

Interracial dating is complicated at Southern. Ryan Lewis, Jacoby's roommate, says most black men would not openly date a white woman on campus. "They would keep it low so nobody knew about it but them," Lewis said. "I've never seen it."

As quarterback, Jacoby often had female students flirting with him. He felt uneasy, caught between the white and black sides of town. Among whites, he said, "everybody just assumed the worst, that I was dating a black girl now because I was at Southern." But even though there were some "gorgeous light-skinned black girls over there," he said, and a couple of women from his classes became good friends, he wasn't attracted. He thinks it was "a cultural thing."

Though college students are confronted with new ideas—sometimes only partially understood—and encouraged to speak out about them, Jacoby felt that when he did, he was criticized. At first, in his African-American literature class, when they discussed slavery, he said he tried to be conciliatory in an oral report. "I would say something like, 'I can't imagine how terrible it must have been, that people could do those kinds of things to other people.' And others in the class made some kind of jokes, but it was like bitter jokes: 'What are you talking about, Marcus? You're one of those whites.' It was like they were saying to me, 'Quit Uncle Tomming.'"

Then he worried he wasn't being true to his white roots. "I felt that I had lost my pride and the respect of friends that I had grown up with," he said. For his next oral report, he decided to speak his mind and said that it was unhealthy for blacks to dwell too much on past racial violence. "There have been tragedies like slavery throughout time," he said. "I don't think one is more important than any other." When he finished, he recalled, "there was an eerie silence and I saw at least three or four people glaring at me."

Increasingly, being in the minority alienated him, made him feel alone. "I learned early on that I was a pioneer in all this and no one else had gone through it and often the best advice I could get was from myself. Because I was the only one who knew the whole situation."

It didn't help that his preoccupied parents were going through a divorce. At one point when he was upset about not fitting in, his mother gave him a copy of *Black Like Me*, the story of a white man in the 1960s who dyes his skin and travels the South to experience being black during segregation. At the time, Jacoby said, "I resented my mother giving me the book. She was just trying to help me understand the other side, but I felt she was almost taking the other side."

Blacks, of course, are much better at being in the minority, since they have far more practice and, usually, no choice. When Jabari Morgan was considering colleges, his father told him he was free to pick Southern or a "white" college, but if he picked white, he had better be prepared. Then he gave him the talk about being in the minority that so many black American men give their sons. "You are going to face being called a nigger," Mo Morgan told Jabari. "Now, are you ready to deal with it? If you're not ready to deal with it, don't go."

The Morgans have a family council of elders that meets regularly to guide their young, and one message emphasized is this: "A black person in America has to be smarter and sharper and work harder to achieve the same things as a white person of the same abilities." Mo Morgan says, as a minority, he understands that "the majority is white, and you have control and you want to keep control."

But Jabari Morgan did not think like his father. He had always dreamed of attending Southern, but for him its great appeal was not as a racial sanctuary. He considered race simply part of the rough and tumble of life, the cost of doing business in a mostly white world. Southern was the place where he might be able to play in the best marching band in America, as his father had before him. He determined very early that the best high school marching bands, like the best college bands, were black, and so he fudged his address in order to attend a nearly all-black Baton Rouge school where the band rocked. He figured that that would give him an edge when he tried out at Southern.

As a marketing major who graduated in May, Morgan fully expects that he will one day work for a big white-controlled corporation. But as a marching band member at Southern for four years, he was in many ways the ultimate insider in the self-contained black-majority culture of the Yard, as Southern's campus is known. All the things that Marcus Jacoby found so irritating were second nature to Jabari Morgan—the music, the dress, the vernacular of put-downs and nicknames that is the campus currency. He loved African-American literature class because the poetry and stories reinforced what his family had taught him about black history.

Like all new band members, Morgan went through hazing. But as part of the majority, he never worried that it was about race. Jacoby, on the other hand, felt so unsettled as part of the minority that he often had trouble sleeping.

Morgan eventually joined a fraternity—a support in its own way as strong as the band's. And, where Marcus Jacoby the minority had no steady girlfriend during his years at Southern, Jabari Morgan the majority began, in his second semester, dating Monique Molizone, an economics major from New Orleans. She had also come to Southern partly for the band—to join the Dancing Dolls, who perform at the band's side.

As much as anything, what got Jacoby through his second year at Southern was a determination to avenge that Heritage Bowl interception, to show everyone—including himself—he could be a champion. He moved through the 1997 season with a passion, working so hard in the weight room that he could now bench-press 350 pounds; running endless drills to improve his foot speed; and doing so much extra throwing that by day's end it took an hour to ice and treat his arm.

Again he was first string, but he had competition. Sam George had returned from academic probation. George was a popular figure on campus, known not only for his hard-partying ways but for his small-man grit on the playing field. Though he was only five foot seven, he had a strong arm and terrific speed. His teammates, responding to his take-charge style in huddles, nicknamed him the Little General. "And," Scott Cloman said, "he was black."

Although Jacoby started, Coach Richardson liked bringing in George when the team seemed flat. Both quarterbacks saw race as the true reason behind the coach's substitutions. Jacoby was convinced that Richardson was giving the black quarterback playing time to pander to the black fans; George was convinced that Coach Richardson—influenced by Coach Orlando—was starting the white quarterback because of favoritism.

George wound up playing in five of twelve games. By Southern's third game, against Arkansas–Pine Bluff, both quarterbacks were bitter. After winning its first two games, Southern was losing to Pine Bluff 7–6 at the half. Coach Richardson decided to replace the white quarterback with the black. Jacoby was devastated; he felt he was a proven winner and should not be yanked for one bad half.

Given his chance, George threw a last-ditch 37-yard pass that tied the game, and threw another touchdown in triple overtime for a 36–33 Southern win. And yet, come Monday practice, Jacoby was the starter again. Now George was frustrated.

Southern had a 9-1 record going into its two final games. A victory in the next game—the Bayou Classic, against Grambling, its archrival—would assure a return to the Heritage Bowl and a chance for Jacoby to redeem himself. His parents and teammates had never seen him so obsessed. He had trouble sleeping and little appetite. His father called Coach Orlando, worried that Marcus's weight was down.

In a journal account of that period, Marcus Jacoby wrote: "I sat down and wrote out a detailed plan of how I was going to get through these last two games, including my political and motivational moves. My survival as a person depended on these last two games. Nobody, including Coach Orlando, knew the amount of outside forces that were pressing on these last two games. I was at a point where I felt that I was crawling on my knees."

He added, "I dreamed of a time when I could just say that I had accomplished something, instead of fighting for respect, fighting in a classroom full of people who disagreed with everything I stood for, and could have a day of true rest."

Before the big game against Grambling, he pleaded with Coach Orlando. "If you don't pull me," Jacoby said, "I guarantee we'll win our next two games."

"You can't guarantee that," the coach said.

"I just did," Jacoby said. Coach Orlando suggested that if Marcus Jacoby played a little more like Sam George, sometimes scrambling out of the pocket, he might be more effective. Jacoby felt that he was being told to become something he was not, but he was so desperate, so nervous about being yanked, that he followed the advice. He ran, and it worked. In a 30–7 win against Grambling, Jacoby threw three touchdown passes and played the entire game. He was named the Bayou Classic's most valuable player.

A month later he achieved his redemption, throwing the winning pass in a 34–28 Heritage Bowl victory over South Carolina State, capping an 11-1 season that earned Southern the black national championship. "I was happier than I had ever been at Southern," he recalled. On the trip back from that game he slept soundly for the first time in months.

The more you achieve, the more is expected. After that 11-1 season, the talk on campus was that Southern would go undefeated in 1998. But in the opener, with the team trailing 7–0 at the half, Jacoby was pulled for George. Southern lost anyway, 28–7.

In practice on Tuesday, Jacoby overthrew a pass to one of his ends, John Forman, who yelled at him in front of everybody. Forman would say later that it was just the frustration of having lost the opener, but to Jacoby it was so much more—the final straw. He was sure that Forman was trying to subvert his control of the team to help George, his roommate. "If you have a choice, you choose black first," Jacoby would later say. "I felt that I was all alone again, on an island by myself. It was like I was right back where I had started two years before, with a lot of the same attitudes against me."

He quit football and Southern.

Coach Richardson was surprised and asked Jacoby to stay. But more recently he said he understood the decision. Because of "the type person he is," the coach said, "it was the best thing for Marcus because it would have killed him." The coach meant that Marcus Jacoby was not emotionally equipped to continue being the solitary white.

When Branch Rickey of the Brooklyn Dodgers wanted to break major league baseball's color line in 1947, he chose Jackie Robinson, not simply because he was a great black ballplayer—there were greater black stars—but because he had experience inside white institutions. Jackie Robinson was twenty-eight that first year in the majors, a mature man who had graduated from UCLA and served in the Army. He knew what it was like to be in the minority.

When Coach Richardson went after Jacoby, he was just looking for a quarterback.

Reporters hounded Jacoby to find why he had left, but he never spoke openly about it. He never mentioned race. In brief interviews, he told them he was burned out, and in a sense this was true. He had burned out on being in the minority. And as a white, he didn't have to be. In those last months at Southern, he often thought about returning to a white life. "You kind of look over your shoulder and see your old life and you say, 'I could go back.'"

There had been such anguish over the Jacoby-George quarterback battle, and all its racial nuances, but at least on the field, in the end, it didn't seem to make much difference. That year Southern, with Sam George at the helm, finished 9–3, once again winning the Heritage Bowl.

A white quarterback at Southern did make people think. Mo Morgan had been against it, but not after watching Jacoby at practices. "I looked at the three quarterbacks that were there, and he was the best at the time. I'm just telling you straight out. It wasn't his ability and I'm not saying he was brighter than the other kids. He just put in the work."

Morgan's son Jabari said he, too, was sorry to see Jacoby go; he liked the idea of a white guy being open to attending a black college. This past year, as a senior, Jabari Morgan reached out to a white freshman tuba player, Grant Milliken, who tried out for the band. He helped him through the hazing. One of Morgan's friends said he had done it because Milliken was white, but Morgan said no, he had done it because Milliken was really good on tuba.

Morgan even helped Milliken create a dance solo full of shakes and shivers and fancy steps, which was performed at halftimes to wild applause. What the crowd loved, said Morgan, was not just that a white guy could dance. "The whole point of letting the white guy dance is that we were saying to the world, 'Hey, you can learn our culture just like we can learn yours.'"

Morgan's father continues to be both fearful of his son's more relaxed attitude about race and a little in awe of it. "He doesn't think it's something he can't overcome," said Mo Morgan, "and you know, I think he's right. You can get caught up in this, and it will screw up your thinking."

One weekend last fall, at the request of a reporter, Jacoby went to a Southern game for the first time since quitting. This was Homecoming Day, and from his seat in the stands he watched Southern seniors and their families being introduced to the crowd at midfield. It could have been his moment. Ryan Lewis, his old roommate, was there, and so was Matt Bushart, the white punter. Bushart's name was called, to applause. Jacoby had read in the newspaper Bushart's saying how much he had enjoyed Southern.

The team had won seven straight games at that point, and so Jacoby was surprised during the first quarter when Southern's starting quarterback was replaced after throwing an interception. Jacoby had always been so sure he'd been replaced with Sam George to pander to fans; now Coach Richardson was using the exact same strategy with two black quarterbacks. In the paper the next day, Richardson said he had just been trying to light a spark under the offense.

After the game, outside the stadium, a large black man spotted Jacoby and, extending his hand, said, "Hi, Marcus, how ya doin'?"

"O.K., Virgil," Jacoby said. "How you doin'?" The two chatted for a moment outside the stadium—the man said he had left school and was working as an account executive for a drug company—then they went their separate ways.

"That was Virgil Smothers," Jacoby said afterward. It was Smothers who had led the aborted strike against Jacoby. "I guess he figures it's all in the past."

It was not all in the past for Jacoby. Though he had moved on—he was now majoring in finance at LSU—his Southern experience still unsettled him. "Just last night I had a dream about it," he said. "Weird dreams. Like some of these people are coming back to haunt me in some way. By these people I mean some of those who I considered friends and who I felt kind of turned on me."

At times he talks about being lucky to have experienced another culture; at others he describes it as "a personal hell." His sister Dana says, "There are some scars that haven't gone away, from the bad things."

After leaving Southern, Jacoby took a while to realize how much pressure he had felt. "I remember one time a few months after I quit—and this was part of the healing process—I said something about country music, that I liked it. And I remember standing around with four white people and thinking, 'Oh, my God, I can't believe I just said that.' And then I caught myself right before I got through that whole thing in my mind and I looked at the people's faces and they were agreeing with me. I went 'Whoa,' I didn't have to apologize for that anymore."

These days, he appreciates walking around anonymously on the mostly white LSU campus. "I got burned out as far as being somebody," he said. "At LSU I've just enjoyed being a part of the crowd."

(Sections of this story about the Morgan family were reported by Kirk Johnson.)

Peter Richmond

When he got a baseball score wrong in a headline he wrote as a *Washington Post* copy editor, people didn't automatically think Peter Richmond (b. 1953) would become a star writer for *GQ* and the author of six nonfiction books. But he did, with a 1989 Nieman Fellowship and stops at the *San Diego Union*, *Miami Herald*, and *The National* along the way. Richmond has written memorably whether his subject was the jam band Phish, the building of the Camden Yards ballpark in Baltimore, or his late father's World War II heroism. Each football season since 2007, he and *Vanity Fair* writer David Kamp have vented about their fate as New York Giants fans on their weekly *Tangled Up in Blue* show for WHDDFM, in Sharon, Connecticut, "the smallest NPR station in the nation." In fall 2013 Richmond began a new adventure, teaching long-form journalism at Moravian College, in Bethlehem, Pennsylvania. One hopes he would put modesty aside and show his students the riveting piece that follows, about the trial of Rae Carruth, a Carolina Panthers wide receiver who was convicted of murder conspiracy charges in the fatal shooting of Cherica Adams, his pregnant girlfriend. Richmond wrote it for *GQ*'s May 2001 issue partly out of outrage and partly out of his long fascination with athletes who think they are beyond the law. He knew he'd hit his target when the story won awards for both sportswriting and crime writing. He offered further thoughts on the piece when it was posted on the website Deadspin in 2013, and they appear here as footnotes.

Flesh and Blood

ONE BY ONE, day by day, they'd glide to the witness stand, this procession of improbable women, a spangled harem of them, drifting into the courtroom and out again, leaving the scent of their perfume and the shadow of their glitter and the echo of their cool. Week in, week out, they never stopped coming.

That was the extraordinary thing. How many there were. The final count stopped short of thirty—that was the number of photographs of women Rae was said to keep in a box at home—but there were more than enough of them to make each and every morning worth my springing out of bed for, worth walking down to the courthouse for, worth getting frisked at the doorway for: in the hope that a new one might illuminate the somber courtroom with its smoked-glass view of the jailhouse across the street.

And sure enough, in the middle of a gray day of testimony filled with the babble of a psychologist or the grunt of a jail guard or the platitudes of a coach, out of the blue Rae's attorney would suddenly say, "The defense calls Dawnyle Willard," and next to me the TV guy would arch an eyebrow at the local columnist—who's this one? what's the angle? lover? friend? cleaned his apartment? helped him jump bail?—and they'd both shrug, because no one had heard of Dawnyle Willard.

Then everyone would turn to the back of the courtroom to get a look at the newest entrant, because we just knew she was going to be beautiful. And honestly, she just about always was.[1]

Dawnyle certainly was. Stately, slim, a dancer. Former girlfriend, now confidante. Wept on the stand, at the pure goodness of the man.

Amber was cool, slim, and fiery and a favorite among those of us who spoke of such things during breaks in the action, although Starlita was easily the most exotic; she looked like an African princess dropped into a southern murder trial. Michelle was the pretty little girl next door. Monique was innocently cute. Tnisha, Rac's current squeeze, was... well, a tad young looking. But she was pretty enough for you to understand why Rae would nod at her each day when, sandwiched by grim bailiffs, he left the courtroom—nodding as if to say, Hey, babe, don't worry: *You're* the one now. And I swear, she believed it.

Sometimes, though, Rae nodded at the woman in the front pew. She was there every day. By some measures, she was the most handsome of all: high forehead, piercing eyes, coiffed and jewelried to the highest. Some newcomers to the courtroom thought she was another female friend. But this was Rae's mother, Theodry Carruth, anchoring the Cult of Rae from the center of the home-team bench.

Really, there was no other way to think of them—other than as a cult—at least not after the mother of one of Rae's former girlfriends took the stand near the end of the trial, and the *mother* was gorgeous.

---

[1] I didn't know the way into the story. I was trying to make silly big-picture observations about sports and society until my editor, Jim Nelson, said to me: "Art"—Art Cooper, who ran *GQ* at the time—"is worried about this story. You have to come up with a new, specific, gripping lede by 5 o'clock. After sitting there for two weeks, what stays with you now?" And I immediately blurted, "These women who testified were all, like, fuckin' beautiful." Four hours later, we had our story.

Not only was she beautiful, but get this: After her daughter testified against Rae, the mother testified glowingly *for* Rae.

And then, as she left the stand, she looked right at Rae—a man facing the death penalty for taking out a hit on a pregnant woman—looked right into his eyes and, all sweet and wet, mouthed the words *I love you.*

As the weeks passed and the women came and went, I would look over at Rae and stare at his profile, which never changed, because Rae never changed expressions, even during the closing argument, when the lead prosecutor played the 911 tape of Cherica Adams's moans: sounds from beyond the grave, all sputtering utterances, atonal syllables so skin-crawling that throughout the courtroom shoulders heaved in sobs. But Rae's face flinched not at all. Animated and emotional and expressive as the women were—weaving and looping their tales of his goodness and his charity—Rae remained a well-tailored sphinx.

And so, day in, day out, I'd ask myself a question. Not what they all saw in him; the first look at Rae explained that: this baby face, the contours all smooth and rounded, the outward downslant of his eyebrows giving him this puppy-dog-swatted-with-a-newspaper look. Girls loved to take care of Rae even before he became a millionaire. No, the question I kept asking myself was this: If Rae Carruth loved women so much, why did he keep threatening to have them killed? How, if he gathered women around him like a cocoon, if he thrived on them and fed on them and drew sustenance from them, could a man get to a point in his life where he routinely considered disposing of them? And how could such a man wind up finding a home—even flourishing—in the National Football League?

Well, because he really didn't like women at all. (He liked to fuck them, and he liked their attention, and he liked the *idea* of them, but he didn't like them.) And because he was accustomed to violence. And because he was making a living in a league in which a man and his basest instincts are encouraged to run wild. Well, he was until recently, anyway; Rae doesn't play football anymore. He's in prison up in Nash County, where he won't have to worry about women and women won't have to worry about him, and as his crime swiftly seeps into the background noise of the culture, we're already starting to act as if we didn't have to worry about Rae Carruth anymore. As if the whole episode were an aberration.

Of course, it's anything but. Take even a cursory look at how Rae Carruth went from first-round NFL draft pick to ward of the state of North Carolina, serving a quarter century of hard time for conspiring to commit the most horrific crime in the history of professional sports, and the question is not how it could happen but when is it going to happen again.

Football is a violent sport, growing far more violent and mean and attitudinal every year, and it has been played by men who have traditionally been violent against their women. This has been the case since Jim Brown, the greatest running back ever to play the game, garnered the first of a half-dozen charges of violence against women, ranging from spousal battery to rape to the sexual molestation of two teenage girls.[2] Brown, who has never been convicted of a single charge, begat O. J., the second-greatest running back, who, at this writing, continues to seek out Nicole's true killers. O. J. begat Michael Irvin of the Dallas Cowboys, who, prior to one of his frequent cocaine-sex bacchanals a few years back, cavity-searched one of his girls a little too hard for the liking of her cop boyfriend, who then took out a hit on Irvin. It wasn't just Irvin who dodged a bullet that time. It was the NFL, which retired Irvin with pomp and circumstance.

[2] Tommy Craggs asked me if I was pathologizing football players in this section—if I was taking the particular circumstances of Carruth and his murder case and suggesting it was pervasively illuminating of NFL culture at large. I don't think so. My point was only that Rae Carruth was miswired, and he entered a profession that only made his kind of psychopathology worse.

No one is born a "bad seed," just as no one is a blank slate at birth who is then completely molded by his environment. We're all born with genetic predispositions that certain environments trigger in different ways. Someone with an alcoholic gene working in a liquor store is stacking the odds. And maybe I'm dipping too much into pop psych, but Rae had a domineering mother who led him at a young age to distrust women, and then he entered an industry in which women's roles are limited to jiggling sex symbols. He never encountered anything that would push back against his misogyny.

As Sally Jenkins so eloquently wrote in a recent *Washington Post* column, NFL players are better citizens than their non-athlete peers. But put simply: The NFL is a bad place for misaligned people, and there's no reason that should be the case. An entertainment corporation pulling in billions of dollars in revenue that employs only a finite number of often-immature young men to whom it is gifting a percentage of those riches has an acute obligation to work with its hires both psychologically and physically. Making a young man an overnight millionaire and then ignoring what kind of fuel you might have just poured on his inner fire is an oversight that might prove, well, fatal.

This year, of course, Super Bowl MVP and murder defendant Ray Lewis, who has twice been accused—but not convicted—of hitting women, commanded headlines and earned full forgiveness at the hands of a most understanding media machine. Wearing a Giants uniform in the same Super Bowl was Christian Peter, a man accused of so many crimes against women in college that public outcry forced the Patriots to drop him within days of drafting him in 1996. Lost in the shuffle but not forgotten, Corey Dillon and Mustafah Muhammad and Denard Walker contributed, each in his own way, to this long-standing tradition. On the day he ran for a record 278 yards, Cincinnati's Dillon, now arguably the game's best running back, was facing charges of striking his wife; after the season, he plea-bargained to avoid trial. His uniform was sent to the Hall of Fame, where it now keeps company with the memorabilia of Brown and Simpson. As for Walker, he played for Tennessee last year after being convicted of hitting the mother of his son. He then declared himself a free agent and was courted by several teams until the Denver Broncos anted up a cool $26 million. Muhammad, a cornerback with Indianapolis, led his team into the play-offs last year after being convicted of hitting his wife. And let's not forget the domestic-assault conviction of Detroit's Mario Bates or former Packer Mark Chmura's troubles surrounding his dalliance with his 17-year-old baby-sitter.

And what about the more subtle misogyny embodied by the late and revered Derrick Thomas of the Kansas City Chiefs, who was killed in a car wreck two years ago? He left behind seven kids by five women, and no will—thus no guarantees of money or consideration for any of the children or any of the women.

The NFL claims it is doing more than ever to educate its recruits. Its preseason three-and-a-half-day symposia are supposed to make its rookies duly aware of their newfound responsibilities to their fans and their leagues and the kids who put their posters on the wall: To avoid the sleaze joints. Steer clear of the hucksters. Grow up quick.

But what is it really doing? When the NFL parades its first-round draft picks to a podium on national television and slathers them in their first frosting of celebrity, its message effectively and immediately neutralizes all the good-behavior seminars. On that day, the commissioner is not only handing each of the players a guarantee of several million dollars; he is also giving them the whispered assurance that the league likes them just the way they are. No need to grow up too fast.

Ultimately, the league refused to ban Ray Lewis and his brutal peers because it needed them on the playing field, and that mandate speaks more loudly than a lecture about good citizenship—especially to a remarkably immature kid like Rae. After all, little boys don't like little girls, and what was Rae Carruth other than an overgrown boy, a bundle of muscle and fiber jerry-rigged to play a game? Of course, most kids grow out of that stuff. It's the rare one who is allowed to harbor his playground sexism until it blossoms into monstrosity.

He came from the place so many seem to come from; only the details vary from kid to kid. Rae didn't grow up with his biological father. As a child, Rae split time among several houses, including his mother's, set in a neighborhood of squalor and dismay on the south side of Sacramento—on an avenue where vandals routinely set cars aflame— and her sister's place in a nicer part of town, absent the bars on the windows. Even then, even before he was showered with privilege, Theodry worried about the sharks and the vultures preying on her son, "the guppy."

This is how she describes him. This is why she describes herself as "the piranha" when it comes to protecting her son. To know Rae Carruth and to understand the course he chose to take, to divine the nature of his particular rebellion—because isn't that what all our adolescent contrarinesses are? rebellion against what was lacquered onto us beforehand?—you must first know Theodry Carruth. There is a hardness and a strength to her, and they seem like the same thing; she seizes the space she is in and commands it from on high.

But if one may be tempted to call Rae's mother domineering, one ought not to, because she will not tolerate being described as overbearing, and she will tell you so. Describe her instead, she warns in a voice that brooks no argument, as simply having been raised by a Southern mother, and then say she is raising her son thusly.

Theodry Carruth's vigilance over her only son's upbringing paid off, at least in the short run: Rae's grades at Valley High School were solid, he stayed out of trouble, and big colleges came calling. In 1992 Rae went off to the University of Colorado. Back on the infernal block on Parker Avenue, Theodry Carruth turned one of the rooms into a miniature shrine where family and friends gathered to sit in mock stadium chairs and watch Rae's games from Boulder. It was called the Rae of Hope room. Neighborhood kids would set it on fire a few years later.

At Colorado, Rae's coach Bill McCartney was a demagogue. On the field, McCartney was known for teams that played hard and thuggishly. Off the field, he was known for the conversation he'd had with God. One day God told McCartney to found the Promise Keepers. Soon thereafter, at McCartney's urgings, tens of thousands of fathers and husbands took to gathering in football stadiums across the land to beat their chests and flagellate their souls and collectively recommit to their gender. The subtext of the Promise Keepers was a patently sexist one, of course: portraying women as worthy beings but regarding them, ultimately, as secondary, as biblical chattel.

But beneath the roar of McCartney's fire and brimstone, his daughter was getting pregnant by two different football players in four and a half years—the first, the star quarterback, wanted her to abort the fetus; the second sired his child during Rae's freshman year. This only proved that when you climb too high in the pulpit, it's easy to ignore the funky stuff going on under your nose. Especially if you're a member of the sinning crowd: McCartney himself quit on his Colorado contract after Rae's third autumn in Boulder. Broke his promise, if you will.

Rae's college athletic achievements were legendary—in one game alone, he had seven receptions for 222 yards and three touchdowns. In 1997 he entered the hallowed fraternity of first-round draft picks under the watchful wink of the NFL. The Carolina Panthers took him as their first selection, number 27 overall. Like all rookies, he would be instructed on how to behave. But like his first-round peers, he knew what had actually just happened: He'd been ushered into a land of entitlement, where the only promise he'd really be held to was the promise he'd shown thus far on the playing field.

The Panthers gave him a four-year contract worth $3.7 million and a $1.3 million signing bonus, and it wasn't so much the amount of money that was stunning but the ease with which it came. Within days of being signed, Rae got a check for $15,000 in the mail from a trading-card company. Just for being Rae. How sweet was that?

He immediately signed it over to his seventeen-year-old girlfriend in Boulder, Amber Turner, and told her to go ahead and set up house for them in Charlotte. Amber was a stylish and precocious beauty, a high school senior (even as a fifth-year college senior, Rae's tastes still tended toward post-adolescence). His girlfriend in high school, Michelle, had been a sophomore when he was a senior, and she'd just turned 18 when Rae got her pregnant on a visit back home from college. He'd waffled about whether or not to have the baby from day to day. Michelle wasn't surprised at his indecision. She says she knew him as a man of many moods. He could be a real joker, or he could be a cipher, or he could even be, in the dark moments, the Devil himself.

Amber Turner knew about the baby back in Sacramento. Amber also knew Rae said the boy might not be his, and even if it were his baby, he said, there were ways to fix the blood tests.

And what of the parents? Amber's mother had no problem with Amber setting up house with Rae in a distant city, right out of high school. She loved Rae, too. He was polite and civilized and kind. He called her Mrs. Turner even after she said he could call her Barbara.

Rae's mom, Theodry, was pleased, too—pleased that her only son would be living in a Southern town with family values. But it wasn't family values that Rae found in Charlotte. It was what all young, wealthy, transplanted men find there, these strangers in a strange land: nightclubs, comedy clubs, strip clubs. Charlotte is full of gentlemen's clubs, peopled by men who are anything but. On the high end, there's the Men's Club, Charlotte's topless palace nonpareil.

The Men's Club, planted right off the interstate, like everything else in a town laid down like a new quilt of plywood and Sheetrock, is a sumptuous palace of fiction. What the Men's Club lacks in poetry it makes up for in excess. The red-felt pool tables are illuminated by hanging lamps ensconced in blue glass. The lobby boutique is filled with expensive clothes for men and women. The kitchen will serve you a fillet medallion sautéed in a mushroom demiglace.

In the center of the place, beyond the sunken bar, is the main stage. But the dancers are not the only attraction; above the stage looms a huge television screen, like Oz's mask, eternally tuned to ESPN, so that the allure of even the most seductive sirens competes with huge images of men being tackled and talking heads blathering about blitzes. In a very real sense, the women at the Men's Club are just another product, with this exception: There is nothing real about them. The tattoos on the soft planes south of the hipbones are frosted over with pancake makeup. Their names are as false as their chests. They are stage actors. They are not meant to be the stuff of reality.

This, of course, explains why Rae sought them out. Because they seemed to be less than real women yet possessed of the necessary female attributes. So that considering their feelings was a less complicated process.

Despite a terrific rookie season on the field—Rae earned a starting position at wide receiver and finished with an impressive forty-four receptions—Rae's home life soon proved rocky. Amber went home after that first season. He found her too possessive: She was jealous of all his other female friends. And there would be many female friends. There was Starlita, whom Rae had so charmed in a barbershop one day that before she'd finished having her hair done, Rae had taken her young son down the street for pizza. Soon Starlita thought Rae was the best thing in Jacobe's life. Rae was worried that Starlita was turning her son into a mama's boy. (Rae always harped on that. And what was Rae if not a mama's boy?) There was Fonda Bryant, who kept a picture of her son on her desk at a radio station Rae visited one day, and before long the boy was spending nights at Rae's. Rae was exactly what the boy needed; Rae was firm about staying away from alcohol and drugs, firm about making sure the boy did his homework. When they played, Fonda couldn't tell who was the kid and who was the adult.

And yet Rae hardly ever visited his own child. He gave Michelle grief about breast-feeding the kid and hugging him so much—he worried she was making Little Rae soft. So Michelle sued him for child support: A judge granted her $5,500 a month. She offered to lessen it if Rae would come home and visit more. He promised. He didn't. In the meantime, Amber went back to Charlotte for a quick visit. She got pregnant. As Rae's responsibilities and missteps threatened to collide, as his little-kid appetites met his stunted ability to cope with adversity, he began to consider a solution both novel and bizarre on the surface but certainly logical in the context of a man who regards his women as disposable and dispensable: Any time he'd get a woman pregnant, he'd threaten her with death.

He didn't carry out all the threats, of course. He was a joker. He just talked about it a lot—about having Michelle and Amber killed.

Like the time Michelle called him in March 1998. She'd been unsuccessful in persuading Rae to come back home to visit their son. Rae had another idea. He suggested the two of them fly east to Charlotte. Fine, she said. I'll rent a car and see the sights while you play with your son.

"Don't be surprised if you get in a fatal car accident," Rae answered, according to Michelle. He spoke very quietly, nearly in a whisper.

"What did you say?" asked Michelle.

"It was a joke," Rae said.

"It's not funny," Michelle said.

"That's why it didn't work out," he said. "You never know when I'm joking."

Back in Charlotte one day, Rae got off the phone, turned to Amber and said, as she recalls it, "Would it be messed up if I had somebody, you know, kill Michelle and my son? Or just my son, so that I wouldn't have to pay her any money? Or if she just got in, like, a car accident, or something happened to her, I could have my son and I wouldn't have to pay her money?"

He said it jokingly. Amber had overheard him talking about the same thing to a friend. Yeah, she said. It'd be messed up, Rae.

So some months later, when Amber called from Boulder to say she was pregnant after her five-day visit and Rae insisted she get an abortion, insisted he was not going to have any more kids by women he had no intention of being with, well, how could Amber be surprised when he said what he said to her?

"Don't make me send someone out there to kill you," Amber remembers him saying. "You know I would."

This one didn't sound funny at all. She had the abortion. Barbara Turner hadn't raised her daughter to be no fool.

Cherica Adams worked in the Men's Club boutique. She also danced under an alias at a different bar—over on the stages of the Diamond Club, a slightly more frayed entry in the topless-club genre, a place where a dancer is likely to be visiting from her home club in Buffalo for the long weekend, to pick up a couple of bucks, leaving the two-year-old back with her grandmother. Cherica Adams was a very attractive, baby-faced young woman who moved with a glittery crowd and felt equally at home backstage at a Master P concert or courtside at the 1998 NBA All-Star Game in Madison Square Garden, where several players, including Shaquille O'Neal, came by to say hello to her.

They never really dated, Rae and Cherica. They had sex a few times. Rae was also having sex with an exotic dancer who was having an affair with Charles Shackleford, a former Charlotte Hornet who happened to be married with three children, but it was Cherica whom Rae got pregnant, in March 1999—exactly one year after he and Amber conceived their second child.

Rae was ambivalent about this one. On the one hand, he kept a new set of baby furniture in a storage facility under his name and took Cherica to Lamaze classes. On the other hand, it was at a Lamaze class that Rae first learned Cherica's last name.

Rae's second season had been a disappointment. He'd broken his foot after a forty-seven-yard catch, and he'd missed most of the year. When Cherica got pregnant, his world began to close in.[3]

He was taking grief from teammates and friends about letting a stripper use him, about her boasting all over town that she was carrying Rae Carruth's baby and wasn't going to have to work anymore. By now Rae's circle of male friends had expanded. Tired of the slick jocks in the Panthers' locker room, he was glad to finally meet some people who were real. This new coterie included a man named Michael Kennedy, who had dealt crack, and a man named Van Brett Watkins, who had once set a man on fire in the joint and stabbed his own brother. Watkins, too, had unusual ways of showing love to his women. He'd once held a meat cleaver to his wife's face.

Frequently injured, no longer a starter, Rae had by now become that singularly sorry football phenomenon: a first-round draft pick gone bust. Taxes and agents had taken half the bonus. He'd invested in a car-title-loan scam that had promised the trappings of easy living—and lost his money. He'd hired former wide receiver Tank Black, later indicted on fraud charges, to manage his money. He'd signed a contract on a new house, but he'd had to pull out when he couldn't get the financing, and the owners had sued him.

And he had hired Van Brett Watkins, for $3,000, to beat up Cherica Adams so she'd lose the baby, but Watkins hadn't delivered.

---

[3]*Sports Illustrated* wrote a story last year about the son. I loved the literary art of the lede, but I didn't love how it completely dismissed/ignored why Carruth did what he did—as if, these 12 years later, it's just assumed that some first-round draft pick can be Satan without ever having been influenced by outside forces. If *SI* is actually going to examine sports, it can't just treat a felon as a "bad seed," then spend 4,000 words telling a feel-good story about a grandmother.

He was tired of being victimized, tired of having these women sucking out his sperm, tired of being rewarded for all his kindness by predators and gold diggers. Tired of taking the ragging. Panicked at the money situation.

So Rae did the only thing he could do, the only option they'd left him.

It's as dark as Charlotte gets, the two-lane stretch of Rea Road a few miles north of the movie theater where Cherica and Rae went that night, in separate cars, and it's so silent, so still in the hour after midnight on a weekday, that if you stop your car in the dip in the road and kill the engine, you can imagine yourself back in the South when the farmland was creased by rambling stone walls and the woods were thick with kudzu.

There are houses here, a few of them, a light or two winking through the trees, but none has a clear sight line to the spot. No one could have known the exact location, even if anyone had been looking, even if someone had been awake and heard the hush of tires on pavement down the road.

No one could have seen Rae's Ford Expedition slowing down in front of Cherica's BMW, blocking her path. No one could have seen Michael Kennedy's rented Nissan Maxima pulling up alongside Cherica.

But they'd have heard the five distinct cracks of the .38, when Watkins sent five metal-jacketed bullets through the tinted glass of the driver's window of the BMW. Four of them hit their target, burrowing through Cherica Adams's lung, bowel, stomach, pancreas, diaphragm, liver, and neck, one of them passing within an inch of her fetus, leaving behind two distinct clusters of star bursts in the glass.

They'd have heard Rae's car pull forward and disappear up Rea Road,[4] and Kennedy making a U-turn to go the other way, and Cherica's BMW weaving down a side street until it crawled to a stop on

---

[4] I went there myself very early on in those weeks in Charlotte that I worked on the story. It was the witching hour. I immediately saw the dip in the road, even felt it: a small valley of 100 yards or so—a shallow dip, but deep enough to make it entirely black; no light from any source. When I turned off the car and stepped outside, the only sound was the clicking of the engine as it cooled down. I could only imagine how loud the sound of gunfire would be in that little pocket of, ironically, pure nature, uninfected by mankind. And yeah, it was creepy. I didn't stay long. I had what I needed.

someone's lawn and she bled out her life onto the front seat. They'd have heard the moans. They *did* hear the moans, in fact; the woman who lives in the house where Cherica ended up that night told me she'd never forget the moans. But she wouldn't give me her name, and she wouldn't open the door more than a few inches, just far enough to flick out her cigarette ashes.

But she did remember one more thing: how after Cherica repeated Rae's license-plate number to the 911 operator, after she pleaded with the operator to save her life, Cherica had had the presence of mind to carefully place the cell phone back on the dashboard.

One other detail of the scene escaped the woman's notice. The way Rae looked back at Watkins, the shooter, in his rearview mirror. As Watkins remembered it, for the briefest moment, their eyes met.

Cherica was conscious when the ambulance arrived at the hospital. Unable to speak, she motioned for a notepad and described the way Rae slowed down in front of her. "He was driving in front of me," she wrote. "He stopped in the road. He blocked the front."

Cherica gave birth to a son named Chancellor, who survived. Then the mother went into a coma from which she never awoke.

Nine days later, at dawn on Thanksgiving, police investigators drove to Rae's house in the Ellington Park subdivision. They rang the doorbell. Rae came to the door naked. A woman was in the bedroom. They arrested him. He made bail. Three weeks later, when Cherica died, and Rae now faced first-degree-murder charges, he skipped town.

They found him lying in the coffin-dark trunk of a gray '97 Toyota Camry in the parking lot of a $36-a-night motel in Tennessee, surrounded by candy bars and two water bottles filled with urine and a cell phone and a couple thousand in cash. His mom had turned him in: Theodry had given him up to the bail bondsman. When FBI agents popped the trunk, Rae kept his eyes closed, and he didn't move.

Soon he opened his eyes, raised his hands, and climbed out. This seemed curious at the time, but it doesn't seem curious anymore. Knowing Rae as we do now, we know that he simply reasoned thusly: If he didn't see them, then the agents weren't there at all.

Michelle Wright watched the trial on television, watched as Candace, Starlita, Dawnyle, Monique, Fonda, and Amber took the stand, and told Little Rae about all the pretty women.

"How many girlfriends did my dad have?" Little Rae asked his mother.

"I don't know, Rae," she answered. "I'm learning just like you."

"But you can't marry that many women, can you?"

"No," said Michelle. "You can't."

The creak of the knee braces Rae wore beneath his pants to keep him from fleeing was the only sound in the courtroom when he was led in to hear the verdicts, one day shy of his twenty-seventh birthday. Out the smoked windows in the back of the courtroom, black clouds huddled on command and great Gothic spills of water tumbled out of the Southern sky as Judge Charles Lamm pronounced the verdict of a jury of Rae's peers: guilty of three of four counts, including conspiracy to commit murder. Innocent of first-degree murder.

The weeping of the women on Cherica Adams's side of the courtroom was immediate and audible and joyous. In a state with no parole, a murder-conspiracy conviction means that Rae will be off the streets for decades. He'll serve nineteen years minimum, twenty-four maximum.

Rae took the news of the verdict the way he'd taken everything for seven straight weeks: with no discernible emotion or expression. Just, as the bailiff led him for the last time past his women, a slight nod—at Tnisha, whose expression was confused, and at Theodry, who was already steeling herself to be strong, and at the rest of the women, who were looking toward him with whatever expressions they could muster.[5]

Rae seemed, if anything, distracted, as if it had just occurred to him for the first time: The only intimate adulation he'd get for the next quarter century would be from men. The women were finally out of his life.

[5]By now I knew that the women had become the story's focus. And I knew Carruth was going to be impassive, and I knew that, journalistically, the man could now be measured by a very specific measurement tool: the reaction of the women who, in different ways, had seen him as something very specifically belonging to them, from mom down to girlfriend, and all in between.

John Ed Bradley

It sounds as though *sportswriter* is being used pejoratively when one says John Ed Bradley (b. 1958) was more than a sportswriter the day he wrote his first sentence for the *Washington Post*, but that isn't the case at all. In the early 1980s the *Post*'s sports section was brimming with talent and every day was a writing contest. Bradley separated himself from his stablemates by employing fictional devices and a poet's touch. The echoes of Faulkner and Hank Williams in his work carried all the way to New York, and soon enough he was writing for *GQ, Esquire*, and *Sports Illustrated*. But novels were his destiny, so he retreated to his native Louisiana and wrote six of them, including *Tupelo Nights* (1988) and *Restoration* (2003). All the while, he was haunted by his memories of playing football at LSU. He had been a tri-captain and an all-Southeastern Conference center in 1979, and then he tried to walk away from his teammates, his alma mater, his old life. Years later, after seeing his former coach on TV, wheelchair-bound and weakened by cancer, he knew he had to do what Hemingway prescribed for the things that trouble you: write about them. The result was Bradley's beautifully melancholy memoir *It Never Rains in Tiger Stadium* (2007). He laid the foundation for it in *SI*'s August 12, 2002 edition with this meditation on the ties that will always bind him to the people and the game that shaped his life.

The Best Years of His Life

IT ENDS FOR EVERYBODY. It ends for the pro who makes $5 million a year and has his face on magazine covers and his name in the record books. It ends for the kid on the high school team who never comes off the bench except to congratulate his teammates as they file past him on their way to the Gatorade bucket.

In my case it ended on December 22, 1979, at the Tangerine Bowl in Orlando. We beat Wake Forest that night 34–10, in a game I barely remember but for the fact that it was my last one. When it was over, a teammate and I grabbed our heroic old coach, hoisted him on our shoulders and carried him out to the midfield crest. It was ending that day for Charles McClendon, too, after 18 years as head coach at LSU and a superb 69% career winning percentage. The next day newspapers would run photos of Coach Mac's last victory ride, with Big Eddie Stanton and me, smeared with mud, serving as his chariot. Coach had a hand raised above his head as he waved goodbye, but it would strike me that his expression showed little joy at all. He looked tired and sad. More than anything, though, he looked like he didn't want it to end.

We were quiet on the flight back to Baton Rouge, and when the plane touched down at Ryan Field, no cheers went up and nobody said anything. A week or so later, done with the Christmas holidays, I went to Tiger Stadium to clean out my locker. I brought a big travel bag with me, and I stuffed it with pads, shoes, gym trunks, jockstraps, T-shirts and practice jerseys. I removed my nametag from the locker. Then I studied the purple stenciling against the gold matte. In one corner someone had scribbled the words TRAMPLE THE DEAD, HURDLE THE WEAK. The source of the legend eludes me now, but it had been a rallying cry for the team that year, especially for my mates on the offensive line.

The last thing I packed was my helmet. I'd been an offensive center, and the helmet's back and sides were covered with the little Tigers decals the coaches had given out as merit badges for big plays. I ran my fingertips over the surface, feeling the scars in the hard plastic crown. There were paint smudges and streaks from helmets I'd butted over the years. Was the gold Vanderbilt or Florida State? The red Alabama or Georgia, Indiana or USC?

When I finished packing, I walked down the chute that led to the playing field, pushed open the big metal door and squinted against the sudden blast of sunlight. I meant to have one last look at the old stadium where I'd played the last four years. Death Valley was quiet now under a blue winter sky. I could point to virtually any spot on the field and tell you about some incident that had happened there. I knew where teammates had blown out knees, dropped passes, made key blocks and tackles, thrown interceptions and recovered game-saving fumbles. I knew where we'd vomited in spring scrimmages under a brutal Louisiana sun and where we'd celebrated on autumn Saturday nights to the roar of maniacal Tigers fans and the roar of a real tiger, Mike IV, prowling in a cage on the sideline. We'd performed to a full house at most every home game, the crowds routinely in excess of 75,000, but today there was no one in sight, the bleachers running in silver ribbons around the gray cement bowl. It seemed the loneliest place on earth.

I was only 21 years old, yet I believed that nothing I did for the rest of my life would rise up to those days when I wore the Purple and

Gold. I might go on to a satisfying career and make a lot of money, I might marry a beautiful woman and fill a house with perfect kids, I might make a mark that would be of some significance in other people's eyes. But I would never have it better than when I was playing football for LSU.

Despite this belief, I was determined to walk away from that place and that life and never look back. You wouldn't catch me 20 years later crowing about how it had been back in the day, when as a college kid I'd heard the cheers. I knew the type who couldn't give it up, and I didn't want to be him. He keeps going to the games and reminding anyone who'll listen of how things used to be. His wife and kids roll their eyes as he describes big plays, quotes from halftime speeches and embellishes a "career" that no one else seems to remember with any specificity. He stalks the memory until the memory reduces him to pathetic self-parody. To listen to him, he never screwed up a snap count or busted an assignment or had a coach berate him for dogging it or getting beat. In his mind he is forever young, forever strong, forever golden.

Standing there in Tiger Stadium, I squeezed my eyes closed and lowered my head. Then I wept.

Hell no, I said to myself. That wasn't going to be me.

I still remember their names and hometowns. And I can tell you, almost to a man, the high schools they went to. I remember how tall they were and how much they weighed. I remember their strengths and weaknesses, both as men and as football players. I remember the kinds of cars they drove, what religions they practiced, the music they favored, the hair color of their girlfriends, how many letters they earned, their injuries, their dreams, their times in the 40-yard dash. In many instances I remember their jersey numbers. On the day last August that I turned 43, I wondered what had happened to Robert DeLee. DeLee, a tight end from the small town of Clinton, La., wore number 43 on his jersey when I was a senior. During my freshman year a running back named Jack Clark had worn the number. Jack Clark, too, I thought to myself—where on earth has he slipped off to? I had seen neither of them in more than two decades.

That was the case with almost all of my teammates. Last summer I attended a wedding reception for Barry Rubin, a former fullback at LSU who is a strength coach with the Green Bay Packers. It had been about eight years since I'd last had a face-to-face conversation with a teammate, and even that meeting had come purely by chance. One day I was waiting in the checkout line at a store in suburban New Orleans when someone standing behind me called out my name. I wheeled around, and there stood Charlie McDuff, an ex-offensive tackle who'd arrived at LSU at the same time I did, as a member of the celebrated 1976 freshman class. A couple of shoppers separated Charlie and me, and I couldn't reach past them to shake his hand. "How are things going?" he said.

"Things are good," I said. "How 'bout with you?"

I felt uncomfortable seeing him again, even though we'd always gotten along well back in school. The media guide had listed him at 6'6" and 263 pounds, but in actual fact he was a shade taller and closer to 275. Even after all these years away from the game he had a bull neck and arms thick with muscle. His hair was as sun-bleached as ever, his skin as darkly tanned.

I paid what I owed and started to leave. Then I turned back around and looked at him again. "You ever see anybody anymore, Charlie?" I said.

"Yeah. Sure, I see them. Some of them. You?"

"Not really."

He nodded as if he understood, and we parted without saying anything more, and two years later Charlie McDuff was dead. My sister called, crying with the news. Charlie had suffered a pulmonary embolism while vacationing with his family at a Gulf Coast resort. He left behind a wife and three young sons. I wanted to call someone and talk about him, and I knew it had to be a player, one of our teammates, and preferably an offensive lineman. But I couldn't do it, I couldn't make the call. Nobody wanted to remember anymore, I tried to convince myself. It was too long ago. So instead I pulled some cardboard boxes out of a closet and went through them. There were trophies and plaques wrapped in paper, letters tied with kite string, a short stack of souvenir programs and a couple of plastic-bound photo albums crowded with news clippings and yellowing images of boys who actually were capable of dying. If Charlie McDuff could die, it occurred to me, we all could.

At the bottom of the box I found a worn, gray T-shirt with purple lettering that said NOBODY WORKS HARDER THAN THE OFFENSIVE LINE.

Charlie had had that shirt made, along with about a dozen others, and handed them out to the linemen on the '79 squad. The year before, we'd lost some outstanding players to graduation, and Charlie had hoped the shirts would inspire us to pull together as a unit. We wore the shirts at every opportunity, generally under our shoulder pads at practice and games. It seems crazy now, but there was a time when I considered stipulating in my will that I be buried in that ratty thing. I was never more proud than when I had it on.

I learned about Charlie's funeral arrangements, and I got dressed intending to go. I started down the road for Baton Rouge, rehearsing the lines I'd speak to his widow and children, and those I'd tell my old teammates to explain why I didn't come around anymore. I drove as far as the outskirts of Baton Rouge before turning around and heading back home.

Are there others out there like me? I've often wondered. Does the loss of a game they played in their youth haunt them as it's haunted me? Do others wake up from afternoon naps and bolt for the door, certain that they're late for practice even though their last practice was half a lifetime ago? My nightmares don't contain images of monsters or plane crashes or Boo Radley hiding behind the bedroom door. Mine have me jumping offside or muffing the center-quarterback exchange. They have me forgetting where I placed my helmet when the defense is coming off the field and it's time for me to go back in the game.

If it really ends, I wonder, then why doesn't it just end?

I suppose I was doomed from the start, having been sired by a Louisiana high school football coach. The year of my birth, 1958, was the same year LSU won its one and only national championship in football, and the month of my birth, August, was when two-a-day practices began for that season. Although my parents couldn't afford to take their five kids to the LSU games, we always listened to the radio broadcasts, usually while my father was outside barbecuing on the patio. He'd sit there in a lawn chair, lost in concentration, a purple-and-gold cap tipped back on his head. Not far away on the lawn I acted out big plays with friends from the neighborhood, some of us dressed in little Tigers uniforms. We played in the dark until someone ran into a tree or a clothesline and got hurt, then my dad would have me sit next to him and listen to the rest of the game, the real one. "Settle down now," I remember him saying. "LSU's on."

When I was a kid I always gave the same answer to adults who asked me what I wanted to be when I grew up. "I want to play football for LSU," I answered. Beyond that I had no clear picture of myself.

Nor could I fathom a future without the game when it ended for me 23 years ago. One day I was on the team, the next I was a guy with a pile of memories and a feeling in his gut that his best days were behind him. I shuffled around in my purple letter jacket wondering what to do with myself, and wondering who I was. Suddenly there were no afternoon workouts or meetings to attend. I didn't have to visit the training room for whirlpool or hot-wax baths or ultrasound treatments or massages or complicated ankle tapings or shots to kill the never-ending pain. If I wanted to, I could sit in a Tigerland bar and get drunk without fear of being booted from the team; I didn't have a team anymore. Every day for four years I'd stepped on a scale and recorded my weight on a chart for the coaches. But no one cared any longer how thin I got, or how fat.

That last year I served as captain of the offense, and either by some miracle or by a rigged ballot I was named to the second team All-Southeastern Conference squad. The first-team player, Alabama's Dwight Stephenson, went on to become a star with the Miami Dolphins and a member of the Pro Football Hall of Fame, and I'd seen enough film of the guy to know I was nowhere in his league. At the end of April, in the hours after the 1980 NFL draft, a scout for the Dallas Cowboys called and asked me to consider signing with the club as a free agent, but by then I'd already shed 30 pounds along with any notion of myself as an athlete. I gave some excuse and hung up. "You don't even want to try?" my father said.

I could've yelled at him for asking, but there was genuine compassion in his eyes. He and my mother were losing something, too. One of their sons had played football for LSU, and where I come from nothing topped that. "It's over," I said.

My father nodded and walked away.

Number 50 was Jay Whitley, the pride of Baton Rouge's Lee High. Fifty-one was Lou deLaunay, then Albert Richardson; 52, Kevin Lair, then Leigh Shepard; 53, Steve Estes and Jim Holsombake; 54, Rocky Guillot. Fifty-five was linebacker S. J. Saia; then after my freshman year the number went to Marty Dufrene, probably the toughest offensive lineman ever to come out of Lafourche Parish. My number was 56. When we left the stadium after games, fans were waiting outside under the streetlamps, some of them with programs and slips of paper to sign. Even a lowly offensive lineman was asked for an autograph. "Number 56 in your program, Number 1 in your heart," I'd write, disgracing myself for all eternity but way too ignorant at the time to know it.

I don't recall how I first learned about what happened to Marty. Maybe it was from a news story about efforts to raise money to help pay his medical bills. Or maybe it was another tearful call from a relative. But one day I found myself punching numbers on a telephone keypad, desperate to talk to him again. Marty was living in LaRose, his hometown in the heart of Cajun country, or "down the bayou," as the natives like to say. His wife, Lynne, answered. "Lynne, do you remember me?" I said, after introducing myself.

"Yes, I remember you," she answered. "You want to talk to Marty? Hold on, John Ed. It's going to take a few minutes, because I have to put him on the speakerphone."

A speakerphone? When he finally came on he sounded as though he was trapped at the bottom of a well.

"Marty, is it true you got hurt?" I said.

"Yeah," he said.

"You're paralyzed, man?"

"Yeah," he said, raising his voice to make sure I could hear. "I broke my neck. Can you believe it?"

It had happened in July 1986, some five years before my call. While in his second year of studies at a chiropractic college then based in Irving, Texas, Marty was injured in a freak accident at a pool party to welcome the incoming freshman class. He and friends were horsing around when a pair of them decided to bring big, strong Marty down. One held him in a headlock, the other took a running start and plowed into him. Marty smashed through the water's surface of a shallow children's pool and struck his head on the bottom, shattering a vertebra. He floated in the water, unable to move or feel anything from his neck down, until his friends pulled him out.

As he told me about the accident I kept flashing back to the kid I'd known in school. Marty had been a lean, powerfully built 6'2" and 235 pounds, small by today's standards but about average for a center in our era. On the field he'd played with a kind of swagger, as if certain that he could dominate his opponent. The swagger extended to his life off the field. Marty liked to have a good time. He spoke with a heavy Cajun accent, the kind of accent that made girls crazy and immediately identified him as a pure Louisiana thoroughbred. Football schools from the Midwest featured humongous linemen brought up on corn and prime beef. At LSU we had guys like Marty, raised on crawfish from the mud flats and seafood from the Gulf of Mexico.

The son of an offshore oil field worker, Marty was an all-state high school center in 1976. He was a highly recruited blue-chipper coming out of South Lafourche High, just as I had been at Opelousas High the year before. Marty had vacillated between committing to West Point and to LSU before he realized there really was only one choice for him. Air Force was the military academy that had tried to lure me before I snapped out of it and understood what my destiny was.

The only problem I'd ever had with Marty Dufrene was that we played the same position, and he wanted my job. Going into my senior year I was listed on the first team, Marty on the second. One day after practice he told me he was going to beat me out. I couldn't believe his gall. "I want to play pro ball," he said.

I shook my head and walked off, thinking, Pro ball? To hell with that, Dufrene. I'm going to see to it you don't even play in college.

Now, on the telephone, I was telling him, "I'd like to come see you, Marty."

"Yeah," he said. "It would be great to see you again."

"I'll do it. I promise. Just give me some time."

"Sure, whatever you need. I'd like to catch up."

But then 11 years passed, and I didn't visit Marty or follow up with another call. Nor did I write to him to explain my silence. How could I tell the man that I was afraid to see him again? Afraid to see him as a quadriplegic, afraid to have to acknowledge that, but for the grace of God, I could be the one confined to a chair, afraid to face the reality that what we once were was now ancient history.

I might've played football, in another life. But in my present one I had no doubt as to the depths of my cowardice.

At some point I decided to turn my back on it all, rather than endure the feeling of loss any longer. Marty Dufrene wasn't the only one I avoided. There were years when I tried to stay clear of the entire town of Baton Rouge. Travelers can see Tiger Stadium as they cross the Mississippi River Bridge and enter the city from the west, and whenever I journeyed across that elevated span I made sure to look at the downtown office buildings and the State Capitol to the north, rather than to the south where the old bowl sits nestled in the trees. I struggled to watch LSU games on TV and generally abandoned the set after less than a quarter. Same for radio broadcasts: I tuned most of them out by halftime. On two occasions the school's athletic department invited me to attend home games as an honorary captain, and while I showed both times, I was such a nervous wreck at being in the stadium again that I could barely walk out on the field before kickoff to receive my award and raise an arm in salute to the crowd.

Love ends, too, and when the girl invites you over to meet her new beau, you don't have to like it, do you?

I received invitations to participate in charity golf tournaments featuring former Tigers players; I never went to them. Teammates invited me to tailgate parties, suppers and other events; I never made it to them. The lettermen's club invited me to maintain a membership; except for one year, I always failed to pay my dues. Even Coach Mac tried to get in touch with me a few times. I was somehow too busy to call him back.

It wasn't until December of last year that I finally saw him again, and by then he was dying. In fact, in only three days he would be dead. Cancer had left him bedridden at his home in Baton Rouge, but even at the worst of it he was receiving guests, most of them former players who came by to tell him goodbye. One day I received a call from an old college friend, urging me to see Coach Mac again. She said it didn't look good; if I wanted to talk to him and make my peace, I'd better come right away.

So that was how I ended up at his doorstep one breezy weekday morning last winter, my hand shaking as I lifted a finger to punch the bell. I wondered if anyone in the house had seen me park on the drive in front, and I seriously considered walking back to my truck and leaving. But then the door swung open and there standing a few feet away was Coach Mac's wife, Dorothy Faye. I could feel my heart squeeze tight in my chest and my breath go shallow. My friend had called ahead and told her I might be coming; otherwise she surely would've been alarmed by the sight of a weeping middle-aged man at her front door. "Why, John Ed Bradley," she said. "Come in. Come in, John Ed."

She put her arms around me and kissed the side of my face. Dorothy Faye was as beautiful as ever, and as kind and gracious, not once asking why it had taken her husband's impending death to get me to come see him again. She led me down a hall to a bedroom, and I could see him before I walked in the door. He was lying supine on a hospital bed. His head was bald, the hair lost to past regimens of chemotherapy, and, at age 78, wrapped up in bedsheets, he seemed so much smaller than I remembered him. His eyes were large and haunted from the battle, but it was Coach Mac, all right. I snapped to attention when he spoke my name. "Come over here and talk to me, buddy," he said.

I sat next to the bed and we held hands and told stories, every one about football. He was still the aw-shucks country boy who'd played for Bear Bryant at Kentucky before going on to build his own legend in Louisiana, and the sound of his rich drawl made the past suddenly come alive for me. I named former teammates and asked him what had become of them, and in every case he had an answer. "Your old position coach was here yesterday," he said.

"Coach McCarty?"

"He sat right there." And we both looked at the place, an empty chair.

"And you're a writer now," he said.

"Yes sir, I'm a writer."

"I'm proud of you, John Ed."

I didn't stay long, maybe 20 minutes, and shortly before I got up to leave he asked me if I ever remembered back to 1979 and the night that the top-ranked USC Trojans came to Baton Rouge and the fans stood on their feet for four quarters and watched one of the most exciting games ever played in Tiger Stadium. "I remember it all the time," I said. "I don't always want to remember it, because we lost, Coach, but I remember it."

"I remember it too," he said in a wistful sort of way.

The Trojans that year had one of the most talented teams in college football history, with standouts Ronnie Lott, Charles White, Marcus

Allen, Brad Budde and Anthony Munoz. They would go on to an 11-0-1 season and finish ranked second nationally behind Alabama, and White would win the Heisman Trophy.

In his bed Coach Mac lifted a hand and ran it over the front of his face in a raking gesture. "They called face-masking against Benjy," he whispered.

"Sir?"

"That penalty. The one at the end."

"Yes, sir. They sure did call it. And it cost us the game."

He swallowed, and it seemed I could see that night being replayed in his eyes: the yellow flag going up, the 15 yards being marched off, the subsequent touchdown with less than a minute to play that gave USC the 17–12 win. "Benjy Thibodeaux didn't face-mask anybody," I said, the heat rising in my face as I started to argue against a referee's call that nothing would ever change.

Coach Mac was quiet now, and he eased his grip on my hand. I stood and started for the door, determined not to look back. His voice stopped me. "Hey, buddy?" he said. I managed to face him again. "Always remember I'm with you. I'm with all you boys." He lifted a hand off the bed and held it up high, just as he had so many years ago after his last game.

"I know you are, Coach."

"And buddy?" A smile came to his face. He pointed at me. "Next time don't wait so long before you come see your old coach again."

Now it is summer, the season before the season, and Major Marty Dufrene, Civil Department Head of the Lafourche Parish Sheriff's Department, motors his wheelchair to the end of a cement drive and nods in the direction of a horse barn at the rear of his 38-acre estate. Five horses stand along a fence and wait for him, just as they do every day when he rolls out to see them after work. "I'm going to be riding before the end of the year," he tells me. "I've got a saddle I'm making with the back beefed up for support, so I can strap myself in. Of course I'm going to have to use a lift to put me in the saddle. But I'm going to do it."

By now I have been with him for a couple of hours, and already the force of his personality has made the chair invisible. After the injury his muscles began to atrophy, and over time his midsection grew large and outsized, his face swollen. But the fire in his eyes hasn't changed. Marty is exactly as I remembered him. "One thing about him," says his wife, "Marty might've broken his neck, he might be paralyzed and in that chair, but he is still a football player."

Their large Acadian-style house stands only a stone's throw from Bayou Lafourche, the place where they met and fell in love as teenagers. Lynne and their 17-year-old daughter, Amy, are inside preparing dinner, and outside Marty is giving me a tour of the spread when we come to rest in the shade of a carport. I reach to touch the top of his shoulder, because he still has some feeling there, but then I stop myself. "Marty, you must've resented the hell out of me," I say.

He looks up, surprise registering on his face. He bucks forward and then back in his chair, and it isn't necessary for me to explain which of my failures might've led me to make such a statement. "No, never," he says. "I saw you as my competition, but I always have a lot of respect for my competition, and I did for you, too. You were standing in my way, standing in the way of where I wanted to be. But even then I knew my role and accepted it. I was going to push you as hard as I could. That was my duty to you and to the team. I looked up to you as a teacher, just as you looked up to Jay Whitley as a teacher when he was playing ahead of you. We were teammates, John Ed. That was the most important thing."

Lynne and Amy serve lasagna, green salad and blueberry cheesecake in the dining room, and afterward Marty and I move to the living room and sit together as dusk darkens the windows. He revisits the nightmare of his accident and the rough years that followed, but it isn't until he talks about his days as an LSU football player that he becomes emotional. "Nothing I've ever experienced compares to it," he says. "That first time I ran out with the team as a freshman—out into Tiger Stadium? God, I was 15 feet off the ground and covered with frissons. You know what frissons are? They're goose bumps. It's the French word for goose bumps." He lowers his head, and tears fill his eyes and run down his face. He weeps as I have wept, at the memory of how beautiful it all was. "It was the biggest high you could have," he says. "No drugs could match it. The way it felt to run out there with the crowd yelling for you. I wish every kid could experience that."

"If every kid could," I say, "then it wouldn't be what it is. It's because so few ever get there that it has such power."

We are quiet, and then he says, "Whenever I have a down time, or whenever I'm feeling sorry for myself, or whenever life is more than I can bear at the moment, I always do the same thing. I put the Tiger fight song on the stereo, and all the memories come back and somehow it makes everything O.K. All right, I say to myself. I can do it. I can do it. Let's go."

Marty and I talk deep into the night, oblivious to the time, and finally I get up to leave. He wheels his chair as far as the door, and as I'm driving away I look back and see him sitting there, a bolt of yellow light around him, arm raised in goodbye.

I could seek out each one of them and apologize for the vanishing act, but, like me, most of them eventually elected to vanish, too, moving into whatever roles the world had reserved for them. Last I heard, Jay Blass had become a commercial pilot. Greg Raymond returned to New Orleans and was running his family's jewelry store. Tom Tully became a veterinarian specializing in exotic birds, of all things. And Jay Whitley, somebody told me, is an orthodontist now, the father of four kids. If they're anything like their old man, they're stouthearted and fearless, and they eat linebackers for lunch.

When the pregame prayer and pep talks were done, we'd come out of the chute to the screams of people who were counting on us. The band would begin to play; up ahead the cheerleaders were waiting. Under the crossbar of the goalpost we huddled, seniors in front. I was always afraid to trip and fall and embarrass myself, and for the first few steps I ran with a hand on the teammate next to me. Arms pumping, knees lifted high. The heat felt like a dense, blistering weight in your lungs. If you looked up above the rim of the bowl you couldn't see the stars; the light from the standards had washed out the sky. Always in the back of your mind was the knowledge of your supreme good fortune. Everyone else would travel a similar course of human experience, but you were different.

And so, chin straps buckled tight, we filed out onto the field as one, the gold and the white a single elongated blur, neatly trimmed in purple.

Wright Thompson

There may be no more Dixie-fried writer currently gamboling about the sports world than Wright Thompson (b. 1976). Whether he's in Ghana, Green Bay, or back home in Oxford, Mississippi, he works with a passion and a commitment to the language that are straight out of the South's literary tradition. "He writes long and often personally," says his friend Chris Jones, of *Esquire*, "and he lays his heart out there, which is a rare thing these cynical days." Thompson's heart is most assuredly on display in "Pulled Pork & Pigskin," his 2007 ode to Southern football for ESPN.com, a work of such fervor and unashamed adoration that even the thickest-headed Yankee can get the picture. Though he's a Missouri grad, the Clarksville native has never stopped being an Ole Miss fan. Thompson's first jobs out of college were covering LSU football for the *New Orleans Times-Picayune* and everything from the Masters to the Kentucky Derby to the Super Bowl for the *Kansas City Star*. Then ESPN brought him aboard to write features and columns for its magazine and website, and Thompson burst to the fore as a free-spirited globe-trotter who wanted a Hemingway life and got it. But you know he'll always be a Mississippi boy when he writes about a pimento cheeseburger "messier than a small-town divorce."

Pulled Pork & Pigskin: A Love Letter to Southern Football

Two friends, both unhinged football fans, got married earlier this year. During the wedding reception, the bride's father somehow got the Ole Miss band to march into the room, a blaring chorus of starched uniforms and shining brass. The groom conducted. The crowd stomped and cheered. You'd have thought folks were celebrating a 12-play scoring drive, not holy matrimony.

Soon after the wedding, I watched video of this event. Immediately, I recognized the feeling deep down in my gut. It's something I've felt in so many cathedral-like stadiums. I closed my eyes, and the familiar notes sent me rushing months into the future, longing for a tailgate that escalates from simmer to burn, for the chill bumps that always come in the moments before kickoff, for the evening breezes rustling the white oaks when the game is done. My body sat in front of a computer screen. My mind was in a stadium. It was only April, and I longed for September.

I missed football season.

As you might have guessed, I live in the South, a little town named Oxford, which means my life is governed by a set of rhythms as familiar as the white-columned mansions up and down Lamar Boulevard. I love air conditioning, and I love cocktails in the gloaming on the City Grocery balcony, and I love a plate of shrimp and grits when the sun finally goes down. I love honking at Faulkner's grave on the way home from the bar. I love cruising 18 miles an hour through campus, the speed limit set in honor of Archie Manning's college number, passing pretty blondes driving foreign cars, courtesy of Daaaaddy, and seeing a boy sporting khakis and an SEC haircut and realizing our fathers looked just like that a half century ago. I love "Dixie" played slow and the Bob Dylan song. I love the magnolias blooming in the late spring and the incandescent heat of the summer but, mostly, I love the insanity of the fall.

The entire South is about ready to explode as summer ends and autumn begins. Football's coming. The preseason magazines appear. Wallet-sized schedules materialize on gas station counters. Meals out are eaten over the soundtrack of folks predicting wins and losses—and not just sports fans with fantasy teams and chicken wing sauce on their chins. No, grandmothers in Chanel and pearls get worked up—I mean *fired up*, brother—about beating LSU.

I love the hope of those preseason predictions. I love 0–0. I love talking about Archie like he played yesterday, because the past isn't dead; it isn't even past. I love game day, the cars hurtling north from Jackson and Biloxi and Vicksburg and Meridian. I love Hermés ties paired with Widespread Panic hats. I love gin and tonic for breakfast and bourbon and Coke for lunch, each faithfully mixed and swilled in those red (or blue) plastic chalices that as a child I simply knew as "Grove cups."

I love "ARE YOU READY?" and all the other SEC football idiosyncrasies, too, because they come from the same kind of passion: Mississippi State's cowbells, the Vol Navy, an Arkansas fan using the Freedom of Information Act, the way the crowd sings along to "Sweet Home Alabama" on a warm Southern Saturday at Bryant-Denny Stadium. In Birmingham, they love the gov'nah, indeed. Me, too, even if I don't know a single thing about him. That's what football can do. It can even make me love Steve Spurrier. That rat bastard, I love him so.

I love most everything about Southern football, but more than anything else, I love for it to begin. This year, the twinges hit hard in mid-July. A work trip takes me to Cayce, near the South Carolina campus, where I find myself sitting at the counter of a local restaurant called the Kingsman. It's one of those places that seems as if it has been there forever, like the planets, or Styrofoam. I order a pimento cheeseburger. The Kingsman's famous for these gobs of cholesterol-laden goodness. They're messier than a small-town divorce, but damn, they're good. A woman works a hot griddle covered in sizzling, dancing meat. Then, apropos of nothing, she turns to a waitress who's calling in an order. The spirit's in her. And it's got to come out.

"Only 52 more days 'til football!" she hollers.

They've both stopped work for a moment. The waitress shakes her head.

"It's 51!" she hollers back.

The wait is almost over.

WINTER AND SPRING

In the winter, when football season lies dormant, we are warmed by our memories. Well, there's recruiting, but memories, too: Catching passes as a young boy in the soft green grass outside Vaught-Hemingway Stadium. Meeting legendary coach John Vaught, for whom it was named. Crying when we heard the story of paralyzed former Rebels cornerback Chucky Mullins whispering, "It's time."

The good people of Louisiana can remedy the boredom of baseball's spring training with memories of the white hot noise in Tiger Stadium—"Chance of rain? Never!"—and the Phil Collins song drifting up and out over the Mississippi River: *I can feel it coming in the air tonight*. Once, the crowd got so loud the seismograph in the geology building a few blocks away registered an actual earthquake. Those corn whiskey-fueled Cajuns literally made the ground shake. Former Tigers quarterback Rohan Davey tried to explain to me once what it was like to run out of the tunnel there. "Everyone is screaming," he said. "Everyone is going crazy. You can smell the bourbon."

In Knoxville, when football season seems like it might never arrive, they can laugh about the fans who've almost sunk a boat in the Tennessee River. They can sing "Rocky Top." In Arkansas, they can let a "Pig Sooie" fly, like a maintenance drink for a boozehound. A few states over, a War Eagle or Rammer Jammer can keep a man (or woman) from going insane. That's a struggle we've been having for generations. Why? Well, there are a thousand theories, many having to do with a lack of any other entertainment, but the one in Tony Barnhart's book about the obsession makes as much sense as any: Dominating at football offers a chance for Southerners to feel equal, a chance to avenge past defeats on the battlefield, which is admittedly bizarre, since no one else in the country ever thinks about the Civil War. In the book, former Georgia coach Vince Dooley describes beating Michigan in Ann Arbor in 1965. "I didn't just hear from Georgia people," he says, "but from people all over the South. To go up there and invade the North and come back a winner was the greatest thing for a lot of people. It was as if we had had a chance to go to Gettysburg again."

So these memories are important, a part of our martial DNA, though some memories are a bit hazier than others. My cousin ran out between the hedges in 2000 after Georgia beat Tennessee for the first time in nine years. He tore off his white dress shirt, ran right over to two players sitting on the Volunteers' bench and screamed, "Go back to Knoxville!" (The family's very proud.) Here's another one I just heard: Two ol' boys were in Baton Rouge, all decked out in LSU gear, tailgating all day. Then, after hours of drinking peacefully next to each other, one guy suddenly jumped the other, quickly getting the upper hand, punching and kicking like a madman. Then he pulled out a knife, apparently to finish the job. Before they were pulled apart, the aggressor screamed at his defeated foe, "I can't believe you named your little girl Auburn!"

Every Southern football fan has a story like that, just like every group has a set of shared experiences. I've never rolled Toomer's Corner after a big War Eagle win, but the people who have will never forget it. *New York Times* sports columnist Selena Roberts sure won't. Today, she's one of the most respected voices in the world of sports. But when she thinks back to her days as a student at Auburn, she can still see the ribbons of white hanging from the trees. She remembers stealing toilet paper from buildings and walking through the knee-deep sea of tissue. "It looks as close as a white Christmas as you can get in the South," she says.

Each school has its legends. There's the time a potential game-winning field goal was blown back by a sudden gust of wind, costing Mississippi State a victory over Ole Miss in the Egg Bowl, removing any doubt which team God himself pulls for (though Alabama fans might argue by quoting Ezekiel 20:29 ... look it up). There's Billy Cannon's punt return which, almost 50 years after he ran into the Louisiana fog, is still played on the radio in Baton Rouge. There's Spurrier reminding us all that you can't spell Citrus without "U" and "T." There's Buck Belue to Lindsay Scott, and if you need an explanation, you've probably never eaten barbecue cooked at a gas station.

These are the stories told in January deer camps and in spring break condos and over graduation weekend grilled cheeseburgers at Rotiers in Nashville. They keep the dream of football alive until winter and spring give way to summer.

SUMMER

There can be no joy of the fall without the brutal heat of June, July and August. Here in Mississippi, it's like you're living inside someone's mouth.

Oxford, as is the case with most college towns, is quiet in the summer. It's resting. The students are gone. The tables are easy to come by. The live music is mellow. You can find parking around the courthouse square. Some restaurants and bars close for a bit to gird for the fall.

We sit inside and make plans, too. My alma mater, Missouri, is coming to Oxford this September (don't tell anyone, but I'm pulling for the Rebels). I've invited all my friends. We've rented an extra house, planned a big party, with a bartender and hot tamales. Planning for the weekend has consumed our summer. We're far from alone. Most every big decision made below the Mason-Dixon Line is made with the distant season in mind.

"I do think that in the state of Alabama," says Crimson Tide die-hard and *Forrest Gump* author Winston Groom, "anybody planning a wedding is gonna get out a schedule, because the worst damn thing you can do is have your wedding on the Alabama-Auburn game or the Tennessee game, because nobody will come to your wedding. They had one here like that, but they put up a big old huge TV at the place where they had the reception. One of those big giant things, about eight feet tall."

He laughs.

"As a matter of fact, in the state of Alabama, I wouldn't even plan a funeral when Alabama is playing Auburn," he says. "You can die, but you're gonna wait 'til Monday."

In the summer, the season is close enough to smell the chicken frying. The good restaurants start taking reservations for ballgame weekends; the City Grocery in Oxford begins June 1. And yet everything is on hold, like a dragster spinning its tires. The tickets haven't come yet. The giant rock-and-roll tour buses sit parked in driveways around the South, many with bumper stickers like, "On the way to see the Kentucky Wildcats play!"

The hardest damn part of the summer is not jumping the gun. Fans are like players: You can't peak too early. Right after the Fourth of July, the hype begins building up steam, with all eyes pointed toward the annual SEC media days in Hoover, Ala.—a three-day extravaganza of all things Southern and football. The South devours newspapers during media days. It was always when the season began for me, first as a fan, then as a beat reporter covering the LSU Tigers for the *New Orleans Times-Picayune*.

Then, soon after that, practice will start, the clacking of pads echoing in the afternoon heat. The closer the season gets, the more the mood of a town changes. Things move a bit quicker, with a little more intensity than the day before. The local hotels are painted. Coeds shop for dresses short enough to get dates to the games but long enough to hide the booze. The luxury condos that set rich fans back upward of a million dollars for six weekends a year are cleaned and stocked. Even the oaks seem different.

"The shadows they cast will change directions," says Widespread Panic drummer Todd Nance, a Georgia alum but a lifelong Tennessee fan. "Outside, the shadows look different. I can always tell fall is coming, and then all the crazy people come to town and go nuts."

One morning, everyone awakens to find football season has arrived on the outskirts of town, a savior, like rain on a parched crop.

It's time.

SUMMER TURNS TO FALL

The jet engines sound like a roaring crowd. A white Cessna Citation, call sign N1UM, revs on the runway, the pilot standing on the brakes, building up the rpm's. Inside, Ole Miss coach Ed Orgeron is poured into a seat, ready to take off for SEC media days. Just before the wheels leave the ground, Orgeron smiles at me. He's almost shaking with excitement. I am, too. Finally, the countdown has ended.

"I knew it was a big day," he says. "Kelly got up and ironed my shirt this morning. It happens one time a year. Media day."

Show time. We fly over northern Mississippi, over the little farms and towns, places with names like Thaxton, Skyline and Shiloh, the brown dirt roads snaking through green fields. Orgeron makes notes: *1. Excited to start camp.* For Coach O, as he's called in Oxford, the smells and the sounds are the things he misses most during the other three, insignificant seasons. Cut grass is his favorite. "There's nothing like a football field in August when you first walk out on it," he says.

In no time, we're on approach to the small airstrip in Bessemer, Ala. Already on the tarmac is the University of Georgia jet, which brought in coach Mark Richt earlier. We'll be parking next to it.

"It's on," Orgeron says. "It's rolling. The energy and the excitement here gets you going. It's sorta like game day."

The Wynfrey Hotel in suburban Birmingham is a zoo. Kenny Stabler is doing live radio. Television cameramen surround players, back-pedaling to catch shots of them walking. Fans press together in the lobby and crowd around the escalator to catch a glimpse of the SEC coaches, most of whom could get elected governor in their state. Kids beg for autographs. One fan musters up the courage to speak to Coach O. I am from a little town in Mississippi, but this guy talks so country that even I am not completely certain I understand.

"I got off at 6 o'clock in the morning waiting for you," he says. "I work for the railroad. My wife's been giving me hell. She's all pregnant."

Orgeron finds his way into the big ballroom. It's packed with Saturday night poets, men like Scooter Hobbs, who's as important in Lake Charles, La., as the *Washington Post* chief political writer is in the District. The room is lit with the glow from 500 laptop computers, reporters' fingers sitting on keys, waiting to praise or to hang.

After hours of questions, the day is over. There's no turning back now. The ease of summer is gone. The pressure of fall has arrived. Before leaving the hotel, Orgeron runs into Richt. I watch the two coaches smile. Today, they are friends. Tomorrow, they will be enemies again.

"Good luck, Coach," Orgeron says.

"You, too," Richt says. "We'll see you at our place."

We ride back to the airport. Richt has left on the Georgia plane, but the Tennessee plane is parked in its place, a big orange "T" on the tail. At least they're here; a few years back, coach Phil Fulmer couldn't come because Alabama fans were threatening to subpoena him if he set foot in the state. Pursuing a defamation lawsuit against the NCAA, they were gonna serve him on the podium.

Longtime Ole Miss sports information director Langston Rogers chuckles.

"Coach Vaught would probably blow that plane up," he says.

The pilots welcome us aboard.

"Y'all enjoy yourselves?" one asks.

"We're still undefeated, baby," Orgeron says, a grin on his face.

It's only 30 minutes back to Oxford, and that smile never goes away. I am ready for toe to meet leather, as a friend puts it, and so is Coach O. Cool air blows from the vents. Tupelo and then Pontotoc flash beneath us, U.S. Highway 78 just a thin trickle of asphalt.

"You spend most of the summer relaxing and all of a sudden... boom!" Orgeron says. "It's energizing. You get a charge from it. Your thoughts immediately change from vacation to football."

Orgeron looks up at us from his seat in the middle of the Ole Miss jet.

"Monday morning," he says. "Lock the doors."

"No interviews Monday," Rogers assures.

"Lock the doors," Orgeron says. "Turn off the cell phones. The vacation's over."

FALL

I close my eyes.

The air smells like sweat and fresh grass. Behind me, Vaught-Hemingway casts shadows over the Ole Miss practice field. Today, they are painting "Rebels" on the outside of the stadium. They are cleaning the inside, stocking it, as if for a long voyage. Big dragonflies circle like fighter jets. The sky is Ole Miss blue. For a moment, I stand there, just letting the sounds of football cover me. A thump of a foot on a ball. Toe to leather. A sudden shriek of a whistle. The screams of a linebacker: "Tall right! Raider! Raider!" A coach screaming even louder: "Tempo! Tempo!" The calm, measured words of the quarterback: "Blue 43 . . . Blue 43 . . . *hut-hut.*"

Orgeron claps and the entire team claps with him, the sun shining off the blue helmets, young men from all over the country, from California to the Mississippi Delta, young men who can never truly appreciate how many hopes and dreams hang on their actions every Saturday afternoon. Orgeron understands. "Nowhere to hide," he yells. "Nowhere to hide today. We're watching everything you do. Everything counts. Let's rock and roll."

I leave practice for a moment, wandering inside the cool belly of the stadium, then out into the bowl, working row by row, section by section, over to my family's seats. Section O, row 61, seats 1–4. There are about a dozen folks in the entire stadium when I sit down, relaxing in the shadow of the upper deck, picturing this place full, and other places like it across the South, imagining what that holy noise will be like. Chill bumps run up and down my arm. The only sound today comes from the gas-powered pressure washers, pushing 3,700 pounds per square inch, making sure this place is spotless when the Missourah Tigers come to town.

I love these seats. I love that Stephen Wiley Vaught sits just a few rows over from us. He was my daddy's college roommate, maybe his best friend in the world, and not long ago he summed up attending the installation of a new Episcopal bishop thusly, without irony: "I haven't seen anything this impressive since Archie Manning's junior year."

I love how people who get it are standing up in their office chairs right now ready to get it on and people who don't are scratching their heads and wondering what in the hell is wrong with these rednecks. I love seeing former Ole Miss coach Billy Brewer jog past with his shirt off. Once, he'd been king of this town. Then scandal, a firing and a lawsuit against the school tore down his throne. But I love that he still comes here. I wonder whether he hears the echoes. I imagine we all do. I think he does for sure. Once, he asked a stranger to sit in the cab of his pickup truck and listen to Elvis Presley sing "Dixie." Yes, he remembers. I love that he's stopped on a concourse, peering down into the heat, watching another coach scream at the Ole Miss Rebels, "No free lunches out here."

Practice comes to a close—just a few weeks until the first game. The town is alive. Classes started last week. Football season's not coming any longer. It's here. A few hours later, I stick my head into the first band practice of the year. "Pride of the South," it reads on the side of the building. They're in a semicircle, starting with flutes and piccolos, working up to the shining sousaphones in the back.

Finally, after months of waiting, it happens. The first slow "Dixie." The name on the sheet music says, "From Dixie with Love." The drums start first. Then an A-flat, an F, a D-flat and we're off. The trumpets and mellophones come in. Then the bass drums, big heavy booms. The snares rattle, the drummers jumping up and down. Rising tidal waves of brass, each reaching higher than the one before, carrying everyone along for the ride.

The band is going full speed, game-day speed, low to the ground and accelerating, a trombone player tapping his foot. Cymbals crash, the notes bouncing around the room, playing a song for our fathers and for our children. I love almost everything about the South. I love the beautiful weirdness of it. I love the burn of catfish right out the grease, and I love the heat of a late-night juke joint, all the songs about heartache and sorrow and pain. I love the mustardy tang of Carolina barbecue on a Sunday afternoon. But right now, I love this moment most.

I close my eyes once more, and I see an ocean of red and blue, grandmothers in Chanel and frat boys in Widespread Panic hats. I see Stephen Wiley Vaught in seersucker and white bucks. I see the green grass of the Grove and the young boys wearing replica jerseys. I see the beautiful scenes of fall in the South, from Lexington to Tuscaloosa, from Fayetteville to Baton Rouge. I see the Vol Navy, and a hand ringing a maroon cowbell, and a cute little girl in pigtails screaming, "Tiger Bait!"

I see football season.

Rick Telander

Rick Telander (b. 1948) was an All-Big Ten cornerback who didn't know how to type when he handed in his first story for Northwestern's student newspaper. He would learn soon enough. Drafted by the Kansas City Chiefs in 1971, he got cut in training camp, wrote about the experience for *Sports Illustrated*, and instantly became a talent to watch. But even Telander's most ardent admirers couldn't have predicted that moving to New York and immersing himself in inner-city basketball would become the basis of his 1976 book *Heaven Is a Playground*, now hailed as a classic by publications as disparate as *SI* and *Playboy*. He eventually joined *SI*'s writing staff, focusing on college football scandals and the NCAA hypocrisy that allows member schools to rake in millions of dollars while often penniless athletes scuffle to survive. Though magazine work looks seductive to newspaper writers, Telander made the reverse trip in 1995 by leaving *SI* to join the *Chicago Sun-Times* as its senior sports columnist. While continuing to write for magazines when time allowed and building his total of published books to eight, he quickly mastered the thousand-word column form. His distinctive sensibility shines in what he wrote for January 1, 2007, a chronicle of his internal struggle with whether or not to knock on the door of a former Chicago Bears star discarded by the game that damaged him. It's the kind of thing journalists do every day, but Telander must decide if the answers he seeks are more important than one man's tortured peace.

Atkins a Study in Pride and Pain

Knoxville, Tenn., January 1, 2007

I DRIVE SLOWLY PAST THE SMALL RED-BRICK HOUSE on the narrow, winding road in the hills outside town.

I pull into a driveway a quarter-mile farther on. A dog barks somewhere. It's a few days before Christmas.

The dog stops. Silence.

I turn the car around, drive past the house again.

I don't know.

The house has its curtains drawn. There are two old cars in the carport, one of them very old, I'm guessing 30, 40 years. Fins. Rusty.

There's a wooden wheelchair ramp that looks weathered and unused leading to the front door. A "No Smoking" sign in the front-door window. Two tiny American flags on the wall next to the carport.

No lights on. No decorations.

Doug Atkins, 76, the legendary Hall of Fame defensive end for the Bears, lives here.

"I don't want to see anybody," he had told me during one of our phone conversations. People had their minds made up about a lot of stuff, he said. Predetermined. The country was going to hell. No middle class. Only rich and poor.

I didn't need to ask which side he fell on.

"I'm doing OK," he had said. "I cracked my hip awhile back. Never got well since then. I can walk with a cane, but it's getting rough. I got sick, and I've been poisoned from some of the medicine they gave me—lead poisoning. They don't put out the truth about medicines. So many crooks in the country nowadays—politicians, oil companies, pharmaceutical companies, lobbyists. A lot of people are worse off than I am. But I don't need to see any reporters."

Everybody knows that football is a rough game, that the NFL is the roughness polished bright and turned into performance art, the brutality into religion, the cracking bones into the percussive soundtrack that suits our times.

But not many know the toll the game takes when the players themselves, the artists, have left the stage.

A shocking number of the men, starting sometimes well before middle age, begin to limp, then hobble, then stop moving much at all.

Dementia, mood disorders, osteoarthritis, surgery, more surgery, pain—the wheel of football repercussion spins and spins.

And often, the longer a man played—meaning the better player he was—the worse his debilitation.

Doug Atkins played 17 years in the NFL, the best 12 for the Bears.

In that time, the long-legged, hickory-tough 6-8, 260-pounder did things that hadn't been done before on the gridiron. A scholarship basketball player at Tennessee as well as an All-America football player, Atkins sometimes jumped over blockers like a hurdler vaulting rolling logs.

He went out for track at Tennessee and won the Southeastern Conference high jump, clearing 6-6. In the NFL, he went to eight Pro Bowls from 1958 to 1966.

"I didn't know what I was doing in the high jump," he said on the phone. "In high school one time, I scissored 6-1½."

All that talent came together on the football field like a rainbow palette.

George Halas, Atkins's coach with the Bears and the man who helped found the NFL, said of the giant from Humboldt, Tenn., "There never was a better defensive end."

But now there's the embarrassment the game has exacted.

Mike Ditka hosts a golf tournament each year wherein Ditka and sponsors earmark money for Hall of Famers in need.

Sometimes it's a payout for surgical procedures or medicine.

Sometimes it's a wheelchair ramp.

One time it was for a tombstone.

"It's pitiful," says Ditka, tearing into the NFL's stingy pension plan for old-timers, the NFL players' union, and all PR aspects of the league. "Rip 'em all, I don't care."

The league's frugal pension plan is complicated, but it's simplified nicely by the fact that the veterans die at a swift pace.

There's a new pension agreement being put into place, but as of last year, NFL players who had reached age 55 might get between $200 and $425 a month.

Enough for aspirin, for sure.

While the current Bears swagger down the road to success and the NFL wallows in money, the old men who helped build the brand suffer in silence, often lame, often nearly destitute, their pride too great to allow pity.

Atkins had mesmerized me when I had asked him, please, just for me, to detail his injuries.

The groin pull that tore muscle off the bone, leaving a "hole" in his abdomen. "My fault," he said.

The big toe injury. The broken collarbone. The leg that snapped at the bottom of a pile. ("I got to the sideline, and it didn't feel right.")

The biceps that tore in half, Atkins's arm hanging limply.

"It's just a show muscle," he said, explaining why he never got it fixed.

"I see these old football players," says Dr. Victoria Brander, the head of Northwestern University's Arthritis Institute, "and every joint is ruined—their toes, ankles, knees, hips, fingers, elbows, shoulders. The supporting structure in the joints is gone. Their spines are collapsed. I see one former star who is bent like a 'C.'

"But they are noble. They played their game because they believed in something. They were warriors. They never complain."

I have gone past Atkins' house four times now. I take a deep breath.

I dial his number on my cell phone.

His wife answers and gives him the phone. I just happen to be in the area, I say. Would he mind if I stopped by, maybe for a minute or two, on the way to the airport?

"Damn it, why do you all keep bothering me?" Atkins yells into the receiver. "I told you I was sick!"

And then the line is dead.

"These guys don't need much," Ditka will say later in barely controlled fury. "Your best players? Ever? Why can't the league give them enough to live out their lives in dignity? Is that so f---king hard?"

I drive on, feeling terrible, feeling cruel. I never should've imposed on Doug Atkins. On his pride.

In the midst of our bounty, I feel lost.

Pat Forde

The game story lies tattered and pitiful in the wreckage of the newspaper business. There is little time for writers racing brutal print deadlines to do more than dash something off, click send, and pray they got the final score right. But a check of the Internet reveals that rumors of the game story's demise are premature. The proof shines brightly in the story that Pat Forde (b. 1964), then of ESPN.com, wrote about Boise State's rollicking, trick-play victory over mighty Oklahoma in the 2007 Fiesta Bowl. He roamed from the happiness on the field at game's end to the press conference to the victors' locker room, spending an hour talking to key figures and even watching a star running back propose to his cheerleader girlfriend. Then Forde composed the story that follows, stylish and rich in detail and the excitement of the moment. "I believe I took two hours to write," he says, "but it might have been two and a half." Whatever the case, it still reached readers before the hasty efforts in newspapers across the country, a bittersweet note considering that Forde spent seventeen honorable years at the *Louisville Courier-Journal*. But there is no going back for him, only forward to his current stand as the national college columnist at Yahoo! Sports. Whether he knows it or not, he honors tradition every time he's the last writer out of the press box, the way he was at the Fiesta Bowl. Red Smith closed his share of press boxes, too.

Broncos Earn Respect With Improbable Victory

Glendale, Ariz., January 2, 2007

AT THE END OF A GAME unlike any college football has ever witnessed, two of the great female icons in American culture staged a harmonic, hypnotic, borderline hallucinogenic convergence.

Boise State introduced Cinderella to Lady Liberty.

A head-to-toe, shining-beacon-to-glass-slipper miracle ensued.

The Broncos culminated an unrivaled string of gusto-laden, do-or-die trick plays with one of the oldest in the book, the Statue of Liberty. And when Ian Johnson grabbed Jared Zabransky's behind-the-back handoff, scooted around the left side and scored two titanic points to beat lordly Oklahoma 43–42 in the Tostitos Fiesta Bowl, magic bloomed in the desert.

"It doesn't even seem real to me," Boise State offensive tackle Andrew Woodruff said, perplexedly rubbing his burr-headed scalp on the field while the Broncos fans roared in the stands.

Reality was further challenged when Johnson followed his winning run with an on-field wedding proposal to his flabbergasted cheerleader girlfriend. But, please, one blockbuster story at a time.

The big picture: The Valley of the Stun was the stage as an indomitable bunch of dreamers in orange pants landed the mightiest populist blow of college football's modern era. They were Hickory High in helmets, George Mason in cleats. They knocked off a gridiron giant one decade to the day after the burial of Pokey Allen, the beloved Boise coach who brought the program up to Division I-A status just 11 years ago.

The doors to the sport's throne room seem thrown open as never before.

Check the plaque at the lady's feet on Liberty Island this morning and see if the familiar sonnet has been changed. See if it now reads, "Give me your non-BCS teams tired of being disrespected, your poor of football budget, your huddled masses of mid-major strivers yearning to play in the grandest bowl games." And see if Lady Liberty is wearing a Boise State jersey today.

The Broncos entered their first Bowl Championship Series game undefeated but unloved in some elitist quarters. The Western Athletic Conference champions were made a steep underdog to the twice-beaten Sooners, and were suspected by some of fraudulence. They carried not just their own quest for nationwide credibility into this game, but the hopes and dreams of every alleged mid-major team that had been snubbed by a system of the rich, for the rich and by the rich.

Boise got its respect by beating the seven-time national champion Sooners in an overwrought overtime. But beyond the big picture was the delicious, utterly improbable manner in which the Broncos did it.

The method was true madness. And true genius. No coaching staff has ever ended a game with so much daring.

Out of conventional offensive options, first-year head coach Chris Petersen and first-year offensive coordinator Bryan Harsin went straight sandlot. They showed a career's worth of guts in calling one gadget play after another, rescuing Boise in a game it first had seemingly locked up, then had seemingly lost.

Asked if there could possibly be anything left in the playbook after this, the 30-year-old Harsin shook his head and smiled.

"No, no," he said. "We threw it all out right there."

They threw it out in the following order:

The last of the 21 points scored in the final 86 seconds of regulation came on a preposterous play: a 50-yard hook-and-lateral pass from Zabransky to Drisan James to Jerard Rabb—a combination that will be the Tinker to Evers to Chance of Boise State lore for the next century or so. Rabb crossed the goal line with all of seven seconds left to play, saving the Broncos from what seemed to be imminent defeat.

Boise practices the play every week in its final full practice before games.

"The guys love it," Petersen said. "We probably run it 10 times because they love it."

So it's a fun play to practice. Whether it's an effective play is another matter entirely.

"Can I say something?" interjected linebacker Korey Hall in the postgame press conference. "It doesn't work in practice usually."

Harsin confirmed this.

"It never works," he said. "Ever."

Pause. Another smile.

"Then we do it and it works."

Zabransky, who looked like he'd lost the game just a minute earlier with a brutal pick-six gift to Oklahoma cornerback Marcus Walker, fired a 15-yard pass to James. The wideout curled just a step or two toward the middle of the field before flipping a lateral to Rabb, who grabbed it and swiftly outflanked the Sooners secondary and sprinted the final 35 yards to the end zone.

It was as shocking a last-gasp play as anything but Cal's five-lateral slalom through the Stanford band. It might also have been the most daring last-gasp call (that worked) of all time.

But it was only the first in Boise State's trick play trifecta.

The next one came when the game was threatening to end with a violent anticlimax. On the first play of overtime, Oklahoma star back Adrian Peterson slashed off left tackle 25 yards for a stand-up touchdown. Suddenly the new life gained by the hook-and-lateral play was in danger of being extinguished.

A designed throwback from tailback Vinny Perretta to Zabransky was aborted on Boise's first play, as Perretta wisely ate the ball for no gain. Five plays later, the Broncos had crept to the Oklahoma 5-yard line, but faced a fourth-and-2.

Harsin went to the trick bag again. Zabransky went in motion to the left. Perretta, at quarterback, took the shotgun snap and rolled right, then lofted a lovely spiral toward the right corner of the end zone. Tight end Derek Schouman cradled it for the touchdown.

But that only made the score 42–41, which left Petersen with a decision: play for the tie or go all-in. Win or lose, in a single play.

Petersen left his kicker on the sideline. Oklahoma called timeout. Boise State's brain trust called the play: Statue Left.

When Zabransky called it in the huddle, confidence flowed.

"We just won this game," receiver Legedu Naanee announced.

"When he said Statue I thought, 'Ohhh, brother, we're going to do it in style,'" Johnson said.

Boise had run the play once before this season, against Idaho, and gained a first down on it. In a credit to Oklahoma's scouting, Sooners linebacker Rufus Alexander said they'd seen the play on tape and had prepared for it.

But they weren't quite prepared enough to stop Boise's perfect execution.

Zabransky took the snap and feigned a throw in the right flat to Boise's three-man bunch formation. As the Sooners flew in that direction, Zabransky calmly stuck the ball behind his back with his left hand—a twist on the conventional handoff he'd convinced Harsin would work earlier in the season.

Johnson then crisply reversed course, circled behind Zabransky and lifted the ball from his grasp. Virtually unimpeded by a bamboozled defense, the nation's touchdown leader crossed the goal line one final time in this dream season.

Bedlam, commingled with outright shock at the audacity of the call, ensued.

Johnson charged to the corner stands where his 56 family members were gathered. He jumped into their embrace, only to bring a banister falling down on him, cutting his leg. Pain was incidental at this moment, though. After hugging his father, the idiosyncratic star runner "started moseying over" to his girlfriend, Chrissy Popadics.

Johnson actually got the idea while attending the Insight Bowl at Sun Devil Stadium last week. One of the Fiesta Bowl committee members, Tyler Hanson, suggested to Johnson that he propose postgame.

"Maybe I will," Johnson told Hanson.

Still, he opted to leave the engagement ring at the team hotel. Just in case things didn't turn out well in the game.

"I didn't want to bring it and then always remember a loss," he said.

In the locker room after the game, Johnson embraced a beaming Hanson, thanking him for his inspiration. Here's the play-by-play from the proposal:

With a national audience watching at home, Johnson dropped on one knee ("I nearly slipped") and asked for her hand in marriage. The poor girl, already delirious over the game's dramatic end, spluttered out a breathless acceptance. Johnson had pulled his finest misdirection play yet.

"I had my hopes up [for an impending engagement], but that was it," Popadics said. "We had talked about it and he said, 'Not for a while.'"

Explained Johnson: "There's no better time than on national TV after the game-winning two-point conversion."

Minutes later, Oklahoma coach Bob Stoops classily jogged up a tunnel to congratulate Johnson. On the victory, I think. Not the proposal.

Johnson's teammates were surprised by No. 41's move. But not shocked.

"I came in with Ian freshman year, and he's a little different guy," safety Marty Tadman said—and when the heavily tattooed Tadman says you're a little different, you're a little different. "You've got to think of the weirdest circumstance he'd do that in, and this is probably it."

No bowl game has ever ended with circumstances this weird, piled improbably upon one another. When the final plot twist had played out and the final trickeration had worked, Boise State had beaten Oklahoma with a magical mix of determination and imagination.

Cinderella joined forces with Lady Liberty. The result was part fairy tale, part American Dream come true.

Michael Lewis

If you follow the money, you will almost certainly find Michael Lewis (b. 1960) there ahead of you. Raised to be a New Orleans gentleman and armed with a degree in art history from Princeton and a master's from the London School of Economics, he went to work for Salomon Brothers as a bond sales-man and ended up writing the best-selling *Liar's Poker* (1989), about greed that was excessive even for the rapacious financial industry. The book marked the beginning of a career in journalism that finds Lewis providing a measur-ing stick for monumental change. He captured the Internet boom in *The Next New Thing* (2000) and the 2008 market crash in *The Big Short* (2010), always managing to explain his subjects in a way that even those of us befuddled by balancing a checking account can understand and actually enjoy. The key to Lewis's success was convincing triumphant mavericks to open their lives for inspection. When he has turned his attention to sports, the characters have proven equally fascinating: a baseball visionary in *Moneyball* (2003), a poverty-bound football prodigy and the well-heeled family who changed his life in *The Blind Side* (2006). It was probably inevitable that Lewis would write about NFL placekickers, a breed apart from their teammates, some hav-ing minimal physical skills, others playing with bizarre handicaps, and most possessed of psyches that require more fine-tuning than European racecars. *The New York Times Play Magazine* turned Lewis loose for its October 28, 2007 issue, and wouldn't you know he tracked down one who *wasn't* bonkers.

The Kick Is Up and It's...
a Career Killer

MY FIRST EXPOSURE to the precarious social status of the profes-sional field-goal kicker came unexpectedly, at a game between the Detroit Lions and the New Orleans Saints on November 8, 1970. There were just two seconds left, and the Saints were losing, which wasn't unusual. The unusual thing was that the game was still close: 17–16. The Saints had the ball, and a field goal would win it—except the ball was in the *Saints'* half of the field, on the 43-yard line. And the record distance the ball would have to travel—63 yards—was only the first of the kicker's problems. He was kicking from a dirt surface churned up like a World War I battlefield. The ball would need to cut through the thick, humid New Orleans air and into the closed end of

Tulane Stadium, where the wind swirled unpredictably. On top of all that, the kicker lacked the most basic requirement for his job: a foot.

His name was Tom Dempsey, and he was born without fingers on his right hand or toes on his right foot. The gnarled stub of his arm jutted from his jersey with an effect, to my 9-year-old mind, so grotesque that even from a great distance my first instinct was to look away. The foot, however, wasn't repellent—less a malformed appendage than the business end of a useful tool. Other professional football teams had kickers. We had a sledgehammer, or the head of a 1-wood, attached to the end of a 260-pound cripple.

Stump! Stump! Stump!

From this distance, the chant that usually accompanied Dempsey's field-goal attempts sounds like an entire stadium full of Americans having fun at the expense of the handicapped. But nobody thought of it that way. Even one of Dempsey's coaches called him Stumpy, and he claimed not to mind in the slightest.

Stump! Stump! Stump!

But on this afternoon in 1970 there was hardly a peep. The bleachers were empty. The Saints had been around for only three years, but already their fans expected them to lose. They still showed up in huge numbers, full of enthusiasm, and hollered at the top of their lungs right till the moment when they saw, once again, that the cause was lost, whereupon they fled. Just a few hours earlier, Tulane Stadium held more than 60,000 supposedly committed fanatics, but as the Saints called a timeout and Dempsey trotted onto the field, I could have thrown a baseball in any direction from our seats under the overhang at the 40-yard line and hit no one but my father and his pal Charles, with whom we went to every Saints home game. Charles's beak-like face— he suffered from anorexia nervosa—was never anything but grim; he seldom actually cheered. Entire sections below us had been vacated, so my father and Charles allowed me to pull us a few rows down, to what struck me as better seats. Along the way, Charles insisted, with total certainty, that Tom Dempsey had no chance of making a 63-yard field goal. He tried, and failed, to distract my father with some boring business topic. Like me, my dad harbored a secret hope.

We weren't the only ones moving closer to the action: everyone who hadn't left was rapidly upgrading to a better view. Somewhere in the stadium another boy about my age, Mike Whitsell, was sitting with his father, Dave, who, as it happened, used to play for the Saints. His dad retired at the end of the 1969 season, and in his final year he was Tom Dempsey's holder. When he saw Dempsey walking onto the field to attempt a 63-yard field goal, he turned to his son and said: "Stumpy can make this! I've seen him make this in practice!" Then he hopped out of his seat and down the rows of benches and over the short fence onto the field—where he raced to a spot right behind the refs at the goal posts. Mike knew his dad adored Dempsey, with reason. When they had him over to the house once, Mike's little brother, age 3, stared for about three seconds at Dempsey's truncated hand and foot, before asking, in a loud voice, "What happened to your feet and your hands?" Dempsey pulled him up onto his lap and said: "Well, when I was standing in line in heaven to get hands and feet, I was last in line. And by the time I got to the front they only had one and a half pairs left." The little boy, completely satisfied with the explanation, said, "O.K.!" and ran off and jumped into the swimming pool.

Now Dave Whitsell was running out to be a part of one last kick by Tom Dempsey. The ball was snapped, Dempsey took his steps and his stump collided with the ball. To me, from my place in the stands, which was closer to the field than I had ever been, the longest field goal ever kicked in the National Football League looked like a wobbly line drive. But just as Mike Whitsell saw his dad hollering at the refs to get their arms up because the kick was good, I heard my father shout:

"Holy shit!"

It was the first time I ever heard my father swear.

The kick, fluttering its way just over the crossbar, was easily the most exciting thing that had ever happened to the Saints, and it would remain the most exciting thing that happened to the Saints for the next three decades. Tom Dempsey had performed a miracle.

And yet what should have been a simple story of football heroism quickly became something else. Immediately, football authorities outside New Orleans, led by Tex Schramm, the president and general manager of the Dallas Cowboys, complained publicly and loudly that Tom Dempsey had cheated: his misshapen foot, in effect, offered him an unfair advantage. A rumor spread that he had fitted his shoe with a steel plate. The most famous player on the Detroit Lions, Alex Karras, was quoted saying that the whole situation was so preposterous he didn't even bother to rush the kicker. The classic playground defense: *He didn't beat us—we didn't try.* The longest field goal ever made in pro football wasn't heroic; it was more like a circus stunt. Even in New Orleans, where you might have thought the kicker would be nothing but feted, a joke circulated at his expense: *Tom Dempsey: made it by half a foot; let's give him a hand.*

From this experience there are several lessons to be drawn. First, you should never leave any game before it's over, because you never know what's going to happen. Second, grown-ups watching sports say a lot of stuff with total certainty when they really don't know what they're talking about. And finally, it is extremely difficult for a field-goal kicker to be a hero. He can perform a miracle, but the world will always find some way to shove him back in his place.

It was this last lesson that I carried with me when I went to Indianapolis to spend time with the kicker for the Colts, Adam Vinatieri. In the 37 years since Tom Dempsey's miraculous field goal, kickers had become more and more accurate. They are thought—possibly wrongly, but nevertheless people say so—to be more and more important to the fate of their teams. Like other professional football players, they quickly become millionaires, though at an average salary of $1.5 million a year they remain among the lowest-paid regulars on the field, after punters. And yet their general social standing has, if anything, declined.

Item: Scott Norwood. At the end of Super Bowl XXV, in 1991, Norwood, who up to that moment has enjoyed a wonderful six-year career, misses a 47-yard field goal for the Buffalo Bills. The Bills lose to the New York Giants, 20–19. Norwood retires after one more season and eventually becomes a real estate agent who spends part of his day selling houses and another part avoiding phone calls from sports journalists seeking either to mine his tragedy for pathos or to get even with him on behalf of the city of Buffalo. A decade after his missed kick, he tells a reporter that he dreads the weeks leading up to the Super Bowl, when his failure is invariably revisited on national television. "A great, great, great kicker was Scott Norwood," Jason Elam, the kicker for the Denver Broncos, says. "And he'll only be remembered for the one that he missed." It's the first of many reminders of the terms of trade between NFL field-goal kickers and everyone else. "People are quick to blame the kicker," an executive with a National Football Conference team says. "If he makes the kick, the coach made a good decision. If he missed the kick, it's his fault. There's virtually no upside, because every kick you're expected to make."

Item: Gary Anderson. In 1998, Anderson, with the Minnesota Vikings, completes the first perfect regular season in NFL kicking history. He attempts 59 extra points and 35 field goals and, incredibly, makes them all. His excellence extends into the postseason, when he drills eight extra points and his first four field goals. But then, in the closing minutes of the NFC Championship game against the Atlanta Falcons, he misses a 38-yard field goal by inches that would have put the Vikings ahead by 10 points and effectively ended the game. The Falcons get the ball back, score a touchdown and go on to win in overtime. The missed kick winds up being not only the single kick that anyone remembers from a great season, but also the one that most football fans remember from Gary Anderson's 22-year career. The man spends 600 million seconds kicking brilliantly in the NFL and winds up being defined by a couple seconds of catastrophe.

Item: Mike Vanderjagt. In 2003, Vanderjagt, of the Indianapolis Colts, becomes the only placekicker ever to follow a perfect regular season with a perfect postseason. (By this point he has already acquired what for a kicker—and only for a kicker—seem to be unseemly airs. After the previous season, on a Canadian cable sports channel, he dares to express faint doubts about the Colts' quarterback, Peyton Manning. Manning responds with ruthless efficiency, calling Vanderjagt "our idiot kicker who got liquored up and ran his mouth off.") By the end of 2005, eight years into his career, Vanderjagt has established himself as the most accurate field-goal kicker in the history of the NFL—a distinction he still holds—by making an astonishing 88 percent of his attempts. Then, late in a 2006 playoff game against the Pittsburgh Steelers, he lines up a 46-yard field goal that could tie the game and send it into overtime. Before the kick, according to Football Outsiders, the best website for football statistics, Vanderjagt made 12 of the 15 kicks that either tied or won a game in its last minute (or in overtime)—a success rate well above the NFL average. Afterward, he is 12 for 16. And he doesn't merely miss; he misses so badly that it is easy to assume total psychological collapse. "It wasn't a Scott Norwood deal where you wondered if he might make it," a member of the Colts' staff tells me. "You knew it was wrong."

Of course it was wrong. This is what kickers do to define themselves: choke under pressure. After the Cowboys acquire Vanderjagt the next season to solve their own kicking problems, their coach, Bill Parcells, makes it clear from the start that he considers him damaged goods. He wonders out loud if anyone could ever recover his manhood after missing such a kick. No one asks whether this is the best way to encourage a kicker's performance; no one wonders if it is perhaps even a bit cruel. Even before the season ends, Vanderjagt has himself a new life story: less than a year after being hailed as the most accurate kicker ever to play the game, and being regarded as an extremely valuable commodity, he is working out by himself on an island off the coast of Florida, wondering if a team might offer him a job. "Next to the quarterback, a coach's confidence wavers so much with who the kicker is," the executive with the NFC team says. "If a linebacker or a running back or a wide receiver has a bad game it's 'Keep him in there. He'll be fine.' If a coach loses just a little bit of confidence in a kicker, you're making a change."

There are many, many more examples of perverse treatment of professional kickers: kickers brought into camp with high expectations and cut after their first NFL game (Justin Medlock, with the Kansas City Chiefs earlier this year), kickers whose exalted reputation collapsed after a single high-profile bad kick in a not terribly meaningful game (Neil Rackers of the Arizona Cardinals on *Monday Night Football* last season against the Chicago Bears) and too many kickers to name who have been quickly dismissed as inherently weak-minded. A kicker in the NFL can be one of two things: the bland technocrat who does what he's assigned to do but who, even when he's exceptionally good, must accept that the coach and the team will be credited for the victory. Or he can be the little choke artist who is very nearly entirely responsible for the loss. For a kicker in the NFL, as the NFC executive put it, there is no upside.

Which brings me to the reason I sought out Adam Vinatieri: he is the exception. Obviously many kickers managed to get to the end of their careers as something other than a goat. But no one else has used the position to become a hero. Vinatieri discovered the upside.

He's the highest-paid kicker in the game, making $2.4 million a year, but he's much more than that. He has kicked his way through some kind of glass ceiling; he has shattered the emotional barrier between football hero and kicker. He's like the first woman in outer space, or the first black man on Wall Street.

In the fourth game of the 2007 season, at home against Denver, Adam Vinatieri started the game by kicking off. He then trailed his team-mates down the field by 15 yards and failed to make contact with anyone. After the kickoff, he ran to the sideline, removed his helmet and found his big practice net. He dragged it, along with five footballs and a ball holder made of white metal, to his favorite spot, alongside the 30-yard line. The whole procedure took three minutes, and while the game raged on he looked less like a player than a man staking out his campsite. Once he was finished, he strolled a few yards to chat with his holder, Hunter Smith. Then he went looking for his baseball cap, which he donned. Then he walked a few yards more and blew several big pink bubbles. A football game, even for an ordinary player, is mostly a lot of waiting around. For a kicker it is virtually nothing but waiting around. "I'm on the field at most about 60 seconds," he says. "I've got to figure out what to do with the rest of the time." When he was younger he simply kicked the ball into the net throughout the entire game, but he's now 34 years old, and his muscles ache if he kicks too much.

Nearly four minutes had elapsed from the game clock when the Colts' offense took the field for the first time. Seeing this, Vinatieri persuaded the TV crew to remove the coiled wire it dumped on his campsite while he was chatting with Smith. As a matter of principle, he substituted his helmet for his baseball cap. "A lot of guys practice in their baseball caps," he says. "For me, whenever I'm working, I put my helmet on." Helmeted, he kicked five balls into the net and then had a drink. But the Colts were stopped, and forced to punt, so his prepara-tion was for naught. Seven minutes of game time had now passed—and roughly 30 minutes of real time—and he could have spent them more usefully reading a book. "It's a real problem," he says. "Once, with New England"—where he was the Patriots' kicker—"I kicked off to start the game and never set foot on the field again."

Hunter Smith and Justin Snow, the long snapper, returned from punting, and Vinatieri joined them on the bench, as far away from the rest of the team as they could be while still remaining within the area designated for players. If Vinatieri stands, his back can tighten up, so instead he sat and watched the game on the JumboTron. When the Colts got the ball back, he would repeat his routine—though not exactly. He insists he's not superstitious, but that's not quite true: he's superstitious about superstition. Every now and then he'll notice, after making a big kick, that he was wearing a certain pair of socks. He'll make sure not to wear the same socks the next time out. "I never want to feel like I have a crutch," he says. Superstition is mental weakness. And mental weakness leads to choking. And choking leads to ... well, it would be a sign of weakness to even think about what it leads to.

On this night, nothing led to anything. The Colts won easily, 38–20, and Vinatieri was called upon only to make five extra points and one meaningless field goal, then kick the ball back to the Broncos. We agreed to meet the next day in the Colts' training facility.

The Indianapolis Colts' locker room is a giant rectangle lined with cubbies and teeming with large, thick-necked men. Big as it is, it fails to hold the entire team. Off the main room, on the other side of a wall, is a row of three more lockers, those of Vinatieri, Hunter Smith and Justin Snow. Over the wall is Mordor; here, in the shire, is where the halflings live. Their lockers are made of the same blond wood, but they are more likely to exhibit signs of a life outside football: pictures of the wife and kids, books. Vinatieri's locker holds several Costco-size boxes of Dentyne Blast, five T-shirts on hangers, a vat of multi-vitamins and two books: *Secrets of the Millionaire Mind* and a Christian work called *Wild at Heart*. NFL people will tell you that field-goal kickers tend to take God seriously.

One funny thing about football players is how different they look in their uniforms. When he's in his helmet and pads and the camera is on, Vinatieri is so transformed that I cannot recall his face. In street clothes he might pass for an actor or a lawyer or maybe even a high school history teacher who still jogs every day around the school track. He is willing to talk about himself and his achievements—the two kicks that won Super Bowls, the improbable 45-yard field goal against the Oakland Raiders in a driving blizzard that sent the Patriots into overtime (and victory, and into the AFC Championship game)—but it's pretty clearly not his favorite thing to do. He is tactically modest and instinctively honest, and he has thought too much about what he does, and how, for his modesty to be anything but false. So he is often torn between his instinct to speak the truth and his wish not to brag. More so than most football players, he starts sentences about himself with "I don't want to say this" and "Don't quote me on this, but—"

Over several weeks of pestering, however, I eventually get from him what I take to be an honest interpretation of his career. In his view, he is no better, physically, than a lot of other kickers both in and out of the NFL. Every year for the past 12 seasons he has found himself in a training camp with a handful of kickers, many of whom have stronger legs than he does. What sets him apart, he is certain, is his character, though he never uses that word. A combination of innate traits and learned skills has rendered him extremely well suited to handle the pressure of the position. "Kicking at this level," he says more than once, "is all about how you handle pressure. We're on an island; everyone is watching us. It's not like some play where only the coaches who can see the film can tell who screwed up. The difference between kickers is, can you do it when the lights are on?"

Ask NFL players and coaches what role in sports is most like being a field-goal kicker and they usually mention golf. That's a fair description of the job—long periods of waiting around punctuated by short, precise swings at a ball—but it doesn't begin to capture its social dimension. When a golfer fails, he fails no one but himself. He doesn't expect to be ridiculed, or to be forced to move to some distant rural place, with an unlisted phone number. Vinatieri suggests a better analogy: the baseball closer. But this is still not quite right: the closer who fails has a chance to redeem himself early and often, doing well tomorrow precisely what he failed to do today. If he has some psychological defect that prevents him from doing the job at all, he isn't drummed out of his profession. He's merely moved to another job in the bullpen. "No one has more pressure on him than a kicker," Vinatieri says, and it's hard to disagree.

Still, I confess my doubts to him. Fans wish to believe that, whatever the sport, a handful of professional athletes respond extraordinarily well under pressure. In baseball, for instance, fans insist on believing that there is such a thing as a great clutch hitter. And while it is impossible to prove that clutch hitting does not exist, it is easy to show that if it exists it is hard to find. There is no evidence in the statistics. The player most commonly cited as a clutch hitter, Derek Jeter, hits just as well in low-stakes situations as he does in high-stakes ones; or, to put it the other way, he hits just as poorly in putatively high-pressure situations as he does in low-pressure ones. A better explanation for clutch hitting is the fan's tendency to superimpose his own weaknesses upon the players. Fanthropomorphism. It's true that many people wilt under pressure; those people never make it to the major leagues. It seems at least plausible that any kicker who collapses under pressure would have been weeded out long before he ever got to the National Football League.

"I think that's 90 percent true and 10 percent false," Vinatieri says. He's not upset that I've suggested he couldn't possibly be special. He's not even irritated. He's just saying exactly what he thinks.

"What's the 10 percent that's false?" I ask.

"Guys fail to control their heart rates," he says. "They hurry. You see a guy moving a little fast. I don't want to say there's two types of people. But I think there are. There are people who like to be in these situations and people who don't. Kickers come into camp every year and you say, 'Jeez, this kid, he's better than me.' Then he gets on the field and the coaches are watching. They may have a nice leg, but they're inconsistent."

If you want others to believe that you are good under pressure, you must first persuade yourself, and obviously he has. But what's odd about Vinatieri's narrative of his career is that he had no evidence for this special talent until he got to the pros. In college, at South Dakota State, he made only slightly more than half of his field-goal attempts, and he missed game winners. Of being good in the clutch, he admits, "I think I might have thought that way about myself, but my stats didn't show it in college." His ability to rise to every occasion failed to manifest itself until 1996, when, as a kicker in the World League of American Football, he received an invitation to training camp from the New England Patriots, then coached by Bill Parcells, the nemesis of field-goal kickers everywhere. "You want to talk about pressure," Vinatieri says. "Every single day of that training camp was about creating pressure for me to respond to. I'd go to kick and Parcells would be doing the ground whammy." That is, Parcells would find the exact spot Vinatieri had groomed for his kick and walk back and forth across it. Then he'd say, casually, "Oh, were you setting up here?" Just before every kick, Parcells positioned himself between the sun and the ball, to throw a shadow over the proceedings.

Vinatieri was signed as a kickoff specialist, but before the third game of the preseason Parcells took Vinatieri aside and said, "I want to see if you got what it takes, or you pack up your [expletive] and go home." That game, he made three field goals, and afterward the team released the veteran kicker Matt Bahr. In the first game of the regular season, in Miami, Vinatieri made one field goal; the next week, against Buffalo, he missed three out of four field-goal attempts in a 17–10 loss. The third week, he missed an extra point. ("At this point he's screaming his brains off at me," Vinatieri says of his coach.) Parcells told the press: "Kicking is a results-oriented business."

The next week, against Jacksonville, he made five field goals, including a game winner. But as far as Vinatieri is concerned, what set him on his path, what showed that he might be different from other kickers, happened at the end of the season, against the Dallas Cowboys. The Patriots were up, 6–0, with less than six minutes left in the first quarter. Vinatieri kicked off. Herschel Walker took the ball, found a seam and bolted down the sidelines. He got all the way down inside the 30-yard line and looked like he was going to score when Vinatieri nabbed him from behind. He didn't shove him out of bounds, either, or get lucky with the old wussy-kicker try; he tackled him hard to the ground. In high school, Vinatieri was a linebacker, and it showed. Right through the slow-motion replay the announcers remained incredulous.

"Vinatieri didn't even have an angle!" Marv Albert shouted.

"The kicker ran him down, Marv!" the color man hollered. "Closing speed! I never thought I'd use that word for a kicker!"

After the game, Parcells sought out Vinatieri in the locker room. "He says to me: 'You're more than a field-goal kicker to this team now. You'll see—the way the guys will treat you will be different now.' And he was right. All of a sudden I wasn't that snot-nose kicker who no one wanted to talk to."

Thus the first step in the rise of this kicker: he proved he could run and hit just like a real football player. He was not an ordinary hobbit. He was Frodo Baggins.

In an office at the Colts' training facility, Vinatieri explained what he actually does for a living. (It isn't tackling: "Ideally, at the end of the year I have zero tackles," he said.) He marked the spot on the carpet, one inch by one inch, then took two deliberate steps back, then two to the side. In a game, he never takes his eyes off that spot. He doesn't watch the center, he said; he watches Hunter Smith, his holder. "His finger is on the spot. When his hand comes up, it's the key to move." The skill of the holder and the long snapper is one reason he chose to come to Indianapolis—as opposed to, say, joining Bill Parcells in Dallas. Dallas was having trouble with its kickers—Vinatieri suspected that this indicated problems with the process. Indianapolis, on the other hand, was a field-goal-kicking machine. "Look, Mike was making 88 percent of his kicks," Vinatieri said, referring to Vanderjagt. "He's a very good kicker. But he's not doing that if they have a crappy holder and snapper."

It was the first hint that anyone but Vinatieri himself should be held responsible for his failure—and that he needs to surround himself with the right people in order to succeed—but when I tried to follow this admission to its logical conclusion, he cut me off. "Don't even ask," he said. "If I miss a kick, it's always my fault. You're never going to get me to say anything else." He resumed the instruction. "The bottom line," he said, "is getting your feet shoulder width." His plant foot, the one that doesn't kick the ball, provides the aim. "It should be aimed in the middle of the upright," he said. "It's like a good golf swing—most of the time you're lined right, you'll hit it in the right spot."

After he gets the position right, most of what Vinatieri thinks about is what he shouldn't do. He shouldn't entertain any thoughts of failure, up to and including the possibly liberating thought that, on a very long kick, no one will blame him for a miss. He shouldn't swing his arms. He shouldn't allow his body to rock back and forth: he starts with his weight forward so his body is stuck in place. "I try to get rid of all the external factors, and keep it as simple as I can," he said. He sees Hunter Smith's hands shift and he moves: step, step, kick. Even after the kick, he keeps his eye on the spot. "Let the crowd tell you it's good," he said. "But most of the time you know if it's good when you hit it."

From snap to kick is a shockingly brief moment. "The goal," he said, "is to be between 1.3 and 1.5 seconds." He's never slow, but every so often he finds himself working too quickly. In practice, a few days ago, he felt it and looked at his holder, Hunter Smith, and said, "That was a little quick." The stopwatch had them at 1.25 seconds.

Theoretically, Vinatieri hits every kick exactly the same way. An extra point in a preseason game is to be treated no differently from a 45-yard field goal to win the Super Bowl. He didn't put it quite this way to me—he wouldn't like the way it sounds, I suspect—but everything he does is designed to eliminate himself from the kick. He controls his body out of a suspicion that he cannot control his mind. In his approach to his job, he is not merely making it as unlikely as possible that he will choke, but also as unlikely as possible that he will be forced to view himself as having choked. (How can you choke when you never change what you do?) The end result is a near-perfect self-certainty, which in turn reassures himself, his fans, his teammates and his coaches—to a greater degree than that of any field-goal kicker in National Football League history.

But what evidence, apart from his three famous field goals, does Vinatieri have that he is actually right about himself? He doesn't pay very close attention to his statistics, he says, and I believe him, because he isn't the sort of person who lies. (Though he does, on occasion, decline to tell the truth.) "I know approximately what they are," he told me, "but they're in the past, so they really don't matter." Since he doesn't know, I asked him to guess: of his clutch field-goal attempts, how many has he made?

"I saw an article somewhere where it said I had made 19 of them," he said.

But how many had he missed?

"I know I boinked one against Kansas City," he said. "In 2003, I think.... So 19 out of 20, or maybe 21."

The actual number is 20 out of 25 with the game on the line and a minute or less on the clock (or in overtime). Adam Vinatieri, in other words, is about as likely to make a clutch kick as he is to make an ordinary kick. And he is not all that more likely to make the clutch kick than the ordinarily good NFL kicker. There are virtual unknowns who have a better clutch record: former Bears kicker Paul Edinger went 9 for 9, for instance. There are kickers famous for choking who were roughly as accurate in clutch situations as Vinatieri. (See Mike Vanderjagt.) As Aaron Schatz at Football Outsiders, who calculated the figures for me, says: "The sample sizes are too small to make a lot out of them. It's not really an analysis of clutch ability as it is an analysis of clutch history. And what separates Vinatieri is that he has almost half again as many attempts as any other kicker. That, and his clutch kicks are so memorable."

In judging Adam Vinatieri as the greatest clutch kicker of all time— and thus exempting him from the scorn and suspicion heaped upon his breed—football culture misses what's most extraordinary about him: not his ability to kick under pressure, but his talent for coping with the crazy world that kickers inhabit. He pretends to accept the lie that he bears complete responsibility for what happens to his kicks while shrewdly letting it be known that those around him can mess things up; he arranges his kicking routine to prevent his mind from playing any role at all; he even genuinely forgets the clutch kicks that he has missed. Adam Vinatieri is obviously a gifted kicker, but he's even more talented at adapting to his environment. Still, he remains at risk. He has made two kicks that won Super Bowls and a third—the so-called Kick in the Snow, a 45-yarder against the Oakland Raiders, which sent the game into overtime—that is perhaps the most legendary of all. ("I still laugh about that kick because it was such a low-percentage kick," he said. "My main thought was 'Don't fall down.'") On these three kicks—a few seconds of playing time—rests the reputation of the most famous clutch field-goal kicker in pro football history. If he misses even one of them, he becomes just another kicker; if he misses all three, he ends up taking early retirement, perhaps envying Scott Norwood for how well football treated him.

Of course, he didn't miss them. He has been spared. And while he seems like the sort of person with the strength of mind to preserve his sense of self no matter what others think, he nonetheless lives in perpetual danger of having his character reappraised in light of the last big kick. When asked how he imagines his career will end, he couldn't find the answer. "That's a hard thing to think about," he said. My NFC executive, who happens to think the world of Vinatieri, says: "Adam Vinatieri's career isn't going to be over until somebody loses confidence in him. And the only way someone is going to lose confidence in him is if he misses a clutch field goal." The only question is: what happens then? Will his miss be forgotten in time, or will it be the sort of kick—say, a chip shot to lose the Super Bowl—that causes everyone to rethink his miracle kick in the snow? In theory, they can never take away from him those kicks he made. But, in practice, they do.

His game against Denver was accident-free. But the game just two weeks before that, against Tennessee, offered an example of just how effortlessly the perception of Adam Vinatieri might change. His first extra-point attempt was blocked. He made his first three field-goal attempts, but the third came out a bit low and, once again, a Tennessee player got a hand on it. "All of a sudden I'm thinking too much," he said. "I'm thinking, 'You got to go a little faster.'" He went a little faster—and missed an easy 36-yard field-goal attempt that would have put the game pretty well out of reach. "You get a field goal or an extra point and somebody gets a hand on it, it gets in your head," the color commentator Dan Dierdorf told millions of television viewers. "Even if that head is on Adam Vinatieri's shoulders." The camera zoomed in on Vinatieri as he walked off the field, wearing the dazed expression of the loser. "I wish I could have that one back," he says now. "It left my foot and I thought, 'Oh, give it back to me.'"

Meghan Crosby tends bar in a New Orleans restaurant called Zeke's, and on one of its walls there is a shrine to the kick her father made 37 years ago. Between framed football jerseys is a black-and-white photograph of the split second after the ball has left his foot. Apart from Dempsey and his holder, Joe Scarpati, it shows a grimacing member of the Detroit Lions, Alex Karras, stretching and diving to block the kick. He doesn't look like he's not trying.

Her father joined me for lunch at Zeke's recently. His hair has gone grey, but apart from that he didn't look much different from his photo in the old Saints program. As he talked over lunch, he hid his hand in various ways—behind a napkin, under the table. But his foot he talked about easily and without prompting. As he warmed to his subject—the Kick—he recalled that under orders from Pete Rozelle, then the commissioner, Tex Schramm phoned him to apologize for saying he had an unfair advantage. "But he didn't really apologize," Dempsey said. "He still thought I had an unfair advantage. I guess if not having any toes is an unfair advantage, I have an advantage." Then there was the matter of the shoe. "Everyone said I had steel in it," he said. "But they X-rayed it. It was just a thin piece of leather." He thought his shoe—created at the insistence of the former San Diego Chargers coach Sid Gillman, for whom Dempsey tried out—may have helped his accuracy but had no effect on his distance. He knew he had that sort of distance the first time he kicked a football, at Palomar College, in Southern California. His coach decided that his current kicker didn't have enough leg to kick off, so he asked everyone on the team to line up and kick a ball off a tee as far as he could. Dempsey didn't think he'd have sufficient control of his shoe, so he took it off and, with his bare foot, kicked the ball out of the end zone. Thus began his career.

His father had consciously raised him to live a useful lie: that it didn't matter one bit that he lacked a hand and a foot. Dempsey suspects that he was born right-handed, but he's not really sure, because his right hand was never usable. He taught himself how to throw left-handed, and even played baseball. But his body was better suited to football, and much of what he did to play it—lifting weights, for example—built great strength in his legs. That strength paid off the year he became Palomar's field-goal kicker and, in his stocking feet, nailed a 65-yarder against Compton City College. At least he thought he nailed it; the refs called it wide. ("Their excuse was it was too high for them to see," he said.) But the Compton City College coach thought it was good, too, and wrote a letter to Vince Lombardi, the coach of the Green Bay Packers, saying he had seen this kid with no foot make a 65-yard field goal. Sight unseen, Lombardi hired Tom Dempsey and put him on a farm team. After a brief time with the taxi squad in San Diego, Dempsey found himself playing for the Saints. That same year, at the end of a game against the Detroit Lions, and with the ball a long way from the goal posts, he overheard his offensive coordinator say, "Tell Stumpy to get ready." And improbable as it seemed to everyone else, he trotted out onto the field without too much concern about the distance.

Thirty-seven years later, a great deal has obviously changed. It's considered bad form even in the bleachers to jeer at physical deformities. (They now mock what they take to be deformities of spirit or character.) Dave Whitsell is dead, as is my father's friend Charles. Tulane Stadium has been razed, and the spot from which Tom Dempsey launched his field goal is a grassy patch below sea level.

And yet some things haven't changed. Tom Dempsey's record stands, for instance. In 37 years it has been tied—by Jason Elam of the Denver Broncos, who was kicking a mile above sea level—but never broken. Field-goal kickers are still defined by the tiniest sliver of their professional career. "I made a lot of big kicks, but all anyone wants to talk about is that one," Dempsey said. And, finally, there is still some faint resistance to the notion that a kicker could ever really do anything great. Brett Favre can throw 10 more game-ending interceptions and fans will still cherish his moments of glory. Reggie Bush may fumble away a championship and still end up being known for the best things he ever does. Even offensive linemen whose names no one remembers are permitted to end their days basking in the reflected glory of having been on the field. Kickers alone are required to make their own cases.

Every so often someone still comes up to Tom Dempsey to put his achievement into perspective. Not long ago, a total stranger approached him wanting to talk about the Kick. "And he said to me," Dempsey recalled, " 'You're really nothing but a one-kick kicker.' And I thought: 'Yeah, but I kicked it once. What the hell did you do?' "

Jeanne Marie Laskas

Unquestionably, the most surprising sentence in this book is: *"I CANNOT FIND MY MULTIPLICITY ESCALATE VOLUME WHIP!"* It also seems safe to say the writer who quotes the cheerleader in that dire situation once would have been this book's most surprising contributor. Jeanne Marie Laskas (b. 1958), director of the Writing Program at the University of Pittsburgh, has spent a goodly portion of her time away from academe doling out advice in *The Washington Post Magazine*, *Reader's Digest*, and *Ladies' Home Journal*. She made her way into more serious realms on the strength of her wit, compassion, and novelist's eye for detail. The author of six books, most recently *Hidden America* (2012), Laskas has graced *GQ, Esquire, Smithsonian Magazine*, and *The New York Times Magazine* with stories about coal miners, migrant workers, hit men, and, much to her surprise, sports. Although she confesses she "knows nothing about any sport in America," she says "sports stories, to me, are just character studies. It's almost better if you're naive, sometimes." Laskas has written memorably about concussions in the NFL, and, as you will discover in this January 2008 *GQ* feature, she took off and flew when her subject was the Cincinnati Bengals' cheerleaders, in whom she found engaging young women alive with hopes and humor and vulnerability. Readers, male and female alike, will wish they'd been there to help find the missing hair gel.

G-L-O-R-Y!

RIGHT NOW ADRIENNE MIGHT BE SICK. It isn't funny. It isn't her stomach so much as her nerves, her heart, her history. Rhoneé, one of her closest cheerleader friends, has her eyes bugged out, standing outside the stall door, *"Adrienne? Adrienne, are you okay?"*

"I'm good," Adrienne is saying. "No, I'm good. I'm good."

She vomits. This is not good. Something is seriously wrong with Adrienne. At pregame practice in the gym an hour ago, she ran off crying—twice. Ran to the bathroom and slammed her fist into the stall door to get ahold of herself, to reclaim herself, to remember who she is: a Ben-Gal. Both times she returned to the gym with a smile, got in formation, front row, left center. "C-I-N!" she roared, "C-I-N! N-A-T-I! LET'S GO!"

She seemed *fine*. She seemed *Adrienne* again, five feet nine, a thoroughbred of a woman, broad shoulders, booming voice, the biceps and forearms of a sailor. She is not the drama queen of the squad, not even close, not one of the girlie-girls, with the super-yummy cleavages and the wee, wee waists and the sugary smiles. She is the iron-willed, no-nonsense, no-curls straight shooter of the squad—six-pack abs, forlorn eyes, too busy with her own too busy life to deal with a lot of crap.

"Is Adrienne okay?" shouts Shannon from the other end of the locker room. Shannon is perhaps best known for her extreme volume of sandy blond hair.

"What happened?" asks Shannon's very best friend and protégée, the demure Sarah.

"Is something wrong?" asks another, as news of Adrienne's nausea filters through the din of cheerleader chatter.

Cheerleaders are all over the place, half-naked, shrieking, sitting, squatting, kneeling in front of mirrors in the panic of an NFL Thursday night. National television! The game starts in just over an hour. This is crunch time, hair-spray time, false-eyelash time, Revlon-Orange-Flip-lipstick time. *"WOULD SOMEBODY PLEASE HELP ME? I CANNOT FIND MY MULTIPLICITY ESCALATE VOLUME WHIP!"* Some cheerleaders are in curlers the size of Budweiser cans. The locker room, reserved just for them, is hardly equipped for the machinery of glamour, and so most have brought their own full-length mirrors, power strips, extension cords, suitcases of makeup, curling irons, hose. *"Try my Bouncy Spray Curl Activator. You can totally glop it on."* The cheerleaders are all scream and shout, jazzed with beauty adrenaline, in thongs and hose and push-up bras, stretching, bopping, bouncing, assisting one another with hair extensions, pasting over tattoos, spraying tans, announcing newly discovered cleavage-engineering solutions—"Duct tape, girls!"—hooting and hollering in a primpfest worthy of Miss Universe.

"We look so awesome."

"Oh, my God, we do!"

Perhaps fittingly, there is a big storm coming, right now a cold front dumping rain and snow on Chicago, moving swiftly east, headed exactly for Cincinnati, promising to turn a balmy sixty-eight-degree evening into instant winter in a way that no one anywhere near Paul Brown Stadium is prepared to believe. *Maybe the storm will be late? Maybe it will get . . . delayed?* Charlotte, the mother superior of the Ben-Gals, the one responsible for all the rules—all the line formations, all the dances, all the praise, all the punishments, all the outfits—has to make a difficult decision: teeny-weeny skirts with white go-go boots and halter tops, or catsuits that hardly provide any better winter cover. The gals vote: catsuits. *"Please! Please! Please!"* They love the catsuits. There is nothing sexier than the catsuits.

"Is Adrienne *okay?*"

"Did you hear she is throwing up?"

"Oh, my God!"

Now, the men. The men are just super. Oh, the men think this whole thing is about them. That is so cute. That is enough to make any Ben-Gal roll her head to one side and get teary with admiration. *That is so sweet!*

Hello, men. Meet the cheerleaders. There are a lot of them. At first they are hard to tell apart in the same way kittens playing with a ball of yarn in a basket are hard to tell apart. Every single one of them you want to pick up and stroke and pinch and poke and take home. How can you *choose?* And what if you did take one home? Think it through. Where would you put the cheerleader? What would you feed it? Would you have time to play with it? Play with it in the way it longs to be played with? Yeah, that is one luscious volume of girl flesh.

The cheerleader is a fantasy. Let it go.

It. The cheerleader is an it. Are you aware that you have been thinking of this person as an *it?* Does that make you a pig? Nah. Or no more so than the next person, but that's not even the point. This is about the cheerleader. She is not trying to get your attention so much as she knows she has it. God, you're easy. You are not the real reason she has been up since five working on her hair, spraying on her tan, squishing her breasts together and forcing them upward into a double-mushroom formation with the assistance of all manner of wired undergarments. Of course, you play a role in it. Of course. When you catch a glimpse. For barely a second on the TV. There on the sideline. Right after some blitz resulting in a crushing sack. She's there for you. Sharing your moment of glee. Bouncing up and down for you with her pom-poms, beckoning you to, yeah, pump-fake your way into her itty-bitty shorts.

Right. She knows you think this way, but there is more to the story: You are sorta beside the point. Oh, your weakness is *precious.*

This is good old-fashioned sex appeal. This is straight-up Marilyn Monroe pinup-girl shtick. Sexy-happy, happy-sexy. It's family-values sex appeal. Other than that, it has nothing to do with you.

People assume a lot. People assume cheering in the NFL is mostly about a girl trying to snag herself a big, beefy, stinkin' rich football player. That is not the case. The Ben-Gals are not even permitted to socialize with players, except at officially sanctioned appearances. This rule is strictly enforced. Zero tolerance. As for football itself, the game, the players, the stats, the formations—that stuff rarely rises to the level of actual conversation. For most of them, this whole thing has nothing to do with football.

Money? No, no, no. This is really, really, *really* not about money, either. People assume NFL cheerleaders are within some vague sniffing distance of the good life, but a Ben-Gal is paid seventy-five bucks per game. That is correct: seventy-five bucks for each of ten home games. The grand cash total per season does not keep most of them flush in hair spray, let alone gas money to and from practice. "We have a rule book that's like *this thick*," Charlotte will explain to any woman interested in becoming a Ben-Gal, holding her hands four inches apart. "If you can demonstrate commitment and dedication and following-the-rules, you're good to go." It is not as easy as it sounds. Practices are Tuesdays and Thursdays at 7 P.M.—sharp—at which time a Ben-Gal must be in full uniform, full hair, full makeup, a state of readiness that can take two hours to achieve. She must then step on the scale. If she is more than three pounds over the target poundage assigned to her by Charlotte, she will have to attend the after-practice "fat camp," doing crunches and running laps for a half hour after everyone else is gone, and she may not be able to cheer in that week's game. There are many other reasons a cheerleader can get benched: If she misses a single mandatory practice, she will not cheer at that week's game. If she misses four practices, she's off the squad. She is permitted just two tardies per season. Within fifteen minutes, it's a tardy, but sixteen is a miss. Two tardies equal a miss. No excuse is greater than another. Death won't get you a free pass, unless it's your own.

Given all the rules and the lack of distinct perks, it is difficult to understand why so many beautiful young women would eagerly and longingly choose any of this.

Charlotte sees it as a gift. Charlotte sees herself as a fairy godmother with a magic wand under which only a few select gals earn the privilege of the wave. "My most precious thing I can do is take a person and give them the tools that the program offers and watch them grasp it and watch them mature," she says. "Now, not everyone does that. But you take a girl like Adrienne. I mean, she was... *whew!* She was kind of... alternate for a while. You know what I mean? And now to watch her mature and develop into the program—she's a real special girl. She's had a hard life. She's the only single mom we have on the squad. Oh, I don't know why I'm talking about Adrienne. I mean she's not *Pro Bowl* yet. But still."

Contrary to popular mythology, not all NFL cheerleaders are bimbos or strippers or bored pretty girls looking to get rich. The Ben-Gals offer proof. Neither a bimbo nor a stripper nor a bored pretty girl would survive the rigorous life of a Ben-Gal. The Ben-Gals all have jobs or school or both. Kat and Sarah are sales reps. Sunshine is a database administrator. Shannon works at a law firm. Tara is a cancer researcher working toward her Ph.D. Adrienne works construction, pouring cement.

They have full and complicated lives. They don't need all this nonsense. They completely crave it.

MEET THE CHEERLEADER: RHONEÉ

This is my second year as a Ben-Gal. The first year, I commuted three hours from Liberty, Kentucky. That's how bad I wanted to cheer. I had never even heard of a switch leap before—where you do a leap and do splits and then switch legs? The first time I tried that, I felt like Peter Pan.

I have a bachelor's in chemistry and a bachelor's in biology. I just finished my master's in public health with an emphasis in environmental-health science. For two years, I worked on a project dealing with air quality within chemical-fume hoods. We came up with something called the smoke-particle-challenge method. I did monoclonal-antibody research for BD Transduction Laboratories. I worked for the U.S. government at the Center for Health Promotion and Preventative Medicine. We did soil sampling, water sampling, at military bases throughout Europe. That was the very best job I ever had.

When I first took my new job at PPD's global central labs, I didn't tell anybody I was a Ben-Gal.

I met my boyfriend when I was 14. He was 16 and I was 14. We took our time. We got engaged in 1998. He asked me to marry him in Paris, at the Eiffel Tower. I was like, "I'm melting!" That's been a long time ago. He's going to have to, you know, renew that. His job takes him to Chicago a lot, so I don't see him a whole lot.

I don't feel 32. I keep telling everybody you're only as old as you feel, and I don't feel 32 at all.

For me the Ben-Gals is about fulfilling a dream. Not many people out there can say they're an NFL cheerleader. I have never been so proud to wear such an ugly color of lipstick.

In Kentucky, cheerleading is big. But when a small-town girl tries out for NFL cheerleading and makes it, that's huge. I made the front page of our local newspaper. Last year I was Miss November in the Ben-Gals calendar. Everyone kept telling me they wanted a calendar. I didn't tell a lot of people I had them. Word of mouth, people asked. I ended up bringing over 350 calendars back to my hometown. This year I'm not a month, but I'm still in the calendar. You feel like a superstar. I had trouble doing the sexy look. They teach you how to do that, to look like you're mad at somebody. This year I don't look mad. Just like I'm halfway smiling. I'm wearing a Rudi Johnson youth size small jersey that they cut up and made into a bathing suit. A youth size small.

The Reindog Parade is this Saturday. There will be 500 dogs dressed like reindeer. I have to be there at one. Judging begins no later than one thirty. The parade starts at two. I'll be walking in the parade with a reindog.

Adrienne comes flying out of the stall. She is not done throwing up but refuses to continue. She will not give in to a day of senseless, stupid puking. She is: Cheerleader of the Week! Okay, that news came days ago. So it's not *news* news, but tonight is the night, and so you could say reality is settling in. This is almost certainly at the center of the nausea Adrienne must conquer.

There are so many things that may or may not happen tonight. The storm may or may not come. The Bengals could score very many touchdowns. The Ravens could be called for holding or do an onsides- whatever kick. All kinds of... *football* things could or could not hap- pen on this electrifying NFL Thursday night. But one thing is certain: Adrienne is going to be Cheerleader of the Week. She'll get her face on the JumboTron during the second quarter. Just her, dancing live, beside a sign listing her name and her hometown and her hobbies—in front of 60,000 people in Paul Brown Stadium—for perhaps five or six or seven seconds.

Okay, listen. Adrienne poured the cement in Paul Brown Stadium. Way before she became a Ben-Gal. When she was just a regular person working under a hard hat in the freezing-cold wind blowing off the Ohio River. *She poured the forms.*

She does not feel worthy to be Cheerleader of the Week, and yet, at the same time, she does. (When in this life does *she* get a turn?) She is looking into the mirror, trying to get color into her cheeks. She is trying to get ahold of herself. *She is a Ben-Gal!* A good Ben-Gal. An obedient Ben-Gal. She stays in her target-weight zone, 144–147, higher than most because of her muscle, her height. She does not smoke. She does not chew gum. She has no visible tattoos or naughty piercings. She curls her hair when Charlotte or Mary tells her to curl it, sprays it when they say it needs to stand taller or wider, slaps on more makeup when they demand bigger glamour. She works as hard as any other Ben-Gal at becoming what the coaches call "the total-package."

But Cheerleader of the Week? It is overwhelming.

"Come here," Rhoneé tells her. "Look in this mirror. Isn't this a great mirror? It makes you look so skinny. It's an awesome esteem booster!"

"All right," says Adrienne.

"Oh, you look awesome," Shannon tells Adrienne.

"You *always* look awesome," Sarah tells her. "I wish I had your abs."

"I wish I had your boobs," Adrienne tells her.

"I wish I had your hair," Rhoneé tells Shannon.

"*Everyone* wishes they had Shannon's hair," Sarah says.

"I wish I had your brains!" Shannon tells Rhoneé.

"Oh, you girls are so awesome," Adrienne says.

Cheerleader of the Week. It is not something most people in the world ever get even close to being. For that matter, most people don't get close to being a regular Ben-Gal—just thirty per year, out of a field of a couple of hundred who try out. Chief among the characteristics required to make the squad—beyond raw dance talent, a degree of physical beauty, a soldierlike level of self-discipline—is a specific consciousness. It is so obvious to those who have it and yet so fleeting, if at all attainable, to others. Ask a person who does not have it why she wants to be a Ben-Gal and she will say things like, "Because I love to cheer" or "I have cheered my whole life" or "For the camaraderie" or blah blah blah.

Now try this same question on a person who has within her the consciousness, the essence of what it is to become a Ben-Gal.

"So why do you want to be a Ben-Gal?"

She will look at you. She will look at you blankly, keeping her smile in place while her eyes tell the story: *What, are you from Transylvania or something?*

"Because it's a *Ben-Gal*," she will say, wondering politely and in her own generous way if you have perhaps suffered some brain injury at some point in your tragic life and if there is anything she can do to help make your world just a tiny bit brighter. Everyone, she thinks, wants to be a Ben-Gal. Pity the president of the United States, the queen of England, the winner of the Nobel Peace Prize, for not having the attributes necessary to become a Ben-Gal. It is difficult to accept that not everyone in this world has what it takes to become a Ben-Gal, and for those people, all she can do is pray.

That's what it takes to become a Ben-Gal. If a woman has any lesser sense of the glory, she will not make it.

Charlotte and her assistants, Mary and Traci, and the captain, Deanna, maintain and constantly feed the glorification. Each Tuesday at practice, they decide who will cheer that week and who will not. Six people per corner, four corners, twenty-four cheerleaders. Six get cut. It depends on weight, glamour-readiness, dance-preparedness, all the factors of the total-package. Each Tuesday, as nonchalantly as possible, Charlotte reveals her choices for those who will cheer and those who will not, for those who have earned a coveted spot in the front of the formation and those who must go to the rear. "Sarah, you are in the back," Deanna will say, or "Shannon, I want you up front." *Nonchalantly.* Because it's stressful enough. It's devastating enough to be left out or put in the back, even though most girls sort of *know*, can sense, can see the signs in Charlotte's eyes or see the way Mary is whispering to Charlotte and nodding and pointing and wondering, *Who told Sunshine she could dye her hair that dark?!?!*

The choosing goes on all season. Everything is about the choosing. Whose picture will make the Ben-Gals calendar? Who will be Miss January? Who will make the front cover and who will make the back?

These choices are revealed Academy Award–style at a special ceremony in September, with slide shows, at a restaurant, with families invited, and lots of hugs and lots of tears, celebration, consolation, grieving.

There is more choosing. There is the biggest honor of all: the Pro Bowl. One cheerleader per season per NFL squad is chosen to attend the Pro Bowl in Hawaii. All season long, the cheerleaders speculate about who will be chosen. Charlotte will tell no one until it is time—she is the decider. No one understands the total-package better than she, herself a Ben-Gal from 1978 to 1989, a Pro Bowler, and a coach for thirteen years.

The choosing is the bait that keeps any Ben worth her Gal reaching toward her total-package goal. And each week there comes this choice: Cheerleader of the Week.

Who among the living would not vomit?

Now, the men. The men are super-adorable. The game has not yet started, and some of the cheerleaders are glamour-ready, so they have left the locker room to sign calendars by the stadium gift shops. "Who-dey!" some of the men chant, soldiers coming to battle, stomping up stadium steps toward nachos, hot dogs, beer. "*Who*-dey!" The idiosyncratic growl is a Bengal original and all the more popular now that the team is actually semicompetitive. Marvin Lewis came in 2003, turned the team around, gave football back to a woefully depressed Cincinnati. From a cheerleader point of view, it's been super.

Who-dey!

The men are dressed in orange and black, some with striped faces, crazy wigs, naked bellies pouring over Bengals pajamas, furry tails hanging from their asses. Soon this platoon rounds a corner, comes upon a table behind which four cheerleaders sit. Daphne, Sunshine, Kat, Tiffany. Glimmery and shimmery kitty-cat babes signing calendars, $10 a pop. The men say OH, MY GOD with their eyes, stop dead in their tracks.

"Who-dey!" the cheerleaders say, all sex and sweetness and growl.

The men suck in air, seem to have trouble releasing it. These gals are, well, *whoa*. These gals are—fuckin' A.

The cheerleaders give a thumbs-up. "Awesome outfits, guys!"

The men look at each other, at face paint, tails, fur. *Oh, sweet Jesus... we look like fucking idiots.*

"Who-dey!" the cheerleaders say.

The men dart away like roosters.

Outside in the parking lot, the men are more serious. Businessmen, banker types, tailgating, bonding. Somebody knew somebody and arranged for two cheerleaders, yeah, two real cheerleaders to come to the tailgate party for 200 bucks. Heh heh. *Where they at? Are they coming? Where they at?*

Holly (blond ringlets) and Stephanie (brunet innocence) arrive.

"Hi!" They have doe eyes and dewy smiles. They wear little string backpacks in which they carry pom-poms. They slip off their backpacks. They slip off their white satin Ben-Gals jackets. "Ooh, it's chilly!" Holly says, revealing her naked arms and abundant bosom. "Ooh, that storm is coming!"

"I've been looking at you girls on the Internet," one of the businessmen says.

"Dude," says his colleague. *"Dude."*

"I'm Holly," says Holly. "Nice to meet you. Thanks for having us."

"You want some beef-barley soup?" one says to her. "Some kielbasy?"

"We have Chips Ahoy," says another.

"I'm good," says Holly.

"We're good," says Stephanie.

The conversation is not flowing. Just what *is* the purpose of this meeting?

The men give up trying to talk to the cheerleaders, turn to one another, laugh, grunt. Holly and Stephanie stand there smiling. Stephanie is shy, is a first-year, is taking lessons from Holly, who is also a first-year but who has so much more experience feeling gorgeous. "Would you guys like to learn a cheer?" Holly asks them.

"Uh, yeah."

"Come on, do it with us."

"Uh, no."

"Well, will you say it if we do it?"

"All right."

Of course, it starts to rain. The men dart under a tarp. Holly and Stephanie stay out in the rain, just a sprinkle, a trickle, a tickle, droplets for the cheeks.

"Let's go Bengals—ooh, aah!" the cheerleaders chant. "Let's go Bengals—ooh, aah!" They spin, throw their heads, offer ass. The men learn the words quickly. "Let's go Bengals—ooh, aah!" The men hold up their beer cans, toast one another. Heh heh.

The cheerleaders finish and wave, taking their jackets and pom-poms with them.

"Well, that was worth it," says one of the men.

MEET THE CHEERLEADERS:
SARAH AND SHANNON

Sarah: I work for Pepsi. I'm pretty much on call twenty-four–seven, so it's stressful. If somebody runs out of Mountain Dew and they're having a sale on it, they're calling me to get out there. I'm like, I know, I know.

Shannon: This apartment is two bedrooms, two baths. We met pretty much through Bath & Body Works in Lexington. We both went to the University of Kentucky.

Sarah: I called Shannon "Miss Hair." I was like, "Do you know Miss Hair?" That was my first meeting of Shannon. We've been best friends ever since then. We're so laid-back. Nothing gets us really fired up too much.

Shannon: I thought it would be awesome to be a Ben-Gal. You just put it way up here. You never really think you can get there.

Sarah: We dared each other to try out. To be an NFL cheerleader, I think every girl dreams.

Shannon: We use a great bra by Victoria's Secret. Body by Victoria Push-up Bra. We all had to get a bra that has a fixture that's real low. It's spandex and it's definitely tight, so it squishes and pulls. And then we have bronzing stuff to make it look more... You do it, like, right here in the V. It makes it look like there's a shadow, so it makes your chest look bigger.

Sarah: Being a female, you gain water weight. You can go in there and think you're so thin, and it'll weigh you five pounds over. It gets frustrating. I eat lots of asparagus.

Shannon: There's, like, seven or eight things on our grocery list. For breakfast it's egg whites and oats—dried oats.

Sarah: People think we're so weird. You have to be very disciplined. And you have to get in that mind-set, because it is hard to follow. Very, very hard to follow. Like, a guy will ask you out on a date on a Wednesday night, and you can't say, "I can't eat, because I have to weigh in tomorrow." But you can't go and not eat, either. So it is hard.

Shannon: I've been in situations with people who think, like, Oh, you're not having fun. Or, Why won't you go out? Because I don't want to eat.

Sarah: I usually say to a guy, "Let's wait until Friday night, because I have four days to get my weight back down after that."

Shannon: You saw us in practice in the short booty shorts and, like, a sports bra or bikini top? That's so they can see your fitness level. The stomach, the legs, the butt.

Sarah: They stand right in front of you with a clipboard. I don't like it, but it's a good idea. It has to be done.

Shannon: It's about glamour, fitness, and always being ready: full hair, full makeup, giving 110 percent.

Sarah: Of course, guys look at it as some type of sex symbol. But I don't think it's a thing that guys want their girlfriend to look like, you know what I mean? It's like a costume. It's not something I think a guy would like to look at every day.

Shannon: Egg yolk is actually what carries most of the fat. I'll usually put one yolk and about six egg whites just to have some fat and not just the protein.

Sarah: This month has been good. I mean, we gained a few pounds, but that helps you start again.

Shannon: I'm not usually this color. I tanned yesterday.

Sarah: If Shannon has her hair up in a ponytail, I swear, ninety-nine out of a hundred people would bet it's fake. It looks so perfect, and it's so big and thick. I bet ninety-nine out of a hundred would think it's fake. It's that good.

Shannon: You want some water?

There's more. For Adrienne, so much more. You have to understand at least one more important beat of the backstory: This is not the first time Adrienne has been named Cheerleader of the Week. The first time, she blew it. She may be the only Ben-Gal in history to screw up so royally. It happened three weeks earlier. Charlotte had told Adrienne, "This is it! You're going to be Cheerleader of the Week!" The night before the game, Adrienne was so excited she could barely sleep. Well, she did sleep. And sleep, and sleep, and sleep.

She awakened to the sound of her phone ringing. It was Missy, calling from the parking lot, where all the other cheerleaders had already gathered. *"Where are you?"* Adrienne hoped this was a bad dream. But, no, it was true. She had overslept. She threw on her clothes and rushed into the stadium, arriving not exactly Ben-Gal ready and more than sixteen minutes late.

"Tardy!"

The Cheerleader of the Week was... *tardy?* She was immediately dethroned. She would not be allowed to cheer, let alone be Cheerleader of the Week, and she would be penalized two games. Hey, late is late. Rules are rules. All the gals, including Charlotte, embraced her, grieved with her, over the tragedy that seemed for her so typical, so many almosts, so much dumb luck, so much stupid, rotten, dumb luck.

"It's my own fault," Adrienne told her teammates on that dismal day. "It's nobody's fault but my own."

For all her mother-superior-style discipline, Charlotte is a kind soul. Now here it is, just three weeks after Adrienne's disaster, and Charlotte is giving her a second chance at being Cheerleader of the Week. Here you go, Adrienne. Your sins are forgiven.

So maybe it's the generosity that is making Adrienne sick. The outpouring of love. The second chance that in so many ways feels like the last. The thought of going out there, in front of all those screaming fans, appearing on the JumboTron in the stadium whose concrete you yourself once poured.

After serious consultation with Mary and Traci, Charlotte has an announcement. "Catsuits!" she bellows out into the locker room that by now is held in tight under a hanging cloud of aerosol. "Okay, girls, *catsuits!*"

"Catsuits!" the women shriek. There is nothing sexier than the catsuits.

Adrienne throws her head in the sink, runs the water at full blast, plunges. "Catsuits!" several tell her. "Catsuits!" They throw their arms around her, leap tiny leaps. "Catsuits!"

"Adrienne, honey, are you okay?"

MEET THE CHEERLEADER: ADRIENNE

My mom was killed. She was murdered by my stepdad. I had just turned 1 year old. I break down sometimes. You can't think: Why me? Things happen for a reason. You just can't think about the unknown.

This right here is a mud mat. It's just so we have a flat area to set our forms on. We poured all this today. We started back in the corner. Last pour, we did over 300 yards.

The finishers finish the concrete and make it look pretty. And the laborers, which would be us, rake it and pull it close to grade. The rod busters are the ones that put all the rebar in. They are just totally rebar. Oh God, I would never want to be a rod buster.

Cement is not the same as concrete. Cement's an ingredient in concrete. Cement is the glue in concrete.

Working with all men, you realize that they really act like girls. They whine and cry. I'm not trying to be stereotypical, but they act different. I don't think of myself as a female at work. I think of myself as an employee. As a guy. Well, I don't want to be a guy. But I let them know: You're not allowed to call me names or treat me like dog crap.

With the Ben-Gals, with thirty girls in one group, you'd think it'd be a bunch of backstabbers, cliques, but it's not like that. They say I'm this role model because I have a little girl I'm raising on my own and I work construction. They say I'm an inspiration. They say that they're amazed I do all this.

I went to college, a full ride in track. I chose criminal justice. Afterward, I took a test in Lexington to become a cop. I got all the way to what they call the "rule of five," when they compare you to four other applicants. I had four speeding tickets, because I commute a lot. That ruined my chances. That kinda bummed me out. I was like, Screw this.

Then I took the county exam and failed by two points. I did bad because the whole time I'm thinking how I'm gonna kill my boyfriend because he made me late. He had my car, didn't get it back to me in time. The whole time I was thinking about him.

I had a change of heart. I decided I didn't want to be a cop. I didn't want someone to have to tell my kids someday that I'd been shot.

In the beginning, when I started working construction, the guys were horrible. The first day, my boss said I was a lawsuit waiting to happen. He made me bust up a twelve-by-twelve slab of concrete alone, with a sledgehammer. Then I had to carry four-by-fours, one after another. But I stuck it out. I've been doing this eight years. My body goes through a lot.

After my mom was killed, my aunt Pam wanted me. She really wanted me. After two years, she hitched a ride to Florida in the back of a truck to get me. People were upset with my grandma for letting me go. Pam was 16 at the time. I call her my mom now. She ended up being a single mom with six kids. I think that's why I am the way I am today, because I was raised on love.

I told Pam I wanted to go on Ricki Lake and find my dad. I said I want to know who made me. She didn't want me to do that, but she talked to my aunts. I met him at a benefit. It was weird. I cried. Like, Wow. We went out to dinner the next night, to F&N Steak House, in Dayton. I ate chicken, and he was so mad. "I bring you to a steak house, and you order chicken?" I didn't want him to think I was money-hungry. He told me how beautiful my mom was, how much he loved her. He said he remembered the last time they made love was 1975, World Series Game 7. He followed newspaper stuff about me through high school but didn't know for sure that I was his.

I don't regret anything that's ever happened. I did get the shit end of the deal with Mom dying, but that was out of my control.

I never get hit on. A lot of my friends say I'm intimidating. Women who are successful or independent, guys are too scared to talk to. Which I hate. Because I'm a person.

My one fear is failing at being a mother. I don't want her to go through the things I went through. I'm afraid she'll be a priss. Her dad spoils her, which I hate because it makes me look bad.

Being a Ben-Gal in general is just awesome.

Being Cheerleader of the Week is awesome.

Taking photos for the calendar was awesome. It's a day that's all about you. Last year I ended up being Miss October. This year I was Miss December. It's heartbreaking when you don't make a month. People say, "Why didn't you get a month?" We don't know. But when you are a month, you feel great. Awesome. Sexy. Amazing. You feel like you're somebody.

Underneath this, I have jeans and long johns. And then I have two long-sleeves on, a sweatshirt, a sweater, and one of the poly sweatshirts that, like, covers you, and my Carhartts. You get cold. Your hands and feet and face and your nose. I'll thaw out later on tonight, like, a couple hours after I'm home I'll start thawing out.

I've always wanted to be a nurse. Ever since I graduated from high school. So I'm just gonna go back and give it a shot. I'm a people person. That's my calling. I get home, and normally I pick up my daughter, and we usually do homework. I have to study. I'm taking chemistry. In a couple years, I should be a nurse. I should graduate in three years. August 3, 2010.

You're not supposed to put a lot of stickers on your hard hat, because sometimes OSHA will think that you're covering up a hole. If these get a hole, you can't use them, because something might land on your head and kill you. But I have this sticker that says HOTTIE. *And* DEWALT *tools. The twin towers—one of the guys from the company, he was killed, so I have a sticker from him. And I have one that says* BITCH GODDESS.

I spit, too, like boys. Oh yeah. Just 'cause, I don't know. Your mouth gets dry or whatever. The guys are like, "Quit spittin'. That's not ladylike." And

I'm like, I'm not a lady at work. Charlotte doesn't know I spit. Charlotte would kill me.

"Who-dey! Who-dey! Who-dey think gonna beat dem Bengals?"

"*Nobody!*"

It is time. The gals have pranced like a pride of lions out of the locker room and are standing in the tunnel, peering out. There are enormous Bengals walking around back here, but the gals notice only one another. They are cold. Sarah is holding on to Shannon for warmth; she always seems to disappear next to Shannon, mostly due to Shannon's hair, currently a celebration, a testament to extremes, curls streaming like Niagara Falls down her back, crashing into the bend of her bottom. "I'm so freezing!" Sarah is saying.

"Get a grip, girl!" Shannon says. "It's showtime!"

The catsuits are sleek, sleeveless, with necklines plunging deep and tight, allowing for blasts of perfectly spherical honeydew breasts. Each gal wears a thin glitter belt around her hips and a pair of white satin wrist cuffs crisscrossed with orange laces. Hair is high, broad, glued in place. Makeup is paint, pasted on thick. Tans are air-sprayed, darker in the V to accentuate the total-package. Perfect. Exactly perfect.

Of course, it might not *really* rain and ruin all their hard work. It might not. The storm is probably still over Indiana or something. It could hold off. The balmy sixty-eight degrees has gone kerplunk to fifty-two. Outside, in the stands, ponchos are starting to come out.

"I don't know about the '80s look, with all this hair," Lauren says. "Do you think we look like poodles?"

"I can't brush my hair after," Tiffany says. "I have to wash it."

"I have to soak it," Brooke says.

"You guys!" team captain Deanna interrupts. "Think how lucky we are to be here, and savor every moment!"

"Sexy, ladies!" Rhoneé shouts. "SEXY!"

"*SEXY!*"

"*Wooo!*"

With that, they fire out of the tunnel like bullets out of the barrel of a gun. One arm up, pom-pom shaking, "Let's Get It Started" blaring, "Who-dey!" "Who-dey!" Fireworks shooting into the night sky. Any one of them could burst into tears of excitement. Some of them will. Adrienne will absolutely not. Adrienne is all game face, determination from a twisted gut. She's on the five-yard line, next to Maja and Tif-fany, all the cheerleaders lined up forming a chute, a welcome path for the football players, who come chugging out like beefy boxcars. "Who-dey! Who-dey!" The gals stand like ponies, one knee up, one arm down. Pom-poms shimmering.

They take to their corners, and the kicker kicks off, and the stadium erupts into "Welcome to the Jungle," Axl Rose crooning his timeless anthem, gals dancing stripper moves with hips, ass, roll head, whip hair. Then they just as quickly retreat into sweet pom-pom action. Sloopy. Feelgood. Hicktown. Worm. Tweety. All the dances have code names.

"We're on Pump, right?"

"*We're on Worm!*"

"Oh, my God!"

Four sets of cheerleaders, one set in each stadium corner, Charlotte and Mary and Traci with walkie-talkies, demanding coordination, demanding precision: "Lines, ladies, *LINES!*"

Six minutes into a scoreless first quarter, most of the hair is… flat. That was quick. That is a shame. But that's okay. At halftime they'll charge back to the locker room and drop to their knees in front of mirrors waiting like lonesome cousins. Hot rollers. Curling irons. Makeup. Spray tan. Primp! There is not much time to re-create perfection, but they'll do their best.

Six-yard line. The football players are trying to pound the ball in. *Come on, football players!* The cheerleaders hold their arms up, smile, keep their arms high, and jiggle their pom-poms, shimmer shimmer shimmer. They have turned themselves into candles burning flames of hope.

A field goal. Okay, we'll take it. Who-dey! "Jungle Boogie." Celebrate with the cheerleaders; watch them bounce like balls.

It isn't until three minutes twenty-six seconds into the third quar-ter that Carson Palmer completes a forty-yard flea-flicker touchdown pass to T. J. Houshmandzadeh, but that is not even the point. The sky has done it, finally opened up—sheets of rain. The gals valiantly bump and grind to "Bang the Drum All Day," the touchdown song, in the glimmery downpour. Forget hair spray, forget makeup. It is all washing off now, washing down, soaking them. Wet cheerleaders! The JumboTron appears itself to experience the orgasm. Exploding wet cheerleaders! The cameras are all over the cheerleaders. The gals are screaming, laughing, howling, forgetting everything. Forgetting the fucking construction site, the man who murdered your mother, the store calling for more Mountain Dew, the chemical-fume hoods and the smoke-particle-challenge method, the men who don't call, and all those egg whites and protein shakes that have made this moment possible. Forget it all! This is it. This is a rain dance, a joy dance, a jet-propulsion explosion of cheerleader love, love to the crowd, love from the crowd, men in striped pajamas, wigs, tails, painted bellies washing clean, oh, those men are super, super-duper adorable. Who-dey drunk.

In the stands cheering for Adrienne is Pam, the woman who hitch-hiked decades ago to Florida to scoop her up. Also, Adrienne's cousin Leslie, her aunt Nancy, her little aunt Sandy, and her regular aunt Sandy—the one who takes the picture. It is the first time they get a picture of Adrienne on the JumboTron. In the picture, Adrienne is smiling and looking up. It's just her face next to her name and her hometown and her hobbies. In that moment, she doesn't even know she is on the JumboTron. She is damp, out-of-her-mind joyful. Free.

Weeks go by, months, a year. Adrienne is looking at the picture. She keeps it in a storage box in her spare bedroom. She doesn't know what else to do with it. She thinks she looks awesome. She thinks she looks like a real girl. She thinks she looks happy. Probably she should display the picture, downstairs with her collection of tiny ceramic angels. She can't believe this is happening.

Nate Jackson

NFL teams always say they want smart players, but when one of those players writes a book that addresses the uncomfortable truths of the pro game, everybody acts like the maiden surprised. We know by now there are no maidens involved. Our education began when Dave Meggyesy, a former St. Louis Cardinals linebacker, spilled his amped-up memories of football's dehumanizing qualities in *Out of Their League* (1970). Peter Gent, battered and cynical but still funny, followed with *North Dallas Forty* (1973), a relentlessly tough novel based on his experiences as a Cowboys wide receiver. In the years since, Pat Toomay, another rebellious ex-Cowboy, and Tim Green, late of the Atlanta Falcons, have maintained the tradition of the player who asks why and then writes about it. The latest to emerge from the NFL with stories to share is Nate Jackson (b. 1979), whose *Slow Getting Up* was greeted by this hosanna from the *New York Times* in 2013: "it's everything you want football memoirs to be but never are: hilarious, dirty, warm, human, honest, weird." Jackson came by his experiences the hard way. Undrafted out of tiny Menlo College, he spent most of his six seasons as a tight end with the Denver Broncos, bouncing between the practice squad and the active roster, making it into only forty-one games, and catching but two touchdown passes. Football beat him up but he loved it. As the following excerpt shows, set in 2009, it was a love that ultimately led him to desperate measures, otherwise known as human growth hormone.

from

Slow Getting Up

A WEEK AFTER BEING CUT, I fly back to Denver to clean out my locker and say goodbye to my friends who work for the team. All of my teammates are gone for the off-season. I'll never see them again. Flip and the guys in the equipment room, Greek and Corey and Trae, and Rich and Crime, and everyone else. They have become my extended family. When I came to Denver, I came alone. All players do in one way or another. The Bronco organization was my lifeline. They were very good to me. I love them. I want to tell them how I feel about my time there. But I don't have the words.

All I can think about is Josh McDaniels not calling me back. I want to run into him in the parking lot. I won't need any words for that. I have a bone to break with him. But Flip tells me that he's not even here. He's in Indianapolis for the combine. Lucky Josh. Not that I don't understand his indifference. He's thirty-two years old. He's just suicide-squeezed his way into the head coaching position of one of the NFL's most venerable institutions, taking over for a future Hall of Fame coach who controlled the entire operation from top to bottom. The last thing he wants to do is waste his time explaining to a backup tight end why he doesn't fit into the plan.

I sit down in my locker for the last time. It was always a bit out of sorts, full of clothes and shoes and tape and gloves, notebooks and letters and gifts. Do I even want these cleats? These gloves? These memories? Yes. I fill up my box. Six years as a Denver Bronco. Six more than most people can say. Still feels like a failure, though. So this is how the end feels? Standing in an empty locker room with a box in my hand? Yep. Now leave.

I get home and call Ryan. He knows that my prospects aren't great. I am an undersized tight end with injury problems and I am pushing thirty. I need to find a team that wants a player with my skill set and won't be turned off by the injuries. That won't be easy, especially because the most recent one hasn't healed. What I couldn't convey honestly to Greek I can to Ryan. There is a problem—a deeper problem—that's affecting my body. It's not simply that my hamstring is shit. The entire functional movement of my body is off. I can feel it with every step I take. Something is amiss.

Ryan sets me up with a biomechanics specialist/physical therapist in San Diego named Derek Samuel. Ryan thinks I'll get along with him. He'll assess my situation and we'll go from there. But I'm afraid this won't be enough. Desperate times, you know the saying. I reach out to a connection I made a year earlier and acquire a supply of human growth hormone, HGH. The drugs come in the mail in a package stuffed with dry ice. I half expect to see the feds storm out of the bushes, guns blazing, as I pull the box off my front porch.

But no feds. Just me and another needle.

It comes with very little guidance as to the quantity and regularity of the shot. I have a conversation with my supplier and he tells me how to do it. Other than that I'm on my own. I will tell no one what I'm doing. I go to the store and buy syringes and start injecting it in my stomach immediately. I am paranoid about every aspect of this decision. I've never used performance-enhancing drugs. Haven't ever even seen them. I take pride in my natural ability and I don't want to taint it. I don't want to test the karmic winds. But I also don't want to taste the death of my football dreams, not like this.

I pack up my Denali and head over the Rocky Mountains, the vials of HGH stuffed in an ice-filled cooler. My time with the Broncos is up. That's for sure. The rest of it will reveal itself eventually. But all men must move along. And they must do it with the feeling that they have left business unfinished, relationships unformed, opportunities untaken. I played for the Denver Broncos. I achieved my dream, which confronted me with a naked truth: the dream has been won, and it is not enough. I leave for San Diego to revive the dream, to give it the fresh air it needs, so that I can leave the game on my own terms.

From the moment I step into Derek's La Jolla office, which connects to a small fitness club, I know I am in the right place. Derek is a six-foot-three former volleyball player at the University of California, Irvine, with a friendly disposition and a freaky knowledge of the human body. He asks me questions and lets me talk. He is interested in what I think and not just what I was told. He is interested in how the treatments I got in Denver affected me, how I responded to them and how I felt about them. He wants to know the backstory so he can make more sense of what he discovers on his own. It is refreshing, truly. For the first time in years I am free to look at my body through my own eyes and to own my own flesh.

After an examination, Derek determines that not only is my hamstring incredibly weak, but my hips are drastically misaligned, my pelvis is tilted forward, and my core strength is very poor. We get to work immediately, realigning my body and strengthening its foundation: the core. This isn't accomplished by snapping it back in place. It takes a soft touch, a gradual redirection of the years of bad habits that I formed while playing football. The body must correct itself. And it must be listened to every day. Derek's genius lies in his ability to hear the human body's cries. But in order to do that, he also has to hear the cries of the mind. He is simultaneously acting as physical therapist and psychotherapist, easing me into a transition I am denying. I think my football days are far from over, yet I rail every day about the oppressive nature of the industry. Between sets of exercises, I go on and on about the meat market of the NFL, the hypocrisy of coaches, the false glamour of fame, and the inevitable meltdown of the players who play football.

He sees many football players in his practice, and knows firsthand what I'm talking about, but he never lays it on me with any air of finality. He is too smart for that. But the fact that I am here at all, seeing Derek for my treatment, means that I have cleared an existential boundary in my pursuit of football absolutism. I have turned my back on the modern philosophy of NFL injury treatment, and in doing so, have taken one more step away from the industry I think I am running toward. Certainly, I am getting superb treatment. But my mind is doing something else. It is picking apart a system to which I have bowed my entire adult life. It is, as a defense mechanism I suppose, finding all of the reasons why I should cash in my chips and walk away. But I can't.

Along with Derek's workouts in La Jolla, I am meeting a track coach at the University of California, San Diego. My first day on the track is a sad realization of how unhealed my hamstring is. To be medically cleared by the Broncos, I had to pass a series of strength and endurance tests. But those tests did not include running. I haven't run since the corner route that tore it three months earlier. And when I try to open up and sprint on the track, I can't. I simply cannot run. Judging by the look on the track coach's face, it's a sad sight. I wish the drugs would fix me already.

I've been hiding the vials in the refrigerator of my friend Billy, who I'm staying with in San Diego. I become a master of refrigerator organization with the express purpose of concealing contraband, wrapped in the folds of my deli meat. Nobody touch my *goddamned turkey*!

When it's shooting time, I get the turkey and retreat to my room, where I mix the active ingredient with the solution, pinch my belly, plunge the needle into my skin, and push the poison into my body. Once again, I imagine the HGH as a fleet of noble warriors. I am doing God's work, after all. There is nothing dishonest about it. HGH is a hormone naturally produced in the body, and my body is starved for it. I am broken. I am unable to perform the sacred task that I was born for. To turn my back on it would be to spit in the face of God. So I draw back the syringe and poison myself again, and again, and again. I don't know what I expect to happen: a miraculous recovery perhaps. A newfound clarity. A bigger dick. But nothing happens. The only noticeable effect is that my body aches viciously. I don't know what this means and I'm too afraid to ask anyone about it, so I assume it is part of the process. My muscles are big and well-defined, perhaps slightly more than normal, but perhaps not. I was always muscular, and I am training like a madman. My body looked the same when I was in Denver shooting tequila instead of HGH. Either I'm not doing it right or my body doesn't like it. And the fact that I'm doing it at all, sneaking around, carrying this secret, makes me feel mentally weak and undeserving of good fortune. Regardless, after a few months of intrastate trafficking and refrigerator espionage, I throw it all away in one dramatic garbage-can dump, and I close the lid. If I am going to play football again, I'll do it clean.

About that time, in April or May 2009, I start receiving calls from Eric Van Heusen, the tight end coach with the Las Vegas Locomotives, one of six teams in the upstart United Football League. The UFL is hoping to steal some of the NFL's thunder. Alternate leagues have been tried in the past and all of them have failed. The branding of the NFL is too good. But the financial backers behind the UFL have an idea that the NFL might implode over the collective bargaining labor dispute and leave the country scrambling to fill the void the NFL's absence created. It is a worthy gamble, I suppose, if you have money to burn.

The Locos have drafted me and now hold my rights. Jim Fassel, the former head coach of the New York Giants, is to be the Locos' head coach and they have already received commitments from a host of former NFL players in limbo, like me. I tell Van Heusen that we'll talk about all of that if the NFL doesn't work out. But I believe it will work out. And when the call comes I'll be ready.

So I keep training. My body stops aching, and thanks to Derek's training methods, I am getting very strong. I feel pretty good considering the hamstring. And I'm getting my stride back on the track. My days consist of four or five hours of training. That's all I do. Ryan tells me to stay ready. Teams have shown some interest and once training camp starts, men will be falling and they'll need a veteran to come in right away and be ready to play. Well then, I'll be that veteran. I'll be ready!

I run sprints on a field that overlooks La Jolla cove; I'm sweating in the San Diego sun and trying to manifest my destiny. When I sprint, I feel vulnerable. I feel like I will snap and collapse into a bag of bones at any moment. But I can sprint. Not as fast as I once could, but fast enough for a tight end. And perhaps the hamstring isn't so bad after all. Perhaps it's healing.

The summer creeps by and I try to stay positive. I convince myself that things will work out if I keep working hard and trust my instinct. Never mind that my instinct, my true instinct, has been screaming at me for years. But I have stopped listening.

One day after workouts I go into an American Apparel store in San Diego and there is a smoke detector beeping. It has a battery that needs to be changed. It's a loud, sustained beep every fifteen seconds. A month later I return to the same store. And still the same beeping. Only now it's two of them. And the same girl is working behind the counter. I buy two T-shirts and as I am paying for them, I ask her about the beeping.

—What beeping?

What beeping? She can't hear it. She's just like me. My body beeps all day long.

Training camps start in late July and I'm not on a team. But I have no other plan. I will train and I will wait. Someone will call. Meanwhile, the therapy sessions with Derek are unearthing more misgivings that I have with the NFL. I rail against what I now see as years of mishandled injuries, against the emptiness of fornicating with the jersey chasers, against my own inability to turn from the game, against my monetary motivations for still wanting to play it, against the media's petty ownership of the players, and against the entire bastardized commercialization of what to me is the most beautiful game on earth. And here is the crux of it: I still believe in the beauty of the game. This above all else is true. But to be a fly on the wall, or to be Derek, is to be struck in the face with how delusional a man scorned by his lover can be. Here I am telling him all the reasons why I hate her, in between sets of an exercise specifically designed to lead me back into her arms. I am sick.

Paul Solotaroff

Paul Solotaroff (b. 1957) learned the hard way about the damage human beings can do to themselves and each other in their quest for perfect bodies. As a scrawny, asthmatic freshman at SUNY Stony Brook on Long Island, he fell under the sway of a bodybuilder who introduced him to a steroid called Deca-Durabolin. Combined with three-hour workouts, it gave him the "shrink-wrapped muscle" he was seeking and sent him down the road to stripping, shadowy sex, and self-administered injections. In time, however, Solotaroff would agree with his father, the critic and writer Ted Solotaroff, that he was living a dead-end life. And yet it proved to be good training for the writing career ahead of him. He got an adrenalized memoir, *The Body Shop* (2010), out of his walk on the wild side, did a tour as a *Village Voice* editor, and was the go-to guy for *Men's Journal* and *Rolling Stone* when a story required an extra dose of testosterone. He has written about boxers, hockey goons, and surfers with Asperger's, but his most significant work has involved the carnage that professional football has left in its wake. At every turn, there are cripples, pill heads, and the victims of too many concussions, but the most dramatic story of all is this one from *Men's Journal*'s February 2011 edition: the suicide of former Chicago Bears star Dave Duerson. Working with extra reporting by Rick Telander, who appears elsewhere in this volume, Solotaroff paints an unforgettable picture of a tragedy even the NFL's public relations machine can't sugarcoat.

The Ferocious Life and Tragic Death of a Super Bowl Star

Dave Duerson set the scene with a hangman's care before climbing into bed with the revolver. The former Pro Bowl safety for the Super Bowl–champion 1985 Chicago Bears drew the curtains of his beachfront Florida condo, laid a shrine of framed medals and an American flag to his father, a World War II vet, and pulled the top sheet up over his naked body, a kindness to whoever found him later. On the dining room table were notes and a typed letter that were alternately intimate and official, telling his former wife where his assets were and whom to get in touch with to settle affairs. He detailed his motives for ending his life, citing the rupture of his family and the collapse of his finances, a five-year cliff dive from multimillionaire to a man who couldn't pay his condo fees. Mostly, though, he talked about a raft of ailments that pained and depressed him past all tolerance: starburst headaches and blurred vision, maddening craters in his short-term memory, and his helplessness getting around the towns he knew. Once a man so acute he aced his finals at Notre Dame with little study time, he found himself now having to dash down memos about what he was doing and when. Names, simple words, what he'd eaten for dinner—it was all washing out in one long wave.

No one had to tell him what those symptoms implied or what lay in store if he stuck around. Once a savage hitter on the best defense the game has ever seen, Duerson filled the punch list for chronic traumatic encephalopathy (CTE), the neuron-killing condition so rampant these days among middle-aged veterans of the National Football League. Andre Waters and Terry Long, both dead by their own hands; John Mackey and Ralph Wenzel, hopelessly brain-broke in their 50s. It was a bad way to die and a worse way to live, warehoused for decades in a fog, unable, finally, to know your own kids when they came to see you at the home.

Among the personal effects Duerson arranged that night in February was the master clue to the act he'd soon commit, Exhibit A in a life turned sideways: his 1987 NFL Man of the Year trophy. It was a testimonial to a former colossus, a player whose brilliance on the football field was a taste of much grander things to come. Future meat-processing magnate and potential congressman, or successor to Gene Upshaw as director of the NFL Players Association—*that* Dave Duerson was all forward motion, the rarest amalgam of outsize smarts and inborn ambition. This version, though—the one slumped in bed with the .38 Special to his chest—this one had run into walls, head lowered, and he, not the walls, had buckled first.

Still, when someone turns a gun on himself, there are bound to be messy questions. Why, given the spate of concussions in the NFL season just past, would Duerson elect to keep silent about his suspected ailment at precisely the moment he should have spoken? Why would a man who knew as much about brain woes as anyone who's ever played the game, having served for six years and read thousands of case files as a trustee on the NFL's pension board, not have sought treatment and financial compensation from the very committee he sat on? And why, bizarrely, did he deny those very benefits to the men who needed them most, brain-dimmed veterans living in pain and squalor and seeking relief from the league?

Perhaps to stanch these questions, Duerson dispatched a blitz of texts in the last couple of hours of his life, some of them making an emphatic plea: Get my brain to the NFL's brain bank in Boston. The meaning of the texts seems plain enough: I'm sick and my mind's failing from all the helmet-to-helmet collisions in 11 brutal seasons in the NFL. Please see to it that my cortex is studied by doctors seeking treatments for brain trauma—and inquire no further about my reasons. It was a grandiose gesture, killing himself at 50 so that current and future players might be spared this horror, and was italicized by a second theatrical stroke: He shot himself through the heart, not the head, to preserve his brain for science.

But the dramatics of the act didn't sanctify him or absolve him of blame for the part he'd played in the suffering of other ex-players. If anything, Duerson's death has become a referendum on his, and his sport's, brutality, a prism through which to finally take a look at the cost of all those hits.

If you're the kind of fan who keeps a mental lineup of ex-players headed for bad endings, Dave Duerson was the last name to make your list. Virtually from birth he'd been a special case, a gold-star guy who didn't bull through problems so much as soar above them. The youngest of four children born to Julia and Arthur Duerson Jr. in working-class Muncie, Indiana, he was as exceptional off the field as he was on it. A big, powerful kid with a nose for the ball and the long-stride speed to get there first, he dominated boys two and three years older in football from the time he hit sixth grade. (He excelled at baseball and basketball, as well.) Even then, though, his dreams were broader than jock stardom. Among friends he talked brashly about owning his own factories and running for the Senate someday. Duerson made the National Honor Society in high school, learned the trumpet and tuba by the age of 15, and toured overseas in an ambassador's band while earning 10 varsity letters.

With his pick of football factories like Texas and USC, Duerson chose South Bend for its glorious campus and network of corporate contacts. "From when I met him in seventh grade, he was positioning himself for a career after football," says Dave Adams, Duerson's teammate at Northside High and his roommate at Notre Dame. He interned at a law firm, then for Indiana Senator Richard Lugar.

"Sports were the springboard," says his ex-wife Alicia, who met him at a bowl game his freshman year. "He made so many plans for such a young age and had the brains to pull it all off. He had a photographic memory, which used to make me mad, because he'd barely study and get A's, where I'd be up a week of nights and be happy to get a B." A four-year starter at Notre Dame and a team captain, Duerson was as proud of his degree in economics as of making All-American, which he did twice.

Duerson was nothing if not complicated. He had, besides ambition and swagger to burn, a deep well of kindness and soul. You could see it in the way he honored Muncie, returning each summer to run a camp for poor kids in memory of a high school friend who'd drowned, and you could hear it later from the teens he sent to college after making it big with the Bears. "Everything he did was a teaching tool," says Michael Gorin, a family friend and retired teacher from Muncie whose son Brandon attended Duerson's camp and went on to play nine years in the NFL. "He had the Super Bowl rings but kept harping on academics. My son says they talk about him at *Harvard*."

Harvard would come later, after Duerson got done playing and commuted to Cambridge for an executive program at the business school. Long before that, though, he got a brawler's education when he showed up at Bears training camp as a third-round pick. He should have gone higher in the '83 draft, but his talk about law school and political aspirations probably set him back a round or two. Buddy Ryan, the great, brutish coordinator of Chicago's 46 defense, loathed rookies, especially rookies with more on their mind than earholing Packers. "He knew I'd gone to Notre Dame and asked if I was one of those doctors or lawyers," Duerson said in an interview he gave last year for a book about Americans turning 50. "I said, 'Yes, sir.' He said, 'Well, you won't be here long, because I don't like smart niggers'"—a comment Ryan has denied making.

Dan Hampton, a Hall of Fame lineman on that absurdly dominant Bears defense, offers a different take. "Buddy didn't care if you were black, white, or green: He wanted smashmouth, and Duerson wouldn't nail guys. In practice, Buddy'd yell, 'That shit ain't cuttin' it! You dive on the ground again, I'm firing you!'"

Duerson submitted to doing it Ryan's way and became a ferocious hitter. He mostly covered kicks his first two seasons and backed up

Pro Bowl safety Todd Bell. Then, in '85, Bell held out for more money, and Ryan had no choice but to start Duerson. "I played through that whole season with [Buddy] telling me that he was rooting for me to screw up," Duerson said in a 2005 interview. "So I became an All-Pro myself." On that banzai unit, which jammed the line with 10 men, Duerson came screaming off the edge on blitzes. In 1986, his second season as a starter, he had seven sacks, a record for defensive backs that stood till 2005. He made the Pro Bowl four years running, a breakout star on a squad of loud assassins. Tellingly, it was Duerson who, with linebacker Otis Wilson, developed the unit's calling card. After an especially vicious shot, they'd stand over their victim, barking and baying like junkyard dogs.

Of course, football has a way of evening things up between preda- tors and prey. In his 11-year run with the Bears, Giants (where he won another Super Bowl, in 1990), and Cardinals, Duerson suffered multiple minor concussions, though he was never knocked out cold. Emerging after games in a pair of dark glasses and wincing against the dusk, he'd complain of nausea and ringing headaches, says his ex-wife Alicia. "Dave would get concussed on the first or second series and play the whole way through, or get a dinger in the second half and be back at practice Wednesday morning," she says. "Dave had one speed, and that was full-out."

In the years to come, he'd have cause to rethink that, at least when it came to his kids. His middle son, Tregg, now a bank analyst in Chi- cago, was a highly regarded prep-school running back who'd go on to play defensive back at Notre Dame. One game in high school, Tregg was dazed from a tackle and wobbled off the field. Watching from the stands, Duerson ran down to the sideline and snatched Tregg's helmet so he couldn't return; at halftime he whisked him off to the hospital to be checked out. Tregg had a concussion. "Just to be on the safe side," says Alicia, "Dave wouldn't let him play for three games."

As his playing days dwindled, Duerson weighed his options, begin- ning with politics. "Both the Republican and Democratic parties in Chicago tabbed him to run for office," says Harold Rice, one of Duer- son's oldest friends and the man who accompanied Alicia and Tregg to Florida after Duerson's death. "Dave wanted to be a difference maker, but realized pretty quick that it wasn't worth the scrutiny."

Rice, who owned a McDonald's, urged him to enter his business instead. Duerson opened a franchise in Louisville, Kentucky, his first year out of football, then got an attractive offer from a McDonald's supplier: There was an ownership opportunity in a meat-processing plant an hour outside Chicago. Duerson bought a controlling stake and, with his contacts and charm, promptly doubled the plant's revenue to more than $60 million a year. He bought himself a huge house in Highland Park, just up the road from Michael Jordan's place, engraved his jersey number, NFL 22, on the driveway pillars, and spent a bundle on exotic cars, including a midnight-blue Mercedes SL 600 with the vanity plate DD22. By then he'd had four kids with Alicia, had local sports talk shows on both radio and television, and was jetting off to Cambridge, Massachusetts, for months at a time for the executive program there. "Dave loved it at Harvard, getting to network with CEOs and bounce ideas off presidents of foreign companies," says Alicia. "When he took us to Europe, it was first class all the way: stretch limos, four-star dining, and—his big dream—flying in the Concorde."

But friction eventually sparked between Duerson and his partner at the plant, who resented his comings and goings. In 2002, Duerson sold his interest to open his own processing plant nearby. It was the first big mistake in a life of shrewd decisions, and caught Duerson flat-footed, stunned by failure.

From the beginning, Duerson Foods had disaster written all over it. He shelled out millions to gut and double the factory's floor space, then borrowed heavily to buy state-of-the-art freezers from a company in the Netherlands. They were impressive to look at but so unsound that he had to postpone opening by six months. He fell behind on his schedule to supply Burger King and Olive Garden, and soon he was leveraged to the hilt. At his swank offices in Lincolnshire, Illinois, employees, some of them relatives, saw a change. His niece, Yvette Fuse, would call Rice in a panic to say that "Dave was berating people, acting mean." Duerson borrowed more, using his house as collateral, and sued the freezer maker. He won a $34 million judgment, but the company filed for bankruptcy and never paid him a dime. By 2006, creditors were raining down lawsuits, and Duerson, broke and heartsick, shut the plant. He'd lost his mother to a heart attack and his house to the finance company, and his father was ailing with

Alzheimer's (he died in 2009). "The pressure on him was phenomenal," said Rice. "It would've taken Superman not to break."

As it turned out, Duerson *had* broken, if briefly. In February 2005, he and Alicia drove to South Bend for a meeting of Notre Dame's board of trustees, of which he was a member. During a small-hours argument at their hotel, he threw her out the door of their room into the hallway wall. Alicia suffered cuts to her head and went to the ER with dizziness and pain. Duerson was charged with several misdemeanor counts and later pleaded guilty to domestic battery. In an interview, he called that night "a three-second snap," but it was played up big in the Chicago papers and forced his resignation from Notre Dame's board of trustees. Alicia, looking back now through the prism of his death, sees a clear demarcation in his conduct. The old Dave, she says, "would never do that; he never showed violence toward me. It was the changes," she says of his new hair-trigger temper, sudden downshifts in mood, and lack of impulse control—all signs of brain trauma.

His missteps, meanwhile, were beginning to throw shade on his fine reputation in the game—a reputation he'd carefully nursed since the day he entered the league. As a rookie in Chicago, Duerson had been chosen by his teammates to be the Bears' union representative. He was the son of a strong labor man at General Motors and "wanted to make things better for the guys," says Alicia.

For more than 60 years, the owners had run roughshod over the players, shackling stars to teams and imposing whatever terms they liked in collective negotiations. Duerson deftly held the Bears together through the bitter 1987 strike and beyond, and became a key adviser to, and close friend of, Gene Upshaw, the union's chief executive. "The two of them traveled together, even during the season, to talk to players about their rights," says Alicia. "Dave believed in the cause with all his heart and set himself to learning about labor laws so he could explain it clearly to the guys."

In 1992 and 1993, the players finally turned the tables in a pair of historic trials in federal court. Duerson was a featured plaintiff in one, and his tour de force performance on the witness stand helped fray the owners' resolve to keep on fighting. "He was so knowledgeable on the facts and spoke them so beautifully that you could really feel the tide start to turn," says ESPN.com legal analyst Lester Munson, who covered the trial for *Sports Illustrated*.

The owners grudgingly cut a deal, awarding free agency and a broad slate of rights to players. Among the key gains was the creation of a board to hear the disability claims not only of active players but of retirees whose injuries prevented them from holding a job. The board was composed of six trustees (three each of management and union members, the latter being appointed by Upshaw), and the disability money, many hundreds of millions of dollars, was funded almost entirely by owners.

Right from its inception, though, an odd thing happened: In case after case before the board, former players were denied assistance or put through a maze of second opinions and paperwork. Men with bent spines and diced joints were told they could still hold a paying job and so were ineligible for aid. Then there were the veterans coming forward in their 40s and 50s with the brain scans of aging boxers who also had their claims voted down by the board. "They made it real clear that they'd fight me to the death, like they did with Mike Webster," says Brent Boyd, a Vikings guard in the '80s who suffers from clinical depression related to brain trauma. (Webster, the Hall of Fame center of the Steelers, was profoundly impaired by CTE and lived out of his truck at times before he died at 50.) "They were supposed to push for us, but were in the owners' pockets. You had to live in a wheelchair to collect."

In 2006, a particularly fraught time in the struggles between veterans and the players' union, Upshaw decided to name his old friend Duerson to the pension board. This seemed a peculiar choice at best: Duerson had been out of the sport for a decade, was tarnished by the recent incident in South Bend, and ran a company that was coming apart. Any doubts about Duerson—and Upshaw's critics had plenty— were quickly ratified by his demeanor. The man who'd been so eloquent in federal court under the grilling of NFL lawyers was barging around town like a pit bull on crank, attacking former players at every turn. At a congressional hearing in 2007 to investigate the ex-players' charges, Duerson started a shoving match with Sam Huff and Bernie Parrish, two former greats speaking out for injured vets. He maligned Brent Boyd to a Senate committee, questioning whether his documented brain woes were actually caused by football. He took to talk radio to disparage Mike Ditka, saying his old coach, who'd raised money for vets, had never cared about his players' health. The worst of it, though, was his sliming of Brian DeMarco, a crippled veteran with several crushed vertebrae who'd gone public about his rejection by the union. Duerson tore into him on a call-in radio show, deriding him as a liar and an insurance fraud, then appeared on a Chicago TV program to ambush DeMarco in person.

His mad-dog behavior was very much in line with the way he voted on claims. Says Cy Smith, the lawyer who won a landmark lawsuit on behalf of Mike Webster's estate: "I get dozens of these files coming across my desk—stark, sad cases of guys really banged up—and the vast majority of these judgments are 6–0 against the players. That's a gross breach of practice by the board and a clear pattern of bias against paying." That Duerson was siding with management—and, apparently, Upshaw—is no surprise to his critics. Says Huff, the New York Giants Hall of Fame linebacker: "Dave wanted Gene's job when he finally stepped down, and was saying and doing whatever Gene wanted, or whatever he thought he wanted." Indeed, Duerson told people he'd been handpicked by Upshaw to succeed him as union chief, a position that paid nearly $7 million a year and was essentially a lifetime appointment. When Upshaw died in 2008, Duerson didn't get the post (attorney DeMaurice Smith did), though he retained his seat on the board.

Whatever Duerson's motives for voting against veterans, they ran counter to a life spent helping others. At Duerson Foods, he'd paid the healthcare premiums for his factory-floor workers and footed the college tuition for kids from inner-city Chicago. That doesn't assuage the retired players he turned down, whose rancor isn't softened by his death. "He caused more suffering personally than all the other board members combined," says Boyd. Adds John Hogan, a lawyer who assists former players with their disability claims: "He really could've changed the story for vets, and done it from the inside without saying mea culpa. He didn't have to indict the system. All he had to do was say, publicly, 'I'm sick, and I need help like these other guys.' "

The last years of his life, Duerson knew he was in decline. He'd gotten divorced from Alicia in 2009 and fled to Florida in glum retreat, dropping out of sight for months on end. (He'd bought the condo, in the twin-tower Ocean One, in Sunny Isles Beach, as a winter house in 2000, but hadn't much used it until he moved in.) On his trips to Chicago to see his kids, he'd complain to Alicia about persistent headaches and frightening spells of blurred vision. "He thought at first he was getting old, but seemed more concerned as time went on," she says. His memory was shot, he wasn't sleeping much, and he had to ask her directions to get around Chicago—a town he'd known cold for 25 years. "He could hide the changes from friends and such, but he couldn't hide them from me. He'd say, 'Remember the time we did such and such?' as if to prove he wasn't fading, but he was."

He was a step above flat broke and trying to hide that, too. He hocked his wedding ring and Rolex watch, unloaded a newer Mercedes and his beloved Harley, and borrowed heavily against the equity in his apartment, though he'd put the place in trust for his four children. Even so, he couldn't make his child-support payments or keep up with his condo fees, and the stress and shame compounded his symptoms and began, it seemed, to derange him.

Says Ron Ben-David, who took over as building manager at the Ocean One towers in 2008: "I called Dave down and asked him politely why he hadn't paid his dues in almost a year. He told me someone had broken into his closet and stolen three paintings he'd bought in Cuba, and unless we reimbursed him the $7,000, he wasn't going to pay the arrears." But Duerson hadn't phoned the cops about his loss or filed an insurance claim, and ultimately paid his back-maintenance fees via wire transfer. A year later, his checks stopped coming again, and again Ben-David called him down. "He said, 'Well, someone stole my paintings. Aren't you going to reimburse me?' And this time they were worth $30,000."

"He was definitely getting worse. I could hear it over the phone," says Alicia. "He was trying to reinvent who he was at 50, and that's hard even when you're thinking straight." Duerson talked a lot about having "irons in the fire"—some deals in the works with Costco and the USDA—but nothing ever seemed to pan out. When he filed for bankruptcy in Florida last year, he showed annual expenditures of $74,000, an income of less than $34,000, and a consulting business whose only assets were the furniture and equipment in his study. His one frail hope, a Hail Mary, was to get hired as a coach in the NFL. Last fall he phoned Steve Zucker, his former agent, and asked him to make some calls on his behalf. At the time, he had several ex-teammates running teams—Jeff Fisher, then with the Titans, Mike Singletary, then with the 49ers, and Leslie Frazier, who'd taken over in Minnesota—all three also proud alumni of that great Bears defense of the '80s. "His plan was to get a position-coach thing or a job in someone's front office," says Zucker, once a Chicago superagent who is now in his 70s and mostly retired. "I talked to him all the time and had no idea. He sounded so positive on the phone."

With the exception of Alicia and a couple of his old cronies, Duerson told no one how grim things had gotten or how badly his symptoms had unhinged him. He holed up in Florida, where he avoided his neighbors. Beyond the occasional visit from one of his kids, the only break in the deepening gloom was a last-chance love affair. He'd met Antoinette Sykes in May 2010 at a business conference in Las Vegas, where he gave a talk to aspiring entrepreneurs about growing and selling a million-dollar company. By summer, he and Sykes, who owns her own PR and marketing firm in Washington, D.C., were speaking or texting 10 times a day and flying to each other's homes for weeklong stays. In the fall, he proudly showed her off to building manager Ben-David, calling her his "angel" and fiancée. They were scheduled to be married in April 2011, when his daughter, who would be on spring recess, could attend.

"What we shared was so sacred and joyful," Sykes said over the phone from D.C. "I knew he had headaches and—and a lump on his skull that he was worried about, but what I'm reading in the papers now about his brain, it's thrown me for such a loop. Maybe he wanted to shield me, but he seemed so excited about spending the rest of our lives together. On our last night, Valentine's, he joked that I owed him 29 more because we'd committed to 30 years of wedded bliss. And then I flew home to pack my things to move down there..." She breaks off, convulsing.

On February 17, Sykes woke up in Washington to a text from Duerson. It began, "My dear Angel, I love you so much and I'm sorry for my past, but I think this knot on my head is the real deal." Sykes called him, heard nothing back, and became frantic as the morning passed. Sometime after two that afternoon, she called Ben-David and asked him to knock on Duerson's door. When no one answered, she faxed him her permission to use a spare key. "I got the door open, but there was a chair wedged against it. That's when I called 911," he says. Paramedics and cops arrived and pushed their way in. "I heard them in the bedroom, yelling 'Sir! Sir! Is everything all right?' Then they asked me to leave," says Ben-David. Duerson was found shortly after 3 P.M. He had shot himself about 12 hours earlier. Apart from the large patch of blood beneath him, the place was immaculate, said Miami-Dade police officers. Veteran detectives, they said they'd never seen a suicide planned and executed so meticulously.

In the months after his death, Duerson has become a wedge for practically anyone with a connection to the sport. The media has mostly lined up with *Time* magazine, which called him "football's first martyr." Ex-players have sourly mocked his sanctification, denying him any credit for calling attention to CTE in death when he could have worked for justice while alive. Even his Bears teammates are badly split: Some are saddened and shocked by his death, while others deem him selfish and arrogant—"political to the end," groused a former lineman. The dissonance was put best by his son Tregg, now 25. "I just wish he'd played baseball," he told the *New York Times* five days after Duerson died. But, he added, sobbing, that his father "was looking for an answer and was hoping to be part of an answer."

At some point, it's hoped, Duerson's motives will matter less than the long-haul impact of his passing. A tremor has gone through the league, deep and wide; players are talking openly about football and brain cells and fretting over their own neural health. "Is it something that I think about? Yeah, absolutely," Baltimore Ravens center Matt Birk told the *Times*. He's one of more than a hundred current and former players who've signed over their brains for postmortem study at Boston University. You'd expect forward thinking from a Harvard grad like Birk, rated the sixth-smartest man in sports by *Sporting News* last year. But the message is getting across to less cerebral types, too. Jim McMahon, the ex-passer and party monster who loved to celebrate touchdowns with ringing head butts, is battling serious memory problems and has also agreed to send his brain to Boston. "What the fuck do I need it for when I'm dead?" he says. That gesture, if not the sentiment, will be part of the answer to the questions Duerson lived and died to raise.

Bryan Curtis

Bryan Curtis (b. 1977) is predictable only in that there seem to be surprises in everything he writes, good surprises, the kind that let readers know they can count on him for a unique take no matter what the subject. Consider the surge in concern over concussions in football from the NFL on down to the youth leagues. It was the youth leagues that fascinated Curtis, a staff writer at the website Grantland and a native Texan whose byline appears frequently in *Texas Monthly*. He wanted to see "how they were processing the news about football. How they were coming to grips with it. How they were, in some cases, ignoring it." Curtis found the perfect team to study in Allen, Texas, outside Dallas—undefeated for years, loaded with prize elementary school athletes who would realize only later that they were saying good-bye to childhood. His story about them, "Friday Night Tykes," appeared in *Texas Monthly*'s January 2013 issue and provided further evidence that he is one of the new century's very best sportswriters. Curtis began his journalism career by writing about the real world for the *New Republic* and *Slate*, first explored the world of fun and games at the *New York Times*' sports magazine *Play*, and returned to the serious side to help Tina Brown, the mercurial former *Vanity Fair* and *New Yorker* editor, launch *The Daily Beast*. While working for Brown, he says, he "sustained repeated concussions."

Friday Night Tykes

I. THE HAWKS

Preteen football players are usually described by other preteen football players with one of three words: "nice," "funny," or, the highest possible compliment, "awesome." Celdon Manning, a running back with the Allen Hawks, is the rare athlete who makes his teammates reach for the *Scholastic Children's Thesaurus*.

"Celdon is very... shy," said Nick Trice, the center.

"He's very... quiet," said Bryce Monk, an outside linebacker.

He is also "so dope" and "so beast," to page further through the twelve-year-old's thesaurus, which is to say he can jump-cut and stiff-arm and cut-block and do things that make his teammates' jaws drop. There was this one play, in the Allen Sports Association Super Bowl this past November. The Hawks were playing the Wild Dawgz for their fortieth consecutive victory and fourth straight league title. Celdon lined up in a Wildman formation with the Hawks leading 27–6. He took the snap and sprinted left. He saw a Wild Dawgz linebacker fill the hole. What was in his mind? As his teammates watched from the sidelines, Celdon jabbed his left foot toward the linebacker's chest and then shifted his body weight to the right, like a metronome. In a split second, he was traveling in the opposite direction, past the defense and toward the end zone.

For four years, the Allen Hawks had been the best youth football team in the most football-mad suburb in Texas—which is to say, the world. In season after season, they'd been so untouchable, so dominant, that trophy-collecting had actually gotten slightly monotonous. "After the first one, I got excited," Eric Engel, a linebacker, told me. "And after the second one, I got excited. After the third one, I was like, okay...." But this Super Bowl had the Hawks' full and undivided attention—it was the last game they would play together. The sixth-graders had grown up together, fought together, gotten their shins skinned together. Next year most would become seventh graders and start playing for their middle school teams. "This is about the Hawks winning on this field for the final time," said their head coach, Kevin Engel (Eric's father), before the game. He sounded like he might cry.

Celdon was one of the few who wouldn't be moving on, since he was actually in fifth grade. While many parents hold their sons back a grade to gain a competitive edge, Celdon's mom, Tracy Wallace, insisted her son play "up." Celdon, who was ten when the 2012 season began, has three older brothers, so he was used to it. "When he was three," Tracy told me one afternoon, "he had a pacifier in his mouth, and he'd get down in a three-point stance." Celdon's dedication to football is fairly ordinary in Allen, a well-heeled suburb of Dallas that made national news in August when the high school opened the doors of a new, $60 million stadium, the largest in Texas devoted to a single school. Celdon was simply a product of that environment. Before every game, his mom made him watch a highlight video called *NFL's Top 10: Football Moves*. The images were burned in his brain. When he had the ball under his arm, Celdon said, he felt he could access those moves as easily as he could make a *Madden 13* player execute a stiff-arm in the video game.

On that run in the Super Bowl, you could see Celdon mentally tapping the buttons. He juked right—*tap*—and the Wild Dawgz linebacker wound up facedown on the ground with his hands around Celdon's shoe. Celdon saw a crowd between him and the goal line. *Tap.* He leaned his body forward so it was at a 45-degree angle and rammed into the defenders.

"Celdon is the best eleven-year-old football player in America," Ronnie Braxton, his trainer, told me. "In *America.*" Celdon isn't the first youth football player to inspire that kind of claim. But when he hit the pile, his powerful legs churning furiously as he wormed his way through the defenders, the assessment seemed indisputable. As the referees pulled everyone off the pile and found Celdon lying in the end zone, his teammates began hopping up and down, and one of the grandmas in the stands rang a cowbell, and the Hawks cheer-leaders—yes, the Hawks have cheerleaders—shook their metallic red-and-black pompoms, and the sound system that Coach Engel had rigged up with two car batteries and an ice chest began pumping out triumphal music, and I abandoned journalistic objectivity to throw my arms in the air and cheer until my throat hurt. How does it feel to watch a running back from the best preteen football team in the most football-mad city in Texas exert his will? It's so beast.

Football isn't supposed to feel like this anymore. We know too much, don't we? We know that if Celdon were to plow his helmet into the pile at the wrong angle, a player could receive a mild concussion. We know that enough mild concussions can cause something called chronic traumatic encephalopathy, which could leave a former youth footballer, a few decades hence, unable to recognize his wife. We know that a thousand former NFL players right now are suing the league for the damage they incurred while slamming themselves into one another on television. We know that when Dave Duerson, a former Chicago Bears safety, killed himself in 2011, he aimed the gun at his chest, so that researchers could study what had happened to his brain.

Whenever football lights up our brains these days, we fear it's turn-ing someone else's to mush. It's a conflict that's playing out not only in the offices of NFL commissioner Roger Goodell but on the side-lines of football fields all across the country, in places like Allen. By any measure, Allen, which has around 80,000 residents, is intensely devoted to football. "It's *ray*-bid down here," Coach Engel said. The high school football stadium that opened in August is not just big and expensive, it's also fully outfitted, with an air-conditioned press box and an HD screen for instant replays. And the residents of this highly Republican community agreed to pay for it with new taxes.

In the city's youth football league, the Allen Sports Association, 1,200 boys play football. In kindergarten, they pull flags out of one another's waistbands. By second grade, they're tackling each other by the legs. By third grade, they're studying elements of the spread offense. By fourth grade, they're glancing at the play charts on their wrists, just like Tony Romo. By the time an Allen boy can read Harry Potter, he has become a football savant. Cullen Perkins, a Hawks tackle, told me he watches Blu-ray game film on his flat-screen in bed at night and writes little notes to himself about what he can do better.

But the wave of concern over concussions hasn't bypassed Allen. When former San Diego linebacker Junior Seau committed suicide in May—aiming his gun, like Duerson, at his chest—moms and dads blitzed the ASA with emails. "There was all this craziness out there that everybody's going to get a concussion and kill themselves like Junior Seau did," Blake Beidleman, the league's commissioner, told me this summer. For the first time in nearly a decade, the number of boys playing football in Allen leveled off.

As the start of last season drew near, however, Allenites didn't abandon football. They doubled down on the things they valued about the game in the first place. They decided that football was important for a boy's growth and essential to the identity of the city and that concussions—which they would try to avoid as best they could—were manageable nightmares.

Allen, like much of the country, decided that it was going to try to save football from modernity. It was going to see if what was primal and brutal about the game could exist in an era of science and safety and lawsuits and attachment parenting. I wanted to see this struggle. I wanted to go to a city where kids practiced football three times a week and played once a week while Mom watched from a lawn chair; a place where they had the best protective gear and the best doctors; where the game was coached the right way and played exquisitely well—even by kids. I wanted to see the sport trying to survive in our new, wised-up universe. And what better way than to spend a season with the Hawks? As Beidleman told me the first time we met, "When somebody in Iowa gets a copy of *Texas Monthly*, they're either going to think that we're crazy or that this is the greatest thing ever!"

II. HELL WEEK

"When we get a chance in football," Coach Engel asked the Hawks, "we do what?"

"Hit!" the Hawks shouted in unison.

"No," Coach said, fighting a smile. "*Breathe*. But 'hit' is a better answer."

It was a hot night in July, and Coach was standing at the top of a steep hill in a park in Allen. The Hawks were at the bottom. Coach had already dubbed the season (on the Hawks' Facebook page) "The Final Flight" and ordered new, $135 uniforms for each boy. He expected not only to win one last Super Bowl but to have a perfect season, which would mean absolutely mud-holing the other ten sixth-grade squads. The Hawks received his expectations with aplomb. Most of them hadn't lost a league game since second grade, and I couldn't find a single one who even remembered that dark day.

"Vertical planks!" Coach called out. The Hawks got into a push-up position and began to crawl up the hill with their arms. Then they crawled down again.

"Backward planks!" Coach called out. The Hawks reversed their posture so that their chests faced the sky. Then they inched up the hill with their arms again. Chris Washington, a running back who was in his first season with the team, lay down on the hill in exhaustion. Coach walked over until he was standing directly over him, and, reluctantly, Chris got up and kept going.

Coach Engel is 42 years old, with carefully combed dark hair and a cherubic face. He wore a baseball cap that said "Violence Solves Problems." He had a pinch of chaw in his lower lip, which he often inserted after polishing off a can of Rock Star Energy Drink. He was not a tyrant. In fact, he is as close to a mensch as a sport like football allows. As a kid in Dumas, he played youth football for the Shamrock Hawks (he named his team in Allen after them). He served in the Navy—he still has "The Star-Spangled Banner" in his white F-150's audio system—and, while he was stationed in South Carolina, married a pretty girl named Pam. Now Coach and Pam and Eric live in a typical Allen red-brick dream house, with leather furniture, thick carpet, and several flat-screen TVs.

During the season, they had Hawks practice three nights a week. Pam coached the cheerleading squad with the help of their older daughter, Nicole, who is 23. The girls performed at halftime, and Coach commanded the players to sit on their helmets and pay attention.

Coach had a literary streak. He'd read George MacDonald Fraser's Flashman novels and had perfected a kind of exurban Texas articulation. "What would you like to eat if there was a bunch of it?" he liked to say, by way of asking a player where he wanted to have lunch. At a restaurant, he'd notice Celdon scraping cream gravy off a chicken-fried steak. "You don't like gravy?" he'd ask. When Celdon, forever quiet, shrugged, Coach would say, "So you'd say you're ambivalent about it."

He'd put the Hawks together like a college team, starting out with a few great players, like the running back Maurice "Mo" Perkins (no relation to Cullen), in kindergarten, and every year, "recruiting" a few more. Recruiting is how you win in Allen. You can't steal a player from another team—any player vacating his squad has to go into the draft, where lousy teams like the Cobras and Cardinals pick first. But Coach could find would-be Hawks who were new to football or, like Chris, the running back, have just moved from out of town. He looked in malls, neighborhoods, everywhere. "I roll with blue Powerade and Now and Laters," Coach liked to joke. He had found Chris chasing a rabbit around his neighborhood.

Coach didn't relish Hell Week, his annual preseason combine. He saw it as a necessary evil. The kids saw it that way too. "He works us hard," Monk told me. "Which is a good thing." Monk was the team's wise guy. Once, during Hell Week, Coach was giving a speech. "Your bodies are changing," he told the team, to which I heard Monk reply, under his breath, "Yeah, we *know*."

"Were those horrible or merely awful?" Coach asked the panting Hawks, who were standing at the bottom of the hill after their backward plank exercises. He told them to jog in place "on two," simulating a snap count. If any Hawk started jogging early, they all had to start over. "Bear crawls up and down the hill!" Coach called. They squirmed along the ground on all fours. "Get off your knees!" Coach said. His sound system was playing the 1812 Overture.

Later, he had the Hawks lie on their backs and raise their feet six inches off the ground. Coach called it "tough bellies." Twelve-year-old cries of agony sounded until everyone's legs were on the grass. You didn't have to be a psychologist to see that the torturous workout endeared the coach to the Hawks and that when the season started in three weeks, the most horrible thing they could do would be to disappoint him.

As the shadows began to get long, Coach gathered the team around and stuck out a meaty fist. The Hawks piled their hands on top of it. They chanted, in voices that were at various stages of puberty,

Hit 'em hard,
Make 'em bleed,
Hawks, Hawks, Hawks!

"You want to see it?" Coach Engel asked me one afternoon. In Allen, "it" is the new football stadium. The *New York Times* and *Time* magazine had already described it with a form of the cliché "Everything's bigger in Texas." On some level, they were right. But as we hopped in Coach's truck, I suspected the stadium represented something more than the culmination of a simple arms race.

Buzz Bissinger's *Friday Night Lights*, published in 1990, is the classic tale of Texas high school football. In his depiction of Odessa, Bissinger unwittingly announced the end of an era. Even by 1990, the locus of Texas football had moved from the cities to the suburbs. The old capitals of Texas football were Odessa and Houston and Dallas; the new ones were places like the Colony and Sugar Land and Allen. Named after Texas secretary of state Ebenezer Allen, the community of Allen was founded in 1872. A local named L. C. "Big Daddy" Summers (in a memoir dictated to his son, Biff) described the town in the thirties as an idyllic farming village on the interurban rail line. But football madness simmered even then. During the forties, Allen High School put together great six-man football teams. According to an account compiled by Tom Keener, a historian at the local library, 1,500 Allenites traveled to see a bi-district championship game in Vernon, in 1948. When asked, "Who's mindin' your store?" an Allen mercantilist replied, "Who's mindin' the *town*?"

If Richardson was the "it" Dallas suburb of the seventies and Plano the eighties, then Allen and McKinney, where you could get cheaper and bigger red-brick houses, have conquered the recent past. And with Whole Foods and Cabela's, not to mention three different semipro sports franchises, Allen doesn't depend on Dallas for anything. "Allen does not like to be called a suburb," Keener told me. "It is the *City* of Allen."

In 1999 Allen High was rebuilt as a college-size, red-brick campus, the city's latest trophy. "It's a yuppie school, let's face it," said Tim Carroll, the director of public information for the Allen school district. And it's growing. Allen claimed fewer than 20,000 residents in 1990 but is pushing 100,000 two decades later. Allen High's enrollment has swelled to 5,500 students, but the city has been loath to build a second high school, because, as numerous residents explained, that would dilute the team's football talent.

The Allen Eagles are good. They won a state title in 2008 under Coach Tom Westerberg. But their stadium on East Main Street was a sad collection of metal bleachers that Allenites derisively called the Double Wide. By 2011, 7,000 fans were squeezing into the Double Wide's seats on Friday nights and another 7,000 were squeezing into temporary bleachers in the end zone. So the city decided to build a new stadium: a grand football palace that would hold 18,000 fans. (In addition to the $60 million for the school's new football field, another $59 million was earmarked for other improvements.) The bond proposal passed with more than 60 percent of the vote.

Allenites are defensive about the stadium's size. They insist that the city did not intentionally set out to build the biggest high school stadium in Texas. Rather, it gave itself a kind of testicular self-examination and concluded that its consuming interest in football ran so deep that building the biggest stadium was unavoidable. "We built it because of the demand," Carroll told me.

Coach Engel pulled his F-150 into the parking lot, and we stared at the stadium. A sign said "Your Bond Dollars at Work"; construction workers scurried in front of the truck. The structure looked like it belonged to a small, well-funded college, with light-pink brick and the words "EAGLE STADIUM" in giant block letters. Two warlike eagle statues stood sentry on either side.

We sat in silence for a moment. Then Coach said, "It's very Reichstag."

III. THE PSYCHOLOGIST

The second-best sixth-grade team in Allen was the Wild Dawgz. For the past three years, the Dawgz had made it to the Super Bowl, only to be routed by the Hawks. The loss in 2011 had been so crushing that the Wild Dawgz had decamped from the Allen Sports Association entirely and reorganized the club in McKinney. Following their departure, a new Wild Dawgz team was formed in the ASA, and as it turned out, these new Dawgz were still the Hawks' biggest competition.

In the second week of the season, the Wild Dawgz were on the schedule. I found Coach Engel at home, pacing nervously. He sat down at the kitchen table, under plaques that said "Praise" and "Faith" and "Love," and punched the keys on his laptop. He'd gone to see the Dawgz play the previous Saturday and shot a couple of hours' worth of video. Taping games is common in Allen. (There was a minor scandal the previous season when a few coaches tried to tape one another's practices.) Coach studied the boys running across his screen and made notes. *Stop the handoff to No. 8. Make sure No. 94 doesn't knife into the backfield and sack Joey on passing plays.* This was mere refresher—he'd already told the Hawks all this stuff at practice.

Eric came downstairs in his jersey. "You ready, bubby?" Coach said. They threw the sound system into the bed of the truck. Between Hawks plays, it would pump out music like the *Jaws* theme, just as at an NFL game. "Nine hundred watts of power," Coach remarked. He flipped on the music and wiggled his butt in ecstasy. Then we hopped in the truck and headed for Lovejoy Stadium, a high school field in nearby Lucas where most of the ASA's sixth-grade games are played.

Before kickoff Coach morphed into a kind of child psychologist, strolling up and down the field where the boys were warming up, planting motivations deep inside the collective preadolescent consciousness. When you coach a team that has won thirty games in a row, Coach explained later, enemies have to be invented. The tricks were transparent even to the players, but they still worked. Coach approached Mo, his running back. "They've been talking about you," he said.

"Who?" Mo said, suddenly very concerned.

"Oh, I hear things through the back channel," Coach said. "'The gap has closed.' 'Mo isn't as fast as he used to be.' Crap like that."

Mo frowned and jogged off. Coach walked over to Monk, who was practicing extra points. The Hawks were the only team in the ASA regularly kicking extra points—an incredibly tough feat for a twelve-year-old. They did it out of boredom.

Coach watched as Monk drilled a 17-yarder. "I told you steroids were a good idea!" he laughed.

Monk backed up 10 yards and nailed another field goal.

"That was Monk*alicious!*"

As we moved on, Coach explained that Monk responded better to praise. If you tore into him, you could lose him.

Joe Crisci, the Hawks' offensive coordinator and father of the quarterback, Joey, was on the opposite side of the field, tending to the offense. It was common in the ASA to have multiple coordinators, just like a pro team, and even an athletic director.

Crisci, who'd played quarterback in high school in California, had designed an incredibly complex offense that incorporated elements of the spread. Some plays he found online; others he reverse engineered from TV. The Hawks' playbook now had around eighty plays. Crisci would call a number from the sidelines, and then Joey would consult the play chart on his wrist. It would have been a complicated system for college players.

"Wing Left 37 Pitch," Crisci said. Joey ran the play.

"Wing Right Fake 38 Pitch Counter."

"I Left Fake 33 Tight End Drag."

Crisci called a Double Wide Left 30 Hitch, a screen pass to Mo. Coach Engel watched proudly. "It's so there," he said. Crisci looked across the field at the Wild Dawgz' coaches. "I'm just showing 'em that because I'm going to do a fake later," he told Coach Engel. That would mean a fake to Mo and then a bomb to the wide receiver.

After the long hours of preparation, the game was anticlimactic. The Wild Dawgz went three-and-out on their first possession. The Hawks blocked the punt and took over at the 5-yard line, and on their first offensive play, Mo, perhaps stung by the anonymous disses Coach had planted in his head, ran to the left and scored. Monk nailed the extra point.

The Hawks were leading 33–6 in the fourth quarter when Engel and Crisci decided to break out their fake. "Coach, you got a stack?" Engel asked. A "stack" meant putting two blockers on one side of the field.

Crisci glanced at his play sheet and yelled, "Forty-six!" Joey looked at his wristband and called the play.

The Wild Dawgz bit all over the fake screen to Mo, and receiver Grayson Ream was wide open when Joey's ball landed in his arms.

The final score was 41–6. The Wild Dawgz coach asked me not to mention the score in my article, because he feared it would hurt his recruiting.

IV. "WHAT ELSE IS THERE?"

An hour and a half before kickoff on a Saturday in September, Celdon answered the door of his red-brick house. (If there are houses in Allen made out of anything else, I didn't see them.) I'd come to watch his famous pregame ritual—or, as some described it, his mom's pregame ritual. Celdon launched right in. "First, I start by taking my Advair," he explained. Celdon had asthma. He held up a purple cylinder and began to suck on it.

"Next, I watch *Top 10: Football Moves*," he said as he turned and walked into the living room. He plopped on a gray couch and turned on the TV. NFL Films music filled the room, and Curtis Martin was running across the screen.

"Turn it up, Celdon!" shouted Tracy when she emerged from her bedroom. She was wearing jeans and a black Beverly Hills Polo Club T-shirt. As we watched Martin stiff-arm a defender, Tracy said, "I always tell him to pick two moves from *Top 10* and apply it in the game."

Tracy has four boys—the others are named Camrin, Colton, and Chase—and all of them are football players. The family had moved to Allen from Lancaster, a nearby suburb, in 2008. That made Celdon a prime recruit who could avoid the draft. One afternoon, an ASA coach saw Celdon and his brothers playing football in the yard. He and Coach Engel showed up at the family's front door around eight o'clock that night. Coach watched Celdon doing cartwheels in his Batman pajamas and, despite having never seen him carry a football, signed him immediately.

On TV, Barry Sanders executed a spin move. "Look at that, Celdon," Tracy said. "Are you looking?"

Celdon nodded and said nothing.

While the video played, Tracy went to the kitchen to prepare the third part of Celdon's pregame ritual. She emerged with a container of PRO Shield, a liquid vitamin supplement whose label, she noted, said "Banned Substance Free." She directed a spoonful into Celdon's mouth, and he gulped it down without taking his eyes off the screen.

About that time, Coach Engel showed up. He is a frequent presence at the house—once, upon discovering that the clothes dryer didn't work, he'd helped Tracy find a new one. Today he was doing some minor electrical repairs. They waved at him.

Then, after Celdon's asthma had been staved off and his brain had been stimulated and his vitamin count had been upped, came part four of the pregame ritual: a massage. Celdon, like a lot of youth football players in Allen, is also a track athlete. "I do the one hundred," he told me. "The two hundred. The four hundred. The long jump. The four-by-one. The four-by-four. I might do the shot put. But I've never run the mile. *Never.*" He and Mo had been members of the ten-and-under state champion 4x100 relay, but Celdon had strained his groin that summer. Tracy, vowing it would never happen again, had bought a handheld massaging device. Celdon lay on his back on a yoga mat while she started massaging his legs. When she got to his quads, Celdon giggled uncontrollably and took the massager and did it himself.

"Smelldon, you ready to do it?" Coach called on his way out the door. "I'll see y'all."

During games, I'd seen Celdon execute his jump cuts, his spin moves, and his other NFL-inspired maneuvers with grace. "But I can't say that he plays at that level all the time," Tracy told me. "He plays at that level for the most part. But in the fourth quarter, he'll start looking at the scoreboard."

What do you think he needs to work on besides concentration? I asked. "His hands," she said.

"I can catch good, Mom!" Celdon said.

"You can catch the ball," Tracy admitted. "But you need to work on catching with your hands and not your body. Go *to* the ball."

Which is why the fifth and final part of Celdon's pregame ritual is hands practice. Celdon and his brother Camrin picked up a football. I thought they'd take it into the backyard, but they began to throw it back and forth right in front of the television that was playing *Top 10: Football Moves*. Camrin is fifteen, a muscular defensive end on the Allen High varsity team, and Celdon shook his hands in pain when he caught the ball.

"Camrin, don't throw it that *hard*," Celdon pleaded.

"Camrin, don't throw it that hard," Tracy repeated.

Camrin gave his mom a skeptical look. "I'm not throwing it hard."

A couple of weeks later, in another large red-brick house a few streets over, Nick, the Hawks' center, said, "I want to try to play professional sports my whole life." It was just before noon on a Sunday. Nick and his mom, Shannon, were arranged on leather couches in front of the flat-screen. Nick was wearing a Cowboys jersey. *Fox NFL Sunday* played on mute in the background.

Like Celdon's mom, Shannon and her husband, Danny, always imagined having sons who played football. Nick came first. Ten years later, Shannon got pregnant again. "When we found out we were having a girl"—that would be Nick's younger sister, who's now two—"we didn't even talk to each other on the way home," she told me. "We didn't know what to do with her." They named her Landry.

They hadn't had such challenges with Nick. He was 22.5 inches long and weighed nine-and-a-half pounds at birth. "When he was little, he couldn't wait to learn to read because he couldn't wait to read the sports section," Shannon said.

"I just read Victor Cruz's book," Nick told me. "Now I'm reading Tim Tebow's book."

"Forget Harry Potter," Shannon said. "He's not interested."

"We started Nick playing football when he was four," Shannon continued, "because we could play him up. That first year in tackle, we told him that for every sack, he'd get ten dollars. And he'd get five dollars for every tackle." She turned to Nick. "How many times did you sack the quarterback the first game?"

"I sacked him, like, four times," Nick said.

"We had to renegotiate his contract when he was four," Shannon said, rolling her eyes.

When Nick was seven, he entered the ASA through the draft. "Unfortunately, he got picked by the Razorbacks," Shannon said. The Razorbacks were a crummy, disorganized team. "I had to get involved," Shannon said, "and get that team disbanded."

Since his team no longer existed, Nick became a free agent rather than a player who had to go into the draft. Coach Engel signed him as a Hawk in 2009, and Shannon became the Hawks' photographer, webmaster, and team mom. "Frankly," she said, grinning at her son, "they're lucky to have him."

Birthright had made Nick and Celdon football players, but the city of Allen took over from there. Like all local boys, in elementary school they had received solicitations from a training outfit called Performance Course. The owner, Geno Pierce, has short-cropped hair and bulging biceps. He's Allen's youth fitness guru, its Billy Blanks and Jack LaLanne. For a fee, he'll pump your kid up. When we met at his office across the street from Eagle Stadium, Pierce was wearing a T-shirt that said "100%."

"Jake, give us a video of the kids," Pierce told his assistant. On a computer screen, we watched elementary-age kids running bear crawls, like the Hawks had done during Hell Week. Nick had spent three summers in Performance Course; Celdon had opted to go with a different trainer who had a similarly intense regimen.

When an athletic Allen boy gets to middle school, he can start attending Performance Course five days a week for seven weeks during the summer. By high school, Performance Course becomes nearly mandatory if you're playing team sports at Allen High. "Jake, give us a high-intensity video so he can see a piece of that," Pierce said. "Watch this!" Another Allen kid—bigger and more muscular, no doubt because of his training—appeared on the computer screen. He was lifting weights and crying out in pain.

Pierce was coaching his youngest son in youth football. But to my surprise, he was agnostic about the game. "Most kids start at a very young age around here," Pierce said. "Now, I don't particularly think they *should* start that early. But I start my kids early. The problem is, if you wait, you get left out. You're almost a victim to the monster."

I asked Pierce if he worried about his kids getting a concussion. "Is it possible?" he said. "Yes. Is it probable? No. I wouldn't let them play if the answer was yes."

"Look at what's going on in this town," Pierce continued. "Sports are important. Parents have a ton of"—he searched for the right word—"resources."

Pierce, like a lot of Allenites, was sensitive about all the national coverage of the new stadium. Beyond the veneer of exotic Texanness—everything's bigger, etc., etc.—he felt something important had been missed. Allen was so passionate about football, and its families were so dedicated to the training required to play the game, that its children were able to take part in a total program that stretched from the crib to the locker room. "If you haven't lived here, it's easy to make rash judgments," Pierce said. "I've been here seventeen years. You don't have to explain anything to me."

He leaned forward in his chair. "Sports," he said, "is a vehicle to raise our kids."

After Nick and Celdon and every other youth footballer complete half a dozen summers in personal training, they'll finally reach the big time: Allen High, the Reichstag. I met the Eagles' head coach, Tom Westerberg, in his office one Friday morning. It was a big, spacious room that a lot of college coaches would envy, with a picture window overlooking the south end zone of the stadium. I noticed that Westerberg's Allen Eagles polo shirt had been manufactured by Nike.

If Allen's parents and personal trainers are the ones who produce an army of young athletes, it's Westerberg's job to manage the herd. The downside to a football-mad town is that everyone expects Junior to play at Eagle Stadium, and there are more Juniors than Westerberg can handle. "I've got an email from a dad whose kid is ten years old," Westerberg said, nodding at his computer. "The dad wants him to play quarterback here, and he wants to know what he can do in the meantime." Westerberg rolled his eyes. He gets more than a few emails like that.

There are around 1,200 elementary-age kids playing football in the ASA. Another 700 play in Allen's three middle schools. At Allen High, Nick and Celdon will find themselves competing for starting positions in a pool of 500 active football players (about one-fifth of the school's male population). The talent is generally so deep that even though Pierce's older son Oliver began the year as the Eagles' starting quarterback, he was replaced mid-season by Kyler Murray, whose dad, Kevin, had been a star at Texas A&M.

I told Westerberg it must be nice to command all that talent while coaches in Dallas were scrounging around for able bodies. "People say, 'Boy, it's awesome to have that,'" he replied. "But I've got to find games for all those kids." According to the rules in Allen, you can't cut a football player, and in middle school, you have to *play* every football player. So even if Celdon and Nick are good enough to start, they'll still have to come out of the game fairly often while lesser players rotate in. (In the fourth quarter, however, all teams play to win.)

For coaches, this was a magnanimous gesture but also a self-interested one. A few years earlier, a quarterback named Alec Morris had trained at Performance Course. He'd worked on his passing. But Morris got lost inside the Allen football machine. The talent in front of him was so good, and so deep, that he didn't start for the Eagles' varsity squad until late in his high school career. Morris is now a scholarship quarterback at the University of Alabama.

"I do see potential in Nick," Shannon said, "but he's got to do the work. He's got to prepare himself for middle school." She turned to Nick. "You've got to suck in some of that passion. You're going to be trying out with thirty or forty people for the same position."

Nick nodded, and Shannon turned back to me. "When he complains about going to practice now, I say, 'Are you going to complain when you go to middle school practice?' You've got to be one hundred percent in, in every way."

Could Nick ever *quit* football? I asked her.

"We pretty much let him make the decision on how much he wants it," she said. "It's up to him."

"What?" Nick said. He'd tuned us out for the NFL pregame show.

"If you came up to Dad and me and said you wanted to quit, would Dad and I be okay with that?" Shannon repeated.

"No," Nick said, and everybody laughed.

Shannon showed me a family photo, a professional shot with three generations of Trices side by side. Nick's 92-year-old great-grandmother, Ivah, was wearing a Cowboys jersey.

"What else is there?" Nick said with a smile.

Shannon nodded her head. "What else is there?"

V. HEAD SHOTS

After the Hawks won their first three games by a combined score of 106–20, I asked the players if it was ever boring rolling over the competition. Ryan Asonganyi, a bespectacled guard who was one of the brainiest Hawks, told me he had simply evolved past watching the scoreboard. "For me, it's like playing a game," he said. "It's not necessarily like we're trying to win."

Their fifth game, against the Cardinals, had that kind of feel. The cool weather of the early season had turned into a fall monsoon, and you could hardly see the opposite sideline. Up 32–0 in the fourth quarter, the Hawks began to pass the ball. It's a quirk of youth football that you pass, rather than run, when you're ahead. On a good day, a thrown ball has about a one in four chance of connecting, whereas if you're handing it to Celdon or Mo, your odds of scoring increase exponentially.

Joey was dropping back to pass when one of the big Cardinals defensive ends began to get chippy. He hit Joey late. He did the same thing on the next play. And on the next play.

Joey came off the field in a rage. "I'm gonna punch him in the face!"

"You punch him in the face," his dad said, "and you'll be thrown out of the league for six months. Be calm."

Joey swallowed his anger and went through the postgame handshake line: "Goodgame, goodgame, goodgame, goodgame...."

I found out later that the referee had thrown the Cardinals player out of the game. When he did that, a woman on the Cardinals' side of the stands flipped him off. The ref threw her out too.

The Hawks were 5-0.

After another win, the 6-0 Hawks were playing the Cobras. You could tell it was October because the Hawks came out wearing pink socks and gloves for National Breast Cancer Awareness Month, just like their NFL counterparts. They rolled up and down the field. Mo scored on the first play from scrimmage on a Pro Left Shotgun 37 Sweep. Then Celdon, playing linebacker, forced a fumble. On the next offensive play, he took a screen pass and jumped right, making two Cobras run into each other; he made another Cobra miss at the 37-yard line, and another miss 2 yards later. As he broke into the open field, he had only a scrawny safety hanging around his waist. Celdon's brain activated—*tap*—and he lowered his body to 45 degrees and left the safety on the ground at the 25-yard line. He looked almost bored tossing the ball to the referee in the end zone.

When the Cobras got the ball back, their quarterback ran right on a scramble toward the Hawks sideline. Just as Celdon and Mo were about to reach him, the Cobras quarterback ran headfirst into his wide receiver, who was blocking for him. There was a sickening crack. The receiver ended up on his back with his hands gripping his face mask.

The Hawks didn't need to be told what to do when a player goes down. They'd seen it last year, when Grayson broke his leg. They made a semicircle around the Cobras' wide receiver and took a knee. The Cobras did the same on the opposite side. It almost looked like a religious ritual was taking place, with supplicants in white and black converging around one fallen man. By this point, he had flipped over onto his stomach and pushed his face mask in the ground.

When I got onto the field, the kid was breathing in low, ragged gasps. "Does your neck hurt?" someone asked him. "Just your head?" He took off his helmet and massaged his temples. His behavior fit to a T the Mayo Clinic's description of a concussion: "confusion or feeling as if in a fog," "seeing stars."

After a minute or so, he caught his breath. And then he hopped up and jogged off the field.

Four plays later, he charged off the sidelines and back to his position. The Hawks said he talked more smack than anyone else on the field. They won 40–0.

Beidleman, the league commissioner, suggested we meet one morning at the Allen Café, one of the few old-time places in a town increasingly dominated by the Cheesecake Factory and P. F. Chang's. Beidleman is a walking boulder of a man, with a shaved head and a tattoo on his right bicep. "I'm livin' at the corner of happy and healthy," he said as he scrunched into a booth. We ordered monster gyro omelets with hashbrowns.

In 2011 Beidleman ran a quixotic campaign for mayor of Allen and lost by 86 percent. But no matter, because he sees his job as ASA commissioner as inherently political. In a sense, Beidleman is a conservative warrior. He is standing athwart football history yelling, "Stop!"

Junior Seau's suicide caused a lot of upheaval among other youth football leagues. Pop Warner, the most venerable youth football organization in America, made a new rule that coaches could use only a third of their practice time on contact drills. Pop Warner further required any kid with concussion-like symptoms—say, the Cobras wide receiver—to get a medical release before he could play again. Beidleman thinks both rules wussify the game too much. At a coaches' orientation that summer, he declared, "There's reasons Pop Warner's not real prolific in the area we're in."

Football, he insisted, is supposed to be a tough, violent game. "I had a fourth grader making a tackle," Beidleman told me. "His hand went through the face mask and up another kid's nose to the first knuckle. When they stopped play, they pulled out the kid's finger, and it was covered in boogers and blood."

"I get an email from a bystander mom saying, 'How do we make the game safer?'" He chuckled. "How do you answer that?" The price football extracts is boogers and blood.

Which isn't to say Allen is a safe haven for nose-gougers. Like his NFL counterpart, Roger Goodell, Beidleman thinks the solution isn't to radically change football but to more closely enforce the rules already on the books. (He made the Cardinals player who took cheap shots at Joey write an essay before he could play again.) Moreover, Beidleman feels that football's battle against modernity has to be fought on grounds other than medical ones. "Our biggest competition is social media and video games and iPhones," he told me. Every kid in Allen—like every kid in Peoria and Seattle and Brooklyn—plays *Madden*. The problem with *Madden* is that it's arguably more fun than real football, it's certainly safer, and it instills a false sense of confidence. Every kid thinks he can catch 40-yard bombs like he can when he's playing as Calvin Johnson in the video game. "Can you imagine a new kid who's never played football lining up against Cullen Perkins?" Beidleman said. Cullen, a Hawks tackle, weighs 195 pounds.

If football is destined to undergo touchy-feely transformations, Beidleman is determined to hold the line. The ASA has mandatory rotations so that every kid gets to play in every game. But Beidleman, who coaches a fifth-grade team called the Warriors, noted, "I fired my own kids from several positions." At the coaches' orientation, Beidleman warned against coaches trying to cut kids who couldn't play. But he also announced that the ASA had done away with end-of-year participation trophies. That made the coaches burst into applause.

In Beidleman's mind, you can build a $60 million high school stadium; you can put your kid in $135 uniforms; you can vigilantly protect against concussions. But football, even when played by children, should still be a sport Tom Landry could love.

VI. THE SUPER BOWL

In eight regular-season wins, the Hawks outscored their opponents 285–20. So the coaches reacted with some alarm when the Hawks gave up 18 points to the Gators in the first round of the playoffs. (They went on to win 30–18.) On the Friday before the Super Bowl, I found the team practicing in Beidleman's backyard, which he'd converted into a 100-yard football field with two stadium lights. He called it Camp Warrior.

The Hawks were facing a Super Bowl rematch with the Wild Dawgz, who hadn't lost since falling to the Hawks in week 2. Coach Engel was worried about their giant defensive end. "Number ninety-four, the Hurst boy," he told the line. "I want you to chop him every now and then. He'll get mad. He'll get frustrated. He may even punch you and get a fifteen-yard penalty." He paused. "You just laugh silently and chop him again."

On offense, the Wild Dawgz had a big, lanky running back, Grant Tisdale, who liked to get loose on a screen pass. "Monkey, the sack-meister," Coach said to Monk, "go get him if he flares out."

"Okey-dokey, artichokey," Monk said. He started calling Tisdale "Ashley Tisdale," after the actress in *High School Musical*, and vowed to do the same thing during the game.

At the end of practice, Beidleman gathered the team for a mock-inspirational speech about winning. If you win, he told the Hawks, "the world is your oyster. You can look your mom dead in the eye and tell her, 'I'll be taking my dinner in my room while I play Xbox. I require a ribeye, medium-rare, with mashed potatoes—no greens.'

"And your father will stand by your side nodding at his wife with the knowing look of, 'You have to do it, babe. He's a winner.'"

An hour later, Coach Engel and Coach Crisci sat on leather chairs at the Engel house. Celdon and Mo were on the floor, and Joey was on the couch. Coach Engel had a surprise: game tape of a scrimmage the Hawks had dropped to a team from Fort Worth. A *loss*. It was his final psychological ploy. The boys immediately protested.

"This game's ugly," shouted Joey. "I don't want to watch it."

"Me either!" said Mo.

Celdon said nothing.

Coach ignored them, putting in the DVD to create a final, annoying flicker of doubt for athletes who never much felt it.

Joey watched the DVD intently. Finally he offered his assessment of why the Hawks had lost: "Dude, something, like, possessed all our minds."

They would never let it happen again.

At three o'clock the next day, Shannon began to cry. Nick could hardly say a word. Shannon tried asking him if he was sad about this last game—this ostensible end of childhood—and Nick just said, "No, Mom. No, Mom."

An hour later, I found Mo at his house, punching the palm of his hand and tapping his feet on the floor. He wanted to run into the end zone.

One of the Wild Dawgz had started talking smack at school, Mo told me. "He said, 'You guys will probably beat us, but not by as much as last time.'"

Mo thought this was the lamest smack talk he'd ever heard.

At six that evening, Coach walked out of his bedroom. His hair was combed neatly to one side, and he was wearing a black visor. He heaved his music machine into the bed of the F-150 for the final time. Eric hopped in the backseat. Coach inserted some chaw.

"Say a command," the F-150 said.

"Bluetooth audio," Coach said. Suddenly the truck was filled with a hard-rock version of "The Star-Spangled Banner."

When we reached the rendezvous point for the Hawks, Coach opened the doors and let the song drift into the night.

After the Hawks had reached Lovejoy Stadium in a honking caravan, after the players had argued about whether the lightning they saw in the distance would get the game canceled (consensus: maybe), after Coach Crisci had made them practice Wing Left 37 Pitch and Hot Left 33 Lead, they huddled around Coach Engel for the last time.

"I'm so jealous," he said. "I'm so jealous. I wish I could be out there.... It's about a football game. It's a football game. We wanna play harder than we ever have." He gave a sly smile. "Y'all ready to do it?"

The Wild Dawgz got the ball first. Tisdale, the running back, ran right. As the Hawks converged on him, Tisdale suddenly planted his feet and threw a pass across his body to a wide-open Wild Dawgz receiver. The receiver ran untouched into the end zone. The Dawgz led 6–0. But when they tried for a two-point conversion, the pass was intercepted, and on the ensuing return, Tisdale hurt his leg. He limped off to the sideline. The game was never really close after that.

Mo got the Hawks' first touchdown. And the second one. Monk missed two extra points wide left. After the second, he was standing on the field with his hands on his knees, breathing hard. "Is Monk hurt?" Coach asked. "I think so," said an assistant coach. But on the next play, Monk knifed into the backfield from his right outside linebacker position and blew up the running back. Monk wasn't hurt. "Monk's *pissed*," one of the other assistant coaches said.

In the fourth quarter, Celdon got the ball. He planted his left foot and moved his body right, lowering his torso and scampering into the end zone. Coach Engel counted down the final seconds with his fingers above his head, and the Hawks said, "Goodgame, goodgame, goodgame..."

The season was over. In a matter of months, the kids would begin funneling into different middle school teams, and eventually to Allen High, with its fierce competition for the few available spots, and then, who knew? To college, maybe, and to the pros if they were good enough. Most, of course, would not be. Most wouldn't be able to live out Nick Trice's dream of playing pro sports their whole lives. Sooner or later, most would have to quit playing football altogether and find a life outside the game. And what about football itself? What would it look like in ten years? In twenty? The Hawks didn't know. What they did know was that most of them would never again get to play together. This was it, the last moment of uncomplicated bliss right on the edge of a big change. I watched as the Hawks embraced their coaches and hoisted their trophies and kissed their moms, and I couldn't help but think that nothing would ever be this easy again.

Roy Blount Jr.

In what he calls the "self-promotional bio, in third person" on his otherwise impeccable website, Roy Blount Jr. (b. 1941) neglects to mention that he wrote "Song to Grits," a poem that speaks to the stomach and the funny bone in a way that is distinctly his. Even with his myriad other accomplishments—author of twenty-three books, panelist on NPR's *Wait, Wait... Don't Tell Me*, star of his own one-man stage show, screenwriter, lecturer, curmudgeon à la Twain, Mencken, and W. C. Fields—the Georgia-bred Blount should have given folks at least a taste of the poem:

> When my mind's unsettled,
> When I don't feel spruce,
> When my nerves get frazzled,
> When my flesh gets loose—
>
> What knits
> Me back together's grits.

Blount's passions and sense of the outrageous made him one of *Sports Illustrated*'s most unpredictable and entertaining writers in the 1960s and '70s. André Laguerre, the magazine's charismatic editor (and Charles de Gaulle's press attaché during World War II), turned him loose to hang out with the Terry Bradshaw-Franco Harris Pittsburgh Steelers for a season, and the result was his first book, *About Three Bricks Shy of a Load* (1974), which became one of pro football's defining texts. When Blount returned to *SI* in emeritus capacity thirty-eight years later, in 2012, one of the first things he did was visit the current crop of Steelers to see if he might have the same chemistry with them that he did with their predecessors. What he discovered informed a dispatch that was funny, wistful, and elegiac. It is also the perfect ending for this book.

Immaculate Memory

I T WAS RAINING AND BLUSTERY before the Chiefs-Steelers Monday-night game a few weeks ago, and the great white tarps on the Heinz Field turf were billowing and swallowing groundskeepers who were struggling to roll them up. From the press box, a vivid tableau. But impersonal. Thirty-nine years ago I knew the head groundskeeper, Steve (Dirt) DiNardo, who once, while the players were getting their keys at a hotel in San Diego, came up behind Mean Joe Greene and told him, in drastically impolitic terms, that he would have to stay in Tijuana. This was when Greene was as forbidding a presence as his nickname implied. He whirled, saw it was Dirt and just laughed.

You had to know Dirt. He liked to drive his Zamboni over loose balls on the field, pooping them around to the exasperation of Jackie Hart, the field manager. Hart himself once slugged Art Rooney Jr., a son of the owner and then the Steelers' head of scouting. Jackie's employment status was unaffected. Artie did throw him into a laundry hamper.

Aw, I'm waxing nostalgic already—and those tarps brought to mind two other stories I heard while hanging around the Steelers in the 1970s. Once, when the Rooneys' friend Squawker Mullen was getting the worst of it from a carnival boxer, various family members engaged the boxer and his carny friends in a "Hey, Rube" that brought down the tent and raged on lumpily under folds of canvas. Then there was the game in Green Bay in which Andy Russell, the Steelers linebacker, saw a fired-up Ray Nitschke dive, miss a tackle and skid headfirst under a sideline tarp. You could see big bulges, Andy said, where the Packers linebacker was kicking and heaving.

Why was I at the Chiefs-Steelers game? Well, Immaculate Reception Day is just around the corner. Usually I observe the anniversary of Franco Harris's game-ending 60-yard deflected-pass touchdown casually, by watching it six or eight times on YouTube while listening to "Pittsburgh Steelers Polka" by Jimmy Psihoulis. But this December 23 is the 40th anniversary of that great turning point in Steelers history. Sure, there's a statue in Pittsburgh International Airport of Franco snagging the ball, and surveyors have determined the exact spot on the site of the old Three Rivers Stadium where he snagged it. (There will be a marker, and a ceremony.) But something more was called for. So my son, Kirven, and I made a pilgrimage to Pittsburgh. He flew in for the Chiefs and Ravens games, and I stayed through the intervening week to see if I could get back in touch with the Steelers.

The Immaculate Reception—which NFL Films and *SI* have deemed the greatest play of all time—gave the Steelers the first playoff victory in their history. It also began Kirven's and my 40-year adherence to, and through, the Steelers. He was four back in 1972, and I was 31. We were watching on TV. When Harris beat the last Oakland defender, cornerback Jimmy Warren, into the end zone, I tossed Kirven into the air. No question now, this was the team to be embedded with.

I was a staff writer at *Sports Illustrated*. André Laguerre, the managing editor, had got the notion that I should hang out with an NFL team for the 1973 season, from training camp through the following year's draft. The Immaculate Reception confirmed my choice of the Steelers. They hadn't been overexposed. They looked to be on the way up. Their town was rich (little did I know) in lore.

And I was divorced. My kids were living mostly with their mother because I traveled so much already. Kirven might have grown up hating the Steelers because of the year his father spent so much more time with them than with him. But he visited me in Pittsburgh. He attended Saturday practice, which was open to relatives and guests back then, and although he was annoyed, at age five, that no one in uniform would chase him, he became a fierce, lifelong Steelers fan. That's one reason I've continued to love the team for all these years.

The Steelers' '73 season ended in the first round of the playoffs. I wrote a book on that team, *About Three Bricks Shy of a Load*. The next year the Steelers won the Super Bowl. They won three more in the next five seasons. I kept going back to cover them and eventually to update the book through the 1980s. Kirven, who after '73 lived with me half the time or more, often came along. Late one night when he was maybe seven, we were at the house of Steelers center Ray Mansfield. I'd heard that somebody had just been traded to the Bengals, but I was fuzzy on who it was. So was Ray. Not even looking up from the Mansfield family dog, on whom I had thought he was asleep, Kirven said, "Coy Bacon." Already he was not only a much better athlete than I but also a more serious football fan.

And a truer Steelers fan. "My love of the Steelers might be the purest thing in my life, just because it's always been there and it's so unquestioned," says Kirven, who develops reality shows in New York City and used to edit video for the NFL Network. "I love the Steelers like a golden retriever loves a tennis ball."

Except that the retriever is not bound by the heartstrings to any particular ball. When a tennis ball goes bad, as the Steelers do from time to time, the retriever doesn't howl, "We suck!"

They're not making fans with quite Kirven's pedigree anymore, because out-of-town media, a status to which I am reduced, are now barred from all Steelers practices. In '73 I was welcomed to everything but team meetings, and one player offered to tape those for me surreptitiously. I declined; I knew if anything interesting went on, someone would fill me in.

Here are some of the rules for people covering the Steelers today:

Media members are prohibited *at any time* from reporting which players take repetitions with the first, second or third team, etc., as well as how many repetitions players take during practice.

Media members are prohibited from blogging or tweeting during practice.

Media members are prohibited from socializing with players or coaches at any time during practice.

At no time will media be permitted to interview members of the Steelers' organization in the lobby or parking lots without prior consent from Steelers p.r.

On the other hand, *Media does have the right to report what they are told by coaches or players.*

Whoop-de-doo. Maybe I'm too sensitive, but these rules chill my ardor to talk to current Steelers. It's like being told you have only certain very limited access to the girls' dorm. I want to say, Hey, I'm a gentleman. And anyway these girls are way too young for me.

Actually, the current Steelers I talk to strike me as too mature. Ryan Clark, the defensive back, is *so* grown up about having to wear a big, uncool-looking special helmet after suffering two concussions in three games. "I'm not afraid of getting hurt," he says. He just doesn't want to miss playing time under the league's concussion rules. "It's a precaution put in place to protect tough people from themselves—take it out of the hands of the players, who would play through anything."

Sensible. Commendably uncrazy. But... one time Joe Greene got so fed up with being held in a game against the Eagles that he grabbed the ball away from the Philadelphia center and flung it into the stands. And walked off. "We watched the ball spiral into the seats," recalled Andy Russell. "It seemed like it took forever. There we were: We didn't have a ball, we didn't have a left tackle. It was like he was saying, O.K., if you won't play right, we won't play at all."

I give today's Steelers credit: They speak of the old ones as if they were gods. "Hanging out with Mr. [Mel] Blount, seeing Mr. Greene, doing signings with them," says Clark, "I actually become starstruck."

"They *repeated* in the Super Bowl," says tight end Heath Miller. Repeated twice, I told him. "They did it *twice*? I can attest to how hard that is—we haven't fared well the years after our Super Bowls."

Defensive end Brett Keisel, he of the big bushy beard: "It's awesome to be around them and to know that we share the same helmet."

I kept wanting a current Steeler to say of the old ones, "We could take 'em." Not that they could.

After the Steelers lost to the Ravens on November 18, Keisel politely told reporters, "It is what it is. They're a good team. We fought hard… and it just didn't work out the way we wanted it."

I don't know. Maybe Steelers could be that trite in my day. But not to *me*. I will still root for today's Steelers. I will still shout, "HEEEATH!" when that excellent performer catches a pass. And I will concede this much: If the Steelers' first Super Bowl team were to come back at playing age today, five current Steelers could hold on to their starting jobs: Miller, quarterback Ben Roethlisberger, linebacker James Harrison (since they're using four now), safety Troy Polamalu and kicker Shaun Suisham.

The head coach? Before I went to Pittsburgh and watched Mike Tomlin with the media, I would have taken him over Chuck Noll. On TV I've seen Tomlin and Roethlisberger with their arms around each other's shoulders on the sideline, following the game together, even when they're down a few points—a much better-looking relationship than Noll's with Terry Bradshaw. But in Pittsburgh I watched Tomlin with the guys who cover the team regularly.

"Are you confident Ben will play again this year?" a local reporter asked. Here is how Noll might have responded, with asperity: "I'm confident that question will be asked again before it is answerable."

Here is how Tomlin answered it, in a downright contemptuous tone: "Next question."

I'm thinking that if Mike is as cool as he seems to be, he should be able to play with reporters a little. Reporters are going to ask annoying questions, like kids on a car trip: "Are we there yet? When will we be there?" That's their job. Those are the questions their readers are asking.

In '73 Ed Kiely was head of public relations. He suggested to a couple of players that they take me to their after-practice bar, the Nineteenth Hole, and the rest is literature. Now Kiely is 94. Three days a week he goes into the Steelers' complex and rides the exercise bike. "Coaches would always be yelling about the press to me," he says, "and I'd say, 'Hey, if you come in here someday and they're not here, get scared, 'cause they're as much of this almost as you are.'"

You'd want to play for Tomlin, though, I guess. As media folk, Kirven and I are allowed to stand on the Steelers' sideline during the last two minutes of the Chiefs game, so that after the final whistle we can get quickly to the entrance to the dressing room. So there we are as the clock ticks down in regulation: Steelers tied with a bad team, and Big Ben is hurt. But you wouldn't know how dull the game has been from the dazzling lights on the sideline. You know the last scene in *Close Encounters of the Third Kind*? Bright like that. "It was like a dream," Kirven says. "I was fairly dispirited going into overtime, but then I'm watching Tomlin stalking to the bench and saying, 'Let's just get this done and we can go home,' and I'm loving him for it."

Linebacker Lawrence Timmons intercepts a pass right in front of us. Steelers win.

"Words can't describe that," Timmons says after the game. "I got butterflies."

"I was shivering," says Kirven, "and I wasn't sure if it was the cold or the thrill."

So, O.K. But nine of Noll's 22 starters are in the Hall of Fame. They were *bodacious*, and acted that way. "We had *gizzards*," defensive end Dwight White (now deceased) told me after he retired. In the current Steelers' grown-up blandness with the press, I kept picking up just a hint of Eddie Haskell.

Maybe I overreacted to all those prohibitions. *Prohibitions*? How can you hang around a football team and give in to a raft of *prohibitions*? I know I had special dispensation in '73, but, hey, I wanted to know what was going on. I would put on Steelers sweats and mess around on the field during practice, catch an occasional pass. I hung with the original Art Rooney and with current offensive coordinator Todd Haley's father, Dick, who was personnel director. I knew that Babe Parilli, the quarterbacks' coach, was going to "resign" before he knew. Rocky Bleier told me what he said to God when he was lying bleeding from multiple shrapnel wounds in Vietnam: "'I'm not going to promise to be a priest. I'm just going to put my life in Your hands, to do whatever You want with it.' I knew at the time that was a pretty chickens--- move. I mean, I could do anything and say, Well, that's what God must want me to do."

Media cannot be prohibited from reminiscing.

After the Kansas City game I visited Dan Rooney in his office. Lucky to catch him, because he's the U.S. ambassador to Ireland now, spends most of his time over there. At 80 he's stooped but still flashes the Rooney twinkle. He's talking about the Immaculate Reception. "Everybody in Pittsburgh is sure they were there for it," says Dan, who was running the team at the time. "They probably saw it on TV"—in fact they couldn't even have done that if they were in Pittsburgh, because before 1973 all home games were blacked out—"but they're sure they saw it here. Even if they weren't alive."

Interesting word choice, *here*. The Immaculate Reception occurred nowhere near Dan's current office but more than four miles away, in old Three Rivers Stadium. That's where, until 2001, the Steelers played and practiced and dressed and lifted weights and watched film and had offices and ate soup and sandwiches in a little kitchen. I don't remember any windows in the Three Rivers offices. The premises had a *noir* quality, leavened by a great deal of laughter. (Come to think of it, that might describe the Steelers' history before the Immaculate Reception.) Dan's office now is almost as bright as the Monday-night sideline.

Today the Steelers play at taxpayer-owned Heinz Field, near where Three Rivers used to be (on the Northside, where Art Rooney Sr. lived his whole life and where his sons grew up), but they do all that other stuff (only with a big cafeteria replacing the little kitchen) on the Southside, over the Hot Metal Bridge across the Monongahela, at a lavish training facility with myriad flat full-length fields that they lease from the University of Pittsburgh Medical Center, which operates a research and rehabilitation facility next door. Once steel mills belched smoke and glowed blast-furnace blood-orange. Now the Steelers share an athletic-medical complex with leading experts on concussions and damaged limbs. The Steel City's economy depends much more on health care than on steel. The tallest skyscraper is called the U.S. Steel Tower, but its biggest tenant will soon be the UPMC. If the Steelers were named for the hot action in town today, they'd be the Pittsburgh Healers.

In fact, there is a kind of continuum to the Steelers-UPMC complex. Smashmouth football feeds research, and vice versa. It's a little bit like the veterinarian and the taxidermist who went into business together. Their motto: Either way, you get your dog back.

The Three Rivers offices were "homier," Dan concedes. "I could walk there from home." And they had Art Sr., the Chief, who died in 1988. He was a man who, once he made your acquaintance, looked almost comically happy to see you again, and his acquaintance was extraordinarily wide. The first thing that struck me about the current offices was, no cigars. The Chief was always smoking one cigar and distributing others. Art Rooney II, Dan's son, who is now team president, says, "I remember when the team plane would land after a victory. Whoever opened the door would be overwhelmed by cigar smoke. When we built Three Rivers, each locker had an ashtray beside it."

Back then, in or around the Chief's office (even in the *lobby*, without p.r. approval), I was introduced to everyone from Billy Conn, the old light heavyweight champion, to Horse Czarnecki, the groundskeeper at Pitt, and Jack Warner, of Warner Brothers. But all a student of Pittsburgh human interest needed was Art's brother Uncle Jim Rooney, who had known many wonderful Pittsburghers.

"She was as fine a lady as I ever knew," Jim recalled one day in the lobby, referring to a local barkeep. "And she ran a tough joint, and nobody ever got out of line. Big, fine woman. Johnny Brown of New Orleens played piano in her place. He was a wonderful man. Sold his body for $120. To the University of Pennsylvania Medical School. All in ones. Came into the place countin' em out. Johnny Brown of New Orleens. Weighed 120 pounds. Dollar a pound. They brought in one of those pianos that play themselves. It put Johnny out of work. He didn't have nothing to do. He got a rock and came in and put it through the piano. Johnny Brown of New Orleens."

"Where is he now?" I asked.

Uncle Jim spread his arms and looked upward. "The University of Pennsylvania Medical School."

Maybe that's where I should be. *Eddie Haskell?* Where do I get off saying that? Did Eddie Haskell ever catch a pass over the middle? Did he ever have a big bushy beard?

Maybe I come off as Ward Cleaver. Or Ward's dad. In the 1943 English movie *The Life and Death of Colonel Blimp*, Clive Wynne-Candy is a fat old blowhard, a veteran of World War I who has been relegated during World War II to a Home Guard command. Having decreed that mock-battle exercises will begin at midnight, he is relaxing in a Turkish bath at 6 P.M. when an impudent young lieutenant bursts in, declares that up-to-date warfare doesn't go by rules, tells Clive that he's fat and has a silly mustache and takes him captive. Clive is outraged. "You have no idea," he sputters before wrestling the lieutenant into the pool, "what kind of fellow I am!" Or was.

Who reminds us of who we are? People who knew us when. I went to see L. C. Greenwood, the former defensive end. L. C. is the one Steeler not in the Hall of Fame who most should be. (No. 2: Donnie Shell.) In the first Steelers Super Bowl he blocked three of Fran Tarkenton's passes, and in the second one he was even better. He had more career sacks than Joe Greene. I wrote in my book that L. C. might leave practice wearing a blue pullover sleeveless suit, brown pantyhose, a shoulder bag and a necklace a lady had given him that said TFTEISYF, which stood, of course, for "The first time ever I saw your face."

L. C.'s various business interests (coal and natural gas marketing, corrugated packaging and fulfillment, etc.) keep him checking computer monitors at his office in nearby Carnegie, Pa., several hours a day; then he plays golf. How does it feel to watch the Steelers now? "I try to be in the gym on Sunday afternoon, so I can watch while I'm working out," he says. "I'm all tensed up. Since I stopped playing, I've never been able to figure this out: the idea that there's nothing I can *do* about it. This player I'm watching is such a great player, what is he thinking? I coulda...." So he sweats it out.

L. C. at 6'6½" is 15 or 20 pounds up from his playing weight, which ranged from 225 to 233. He says, "These kids are too big! I looked at one of them, 350 pounds. That's too big to be an athlete. They just walk into the weight room, and walk out on the field. How the hell are you going to bend over?"

Yeah! Giants walked the earth in my day, and they could also run the earth. Case in point, the Immaculate Receptor himself. When Franco Harris was 32 and still carrying a football for a living, he told me, "The hole is never where it's supposed to be." Now at 62 he tells me, "I loved playing football. Now I love business. The competition changes all the time—where's the opening?" Franco's bakery business sells nutrition-laden, trans-fat-free doughnuts to public schools and retail outlets. In another venture he markets workout towels and, for the military, socks made of bamboo viscose and silver nanoparticles, which you can use for 60 days before they smell bad. And he chairs the board of directors of the Pittsburgh Promise, which provides (with seed money from the UPMC) college scholarships of up to $10,000 a year to all students at Pittsburgh public schools who achieve a 2.5 average and a 90% attendance record.

Franco studied food science at Penn State. "Twelve years ago," he says, "I knew I was going to have trouble with inflammation and trouble with my brain," so he became a vegetarian. Now he'll eat a little chicken or fish. And every morning, for 12 years, he has eaten blueberries. His joints and his brain are O.K. so far.

Yeah!

"Maybe I should write this whole story as an apology to you, because the current Steelers aren't what they were in my day," I told Kirven. "Not that I'm trying to compete, I'm just being—"

"Passive-aggressive," said Kirven. For the first 58 minutes of the Ravens game we sat in the stands, way up above the end zone, with other fans. In my day Steelers fans were just beginning to sense that their team could actually win, and they were beside themselves. They organized their own subgroups: Gerela's Gorillas (led by a man in a gorilla suit) for the kicker, Roy Gerela; Dobre Shunka, said to be Polish for *good ham*, for Jack Ham; and Franco's Italian Army, once blessed in person by Frank Sinatra. Now what Steelers fans do is wear Steelers stuff. In fact, I did not see on the streets of Pittsburgh, in the course of a week, six or eight people go by before at least one appeared wearing a Steelers jersey or shirt or hat. And on game days... how shall I describe it? Once I was on a clothing-optional beach in France. You would see a naked person changing a tire, a naked person wiping a baby's nose, a naked person shaking her finger at a misbehaving dog. So it was in Pittsburgh on game day, only instead of naked people, it was Troy Polamalus. Here a Polamalu bonking into a revolving door, there three Polamalus throwing a Frisbee. "Nice dog," you say to a Polamalu walking a hassling pug.

"You should see him in his Polamalu sweater," the walker replies.

Polamalus everywhere but on the field. The electrifying safety is injured; Roethlisberger is injured; so many wide receivers have been injured that the team will resort to signing 35-year-old former Steeler Plaxico Burress. This has had an effect on the Steelers' play. Wave our Terrible Towels as we might, as the Huge Electronic Screen commands us to GET ENERGIZED, eventually somebody is going to spill his beer on himself so he has to stop yelling "Get funky!" and go get two more beers just in case. In his absence we notice that the Huge Electronic Screen is yelling DEE-FENSE! louder than the crowd is.

And the Steelers lose to Baltimore 13–10. Playoff chances fading. Kirven and I are in the locker room. Reporters surround backup quarterback Byron Leftwich, who stepped up for the injured Roethlisberger but failed, after a great start, to carry the day. Off to the side, an insecure rookie receiver, David Gilreath (whom the Steelers will cut in a week), is trying to reach around reporters to get at his locker.

Kirven: "I asked him about Leftwich's feeble pass to him when he was wide open, and how he slipped trying to come back for it. He said in college he would have come back more aggressively, but he trusted Byron's arm. Neither of us knew that Byron had broken ribs at the time—he was with the throng of reporters, admirably refusing to use those ribs as an excuse. You remember, when he was asked if he surprised himself running for a touchdown, he said, 'I'm not a slow quarterback. I'm just the slowest black quarterback.' And Gilreath asked me, 'Do you think I should have caught it?' in such a tender way that I assured him he couldn't have." That's my boy. Human interest.

Here's one last nostalgia-cutter: Joe Gordon was Ed Kiely's No. 2 in the old days. "The most important game after the Immaculate Reception," Joe says, "was the Steelers beating Oakland out there in '74. John Madden had said the Super Bowl had already been played the week before when [the Raiders] beat Miami."

Oh, I remember. We kicked Raiders butt 24–13 to win the AFC title, and when we flew back into the Pittsburgh airport, wow, it was full of Steelers fans. It was like being welcomed into Heaven. It doesn't get any better than that, right? Well, but here's Gordon:

"Twenty years later, I tried to find a tape of that game. Finally a guy in the Greensburg area said he had one. I bought four copies from him. You could not believe how slow it was. We're always in standard formations, occasionally a fifth back. And the speed of it compared to today—it was like slow motion! I only watched 10 minutes of it, and I haven't looked at it since. Better off reading about it."

Noted.

Sources and Acknowledgments

Great care has been taken to locate and acknowledge all owners of copyrighted material included in this book. If any such owner has inadvertently been omitted, acknowledgment will gladly be made in future printings.

Grantland Rice, from *The Tumult and the Shouting* (New York: A. S. Barnes & Co.), 1954. Copyright © 1954.

W. C. Heinz, The Ghost of the Gridiron. *What a Time It Was* (New York: Da Capo, 2001). Reprinted by permission of Gayl B. Heinz for the Estate of W. C. Heinz.

Myron Cope, from *The Game That Was* (New York: World Publishing, 1970). Copyright © 1970 by Myron Cope. Copyright © 1974 by Thomas Y. Crowell. Reprinted by permission of HarperCollins Publishers.

Shirley Povich, The Redskins' Longest Day. *All Those Mornings . . . At the Post* (New York: PublicAffairs, 2005). Copyright © 2005. Reprinted by permission of the Washington Post Co.

Red Smith, The Most Important Thing; The Lost Cause. *Out of the Red* (New York: Knopf, 1950). Copyright © 1950. Reprinted by permission of Terence Smith and Catherine O'Meara.

Frederick Exley, from *A Fan's Notes* (New York: Random House, 1968). Copyright © 1968 by Frederick Exley. Reprinted by permission of Random House, an imprint and division of Random House LLC. All rights reserved.

Stuart Leuthner, from *Iron Men* (New York: Doubleday, 1988). Copyright © 1988 by Stuart Leuthner. Reprinted by permission of Doubleday, an imprint of the Knopf Doubleday Publishing Group, a division of Random House LLC. All rights reserved.

Gary Smith, Moment of Truth. *Going Deep* (New York: Sports Illustrated Books/Time Inc., 2008). Copyright © 2008 by Time Inc. All rights reserved. Reprinted by permission of *Sports Illustrated*.

Frank Deford, The Best There Ever Was. *Sports Illustrated*, September 23, 2002. Copyright © 2002 by Time Inc. All rights reserved. Reprinted by permission of *Sports Illustrated*.

John Schulian, Concrete Charlie. *Sports Illustrated*, September 6, 1993. Copyright © 1993. Reprinted by permission of John Schulian.

David Maraniss, from *When Pride Still Mattered* (New York: Simon & Schuster, 1999). Reprinted by permission of Simon & Schuster Publishing Group. Copyright © 1999 by David Maraniss. All rights reserved.

Jimmy Cannon, Greatness. *Nobody Asked Me, But . . . : The World of Jimmy Cannon*, ed. Jack Cannon and Tom Cannon (New York: Holt, Rinehart and Winston, 1978). Copyright © 1978 by The Estate of Jimmy Cannon. Reprinted by arrangement with Henry Holt and Company, LLC.

Jimmy Breslin, . . . The One Last Good One That Wasn't to Be. *New York Herald Tribune*, December 13, 1964. Reprinted by permission of SLL/ Sterling Lord Literistic, Inc. Copyright © 1964 by James Breslin.

George Plimpton, from *Paper Lion* (New York: Harper & Row, 1966). Copyright © 1963, 2006 by George Plimpton. Reprinted by permission of Little, Brown and Company. All rights reserved.

Dan Jenkins, An Upside-Down Game. *Sports Illustrated*, November 28, 1966. Copyright © 1966 by Time Inc. All rights reserved. Reprinted by permission of *Sports Illustrated*.

Jerry Izenberg, A Whistle-Stop School with Big-Time Talent. *True*, September 1967. Copyright © 1967. Reprinted by permission of Jerry Izenberg.

Jerry Kramer and Dick Schaap, from *Instant Replay* (New York: World Publishing, 1968). Copyright © 1968 by Jerry Kramer and Dick Schaap. Reprinted by permission of Doubleday, an imprint of the Knopf Doubleday Publishing Group, a division of Random House LLC. All rights reserved.

Jennifer Allen, from *Fifth Quarter: The Scrimmage of a Football Coach's Daughter* (New York: Random House, 2000). Copyright © 2000 by Jennifer Allen. Reprinted by permission of Random House, an imprint and division of Random House LLC. All rights reserved.

Al Silverman, Gale Sayers: The Hard Road Back. Al Silverman, ed., *The Best of Sport, 1946–1971* (New York: Viking, 1971). Reprinted by permission of Al Silverman.

Jim Murray, Don't Look Now . . . but the Funny Little League is No. 1. *Los Angeles Times*, January 13, 1969. Copyright © 1969. Reprinted by permission of the Los Angeles Times.

Larry Merchant, from . . . *And Every Day You Take Another Bite* (Garden City, NY: Doubleday, 1971). Copyright © 1971. Reprinted by permission of Larry Merchant.

Arthur Kretchmer, Butkus. *Playboy*, October 1971. Copyright © 1971 by *Playboy*. Reprinted by permission. All rights reserved.

Paul Hemphill, Yesterday's Hero. *Lost in the Lights* (Tuscaloosa: The University of Alabama Press, 2003). Copyright © 2003 by The University of Alabama Press. Reprinted by permission.

Gary Cartwright, Tom Landry: Melting the Plastic Man. *Texas Monthly*, November 1973. Copyright © 1973. Reprinted by permission of *Texas Monthly*.

Tom Archdeacon, Smith Hates for It to End Like This. *Miami News*, January 22, 1979. Copyright © 1979. Reprinted by permission of Tom Archdeacon.

Richard Price, Bear Bryant's Miracles. *Playboy*, October 1979. Copyright © 1979 by Richard Price. Reprinted by permission of Richard Price.

Rick Reilly, A Matter of Life and Sudden Death. *Sports Illustrated*, October 25, 1999. Copyright © 1999 by Time Inc. All rights reserved. Reprinted by permission of *Sports Illustrated*.

Leigh Montville, A Miracle in Miami. *Boston Globe*, November 24, 1984. Copyright © 1984. Reprinted by permission of Globe Newspaper Co.

H. G. Bissinger, from *Friday Night Lights* (New York: Da Capo, 1990). Copyright © August 11, 2000, by H. G. Bissinger. Reprinted by permission of Da Capo Press, a member of the Perseus Books Group.

Mark Kram, No Pain, No Game. *Esquire*, January 1992. Copyright © 1992. Reprinted by permission of Mark Kram Jr.

Charles P. Pierce, Legends of the Fall. *Sports Guy* (New York: Da Capo, 2001). Copyright © December 28, 2000, by Charles Pierce. Reprinted by permission of Da Capo Press, a member of The Perseus Books Group.

Ira Berkow, The Minority Quarterback. *The Minority Quarterback, and Other Lives in Sports* (Chicago: Ivan R. Dee, 2002). Reprinted by permission of Ivan R. Dee.

Peter Richmond, Flesh and Blood. *GQ*, May 2001; author's comments in footnotes: http://thestacks.deadspin.com/rae-carruth-the-women-who-loved-him-and-the-one-he-wa-747347792. Copyright © GQ/ Peter Richmond/Condé Nast. Reprinted by permission.

John Ed Bradley, The Best Years of His Life. *Sports Illustrated*, August 12, 2002. Copyright © 2002. Reprinted by permission of John Ed Bradley.

Wright Thompson, Pulled Pork & Pigskin: A Love Letter to Southern Football. ESPN.com, August 2007. Copyright © by ESPN.com. Reprinted by permission of ESPN.

Rick Telander, Atkins a Study in Pride and Pain. *Chicago Sun-Times*, January 1, 2007. Copyright © 2007 by Sun-Times Media. All rights reserved. Reprinted by permission and protected by the Copyright Laws of the United States.

Pat Forde, Broncos Earn Respect With Improbable Victory. ESPN.com, January 2, 2007. Copyright © by ESPN.com. Reprinted by permission of ESPN.

Michael Lewis, The Kick Is Up and It's . . . a Career Killer. *Play*, October 28, 2007. Copyright © 2007 by The New York Times. All rights reserved. Reprinted by permission and protected by the Copyright Laws of the United States.

Jeanne Marie Laskas, G-L-O-R-Y! *GQ*, January 2008. Copyright © GQ/ Jeanne Laskas/Condé Nast. Reprinted by permission.

Nate Jackson, from *Slow Getting Up* (New York: HarperCollins, 2013). Copyright © 2013 by Nate Jackson. Reprinted by permission of HarperCollins Publishers.

Paul Solotaroff (with Rick Telander), The Ferocious Life and Tragic Death of a Super Bowl Star. *Men's Journal*, February 2011. Copyright © 2011 by Men's Journal LLC. Reprinted by permission. All rights reserved.

Bryan Curtis, Friday Night Tykes. *Texas Monthly*, January 2013. Copyright © 2013. Reprinted by permission of *Texas Monthly*.

Index

ABC, xvii, xx, 119, 135
Adderley, Herb, 137
Agajanian, Ben, 43
Alabama, University of, xix, 52,
    114, 121, 229–45, 333, 338,
    342, 345–46, 348, 428
Albert, Frankie, 68
Albert, Marv, 370
Alexander, Kermit, 160
Alexander, Rufus, 358
Allen, George, xiv, 144–54
Allen, Jennifer, xiv, 144–54
Allen, Marcus, 337–38
Allen, Maury, 91
Allen, Pokey, 356
Allen Eagles, 420, 427
Allen Hawks, 413–34
Ameche, Alan, 66, 68
American Football League, xvi,
    81, 121, 142, 167–69, 175–78
Anderson, Donny, 136–37, 139–
    40, 143, 195
Anderson, Eddie, 127
Anderson, Gary, 364
Anderson, Tom, 206–8
Andrie, George, 138
Andros, Plato, 41
Antonopulos, Steve, 396
Apisa, Bob, 117
Archdeacon, Tom, xiv, 224–28
Arizona Cardinals, 365
Arkansas, University of, 39–41, 52
Arkansas, University of, at Pine
    Bluff, 309
Army (U.S. Military Academy),
    xiv, 1–3, 28, 31–33, 114
Ashley, Norman, 50
Associated Press, 6
Atkins, Bob, 133
Atkins, Doug, 351–54
Atkinson, Al, 171
Atlanta Falcons, 364, 395

Auburn University, 235, 344–46
Axthelm, Pete, 173
Azzaro, Joe, 118

Bahr, Matt, 370
Baker, John, 97
Baker, Moon, 9
Baltimore Colts, xiii, xv–xvi, xx,
    44, 65–70, 85, 167–69, 177–
    78, 193, 198, 215, 280, 283
Baltimore Memorial Stadium, xi
Baltimore Ravens, xx, 303, 412,
    436, 439, 444–45
Bannerman, Dave, 31
Barnes, Ernie, 280
Baron, Sherry, 282
Bass, Tom, 280
Bates, Mario, 318
Baugh, Sammy, 68, 207, 209
Baughan, Maxie, 75, 80, 82
Baylor University, 53
Baynham, Craig, 183
Baysinger, Slats, 31
Beach, Walter, 100
Beasley, John, 181
Bednarik, Chuck, xvi, 71–84
Beidleman, Blake, 416, 430–32
Bell, Todd, 405
Belue, Buck, 345
Bengtson, Phil, 195, 197
Benirschke, Rolf, 247–50, 252–58
Bergin, G. Frank, 28–29
Berkow, Ira, 294–313
Berry, Raymond, 66, 68
Bicknell, Jack, 261–62
Bidwell, Bill, 42
Bidwell, Charles, 42
Birk, Matt, 412
Bishop College, 133
Bissinger, H. G., xvii, 363–71, 419
Blackwood, Lyle, 251
Blanchard, Doc, 114

Blanda, George, xvi, 172
Blass, Jay, 340
Bledsoe, Drew, 74
Bleier, Rocky, 118, 440–41
Blount, Roy, 435–46
Boise State University, 355–59
Bolin, Bookie, 100
Boston College, xiv, 259–62
Boston Globe, xviii, 259
Boston Herald, 285
Bourguignon, Dick, 88
Bowden, Bobby, 290
Bowman, Kenny, 140, 142
Boyd, Brent, 408
Bradley, John Ed, xiv, xviii,
    328–40
Bradshaw, Terry, 173, 435, 439
Brady, Tom, xix
Braggs, Byron, 237–38
Braisher, Dad, 136
Brander, Victoria, 353
Brettschneider, Carl, 105, 108,
    110
Brewer, Billy, 349
Britton, Earl, 9, 11
Brooks, James, 252, 256
Brooks, Sid, 249
Brookshier, Tom, 75, 81
Brown, Bob, 184, 196
Brown, Elmer, 55
Brown, Jim, xiii, xvi, 48–49, 54,
    58–63, 72, 91–93, 97, 99,
    317–18
Brown, Paul, 40, 82, 85, 92
Brown, Robert, 270
Brown, Roger, 104, 107–8
Browner, Joey, 273–78, 282, 284
Brown University, 12
Brumbaugh, Carl, 15
Bryant, Paul (Bear), xix, 52, 85,
    133, 207, 222, 229–45, 337
Bryant-Denny Stadium, 240, 342
Buchanan, Junius, 120, 123
Buchanon, Willie, 249
Buckley, William F., 174
Budde, Brad, 338

Buffalo Bills, 295, 363, 370
Buffone, Doug, 182, 194
Bull, Ronnie, 158, 164
Bullock, Matt, 11
Bullock, Tom, 31
Burke, Randy, 283
Burns, Jerry, 274
Burress, Plaxico, 445
Burroughs, Don, 82
Bush, Reggie, 376
Bushart, Matt, 305–6, 312
Butkus, Dick, xvii, 75, 157–58,
    177, 179–202
Butler, Sol, 21
Butler University, 10, 12
Byrd, Ben, 208

Cadile, Jim, 196
Cafego, George, 206–8
Caffey, Lee Roy, 188, 197
California, University of, at
    Davis, 247
California, University of, at Los
    Angeles, 121
Camden Yards, 314
Camp, Walter, xviii
Canadeo, Tony, 88
Cannon, Jimmy, xii, 91–93, 167,
    345
Carideo, Frank, 127
Carlisle Indians, xiv
Carolina Panthers, xx, 314, 320
Carpenter, Louis, 40
Carpenter, Preston, 40
Carruth, Rae, xx, 314–27
Carson, Ted, 31
Carter, Virgil, 160
Cartwright, Gary, xiii, xv, 112,
    213–23
Cavender, Regis, 117
CBS, xvi, 38, 123, 137, 274
Cefalo, Jimmy, 255
Chandler, Don, 44, 135
Chandler, Wes, 248, 250, 252,
    256
Chavez, Brian, 264–66, 270–71

Chicago, University of, 10–12
Chicago Bears, xvi, xix, 6–7, 13–15, 23, 25–27, 30, 39, 41–42, 85, 97, 120, 144, 149, 155–66, 173, 179–202, 279, 351–54, 365, 373, 401, 404–5, 407, 411–12, 415
Chicago Cardinals, 14, 38, 40–44, 180, 202
Chicago Daily News, 71
Chicago Sun-Times, 71, 351
Chicago Today, 158
Chicago Tribune, 10
Chippewa Falls Marines, 23
Chmura, Mark, 318
Christian, Ivory, 264, 271
Christy, Earl, 169
Cifers, Ed, 206
Cincinnati Bengals, xiv, 257, 318, 377–94
Citadel, 210
Citrus Bowl, 291
City Park Stadium, 131
Clark, Dutch, 17
Clark, Jack, 330
Clark, Ryan, 438
Cleveland Browns, xvi, 38, 40, 44, 60, 71–72, 82, 85, 91–94, 96–97, 99–101, 120, 128, 221–22, 280
Cloman, Scott, 299, 302, 304, 308
Cody, Ed, 163
Colgate University, 54
Collier, Blanton, 92
Colorado, University of, 319–20
Columbia University, 32, 116
Comer, Chris, 267
Comiskey Park, 41
Compton City College, 375
Concannon, Jack, 173, 183–84, 188–90, 194–98
Conerly, Charlie, 43–45, 76
Conjar, Larry, 118
Cope, Myron, xii–xiii, xvii, 17–24
Cornish, Frank, 160
Corydell, Don, 247, 250, 253, 257

Cosell, Howard, xvii, 76
Costello, Vince, 94, 97–98
Cotton Bowl, xiii, 44, 47–50, 53, 56–59, 61, 63, 219
Crow, John David, 60
Crowley, Jim, 1, 3
Cruz, Victor, 425
Cuozzo, Gary, 182–84
Curran, Pat, 247
Curtis, Bryan, xviii, 414–34
Curtis, Chuck, 50, 53–54, 56–58, 60–64

Dallas Cowboys, xiii, xvii, 44, 75, 135–41, 195, 213–28, 278, 280, 283, 317, 333, 362, 365, 370–71, 395
Dallas Morning News, xviii
Dallas Times Herald, 112
Daugherty, Duffy, 114, 116
Davey, Rohan, 343
Davis, Glenn, 114
Davis, Willie, 120, 123, 129
Dawson, Len, 123
Dayton Daily News, 224
DeBerg, Steve, 276
Decker, Quinn, 210
Deford, Frank, xiii, 47, 65–70
DeLaunay, Lou, 333
DeLee, Robert, 330
DeMarco, Brian, 409
Dempsey, Tom, 172, 361–63, 374–76
DeNiro, Gary, 238–39
Denver Broncos, xx, 246, 318, 363, 366–67, 374, 376, 395–97
Dess, Darrell, 100
Detroit Lions, xvi, 80–81, 102–11, 171, 185–91, 280, 318, 360–63, 374–75
Dierdorf, Dan, 279, 374
Dike, Buddy, 49, 58, 62
Dillon, Corey, 318
DiNardo, Steve, 435–36
Ditka, Mike, 144, 149, 279, 353–54, 409

Donovan, Artie, 66
Dooley, Jim, 157, 185, 190, 194–95
Dooley, Vince, 344
Dorais, Gus, 1
Douglass, Bobby, 190
Dowler, Boyd, 137, 139
Duerson, Dave, xx, 401–12, 415–16
Dufrene, Marty, 334–36, 338–40
Duhe, A. J., 249
Dupre, L. G., 66

East 26th Street Liberties, 21
Ebbets Field, 2
Eckersall, Walter, 10
Eddy, Nick, 115
Edinger, Paul, 373
Edwards, Glen, 248, 253
Egg Bowl, 345
Elam, Jason, 363, 376
Elenburg, Possum, 52, 56
Engel, Kevin, 414–16, 417–25, 432–35
Enis, Hunter, 55–56
Erickson, Bud, 102–3, 110
ESPN, 135, 246, 263, 279, 341, 355
Esquire, xvii, 141, 272, 285
Estes, Steve, 334
Evans, Vince, xix
Ewbank, Weeb, 85, 175
Exley, Frederick, xiv, 34–37

Farmer, George, 195–97
Farr, Mel, 188–89
Fassel, Jim, 399
Feathers, Beattie, 210
Fichtner, Ross, 99
Fiesta Bowl, 355–59
Finney, Dick, 51, 57
Fisher, Jeff, 411
Flanagan, Ed, 188, 191
Florida, University of, 286, 292
Florida A & M University, 121
Florida State University, 290
Flutie, Doug, xiv, 259–62

Football Outsiders, 364, 373
Forde, Pat, 355–59
Forman, John, 310
Fort Worth Press, xv, 112, 213
Fouts, Dan, 247, 250–53, 256–57
FOX, 38, 425
Franklin, Andra, 251
Franklin Field, 12, 73, 82
Frazier, Leslie, 411
French, Walter, 2
Frick, Ford, 12
Fugett, Jean, 280
Fulmer, Phil, 348

Gabriel, Roman, 145, 152
Gaines, Gary, 264, 269, 271
Galiffa, Arnold, 31
Galimore, Willie, 162
Gallico, Paul, 102
Gannon, Chip, 30
Garrard, Allen, 51
Garrison, Walt, 223
Gent, Peter, 216, 220–21, 278, 283, 395
Gentleman's Quarterly, xvii, 71, 285, 314, 377
George, Bill, xvi, 74–75
George, Sam, 299, 302, 308–12
Georgia, University of, 230, 344, 347–48
Gibbons, Jim, 108–9
Gibron, Abe, 189–90, 193–94, 199
Gifford, Frank, xvii, 34, 36–37, 75–78, 81–82, 86, 100, 218, 279
Gillingham, Gale, 136, 139–40, 198
Gillman, Sid, 375
Gilmore Stadium, 14
Gilreath, David, 445
Gipp, George, 1–2
Gladieux, Bob, 115
Goeddeke, George, 115
Goode, Irv, 226
Goodell, Roger, 415, 431
Gordon, Dick, 188–89, 195, 197

Gordon, Joe, 445
Gordon, Larry, 257
Gordy, John, 105
Graham, Otto, 68
Grambling College, 119–34,
    309–10
Grange, Red, xii, xiv, 4–17, 206
Grantham, Larry, 169, 175
Green, Cornell, 221
Green, Ernie, 92
Green, Tim, 395
Green Bay Packers, xvi–xvii, 4, 17,
    22–24, 40, 73–74, 82, 85–90,
    96, 120, 123, 135–43, 152–53,
    159, 162, 171, 187, 193–200,
    215, 218–20, 318, 330, 375,
    404, 436
Greene, Joe, 435–36, 438, 443
Greenwood, L. C., 443
Gregg, Forrest, 136, 138, 140
Greggs, Isaac, 301, 304
Grier, Rosey, 60–61, 147
Griffith Stadium, 25
Gross, Milton, 170
Groza, Lou, 40
Guillot, Rocky, 334

Hackett, Willie, 288
Halas, George, 14, 26–27, 85, 184,
    353
Haley, Dave, 118
Haley, Dick, 440
Haley, Todd, 440
Hall, Harry, 10, 12
Hall, Korey, 357
Hamilton, Norman, 54, 62
Hampton, Dan, 404
Hampton, Dave, 195
Hanner, Dave, 39–40
Hanratty, Terry, 115–16
Hanson, Tyler, 359
Hardt, Henry B., 54–55
Hardy, Kevin, 117, 160
Harlow, Dick, 30
Harper, Jesse, 1
Harris, Duriel, 249–50

Harris, Franco, 435–36, 444
Harris, James, 133–34
Harris, Phil, 222
Harrison, James, 439
Harsin, Bryan, 356–57
Hart, Doug, 197
Hart, Jackie, 436
Harvard University, 28–30
Haskell, Eddie, 440, 442
Hawkins, Alex, 68
Hawkins, Bill, 31–32
Hayes, Lionel, 303
Hayes, Woody, 133, 238
Hays, Harold, 160
HBO, 65, 170
Hearne, Nate, 268–69
Heinz, W. C., xii–xiii, 4–16, 155
Heinz Field, 435, 441
Heisman Trophy, 286, 338
Hemphill, Paul, 203–12
Heritage Bowl, 303–4, 308–11
Herman, Dave, 172
Hilgenberg, Wally, 181
Hill, Lloyd, 268
Hirsch, Crazylegs, xxi
Hoag, Phil, 118
Holman, Willie, 198
Holsombake, Jim, 334
Holub, E. J., 81
Hooser, Hobart, 39
Horney, John, 117
Hornung, Paul, 82, 137, 142, 219
Hoskins, Neil, 53
Houston Oilers, xvi, 120, 129, 142
Howard University, 304
Howell, Jim Lee, 43, 218
Howell, Mike, 120
Howley, Chuck, 141
Huff, Sam, xvi, 74, 77, 82, 93, 164,
    193, 408–9
Hull, Mike, 158
Hyde, Frankie, 55
Hyland, Bob, 136

Illinois, University of, 5–13,
    15–16

Illinois Memorial Stadium, 10
Indianapolis Colts, 318, 363–64
Inside Sports, 34, 37
Insight Bowl, 359
Iowa, University of, 10, 12, 127
Irvin, Cecil, 14
Irvin, Michael, 317
Izenberg, Jerry, 119–34

Jackson, Levi, 28
Jackson, Nate, xx, 395–400
Jackson, Randy, 160
Jackson Memorial Stadium, 288
Jackson State University, 121
Jacobs, Don, 235–36
Jacoby, Marcus, 294–99, 301–13
James, Dick, 99
James, Drisan, 357
Janowicz, Vic, 40
Jenkins, Dan, xiv–xv, 112–18
Jeter, Bob, 196
Johnson, Charley, 226
Johnson, Gary, 251, 253
Johnson, Ian, 355–56, 358–59
Johnson, Jimmy, 262
Johnston, Jimmy, 27
Joiner, Charlie, 248, 252, 257
Jones, Chris, 341
Jones, Clinton, 117, 183
Jones, Deacon, 145, 152
Jones, Leroy, 256
Jones, Ralph Waldo Emerson,
   121–24, 126, 128, 130,
   133–34
Jordan, Lee Roy, 136–37, 142, 220,
   234
Justice, Ed, 27

Kahn, Roger, 155
Kaine, Elinor, 174
Kansas, University of, 52
Kansas City Chiefs, xvi, 81, 120,
   123, 223, 276, 318, 351, 365,
   372, 435–36, 440–41
Kansas City Star, 341
Karras, Alex, 280, 362–63, 374

Katcavage, Jim, 43
Keck, Lorraine, 88–89
Keisel, Brett, 439
Kelcher, Louie, 251, 253, 257
Kenary, Jim, 30
Kenney, Dick, 117
Kent, Joey, 286
Kentucky, University of, 288, 337,
   346
Kiely, Ed, 439–40, 445
King, Linden, 249
King, Phil, 97
Kinnard, Billy, 59
Klein, Gene, 281
Knafelc, Gary, 90
Knoxville Journal, 206, 208
Kostelnik, Ron, 136
Kotal, Eddie, 119, 121–23
Kram, Mark, 272–84
Kramer, Jerry, xvii, 135–43, 217
Kretchmer, Arthur, xvii, 179–202
Kuechle, Ollie, 18
Kurek, Ralph, 158

La Crosse Loggers, 23
Ladd, Ernie, 120, 129–30
Lair, Kevin, 333
Lambeau, Curly, 18, 22–24
Landry, Tom, xiii, 44, 75, 213–23,
   226, 432
Lane, Night Train, xxi
Lardner, John, xv, 112, 155
Lardner, Ring, 1–2, 112
Laskas, Jeanne Marie, xiv, 377–94
Las Vegas Locomotives, 399
Layden, Elmer, 1, 3
Layne, Bobby, 68, 171
Lazzaro, Paul, 30
Leatherman, Lonnie, 62
LeBeau, Dick, 189
Lee, Richie, 133
Leftwich, Byron, 445
Lemm, Wally, 44
Leuthner, Stuart, 38–45
Levias, Jerry, 60
Lewin, Leonard, 170

Lewis, Danny, 107
Lewis, Michael, xiv, 360–76
Lewis, Ray, xx, 318–19
Lilly, Bob, 137, 139–40, 223
Lipscomb, Big Daddy, 66, 280
Livingston, Andy, 162
Lombardi, Vince, xvii, 4, 45, 82, 85–90, 135, 141–42, 152, 158–59, 164, 187, 189, 195, 197, 217–20, 375
Long, Terry, 402
Los Angeles Coliseum, 152
Los Angeles Rams, xxi, 81, 90, 121, 144–48, 150–53, 226
Los Angeles Times, xviii, 167, 246, 282–83
Lott, Ronnie, 273–75, 337
Louisiana State University, xiv, 300–1, 312–13, 328–44, 346
Louisville Courier-Journal, 355
Lovejoy Stadium, 421
Lucci, Mike, 185, 188–89
Luckman, Sid, 68
Lujack, Johnny, 114
Lundy, Lamar, 145, 152
Luther, Ed, 254–56
Lyles, Lenny, 68
Lynch, Jim, 117

MacDonald, Mark, 259–60, 262
Mackey, John, 68, 402
Madden, John, xx, 38, 274, 279, 431, 445
Mailer, Norman, 172
Mandell, Arnold, 276, 278, 281
Manders, Dave, 216
Manning, Archie, 285–93, 349
Manning, Celdon, 413–15, 418, 423–30, 432–35
Manning, Eli, 285–86, 289
Manning, Peyton, xix, 285–87, 289–92, 364
Mansfield, Ray, 437
Mara, Wellington, 218
Maraniss, David, xvii, 85–90
Marchetti, Gino, 66–67, 280

Marshall, George Preston, 25
Martin, Orthol (Abe), 48–55, 57–59, 61, 63
Maryland State University, 121
Mason, Tommy, 162
Matson, Ollie, 41
Maule, Tex, 176
McCartney, Bill, 320
McClendon, Charles, 328, 336–39
McClung, Willard, 47, 55
McDaniels, Josh, 395–96
McDonald, Ric, 251, 257
McDonald, Tommy, 81
McDougal, Jerrod, 263, 270–71
McDuff, Charlie, 331–32
McEwan, John J., 1–2
McIlwain, Wally, 10–11
McKay, John, 237
McKloskey, Ruth, 88–89
McMahon, Jim, 412
McNair, Kirk, 231, 240, 244–45
McNally, John Victor (Johnny Blood), xii–xiii, 17–24
McRae, Bennie, 163
Medlock, Justin, 365
Meggyesy, Dave, 180, 280, 395
Melton, Jim, 39
Mendoza, Chico, 63
Men's Journal, 401
Mercein, Chuck, 136–37, 139–40
Merchant, Larry, 170–78
Meredith, Don, xvii, 137, 216, 220–22
Messerschmidt, Al, 257
Miami, University of, 53, 259–62
Miami Dolphins, 246–58, 333, 445
Miami News, 224
Michaels, Lou, 177
Michigan, University of, 10–12, 32, 127, 286, 290, 344
Michigan State University, 112–18
Miles, Boobie, 263, 267–69
Miller, Don, 1, 3
Miller, Heath, 439
Miller, Tom, 88
Miller, Virgil, 54

Milwaukee Badgers, 17, 21
Minnesota Vikings, xi, 180–85,
    187, 272–74, 364, 408, 411
Mississippi, University of, 56–57,
    59, 286, 288–91, 341–42, 345,
    347–50
Mississippi State University, 342,
    345
Mitchell, John, 51
Moffie, Harold, 30
Molinski, Ed, 206
Monday Night Football, xvii, xx,
    76, 379, 365
Montgomery, Ross, 156, 158, 165
Montville, Leigh, xiv, 259–62
Moore, Lenny, 49, 60–61, 66, 68
Morgan, Jabari, 300–1, 307–8, 311
Morgan State University, 121
Morrall, Earl, 168, 177
Morris, Alec, 428
Morris, Johnny, 158
Morris, Jon, 279
Morrison, Joe, 100
Morton, Craig, 221
Mudd, Howard, 182, 186
Muhammad, Mustafah, 318
Muncie, Chuck, 248, 257
Munoz, Anthony, 338
Munson, Bill, 188–90, 198
Munson, Lester, 408
Murchison, Clint, Jr., 223
Murray, Jim, 112, 167–69
Mutscheller, Jim, 66

Naanee, Legedu, 358
Nack, William, 47
Nadherny, Ferd, 30
Nagurski, Bronko, 15, 206
Namath, Joe, xvi, 168–78, 205,
    234–35
Nathan, Tony, 249–51, 253
National Collegiate Athletic
    Association, xix, xxi, 55, 116,
    294, 348, 351
National Football Hall of Fame,
    6, 76, 80, 144, 149, 206, 208,

210, 225, 257, 318, 333, 352–
    53, 396, 404, 408–9, 440, 443
National Football League, xiv,
    xvi, xix–xx, 21, 25, 34, 38,
    60, 71–73, 80, 82, 84–85,
    119–21, 144–46, 149–52, 160,
    167–69, 176–78, 180, 195,
    217, 246–47, 256–57, 273–74,
    277–79, 281–82, 286, 316–18,
    320, 333, 352–53, 360, 362–
    65, 367–69, 372, 377, 380–82,
    385, 395–402, 410, 413, 415,
    421, 424, 428–29, 431, 437
National Professional Football
    League, 13
National Sports Daily, 65, 285
Navy (U.S. Naval Academy), 28,
    31–33
NBC, 38, 123, 135
Neale, Earle, 80, 84
Nebraska, University of, 10, 12,
    114
Neidert, John, 199
Nelson, Lindsey, 5
Nevers, Ernie, 17
New England Patriots, 38, 74, 318,
    366, 368–70
Newman, Ed, 254, 257
Newman, Marvin E., 46–47,
    58–69, 61
Newman, Will, 292
New Orleans Saints, 360–63, 374
New Orleans Times-Picayune, 341,
    346
Newsweek, xv, 112, 135, 173
Newark Star-Ledger, 119
New York Daily News, 47
New York Giants, xvi–xvii, 14,
    22–23, 34–38, 42–45, 67,
    75–77, 81–82, 91–101, 170,
    181, 197, 215, 218, 314, 318,
    363, 399, 405, 409
New York Herald Tribune, 1, 28, 94,
    119, 135
New York Jets, xvi, 167–78, 280
New York Journal-American, 91

New York Post, 91, 170
New York Sun, 4
New York Times, 28, 176, 294, 344, 360, 395, 412, 419
New York Yankees (football team), 13, 98
Neyland, Bob, 206, 209
NFL Films, xvi, 75, 251, 277, 423, 436
NFL Network, 144, 437
NFL Players Association, 283, 402, 407–9
NFL Sunday, 425
Nitschke, Ray, xvi, 193, 197–98, 436
Nolan, Chuck, 218–19
Noll, Chuck, 81, 439–40
Nomellini, Leo, 81
North Carolina State University, 210
Northwestern State University, 299, 301–2
Northwestern University, 10, 351, 353
Norwood, Scott, 363–4
Notre Dame, University of, xii, xiv, 1–3, 10, 20–21, 60, 112–18, 127, 229, 237, 403–5, 407

Oakland Raiders, 120, 142, 280, 368, 373, 436, 445
O'Bradovich, Ed, 97, 188, 194, 197–98, 201
O'Brien, Coley, 115, 118
O'Donoghue, Don H., 161
Offen, Neil, 170
Ohio State University, 10, 12–13, 40, 49, 238, 286, 291
Oklahoma, University of, 41, 355–59
Okoye, Christian, 276–77
Olejniczak, Dominic, 87–88
Olszewski, Johnny, 41
Orange Bowl, 175, 225, 247, 250–51, 254, 259–62
Orgeron, Ed, 347–49

Orlando, Mark, 294, 302–3, 305, 309
Orr, Jimmy, 68
Osborne, Jim, 184
Osmanski, Bill, 27
Ozee, Jim, 50, 62

Palomar College, 375
Parcells, Bill, 365, 369–70
Pardee, Jack, 145, 152
Parilli, Babe, 440
Parks, Billy, 216
Parrish, Bernie, 100–1, 280–81, 408
Parseghian, Ara, 113–16, 118, 237
Patrick, Frank, 196–99
Paul Brown Stadium, 378, 383
Payne, Chad, 270
Payton, Walter, xix, 73
Peay, Francis, 197–98
Pellegrini, Bob, 71, 81
Pennsylvania, University of, 12, 74, 80
Pennsylvania State University, 5, 49–50, 60
Percival, Mac, 195
Permian High School, 263–71
Perretta, Vinny, 358
Peter, Christian, 318
Peters, Floyd, 104, 109
Petersen, Chris, 356–58
Peterson, Adrian, 357
Phelan, Gerard, 259–62
Philadelphia Daily News, xviii, 47, 71, 170
Philadelphia Eagles, xvi, 14, 71–84, 209–10, 226
Philadelphia Municipal Stadium, 30
Philbin, Gerry, 169
Piccolo, Brian, 155–56, 158–59, 165
Pierce, Charles P., 285–93
Pietrosante, Nick, 105–6, 109
Pihos, Pete, 80
Pittsburgh Post-Gazette, 17

Pittsburgh Steelers, 17, 23–24, 42, 81, 92, 97, 225, 364, 408, 435–46

Playboy, xvii, 174, 179

Plimpton, George, xvii, 102–11

Polamalu, Troy, 439, 444–45

Pollard, Harold (Toad), 56–58, 62–63

Polo Grounds, 1, 3, 14, 34–35, 37, 76

Povich, Shirley, 25–27

Prairie View College, 121

Price, Peerless, 285–87, 292

Price, Richard, 229–45

Pro Bowl, 80, 149, 199, 352, 401, 405

Pugh, Jethro, 136, 138, 140

Pyle, Charles C., 13

Rabb, Jerard, 357

Rackers, Neil, 365

Ramsey, Jones, xv

Ray, John, 117

Raye, Jimmy, 117–18

Raymond, Greg, 340

Real Sports, 65

Reeves, Dan [Dallas Cowboys], 139

Reeves, Dan [Los Angeles Rams], 144–45, 147, 150–51, 153–54

Reilly, Rick, xiv, 246–58

Rentzel, Lance, 216

Reston, James, 172

Retzlaff, Pete, 81, 83

Rice, Grantland, xii–xiii, 1–3, 12, 167

Rice, Jerry, 277

Rice University, 53

Richards, Ray, 42

Richardson, Albert, 333

Richardson, Jeff, 116

Richardson, Pete, 295–99, 302–4, 308–12

Richmond, Peter, xx, 314–27

Richt, Mark, 347–48

Richter, Les, 75

Ringo, Jim, 199

Robert F. Kennedy Stadium, 162–63, 166

Roberts, Selena, 344

Robinson, Eddie, 120–34

Robustelli, Andy, 43, 96

Rockne, Knute, 1–3

Rockwell, Tod, 11

Roethlisberger, Ben, 439, 445

Rogers, Langston, 348

Rooney, Art, Jr., 436, 442

Rooney, Art, Sr., 436, 440–42

Rooney, Dan, 441–42

Rose, Joe, 248, 250–51

Rose Bowl, 114

Rozelle, Pete, 164, 173, 279, 374

Rozy, Ed, 158–60

Rubin, Barry, 330

Runyon, Damon, 12, 91

Russell, Andy, 436, 438

Ryan, Buddy, 404–5

Ryan, Frank, 92, 100

Sabol, Ed and Steve, xvi

Saia, S. J., 334

St. John's University, 24

St. Louis Cardinals (football team), 14, 225–26, 395, 405

Saldi, Jay, 226

Sample, Johnny, 177, 280

Samuel, Derek, 396–400

San Diego Chargers, 185, 246–58, 276, 278, 280–81, 375, 416

San Francisco 49ers, 81, 90, 160, 182, 218, 411

Sann, Paul, 5

Sauer, George, 177–78

Sayers, Gale, 155–66, 200

Scarpati, Joe, 374

Schaap, Dick, xvii, 135–43

Schatz, Aaron, 373

Schenkel, Chris, 86

Schmidt, Joe, xvi, 74, 104, 185

Schnelker, Bob, 43

Schoen, Tom, 118

Schouman, Derek, 358

Schramm, Tex, 216, 225, 362, 374–75

Schubach, Fred, 66
Schulian, John, xi–xxi, 71–84
Scott, Lindsay, 345
Seals, George, 160, 163
Seau, Junior, 416, 430
Sellers, Ron, 216
Selmon, Lee Roy, 276
Seymour, Jim, 116, 118
Shaw, Buck, 71, 82
Shaw, George, 66, 76
Shaw, Pete, 251, 254
Shealy, Steadman, 234–35
Shecter, Leonard, 170
Shell, Donnie, 443
Shepard, Leigh, 334
Sherman, Allie, 92–93, 96–97
Sherrod, Blackie, xv, 112
Shibe Park, 14
Shields, Billy, 256–57
Shinnick, Don, 193–94
Shires, Abe, 206
Shoals, Roger, 188
Shrake, Edwin (Bud), xv, 112, 213
Shula, Don, 247–50, 253, 255,
    257
Shy, Don, 195
Sievers, Eric, 255–56
Silverman, Al, 155–66
Simpson, O. J., 237, 317–18
Singletary, Mike, 411
Skorich, Nick, 74, 81
Skoronski, Bob, 88, 90, 136, 138
Small, Gerald, 251, 255
Smith, Bubba, 112–16
Smith, Cy, 411
Smith, DeMaurice, 409
Smith, Gary, xiii, xviii, 47–64
Smith, Hunter, 366–67, 371–72
Smith, Jackie, 224–28
Smith, Red, xii, 28–33, 167, 294,
    355
Smith, Tody, 216
Smith, Vitamin T., xxi
Smothers, Virgil, 302–3, 312
Snell, Matt, 171
Snow, Justin, 367
Solotaroff, Paul, xx, 401–12

South Carolina State University,
    310
South Dakota State University, 369
Southern California, University
    of, xvii, 36, 50, 237, 273,
    337–38
Southern Methodist University,
    53, 60, 221
Southern University, 121, 129,
    294–312
Spartan Stadium, 118
Sport, xvii, 135, 155, 203
Sporting News, 412
Sports Illustrated, xiii, xv–xviii,
    17, 47, 65, 71, 112, 155, 167,
    176, 186, 246, 259, 263, 272,
    279, 285, 324, 328, 351, 408,
    435–37
Sports Reporters, 135
Spurrier, Steve, 343, 345
Stabler, Ken, 234–35, 347
Stagg, Amos Alonzo, 11, 230
Stanton, Eddie, 328
Starr, Bart, 82, 136–42, 178, 195–
    98, 200
Staubach, Roger, 223, 225, 227
Stephenson, Dwight, 333
Stone, Ed, 158
Stoops, Bob, 359
Strachan, Steve, 260
Stringley, Darryl, 280
Strock, Don, 248–51, 253, 256
Stuhldreher, Harry, 1, 3, 20
Stydahar, Joe, 41–42
Suffridge, Bob, 203–12
Suisham, Shaun, 449
Summerall, Pat, 38–45
Sunde, Milt, 183
Sun Devil Stadium, 359
Super Bowl, xiv, xvi, xviii–xx, 34,
    38, 123, 144, 167–69, 176, 213,
    215–17, 224–28, 257, 300, 318,
    341, 363, 367, 372–74, 401,
    404–5, 437, 439, 443, 445
Sweatt, Greg, 271
Swink, Jim, 52, 57, 62
Syracuse University, 5, 60–63

Tadman, Marty, 359
Tampa Bay Buccaneers, 276
Tangerine Bowl, 328
Tarkenton, Fran, 173, 181, 280, 443
Tatum, Jack, 280
Taylor, Altie, 188–90
Taylor, Jim, 73, 82
Taylor, Joe, 182
Taylor, Lawrence, 73
Taylor, Otis, xvi
Taylor, Roosevelt, 120
Tebow, Tim, 425
Telander, Rick, 351–54, 401
Tennessee, University of, 203, 205–7, 209–11, 245, 285–86, 289–92, 344–46, 348, 352
Tennessee State University, 121
Tennessee Titans, 318, 374, 411
Texas, University of, xv, 50, 121
Texas A & M University, 52–53, 57, 60, 290
Texas Christian University, xiii, 46–64, 156
Texas Monthly, xv, xviii, 213, 413, 417
Texas Tech University, 53, 56
Theismann, Joe, 279
Thibodeaux, Benjy, 338
Thomas, Aaron, 95–96
Thomas, Derrick, 318
Thomas, Duane, 216, 220
Thompson, Wright, xviii, 341–50
Thorne, Samuel, 3
Thornhill, Charlie, 116
Thorpe, Jim, xiv, 205–6
Three Rivers Stadium, 436, 441
Thurston, Fuzzy, 135, 142–43, 187
Tiger Stadium, 329–30, 336–37, 339–40, 343
Time, 412, 419
Timmons, Lawrence, 440
Tittle, Y. A., 94–101
Tomlin, Mike, 439–40
Toomay, Pat, 395

Towler, Deacon Dan, xxi
Townes, Willie, 138–40
Trammel, Pat, 235
Trippi, Charley, 40–41, 80
Trowbridge, Fred, 88
True, 4, 119
Tulane Stadium, 361, 376
Tully, Tom, 340
Tunnel, Em, 218
Turner, Cecil, 198
Turner, Robin, 124–27, 129
Twentieth Century, xvi
Tyne, Phil, 250

Uecker, Vernon, 55
Underwood, John, 279
Unitas, Johnny, xiii, xxi, 65–70, 178, 198
United Football League, 399
Upshaw, Gene, 402, 407–9

Van Brocklin, Norm, 68, 76, 81–83, 168
Van Buren, Steve, 80
Vanderbilt University, 1
Vanderjagt, Mike, 364–5, 371, 373
Van Heusen, Eric, 399
Vaught, John, 343, 348
Vaught-Hemingway Stadium, 343, 348
Vermeil, Dick, 74, 79
Vigorito, Tommy, 253
Vinatieri, Adam, 38, 363, 365–74
Von Schamann, Uwe, 248, 250–51, 253, 255

Wake Forest University, 156, 328
Walker, Denard, 318
Walker, Marcus, 357
Walker, Mickey, 100
Ward, Al, 215, 223
Warner, Glenn Scobey (Pop), 230, 430–31
Warren, Jimmy, 436
Washington, Gene, 117, 182

Washington, Kenny, 121
Washington Post, xviii, 25, 85, 314, 317, 328
Washington Redskins, 25–27, 144, 157–59, 164–66, 226
Waters, Andre, 402
Webb, Jack, 51
Weber, Chuck, 72, 77
Webster, George, 113, 116
Webster, Mike, 408–9
Wenzel, Ralph, 402
Werblin, Sonny, 175–76
Westerberg, Tom, 420, 427
Wheelwright, Ernie, 98–99
White, Charles, 337–38
White, Dwight, 440
White, Ed, 183, 257
White, Quincy, 266
White, Reggie, 74
Whitley, Jay, 333, 340
Whitlow, Bob, 103–4, 106
Whitsell, Dave, 362, 376
Wickhorst, Frank, 9
Wietecha, Ray, 44, 138
Wilbur, John, 216
Wilkerson, Doug, 256–57
Wilkinson, Bud, 174
Williams, Chris, 302, 305
Williams, Fred, 39
Williams, Joe, 51, 53, 62
Williams, John, 303–4
Williams, O'Day, 53
Williams, Pete, 31
Williams, Willie, 120
Wilson, George, 109–10

Wilson, Larry, 226
Wilson, Otis, 405
Winchell, Mike, 264–65, 268, 270–71
Winslow, Kellen, 246–49, 251–58
Wisner Stadium, 103
Wood, Gary, 96, 101
Wood, Willie, 197
Woodley, David, 248, 257
Woodruff, Andrew, 356
Woodruff, Bob, 206
Woodward, Milt, 176
Woodward, Stanley, 119
World League of American Football, 369
Wrigley Field, 14, 42, 181, 184, 186, 188, 196
Wyatt, Bowden, 206

Yale Bowl, 170
Yale University, 12, 28–30
Yankee Stadium, 35, 44, 67, 76, 114
Yaras, Miki, 283
Yardley, Jonathan, xiv
Yary, Ron, 184
Yost, Fielding, 10
Younger, Paul (Tank), xxi, 121–23, 126–27

Zabransky, Jared, 355, 357–58
Ziegel, Vic, 170
Zimmerman, Paul, 170
Zucker, Steve, 410–11
Zuppke, Bob, 8–12, 15

This book is set in
9.5 point ITC Stone Serif, a face designed
for digital composition by Sumner Stone in 1987 as part
of the ITC Stone font family, an endeavor undertaken in response
to the difficulty of mixing different type styles on one page or in one
design. The paper is an / / / / / / / / acid-free, offwhite stock
produced by Glatfelter and meets the requirements for permanence of the
American National Standards Institute. Design and composition by
Publishers' Design and Production Services, Inc. Printing and
notch adhesive binding by Edwards Brothers
Malloy, Ann Arbor.